MUTUAL CONTEMPT

MUTUAL CONTEMPT

Lyndon Johnson, Robert Kennedy,
and the Feud That Defined a Decade

JEFF SHESOL

W. W. NORTON & COMPANY
New York   London

For information about permission to reproduce selections from this book, write to
Permissions, W. W. Norton & Company, Inc., 500 Fifth Avenue,
New York, NY 10110.
The text of this book is composed in Bembo with the display set in Palatino.
Composition by JoAnn Schambier.
Manufacturing by Quebecor Printing, Fairfield Inc.

Library of Congress Cataloging-in-Publication Data

Shesol, Jeff.
    Mutual contempt : Lyndon Johnson, Robert Kennedy, and the feud that
defined a decade / Jeff Shesol.
        p. cm.
    Includes bibliographical references and index.
    ISBN 0-393-04078-X
    1. Johnson, Lyndon B. (Lyndon Baines), 1908–1973. 2. Presidents—United
States—Biography. 3. Kennedy, Robert F., 1925–1968. 4. Legislators—United
States—Biography. 5. United States—Politics and government—1963–1969. I.
Title.
E847.2.S48 1997
973.923'092—dc21
[B]   97-710   CIP

W. W. Norton & Company, Inc., 500 Fifth Avenue, New York, N.Y. 10110
http://www.wwnorton.com

W. W. Norton & Company Ltd., 10 Coptic Street, London WC1A 1PU
1 2 3 4 5 6 7 8 9 0

To my parents, Susan and Barry,
and to Nancy

CONTENTS

Acknowledgments

This book, like every other, is a team effort. I am deeply indebted to the Johnson and Kennedy associates who agreed to be interviewed and were so generous with their time and recollections: David Black, Liz Carpenter, George Christian, Clark Clifford, Joe Dolan, Peter Edelman, Daniel Ellsberg, Myer Feldman, Grenville Garside, William Geoghegan, Nicholas Katzenbach, Lawrence Levinson, Ron Linton, Frank Mankiewicz, Harry McPherson, Melody Miller, Matthew Nimetz, DeVier Pierson, George Reedy, Walt W. Rostow, the late Dean Rusk, Pierre Salinger, Arthur M. Schlesinger, Jr., Theodore Sorensen, Stewart Udall, Jack Valenti, William vanden Heuvel, Adam Walinsky, Lee White, and Roger Wilkins. Their stories added nuance to my picture of an often stark conflict.

I am grateful to the staff of the Lyndon Baines Johnson Library in Austin for their tireless assistance. Charlene Burgess, Tina Houston, Mary Knill, and E. Philip Scott were especially helpful, and Claudia Anderson and Linda Hanson helped to orient me—no small task—in the library's vast holdings of oral histories. The Lyndon B. Johnson Foundation generously funded my extended stay in Austin. The John F. Kennedy Library in Boston showed similar generosity by providing a Kennedy Research Grant, and William Johnson and Stephen Plotkin guided me through the Robert F. Kennedy Papers. Staff members at the Library of Congress, the National Archives, and the Martin Luther King Public Library in Washington were also helpful.

Old friends and new acquaintances gave support of every kind. Dan Buck, Andrea Camp, Joe Dolan, Paul Kirk, Dick Schmidt, Patrick Shea, and Amanda Smith provided valuable contacts and sources. Stan Oliner of the Colorado Historical Society helped to uncover grants and other resources. My uncle, David Pliner, put cutting-edge printing technology at my disposal to produce manuscripts bound and unbound, and always at the eleventh hour. Creators Syndicate—particularly Laura Mazer, Rick Newcombe, Mike Santiago, Katherine Searcy, Anita Tobias, and Anthony Zurcher—was supportive even when deadlines were stretched.

Many friends became, in many different ways, important contributors: Jeff Dolven, David Greenberg, Francesco Lecciso, Nader Mousavizadeh, Ed Pallesen, David Sartorius, and Len Stark read portions of the manuscript and offered thoughtful and always tactful commentary. In 1991, Brown professors Patricia Herlihy and the late William McLaughlin read my senior thesis—in effect, an early draft of this book—and wrote comprehensive critiques. Sean Hartgrove, David Krovitz, and Jay Strell provided counsel and companionship from the beginning. Richard Halstead, Jon Levitsky, Eric Liu, Jesse Malkin, and Sophie Oltiványi contributed helpful ideas I have done my best to incorporate. Brian Floca, Brian and Elle Ohleyer, and David Whitney in Massachusetts and Carol deOnis in Texas were my Boston-Austin connections, and showed me true Yankee and Southern hospitality, respectively. Brian Ohleyer, to whom I am indebted for so much more than that, told a good Johnson story and lived every bit as expansively, announcing his presence in a room, and in our lives, like LBJ bursting into a tea party of "Kennedy ladies." He is deeply, badly missed.

I am especially grateful for the invaluable help and encouragement of three Bancroft Prize–winning historians. Arthur M. Schlesinger, Jr., took time away from other projects to read a manuscript that must have arrived at his door with a discomfiting thud; he was forthcoming with encouragement and helpful criticism, and I am profoundly thankful for both. I am also lucky to count Robert Dallek as friend and mentor. His greatest contribution to this book—in addition to anecdotes, sources, and tapes—was the complex understanding of LBJ his own work has engendered. James T. Patterson, in 1990, scribbled three hopeful words in red pen in the margin of a thesis proposal: "Should be interesting." Since then, he has guided this project through its every stage, from honors thesis to manuscript to final product, and always with the gruff candor and warm humor he shows his students at Brown University. What is best in this book bears his imprint.

My editor, Starling Lawrence, endowed this book with his experience, his critical eye, and his wit. He saw from the beginning that the story of Johnson and Kennedy is far more than a good brawl. Patricia Chui responded to all my queries with humor, patience, and good judgment.

I also wish to thank Henning Gutmann for investing both his enthusiasm and his confidence in this project. And Rafe Sagalyn, my agent, was the first to say, "it's a book." As usual, he was right, and I owe him countless debts of gratitude.

Through a process that was by turns exciting and imposing, my parents, Susan and Barry, my brother, Robert, and my grandparents, Lawrence and Ann Shesol, sustained me in countless ways, boosting my confidence and offering more title ideas than a thesaurus. To my family I offer the deepest thanks and love for a lifetime of that kind of support. And to Nancy O'Neill, who learned that there is truly a Johnson or Kennedy anecdote for every occasion, who edited my words with patience and skill, and who continues to enrich my life with her special grace, I offer love and gratitude that I cannot begin to express.

Two stars keep not their motion in one sphere.

—Shakespeare, *Henry IV, Part 1*

MUTUAL
CONTEMPT

Introduction

Lyndon Johnson and Robert Kennedy loathed each other. "This man," Kennedy said of Johnson, " . . . is mean, bitter, vicious—an animal in many ways." Johnson considered Kennedy a "grandstanding little runt." Their mutual contempt was so acute, their bitterness so intense and abiding, they could scarcely speak in each other's presence. When they did speak, cordiality quickly gave way to uneasy silence or a shouting match. Alone or with friends and assistants, each man ranted and obsessed, sulked and brooded about the other. Kennedy and Johnson spent the 1960s listening for footsteps, looking over their shoulders, making few important decisions without first considering the feud.

Politics, of course, is full of heated rivalries. The rancorous debates of the 1990s have buried the romantic (or cynical) notion that political differences can be finessed by an after-hours whiskey among gentlemen. Still, Bill Clinton and Newt Gingrich are no Johnson and Kennedy. The rivalry between LBJ and RFK was of a different magnitude—and of greater importance—than any of the postwar era. Their antagonism spawned political turf battles across the United States. It divided constituencies the two men once shared and weakened their party by forcing its members to choose between them. It captivated the newly powerful media that portrayed every disagreement between Johnson and Kennedy as part of a prolonged battle for the presidency or a claim on the legacy of the fallen JFK. It helped propel one man to the Senate and drive the other from the White House.

Lyndon Johnson and Bobby Kennedy were a study in contrast—so dissimilar in background, character, and even appearance that they seemed natural antagonists. It was as if one were designed to confound the other.

Six feet three inches tall, Johnson towered over Kennedy, crowding him, threatening to back him across a room. Kennedy, half a foot shorter, was solid but slight; perpetually hunched, he kept his distance. Johnson, bedecked in gold rings, watches, and cufflinks, gloried in newfound wealth. He was immaculately, almost dandily, groomed. The rumpled Kennedy seemed embarrassed by his own trust fund ("You're lucky you've been born poor," he told a friend, cryptically). Kennedy spoke in monosyllables that some perceived as shyness, others as diffidence. He was often witty but never sparkling. Johnson delivered monologues, great torrents of effortless, endless, earthy language. From Kennedy's childhood, it was bombastic boors—people like LBJ—who drove Bobby out of a room and into his shell, muttering words of disapproval. Johnson trafficked in tall tales; Kennedy despised "liars."

It was an elemental clash of personalities—"a matter of chemistry," as Johnson put it in his memoirs. It was also generational. LBJ and RFK bracketed the era of the Second World War. Though Johnson survived a brief firefight during a congressional junket and Kennedy volunteered for the Navy, neither man saw real combat; during the unifying experience of the era they were observers, not participants or brothers-in-arms. To Johnson, born in 1908, Bobby was a "snot-nosed kid." To Bobby, seventeen years younger, Johnson was an anachronism.

Culture as much as chemistry divided the two men, and the socioeconomic chasm between them was wider than any generation gap. Johnson often stressed his humble roots, but he also boasted of an impressive Southern heritage. "Listen, goddammit," he once said, "my ancestors were teachers and lawyers and college presidents and governors when the Kennedys in this country were still tending bar." Though the Johnson family's fortunes swung erratically between comfort and poverty, they considered themselves something better than average Hill Country folk. Lyndon's father, Sam, was a shrewd political maverick and state legislator. His mother, Rebekah, read Browning and Tennyson and political biographies. The Johnsons earned a certain notoriety (both respect and ridicule) in the Hill Country of Texas, but of course the Hill Country, during Lyndon's youth, was about as isolated a place as one found in the vast United States; in the Age of Radio, the Hill Country was largely without radios and entirely without electricity.

In the boyhood homes of Robert Francis Kennedy, electricity was taken for granted. There were homes in Bronxville, Hyannis Port, and Palm Beach—each one a marker of status and very public success. By 1938, Bobby's father, Joseph, was U.S. ambassador to Great Britain and his winsome brood were well known to any reader of *Life* magazine. Compared to the Johnsons, one of whom fought in the Revolutionary

War, the Kennedys were newcomers to the United States, part of the Irish influx of the mid-nineteenth century. But even when the Kennedys were "tending bar" in turn-of-the-century Boston (Bobby's grandfather, Patrick J. Kennedy, was a saloonkeeper), they were prospering and dabbling in politics (he was also a ward boss). Bobby's mother, Rose, was the daughter of John F. "Honey Fitz" Fitzgerald, a former congressman and mayor of Boston. Bobby's political heritage was as deeply felt as LBJ's, though the Kennedy family mantle fell predominantly on the shoulders of Bobby's older brothers, Joseph Jr. and John. The young Kennedys shared a grand sense of possibility and entitlement: "my father," Bobby recalled, "used his money to free us."

Both LBJ and RFK were weaned on politics, but politics of different sorts. As a child, Lyndon Johnson dogged his father's footsteps at the state legislature in Austin; he watched the long floor debates intently, springing up occasionally to wander the halls of the power elite. He loved campaigning, handing out literature at rallies and listening as his father chatted with farmers about crop yields and pending legislation. The younger Johnson was no less a politician: gregarious and ambitious in school, he "could reason you right out of your shoes," recalled a classmate. "If he wanted something, he knew how to go about getting it. . . . They should have named him the great persuader." Later, LBJ delighted in the sweaty personal tangle of local politics; there was little doubt he would end up in Austin, if not Washington.

Bobby's grandfather Honey Fitz had thrived in the ethnic hothouse of Boston politics. But Joseph Kennedy disdained the stereotype of the Irish politician—all blarney and backslapping—that his father-in-law epitomized. Joseph Kennedy's horizons were broader than Boston, and his ambitions for his boys were bigger. When Joe was at home, mealtime at the Kennedy household became a nightly forum on global affairs. "I can hardly remember a mealtime," Bobby later wrote, "when the conversation was not dominated by what Franklin D. Roosevelt was doing or what was happening in the world." Bobby did less of the talking than Joe Jr. or Jack, but he absorbed much that was said: one of his classmates at Milton Academy recalled that Bobby was better informed about international politics than any of his peers.

Predictably, both Johnson and Kennedy made it to Washington— Johnson first, as a congressional aide in the early 1930s. He climbed the ladder quickly, from aide to congressman to senator by 1949. Kennedy arrived in 1951, taking a job at the Justice Department after rejecting a run for Congress from Connecticut. For a time, they lived minutes from one another in northwest Washington and worked ten blocks apart on Pennsylvania Avenue; but they inhabited different worlds. Bobby

Kennedy was interested in public affairs but not so much in electoral politics. Politically he was (like JFK) a moderate Democrat, closer in ideology to northern, urban Republicans than to the liberal wing of his own party. Bobby was more a moralist than an operator, better suited to criminal investigations than Capitol Hill intrigue. And unlike John Kennedy, who treated fellow politicians with affable indifference, Bobby wore his contempt openly. "You can't get any work out of a politician," Bobby groused after running JFK's successful campaign for Senate in 1952. An interviewer observed that Bobby pronounced the word "politician" as if it were something "unclean and unwanted." Politics was the dirty business Bobby did for his brother. It was, Bobby later scoffed, "a hell of a way to make a living."

In Johnson's view, politics was the *only* way to make a living, and he reveled in it. Politics for Johnson was a personal art, and from his first days in Congress friends noted LBJ's unusual desire—and ability—to win people over. "You couldn't help but like him," one recalled. Johnson cultivated his colleagues and savored their company. To woo them or to conquer them, Johnson had to *know* them, had to understand their fears and desires. This he did masterfully, emerging during the course of the 1950s as the most powerful politician on Capitol Hill. Johnson stepped nimbly between the liberal and conservative wings of the Democratic Party, walking the line between his activist, New Deal instincts and conservative Southern constituency. "On many important occasions," recalled one House member, "it was impossible to know why he had voted a certain way, whether it was from conviction or political considerations." For Johnson this was a false distinction. While Bobby Kennedy's universe was starkly black-and-white, Johnson's was a broad band of muted grays.

What little they had in common only drove them farther apart. Both Johnson and Kennedy were vulnerable, volatile men. Bobby had always been sensitive, his sister Eunice recalled. The seventh of nine children, bullied by his older brothers, Bobby "got hurt easily. . . . He just either would look mad or he'd be a little sarcastic and talk back to you." But the Kennedys did not coddle children; the most vulnerable among them was the least likely to show it. By adulthood Bobby emerged as the toughest and most quick-tempered of the bunch. "Just fierce!" remembered a childhood friend. In 1954, as the Kennedys played touch football in a Georgetown park, a baseball landed on the field. A group of graduate students were hitting fly balls from the other end of the park, and the balls continued to rain upon the Kennedys until Bobby's younger brother Edward exchanged angry words with one of the students. A fight was coming. Bobby, far smaller and lighter than either Ted or his opponent, leaped between them, lunged at the student, and fought him in a bloody brawl until they both collapsed in exhaustion. Thankfully, the incident did not make the newspapers. But Bobby's public reputation as a brawler of one kind or another dogged him for the rest of his years.

Johnson, too, was easily wounded, and was more likely to show it than Kennedy. As a child, Lyndon greeted the slightest reprimand, rejection, or injury with howls of pain and pleas for sympathy. Even in the prime of his career, LBJ's self-pity was bottomless. On occasion he lashed out, like Kennedy, when upset; Johnson thought nothing of giving an aide or peer a vicious tongue-lashing in public. More often, though, Johnson sulked and sought reassurance. He bristled at the gentlest mockery, particularly of his background. At a radio and television correspondents' dinner in 1956, LBJ wore a new tuxedo, gray silk with black lapels. Senator Clinton Anderson of New Mexico pointed at Johnson's suit and chortled, "Every damned time you bring one of these rich Texans up here and introduce them to civilization, he goes completely hog-wild!" LBJ stood stone-faced and indignant. Cracks like these meant he was not being taken seriously, and despite a raucous sense of humor Johnson had never shown an ability to laugh at himself.

Johnson was vain, capricious, and occasionally cruel. Kennedy was curt, prickly, and thin-skinned. But they were also deeply compassionate, and there were other, more salutary similarities. LBJ and RFK shared a heartfelt concern for the disadvantaged—based, in part, on their common (if somewhat improbable) self-identification as underdogs. Kennedy was never as hard and pitiless as his early public image: once a "victim" himself in the rough-and-tumble of a competitive family, Bobby often rushed to the aid of "misfits." Despite his privileged upbringing, Bobby was, in one classmate's recollection, "an underdog in sports, with studies and girls, and as a Catholic." As Kennedy matured politically and personally, he emerged again as a zealous defender of the disenfranchised.

LBJ's populism was his father's legacy. Sam Johnson took up unpopular causes, defending tenant farmers against wealthy landlords and shielding German-Americans from prevailing prejudices. Part of this was posturing; Sam was at heart a political pragmatist, and so was Lyndon. When LBJ's constituents got what they wanted, so did he. Power was his reward for public virtue. But Johnson had also deeply imbibed the pieties of his upbringing: duty, sacrifice, and service. "Some men," Johnson reflected late in life, "want power simply to strut around the world and to hear the tune of 'Hail to the Chief.' Others want it simply to build prestige . . . and to buy pretty things. Well, I wanted power to give things to people—all sorts of things to all sorts of people, especially the poor and the blacks." In fact LBJ wanted power for all these reasons.

Both men were extremely ambitious, though there was little reason, through much of the 1950s, to expect those ambitions to clash. The first exchange between Johnson and Kennedy was perfectly cordial. In October 1957, when the Soviet Union launched its Sputnik satellite, Senate Majority Leader Johnson made reference to RFK, then the aggressive chief counsel of a Senate investigative committee. "A successful investigation of Sputnik could only take place," Johnson observed, "if [it] had someone like young Kennedy handling it." Bobby recorded Johnson's comment in his diary, adding, "Am very pleased with myself."

In 1959, though, their careers collided. By year's end, Lyndon Johnson and Bobby Kennedy were combatants in the race for the Democratic nomination for president—Johnson on his own behalf, Kennedy on his brother John's. By January 1961, LBJ and RFK were bitter rivals in a battle for power within the Kennedy White House. A scant one thousand days later, they were competitors for the legacy of the martyred JFK, dueling heirs to the Kennedy throne. And finally, for two brief but brutal weeks in March 1968, Lyndon Johnson and Bobby Kennedy were contestants for the leadership of the Democratic Party and the presidency of the United States.

The story unfolds like a Greek tragedy played out on a nation's center stage. The protagonists are flawed, very human men, and their conflict illuminates not only their characters but their era. As historical figures, Johnson and Kennedy are forever entangled: one cannot fully comprehend either man without considering his relationship with the other. Their antagonism was, from the beginning, very personal, but it was also a complicated blend of politics, ideas, ambitions, and anxieties. Kennedy's challenge to Johnson says much about his own evolution as a public figure. LBJ's nervous response to the "Bobby problem" speaks volumes about the Johnson presidency. This became the defining relationship of their political lives.

Nor can one fully comprehend the 1960s without considering the Johnson-Kennedy feud. The issues that wrenched these two men apart—Vietnam, race, poverty—were at the heart of many personal and political cleavages in those years of division. But Johnson and Kennedy were not, like student demonstrators or civil rights workers, peripheral or anonymous figures. After John Kennedy's assassination, they were the political titans of the decade. They not only responded to issues but also shaped them. From the war in Vietnam to the war on poverty, from the "problem of the cities" to the collapse of the Democratic coalition, the major events of the sixties bear the imprint of this personal rivalry.

Politics, too, bore its mark. Johnson and Kennedy personalized, embodied, and crystallized growing rifts among Democrats. Their feud was, in large part, an ideological and generational struggle for the soul of the Democratic Party and the future of American liberalism. Would liberals, like LBJ, continue to represent unions, federal paternalism, and globalism? Or would they move with RFK toward "a newer world"—a broader coalition, more decentralized decision-making, and "empowerment" of the underprivileged? These tensions linger: the long shadow of the Johnson-Kennedy feud looms above today's clash between "Old" and "New" Democrats. Johnson and Kennedy's struggle for power, a focal point of the Democratic search for identity, is a lens through which to examine these larger divisions.

Kennedy's friend and assistant Edwin Guthman warns that "anyone who writes with certainty about Bob's relationship with Lyndon Johnson does so at his own risk. . . . There are no balanced views, no neutral observers—only partisans." The flood of literature on Kennedy, Johnson, and the 1960s has largely proved Guthman right. Contemporary accounts leave much to be desired. Observations are scattered, limited by personal experience, and colored by loyalty or nostalgia. Memoirs, however vivid, offer only threads of the story. Comprehensive biographies of LBJ and RFK also disappoint on the subject of the feud. The feud is mentioned—as it must be—but is distilled or slighted by biographers with the burden of presenting a life *in toto*.

This book is the first history of the Johnson-Kennedy relationship in its own right, not as part of a larger study or biography. It draws together scattered strands of the story. It also endeavors to lift the shroud of bias and transcend the partiality or sentimentality affecting so much of the work on these two men and the 1960s. Only by integrating new and old material, by focusing on a distinct period of nine years (1959–1968), and by placing the feud in the context of not one life but two can the relationship of LBJ and RFK be properly understood and its impact determined.

In 1961, after a White House dance, a group of officials gathered upstairs for a late-night batch of scrambled eggs. In the kitchen, Vice President Lyndon Johnson accosted Attorney General Robert Kennedy. "Bobby, you do not like me," Johnson moaned. Bobby recoiled; the situation was painfully awkward for everyone, but the vice president was unrelenting. "Your brother likes me," Johnson went on. "Your sister-in-law likes me. Your Daddy likes me. But *you don't like me*. Now, why? Why don't you like me?"

It remains a central question, charged with emotion and invested with significance. Its answer reveals a great deal about two men, their times, and the nature of power.

CHAPTER 1

Prelude to
a Feud

In the late autumn of 1959, Senator John Kennedy dispatched his younger brother, Robert, to the Texas ranch of Lyndon Baines Johnson.

Bobby Kennedy's visit to the Senate majority leader had the appearance of a political ritual, a deferential nod to a party elder. It was not. In the pursuit of the 1960 Democratic nomination for president, Johnson was not John Kennedy's potential patron but his potential rival. Bobby Kennedy, as his brother's campaign manager, traveled to Texas not to seek Johnson's blessing but to size up his ambitions.

Arriving at the ranch, Bobby aimed his brother's questions at Johnson with the grim precision of a prosecutor. Was Johnson in or out? Whose side was he on? Johnson, in a long and rambling talk, left Bobby with three clear impressions: that LBJ would not run for the presidency, would neither help nor harm John Kennedy's candidacy, and would do all he could to deny a third nomination to Adlai Stevenson, who, despite successive debacles in 1952 and 1956, was making it known in Washington that he wanted another chance. Johnson seemed resolute; Kennedy placed considerable faith in his promises.

In time, LBJ was to break all three.

Bobby Kennedy's overnight stay was amiable, by all accounts, but marred by a disturbing incident. Johnson insisted that the two men hunt deer; with political guests it was his custom, a frontier ritual. Kennedy dutifully marched through the woods of the LBJ ranch, carrying a borrowed shotgun. He stopped short and fired at a deer. The gun's powerful recoil threw Kennedy backward, knocking him to the ground and cutting his brow. The towering Johnson reached down to help Kennedy to his feet. "Son," he told Bobby dismissively, "you've got to learn to handle a gun like a man."

Johnson's withering disdain was an assertion of his political primacy. He might—for now, at least—have stepped out of John Kennedy's path to the White House, but Johnson would not bow before the vaunted Kennedy "machine." Even on the sidelines LBJ would continue to cast a very large shadow on the race. His patronizing tone toward Bobby reflected Johnson's assessment—a reckless one, events would show—of the Kennedys' political acuity.

Johnson was soon to regret his flippancy. But now, in 1959, his advantage over Kennedy was beyond question. The thirty-four-year-old Bobby was, after all, almost young enough to be Johnson's "son." He had held no elective office, only staff positions in the Senate—Johnson's Senate. He was the younger brother of a "playboy" senator who was widely liked and even envied by LBJ and his colleagues, but hardly feared. It was Robert Kennedy who now lay prostrate before Johnson, not the reverse. To the Senate majority leader, in 1959, it must have seemed the natural order of things.

Never had a majority leader dominated the Senate more fully than Lyndon Baines Johnson. With his overpowering persona and ambition, organizational skill, and manic, restless devotion to the task, he molded Senate Democrats into a surprisingly unified force during the Eisenhower years. He infused the Senate with an energy and relevance it had lacked since the days of the New Deal.

Johnson's ascent was quick and unconventional. Entering the Senate in 1949 after a controversial election and twelve years' service in the House, LBJ found his ideal environment. "Mr. Johnson took to the Senate as if he'd been born there," recalled Walter Jenkins, one of LBJ's closest aides. "From the first day on it was obvious that it was *his* place." Johnson secured a largely ceremonial, procedural post and transformed it into a focus of unprecedented reach and power—just as he had done in the Little Congress (a mock House for congressional secretaries) after his arrival in Washington in the early 1930s. Halfway through his first Senate term he was minority leader, and in 1955, following the Democrats' narrow victory in the 1954 midterm elections, Lyndon Johnson became the youngest majority leader in American history.

Johnson's hold over his colleagues depended largely on his skillfully overbearing personal style. Political observers tagged it "the Johnson Treatment," and it was a whirlwind of emotions almost paralyzing in its intensity. "Its tone," observed columnists Rowland Evans and Robert Novak, "could be supplication, accusation, cajolery, exuberance, scorn, tears, complaint, the hint of threat. It was all of these together." Johnson bent his colleagues backward, physically and figuratively, under his enormous frame and by the sheer force of his will. Senator Hubert Humphrey of Minnesota would slink from a room, pleading for a cigarette break, to escape a face-to-face encounter with LBJ.

The Johnson Treatment was partly intuitive and partly the product of discreet calculation. LBJ's understanding of senators' individual vulnerabilities was innate, but he also scripted, rehearsed, and contrived seemingly spontaneous encounters in Capitol corridors. "Johnson knew how to woo people," remembered Humphrey, the frequent object of LBJ's attention. "He was sort of like a cowboy making love. . . . He knew how to massage the senators." Johnson knew whom to nurture, whom to threaten, and whom to push aside. The whole chamber seemed subject to his manipulation. "He played it like an organ," exclaimed *Time*'s Hugh Sidey. "Goddamn, it was beautiful! It was just marvelous."

Johnson's mastery of the Senate required more than a powerful personality; his knowledge of policy and procedure were superlative. He wielded an arsenal of statistical information, fishing through his large pockets for crucial memos or clippings. He followed and orchestrated the chamber's every activity from bill markups to floor votes. Pacing tirelessly in his enormous, ornate office, a cigarette in one hand and a telephone—always a telephone—in the other, LBJ worked his dedicated staff to the limits of physical and mental exhaustion, demanding that they match his own relentless pace. Many did not; even an articulate Texan who did, Harry McPherson, thought Johnson's use of his staff "callous and wasteful." LBJ seemed to regard the men around him, whether staff members or senators, "as fungible parts of an army whose purpose was to serve, equip, and sustain its general in his infinite tasks." Their reward was a smothering embrace—and the near-constant exhilaration of progress.

All of the decade's significant domestic reforms bore the LBJ brand. In Sidey's view, Johnson and his fellow Texan Speaker of the House Sam Rayburn "literally ran the country" in the 1950s. "They *were* the President and the Vice President. . . . Christ, [Ike] didn't run the government." Yet Johnson maintained great respect for both the president and his office. LBJ's leadership was expressly bipartisan and nonconfrontational—in his words, the "politics of responsibility." On foreign matters, Johnson backed the president and former general unquestioningly. Domestically, while Republican senators bickered openly about their agenda, Johnson's Democrats—despite considerable divisions—secured important reforms in Social Security, housing, and agriculture and on the minimum wage.

Johnson's success derived from his great flexibility. The essence of Lyndon Johnson's legislative strategy, the complement to the Treatment, was what Evans and Novak called the Procedure: "On any major piece of legislation, never make a commitment as to what will pass; determine in advance what is *possible* under the best of circumstances for the Senate to accept; after making this near-mathematical determination, don't reveal it; keep the leader's intentions carefully masked; then, exploiting the Johnson Network, start rounding up all detachable votes; when all is in readiness, strike quickly and pass the bill with a minimum of debate." Unlike his more liberal colleagues, Johnson took a pragmatic view of consensus-building: he saw it not as the lowest common denominator but as the maximum acceptable to the majority. It was a strategy perfectly attuned to the dynamics of divided government. Ideological rigidity invited defeat.

"These were glory years for Johnson; well he knew it; much did he desire that others know it as well," Daniel Patrick Moynihan recalled. Others did know it, and LBJ's fellow Democrats were effusive in their praise. "I'm bursting with pride over the magnificent job you did in this Congress," Clark Clifford, a Missouri lawyer and former counsel to President Harry Truman, wrote to Johnson in 1958. "When I contemplate what would have happened up there without you it makes me believe that a beneficent God has an interest in our destiny."

LBJ's status as congressional colossus was underscored by his landslide reelection in 1954, which freed him from most of the snags of Texas politics. Johnson remained a tireless booster of his state's fortunes, but with his base now secure, he shifted his emphasis toward advancing national issues and minimizing his own political liabilities. Johnson's persuasive powers diffused as the size of his audience expanded, and he knew it. He strove to improve his public speaking and press relations, and did so, becoming increasingly confident with crowds and reporters. Yet the cool mastery of television that came naturally to some of his younger colleagues, like John Kennedy, eluded LBJ.

If any ambition surpassed Johnson's reach, it was this yearning to be a truly national figure. Northern liberals could not but acknowledge Johnson's legislative prowess. His Southernness, however, invited their suspicion, indifference, or hostility. In response, Johnson evoked the standard of their mutual hero Franklin D. Roosevelt and advocated a renewal of the New Deal—expanded farm subsidies and Social Security coverage, and investment in infrastructure and economically depressed areas—and pursued it effectively in Congress. In the wake of the Soviet Union's successful launch of the Sputnik satellite in late 1957, Johnson further heightened his national profile by pressing for the creation of NASA and revitalizing America's scientific and technical education.

Yet a formidable obstacle—civil rights—blocked Johnson's entry into the Democratic mainstream. Johnson was a Southerner, and liberals eyed warily his voting record on this, the nation's most intractable issue. LBJ had remained aloof from Southern segregationists, shrewdly refusing to sign the Southern Manifesto (protesting the Supreme Court's 1954 *Brown* decision to desegregate the nation's public schools). But in twenty years of public service, Johnson had voted against every civil rights measure he faced. Now, concerned for his party, his region, progressive government, and his political career, and—not least—by the plight of America's blacks, Johnson labored in 1957 to pass a civil rights act, the first such legislation since Reconstruction. Liberals like Eleanor Roosevelt derided the act as toothless "fakery." Still, Johnson's sponsorship was clear and the political triumph was his.

By the late 1950s, then, Lyndon Johnson had promoted himself ably but remained largely untested in the national arena. His supporters, still mostly Texans, believed he had transcended the limits of Senate and regional politics. Johnson had, at the very least, entered the political calculations of every contender for his party's nomination in 1960. As the 1950s drew to a close, LBJ could look back at a litany of legislative victories and a remarkably rapid ascent to the heights of political power. He was only fifty-two years old. The path to the presidency, Johnson was coming to think, might pass through his enormous oak door.

But 1959 found LBJ in low spirits. His characteristic displays of gregariousness and confidence masked a deep ennui and frustration. The heady days of the mid-1950s were clearly over, and the Senate, Johnson's vocation, passion, and religion, seemed to be turning on its master. Liberal Democrats, their ranks swelled by the 1958 elections, were growing restless and resentful of his conciliatory tactics. Their praise gave way to backbiting. They accused Johnson of dictatorship and of accommodating the Republican agenda. Conservative Democrats added their voices to the discord, emboldening the once agreeable Eisenhower to strike down some of Johnson's initiatives with his veto. Across the aisle, Republicans achieved unity and discipline under the able leadership of Everett Dirksen. Johnson's renowned control of the Senate was slipping.

As 1960 approached, the growing presidential ambitions of Johnson's colleagues further loosened his hold. Even lesser rivals like Senators Joseph Clark of Pennsylvania, Albert Gore of Tennessee, Eugene McCarthy of Minnesota, Patrick McNamara of Michigan, Edmund Muskie of Maine, and William Proxmire of Wisconsin, smelling Democratic victory in 1960, joined a once small band of liberal critics like Tennessee's Estes Kefauver and Illinois's Paul Douglas in regular and open defiance of their party leader. LBJ's major rivals—Kennedy, Humphrey, and Missouri's Stuart Symington—refrained from personal attacks, but their increasing cries for stronger action on social issues threatened to drown out Johnson's tired mantra of "responsibility." In the Senate itself, these men posed little challenge to Johnson's primacy; it was not his job they were after. The leadership they sought was that of the national party, which they pursued with far-flung speeches and courtesy calls. Johnson, meanwhile, had done little during the 1950s to extend his web of loyalty and patronage outside Washington.

The Senate, simply put, was no longer fun. In fact, it was downright mutinous. When liberal Democrats challenged their leader's right to select the party's Senate Policy Committee in January 1960, Johnson told his aide George Reedy that "everybody in the Senate could go commit a biological improbability. . . . Screw 'em all, I'm sick and tired of this kind of nonsense." The resolution failed, 51 to 12, but Johnson was stung, bitterly. Plagued by fears of another heart attack (he had nearly died in July 1955), Johnson began to consider a shift in career, even mumbling to intimates about retirement. More seriously, he entertained notions of running for president.

Should he retire from politics? Or should he seek its biggest prize? Johnson gave profoundly mixed signals. As early as 1956, he told his friend Jim Rowe flatly that Texans and Southerners must face facts. Their power base was in the Senate, not the White House. LBJ's calculus was simple: he would not run because he could not win. He would not distract himself with quixotic power plays. Yet he followed each such decision with more plotting for the presidency, more sounding out of schemes and strategies.

Each move negated the last. Indecision paralyzed LBJ. In the fall of 1958, Rowe urged him to begin a full-fledged campaign immediately; his opponents were already mobilizing. Again, Johnson seemed to long for the presidency: "He wanted it so much his tongue was hanging out," Rowe believed. But Rowe's appeals to vanity and patriotism were futile. Johnson held back, afraid of failure. By January 1959, Rowe had tired of Johnson's equivocation and reluctantly joined the Humphrey campaign.

Johnson's reticence was born of more than tactical concerns. Was his personal style, he wondered, so uniquely suited to the workings of Congress that it rendered him unfit to be president? He worried aloud that his Procedure and Treatment would be ineffective in the Oval Office. "I don't want to get a bug in my mouth that I can't swallow," a falsely modest Johnson told an office visitor. "I don't have the disposition, the training or the temperament for the presidency." Memories of his heart attack weighed upon him. "There are times when my heart feels like lead. It's as if it's pushing down," he told a reporter, cupping his hand to his chest. Past political scares loomed, as well: Johnson could not forget his narrow loss of the 1941 Senate election and his narrower, disputed victory in 1948—the eighty-seven-vote margin that earned him the nickname "Landslide Lyndon."

Nor did Johnson wish to forfeit his Senate seat in a failed race for the presidency. During the spring of 1959, he orchestrated a change in Texas law to permit officeholders to run simultaneously for Senate and the presidency or vice presidency. He also arranged to advance the state's Democratic primaries from July and August to May and June, giving Texas more weight in the nominating process. Both LBJ and the state legislature were protecting themselves from an unsuccessful bid. Johnson denied authorship of the bill, but it surprised no one that the senator's surrogates privately referred to it as the "LBJ Law"—not the "Ralph Yarborough Law" (for Texas's junior senator).

While publicly disavowing any such intentions, LBJ began quietly spreading national campaign funds and collecting information for the approaching primaries. He scattered campaign funds in the key battleground of West Virginia, strengthening his ties with Senator Robert Byrd, already an ardent Johnson man. He quizzed his Republican friend New Hampshire Senator Styles Bridges about the crucial early primary in Bridges's state. He spoke often in the Northeast, bragging to colleagues of the "fine receptions" he received. When Georgia Senator Herman Talmadge predicted Johnson would not secure even fifty delegates in the country's five most populous states, LBJ bet him a hat he would earn more.

The open secret of Johnson's candidacy complicated his political relationships. In late 1959, Governor Edmund "Pat" Brown of California appeared on NBC's *Meet the Press*. Toward the show's end, a reporter asked, "What about Lyndon Johnson for President?" Brown diplomatically noted his respect for the majority leader, but added that LBJ's regional baggage—segregation, his ties to the oil industry—rendered him too conservative for most Democrats. Pressed by the panel of reporters, Brown candidly deemed Johnson unable to win. As the show ended and the studio lights dimmed, an assistant ran toward Brown with a phone. Johnson waited on the line, and he was livid—not at Brown's implication that he was weak on civil rights or the captive of oil interests, but at the suggestion that he was not a winner. The next time they talked, Johnson was more conciliatory. For months he pursued the governor doggedly, switching from sweet talk to intimidation and back again.

LBJ's strategy, if it could be called such, seemed muddled. But it had its own deliberate logic: "All this talk about my candidacy is destroying my leadership," he told Sam Rayburn. "I'm trying to build up a legislative record over there. The Senate already is full of presidential candidates. If I really get into this thing, they'll gang up on me and chop me up as a leader so that I'll be disqualified for the nomination." In effect, Johnson was pursuing the presidency by *not* pursuing it. His noncampaign encouraged his opponents to chop up one another, thus underscoring his reputation as a careful, mature leader. While they bickered among themselves, he would keep focused on his next legislative accomplishment.

Throughout 1959, Johnson and his aides thought his strategy was working. Despite his disclaimers, LBJ remained a contender because, as George Reedy told him, "you are the only national Democratic leader who has a record of achievement." Johnson also fancied himself the only Democrat acceptable to Southern and Western conservatives as well as northern New Dealers. Betting on his moderate record of bipartisanship and "liberal nationalism," he hoped for a draft or deadlock.

Johnson's was a convention-based, not a primary-based, strategy. It demanded patience and the most discreet of machinations. It was as much the product of cautious deliberation as of self-doubt. Either way, Johnson's inconsistency baffled his opponents. By the end of 1959, he had generated enough confusion to warrant Bobby Kennedy's political "fishing expedition" at the LBJ Ranch.

At the time of his visit to the ranch, Bobby Kennedy could boast of few accomplishments to match those of the Senate majority leader. Yet Kennedy arrived in Texas that autumn not merely as the emissary or sibling of a senator but as an emerging political figure in his own right. The 1950s had marked the arrival of Robert Kennedy, and if they were not his glory years they were certainly heady ones.

A young lawyer with no courtroom experience, Bobby Kennedy came into his own within Lyndon Johnson's arena, the U.S. Senate. Kennedy was quickly schooled in the vulgarity of Senate politics. In 1953, Senator Joseph McCarthy of Wisconsin, a Republican, assumed control of the low-profile Committee on Government Operations. Naming himself chairman of its Permanent Subcommittee on Investigations, McCarthy obtained the power, rarely exercised, to scrutinize "government activities at all levels." McCarthy took a hand in hiring staff, stocking his subcommittee with loyal supporters. At the urging of Bobby's father, Joseph P. Kennedy, McCarthy named the twenty-seven-year-old RFK as assistant counsel. Joe Kennedy had sought the position of chief counsel for Bobby, but McCarthy gave the job to the more experienced Roy Cohn, a hotheaded and often tormented New York lawyer.

McCarthy and Cohn quickly plunged into a vociferous, clumsy search for subversives in the State Department and the Voice of America. Whether the early stages of McCarthy's brutal crusade troubled Bobby is unclear; at the very least, he shared McCarthy's concern about Communist activities in the United States. Kennedy's nascent political ideology had been largely informed by his father, who imparted to his sons a vague economic liberalism and zeal for public service but no great interest in civil liberties. Most likely, Bobby gave the matter little thought. As assistant counsel he was occupied with the more mundane, if potentially explosive, issue of trade between America's allies and Communist China—a subject of increasingly ominous speculation in Congress. His shirtsleeves rolled up past his elbows, his tie loosened, Kennedy pored over Maritime Commission records and the Lloyd's of London shipping index with single-minded intensity. In July 1953, Doris Fleeson, an ascerbic liberal columnist, accorded Kennedy's interim report "much more credence . . . than normal for anything to which Senator McCarthy's name is attached."

Yet the gap between Bobby's exactitude and McCarthy's recklessness was widening. Roy Cohn's petulance had been troubling enough to RFK; now, Cohn brought a friend, an equally rash young millionaire, G. David Schine, onto the subcommittee as an unpaid "chief consultant." Schine's only credential was a thin tract on psychological warfare. Schine and Cohn outdid even McCarthy in half-cocked zealotry, running to Europe to purge U.S. Information Service libraries of "suspect" materials. Bobby blamed Cohn for McCarthy's mounting troubles but also McCarthy for encouraging him. When the senator placed Cohn in charge of the entire subcommittee staff, Kennedy protested and resigned.

"McCarthy was out of his mind to go along with them [Cohn and Schine]," Bobby told his friend Ed Guthman three years later. "But he was intoxicated—driven—by all the publicity. . . . It had to end in disaster, but Joe couldn't see it." It was an unusually candid admission. Bobby did not admire McCarthy, did not respect his methods, but would not speak ill of him. He kept his deep ambivalence toward McCarthy closely guarded. As McCarthy sank deeper into self-made ignominy, something in McCarthy's role as the underdog continued to appeal to Bobby; something in McCarthy's complexity intrigued him. McCarthy "wanted so desperately to be liked," Bobby said later. "He was sensitive and yet insensitive. He didn't anticipate the results of what he was doing. He was very thoughtful of his friends, and yet he could be so cruel to others."

Kennedy returned to the subcommittee staff in January 1954 on the opposite side, as minority counsel. He fixed his animus on Cohn and

Schine, helping to make a mockery of Cohn (and, indirectly, McCarthy) in public hearings on a particularly egregious case of Red-baiting. During the Army-McCarthy hearings, from April to June 1954, Kennedy distanced himself further from the self-destructing senator. Sitting behind the minority members, quietly scribbling notes for their use, Bobby was a discreet participant at the hearings. Yet he had his moment. Bobby fed a steady stream of questions to Senator Henry "Scoop" Jackson of Washington as Jackson, in some eleventh-hour political posturing, interrogated McCarthy on Schine's qualifications. Kennedy's cutting questions laid bare the obvious absurdity of the "Schine Plan" of psychological warfare and brought forth waves of laughter from the crowd. Committee members erupted in fits of giggles.

Sitting by his patron, Cohn seethed. His attempt at rebuttal cut short by the chairman's gavel, Cohn headed straight for Kennedy. "Tell Jackson we're going to get him on Monday," he snapped, thrusting a file folder like a weapon into Kennedy's face. "We've got letters he wrote to the White House on behalf of two known Communists."

"You tell him yourself," said Bobby curtly. His blue eyes turned dead cold in what friends later called "the look." "Don't threaten me. You've got a ———— nerve threatening me."

"Do you want to fight right here?" Cohn, hysterical, began to swing at Kennedy, but bystanders stepped in before punches were thrown. Kennedy walked away wearing a taut grin of contempt, a brief moment of relish at Cohn's undoing.

By 1955, McCarthy, too, had self-destructed. In 1956, Kennedy, after a disappointing but educational stint in Adlai Stevenson's second presidential campaign, moved on to a more fruitful field of inquiry: labor racketeering. Burgeoning union coffers and pension funds presented easy takings to shady union leaders and mobsters. A Senate investigation earlier that year offered a menacing glimpse of the creeping corruption, intimidation, and brutality infecting American labor. In January 1957, the Senate created the Select Committee on Improper Activities in the Labor or Management Field—the Rackets Committee, as it became known—and named John McClellan of Arkansas as chairman.

Even Kennedy, eagerly taking the position as chief counsel over his father's vehement objections (a racketeering probe being, at best, an inauspicious beginning to John Kennedy's courting of labor support for 1960), could not have foreseen the growing scope and significance of the investigation. What began tentatively as an inquiry into embezzlement became by 1959 one of the most sweeping and productive investigations in the Senate's history.

The counsel's office, the nerve center of the probe, had the unkempt air of a secondhand bookshop. Loose piles of documents cluttered the floor. Adding to the mess were the thousands of letters that flooded in weekly. Often anonymous, usually written in haste and fear, these letters testified to rigged union elections and stolen pensions, to beatings and intimidation, even to acid-throwings and murder. Kennedy was drawn in quickly, completely. Guthman, one of his assistants, noticed how instinctively Kennedy identified with the union rank and file, cheated by criminals and betrayed by their own leaders. But their distress symptomized a larger disease: from the beginning, as Guthman remembered, Bobby was "more concerned with what corruption, dishonesty and arbitrary use of power were doing to the democratic process and individual morality than he was with the specifics of the crimes that were being uncovered."

Yet Bobby's energy and wry levity broke the solemn weight of the committee's task. His staff appreciated his spirit. Young and dedicated— and numbering more than a hundred by 1958—they worked feverishly to match their tireless principal. Kennedy set an "unbelievable pace," remembered a staff member. One night during the investigation of Teamsters leader Jimmy Hoffa, Kennedy and his assistant Pierre Salinger left their Senate office at 1:00 A.M. Driving by the Teamsters' grand marble headquarters, they noticed the yellow glimmer of Hoffa's office lights. Kennedy turned the car around. "If he's still at work, we ought to be," he said, and they worked for two more hours. (After hearing this story, Hoffa took a special glee in leaving his office lights burning long after leaving for a restful night's sleep.)

Kennedy forged many of his closest bonds—with men like Salinger, Guthman, John Seigenthaler, and Kenneth O'Donnell—in this crucible. "I've seen a lot of counsels here," reflected LaVern Duffy after twenty-five years on the Government Operations Committee. "There was no one like him. He had an uncanny ability to get people to do more than they thought they could do. He didn't do this by bringing pressure on them. It was because they wanted to please him. He gave people a sense of personal interest in themselves, their work, their families. This was his secret. He never got mad except when someone lied to him. He couldn't stand that."

When Teamsters president Dave Beck lied to him and the Rackets Committee, Kennedy couldn't stand that, either. Beck, suspected of larceny and misuse of union funds, appeared before the committee in March 1957. He was smug with self-assurance. Barry Goldwater and other Republican senators offered friendly queries, dispatched by Beck with statesmanlike cool. As the first day ended, Bobby Kennedy leaned forward, barking out a staccato of detail, quickly overwhelming Beck.

Unlike the McCarthy hearings, these were not "fishing expeditions"; Kennedy rarely asked a question whose answer he did not already know, and it showed. This was the public's first introduction to the Kennedy manner: rapid, relentless, pointed questioning. Beck pled the Fifth Amendment sixty-five times before the hearings ended.

A *Chicago Daily News* reporter praised Kennedy for just "about the finest job I've ever seen on Capitol Hill. If ever Providential justice was ladled out in the Caucus room, you did it that day." Beck's unraveling at Kennedy's hands set the Teamsters president on the path to prison. The swift, crushing collapse of one of labor's most powerful leaders shot the Rackets Committee—and its thirty-one-year-old counsel—into national prominence and significance.

The hearings were a test and a competition of sorts for Robert Kennedy. As he himself admitted, "My biggest problem as counsel is to keep my temper. . . . To see people sit in front of us and lie and evade makes me boil inside. But you can't lose your temper—if you do, the witness has gotten the best of you." By his own standards, Kennedy was succeeding. He felt fulfilled and relevant, engaged in a cause of moral and political consequence.

Some political observers shared Kennedy's sense of a moral crusade; more were simply impressed by his stern but respectful demeanor in the televised hearings. Privately, his rare candor disarmed most reporters. No one failed to notice, as the *Cleveland Press* pointed out, that "this is Bob Kennedy's show so far." When Kennedy was in Seattle to interview witnesses during the Beck hearings, passersby shouted greetings and congratulations, or stopped to urge him solemnly to "keep going." Kennedy, surprised and quietly thrilled by the reception, waved shyly and mumbled his thanks. The public seemed to agree with the *Kansas City Star* that Kennedy had "by his own intelligence, initiative and courage established himself as a real 'comer.' "

But to many others, Kennedy had revealed himself as a vicious, opportunistic zealot, eagerly trampling civil liberties to carry out personal vendettas. A Berkeley professor wrote Kennedy to decry his "juvenile antics" and suggest that he call his memoirs *Profiles in Bullying*. A correspondent of John Kennedy's compared Bobby's "brow-beating, badgering and attempts to bulldoze the witnesses" to the "same insolent and overbearing manner which was the downfall of Senator McCarthy." A caricature of "ruthless Bobby" emerged and never entirely faded.

Jimmy Hoffa, the Rackets Committee's next target, shared this view of RFK and promoted it: Kennedy "got his jollies playing God," he bellowed. But Hoffa was developing his own public relations problems. His dictatorial hold on the Teamsters and his ties to mob figures were drawing considerable suspicion on Capitol Hill. If "it was the investigation of Beck that opened Kennedy's eyes," Guthman recalled, "it was the investigation of Hoffa that revealed to him the depths of the corruption, venality and violence in the ranks of labor and management." Each found the other a perfect antagonist: to Kennedy, Hoffa was a kingpin who exploited and brutalized honest workers for his own gain; to Hoffa, Kennedy was a pampered, insolent brat who had inherited everything and worked for nothing.

Like Beck's, Hoffa's trademark cocksureness quickly faltered under Kennedy's public scrutiny, but Hoffa proved a more elusive witness. Beginning in the summer of 1957, reconvening the following spring, and interrupted by the testimony of countless thugs and mobsters, the Hoffa hearings were lengthy and brutal, leaving both sides enervated. "Look at him, look at him!" a smirking Hoffa yelled at Kennedy one long afternoon. "He's too tired. He just doesn't want to go on." "I am mentally fatigued," Bobby admitted in a personal note. "This year seems to have been tougher than last. . . . I feel like we're in a major fight. We have to keep going, keep the pressure on or we'll go under."

By 1959, Kennedy was drained and disillusioned. The committee's shocking revelations—including, for the first time, strong evidence of an organized criminal underworld—seemed to have little impact. "Candor compels me," Kennedy wrote in June, "to say that in the months since the committee began to work, conditions in the labor and management fields have actually grown worse." Hoffa flaunted his acquittals in the courts. Worst of all, two years of intensive investigations had produced only three convictions by the Justice Department. Kennedy's tedious, exhausting efforts seemed to have been largely in vain.

He turned to a legislative solution. At Bobby's insistence, John Kennedy and Senator Sam Ervin of North Carolina drafted a bill providing for fair and supervised labor elections. Fighting a coalition of business, Teamsters, and the Eisenhower administration, Senator Kennedy forged a compromise between his bill and the House's more severe (and thus less acceptable) Landrum–Griffin bill. When the resulting piece of legislation passed, Robert Kennedy proffered his resignation on September 10, 1959, ending his participation in one of the longest, most publicized congressional investigations in history. He had directed the questioning of more than fifteen hundred witnesses over nearly three hundred days of hearings. In holding the spotlight for more than two years, he had become something more than Joe Kennedy's son or Jack Kennedy's brother. But once again, as Bobby drifted back toward politics, his career merged with that of JFK.

Their paths had never been entirely distinct. Fiercely clannish, Bobby had not really tried to shake free of his role as kid brother. As a public perception it lingered: the Rackets Committee hearings may have been "Bobby's show," but newsreels rarely caught him alone. Bobby lit into witnesses, holding the microphone and owning the spotlight, but John Kennedy, a committee member, sat quietly beside him, sagely reclining in his chair.

This TV image—cool Jack, fierce Bobby—was a telling study in contrast. The brothers were dramatically different personalities. "Jack Kennedy is the first Irish Brahmin," Massachusetts Governor Paul Dever observed. "Bobby is the last Irish Puritan." Even as a child, Jack had been wry, reflective, coolly remote; Bobby had been earnest, engaged, explosive. Jack had accepted his own chronic sickliness with a shrug, affecting droll indifference; otherwise, he breezed carelessly through adolescence and early adulthood. Bobby, healthy and full of vigor, seemed steeled for struggle. As his Milton classmate David Hackett recalled, Bobby "was neither a natural athlete nor a natural student nor a natural success with girls and had no natural gift for popularity. Nothing came easily for him. What he had was a set of handicaps and a fantastic determination to overcome them."

Bobby considered himself an underdog—in class, on the playing field, as a Catholic—and sought out others like himself. His identity as a "black Irishman" remained undiluted by Harvard or, for that matter, the Court of St. James's. His ethnic identity, if affected at all by either experience, was hardened; he did not assimilate easily. While Jack detached himself somewhat from his father and his faith, Bobby assumed the Irish-American burden solemnly. This was not lost on Joe Kennedy, who turned to Bobby, not Jack, with family matters. Joe saw himself in his younger son: "Bobby's a tough one," he told a reporter admiringly in 1957. "He'll keep the Kennedys together, you can bet."

But keeping the Kennedys together demanded that the brothers close the gap of personality and experience between them. The union occurred relatively late. Bobby's absorption in his brother's life and career began only in adulthood. Until the 1950s, the two men were not even well acquainted, for Jack was away—at school and at war—while Bobby matured. They saw each other only at family gatherings. Eight years apart in age, Jack and Bobby "were really different generations," reflected Lem Billings, Jack's childhood friend.

Not until the autumn of 1951, during a seven-week trip from Israel to Japan, did the brothers connect as adults. But it was JFK's 1952 Senate race that truly brought them together. "The campaign," as Kenneth O'Donnell remembered, "began as an absolute catastrophic disaster." Joseph Kennedy kept a heavy hand on the operation, consorting with political has-beens and brooking no challenges to his authority. O'Don-nell, then a campaign worker, beseeched Robert Kennedy to leave his post in the Criminal Division of the Justice Department to rescue the campaign. Bobby was only twenty-six, but he understood the new pol-itics of Massachusetts, he had a talent for organization, and—most important—he could stand up to his father.

Bobby did not relish a family squall. He was wrapped up in his first heady investigation; the work thrilled him. Having no wish to leave Washington, he lashed out at O'Donnell in anger and frustration, feign-ing ignorance: "I don't know any of the players and I'll screw it up. . . . I just don't want to come."

"Unless you come," O'Donnell insisted, "I don't think it's going to get done."

Bobby went, reluctantly. "He was the most unhappy fellow that you ever saw in your life," recalled O'Donnell. But no one questioned Bobby's dedication. Working eighteen-hour days and shedding a dozen pounds, he organized an unconventional network of ethnic and profes-sional support that largely bypassed the traditional Democratic organiza-tion. Brusque and impatient with machine politicians, he was not in politics to win friends; the niceties of politics were an impediment and a bother. "If you're not going to work, don't hang around here," Bobby snapped at a senior labor leader chatting amiably at campaign headquar-ters. "Politicians do nothing but hold meetings," Bobby grumbled later. "You can't get any work out of a politician." Among volunteers he was more patient and trusting. Bobby listened to them, valued them, and stirred them to action. In the end, John Kennedy won the seat by a mar-gin of seventy thousand. His brother won an admiring legion of "Bobby Kennedy guys."

Bobby's political acumen impressed his older brother. "I don't think [Jack] was aware that Bobby had all this tremendous ability," said Lem Billings. As Bobby's latent talents blossomed, the brothers grew closer. Loyalty and shared ends were absolute. Socially distinct, temperamental-ly opposite, John and Robert Kennedy were politically symbiotic.

Through most of the 1950s, though, RFK was too consumed by investigative work to invest much energy in John Kennedy's Senate career. Bobby remained a valued political adviser, but "had almost noth-ing to do with the operations of the John Kennedy Senate office," as Myer "Mike" Feldman, a legislative assistant to JFK, explained later. Bobby dashed in and out of the office, eyes straight ahead, a fleeting pres-ence, leaving little impression on his brother's staff. He reminded one visitor of a disheveled paperboy. Lee White, another of the senator's aides, "didn't think of him as a political genius, but I had no reason to think anything else about him, either. He was not unfriendly; he was just not communicative or a 'hail fellow well met.' " Bobby displayed a seriousness of purpose and a fierce devotion to his brother's fortunes; little more. If he was an alter ego, as other advisers maintained, he was uncommonly discreet about it.

Indeed, freewheeling, expansive political strategy sessions were no more John's style than Bobby's. When the brothers talked politics, they did so in hushed tones, with only Feldman or JFK's closest aide, Ted Sorensen, present. And when they talked, they talked about 1960.

Since 1900, the United States had elected only one standing senator, Warren G. Harding, to the presidency. But John Kennedy, unlike previous contenders from the chamber, was not a member of the Senate "club." Nor had he ever sought to be. Joining the club, Kennedy told columnist Joseph Alsop, meant making shameful deals without betraying a hint of shame. Kennedy smiled sardonically; cynical bluster did not gush easily from this man of well-developed irony. Kennedy, as Harry McPherson recalled him, was elusive, less interested in the self-important spectacle of Senate business than with "other worlds outside the chamber"—social and intellectual orbits beyond the reach of Kennedy's parochial colleagues, whose conventions he regarded with vague bemusement. But John Kennedy's easygoing affability, his famous playboy charm, and his casually worn wealth made him an object of general affection, despite (and possibly because of) the fact that most senators regarded him a lightweight, a dilettante dabbling in politics.

John Kennedy's obvious popularity outside Capitol Hill drew disdainful but wary glances from rivals as 1960 approached. From the moment of his explosive national arrival in 1956, when he barely lost the vice presidential nomination to Estes Kefauver, observers correctly assumed that Kennedy—audacious as it might seem to congressional power barons—was plotting for the White House. After JFK's disappointment in 1956, Bobby offered consolation: "You're better off than you ever were in your life, and you made the great fight, and they're not going to win. You're going to be the candidate next time."

In the months after Stevenson's second loss to Eisenhower it began to seem that JFK might well be the candidate in 1960. Abraham Ribicoff, senator from Connecticut, and John Bailey, the highly efficient chairman of the state's Democrats, began a public drive for JFK. But endorsements were hard to extract from skeptical party leaders. "If the Convention ever went into the back rooms," Ted Sorensen said several months later, "he'd never emerge from those back rooms." Kennedy was not exactly the dark horse his advisers claimed, but it was clear that the primaries, carefully selected, were his proving ground. Only widespread voter support would jolt the Democratic establishment into support of a young, Northeastern, Catholic senator; only a series of stunning victories could convince many Northern party bosses—mostly Catholics themselves—that Kennedy's effort was not, like Al Smith's in 1928, doomed from the beginning.

No gloom of predestination blighted the Kennedy camp, however. Bullish confidence drove the effort throughout 1959. "We knew how it would turn out, that we could meet them [JFK's weaknesses] and lick them," said Ted Sorensen after the fact. Surely the challenge demanded a larger leap of faith than Sorensen remembered; but at the very least, there was no hand-wringing about whether to make the effort. When John Kennedy's closest advisers gathered in Palm Beach in April 1959 to draw up "the final assault plan," in Theodore White's words, they were preoccupied not by "the Yes or No of the Presidential strike, but the HOW: which levers, in what manner, must be pressed . . . to bring about the occupation of the White House."

The how was Bobby Kennedy's domain. Patiently and determinedly he laid the groundwork for his brother's challenge. At the 1956 Democratic Convention in Chicago, Bobby had scurried among the delegates, an anonymous blur, trailed by the dark and lanky Ken O'Donnell. "Bobby and I ran around like a couple of nuts and tried to make believe we were busy" collecting support for JFK's vice presidential bid, O'Donnell said later. Their efforts, he judged, were "a joke; we didn't know two people in the place." But Bobby was busily surveying and absorbing the workings of national organization. Sorensen remarked that Bobby was his brother's "first and only choice for campaign manager." RFK could be "trusted more implicitly, say 'no' more emphatically and speak for the candidate more authoritatively than any professional politician."

By October 1959, when sixteen of JFK's most important advisers gathered on a crisp Hyannis Port morning to flesh out the campaign structure, Robert Kennedy had finished *The Enemy Within,* his book on the Rackets Committee, and submerged himself completely in the campaign's mosaic of colored labels and files and indices. What mattered most, along the punishing road to the convention in Los Angeles, was the delegate count. While Sorensen—the candidate's "intellectual blood bank," as JFK put it—focused broadly on the big picture of national politics and policy, Bobby organized the gritty work of visiting remote party headquarters and assessing and courting delegates. Across the nation, local committees consolidated traces of Kennedy support; surrogates fed RFK a comprehensive census of players and factions.

But Robert Kennedy was too valuable a resource to keep at campaign headquarters. Again he showed his rapport with volunteers, especially women, minorities, and the young. Bobby's "genius as manager," Arthur Schlesinger observed, "lay in his capacity to address a specific situation, to assemble an able staff, to inspire and flog them into exceptional deeds and to prevail through sheer force of momentum." Yet his seasoning in political circles had not tempered his impatience with machine pols. He thought them phonies and showed it in his forbidding glare; they thought him malevolent and grumbled sorely among themselves. Both Kennedy brothers shared this suspicion of, or contempt for, what John Kenneth Galbraith called "the baroque tendencies of politics"—its equivocations and petty deceits. But while John Kennedy was controlled and conciliatory, Bobby erupted in petulant flashes of anger.

"Bob came out of that campaign," said Ron Linton, an ebullient young assistant to Salinger, "labeled as heartless, cold, hard, the axman." But Bobby's reputation—and the behavior that prompted it—was at odds with his private persona. One on one, Linton observed, Bobby was "sensitive and caring . . . a very warm, interested personality." He "did not particularly enjoy chopping people down, but if you weren't performing, [he was] not going to be nice to you." Bobby's standard of performance was exacting. When his campaign aides, stationed in Los Angeles well in advance of the national convention, spent an afternoon unwinding at Disneyland, RFK summoned his coordinators at headquarters early the next morning. Standing on a stool, he glared peevishly at his team. "It has come to my attention," he said, "that some of you think Disneyland is more important than nominating the next president of the United States. Those that do can just resign." Amusement parks, after all, were about amusement. Campaigns were about winning. Bobby Kennedy was not likely to confuse the two.

As Robert Kennedy advanced the how of his brother's candidacy in early 1960, Lyndon Johnson sat in a spacious office in the Capitol, ruminating endlessly on the telephone, teetering between yes and no. Whatever Johnson's regional liabilities, whatever his deficiencies in public charisma, an early and energetic effort would almost certainly have assured him his natural place among leading contenders. Yet Johnson continued to agonize. Through the spring of 1960, he firmly opposed any direct efforts while sanctioning "covert" activities by his surrogates. He listened patiently to reports by advance men who were trumpeting his name to delegates across the country, then upbraided and disavowed them.

Month after month, Johnson declared himself unsuited for the presidency, unlikely to win it, unlikely to survive it. He shunned the pri-

maries. He denied any ties to Citizens for Johnson, a group of his closest political allies. "I know nothing about it, Bill," Johnson told the AP's
Bill Arbogast, who had just reported the imminent opening of a Citizens
for Johnson headquarters in Washington. "I thought that was a very irresponsible story and I wondered where it came from."

"You know where it came from," Arbogast replied.

Johnson insisted he knew nothing about it. "I would think if I were
getting ready to launch a big headquarters and bring a big carnival to
town, I would know something about it."

"Good Lord, you know where I got it, don't you?" Arbogast repeated.

"No, I never heard of it."

"From Sam."

Sam Rayburn's stories were hurtful, Johnson complained. The news
was energizing his supporters, who were "giving me hell for not
announcing it to them." LBJ wished his friends would stop speaking to
reporters. "The Speaker talks to them and tells them I ought to be doing
this this way and that that way . . . and it gets in the paper and I spend
all the rest of the day denying it." Johnson blocked the opening of the
campaign headquarters. "Just let me do it my way!" he roared when
questioned by his confused enthusiasts.

Johnson's champions chafed with frustration. Convinced JFK's support was thin, they "wanted to get out and really fight," remembered
George Reedy. Reedy, Walter Jenkins, and the up-and-coming Texas
politician John Connally phoned delegates but garnered little more than
expressions of goodwill. With no commitment from Johnson, otherwise
sympathetic delegates pledged their support to JFK, at least for the first
ballot. Speaker Rayburn and Senate Secretary Bobby Baker, both out-
and-out Johnson men, agreed their friend was making a critical mistake.
"I've already done everything but hold a gun to Lyndon's head," the old
Texan scowled to Baker. "Lyndon's using his friends to raise money and
court delegates, and he's making them as well as himself look silly by
declaring himself a noncandidate. He ought to shit or get off the pot."

For all Johnson's dissembling, though, few savvy observers doubted
that he was—albeit tentatively—on the pot. His *de facto* candidacy was
poorly concealed. Local Texas politicians, eager to crash the national
party, loudly and gleefully subverted Johnson's careful machinations in
Washington. Mixing rowdily in Democratic circles in their ten-gallon
hats, yellow rose lapel pins, and whooping "All the way with LBJ," they
were so identifiably Texan they seemed straight from central casting.
Reporters deemed them the "noisemakers." They may have done LBJ
more harm than good. In Washington, Jim Rowe derided them as "a
bunch of . . . incompetent[s] . . . fouling things up around the country."

As summer approached, Johnson ordered Reedy, Jenkins, Connally, and others to clean up the mess.

Johnson's opponents noted his approaching, if stumbling, challenge. As early as February 1960, Bobby Kennedy declared publicly that "Senator Humphrey is our big rival now, but over the long run I expect Senator Johnson to be the principal opposition." Humphrey, too, thought Johnson's entry inevitable. If so, what held Johnson back? Why not openly enter the race and make a contest of it? Some aides blamed LBJ's fear of defeat, of gambling and losing it all. While accusing his advisers of feeding him "'can't win' bullshit," Johnson was the greatest handwringer in his own camp. Victory was certainly far from assured. And the costs of a protracted, public campaign were daunting: "Johnson had a lot to lose by throwing his hat flamboyantly into the ring when he had been king of the Senate," reflected Liz Carpenter, a Texas journalist and an eager campaign volunteer. More bizarrely, Johnson spoke of a conspiracy of "red hots"—labor, big-city machine pols, limousine liberals—out to humiliate or destroy him because he was "a Texan rather than a Harvard." Johnson's other fears—of winning a job that ill suited him or might even kill him—were better grounded.

In fact, Johnson's noncampaign was only partly the product of ambivalence. It was also rooted in his role in the Senate and his misreading of national politics. Johnson was not, as he wished to be, a national figure. Yet neither was Johnson, as he feared, a Texas provincial. After thirty years in the nation's capital, he was a Washington provincial, an avatar of the capital's peculiar brand of insularity. "America, to Johnson, was a vast power grid, whose dynamo was in Washington—its armature running between the Capitol and the White House," Harry McPherson explained. Omniscient in the Senate chamber, Johnson was myopic outside it. McPherson summed up the majority leader's paradox: "Power outside the Senate did not follow from power within, and vice versa.... Indeed there were times when they seemed mutually exclusive. The very absorption in legislation, in committee work, and in negotiating, that helped to make a man important within the Senate, made him less sensitive to what was happening in the country."

LBJ based his campaign in 1960 on this miscalculation and got—as Humphrey recalled—"a real awakening in American politics, a shock." Assuming that senators and congressmen controlled their states' delegations, Johnson expected that in the end, delegates and electoral votes would flow to him as a natural prerogative of his power. They did not. In the Kennedy camp, Ken O'Donnell imagined the astonishment of Johnson and Rayburn "as they suddenly started to realize that these fellows they were relying on really had no political clout at home." The majority leader discovered that governors, national committeemen, and party chairmen—not senators—controlled a state's political apparatus.

"Even I knew better," recalled McPherson. If Johnson did, too (as McPherson believed), he nonetheless relied upon legislators as the only forces under his firm command. Johnson was bound to the leader's chair. Political sojourns cost him more dearly than they did his competitors. Johnson felt trapped, and his resentment showed. As he fumed at Bobby Baker on the eve of the convention, "Jack Kennedy and other senators can go gallivantin' around the country kissin' asses and shakin' hands when they want to. But if I'd done it, the Senate business wouldn't have gotten done and the press would have crucified me for running out on my job." Legislative accomplishment, after all, was the bedrock of his candidacy, the basis for his claim to the presidency. If Johnson didn't "mind the store," no one would. The blame, like the responsibility, would be his alone.

Out of necessity, then, Johnson clung to the faith that public service (seemingly) for its own sake would be rewarded. This belief—like Johnson himself—struck Kennedy's campaign staff as a quaint anachronism. In Fred Dutton's view, Johnson was playing outmoded "manipulative politics" to Kennedy's modern "mass media politics." While LBJ courted deal-makers, Kennedy was courting *Life* magazine. And while Johnson's power brokers schemed, John Kennedy was wrapping up the Democratic nomination.

In March, a frustrated George Reedy typed a memo that he asked LBJ to read and then destroy. Reedy urged "a hatchet job" on Jack Kennedy. Others would continue the barrage on Kennedy's youth and religion, Reedy argued, so Johnson should focus on Kennedy's family name—and promote the idea that Joseph Kennedy was buying his son the Oval Office. *"Americans would bitterly resent the concept that the White House is a plaything to be handed out as a Christmas present,"* Reedy wrote.

Johnson demurred. Slurs and insinuation, though he had used them in the past, did not befit a self-professed builder of consensus. Besides, Johnson had no particular animus against Kennedy. Throughout the 1950s, Johnson treated JFK genially, playing the distant but fond uncle— a bit patronizing, a bit envious, a bit protective. When Kennedy underwent back surgery in the fall of 1954, Johnson asked JFK's father, Joseph, to "tell him for me how much we all love him." He wrote the recuperating Kennedy that Senate business would "go even better if I had my strong right arm, Jack Kennedy, on tap."

Much of this, of course, was the rote warmth of the career politician. But the wry young Kennedy intrigued Johnson, who spoke of JFK to

Walter Jenkins with affection and a "very healthy respect." It was a respect tinged with ambivalence. Was Kennedy apprentice, asset, or adversary to LBJ? In a sense Kennedy was the anti-Johnson; his strengths matched Johnson's perceived inadequacies. Johnson had attended Southwest Texas State Teachers College; Kennedy had gone to Harvard and published his senior thesis, *While England Slept.* Johnson, granted a Silver Star under dubious circumstances, revered Kennedy's heroics in the Pacific. In Lyndon's view, one aide recalled, "Jack was doing these incredibly brave things on that wonderful torpedo boat, medals all over, while all he [Johnson] did was sit in Melbourne, Australia" as a member of a congressional delegation. Kennedy's womanizing, too, aroused Johnson's (and many other senators') admiration: "Is ol' Jack gettin' much pussy?" Johnson once whispered to Bobby Baker. In the 1950s, Johnson often marveled, wide-eyed, at Kennedy's smooth orchestration of yet another tryst.

Johnson, accustomed to alliances with senators he considered near equals in power—Richard Russell of Georgia, Robert Kerr of Oklahoma—took an uncommon interest in the junior senator from Massachusetts. Johnson cultivated Kennedy, nurturing his career, grandly bestowing him favors. And as he pulled Kennedy closer, Johnson empowered him, boosting Kennedy's political stock by choice assignments. Still, LBJ was careful not to let him rise too quickly. Johnson dispensed lesser appointments but repeatedly denied Kennedy a prized and prominent seat on the Senate Foreign Relations Committee. In a more striking gesture of goodwill, Johnson delivered the Texas delegation to the "Kennedy for VP" drive at the 1956 Democratic Convention. "Texas proudly casts its vote for the fighting sailor who wears the scars of battle," Johnson declared on the convention floor. Days later, in a letter to Jack, Johnson unabashedly described the balloting as "one of the proudest moments of my life. . . . I can never go wrong backing Jack Kennedy."

Nor could Johnson go wrong undermining Estes Kefauver, Kennedy's opponent in vice presidential bidding. Johnson's generosity stemmed mostly from long-held contempt for the Tennessee senator, but LBJ also had an eye toward future ties to the Kennedys. A gesture to Jack Kennedy was also a gesture to his wealthy father. Recuperating by poolside after the convention, Johnson wrote Joe Kennedy to tell him "how proud I am of the Democratic Senator from Massachusetts. . . . In my opinion, that session of the Convention lighted the brightest lamp of hope for a truly great Democratic Party. I hope we can talk about this sometime when you are in Washington."

Johnson's letter also included an apology of sorts for his own native-son bid for the presidential nomination. "I have been thinking of a lot of things," Lyndon wrote Joe, "one of them being that phone call from you in October last year. You said then that you and Jack wanted to support me for President in 1956. . . . I told you I was not interested and it occurs to me that you may be somewhat mystified about my activities in Chicago last week. When I see you I will explain how they involved a local political situation here in Texas and were not inconsistent with what I told you last October."

"Last October" referred to the most unusual twist in Johnson's relationship with the Kennedys. In the autumn of 1955, Joe and Robert Kennedy met at an elite New York restaurant with Tommy Corcoran, a former aide to FDR and by the 1950s a mentor to Johnson. Joe made a striking offer: if Johnson would publicly announce his candidacy for president and privately pledge to take Jack Kennedy as his running mate, "I have friends who'll help finance the ticket," Joe promised. Corcoran carried the proposal to the LBJ Ranch in October, but returned to the Kennedys empty-handed. Johnson had denied any presidential ambitions. Joe was disappointed; Jack was unsurprised but curious about Johnson's hidden agenda. "Young Bobby," Corcoran recalled, "was infuriated. He believed it was unbelievably discourteous to turn down his father's generous offer."

Johnson saw Joe's offer as less magnanimous. As Corcoran conveyed to LBJ, Joe sought to make his son president in 1960, not vice president in 1956. Joe believed LBJ a likely loser to the popular Eisenhower, but thought a respectable showing by a Johnson-Kennedy ticket would position Jack nicely for the next presidential election. Yet Johnson had no wish to be Jack's stalking horse. Johnson, too, was looking toward 1960. That, he told intimates, would be the proper moment for a Johnson-Kennedy "dream ticket."

After 1956, however, Jack Kennedy would not be so easily relegated to second place. Kennedy was clearly a rising star whose fortunes could, perhaps, boost Johnson's own. Yet he appeared increasingly inclined to leave Johnson behind. Sensing the changing dynamic between them, Johnson became solicitous, even fawning. In January 1957, after toying with Kennedy's hopes for three years, Johnson finally placed him—again over Kefauver—on the Foreign Relations Committee. Columnist Doris Fleeson thought the appointment "the opening gun of . . . a Johnson-Kennedy ticket" for 1960. Later that year, LBJ gave special honor to Kennedy's efforts on behalf of the 1957 Civil Rights Act. "If they want to look for that courage they talk about," Johnson said, in a nod to JFK's *Profiles in Courage,* "they ought to look [at Kennedy]."

By 1958, however, pre-presidential jostling brought old resentments to the surface and created new ones. Kennedy, Johnson groused to columnist Arthur Krock, was ungrateful. Johnson claimed he had given Kennedy all the plum committee assignments, but Kennedy's backbiting staff was never satisfied. As Kennedy toiled to build a substantive legislative record to present to voters, Johnson let him struggle and spin. When Kennedy strove to pass bills on unemployment compensation and foreign aid, the majority leader stood aside.

The two senators remained outwardly cordial, but there was no disguising the fact that, as Kennedy aide Ralph Dungan stated, "they were contenders after a very big prize." And Kennedy's very ambitions offended Johnson's notion of political rank. Kennedy was popular, yes, but he was not *worthy*. Not of the presidency; not now, at age forty-two. He was not seasoned or accomplished or feared. Kennedy was no Lyndon Johnson.

Johnson began to savage his opponent in political circles. A conversation in March 1958 with Massachusetts Congressman Thomas "Tip" O'Neill revealed Johnson's scant regard for Kennedy's claim to the presidency. "You and I know the boy can't win," Johnson told O'Neill conspiratorially, referring to Kennedy only as "the boy," never by name. "He's just a flash in the pan. He has no record of substance." Johnson scoffed at O'Neill's first-ballot pledge to Kennedy. "Tip, I want you with me on the second ballot," he implored. "That boy is going to die on the vine." Over their regular cocktails with President Eisenhower, Johnson and Sam Rayburn ridiculed Kennedy as an overeager dilettante. Kennedy, they sneered, was barely a senator, let alone a presidential contender.

Johnson avoided voicing his opinion publicly, hoping instead that Hubert Humphrey could stop Kennedy in heavily Protestant West Virginia. Led by Senator Robert Byrd, Johnson's loyalists toiled for Humphrey—and against Kennedy—in the weeks before the state's May primary. In fact, it had been Johnson's men who encouraged Humphrey to enter the primary in the first place. By May 10, however, an aggressive Kennedy effort overwhelmed what had been a comfortable lead for Humphrey. Kennedy's victory jolted the political landscape. Humphrey withdrew. If Lyndon Johnson—as Bobby Kennedy had predicted—was JFK's only obstacle to the nomination, he was not an imposing one.

Inevitability bred cockiness. At the Washington premiere of *Guys and Dolls*, Bobby Kennedy introduced his show business friends to LBJ's associate Bobby Baker. "This is Little Lyndon Johnson," Baker recalled Kennedy saying. "You should ask him why Big Lyndon won't risk running in the primaries against my brother. They're supposed to make 'em tough down in Texas, but Big Lyndon doesn't look so tough to me."

Big Lyndon, meanwhile, was despondent one moment, defiant the next. "What are the possibilities? Are any left?" Johnson demanded of

Jim Rowe after West Virginia. Rowe suggested that Johnson encourage Adlai Stevenson to challenge Kennedy, thus opening the race for LBJ. Encouraged by Stevenson's mixed signals and unwilling to challenge Kennedy himself, Johnson clung to this hope. At other times, though, he insisted he would win the nomination on the merits: West Virginia had placed "this Catholicism thing in the background," Johnson told a friend, and "now they will start looking to see who's qualified. Nobody has ever examined Kennedy from that standpoint. It's kinda like, who's the home run hitter."

Still, Johnson remained a reluctant batter. He appeared more widely and frequently on his own behalf and stepped up his pursuit of delegates. Mocking the primaries as "beauty contests," Johnson insisted that "when it gets down to the nut-cuttin' [Kennedy] won't have the old bulls with him." But with the convention a mere two months away, Johnson's words rang hollow and his noncampaign sat stalled at a critical threshold. It was time for a shift in strategy. Desperately, scenting opportunity and fearing further embarrassment, Johnson mounted a "stop Kennedy" drive.

It was his last remaining hope for victory, and Johnson undertook it with relish. He went on the attack, making JFK and the Kennedys targets of his public and private ridicule. Echoing Reedy's strategy, Johnson's men accused Kennedy of buying votes in West Virginia and Oregon. America, Johnson said repeatedly, needed an experienced leader, a man "with a touch of gray in his hair." When the Soviet Union shot down an American U-2 spy plane, capturing its pilot, Johnson took the opportunity to lecture "Sonny Boy" on foreign policy. Johnson's aides, meanwhile, without the explicit consent of their principal, began a chorus of loud whispers that a Catholic candidacy was a doomed one. Johnson himself only reinforced the prejudice, attributing it with a shrug to politics: "None of these big-city leaders in New York, New Jersey, or Illinois want Kennedy. Most of them are Catholics and they don't want a Catholic heading up the ticket," LBJ told the columnist Drew Pearson. As June passed into July, Johnson supporters drew attention to Kennedy's thin Senate record and poor attendance at important votes. "Where Was Kennedy?" asked a Johnson memo. "He's smart enough," Johnson said, "but he doesn't like the grunt work."

More ominously, Lyndon and his men began to drop hints about Kennedy's health. In a conversation with Peter Lisagor of the *Chicago Daily News,* LBJ described John Kennedy as a "little scrawny fellow with rickets" and a host of other unknown diseases. "Have you ever seen his ankles? They're about so round," Johnson said, tracing a petite circle in the air with his finger. Publicly, LBJ remained above reproach, generously offering that all candidates had surely entered the race with their doctors' blessings.

Johnson's surrogates, however, finally blurted the unspeakable truth about John Kennedy's health. In Los Angeles, on the eve of the convention, John Connally and India Edwards, a Democratic *grande dame,* prepared to rebut charges against Johnson's well-being. Whisperings from the Kennedy campaign about Johnson's "heart condition" were fueling press speculation about LBJ's fitness for the presidency. "Don't you think it's time that we said something about Kennedy's health?" Connally asked Edwards. "Yes, I do," she agreed, adding, "John, let me do it. I have no career ahead of me, and you're a young man. It will cause a terrible stink."

Edwards based her allegations on well-established rumors. Among journalists and Johnson workers, hushed suspicions of a Kennedy mystery illness blossomed into sensational cries of a Kennedy cover-up. A "reliable" source told Edwards he had been present at a governor's mansion during a JFK campaign stop; Kennedy, this source insisted, had forgotten his cortisone and lapsed into a coma—until a state trooper rushed medicine to Kennedy's bedside under cover of night. Pursuing the matter with several physicians, Edwards extracted the diagnosis she was seeking. On July 4, she publicly declared that John Kennedy had Addison's disease, a disorder of the adrenal glands—and that Kennedy "would not be alive today if it were not for cortisone." Edwards and Connally urged a public evaluation of Kennedy's physical fitness for the presidency.

The news was explosive. According to Edwards, Johnson lashed out at her for this brazen bit of freelancing. An incredulous press corps regarded her charges as unusually underhanded; the *New York Times* buried the story on page 19. In the Kennedy camp, "it was as though a bomb went off," said Clark Clifford. Bobby Kennedy called a quick press conference to deny unequivocally that his brother had "an ailment classically described as Addison's disease," decrying "any statement to the contrary [as] malicious and false." A trumped-up medical report pronounced the candidate's health "excellent"—"superb," even—and attributed any "adrenal insufficiency" to JFK's "wartime experiences of shock and continued malaria." "Evidently," Bobby concluded, "there are those within the Democratic party who would prefer that if they cannot win the nomination themselves they want the Democrat who does win to lose in November."

Edwards's outrageous charges were, in fact, completely true. Since 1950, doctors had been administering cortisone to JFK—by injections, pills, and pellets implanted in his thighs. His father, Joe, had long concealed emergency stashes of medication in safety deposit boxes across the globe. As an adult, John Kennedy had received the last rites of the Catholic Church at least four times. According to biographer Richard Reeves, cortisone—and a host of other drugs, consumed daily, even hourly—kept Jack Kennedy alive. But Addison's could, at least, kill his campaign. Candor was out of the question. Smiling broadly, boasting of his own "vigor," Kennedy would blithely outlast the mud-slinging which he regarded as part of the game of politics.

Jack Kennedy implicated not LBJ but the Texan's overzealous aides, and rarely spoke of the matter again. To JFK's campaign staff, however, it was a "low blow" not to be forgotten. The most livid among them was Bobby Kennedy. Publicly, he echoed his brother: "I am confident," Bobby told the press, "that Senator Johnson will repudiate the irresponsible statements . . . which were undoubtedly made without his knowledge or consent." Bobby's famous zeal for truth-telling was taking second seat to his brother's political fortunes. Bobby denounced Edwards's charges as dirty slurs, off-limits even in a hard-hitting campaign. But Bobby did not blame Edwards. Unlike Jack, Bobby blamed Lyndon Johnson.

At one o'clock the next afternoon, July 5, a somber and self-assured Lyndon Johnson stood in the New Senate Office Building and finally declared himself a candidate for president. The *New York Times* dismissed Johnson's grand performance as "no surprise to anyone." It was too late and Johnson knew it. Delegates were already assembling in Los Angeles for the Democratic Convention; Johnson spent a scant two days campaigning before arriving there himself, on July 8. After meeting with Humphrey and Governor Robert B. Meyner of New Jersey, LBJ told intimates that "it is all over with. It is going to be Kennedy by a landslide."

Johnson's delegates, meanwhile, held fast to their illusions. Arriving in Los Angeles full of imprudent confidence and self-importance, the Texans expected the best of everything, perks worthy of the Senate majority leader and his men. To their horror, they were assigned to "the sorriest, nastiest [hotel] I've ever seen," complained delegate Jake Jacobsen. Their Massachusetts counterparts, meanwhile, luxuriated among Democratic luminaries (including LBJ) at the Biltmore Hotel. This contrast conveyed John Kennedy's control as succinctly as the delegate count. At a party convention, votes may be the currency of power, but hotels, cars, and floor passes are its symbols. And Johnson's men, Jacobsen complained, "were short of everything."

Most important, Johnson was short of delegates. By his own generous estimate, he trailed Kennedy by a hundred—a daunting though surmountable margin. But as the convention began on July 11, Johnson appeared resigned. In LBJ's Biltmore suite, Johnson and Jim Rowe swallowed their dinners in silence as the image of Idaho Senator Frank Church, the keynote speaker, flickered on the television screen. Johnson turned to Rowe. "I don't see how we can stop this fellow [Kennedy], do you?" Johnson said quietly. Rowe did not.

Face to face at last with the vaunted Kennedy "machine," LBJ saw the folly of his own exertion and, embarrassed and exhausted, simply wanted to "get it over with," in George Reedy's words. Yet the heat of Johnson's recent rhetoric had obligated him to a coalition of the discontented—a considerable if unruly mix of anti-Kennedy forces, Johnson loyalists, Southerners, and congressional leaders. They compelled a drive to the last. Johnson's pride, too, bristled at the thought of losing to Kennedy. "I can't stand to be pushed around by that forty-two-year-old kid," Johnson sneered to Adlai Stevenson. Frustration and resentments burst to the surface; Johnson and his aides continued to lash out, viciously, personally. In the last days before the convention, a Johnson man called journalist Theodore White and said, "I think you should know that John Kennedy and Bobby Kennedy are fags."

"You're crazy," White said, laughing.

The aide was insistent. "We have pictures of John Kennedy and Bobby Kennedy in women's dresses at Las Vegas this spring at a big fag party. This should be made public." White said he would do so as soon as he had the pictures in hand. "I'll get you the pictures in twenty-four hours," the man assured. No pictures ever arrived. According to Salinger, the caller (whose identity neither Salinger nor White disclosed) occupied a high post in President Johnson's administration by 1964.

LBJ and his men continued to assail Jack Kennedy's youth, his inexperience, even his Catholicism. But Johnson reserved his ugliest public words for other members of the Kennedy family, whose many members seemed to pervade even the quietest corners of the convention hall. On July 8, echoing charges by former president Harry Truman, LBJ raised the sinister specter of convention "rigging." "Is this convention open or has the outcome been determined somewhere in a back room?" an indignant Johnson wondered aloud en route to Los Angeles. LBJ referred to a *New York Times* article in which Robert Kennedy predicted the nomination would be settled by Monday at noon—five hours before the convention's official opening. "There are countries in the world where such pure arrogance is customary in politics," Johnson declared piously. "This is not that kind of a country."

Later that afternoon, Bobby Kennedy charged mysteriously that Teamsters locals in Los Angeles had been ordered to "whoop up" the flagging Johnson campaign. It was a curious implication, especially in light of the antagonism between Lyndon Johnson and organized labor. That day, in fact, George Meany, president of the AFL–CIO, had begun inciting delegates to bar LBJ from the ticket, loudly decrying "intimidation" by the "Johnson operation" in the Senate. But Jimmy Hoffa's Teamsters were union rogues, expelled from the AFL–CIO, and no one seemed more qualified to comment on their activities than the Rackets Committee's Bobby Kennedy. LBJ vehemently denied any relationship with Hoffa. Johnson was weary, too, of the Kennedys' attempts to "smear candidates through guilt by association. . . . It is a tactic used by the late Senator [Joe] McCarthy and it shows up repeatedly at this convention."

It was a masterful statement, at once condemning the politics of insinuation and putting them to use. LBJ pointed obliquely to Bobby Kennedy's known association with Joe McCarthy, an object of Johnson's public contempt. Senator Johnson had gone on the record early against McCarthy. In July 1949, LBJ joined several other powerful members of the Senate Armed Services Committee in defending Raymond Baldwin, a Connecticut Republican, against McCarthy's accusations. Two years later, when McCarthy charged General George Marshall with aiding the Communist drive for world domination, Johnson led a group of Democratic senators who favored a direct confrontation with the Wisconsin senator. Mostly, Johnson kept silent, conscious of McCarthy's widespread support in Texas and awaiting an opportune moment to attack; McCarthy, after all, was doing plenty to destroy himself. In Baker's recollection, Johnson considered McCarthy little more than "a loud-mouthed drunk," but kept well clear of him: "you don't get in a pissin' contest with a polecat," Johnson declared.

In 1954, McCarthy, weak and bloodied by the Army hearings, gave Johnson his opportunity. LBJ helped handpick the members of the censure committee and set a moral tone for the debate: breaking his party's silence, he announced, "Each of us must decide whether we approve or disapprove of certain actions as standards of Senatorial integrity. I have made my decision." The censure vote, though a foregone conclusion, was one of Johnson's finest moments. During the debate, he stalked the Senate floor and bore down upon squeamish Democrats, losing only one Democratic vote: John F. Kennedy of Massachusetts, who lay in a Boston hospital bed recuperating from two serious spinal operations.

No one had expected Kennedy to show for the debate, but the fact that he failed to vote by proxy did not surprise LBJ. Massachusetts was more pro-McCarthy than even Wisconsin. And then there was the senator's brother. In Johnson's words, Bobby was a "liberal fascist," "one of McCarthy's toadies." Even after Bobby's split with McCarthy, his status as minority counsel on McCarthy's committee was seen as evidence of undying loyalty. As Liz Carpenter put it, Johnson's abiding memory of Robert Kennedy in the 1950s was of "a fallen-away Kennedy . . . kissing Joe McCarthy's ass."

If Johnson was resigned to defeat, making hollow gestures to please his well-wishers, he was striking with convincing venom. In his only memorable statement of the entire convention, Johnson implied that Joe Kennedy, as Franklin D. Roosevelt's ambassador to Great Britain, was a Nazi appeaser. "I was never any Chamberlain umbrella policy man," Johnson told Washington state delegates hours before the balloting. "I never thought Hitler was right." Years later, Bobby Kennedy spoke of the comment with bile barely diminished.

Each bitter thrust, however, came to nothing. They revealed Johnson's campaign for what it was—vain, scattered, desperate. In a final, sad gambit, Johnson invited Jack Kennedy to debate in front of the Texas and Massachusetts delegations on July 12. He was deftly deflated by Kennedy's dry wit. Johnson, earnest and uptight, deconstructed his opponent's absenteeism and his record on agriculture and civil rights; Kennedy, by now confident of victory, smiled bemusedly and beneficently. "I don't think Senator Johnson and I disagree on the great issues that face us," he demurred. JFK returned to his chair on the dais, exchanging sly grins and whispers with Bobby, who sat at his side. John Kennedy's remote magnanimity seemed the stuff of real leadership compared to Johnson's schoolmarmish harping about quorum call attendance. "My God," observed political scientist John Roche, "Jack made mincemeat of him."

Privately, and with equal futility, Johnson continued to press Adlai Stevenson to stop Kennedy. Fearing that the collapse of the Stevenson drive would prompt a surge of delegates to carry Kennedy to victory, LBJ urged Stevenson to hold on to his eighty to a hundred delegates. "If I don't get it, it will be you," Johnson had promised Adlai in May, and now he pushed Minnesota Senators Hubert Humphrey and Eugene McCarthy to throw (temporary) support to Stevenson. Meanwhile, Johnson's minions scattered across the convention floor, fomenting a first-ballot Stevenson "boom," encouraging notions of the two-time loser as a "port in the storm."

It was an artless and transparent ploy. Johnson had now broken all three of the promises he had made to Bobby Kennedy the previous autumn: having entered the presidential race and attacked JFK, he was now aiding Stevenson, the man he had solemnly pledged to deny the nomination at all costs. Bobby Kennedy was incensed. He was, by now, incapable of even superficial convention banter with his adversaries. "He had that look on his face," remarked journalist Murray Kempton; it was a look that expected—perhaps invited—confrontation. Bobby Baker saw the look at breakfast at the Biltmore, where he encountered Bobby Kennedy. When Baker suggested mildly that Ted Kennedy had been perhaps "a bit rough" in suggesting that Johnson had not fully recovered from his 1955 heart attack, Bobby Kennedy's face flushed red. "You've got your nerve," he snapped, clenching his fists, leaning forward threateningly. "Lyndon Johnson has compared my father to the Nazis and John Connally and India Edwards lied in saying my brother is dying of Addison's disease. You Johnson people are running a stinking damned campaign and you're gonna get yours when the time comes!" According to Baker, Kennedy narrowed his eyes, slapped three one-dollar bills on the table, and stormed off.

The public perception of Bobby as brawler, as Jack's fixer, was calcifying. "Whenever you see Bobby Kennedy in public with his brother, he looks as though he showed up for a rumble," a reporter observed. In political circles, Kennedy did not help his own reputation by strong-arming powers like Governor Pat Brown of California. "I want you to release that [California] delegation today, and I want you to come out for my brother," Kennedy demanded, his words clipped and impatient. Brown was shocked by Bobby's impudence. He held his delegates for three more days.

At their headquarters in room 8315, however, Kennedy's staff found Bobby's presence uplifting and galvanizing. Standing on a chair to project his nasal, boyish voice, Bobby displayed total freedom from illusion. He demanded not optimism but precision. On Wednesday morning, the day of the nomination, Bobby's delegate count showed 740. It was twenty-one short of victory. "We can't miss a trick in the next twelve hours," he told the group. "If we don't win tonight, we're dead."

On the night of July 13, as the first few delegations eased into the Kennedy column, LBJ was the only major politician who appeared genuinely shocked. He spat irrelevant orders at aides and slammed down telephones. He cursed and sulked. Still, at other moments, he seemed to one aide "gay, relaxed and possibly relieved." And finally, he sat dejectedly in his suite, wearing a sports shirt, slacks, and house slippers, staring sullenly at the returns. Before the indignity was complete, Johnson stood and announced to the handful of friendly reporters that he was going to bed. He missed no all-night political maneuvering or secret brokering; those who remained awake watched Kennedy's delegate count rise to a convincing 806. Johnson received 409. His Stevenson boom sputtered at 79½.

The only intrigue to be found at the convention, then, was in John Kennedy's selection of a running mate. And Lyndon Johnson, by all accounts, was out of the picture entirely.

CHAPTER 2

The Affront

"Time and years will eventually hammer the conflicting recollections of the participants into a commonly accepted truth, which will then become the final truth," wrote Theodore White in 1961. But more than thirty-five years later, the only final truth about the selection of Lyndon Johnson as the Democratic vice presidential nominee is that it shattered, irreparably, the already fragile relationship between LBJ and Bobby Kennedy. It doomed any attempts to reconcile these two men, their ardent allies, or even their ideas. And it bred resentments that Johnson and Kennedy carried to their graves.

It was all based on a misunderstanding, though hardly a simple one. The story of the 1960 Democratic National Convention—and the real beginning of the Johnson-Kennedy feud—is a convoluted chronology of misreadings, miscommunications, and missed connections. Contrary to White's expectation, the "conflicting recollections of the participants" still conflict. The burgeoning stacks of memoirs and histories of the Kennedy years have muddled the picture further, creating new contradictions and casting doubt upon common assumptions. "There were only three persons who knew the whole story, and now one is gone," Bobby told a friend after the assassination of JFK. "I guess it will have to wait until Lyndon and I write our memoirs." And those versions, he conceded, would probably differ.

In the vast tapestry of conflicting accounts there are, however, common threads. What emerges clearly is that John Kennedy, prior to his own nomination, gave only cursory consideration to the vice presidency. And when Kennedy did think about running mates, he rarely thought of Lyndon Johnson.

Two of Kennedy's aides did, however. In June, a month before the convention, press secretary Pierre Salinger confessed a "hunch" to Earl Mazo of the *New York Herald-Tribune* that the Democratic ticket would be Kennedy-Johnson. Mazo read the hunch as a deliberate leak of inside information; it was not. In fact, there was no serious internal discussion of the vice presidency until June 29, when Ted Sorensen submitted to John and Robert Kennedy a one-page memo—an outline, really—titled "Possible Vice Presidential Nominees." Lyndon Johnson topped the list. The majority leader "helps [the ticket] with farmers, Southerners and Texas," Sorensen wrote, adding that LBJ would be "easier to work with in this position than as majority leader." Among other possibilities, Sorensen named Senators Hubert Humphrey and Stuart Symington, both Midwesterners. Governor Orville Freeman of Minnesota and Senator Henry "Scoop" Jackson of Washington State were worthy of consideration though "handicapped by being young and too much like JFK (we don't want the ticket referred to as 'the whiz kids,' etc.)."

In recommending LBJ, Sorensen had in mind a curious encounter with Bobby Baker earlier in June. Meeting Sorensen by chance at a social gathering, Baker, who was given to loud predictions of a Johnson-Kennedy ticket, conceded that the ticket might, after all, read "Kennedy-Johnson." "That would be wonderful, but I doubt very much that the second man on that ticket [LBJ] would agree to it," Sorensen responded. "Don't be too sure," Baker replied mysteriously, and encouraged the Kennedy campaign to pursue the possibility.

Whether Baker was acting on his own initiative or Johnson's was unclear. The question went unexplored in the remaining weeks before the convention. Sorensen and John Kennedy kept this intriguing political intelligence between themselves; they did not share it with Kennedy's top political aides Ken O'Donnell and Larry O'Brien, or even with Bobby Kennedy. Nor did Sorensen's memo evoke a response; it was still too early.

As the convention drew closer and Johnson's attacks grew more visceral and brutal, Baker's proposal seemed more and more implausible. Reconciliation between Johnson and the Kennedys seemed increasingly impossible or, at least, distasteful. Few, anyway, believed an ego of Johnson's girth could be squeezed comfortably into the ticket's second seat. John Kennedy intimated he would pick Humphrey or another Midwesterner; through Clark Clifford, Kennedy also made strong gestures to Symington. Journalists focused on Symington, Jackson, and Freeman. By the time of the convention, Salinger, if asked, would have changed his prediction to Kennedy-Symington. Lyndon Johnson, remembered Arthur Schlesinger, became "the one name that no one ever mentioned."

This was not exactly true. Fed largely by LBJ, press speculation continued about a Kennedy-Johnson ticket. In Washington on July 3, reporters asked LBJ if he might accept the second spot. "Well, that is a very iffy question," Johnson began, "and I wouldn't want to have it even thought that I would refuse to serve my country in any capacity, from running the elevator to the top job, if I felt that my services were needed." The next day he was less coy: "I have been prepared throughout my adult life to serve my country in any capacity where my country thought my services were essential."

If JFK noticed these signals he did not heed them. Arriving at New York's Idlewild Airport from Hyannis Port on the night of July 8, JFK was asked if he would consider Lyndon Johnson as his running mate. "Certainly," Kennedy said, "although I don't think he's interested in that at the moment." Meanwhile Bobby Kennedy and his campaign staff, now in Los Angeles, were taking pains to convince liberals and organized labor that Johnson was off JFK's short list. Humphrey was off, too: he had sided with Stevenson. John Kennedy renewed his overtures to Symington's liaison, Clark Clifford, and told Clifford in the days before the balloting that he had reached a "final decision" for Symington. Clifford privately "wondered how many others were being told the same thing"; rumors were circulating that Bobby Kennedy had promised the vice presidency to four or five men.

Bobby in fact had made promises to no one. His own list was short: Symington and Jackson. Symington was palatable, labor's choice, but Bobby preferred Jackson, the young senator dismissed by Sorensen as "too much like JFK." Like Jack Kennedy, Scoop Jackson was an ambitious outsider in the Senate. Jackson was liberal on domestic issues and tough on foreign affairs; he was an expert in the more arcane aspects of national security. "He did not disturb or excite, but he was consistently reasonable," Harry McPherson later observed. Kennedy campaign workers believed Bobby to be a "Jackson man."

On July 9, at Kennedy headquarters in the Biltmore, Bobby ate a late lunch of a turkey sandwich and a glass of milk and discussed Jackson with Ed Guthman, a Seattle journalist. "He's my choice," Bobby said, "and Jack likes him. . . . Scoop would help us in the West, but between now and Thursday he is going to have to convince some of the Midwestern and Eastern leaders . . . that he can help the ticket the most. We've told him that, and he understands it. I hope he can do it." Gestures to Symington might be written off as attempts to flatter him out of the presidential race (he still held nearly a hundred delegates), but Bobby's interest in Jackson seemed heartfelt. On Wednesday, though, Bobby cautioned Washington state delegates that his personal preference "is not going to determine who is selected" as the vice presidential nominee.

It was a prescient comment. By Wednesday, unknown to the frantically busy Bobby or other top campaign aides, JFK's thinking on the vice presidency had become increasingly blurred. Tentatively but inexorably, John Kennedy had begun to move toward the selection of Lyndon Johnson. Kennedy had long considered Johnson the man most qualified to be president, the man, as Kennedy told national security expert Walt Rostow in 1958, with "the most legitimate claim in the party for the nomination"—more legitimate than his own. Yet Johnson was unelectable to the highest office. No Southern man was going to win the presidency, Kennedy told Rostow. "It's too close to Appomattox."

Still, Johnson's regional appeal and political gravitas made him a considerable asset to any ticket; Sorensen had been right. On Sunday night, July 10, Kennedy mentioned offhandedly to *Washington Post* publisher Philip Graham that if LBJ was willing to accept the vice presidency, Kennedy just might offer it. The bitterness of an ugly contest was being subsumed by political expediency.

At Kennedy's suite the next night, July 11, Graham and columnist Joseph Alsop made an eloquent, detailed pitch for LBJ's electoral strengths. Kennedy agreed immediately—"so immediately," Graham wrote days later in a lengthy memorandum, "as to leave me doubting the easy triumph." Pressing his point, Graham urged Kennedy not to court or expect rejection but to persuade LBJ to join the ticket. This, Kennedy assured, was his intention, and he noted that Johnson would bolster the ticket nationally in ways that Symington could not. "Joe and I were a bit shaken by his positiveness," Graham wrote, since "Bobby had told me earlier that Johnson would not be considered." But the two men left Kennedy's suite convinced that JFK had resolved to pick Johnson.

Johnson had other advocates, including some Eastern governors and urban machine pols. On Tuesday evening, July 12, Tommy Corcoran caught JFK alone in an elevator and apologized for Johnson's slurs against Joseph Kennedy. "We've got to patch up this split between you and Lyndon," Corcoran recalled saying. JFK listened, amused. They had reached his floor, and the elevator door slammed repeatedly on Corcoran's foot as he held it open. "I don't blame you for hating him tonight," Corcoran continued, "but I'm talking politics." He stressed a Kennedy-Johnson ticket as a means to win the South, finesse the religious issue, and bring the party together.

"Stop kidding, Tommy," Kennedy said. "Johnson will turn me down." Corcoran asked for Kennedy's permission to pursue the matter with LBJ. Kennedy smiled and nodded. "Tommy, you have peculiar abilities," he said, and stepped out into the corridor.

Corcoran was quickly vindicated. That same evening at Chasen's restaurant, at a United Steelworkers buffet supper, Congressman Tip

O'Neill passed along a crucial signal from the Johnson camp: if Kennedy wanted Johnson, Johnson would not turn him down. Kennedy and O'Neill, lit by spotlights and surrounded by a thin police cordon and several hundred onlookers, stood and talked on the sidewalk outside Chasen's. "Of course I want Lyndon Johnson," Kennedy said, apparently delighted. "The only thing is, I would never want to offer it to him and have him turn me down; I would be terrifically embarrassed. He's the natural. If I can ever get him on the ticket, no way can we lose."

Twenty-four hours later, as John Kennedy claimed his party's nomination, many of Lyndon Johnson's staff packed their bags. "We thought our party was over," Walter Jenkins remembered. There was little talk within his camp of the vice presidency, though rumors filtered in from several different sources that Kennedy was about to offer the second spot to LBJ. Johnson appeared nonplussed. When the Missouri delegation switched its first-ballot votes to Kennedy, Johnson sniffed a deal; "There's your vice president," he said in reference to Symington. But when he learned that the midnight edition of California's Knight Newspapers counted him out of the vice presidential race, LBJ was quietly enraged. He was convinced Bobby Kennedy had planted the story to humiliate him.

Did Johnson want the vice presidency? Or did his dignity demand no more than an offer, the right of first refusal? On Monday, learning of Phil Graham's conversation with Kennedy, LBJ seemed to dread an offer: "Shit!" he said, and did not elaborate. But on Wednesday night, when Tommy Corcoran sought Johnson's permission "to work out the option" with JFK, the majority leader shrugged his shoulders. "Only if Sam goes along with it," Johnson told Corcoran. "He hates Kennedys."

The speaker snapped at Corcoran. "No, I won't go along with it," he said. "I wouldn't trust Joe Kennedy across the street. He'll double-cross us sure as hell." To all present, Rayburn loudly declaimed his vehement opposition to a Kennedy–Johnson ticket. LBJ later maintained that at 2:00 A.M. Rayburn directed him flatly not to accept the vice presidency. "Don't get caught in that trap. Don't accept," the speaker allegedly told him. But the next morning, July 14, Rayburn declared himself a convert. Someone—either Connally, Graham, or Congressmen Hale Boggs and Wright Patman, depending on the account—had convinced him, apparently, that only a Kennedy-Johnson ticket could beat Richard Nixon. To the shocked Texans who gathered in Johnson's suite, Rayburn shrugged his shoulders. "I'm a damn sight smarter than I was last night," he said sheepishly.

Johnson was Rayburn's political protégé; he rarely acted without the old Texan's approval. The speaker's "conversion" therefore cleared Johnson's path to the vice presidency. But "it is inconceivable," as Johnson's biographer Robert Dallek writes, "that as astute a politician as Rayburn needed instruction on what Johnson's presence on the ticket would mean." On the night of Kennedy's victory, after all, Rayburn had been quietly propagating rumors of a Kennedy offer—even personally urging Kennedy to choose LBJ. If Rayburn's obstinance was a ruse, as it appears in fact to have been, it was a crucial and carefully constructed one. In the ashes of Johnson's presidential bid, any eagerness for the vice presidency would have appeared unseemly, if not shameful or outrageous. LBJ and Connally had filled campaign coffers by promising to win the presidency; under no circumstances, they promised, was the vice presidency an option. "Texas is going to be very unhappy if I take it," LBJ told John Connally on Thursday morning. This was an understatement. Yet if a reluctant Rayburn could be convinced, other Texans, though embittered, would follow.

Stubbornly proud, Johnson was hardly more eager than his supporters to see his name second to anyone's on the November ballot. But equivocation suited yet another purpose: if Johnson appeared reluctant, he might win promises of expanded vice presidential powers. These, Johnson may have reasoned, would be his due as a powerful majority leader and a crucial element in a Kennedy victory.

But what could a powerful majority leader gain by becoming vice president, even an unprecedently influential vice president? This, to Johnson's partisans, was the crux of the matter. After the heady 1950s, when LBJ dominated Capitol Hill and showered patronage and prestige upon his constituents, the vice presidency could seem only a massive step down, an emasculation. The office which John Nance Garner, FDR's Texan vice president, had famously derided as worth less than "a pitcher of warm spit" was, to men like LBJ, an object of derision.

From the vantage point of 1960, however, Johnson's choice was not between the vice presidency and control of the Senate. The majority leader had lost his hold; Democrats were far less pliable than they had been in the mid-1950s. Johnson's effectiveness as leader was "finished," Senator Theodore F. Green of Rhode Island told Tommy Corcoran. And if Johnson shrugged off his party's standard by refusing to run with Kennedy, LBJ stood to lose what remained of his authority, if not his leadership itself; his perceived culpability in a Kennedy loss could cripple him. Neither did he relish being majority leader after a Kennedy victory. A Democratic majority leader under a Democratic president could expect to run legislative errands for the White House. Johnson would be "constrained," said Texan Jack Valenti, "fettered, on [a] leash." He would take the blame for Kennedy's legislative failures and little credit for his own successes. If a Kennedy-Johnson ticket lost, though, LBJ could return to the Senate valiantly, as a paragon of self-sacrifice and party loyalty and with a strong claim to the nomination in 1964.

And what of a Kennedy-Johnson victory? "Power is where power goes," Johnson told Jim Rowe the night of Kennedy's nomination, and seemed to believe it. LBJ had transformed offices before, transcended their boundaries, generated and sustained his own authority. "He was thinking," a friend explained, "that he could run Congress from the vice presidency." Perhaps he sensed that a Kennedy White House, unlike its predecessor, would be a center of activism. It was implicit in Kennedy's campaign rhetoric, the call for change: "We can do better." The vice presidency was the closest Johnson, for the time being, could get to the action.

If not, if the vice presidency brought only obscurity and political atrophy, it might, at least, be a peaceful denouement to an exhausting political career. This was Lady Bird's hope, if not LBJ's. Johnson's tight control of his colleagues and institution in the 1950s had exacted a heavy cost; it nearly killed him in 1955. Lady Bird feared the pace and relentlessness of the majority leadership and her husband's inability to invest any less than his whole self in the job. She expected that the next heart attack would kill him.

Escape from the Senate may have also offered Johnson an escape from sectionalism. His previous attempts to transcend his Texan or regional identity had foundered; now the vice presidency offered Johnson an opportunity (perhaps his last) to become a truly national leader, to liberate himself from what Arthur Schlesinger called "the Texas trap." Yet national office, or national candidacy, was not an abandonment of his roots. LBJ felt deeply responsible for the South and its future in American politics. As Schlesinger recalled, Johnson "used to lament the fact that so much southern political energy was diverted from constructive channels to the defense of the past . . . fighting for lost causes." To remain in the Senate and adopt anything but a subservient pose to a Kennedy White House would be to assume *de facto* leadership of a reactionary force, a Southern conservative faction in opposition to a liberal administration. The prospect appalled him. LBJ wanted integration and acceptance of the South into the party, and only by placing a Southerner on the ticket could the Democrats halt a Southern retreat into a backward bitterness.

In the late hours of July 13 and early the next morning, these concerns pressed upon Lyndon Johnson. He weighed the agonies of running a recalcitrant Senate against the indignities of running nothing much at

all. He thought of health and pride and loyalty. Disconsolate, he awaited
Kennedy's offer and slouched toward acquiescence.

In the Kennedy suite, it was not altogether clear that an offer was imminent. Overwhelmed by the excitement of victory—on the first ballot,
no less—Kennedy advisers found it difficult to focus on the thorny and
less glamorous matter of the vice presidency. Joe Kennedy dropped by
and urged Jack to pick Lyndon Johnson, but the candidate appeared
irresolute and went to bed at 2:00 A.M., leaving advisers with the impression that only Symington and Jackson were being considered. Neither
John nor Bobby said a word about LBJ.

Thus began, in Bobby's view, "the most indecisive time we ever had,"
a period hopelessly snarled by confusion, miscommunication, and
murky, mixed intentions. Jack "thought how terrible it was that he had
only twenty-four hours to select a vice president. He really hadn't
thought about it at all." According to Bobby, it was only after the presidential nomination, the night of July 13, that they learned Johnson was
interested in the vice presidency. And yet JFK had been receiving signals
for days. Unless Bobby's recollections are wholly inaccurate, which
seems unlikely, it appears that he knew nothing of Rayburn's, Graham's,
or others' overtures on Johnson's behalf. "Well, we couldn't believe [LBJ]
would [want the vice presidency]," Bobby said later, speaking more for
himself than for his brother, "but Jack decided that he'd go down and
talk to him about it anyway."

At 6:30 A.M. on July 14, Pierre Salinger stepped across the hall from
his suite into Bobby Kennedy's. Ken O'Donnell stood outside the bathroom, where Kennedy was bathing. "How many electoral votes are we
gonna get if we capture the East, Northeast, and the solid South?" Bobby
shouted from the bathtub. The solid South included Texas. "Are you talking about nominating Lyndon Johnson?" Salinger demanded. "You're
not going to do that."

"Yes, we are," Bobby said matter-of-factly. JFK was heading to Johnson's suite at 10 A.M. to make the offer. At this news, the two advisers
exploded. O'Donnell "violently protested" Johnson's presence on the
ticket; he had not forgotten the ugliness of the Johnson campaign.
Salinger expounded on Symington's virtues. Bobby calmly cited Johnson's unique strength in the South. Then, rising from the tub, he dried,
dressed, and excused himself to conduct a morning meeting.

Had Bobby been converted to a Kennedy-Johnson ticket? It seems
highly unlikely, for as Bobby later explained, Johnson had "said some
rather nasty things—or his people had—and we hadn't really gotten over
that." Bobby spoke for Salinger and O'Donnell and especially for himself,
revealing an antipathy that ran deeper, predating the campaign. *Time's*

Hugh Sidey recalled Robert Kennedy's "contempt for Johnson as majority leader. Bobby Kennedy had a theory . . . that Lyndon Johnson was not
a majority *leader* . . . he was a man who took advantage of just the right
climate in American politics"—the weak Eisenhower presidency. But by
the morning of July 14, 1960, Bobby knew an overture to Johnson was
imminent and seems to have been preparing or warning his like-minded
advisers. He was not going to undercut his brother's decision.

Shortly after 10:00 A.M., John Kennedy traced the two flights back up
from Johnson's suite to his own. He arrived, according to Bobby, in a
panic of misgivings. "You just won't believe it. He wants it," the dazed
Jack told his brother.

"Oh, my God!" Bobby exclaimed.

"Now what do we do?"

Bobby later told Arthur Schlesinger that "the idea that [JFK would]
go down and offer him the nomination in hopes that he'd take the nomination is not true. The reason he went down . . . [is] because there were
enough indications from others that he [Johnson] wanted to be offered
the nomination. But [JFK] never dreamt that there was a chance in the
world that he would accept it."

Bobby's case is not persuasive. It is hard to fathom that John Kennedy,
after clear signals from Rayburn, Graham, O'Neill, and Corcoran, could
possibly have been surprised by Johnson's answer. JFK, after all, had earlier told O'Neill that he would be "embarrassed" if Johnson rejected an
offer. It is impossible to conceive that John Kennedy "never dreamt" of
the alternative.

It is also doubtful that, as Bobby argues, JFK offered the vice presidency only to appease Johnson's self-importance and without any
"hopes" that LBJ would accept. Graham, Alsop, and O'Neill clearly recall
encounters with JFK in which he convincingly sang the praises of a
Kennedy-Johnson ticket, impressing others with his "positiveness." Hale
Boggs thought it obvious, despite the political chaos, that JFK considered Johnson essential to victory. Tip O'Neill thought JFK "delighted"
at the prospect of a Kennedy-Johnson ticket.

The accounts seem irreconcilable. What can explain Bobby's puzzling
version of events? It is tempting to dismiss it as fabrication. By 1965—
the year of Robert Kennedy's talk with Schlesinger—Bobby's relations
with LBJ had grown so openly hostile that his objectivity could be questioned. The chaos of the 1960 convention may also have obscured his
vision and blurred his memory. As Theodore White writes, "it is a trap
of history to believe that eyewitnesses remember accurately what they
have lived through."

Yet Bobby's version emerged in a series of private, sealed oral history interviews with historians and trusted friends Schlesinger and John Bartlow Martin. Over the course of eight conversations, spanning a full year, Bobby's story was consistent and emphatic: under no circumstances, he insisted, again and again, was JFK's offer either intended or expected to be accepted by LBJ. This account cannot responsibly be dismissed as duplicity. It is more believable that Robert Kennedy, who despised LBJ even in 1960, remembered events as he saw them.

As Sorensen suggests, some inconsistencies amount to "a question of semantics." John Kennedy was *inclined* to invite Johnson on the ticket; he *suspected* Johnson wanted to be on the ticket—but by Thursday morning, he remained confused and noncommittal. Until he talked with Johnson personally, Kennedy could not truly believe that the majority leader—despite any assurances—would willingly accept such a profound diminution of power. If this is the case, Kennedy's 10:00 A.M. visit constituted neither a genuine offer nor a *pro forma* offer, but a feeler. In other words—Bobby's words—JFK went to Johnson's suite simply "to talk to him about it." "I didn't really offer the nomination to Lyndon Johnson," John Kennedy told reporter Charles Bartlett a few days later, off the record. "I just held it out to here"—he poised his hand two or three inches from his pocket, implying that Johnson snatched the opportunity.

Each protagonist, then, interpreted the Kennedy-Johnson meeting as he wished. Johnson expected an offer, wanted an offer, and perceived one in Kennedy's vague inquiry. Johnson's affirmative response revealed his own assumption, as Bobby Baker recalled, "that Jack Kennedy's offer at the morning conference was as firm as could be."

John Kennedy, however, appears to have wanted only to determine LBJ's state of mind and to make a final choice shortly thereafter; but found, to his discomfort, he had inadvertently committed himself to a running mate he was not certain he wanted, a running mate who might inspire a revolt by liberals and labor. JFK was trapped. It was this shock that Bobby witnessed upon Jack's return.

And Robert Kennedy—in favor of Jackson or Symington; resentful, distrustful, and unforgiving toward Lyndon Johnson; never dreaming that Johnson might want the vice presidency; and very possibly unaware of JFK's flirtations with the Johnson circle—saw in his brother's actions a feeler or *pro forma* offer gone horribly awry.

What followed was chaos. "We both promised each other that we'd never tell what happened," Bobby recalled, "but we [RFK and JFK] spent the rest of the day alternating between thinking it was good and thinking that it wasn't good . . . and how he could get out of it." Their initial misgivings were compounded by a staff which, once informed, stormed on the verge of insurrection. Salinger was outraged; O'Donnell was almost hysterical. Turning on Bobby, O'Donnell denounced the choice of Johnson as a "disaster" and told JFK it was "the worst mistake" he ever made. "In your first move after the nomination, you go against all the people who supported you," he said. O'Donnell, JFK's liaison to labor, "was so furious that I could hardly talk. I thought of the promises we had made to the labor leaders and the civil rights groups. . . . I felt that we had been double-crossed."

Taut with anger, John Kennedy whitened and composed himself. He protested stiffly that his offer had not been accepted. "Did it occur to you," he pointed out, "that if Lyndon becomes the vice president, I'll have Mike Mansfield as the leader in the Senate, somebody I can trust and depend on?" The argument won few converts other than Bobby Kennedy.

At 11:00 A.M., labor leaders filed into Kennedy's suite. JFK's relations with organized labor had never been particularly comfortable; in June 1959, when Kennedy gave the annual Jefferson-Jackson Day speech in Seattle, most labor leaders boycotted the dinner, upset by his sponsorship of labor reform and by Bobby's work on the Rackets Committee. Now, Jack Conway told them pointedly that the nomination of LBJ would backfire. "Bob," he warned, "don't do it. Because if you offer it to him, he'll take it. We've come a long way. . . . If you do this, you're going to fuck everything up." Bobby looked shaken. They had already done it.

By this time, word of an impending Johnson nomination had reached the convention floor. "All hell broke loose! They were just up in arms," Hubert Humphrey said of his fellow liberals. The normally sanguine Arthur Schlesinger lit into Phil Graham with such ferocity that Graham's wife, Katharine, had to pull them apart. New Mexico Congressman Stewart Udall ran from delegation to delegation "putting out fires," promising his liberal friends that a Kennedy-Johnson ticket was the surest route to victory. It was a difficult pitch. Negro leaders cried "sell-out"; the D.C. delegation, infuriated by rumors of Johnson's selection, threatened hollowly to tear the convention apart. As word of the spreading liberal revolt reached JFK's suite, Robert Kennedy in particular saw the choice of Johnson as a grave mistake.

Johnson had his own fires to quench. Few Texans had even considered that LBJ might take the vice presidency. Now, most felt deserted and sick at heart, just as bitter as the Kennedy supporters. "Who'd want to be Vice President for that man?" Jake Jacobsen demanded. Juanita Roberts, Johnson's secretary, was not the only one to characterize the ticket as upside down. In Johnson's suite, political leaders gathered to voice their support or outrage. Robert Kerr was so livid that upon confirmation of the bad news, he reportedly slapped Bobby Baker in the face. "Get me my .38," Kerr yelled at Baker, LBJ, and Lady Bird. "I'm gonna kill every damn one of you. I can't believe that my three best friends would betray me." Eventually, either Rayburn or Baker converted Kerr, who apologized to the Johnsons for "los[ing] my head."

Meanwhile, the two Kennedy brothers sat alone inside Jack's suite in utter indecision. "Jack changed his mind back and forth, as I did . . . at least six times," Bobby remembered. "The problem was, if it wasn't a good idea, how you'd get [Johnson] out of it. Secondly, if you *did* get him out of it, how bitter would he be?" Shortly after 1:00 P.M. they decided to talk Johnson off the ticket "because Jack thought it would be unpleasant to be associated with him." The best outcome, they decided, was "if he could get him to withdraw and still be happy." It was Bobby's duty to coax Johnson off the ticket, to undo "the terrible mistake."

The accounts of Robert Kennedy's subsequent visits to the Johnson suite—three visits in all—are jumbled and contradictory. What remains clear is that each trip generated a wider wake of confusion and disaffection. When a phone call heralded Bobby's first visit, Johnson told his advisers, "Whatever it is, I don't want to see him." Bobby arrived at Johnson's suite at about 1:30 P.M. and was ushered into a side room by Rayburn and Connally. Phil Graham, arriving fifteen minutes later, was tugged into a separate bedroom by an insistent LBJ. Johnson and Graham sat on the bed with Lady Bird, "about as composed," Graham recorded, "as three Mexican jumping beans." Johnson said that Bobby Kennedy was making a final offer of the vice presidency. It was time for a final decision.

Bobby's "final offer" was largely a pretense. In fact he was testing Johnson's commitment to the ticket, "just sort of to feel him out." Bobby complained to Connally and Rayburn—a bit disingenuously—that the Kennedys were in danger of losing control of the convention to a labor revolt. According to Connally, Bobby added that "Lyndon just can't accept this nomination. It was a mistake." He asked whether Johnson might be interested in becoming party chairman. "Shit!" answered Rayburn. Connally called the threat of revolt "ludicrous." In that case, Bobby said, he wished to express his brother's final offer to LBJ in person. Rayburn stormed out of the room.

At about 2:30, Graham sat nervously in a vacant room with Jim Rowe, hastily dialing the nominee's private number. After a seeming marathon of excruciating delays, Graham reached JFK and outlined Johnson's position: he did not want the vice presidency, would not negotiate for it, but would take it if Jack—and only Jack himself—drafted him. Kennedy seemed preoccupied. He grumbled that the convention was a mess and seconded his brother's concerns about the liberals. "No one has anything against Symington," he told Graham, who reminded him that earlier in the week Kennedy himself had something against Symington. JFK muttered agreement and asked for three minutes to make a decision.

A few minutes later, at 2:45, Graham called him back and was struck by Kennedy's utter calm. "It's all set," Kennedy said. "Tell Lyndon I want him." Handing the phone to Rowe, Graham raced to Johnson's suite with the news.

Meanwhile, by Connally's account, Bobby Kennedy was back in LBJ's suite. Rayburn again refused to meet with him. Alone with Connally, Bobby reiterated that Walter Reuther and other labor leaders had never forgiven Johnson's vote for the Taft-Hartley bill (which restricted union power) in 1947 and were threatening to disrupt the convention. "Bobby, there is no point in your talking to me, or to Lyndon," Connally remembered saying. "Your brother came down here and offered him the vice presidential nomination, and Johnson accepted. Now if he's changed his mind . . . he's going to have to call and ask him to withdraw, because Johnson is not going to do it himself. Don't kid us that you can't control this convention. Those are your delegates out there." Connally added pointedly that in the future, LBJ would deal with one Kennedy only—Jack. Backpedaling again, Bobby promised that JFK would soon phone Johnson with his final offer, and left the suite.

Thirty minutes passed without a call from Jack Kennedy. Johnson was getting edgy. Again he dispatched Graham to contact JFK, who, it turned out, had lapsed again into indecision. On the phone with Graham, Kennedy dwelt upon the opposition to LBJ. "You ain't no Adlai," said Graham—a reference to the famously irresolute Stevenson. Kennedy agreed. The matter was settled: his choice was Lyndon Johnson.

JFK had assumed his first conversation with Graham was confirmation enough, but now he called to assuage the anxious and disgruntled Johnson. As LBJ cradled the telephone, Lady Bird and Rowe sat on the bed, so close to Johnson they could hear Kennedy's voice in the receiver. Kennedy read a press release on the vice presidency to Johnson, who uttered only one, plaintive question: "Do you really want me?"

"Yes," Kennedy replied.

"Well, if you really want me," Johnson said, "I'll do it."

Half an hour later, at about 4:00, Bobby Kennedy returned a third time to Johnson's suite. This time, Bobby met with Lyndon Johnson himself. This time, Bobby recalled, "I went down to see if I could get him to withdraw."

Bobby and Lyndon sat alone on a couch in Johnson's suite. "There's going to be a lot of opposition" from liberals and labor, perhaps even a floor fight, Bobby said. This was what he had rehearsed with his brother. Bobby asked a second time: Wouldn't Johnson prefer the chairmanship of the Democratic National Committee to the nomination? The chairman, as both men knew, dispensed patronage with a far freer hand than the vice president or even the majority leader. At the controls of the party machinery, LBJ could place Johnson men in party organizations across the country—and lay the foundation for a future run for the presidency.

Johnson looked up, wounded, and refused to budge. It was a masterful performance of Texan dramatics. Bobby said later that Johnson

> is one of the greatest sad-looking people in the world. You know, he can turn that on. I thought he'd burst into tears. . . . He just shook, and tears came into his eyes, and he said, "I want to be Vice President, and if the President [JFK] will have me, I'll join him in making a fight for it." It was that kind of conversation.
>
> I said, "Well, then, that's fine. He wants you as Vice President if you want to be Vice President, we want you to know."

In a room down the hall from Johnson's suite, at this very moment, Graham, Connally, and Rowe were trying to track down Bobby Kennedy. Several Southern governors were demanding changes in the list of seconding speakers for LBJ—Bobby's domain. Bill Moyers, Johnson's young appointments secretary, burst in. "Graham, my God, Bobby is in the room!"

"I'll be along in just a minute," Graham replied.

"That won't do," Moyers yelled, and dragged him by the arm through a phalanx of newspapermen and into the entrance hall of the Johnson suite. The room was a tumult, a din of confused and affronted aides. Johnson himself was extremely agitated, "about to jump out of his skin," ranting to Graham that Bobby Kennedy was trying to pry him off the ticket. "Call Jack Kennedy and straighten out this mess!" Rayburn barked at Graham. If this was the product of the "smooth Kennedy machine" described breathlessly by the press, Bobby Baker was underwhelmed. "Hell," he thought as Graham dialed the extension, "they're as confused as we are."

"Jack," Graham said into the phone, "Bobby is down here and is telling the speaker and Lyndon that there is opposition and that Lyndon should withdraw."

"Oh," Jack replied serenely, "that's all right; Bobby's been out of touch and doesn't know what's happening." He instructed that LBJ make a statement right away, and then talked for a moment to Johnson, who was sprawled across the bed. "Yes . . . Yes . . . Yes . . ." Johnson mumbled and handed the phone back to Graham. JFK chatted amiably to Graham "as though we were discussing someone else's problems." Baker, meanwhile, tugged an utterly exhausted Bobby Kennedy back into the room.

"Bobby, your brother wants to speak to you," Graham said, thinking himself a character in an increasingly absurd melodrama. According to Graham, Bobby took the phone, listened a moment to JFK, and said, "Well, it's too late now," before half slamming down the receiver. Robert Kennedy remembered no such phone call. If it took place it was the sort of conversation he might have wanted to forget.

As the rest of Johnson's entourage filed out into the hallway, Bobby turned to Jim Rowe. "Jim, don't you think it's a terrible mistake? It should have been Symington or Jackson." Rowe objected, but Bobby was not really listening. "If we weren't so tired, this wouldn't have happened," Bobby said vacantly. He repeated himself to nobody in particular.

Lyndon and Lady Bird Johnson stood in the entrance hall of their suite looking, in Graham's view, like survivors of an airplane crash. "I was just going to read this on TV when Bobby came in," Johnson said, holding up a hastily typed statement. "Now I don't know what to do."

"Of course you know what you're going to do," Graham volunteered ("with more ham than I ever suspected myself of," he wrote). "Throw your shoulders back and your chin out and go out and make that announcement. And then go on and win. Everything's wonderful." And as Bill Moyers led them into the exploding flashbulbs and klieg lights, the Johnsons swelled with hollow cheer and confidence for the cameras.

John Kennedy had changed his mind while Bobby was trying to change Johnson's. The nominee decided a reversal would do him more damage than an anti-Johnson revolt. "I just got a call from Clark Clifford . . . saying that this [indecision] is disastrous, you've got to take him," Jack explained when Bobby returned from Johnson's suite. There was more: as Bobby recalled, JFK had concluded that Johnson "would be so mean as majority leader that it was better having him as vice president, where you could control him." And "particularly after you had offered him the job, then it would have been disastrous to have that affront and withdraw it."

As it turned out, it was disastrous just to attempt to withdraw it. In the wake of Bobby's last visit, a pall hung over the Johnson suite. Lady Bird was in tears. LBJ returned from his press conference sour-faced and seething. Yet he did not blame John Kennedy as the agent of his stinging repudiation; the villain, Johnson believed, was Bobby Kennedy— Bobby, who opposed Johnson from the beginning; Bobby, who sided with labor against him; Bobby, who ruthlessly tried to humiliate him. In

Baker's recollection it was Bobby, not Jack, whom Johnson denounced as "that little shitass" and a score of epithets more coarse.

Johnson's friends joined in the recriminations. Connally seconded LBJ's suspicion that Bobby was the mastermind. JFK was too "practical [a] fellow," Connally said, to make an offer without expecting it to be accepted. Joe Alsop believed that Bobby took the initiative to talk Johnson off the ticket and that Jack, seeking to avoid "an exhausting fraternal argument during an already stressful time," placated Bobby by allowing him to do so. Even Graham, who remembered John Kennedy's last-minute qualms and "mind-changing" more clearly than anyone, could not believe JFK had authorized Bobby's inept political maneuver. Graham instead imagined that Bobby was fulfilling a promise to liberal delegates to deny Johnson the nomination. "My guess," Graham concluded in his memorandum, "is that he made that assurance on his own and tried to bring it about on his own."

In later years, Bobby Kennedy was incensed, "flabbergasted," by the Graham memo. "Phil didn't know us then as he knew us later," he told Kay Graham after her husband's suicide in 1963. Bobby argued that when he had left the Kennedy suite to meet with Johnson, the two brothers had been in agreement: if Johnson seemed amenable, Bobby should ease him off the ticket. But once plunged into the labyrinth of crowded hallways and snarled communications, Bobby did indeed fall "out of touch" and was betrayed, however unintentionally, by his own brother. This was perhaps too painful to admit, but the alternative was unthinkable. "Obviously," Bobby said to Arthur Schlesinger, "with the close relationship between my brother and I, [I] wasn't going down to see if he would withdraw just as a lark on my own—'My brother's asleep so I'll go see if I can get rid of his vice president.'"

Although Bobby's self-justifying claims cannot be verified, they make more sense than LBJ's conspiratorial account. At conventions, as George Reedy explained, "people become extremely emotional. They have a tendency to believe things that they would never believe . . . in their calmer moments." Johnson had a tendency to believe such things even in his calmer moments. And in the distorting heat of Los Angeles, and forever afterward, LBJ was absolutely convinced that Robert Kennedy had acted alone, with premeditated spite, to destroy his political future.

On Thursday, July 14, 1960, Lyndon Johnson was nominated as John Kennedy's running mate. The party's liberals sullenly acquiesced, their anger spent, in large part, on Bobby Kennedy late that afternoon. By the time Bobby and O'Donnell walked into Walter Reuther's suite to break the final news to labor leaders, they had already been upstaged by Johnson's televised announcement moments earlier. Before Bobby could explain himself, Reuther exploded in a profane fury. O'Donnell didn't think "Robert Kennedy ever was so savagely attacked in his life. . . . I mean, they just murdered him. . . . They were just so bitter it's unbelievable." They felt, as Bobby did, bruised and betrayed by the choice of LBJ.

Thursday evening, at the ornate Spanish mansion rented by Joe Kennedy, Bobby sat on the telephone, glumly stage-managing the nomination he had been sent to undo only hours before. "Yesterday was the best day of my life," Bobby told Charles Bartlett, "and today is the worst day of my life." Bartlett thought Bobby was "in near despair." Jack Kennedy, in low spirits himself, was reading the *New York Times* spread across the trunk of a car. The sun was setting and Bobby's children splashed around in a fountain in front of the house. Other than the children, the only one unaffected by Bobby's pervasive gloom was his father, who stood in the doorway, his hands behind his head, posing grandly in a velvet smoking jacket. "Don't worry, Jack," he said. "In two weeks they'll be saying it's the smartest thing you ever did."

That night, however, tensions remained close to the surface. After LBJ's nomination, Pierre Salinger returned to his office and was besieged by calls from reporters. They wanted confirmation of a story by John S. Knight, publisher of Knight Newspapers, contending that LBJ had forced his way onto the ticket. Knight based his story on an alleged conversation between Robert Kennedy and LBJ. Salinger called to check the story with Bobby, who vehemently denied it. Salinger issued a standard denial and went to sleep.

An hour later he was awakened by a phone call from Bill Moyers, who handed the phone to a highly agitated Sam Rayburn. The speaker demanded a denial be released under John Kennedy's name, not his press secretary's, and ordered Salinger to awaken JFK and have him call Knight to squelch the story. Rayburn said that Lyndon Johnson was "extremely disturbed" by the rumors and wanted the story killed—now—before it gained wide currency.

Salinger called Bobby back, waking him this time. "Bob was extremely loath to call Senator Kennedy as the senator had had a particularly tough day," Salinger recalled. He and Bobby patched together a statement under John Kennedy's name. Bobby himself called Knight and explained that he had not, in fact, spoken with Johnson before Jack offered the vice presidency. Meanwhile, Salinger called Moyers and Rayburn to read them JFK's statement and assure them Knight had been contacted. Salinger did not say by whom, nor did they ask. In the end, the statement proved enough to quiet the speaker and stifle the damaging story.

The injurious events in Los Angeles marked an inauspicious beginning to a presidential campaign. Jim Rowe expected more of the same from RFK. He urged LBJ to maintain an independent campaign staff in order to "handle" that "ruthless son of a bitch." Bobby had a habit of lashing out at his political seniors, and Rowe told Johnson to keep his distance and appoint John Connally as his campaign manager. Only Connally could "be fully as 'hard nosed' as Bobby."

By the end of July, though, when Kennedy's and Johnson's advisers met in Hyannis Port to discuss campaign strategy, passions had cooled substantially. All participants focused on the challenge before them. Later, disgruntled Kennedy aides would murmur that Johnson had been too loud and overbearing during the talks, but on Cape Cod, both John and Robert Kennedy seemed pleased by LBJ's enthusiasm. "Lyndon was just as anxious to be elected as we were, so we worked together," explained Mike Feldman, who served as liaison (along with Jim Rowe) between the two staffs. There was little friction. Feldman and Rowe got along comfortably; so did Salinger and George Reedy, the press secretaries.

The campaign, in large part, was not one but two: "Our paths only crossed a few times," Reedy said later. Sometimes Jim Rowe wondered whether lines between the two campaigns had been severed too completely, but the arrangement kept a lid on simmering resentments. Between July and November, the most embittered antagonists of the convention drama, Lyndon Johnson and Robert Kennedy, were rarely in the same state or even the same region.

One of the greater gestures toward campaign unity was made, ironically, by their wives, Lady Bird Johnson and Ethel Kennedy. The Kennedy campaign decided to export the family's "tea parties," which had proved so successful in Massachusetts since the 1940s, to Texas. In August 1960, the "Kennedy girls"—an entourage of wives, sisters, and cousins—embarked upon a statewide tour of Texas. Liz Carpenter, Lady Bird's campaign manager, aimed to "usher [them] into Texas" with a wirephoto of Ethel Kennedy and Eunice Kennedy Shriver in cowboy hats. On the morning of August 29, LBJ arrived on the tarmac at Washington Airport to pass out the hats and bid the women farewell. "Well, the two Kennedy girls were great and gay," Carpenter remembered, "but they sure didn't want to put on Texas hats. I kept thinking . . . if we had been up in Boston we would have been glad to put on a derby or a homburg. But they practically sat on them. I kept making them try to throw the hats up in the air and they were embarrassed." The Kennedy women, white hats matching white gloves, stood with Lyndon and Lady Bird and smiled gamely for the cameras. Ethel's hat fit snugly, but Eunice's teetered unsteadily on the back of her bouffant hairdo.

Eunice in particular was amused by "funny-named towns" like Happy, Texas. "These towns couldn't possibly have these names. You've made them up," she protested. Sporadic tensions arose over hotel arrangements or the duration of the "get-acquainted" parties, but Ethel in particular was warm and gracious to her hosts. "We loved every minute with you," Ethel wrote Lady Bird two days after leaving Texas. After the November victory, Lady Bird replied that "your sense of humor made it all the more pleasant. Tell 'Bobby who sent me' that you left Texas full of admirers and anytime he wants to do something about Mr. Hoffa, you are entitled to make the announcement."

Between their husbands, however, the spirit of harmony was tenuous. On the campaign plane, Bobby Kennedy tugged the coat of Peter Lisagor as the reporter walked down the aisle. "I hear that you have an interesting story to tell about how Lyndon Johnson feels about Jack," Bobby said. Lisagor demurred. "Well, I do, Bob, but I don't see why I should tell that story now. . . . You're all bedfellows." When Bobby beseeched him repeatedly, Lisagor relented and described his conversation with LBJ. In recounting it for Bobby Kennedy, "I don't think I left out a single word, four-letter or otherwise," Lisagor remembered.

He told Bobby about a flight on Johnson's private plane in July, just before the convention. Lisagor and LBJ were returning from Oklahoma City after filming a special edition of *Face the Nation*. When Lisagor asked LBJ about the Kennedys, he was shocked by Johnson's instant "enmity and hostility." Mocking JFK as scrawny and disease-ridden, Johnson said that "if he ever got elected, his father, old Joe Kennedy, would run the country."

As Lisagor finished his story, Bobby turned to the window. He was silent for a moment. "I knew he hated Jack," Bobby said, "but I didn't think he hated him that much." Lisagor wished he had kept the story to himself.

During the fall campaign, however, Bobby took no issue with Johnson's conduct. Forceful and exuberant on the stump, Johnson was granted broad freedom of action and he responded quickly to any directions from Bobby or the main campaign staff. When Bobby called in October to say he was going to urge the release of Martin Luther King, Jr., from a Georgia jail, thus placing Johnson in a difficult position down South, LBJ responded gracefully to the warning. "Tell Jack that we'll ride it through down here some way, and at least he's on the side of right," he said.

Privately, Johnson was less confident. His terror at the thought of losing Texas sparked an often violent temper on the campaign trail. He lashed out at aides at the slightest provocation. "Why his staff did not kill him I do not know. They almost did several times," Jim Rowe told Hubert Humphrey after the campaign. Publicly, though, Johnson was an impeccable performer, lauding JFK and "the Boston-Austin Axis," decrying anti-Catholic prejudice, and joyfully attacking Nixon. Johnson proved invaluable to Citizens for Kennedy and Johnson, whose primary function was to broaden the base of electoral support; and LBJ worked hard indeed to attract the independent, conservative, and business vote. In a dynamic five-day whistlestop tour of the South in October, LBJ (in a train tagged "the Cornpone Special" by gently mocking journalists) covered 3,500 miles and eight states and delivered sixty speeches.

By election day, Johnson had vindicated his place on the ticket in stunning fashion. Even his Texan advisers had to concede that JFK had been "outthinking" Johnson's parochial supporters by recognizing LBJ's importance to the Democratic ticket. The Kennedys, too, were pleased and relieved. Bobby wrote Johnson in late October that "we are getting outstanding favorable reaction to your speeches wherever you go. There is no question but what these speeches are making a major difference."

In the end, most Kennedy advisers agreed. On November 8, 1960, John Kennedy won the presidency by a scant margin of the popular vote; he carried Texas, barely, and six more states of the old Confederacy. Robert Kennedy called the Johnsons' suite at the Driskill Hotel in Austin. "Lady Bird carried Texas," he said gallantly.

Whether or not the Johnsons were crucial to the victory cannot be proved, but LBJ was not shying from the credit. As he watched the televised returns come in from the South, Johnson turned to Liz Carpenter and said, "That Minnesota boy couldn't have carried this ticket, could he?" (He referred to Orville Freeman, another contender for the vice presidential nomination.) But as LBJ sat in his suite at the Driskill, his pride was soured by gloom. After midnight, when his election as vice president was apparent, Johnson, Lady Bird, the Connallys, and other friends walked across Seventh Street to an all-night café. "There was no jubilation. Lyndon looked as if he'd lost his last friend on earth," remembered one of his secretaries, who was appalled by LBJ's uncharacteristically rude behavior.

There was no victory celebration at his hotel; the election was too close, the votes tallied too late. At 7:00 the next morning, when the TV reports began again in earnest, Liz Carpenter walked into the living room of the suite. It was littered with coffee cups and cigarette butts, souvenirs of last night's nervousness. There, amid the rubbish, Johnson sat alone, staring at the television. His unhappiness at winning the vice presidency was palpable. Of his many political victories, this was the least welcome.

Johnson's active role in the campaign, however, heralded a brighter future. "If Jack Kennedy gets elected," he promised in late October, "you can be sure that the man closest to the President will be the man closest to the Senate. I'm going to be a working Vice President."

CHAPTER 3

The Vice President and the Assistant President

"I am vice president," wrote John Adams, the first to inhabit the office. "In this I am nothing. But I may be everything." In January 1961, as Lyndon Johnson left the Senate for the vice presidency, his future held the dim but tantalizing promise of the presidency, of "everything." But in the meantime LBJ would not resign himself to nothingness. It was not his nature. Throughout his life Johnson had assumed positions with no inherent power base and infused them with irrepressible energy, drive, and ambition: as assistant to President Cecil E. Evans of Southwest Texas State Teachers' College, as speaker of the "Little Congress" of staff members in the 1940s, and as party whip and leader in the 1950s, power seemed to flow to him and issue from him naturally. In Johnson's political ascent, power was the constant; public offices were quantities to be stretched, exploited for public and personal gain, and, ultimately, discarded along the climb. If this was arrogance, it was well grounded. Lyndon Johnson was never nothing; and if the vice presidency meant little today, that could not be the case for long.

The press accepted Johnson's bold claim with little skepticism. On the eve of the inauguration, *U.S. News & World Report* exclaimed that "the vice presidency is to become a center of activity and power unseen in the past." The magazine foresaw "important assignments" for LBJ in foreign affairs, especially in the explosive Cuban situation. Undoubtedly, President Kennedy would rely heavily upon the negotiating skills of his brilliant second, Lyndon Johnson, "a new kind of vice president." And LBJ, surely, would demand no less. "The restless and able Mr. Johnson is obviously unwilling to become a ceremonial nonentity," Tom Wicker rightly predicted in the *New York Times*. Johnson's former Senate colleagues agreed, assuring reporters that LBJ "will be very important in the new Administration—and much utilized." Headlines heralded Washington's new "Number 2 Man."

Cheered on by the press, Johnson acted quickly to construct himself a new kind of vice presidency. In late December, only weeks before his inauguration, LBJ summoned Bobby Baker to the "Taj Mahal," the leader's palatial quarters in the Capitol Building. Johnson seemed newly energized, almost giddy. "Bobby, I've been thinking about where I can do Jack Kennedy the most good," he said, according to Baker. "And it's right here on this Hill, the place I know best. . . . All those Bostons and Harvards don't know any more about Capitol Hill than an old maid does about fuckin'." Johnson swept his arm around him in a broad arc, his eyes shining: "I'm gonna keep this office and help Mike Mansfield and Hubert Humphrey pass the Kennedy program. It's gonna be just the way it was! You can keep on helpin' me like you've always done."

Baker shifted uncomfortably in his seat. And when the vice president-elect outlined his plans to attend—and preside over—meetings of the Senate Democratic Caucus, Baker was "astonished and horrified." Could Johnson be so blind to the traditions and prerogatives of his own Senate? Could he be so deluded as to imagine that a member of the executive branch could control the legislature; that his former colleagues would cede their new powers to their old master? The scheme was ludicrous. It was a breach of the constitutional separation of powers and anathema to those who had long suffered the Treatment. Baker hoped that Johnson was simply assuaging his own endangered ego, consoling himself with the sound of his own voice. Yet as Johnson chattered manically, Baker realized he was serious. The vice president-elect seemed not to hear Baker's cautious interjections; LBJ drummed his fingers impatiently and pressed onward. "Do a little pulse-taking," he ordered Baker. "Let me know what you hear."

Baker heard little, if any, encouragement. Though reluctant to upbraid a man known as Johnson's personal aide, senators voiced a measured disapproval that thinly veiled their deep resentment. Baker's soundings only fueled apprehensions about the continued pressure of Johnson's heavy hand. Mike Mansfield, the incoming majority leader, owed his rise in the party solely to Johnson; he had already demonstrated his fealty to LBJ by agreeing to keep Baker as Senate secretary and to grant Johnson a continued lease on the Taj Mahal. The new leader's deferential manner worried liberals; they feared he would continue to bow to his overpowering predecessor.

Johnson was uninterested in Baker's findings. He had done his own pulse-taking, had corralled Humphrey and Mansfield and others at the Statler Hotel and refused to be dissuaded. Humphrey thought it perfectly obvious that the plan was doomed, but held his tongue. Johnson, he reflected, was not a man to whom one said no.

Despite Johnson's signals, few senators anticipated the extent of his power grab. On January 3, 1961, the Senate's sixty-four Democrats gathered for a routine conference to precede the new Congress. After pausing to shower plaudits upon the passing tenure of Lyndon Johnson, who responded with evident pleasure, the Democratic senators elected Mansfield their leader. There was no discussion or dissent. Then Mansfield rose, thanked his colleagues, and immediately proposed that Johnson be invited to preside over all future caucus meetings.

Mansfield was suggesting no less than that Johnson continue as the Democrats' *de facto* leader. The senators were stunned into silence. Then, one after another, five men rose to denounce the motion. First to object were two liberals, Joseph Clark and Albert Gore. "We might as well ask Jack Kennedy to come back up to the Senate and take *his* turn presiding," Gore snapped. This was no surprise. Gore had long chafed under Johnson's leadership and openly relished his departure. But when three valued friends and Senate insiders—Clinton Anderson, Olin Johnston, and Willis Robertson—rose to protest Mansfield's motion on constitutional grounds, Johnson's expression changed from outrage to despair. These men's dissent, though tempered by praise of Johnson's leadership, made it bitterly clear: Johnson was now an outsider. His continued presence was unacceptable.

As the objections mounted, there was an embarrassed tone to the debate; it was a dressing-down of leaders old and new. Only under Mansfield's threat to resign did the caucus uphold his motion, 46 to 17. If this could be called a victory, it was hardly to be cherished. The number of opposing votes registered the depth of discontent. Mortified, Johnson darted from the caucus room to which he would never return as vice president.

Moments later, Johnson stalked the Taj Mahal in a paranoid rage. "Those bastards sandbagged me," he fumed to Bobby Baker. "They'd plotted to humiliate me, all those goddamn red-hots and troublemakers. If they didn't want me all they had to do was say so privately to me or to Mike Mansfield. Hell, we didn't pull any big surprise on 'em! But no, they had to humiliate me in public." Over drinks, Baker spoke soothing words, but LBJ was inconsolable. "Now I know the difference between a caucus and a cactus," Johnson reportedly groused. "In a cactus all the pricks are on the outside."

That afternoon, Lyndon Johnson forfeited the Senate seat he had reclaimed in November under his state's "LBJ Law." He was finished on Capitol Hill. And as he moved westward along Pennsylvania Avenue, the new vice president, shamed and chastened, clung to each of the seventeen "no" votes as an individual act of betrayal. Lyndon Johnson was profoundly, permanently wounded by the caucus vote. It was more than a temporary setback; it was a stinging repudiation that would cloud his vice presidency and shape it as well.

Stripped of legislative ambitions, Johnson began to probe the boundaries of his executive authority. Shortly after taking office, he asked the Justice Department to explore the constitutional parameters of his office. Was the vice president circumscribed in his supervision of particular federal agencies? Surely, Johnson hoped to test and stretch his authority, but his inquiry had an undertone of caution. President Kennedy, unlike Mansfield, would not be bullied; in the narrow corridors of the White House, flanked by ardently protective Kennedy aides, Johnson would have to step carefully. Nicholas Katzenbach, the new assistant attorney general, sent LBJ a long memo delineating the vice president's powers, finding that the office was endowed with more executive authority than generally presumed. A supervisory role, Katzenbach concluded, was not at all improper.

Soon thereafter, a Johnson aide drafted an executive order granting the vice president "general supervision" of a broad span of government activities, including the National Aeronautics and Space Administration (NASA). Reports, plans, and proposals traditionally sent to the president would go instead to Lyndon Johnson. After receiving the signature of President Kennedy, the order was to be distributed to certain federal agencies and departments to ensure compliance. Such a grant of powers, if approved, would have been unprecedented. Even Johnson was a bit struck by its audacity. Yet he approved it, however warily, and forwarded it to the president.

John Kennedy was astonished and bemused. He ignored the order. And Lyndon Johnson, now twice rebuffed, did not press the issue. The proposed order was not, like Mansfield's motion, the product of eager and wildly optimistic plotting by Johnson himself. Rather, this second and equally clumsy reach for power may well have been the initiative of overzealous aides used to acting on Johnson's behalf and with his tacit approval.

Either way, the White House staff regarded Vice President Johnson with heightened suspicion. In the halls of the West Wing, some muttered the name of William H. Seward, Abraham Lincoln's secretary of state, who persistently sought to claim presidential powers as his own. President Kennedy's men were a loyal, protective lot. Though diverse and occasionally fractious, the group was bound by a total commitment to the president. And none among them was more committed, protective, or loyal than the president's brother, Bobby.

In the first days after the November election, Robert Kennedy, JFK's triumphant campaign manager, emerged quickly as chief of staff of the transition. "It is Bobby . . . who will be the new man-to-see in Washington," *Newsweek* reported in mid-November. Drawing on his vast campaign contacts, Bobby performed most of the recruiting for the new administration. His own role in a Kennedy administration, however, was in doubt. He resisted what seemed a natural position on his brother's White House staff, insisting that "I had to do something on my own, or have my own area of responsibility. . . . It would be impossible with the two of us sitting around an office looking at each other all day." The brothers' roles during the campaign had been coordinated but distinct; Bobby considered that preferable to "working directly for him and getting orders from him as to what I should do that day."

With his brother's future secure (at least until 1964), Bobby was momentarily adrift. Briefly, he considered a run for JFK's Senate seat or for governor of Massachusetts, or perhaps a college presidency before a return to public service. At Hyannis Port just after the election, John Kennedy suggested the Department of Justice. "I said I didn't want to be Attorney General," Bobby recalled. "In the first place, I thought nepotism was a problem. Secondly, I had been chasing bad men for three years and I didn't want to spend the rest of my life doing that." In addition, escalating pressures on civil rights were certain to demand federal intervention; as a visible and activist attorney general, Bobby would surely inspire talk of the "Kennedy brothers," thus personalizing the conflict. Yet the appointment was compelling. A law school classmate of Bobby's suspected he was "dying to do it" but fearful of bringing great criticism upon President Kennedy.

"You've got to be cabinet," their father maintained, and by this he meant attorney general. (In 1959, Eunice Kennedy Shriver joked, "Bobby we'll make Attorney General so he can throw all the people Dad doesn't like into jail. That means we'll have to build more jails.") Like Bobby, though, John Kennedy was worried about the public reaction. In mid-November, the *Times* took aim at a Kennedy trial balloon: "It is simply not good enough," the editors argued, "to name a bright young political manager, no matter how bright or how young or how personally loyal, to a major post in government." The president-elect, in a moment of doubt, enlisted Clark Clifford to persuade Joseph Kennedy to drop the idea. Clifford failed. "It's the only thing I'm asking for and I want it," Joe insisted.

Prodded in one direction by their father, pulled in the other by their own ambivalence, the two brothers vacillated "almost like we did on the Vice President," Bobby recalled. But in the end their father had his wish. "I need to know that when problems arise I'm going to have somebody who's going to tell me the unvarnished truth, no matter what . . . and Bobby will do that," JFK explained to Bobby's friend John Seigenthaler. Bobby would also be a strong, honest point man on civil rights. "So, that's it, General," Jack told Bobby. "Let's go." Thus ended Robert Kennedy's brief flirtation with independence.

"Don't smile too much or they'll think we're happy about the appointment," Jack told Bobby on the day of the announcement. The press, predictably, was skeptical. While a few journalists lauded Bobby's credentials and tough public persona, others cited them as evidence of his unfitness for the job. Alexander Bickel of *The New Republic* characterized Robert Kennedy as having run roughshod over process—the foundation of justice—in his stampede toward desired results on the Rackets Committee. "In his brief but highly visible professional career," Bickel concluded, "Mr. Kennedy has demonstrated specific grounds of disqualification."

Surprisingly, perhaps, Lyndon Johnson disagreed with the critics. His view of Robert Kennedy had not softened during the campaign or since; among friends, he still derided Bobby quite loudly as a "snot-nosed little son-of-a-bitch." Bobby Kennedy, Johnson told Bobby Baker, was laughably underprepared to lead the nation's law enforcement effort and was sure to politicize the Justice Department.

Yet Bobby's placement near the center of power could not have surprised Johnson or anyone; and on principle, LBJ defended the president's right to select whomever he wished, even family. "Unless there's over-whelming evidence for cause against a president's nominee," Johnson lectured Baker over drinks one evening in January, "the Senate ought to confirm him." Begrudgingly, Johnson conceded Bobby's competence. "It's a different matter if some ol' boy hasn't got sense enough to pour piss out of a boot, but I don't think you can say that about Bobby Kennedy. He may be a snot-nose, but he's bright," he said. And there was only so much damage Bobby could do under his brother's watch: "I don't think Jack Kennedy's gonna let a little fart like Bobby lead him by the nose. If I learned anything last year, it's that Jack Kennedy's a lot tougher, and maybe a lot smarter, than I thought he was."

As Baker refreshed their drinks, Johnson explained gloomily that the anxious president-elect had asked him to shepherd Bobby's nomination through the confirmation process. Ominous rumblings were emanating from Southerners on the Judiciary Committee; could Johnson help "tone down the Dixiecrats"? He would try, but with little enthusiasm. Johnson noted sarcastically that Joe Kennedy had forced the appointment on JFK. "Well," Johnson added, betraying his bitterness at his own defeat, "since the old bastard bought the office I guess he's got a right to get his money's worth."

Johnson could laugh, but in a perverse twist of irony, Bobby Kennedy's confirmation had become nearly as important to Lyndon Johnson as to Joe Kennedy. Bobby's confirmation, placed upon Johnson's shoulders, was the first gauge of the vice president's usefulness to the administration. LBJ had proved his worth admirably during the campaign, but that meant little now; political capital was renewable only by continual, concerted effort. "We've got to make a real crusade out of this," Johnson told Baker, "because it's the first thing he's asked me to do, and it's very personal with him." Now, it was personal with Johnson as well.

"I want you to lead all our Southern friends in here by their ying-yangs and let me work on 'em," Johnson directed Baker. "I'm gonna put it on the line and tell 'em it's a matter of my personal survival." It was the truth, and a far more effective tactic than singing Bobby's praises to disbelieving senators. Sharing and indulging their animosity toward Bobby Kennedy required little play-acting. It gave Johnson a certain credibility on the Hill, where his standing was uncertain in the aftermath of the caucus vote. This time, however, Johnson presented himself as no more than an emissary for the administration, well within his bounds as vice president.

Johnson recommended the Treatment. Gripping the lapels and tapping the chests of disgruntled senators, Johnson leaned forward and *pushed*. If I can't confirm the president's brother, I'll be ruined before I start, Johnson warned them. And the next time *you* come begging for a dam or a bridge or a judicial appointment, well, you can be damned sure the president won't lift a finger to help.

Among oil-state senators, Johnson was more conciliatory. If they took care of the president, why, the president would take care of them. With a wink, Johnson reminded other senators that RFK was young and inexperienced. "Why, don't you know Bobby Kennedy won't get to go to the bathroom unless Jack Kennedy feels like takin' a pee?" The statement belied everything Johnson believed about the events of July, but he continued with fervor: "If Bobby's rejected and some tough old lawyer who wants to impress the president gets the job, we could have ten times more trouble out of him than we'd have with a baby brother!"

Other senators were more intractable. In Johnson's words (according to Baker), his old mentor Richard Russell of Georgia was "absolutely shittin' a squealin' worm" about the appointment of a "kid" as attorney general. It was unlikely, though, that any nominee would have won Russell's support. With an eye toward the next, inevitable civil rights conflagration, Russell had no desire to be on record as having voted for an attorney general—any attorney general—who might well send federal marshals into the heart of Georgia. Preparing for an open fight, Russell found himself confronted by the wheedling, cajoling face of Lyndon Johnson. Johnson warned that Bobby's confirmation could not be stopped. He said, "It can be by a big margin and everybody can feel good, or it can be close and embarrass everybody. Now, what good will it do me if Dick Russell—*the best friend I've got in the whole world*—gets up and snorts and fusses and embarrasses me and the president and the president's brother and his mama and daddy?" Russell wavered; for Johnson's sake, only, he would refrain from snorting and fussing.

Thus pacified by LBJ and wary of offending a new president, senators adopted a generally civil tone during the Senate hearings. And Bobby Kennedy—summoned into the cavernous hearing room of the Judiciary Committee on January 13, 1961—was deferential but resolute. He had prepared intently for the questioning. Pressed, predictably, about his inexperience, Bobby responded firmly: "In my estimation I think that I have had invaluable experience. . . . I would not have given up one year of experience that I have had over the period since I graduated from law school . . . for experience practicing law in Boston." When Roman Hruska of Nebraska chided that Kennedy had never even negotiated a civil settlement, Kennedy was unmoved. "I doubt if I am going to be doing that as Attorney General," he said disarmingly. The committee unanimously recommended his confirmation.

Kennedy's poise had not, however, clinched the matter. Though his confirmation was now a certainty, a divided Senate vote would greatly embarrass the administration. Behind the scenes, Johnson lobbied tirelessly for a voice vote rather than the traditional roll-call vote. Its virtue, for both sides, was anonymity: senators voting to confirm could do so without inciting their constituencies; those in opposition could avoid personally provoking the White House. Under pressure from Johnson, Jim Eastland, the obstinate chairman of the Judiciary Committee, finally agreed to the procedural change. And in the end, though Dick Russell could not resist bellowing a spiteful nay, the ayes had it by a large margin.

Johnson's advocates credited him with saving Bobby Kennedy's confirmation. They probably overstated their case. The confirmation, though a delicate and inflammatory matter, was probably never in doubt; few senators would have risked openly incurring the wrath of a new president by rejecting his brother and alter ego. Yet neither was it "clear sailing," as Arthur Schlesinger contends, as soon as Bobby sat before the committee. Johnson, acting on principle and to preserve his own political viability, helped clear the rough road toward confirmation and thus saved President Kennedy from an early, perhaps costly, setback.

In doing so, the vice president placed Robert Kennedy squarely between himself and the political role he so coveted in the new administration.

As if to compensate for his own lack of practical legal experience, the new attorney general, the youngest since 1814, assembled what some observers described as the most able, professional cabinet department since the New Deal. Taking Byron White as his chief deputy, Robert Kennedy collected the sharpest lawyers of his generation—a group bound by Ivy League education, by war experience, and, more important, by a deep commitment to social justice and a progressive, ends-oriented jurisprudence.

Bobby Kennedy's men were not ideologues or partisans; they shared with their principal a deep respect for the cautious, incremental nature of legal reform. Neither were they political functionaries. Only White— who attended Oxford and Yale Law School and clerked for Chief Justice Frederick M. Vinson—had been active on John Kennedy's behalf in 1960. The politics of the Justice Department were insulated by the attorney general's personal staff—John Seigenthaler, Edwin Guthman, and Joseph Dolan. Among a remarkable group of assistant attorneys general were Nicholas Katzenbach at the Office of Legal Counsel, Burke Marshall (Civil Rights), and Ramsey Clark (Lands). Even Alexander Bickel, the scalding critic of the attorney general's appointment, corrected his judgment of RFK: "One immediately had the sense of a fellow who wasn't afraid of having able people around him and indeed of a fellow who had a vision of public service that would have done anyone proud."

Service meant action. "Bob never pauses to regroup and say, 'Now what shall we do?' " said Joe Dolan. "When he is saying, 'What shall we do now,' he is doing something." A sense of *movement* pervaded the attorney general's policies and his management style. Civil servants described an electric charge in the once musty air of the Justice Department; Bobby roamed widely, curiously, through its corridors, poking his head into random offices and chatting with employees who had long toiled in obscurity, never meeting an attorney general. In his enormous, staid, walnut-paneled chambers, Bobby reproduced the informal and cluttered air of his cramped Senate quarters of the 1950s. With his top assistants, whom he consulted freely, Bobby was direct in his questioning, willing to listen, and confident in their judgment. Bobby demanded versatility, not specialization, in his deputies. In a crisis, said Bill Geoghegan, "titles meant nothing . . . job descriptions meant nothing." And in quieter times, a tax lawyer might find himself with a civil rights assignment simply because he had wandered past Bobby's office.

Archibald Cox, Kennedy's solicitor general, found RFK far from the rigid dogmatist of public caricature. Bobby rarely second-guessed decisions but was quick to reconsider his initial views in light of new information. Occasionally, though, the old abruptness resurfaced. Evasiveness infuriated him. So did ill-preparedness. "His face," said one department official, "when it lacks that boyish, photogenic grin, is not a pleasant sight. It has a certain bony harshness and those ice-blue eyes are not the smiling ones that Irishmen sing songs about." Kennedy's anger boiled close to the surface; his face grew taut and red, his voice clipped, but he was not given to outbursts. In general, recalled John Douglas of the Civil Division, Bobby "treated people decently . . . he didn't duck or try to shift blame. He didn't say one thing in private and another in public. He never let his subordinates down. He stood up for them, followed their careers and interests, tried to help them, looked for the best in them, and usually found it. . . . He was the most fastidious man in public life I ever met in his personal relationships." The attorney general inspired deep respect and an almost fanatical devotion. His Justice Department became less a professional order than a secular brotherhood.

Protective of his own domain, Bobby was less respectful of others'. His attention was rarely fixed for long on the departmental agenda— civil rights, juvenile delinquency, and organized crime—and, as international tensions flared, his bailiwick broadened significantly. In April 1961, a band of twelve hundred Cuban exiles, trained and instigated by the CIA and the Joint Chiefs of Staff, invaded Cuba in an attempt to overthrow Fidel Castro. The resulting catastrophe drew Robert Kennedy into the management of foreign affairs.

While President Kennedy received reports of the growing debacle on the shores of the Bay of Pigs, Bobby paced angrily in the cabinet room, mumbling, "We've got to do something. We've got to do something." A day earlier Bobby had bristled at any suggestion that the invasion plans were ill-conceived, reminding a concerned Arthur Schlesinger that proper protocol was to support the president, period. Today Bobby stopped short and glared at his brother's advisers. "All you bright fellows have gotten the president into this," he shouted, "and if you don't do something now, my brother will be regarded as a paper tiger by the Russians."

John Kennedy's foreign policy advisers, during the coming years, were to reckon with much more of this. Beginning with the Bay of Pigs crisis, Robert Kennedy emerged as his brother's chief counsel and frequent surrogate. He attended all key meetings, listening and rarely interjecting—though when he did interject, he spoke frankly and often callously. At a National Security Council (NSC) meeting on April 27, 1961, Under Secretary of State Chester Bowles aroused Bobby's ire by explaining that Castro was lodged securely in power unless the United States launched and led a full-scale invasion of Cuba. "This is worthless," Bobby exploded, slamming his copy of Bowles's report on the table and ranting for a full ten minutes. "You people are so anxious to protect your own asses that you're afraid to do anything. All you want to do is dump the whole thing on the president. We'd be better off if you just quit and left foreign policy to someone else," he yelled at Bowles, leaving little doubt as to the identity of that someone else.

As Bobby Kennedy upbraided Bowles, the president sat in silence, unmoved, rapping the metal band of a pencil eraser against his front teeth. Presidential aide Richard Goodwin, sitting on the room's periphery in wonderment, realized that the rage he was witnessing was John Kennedy's—channeled with precision through Bobby. The outburst spoke volumes about the brothers' relationship. Bobby's intensity was a valuable tool: time and again JFK watched as Bobby turned his wrath upon some poor wretch of an aide; later, the president disowned Bobby's behavior (but not his message) with a shrug and a sympathetic laugh to the beleaguered party. Only with this tacit endorsement could Bobby behave as he did; only a president's brother could get away with it. At dinner at the home of Averell Harriman, the former New York governor and now JFK's assistant secretary of state for Far Eastern affairs, Bobby pressed Harriman for updates on anti-Communist activities in Eastern Europe. Harriman explained he was looking into the situation. Turning on the seventy-year-old "wise man" with an icy, indolent glare, Bobby said, "Well, get on it, Averell. See that you do it tomorrow." To journalist Rowland Evans, who attended the dinner, this was a perfect (if unneeded) reminder of Bobby's political insensitivity. Bobby "couldn't have cared less if [Harriman] had been the Maharajah of Jaipur. . . . Bobby was giving an order, and it happened to be Averell Harriman; it could have been anybody."

Harriman, indulgent and fond of his political junior, was unruffled. In fact, he admired Bobby's intolerance and impatience. Government foot-dragging enraged Bobby, as did most things—"Oh, everything!" Harriman recalled approvingly. "All procedures! . . . Everything having to do with everything in government." Bobby's temper was not, however, indiscriminate; as the Bay of Pigs clashes showed, Bobby was most incensed by anything or anyone with the potential to disappoint, damage, or embarrass John Kennedy. Bobby was fiercely, vigilantly protective. When Soviet Premier Nikita Khrushchev sent the president a gift of wine, Bobby had the FBI examine it for poison or personality-altering drugs. (None was found, though the wine was "consumed in the examination.")

But Robert Kennedy was more than a watchdog; he was a candid, incisive analyst who could be trusted fully to pursue any project to its end, with a clear eye to the president's interest. His power and value derived, obviously, from his uniquely close relationship with the president. The two did not always agree but their understanding was implicit, their language a series of coded grunts and seemingly telepathic signals. Bobby was invaluable to President Kennedy in a way his other advisers could never be, and they adjusted accordingly: in meetings of the cabinet and NSC, participants appealed to the attorney general as a powerful ally. They knew that unlike those of most other cabinet members, Bobby's direct phone line to the president was busy every day. Democratic National Chairman John Bailey recalled, "If Jack Kennedy wanted to be in the room with only one man, that man was Bobby. He wasn't just Number Two. He was Number One-and-a-Half."

Once President Kennedy asked an adviser, "Do you want the opinion of the second most powerful man in the world?" and gestured toward his brother. In the president's eyes, Bobby's worth rose as others' declined. The Bay of Pigs debacle left the president profoundly disillusioned by government and military careerists. Briefly he considered replacing the director of central intelligence, Allen Dulles, with Robert Kennedy, but Bobby cautioned that the appointment would end the president's plausible deniability of the CIA's more unsavory activities. The president instead paired Bobby with General Maxwell Taylor to examine, comprehensively, the course of the Cuban disaster. It was an education for Bobby, who plumbed the depths of the Agency and emerged a zealous advocate of its covert capabilities.

On June 13, 1961, Robert Kennedy and Taylor submitted an expansive, 154-page analysis of the Bay of Pigs invasion. Their report was measured in tone. It took issue not with the invasion's inception but with its development and execution. Castro, they determined, was indeed a "real menace," a "dangerously effective" Communist force in the hemisphere, threatening to disrupt the shaky democracies of Latin America. The attorney general seemed to have absorbed the institutional ethic of the CIA. Commenting on the investigation, Bobby assured that the United States "will take action against Castro. It might be tomorrow; it might be in five days or ten days, or not for months. But it will come."

As the affair ended and the months passed, Bobby Kennedy's foreign policy concerns diversified, ranging from Berlin, where he urged his brother to dispatch General Lucius Clay, to Vietnam, where he advised a "sharp step-up." But Cuba was a constant; it became Bobby's personal obsession. Beginning in November 1961, Bobby oversaw a regular gathering of White House advisers, labeled "Special Group (Augmented)," dedicated to ridding Cuba of Castro by a gradual escalation of insurgency. "My idea," Bobby noted to himself at the inception of Mongoose, the operational wing of SG (A), "is to stir things up on island with espionage, sabotage, general disorder, run & operated by Cubans themselves. . . . Do not know if we will be successful in overthrowing Castro but we have nothing to lose in my estimate." As his brother's *de facto* czar of Cuban affairs, Bobby acted with rash impunity: "Get off your ass on Cuba!" he shouted at generals and advisers.

Robert Kennedy's expanding reach and his brusque, if not brutal, manner raised hackles in the White House. If JFK valued Bobby as a catalyst and a watchdog, many others considered him an irritant and a micromanager. Unlike Bobby's subordinates at Justice, who described him as cool-headed in a crisis, Secretary of State Dean Rusk considered him petulant and reactionary—dangerously so. But it was Bobby's intrusiveness that truly rankled Rusk. "My understanding with President Kennedy," Rusk explained later, "was that we would try to find ways" to let Bobby express his "considerable interest in foreign policy . . . but that there would be no confusion about who was Secretary of State." The president often joked with Rusk about Bobby's "exuberance" and the need to keep Bobby on a tighter leash.

Robert Kennedy's more exuberant ideas were easily dismissed. When he proposed that American businessmen abroad demonstrate in the streets, meeting Communist-organized protests with their own, it was clear to the rest of the cabinet that corporations and foreign hosts alike would chafe at such an openly political role for American business. It was, at best, a half-baked notion. But the brothers' professional relationship had always been predicated on this unrestrained flow of ideas, however tentative or ill-formed. Most often Bobby's ideas were mulled over, refined, and implemented.

Beyond the president's watchful eye, however, tensions were not easily defused. Rusk's personnel battles with Robert Kennedy showed that an "understanding" with the president did not necessarily imply an understanding with the attorney general. Like the China hands drummed out of the State Department by the insistent beat of McCarthyism in the 1950s, Cuba experts were marked by suspicion after the Bay of Pigs. Bobby, Rusk recalled, was "very sensitive" on this point:

these men were not fit for promotion in his brother's administration. Rusk considered them honorable public servants who should not be penalized for larger policy failures. Asked later whether he had encountered any "latent McCarthyism" while staffing his State Department, Rusk pointed the finger at a "ruthless" RFK.

"Let Bobby have his say on these matters because he is very much interested in them," JFK told Rusk in 1961. "However, if he ever gets in your way, let me know and I'll take care of it"—which he did, quickly, on several occasions. Similarly, when General Clay reluctantly agreed to serve as ambassador to West Berlin in August 1961, he did so with one condition: under no circumstances would he work with Robert Kennedy. John Kennedy laughed. "I understand," he said. Again, the dichotomy was reinforced: Bobby the rogue, Jack the restraining hand.

At the same time, aided by sympathetic White House staffers, Bobby was enjoying a rehabilitation of his public reputation. Gone were reports of a callow youth rising far above his abilities. In January 1962, *Life* pronounced him "a political phenomenon such as never quite existed before. . . . As Attorney General he polices the practices of both labor unions and corporations, enforces the desegregation of the South and presses the battle against Big Crime. And as the President's brother, confidant and most trusted adviser he reflects the power and prestige of the White House as nobody, including Harry Hopkins and Sherman Adams, ever reflected it in the past." Only six months into John Kennedy's term as president, *U.S. News & World Report* proclaimed Bobby the "number two man in Washington . . . second only to the president in power and influence." He was the "Assistant President."

His expanding role in domestic and international affairs was not concealed by the White House; it was trumpeted. "Nothing big goes on without Bobby being in on it," a staff member boasted to *Life*. Based on "insider reports," *U.S. News* outlined RFK's legerdemain: international diplomacy, counterintelligence, national military strategy, politics, and even agriculture. Bobby was one of the few "who really [make] foreign policy." Some officials sought to underplay Bobby's unofficial role as global ambassador, but his travels—to Japan, Indonesia, Thailand, Italy, West Germany, and France, among other countries—placed Rusk and the State Department in his shadow.

Journalists were quick to underscore the political significance of the attorney general's ascent. As early as February 1962, *U.S. News* was reporting Bobby's frequent mention in Washington as a contender for the 1968 Democratic presidential nomination and detecting political calculation behind the "building" of his image as traveling statesman. Whatever Robert Kennedy's aims—the Senate, the Massachusetts governorship, or the presidency—he was seen as "running the political show" and positioning "Bobby's men" throughout the government. It appeared a vast political intelligence operation, a virtual shadow administration: his campaign loyalists, according to one official, "are posted all through the government. They are ready to give him an instant report on any phase of the government's activities—from the Agriculture Department to the Peace Corps. When he wants to know what's going on in a department, he can call his own man."

One thing, at least, was apparent to all. Robert Kennedy's public career was on an upward path; his political capital was skyrocketing: "Up, way up," gushed *Time*.

Lyndon Johnson's decline was as swift and merciless as Robert Kennedy's rise was meteoric. During the last six years of Eisenhower's presidency, LBJ had been widely and accurately considered the second most powerful man in government. No one made that claim again after Johnson's first few months as vice president. While RFK captured the headlines and the title of "number two man," the few stories on the vice president referred delicately to his "changed role." Others asked more bluntly: "Whatever happened to Lyndon Johnson?"

Certainly, Johnson had approached the vice presidency with unrealistic expectations—fed by his staff, the press, and his own inflated rhetoric. Now, rebuffed by the Senate and the White House in his scramble for power, Johnson was relegated—and relegated himself—to the periphery of the New Frontier. Reflecting later upon his own role during John Kennedy's thousand days, Johnson remembered "trips around the world, chauffeurs, men saluting, people clapping [and] chairmanships of councils, but in the end, it is nothing. I detested every minute of it."

As recently as the inauguration, it had seemed impossible, counterintuitive; now, it was undeniable: Lyndon Johnson was nothing. He was nowhere. He was a superfluous man, a spectral presence, a vague reminder of campaign unpleasantries. Among the press corps and within the administration, Johnson was scarcely mentioned or noticed. New Frontiersmen looked ahead and envisioned a Kennedy era, a political and cultural renaissance stretching eight years—sixteen, perhaps, if Bobby ran in '68—into the future. Lyndon Johnson and the old politics he represented were forgotten.

The void in Johnson's life was considerable. He filled it as best he could with trivialities. He contrived a sad charade of a man with something to do. Charlie Boatner, a Johnson aide, remembered the manic pace the vice president struggled to maintain, as if to convince himself of his own relevance. Boatner lived in a spare room at the Johnsons' home at 4040 52nd Street, "The Elms," in late 1961. Every night, when the Johnsons returned from yet another ceremonial event, LBJ summoned Boatner into the master bedroom. Boatner learned to bring a pencil and notepad, for the vice president would then unleash a torrent of questions, demands, concerns, and tasks for the following day. The 11:00 news provided a brief respite before Johnson resumed his monologue, talking as he undressed, talking as he climbed into the bed while Boatner sat furiously transcribing the whims which tumbled forth, endlessly, stream-of-consciousness, from the vice president. Inevitably LBJ would talk himself to sleep and Boatner would creep back to his own bedroom. The next morning, "just as regular as rain," Boatner recalled, LBJ would knock on the door—"Charlie, you awake?"—and barge into the room with two cups of Sanka. Sitting down on Boatner's bed, LBJ would sip his coffee and begin right where he had left off the night before. It was a convincing affectation of urgency; but Johnson, Boatner judged, was doing no more than trying to keep informed.

As majority leader, Lyndon Johnson had welcomed a constant stream of visitors into the Taj Mahal, greeting each one with great, effusive cheer but always making clear that important business was pressing. Johnson ushered lingerers quickly out of the room. As vice president, however, the gaps in Johnson's schedule were broad and intolerable; they taunted him with his impotence. Yearning for company, flexing his expansive personality like a muscle in danger of atrophying, Johnson picked up the telephone and railed to anyone about anything. If the matter at hand, however obscure, concerned Texas, Johnson treated his listener to a meandering historical journey, beginning in the 1930s and working, almost month by month, toward the present.

At the receiving end, government officials sat frozen on the line, often for thirty or forty-five minutes, terrified to interrupt Johnson's diatribe and wishing that he would stop and let them get back to work. Adam Yarmolinsky, Secretary Robert McNamara's assistant at the Pentagon, was baffled by LBJ's attention: "I was no particular confidant of his," he recalled. Yarmolinsky came to understand the length of Johnson's "endless" ramblings as a measure of his underutilization as vice president.

"No one knew quite what to do with him," Clark Clifford recalled. One of the few to grapple actively with the question was President Kennedy. "I don't know what to do with Lyndon. I've got to keep him happy somehow," he repeated frequently to columnist Arthur Krock. Kennedy understood that the vice presidency was unpleasant, frustrating, a "non-job." He predicted difficulty for LBJ from the beginning. But he was extremely concerned that Johnson be treated with dignity.

To avoid conflicts between the presidential and vice presidential staffs, Kennedy granted Johnson easy access to the Oval Office and dealt with LBJ directly. He tolerated no word of disrespect toward his vice president. "I want you to know one thing," the president told his close adviser Ken O'Donnell in 1961. Johnson "thinks he's ten times more important than I am . . . but he thinks you're nothing but a clerk. . . . You have never been elected to anything by anybody, and you are dealing with a very insecure, sensitive man with a huge ego. I want you literally to kiss his fanny from one end of Washington to the other." Kennedy joked that O'Donnell was in charge of the care and feeding of LBJ.

If so, O'Donnell was a poor choice. As a custodian of the vice president's well-being, O'Donnell was indifferent and offhandedly cruel. He demanded that every request LBJ made of the Pentagon, however mundane, be cleared first by the White House. He had no time for Johnson whatsoever, "wouldn't give him the time of day," said another presidential aide. Open disparagement of LBJ was rare, but O'Donnell's demeanor typified what Johnson's staff perceived as a "loose contempt" for the vice president by the White House staff. Though John Kennedy conducted himself as president with a certain humility, his senior staffers struck Charles Bartlett as "enormously impressed with themselves," and O'Donnell, closest to the president, was the most impressed. In Bartlett's view, O'Donnell's arrogant disregard conveyed one simple, gleeful fact to the vice president: "We're it and you're not." Robert Kennedy communicated as much when he barged in and interrupted Johnson's private meetings with the president, launching into what he considered to be far more important business without so much as a nod of apology toward LBJ.

Bobby did not require important business to cut off the vice president. Once when President Kennedy had to leave a White House meeting with civil rights leaders he asked LBJ to wrap things up. Bobby listened silently. After a few minutes Bobby looked up and motioned for Louis Martin, an official of the Democratic National Committee, to come over. "I've got a date, and I've got to get on this boat in a few minutes," he whispered in Martin's ear. "Can you tell the vice president to cut it short?" Martin was "absolutely thunderstruck." Having no wish to step between these two combatants, Martin returned to his seat and did nothing. Bobby motioned again. "Didn't I tell you to tell the vice president to shut up?" he snapped. Martin edged uneasily around the table to stand beside LBJ, who was now quite happily mid-monologue. Martin whispered in his ear, "Bobby has got to go, and he wants to close it up." Johnson glared up at Martin and did not pause for a moment. Martin slunk back to his seat. "I thought surely this was the faux pas of the year, as far as I was concerned . . . and I was really sick." Johnson continued for another ten or fifteen minutes and then ended the meeting on his own timetable.

If John Kennedy could not entrust Johnson's dignity to Bobby or the White House staff, he could, at least, insist that they keep Johnson generally informed on issues and apprised of all major meetings, ceremonies, parties, and dances. The president's instructions were clear: at meetings of substance, Johnson's invitation was automatic.

The policy proved difficult in practice. Early in his presidency, JFK sat in the cabinet room surrounded by advisers discussing a message to Congress. The meeting had barely begun when Kennedy paused and glanced around the table. "Where is the vice president?" he demanded. Kennedy's men looked at him blankly. They had forgotten to notify Johnson of the meeting. Angrily, Kennedy restated his policy: "Don't let this ever happen again," he said. "You know what my rules are, and we will not conduct meetings without the vice president being present." The president struggled to set the example himself, and wanted it known that he was doing so. "President Kennedy," *Time* reported in February 1962, "is tireless in his efforts to keep Lyndon Johnson busy—and happy. . . . [Kennedy is] going out of his way to please and placate Johnson."

It was a bit of an overstatement. Despite President Kennedy's intentions, Lyndon Johnson was often excluded as events heated up and the pace within the White House quickened. It happened more by accident than by design; Johnson was regarded less as an interloper than as an "extra wheel." In the summer of 1963, at Robert Kennedy's suggestion, the president held a series of meetings with groups of Southern leaders to discuss the inequality of opportunity facing black Americans. Lee White, the president's top assistant on civil rights, invited separate gatherings of leaders in labor, education, religion, and business. "Look," the president instructed White, who was preparing administration officials for the meetings, "you work with Lyndon Johnson and make sure that he knows about all these things. I want him here. I think he can do a lot. First of all, he's pretty damned smart. And second of all, he's a Southerner and he's got a better speaking voice [to] a lot of these people." The president's instructions, White recalled, were "just as clear as a damned bell."

The affable White, who bore no malice toward the vice president, was the staffer least likely to offend him; but of the eight meetings, there were two or three occasions when he forgot—"just forgot!"—about Lyndon Johnson. In the frenzied final minutes before a meeting, as secretaries recorded White's last-minute memo on madly chattering typewriters,

Johnson was far from White's mind. On more than one occasion, just moments before a gathering, White rushed into the Oval Office bearing a handful of carbon copies of the president's talking points. After the memo was distributed, LBJ stood empty-handed. White had forgotten to print him a copy. Johnson was entitled to one, of course, but too ashamed to ask. Instead, the big man sidled up to the short, stout White and peered silently over his shoulder.

Once White failed even to invite Johnson to the conference (LBJ was rarely given more than five minutes' notice, even for cabinet or NSC meetings). Later that day, sounding angry and "very, very hurt," Johnson called White to protest. "It was a terrible thing," a chagrined White recalled, noting in his own defense that when one is on deadline for the president of the United States, he becomes a bit blind to protocol.

Whenever Johnson failed to receive or respond to an invitation, JFK had Bobby Kennedy phone the vice president as a sign of his personal concern. But other times, Johnson slipped the mind of even the conscientious president. Charles Bartlett, passing along murmurs that Johnson was feeling neglected in foreign policy matters, asked the president, "Why don't you call Lyndon more often and ask his opinion?" Kennedy appeared struck by the question, then apologized. "You know," he said, "it's awfully hard, because once you get into one of these crunches you really don't think of calling Lyndon because he hasn't read the cables. . . . You want to talk to the people who are most involved."

Yet even when present at White House meetings, LBJ was hardly involved. Gloomily, he sat at the president's side in virtual silence, volunteering nothing, uttering no more than a syllable or two in response to a direct question from JFK. Johnson remembered the vocal dissent of Franklin Roosevelt's Texan vice president, John Nance Garner, and judged it inexcusable; he also recalled Eisenhower's resentment of Nixon's discreet pressures on policy. Both men had been edged out—Garner out of office and Nixon out of the inner circle. Kennedy tried to draw Johnson into the debate, but as a matter of principle and political instinct, Johnson remained silent, providing no fodder for rumors of a split between himself and the president. Instead, if he felt strongly on an issue, he broached it privately with Kennedy. He did so only rarely.

Neither did Johnson make much of his institutional responsibilities. As a gesture to LBJ's desire for an expanded executive role and to find some outlet for Johnson's capabilities and pride, Kennedy appointed him as chairman of the President's Committee on Equal Employment Opportunity, the Peace Corps advisory board, and the National Aeronautics and Space Council. The press, as usual, made bold predictions about the vice president's will and ability to dominate these important-sounding agencies. Many political observers agreed that Johnson would seize the opportunity to become the administration's expert on space policy, one of JFK's top priorities for the 1960s. He did not. In March 1961, NASA observers told Tom Wicker of the *New York Times* that "Mr. Johnson's hand, if it has been laid upon that organization at all, has been light indeed. . . . Mr. Johnson's activities and influence there are scarcely visible."

On March 7, 1961, the White House issued an executive order establishing the President's Committee on Equal Employment Opportunity (CEEO). The vice president was its chairman; the attorney general and the secretary of labor, Arthur Goldberg, were among its members. The CEEO, not the space council, was to be Johnson's primary day-to-day responsibility, and it was one Johnson was not sure he wanted. Created to prevent racial discrimination by corporations holding government contracts, the committee was an experimental body, the first official federal commission of its kind. As a Southerner, Johnson would make an attractive target for liberal critics of the committee's assuredly slow pace. But this risk carried with it an opportunity to bolster his record on civil rights.

Johnson relished the chance to improve his image and to combat discrimination. Once on board, he threw himself into the committee's work enthusiastically. Even while touring Afghanistan, LBJ phoned Goldberg with ideas for the committee. Johnson's energy was manic but sporadic; at times he seemed disengaged from the committee's activities. Still, the vice president took consistent pride in its achievements, which included a "Plans for Progress" agreement with eighty-five firms holding government contracts, and a "Plans for Fair Practices" pact with 117 international unions and 300 local AFL-CIO affiliates.

Plans for Progress was the creation of President Kennedy's close friend Robert Troutman, an Atlanta attorney. Troutman's idea was to enlist the active support of large corporations. "I think this can be one of the most important things we will be able to do this term," JFK wrote his vice president. "I feel that anything that can be done to promptly expand this to other companies . . . will prove to be very beneficial." Johnson agreed; Troutman's plan appealed to his conciliatory nature. As chairman, Johnson was reluctant to cancel the contracts of offending corporations and did so only when mediation failed. Johnson was, as always, a skilled negotiator. When airlines were loath to hire more black stewardesses, for example, Johnson simply placed a phone call to the company executives and won the concession. The mere threat of enforcement was enough, believed George Reedy, LBJ's chief aide on the committee. Voluntary compliance was yielding "rather sizable" achievements.

Without legislative support, though, the CEEO lacked real authority. It was not going to come from the Senate, where LBJ's old colleagues pressured him against an aggressive pursuit of the committee's mandate. As far back as the Truman years, Senator Richard Russell had slashed federal funds allotted to contract compliance; now he curtailed the activities of Johnson's CEEO. Other Senate critics kept a tight fist on appropriations.

Within the White House there was a bit of tinkering with the CEEO's jurisdiction; throughout 1961, aides drafted a planned executive order on "Extending the Authority of the President's Committee . . ." Memos circulated between the White House and the Justice Department, back and forth for nine months, among Harris Wofford, President Kennedy's special assistant on civil rights, and Burke Marshall, Ted Sorensen, Lee White, Nick Katzenbach, and others. At no point did a copy reach the vice president, the order's chief beneficiary. In fact, as Wofford told White, the CEEO's executive director, John Feild, "has delayed processing it through the Vice President for internal Committee reasons."

Those reasons were, most likely, ideological. Johnson's CEEO was considerably more forward-looking than a similar committee under Vice President Nixon, but was far from militant. "Let's make it *fashionable* to end discrimination," he urged his more "red-hot" committee members. He convinced few of them. In May 1962, Johnson sought to undercut the liberal Feild and stifle the growing internecine conflict by interposing his own man, a politically moderate black lawyer, Hobart Taylor, Jr., as executive vice chairman of the CEEO.

While Taylor clashed with Feild, Johnson was fighting to preserve his own authority. In the press, "sources" were calling the committee a "publicity vehicle" for Lyndon Johnson or an appeasement of Southern congressmen that left heavy industry untouched. Herbert Hill of the NAACP called Plans for Progress "one of the great phonies of the Kennedy administration's civil rights program." Housing representative Jack Conway thought Johnson and Taylor "were selling out the program at a pretty rapid rate." And within the administration, JFK's leaders on civil rights and employment policy, Robert Kennedy and Willard Wirtz (Goldberg's successor as labor secretary), began to suspect that the CEEO was producing more "Plans" than "Progress."

Johnson had hoped for the attorney general's support. He would not be going far without it. When the president granted Johnson stewardship of the CEEO, LBJ immediately wrote to Bobby Kennedy, forwarding the executive order and adding, "I am looking forward to cooperating with you in achieving [the] objective" of ending discrimination in hiring. Bobby was a member of the committee, and Johnson was careful to keep him duly informed. In May 1962, the attorney general thanked Johnson for forwarding a report on Negro government employment. "It certainly shows that some progress has been made," Bobby replied tersely. But it was clear he did not share the apparent enthusiasm of his brother, who wrote Johnson only three months later that Troutman's latest results "are most impressive" and worth pursuing. "I am satisfied," the president added, "that a great deal of the criticism of the Plans for Progress resulted from completely irrelevant factors quite unrelated to the merits of the program." In reality JFK was unsatisfied; he blamed Johnson for the Plans' failings but let him be for fear of offending him. Bobby had no such fears and had never put any faith in Plans for Progress; he thought "it wasn't worth a damn," in Katzenbach's words. Specifically, Bobby shared organized labor's suspicion of "voluntary compliance" as an empty slogan that let business off the hook. It was nothing personal; Troutman, after all, was his brother's close friend. But the administration was either going to get tough or it was not. Plans for Progress was equivocal and naive. The real emphasis, Bobby believed, must be on enforcement.

Bobby's concern extended to the CEEO as a whole. Not once had the committee canceled a work agreement with any of the 25,000 all-white companies doing business with the federal government. "What the hell are they doing over there?" he demanded of White, JFK's liaison to the committee. Bobby did a bit of exploring himself, sitting in on committee meetings. He preferred to send his delegate, John Seigenthaler, and thought his time better spent elsewhere, but Bobby wanted Johnson to know the attorney general was not hostile toward him or the CEEO, and that he appreciated Johnson's service to the administration. Bobby made a public show of deferring to the vice president, speaking up quickly when he agreed with Johnson's statements. But Johnson did not reciprocate the sentiment, thin as it was. Seigenthaler had the uneasy feeling that Bobby's appearances were raising eyebrows and tensions among the Johnson staff.

It was not Bobby's attendance but his interference that irked the committee and its chairman. Adjustment of CEEO policy was made by the White House, not LBJ, and often bore the stamp of the attorney general. Bobby gave instructions and then steered clear of any complications. Those belonged to Johnson—as did the blame for any policy failure. "It was things like this," reflected Hobart Taylor, "that [explain] why so many people in government did not like Bobby."

As Bobby looked closer at the CEEO, it was true, he was growing frustrated, and he began poking and prodding; the committee was full of good talkers, he told Seigenthaler, but they didn't know a thing about action. They spoke in bland generalities and then issued them as press releases. "There was an awful lot of propaganda put out," Bobby recalled later, "but when we started making an analysis, we found it really hadn't accomplished a great deal." Troutman's program was not a failure, exactly; it had sparked some marginal progress. But in Bobby's view it was being oversold. In private meetings with the attorney general, Wirtz and several other committee members went a step further, denouncing Plans for Progress as "a real fraud"; either Troutman had duped Johnson, or Johnson, with a wink toward his Southern friends on the Hill, had let himself be duped.

For two years, the CEEO offered moderate gains and mild reassurances concerning Negro employment. In the summer of 1962, President Kennedy gave Bobby the go-ahead to survey government-contracted firms that still had no Negro workers. "The number," Bobby said, "was shockingly high." And in 1963, an investigation by Wirtz revealed that 25,000 of 35,000 companies with federal contracts still employed no Negroes. Bobby rifled through corporate questionnaires, page after page bearing the same figure: zero. Companies boasting what the CEEO called "100 percent gains" were often revealed to have increased their number of black employees from one to two.

Robert Kennedy was outraged and terrified. If the facts became known, there would be scandal. His brother's administration, so publicly proud of its progress, would be savaged by liberals and the press. And with an election year approaching, the CEEO's failures would belong not to Lyndon Johnson but to John Kennedy. "It was a matter of great concern to me," Bobby recalled, ". . . not just because I was so worked up about the Negroes [not] getting jobs, but because I could just visualize this coming out." What had begun as a clash over policy was becoming political and deeply personal.

In Bobby's final analysis, the main problem was not Plans for Progress or even the weakness of the CEEO. The problem was Lyndon Johnson. The CEEO "could have been an effective organization . . . if the vice president gave it some direction," Bobby said later. He echoed the committee's bad press: "It was mostly a public relations operation" and "very badly managed." Johnson's staff, said RFK, was taken in by its own hype. And Hobart Taylor, Johnson's executive vice chairman, "was an Uncle Tom."

According to Robert Kennedy, the president was every bit as infuriated by the real statistics on equal opportunity. "Oh, he almost had a fit. And he said . . . 'That man can't run this committee. Can you think of anything more deplorable than him trying to run the United States? That's why he can't ever be president.' " The brothers wondered aloud how Johnson had ever run the Senate; he couldn't even manage this small operation.

Ironically, the operation was about to become larger. After April and May 1963, when a series of civil rights demonstrations in Birmingham, Alabama, erupted into riots and shockingly brutal police assaults, the Kennedy administration cast about desperately for any area where it could act more strongly on civil rights. Lee White had held on to the draft executive order for an expanded CEEO since 1961. Now it won the president's hurried assent. The CEEO's domain was to stretch beyond government contracts to highway and other programs which received even a portion of federal funds.

White finalized the order on a Sunday amid a flurry of consultations—and again, he lost LBJ in the confusion. "I checked with every damned guy in government, I think, except Johnson! There was nothing deliberate about it. . . . There's no goddamned rational explanation for it," White explained later, "except in my mind . . . he wasn't part of the machinery."

Johnson was quietly devastated. "I've never seen a more surprised, disappointed and annoyed guy than Lyndon Johnson when the President of the United States issued [the] executive order changing the jurisdiction of his committee," observed White. There was nothing to do but accept the indignity with good grace—"about as good as a guy can when he gets a mackerel in the face!" White exclaimed contritely. But Johnson made it very clear: he was pained by the slight.

It would not be the last or the deepest cut. Birmingham had energized the federal civil rights effort; and the attorney general, finally confronting the brutality of racism, was simmering with rage. Burke Marshall, Bobby's assistant attorney general for civil rights, described the charged political environment of May 1963:

> The country was in absolute turmoil because of Birmingham; . . . black people, white people, everybody was on [JFK's] neck. So Robert Kennedy was trying to do all sorts of things; he was trying to persuade businessmen to open their restaurants and theaters; he was trying to get this [civil rights] legislation underway; he was trying to get church groups and educators and labor people stirred up about this and doing something within their own constituency. And so he was very impatient.

On all fronts, RFK was pressing for fast action. But when the CEEO met on May 29, 1963, he learned that out of two thousand federal employees in Birmingham, only fifteen were blacks—1 percent in a city that was 37 percent black. Bobby sent Marshall down to Birmingham to survey the situation. "I'd gone into . . . every federal office," Marshall said later, "and you couldn't even find a Negro sweeping the floor."

In the wake of the riots, attendance at the next CEEO meeting was unusually high. Johnson and Hobart Taylor sat at the head of the conference table; the rest of the committee flanked them in a semicircle, with staff behind them in a row. The room was full. Mid-discussion, Robert Kennedy charged into the room, trailed by Burke Marshall and very obviously ready to explode. Immediately Bobby peppered the committee with questions about progress in Birmingham, about the city's defense industries, about employment patterns and compliance reports. What agencies had how many Negroes? How many vacancies were there? Who was doing what to improve the situation?

Johnson, struggling for control of his own forum, called on NASA Director Jim Webb to give a report. Webb was Johnson's man at NASA and, in Bobby's private view, a poor choice and "rather a blabbermouth." Today, however, Webb gave a measured, optimistic presentation, and Johnson congratulated him warmly on NASA's fine progress. Bobby stood again, his face reddening. He turned toward Webb and demanded to know why, with $3.5 billion in contracts, NASA had only two men working on equal employment. Webb, shocked and disoriented, turned helplessly to his staff. If anything infuriated Robert Kennedy, it was a lack of preparation; he lashed out like a bitter prosecutor. As Bobby pressed harder, Webb grew more and more vague. A pall of embarrassment covered the room.

Bobby turned now to Hobart Taylor and asked again about compliance reports. A new form was being developed, Taylor assured him. "Where is the form?" Bobby snapped. It was being processed by the Budget Bureau. "Where in the Budget Bureau?" Bobby offered to expedite it—insisted, really. Taylor was becoming visibly upset now, straining to keep a level tone: "Mr. Attorney General," he protested, "I don't believe I need your help. . . . It really won't be necessary."

Lyndon Johnson was sunk deeply into his chair, his eyes narrowed to mere slits. He watched the dressing-down of Taylor, his dear friend from Texas, his man at the helm of the CEEO, with obvious rage and discomfort. Finally, Johnson cut in: "This is our position, Mr. Attorney General," he declared firmly, and delivered a careful and thorough review of the committee's work. Bobby fired a few impatient questions at LBJ. "It was a brutal performance, very sharp," recalled Jack Conway, who attended as a representative of the federal housing agency. "It brought tensions between Johnson and Kennedy right out on the table and very hard. Everybody was sweating under the armpits."

Johnson's voice grew quieter, more deliberate, in response. "He went over the whole thing again like a father explaining something to a small child," remembered Marjorie McKenzie Lawson, a committee member. Johnson's face was red, his voice barely audible, but his controlled manner struck Lawson as "more dignified . . . than Bobby, who was beginning to be shrill."

Kennedy turned away from Johnson and asked another member about the committee's apprenticeship program. The man fumbled through his materials, began to answer, but Kennedy had had enough. "Finally," Conway recalled, "after completely humiliating Webb and making the vice president look like a fraud . . . [Bobby] got up. He walked around the table . . . shook my hand . . . and talked to me for about thirty seconds about how things were going here, there, and every place, and then he went on out."

There was a moment of profound silence. Lyndon Johnson recommenced his meeting.

In the days that followed, Kennedy loyalists gleefully spread the story of Johnson's embarrassment. LBJ and RFK aired their grievances privately. "Bobby came in the other day to our Equal Employment Committee and I was humiliated," Johnson complained to Ted Sorensen on the telephone. "He took on Hobart [Taylor] . . . and he just gave him hell" about Negro employment in Birmingham. It was not just embarrassing, Johnson implied; it was grossly unfair to a committee with minimal powers. "Obviously, the president and the attorney general can get twenty-six or twenty-six hundred" jobs for blacks if they demanded it. "But the only way we can tell [corporations to comply] is [by removing] them from the civil service register. . . . We can't *make* them do anything." Years later, LBJ was still embittered by the experience. "We couldn't just go out and wrestle with the fellow [the corporation] and say, 'You've got to do this or we'll do something to you.' We tried to lead them with persuasion because that's all the power we had."

If that was all the power the CEEO had, Bobby decided, he would bypass it altogether. In July, he wrote the president that his civil rights advisers "were having a difficult time with Johnson and the committee because of his oversensitivity [to] any outside criticism. One of the great problems has been the fact that this committee has not really accomplished what . . . the press releases would indicate . . . , the result being a stepped-up effort which Burke [Marshall], Bill Wirtz and I have had to undertake with a great deal of care."

Committee members might well have disputed that last point. Just after the meeting, Marshall and other Justice Department officials called the aggrieved Hobart Taylor and asked him please to overlook the whole affair. There would in fact be no future clashes or any cause for them, since the CEEO was being gradually supplanted. Secretary Wirtz, since the autumn of 1962, had largely ignored the committee in favor of more powerful government agencies which held the majority of contracts with private industry. And Robert Kennedy's Justice Department, armed with the (albeit limited) machinery of LBJ's Civil Rights Acts of 1957 and 1960, continued to confront discrimination with vigor. Once, Johnson had controlled the entire Senate; now, weighed down by controversy and diminished expectations, he had lost control of a mere presidential commission.

In Johnson's battle with Robert Kennedy over the direction of the CEEO, some, like Lee White, detected jockeying for leadership of the civil rights effort. But it was hardly a contest. For the attorney general, this was the time of Birmingham and Oxford, of Freedom Rides and marches on Washington, a time of managing crises and making history. The vice president's CEEO, inherently weak and weakened further by his conservative approach, was obscure and ultimately irrelevant. Still, fueled by policy differences and personal antagonism, the committee sparked what Bobby called "the sharpest disputes I ever had with Vice President Johnson." They were not to be forgotten by either man.

CHAPTER 4

Two
Heirs Apparent

John Kennedy's Washington offered little to Lyndon Johnson beyond humiliation, loneliness, and ennui. When Sam Rayburn died in November 1961, Johnson felt cut from his moorings. "He was crushed by the loss at a time when he felt very much adrift and sorely needed an anchor," Bobby Baker observed. "The Capitol," Johnson mourned, "will be a lonely place without [Rayburn]."

Johnson's eagerness to leave the country surprised no one. In less than three years as vice president, LBJ made eleven trips and visited thirty-three countries. Overseas, Johnson regained a certain vitality and sense of purpose which flagged at home. His first trip set the pattern: in Senegal to celebrate the country's independence, Johnson stormed the streets and marketplaces like a candidate for office, leading his entourage through the muddy, smelly streets of a fishing village, stepping over chickens and pigs to shake hands effusively with village lepers while the American ambassador sat impatiently in his limousine. That night, Johnson slept at the embassy, but only briefly. He upset the ambassador's wife by staying awake until the early morning, reading messages and cables and talking back and forth to the United States. Thereafter, Johnson—and his portable communications station—stayed at a hotel.

From Africa to Italy, Great Britain, Greece, Cyprus, Jamaica, and Israel, the image was the same: Lyndon Johnson, looking misplaced and unnaturally large, sweating profusely in shirtsleeves and passing out souvenir pens to enthusiastic crowds. Johnson's exuberance, painfully suppressed in Washington, exploded outward on these travels. He delighted foreign audiences, establishing a genuine rapport with masses of peasants everywhere. Johnson did less well with members of the Foreign Service. Preceding his arrival at any host embassy was an extensive and nettlesome checklist of requirements, always including an oversized bed to fit LBJ's lengthy frame. He changed plans at whim and left embassies scrambling in his wake. He did, however, bring his own limousine, an ample supply of Cutty Sark whiskey, and a custom shower head with a fine needlepoint spray.

Still, embassy cables testified to LBJ's valuable performance, and the president registered approval by sending Johnson not only on goodwill tours but on important missions. When Kennedy dispatched Johnson to Southeast Asia in the spring of 1961, the vice president carried clear instructions from the White House endowing the trip with greater authority and giving LBJ freer license to act as the president's representative. In the midst of a bloody Communist insurrection in Laos, LBJ was reluctant to go to Saigon, the capital of neighboring South Vietnam, but JFK insisted. Kennedy intended to demonstrate America's commitment to democracy in the region. To heighten the trip's prestige, Kennedy sent along his sister and brother-in-law, Jean and Stephen Smith. Administration officials joked that Johnson was joining them to watch a little Kennedy diplomacy.

Johnson did, however, carry a substantive agenda of his own. During his meeting with South Vietnamese Premier Ngo Dinh Diem, Johnson tried, at President Kennedy's instructions, to persuade the corrupt and authoritarian regime to enact social and fiscal reforms. Diem was conciliatory but remote. When Johnson returned to Washington in May, he was rumored to have been charmed into complaisance by Diem (Johnson had toasted him with champagne as "the Winston Churchill of Asia"), but in his thorough and thoughtful report to President Kennedy, LBJ was equivocal in his view of the increasingly autocratic premier. Diem, wrote the vice president, had "admirable qualities" but was cloistered from his people and surrounded by incompetents. Neatly and matter-of-factly, LBJ assessed America's vital interest in Southeast Asia and concluded that "there is no alternative to United States leadership" in the Pacific. Johnson predicted "very heavy and continuing costs . . . in terms of money, of effort, and of United States prestige." Was America prepared to meet the challenge? Given the price of failure, the vice president urged "a clear-cut and strong program of action."

Johnson's analysis was concise and forward-thinking, but at heart his worldview smacked of parochialism. Inexperienced in foreign affairs, the vice president did not work hard at developing any new insights. He shied from men his aide George Reedy classed as "remote" or "otherworldly types" and preferred pressing the flesh of the masses to probing the perspective of diplomats. This was not entirely a liability: days after his return from Asia, in an extemporaneous address to the Advertising

Council, LBJ railed less against the snares of geopolitics than the wages
of poverty and human neglect, of poor education and inadequate health
care. He movingly described his youth amid Texan poverty, compared it
to the deprivations of the third world, and spoke passionately of the
progress that could be made in one man's lifetime. Kennedy's national
security adviser Walt Rostow later called it "the single best speech on
foreign aid I've ever heard by anyone."

More important, LBJ was a vivid embodiment of American goodwill
abroad. JFK used him accordingly. In August 1961, three months after
LBJ's Southeast Asian trip, cold war tensions erupted when the Communist government of East Germany began erecting a cinder-block-
and-concrete wall between East and West Berlin. Kennedy wanted his
vice president in West Berlin to greet arriving American troops, inspect
the wall, and assure Berliners they were not forgotten. But Johnson had
no wish to be a symbol for anything in Berlin. The situation was explosive; Johnson feared war—and damage to his political career—and
refused to oblige.

It was an inauspicious moment to show backbone. Johnson was setting himself up for reproof and Bobby Kennedy was quick to deliver it.
Bobby served LBJ with a presidential command to pack his bags for
Berlin. Incredibly, Johnson refused again, ensuring another unpleasant
exchange with a man who considered a raised eyebrow at a presidential
order an act of insubordination.

Johnson, disgruntled and nervous, flew to Berlin with no real choice
in the matter. But in the supercharged atmosphere of the divided city, he
quickly forgot his qualms. He acquitted himself brilliantly, delivering a
rousing speech before a special session of the West Berlin parliament and
saluting American troops as they entered the city. Still, his reluctance to
go—indeed, his cowardice in trying to wriggle out of an important
assignment—had cost him dearly in the White House. And true to
form, Johnson blamed not himself but Bobby Kennedy, once again the
harbinger of his humiliation.

At home, President Kennedy was determined to include LBJ in matters
of national security. In 1961, when bad weather delayed Air Force Two,
stranding Johnson in a holding pattern above Washington, Kennedy
shelved important matters until his arrival. "Put that issue aside, and we'll
meet later this afternoon when the vice president is here," he told his
advisers. Kennedy wanted Johnson to share in the responsibility—or liability—for decisions and to be prepared, at any time, to assume the presidency. But Kennedy's deference was mostly a matter of protocol.
Johnson's extensive travels meant little in terms of real influence; he

made trips but not foreign policy. Secretary Rusk, at his own initiative, assigned a Foreign Service officer to brief LBJ on international affairs and to serve as liaison to the State Department. Johnson embraced the idea and excitedly received daily intelligence reports, telegrams, and State Department summaries. "He absorbed briefings in expert fashion," Rusk remembered. But Rusk said nothing of Johnson's contributions to policy-making; if there were any, they were slight and undocumented.

LBJ tried in vain to exploit his peripatetic image by portraying himself in the press as a foreign policy strategist. When the president tried to absolve Johnson of blame for the first Cuban crisis by stating publicly that LBJ had participated in all major administration decisions "with the exception . . . of the Bay of Pigs," Johnson was upset at the perceived slight. He had, of course, attended almost none of the meetings on the plan, which he regarded with a vague skepticism; according to Rusk, Johnson considered the invasion a "harebrained scheme." In its immediate aftermath, LBJ tried to avoid committing to a new course of action, thus irritating the attorney general. "We had the impression," Bobby wrote of his colleagues on the NSC, that Johnson "was just trying to get off it himself." Inspired by this "slight flare-up" with Johnson, Bobby took aside the secretaries of defense and state and lectured them that "the important matter was to stand firm and to not try to pass the blame off to somebody else. This could lead only to bitter recriminations and even more disaster."

Now, bizarrely, Johnson tried for days to convince reporters that he had in fact been integral to planning the debacle. At the same time, with no appreciation for the contradiction, mysterious "White House insiders" leaked that the Bay of Pigs crisis had taught JFK to value his vice president's "practical" advice on foreign affairs over his other counselors'.

If the vice president had any practical wisdom to offer he was keeping it to himself. In meetings of the National Security Council, Johnson maintained a "general policy of never speaking unless the president asked me [to]. . . . I never thought it would be appropriate or desirable to debate differences of opinion in open meetings," LBJ said later. When, on rare occasions, his enthusiasm got the better of him, he was sternly corrected. During the Bay of Pigs crisis, Johnson asked whether the Joint Chiefs had in fact recommended what they had been quoted as recommending, since it contradicted what they had told him privately. "The President," Johnson remembered, "showed some irritation and said of course they had. . . . It was an embarrassing situation." Johnson retreated into what one participant called "a listening role."

LBJ was damned either way. If his comments inspired irritation, his silence invited mockery—particularly from Robert Kennedy. In private meetings, the attorney general and the president "used to laugh about it." According to Bobby, JFK asked Johnson's views just to elicit his standard evasions, a private joke between brothers. On serious matters like the Cuban missile crisis, Bobby said, the president stopped consulting Johnson altogether.

When, on October 16, 1962, aerial photographs confirmed the Soviet placement of surface-to-surface ballistic missiles in Cuba, President Kennedy hastily convened an *ad hoc* group called the Executive Committee of the NSC, or ExComm. This was the defining—and, some feared, the last—crisis of the nuclear age. It was also a defining moment in the life and relationships of Robert Kennedy. For Bobby, the tense, freewheeling discussions of the ExComm were the test of mental toughness and moral fiber that the Second World War, disappointingly, had not been (Bobby spent its last months in officer training school at Harvard). By October 28, when the Soviets agreed to withdraw their missiles from Cuba, Bobby had developed lasting, fundamental impressions of the ExComm members. For some men, like Secretary of Defense Robert McNamara, he felt the camaraderie and respect of brothers-in-arms. For others, like Rusk, Bobby developed a new disdain. The most profound among these impressions was Bobby's utter contempt for Lyndon Johnson.

Johnson rarely attended ExComm meetings, where Bobby was a constant and crucial presence. In the first days of the crisis, when most ExComm members pushed for bombing the missile installations, the attorney general was wary. "You're going to kill an awful lot of people," he cautioned, "and we're going to take an awful lot of heat on it." It would invite a precipitate response in Turkey or Iran by the Soviets. Even worse, Bobby said, a preemptive air strike or "sneak attack" was un-American; it was "Pearl Harbor in reverse," an affront to American ideals.

It was, ironically, just the sort of reckless action others expected from Robert Kennedy. Participants were surprised by his restraint. "I had always had a feeling," observed Under Secretary of State George Ball, "that Bobby had a much too simplistic and categorical position toward things . . . that you always acted decisively and you always went in and damned the torpedoes. . . . But he behaved quite differently during the Cuban missile crisis," when he was "very useful" and surprisingly cool-headed. As the days passed and tempers escalated, Bobby helped defuse tensions between members of the group by moving the discussion forward or cracking an occasional wry joke. In McNamara's view, it was Bobby who kept the ExComm focused on the big picture, the implications of their actions in strategic and historical terms.

Not all were impressed by the attorney general's performance. Rusk thought him overemotional in contrast to more seasoned strategists. (The feeling was mutual: Bobby thought Rusk on the verge of breakdown at several points.) The very presence of the president's younger brother in the highest councils of war and peace offended those who had preceded him there and now presided as "wise men." Dean Acheson, Harry Truman's secretary of state, sneered at what he considered Bobby's infantile moralism, his historical ignorance. Cuba, Acheson huffed, was no Pearl Harbor; but if Bobby's advice was heeded it might become a "Munich," a reference to Chamberlain's appeasement of Hitler in 1938.

Bobby's unstated but obvious role as the president's eyes and ears whenever JFK was absent also rankled his seniors. The attorney general was further given to occasionally baffling and contradictory observations. Official notes of the October 18 meeting paraphrase this strange interjection: "in looking forward to the future it would be better for our children and grandchildren if we decided to face the Soviet threat, stand up to it, and eliminate it now. The circumstances for doing it at some future time were bound to be more unfavorable."

Eliminate the Soviet threat? It was a curious rhetorical flight and fodder to his critics. Yet such lapses were rare. With some consistency and little support from his colleagues, Bobby argued for a "quarantine"—a military euphemism for a blockade, which was, by international accord, an act of war. Acheson pushed for a showdown with the "madman" Khrushchev; most others supported bombing as the only way to rid Cuba of Soviet bases. Still, as the attorney general argued with relentless passion for a naval quarantine, decrying air strikes as un-American, he won converts and helped build a consensus. Gradually, the major players—Rusk, McNamara, and McGeorge Bundy, the president's special assistant for national security affairs—agreed that a blockade was the best course, a nonviolent action that preserved global goodwill and gave Khrushchev time to assess his options coolly.

At the morning meeting on Saturday, October 20, President Kennedy decided in favor of a quarantine. He turned to Vice President Johnson for his thoughts. "You have the recommendation of your secretary of state and your secretary of defense," Johnson said. "I would take it." Johnson was hardly in a position to argue; not only was he averse to open dissent, but he had also missed most of the preceding discussion. Four days earlier, at the first meeting after photo confirmation of the Soviet missiles, Johnson had made his one real contribution to the talks thus far, conceding that Congress must be ignored in the interest of secrecy. "I realize it's a breach of faith," Johnson said with regret, "but we're not going to get much help out of them."

Johnson then cast his lot with the hawks, who seemed, for the moment, to predominate. "I would like to hear what the responsible commanders have to say. I think the question with the base is whether we take it out or whether we talk about it, and both alternatives are very distressing. But of the two, I would take it out."

The president seemed a bit staggered: "Well, uh, the, uh——"

"Assuming the commanders felt that way," Johnson repeated carefully.

His inclination was clear, however: "Take it out." These were surprisingly strong words for the vice president, and perhaps he regretted them; thereafter he was either silent or absent. When President Kennedy pushed him that evening for his thoughts, Johnson mumbled, "I don't think I can add anything." LBJ struck Ted Sorensen as being upset at himself.

"Lyndon Johnson never made any suggestions or recommendations as to what we should do at the time of the Cuban missile crisis," Robert Kennedy complained later. "He was displeased with what we were doing although he never made it clear what he would do." According to Bobby, as the nuclear confrontation reached its climax the following Saturday, Johnson did no more than indicate displeasure with the president's policy. "He was shaking his head, mad," Bobby recalled.

The vice president did, in fact, make an important contribution to the discussion on the last Saturday of the crisis, October 27. In a long, enervating meeting, the ExComm discussed two messages sent by Khrushchev to President Kennedy. The first, received on October 26, contained what Bobby perceived as "the beginnings, perhaps, of some accommodation, some agreement." The second, received the following morning, was more formal and intractable; it seemed to have been written by the Soviet Foreign Office rather than Khrushchev himself. The second letter carried a new and deceptively simple condition: the USSR, it said, would remove its missiles from Cuba if the United States "remove[d] its analogous means from Turkey."

These new terms, released publicly by the Soviet Union, posed a terrifying dilemma. The American Jupiter missiles in Turkey were obsolete, easily replaced by Polaris submarines in the Mediterranean. President Kennedy had in fact pressed for their removal more than a year earlier, but in light of Turkish objections the State Department dropped the matter. Now, raised by the Soviets as a quid pro quo, removing the Jupiters would be interpreted as a weakness of resolve and a sacrifice of Turkish (and European) security; it would destroy JFK politically and very possibly shatter the NATO alliance. The president was angry and frustrated. The Jupiters, in Bobby's words, were "hostages of the Soviet Union . . . [and] it was our own fault."

By now it was clear that the quarantine had failed. The only alternative to a missile swap was an invasion or massive strike on Cuba. This, all agreed, risked a retaliatory Soviet attack on Turkey or even Berlin—demanding a NATO response and very possibly prompting a third world war. In the eyes of the world, could the United States justify a costly war over "antiquated and useless" missiles in Turkey? Would not a trade, in retrospect, seem humane and reasonable?

By midafternoon on October 27, Bobby Kennedy and several aides had become convinced that the United States should respond to Khrushchev's first letter, ignoring his second—and the Turkish missiles. The ExComm got to work drafting a response. Meanwhile, Rusk reported that an American U-2 plane had been shot down, its pilot killed, while surveying the Cuban bases. Tensions were escalating, fueling the war plans of the hawks. The president left the room to discuss troop movements with General Lyman Lemnitzer, commander of U.S. forces in Europe.

Now, shockingly, passionately, Vice President Johnson began to speak. Why, he asked, if the United States was willing to give up its Jupiter missiles in Turkey, was it not prepared to trade them for withdrawal of the Soviet missiles in Cuba? George Ball agreed; last week, after all, the United States had been prepared to withdraw the Jupiters if it seemed likely to save Berlin. Johnson saw an opening and pressed his point. Khrushchev's offer, he said, was what they'd been waiting for: "We were afraid . . . he'd never offer this, that what he'd want to do was trade [the Cuban missiles for] *Berlin*."

The meeting broke up. The vice president remained in his seat, speaking in hushed tones with Dean Rusk and Treasury Secretary Douglas Dillon. As the conversation turned to the surveillance problem, Johnson began to get edgy. "I've been afraid of these damned flyers ever since they mentioned them," he said, referring to the U-2 reconnaissance flights. "Just an ordinary plane goin' in there at two or three hundred feet without arms or an announcement . . . Imagine some crazy Russian captain . . . " Johnson trailed off. "He might just pull a trigger. Looks like we're playing Fourth of July over there. . . . I'm scared of that, and I don't see what you get for that [aerial] photograph." If the flyovers were intended to scare the Cubans, he said, they were having the reverse effect—terrifying the cabinet and escalating tensions. It was just like using scare tactics in the Senate: "Every time I tried to put a monkey on somebody else's back I got one [on mine]," Johnson exclaimed.

LBJ was equally concerned about agitating the American public. "You're going to have a big problem right here in a few more hours, in this country," he warned. "What are you doing? The president made a fine speech. What else have you done?"

"They want more action?" Rusk asked.

"They don't know what we're doing," Johnson replied. He had shed his reserve; he was showing his irritation. "They see that there are some ships coming through. There's a great feeling of insecurity." A deal-maker like Johnson saw the opportunity for compromise and did not want to let it slip. By backing this deal—a missile swap—LBJ seemed to have come full circle from his knee-jerk response of last week. Now, when Llewellyn Thompson suggested a surgical strike on one SAM site, LBJ mocked him gently. "You warhawks ought to get together," he said, neatly removing himself from their ranks.

President Kennedy reentered the room, and Johnson, invigorated by his own participation, cogently reviewed the alternatives. "We can't very well invade Cuba," Kennedy interrupted, "when we could have gotten them out by making a deal on the same missiles in Turkey. If that's part of the record, I don't see how we'll have a good war." No one was sure that this was a decision. Yet without knowing it, John Kennedy had echoed the rare counsel of his vice president.

During the next two hours, between ExComm meetings, Robert Kennedy met with Soviet Ambassador Anatoly Dobrynin and delivered a copy of the American letter. When Dobrynin raised the question of the Turkish missiles, Bobby explained that the president had long sought their removal; and though the United States could not accept a quid pro quo, the Soviet Union could be quite certain that after the crisis was resolved, the Jupiters would simply disappear. Dobrynin, however, was not optimistic. "The Politburo," he said, "is too committed to back down now."

The ExComm reconvened at 9:00 P.M. There was more war talk. The president agreed to call up Air Reserve squadrons to prepare for invasion; NATO and the Turks, he said, should be warned of impending "disaster." The group discussed the likelihood of more attacks on American U-2s. "We're going to get shot at tomorrow," Bobby declared. Should the United States shoot back? McNamara believed so, but the president was determined to hold off until the Soviets replied to his letter.

Bobby turned to McNamara as the men stood to leave. "How are you doing, Bob?" Kennedy asked.

"Well, hard to tell. You have any doubts?"

"Well, I think we're doing the only thing we can do," Bobby said.

Bob McNamara did not think so. "We need to have two things ready, a government for Cuba, because we're going to need one . . . and secondly, plans for how we're going to respond to the Soviet Union in Europe, because sure as hell they're going to do something there."

"Suppose we make Bobby mayor of Havana?" someone added gamely, but it was late, and nobody laughed.

The Soviet response came the next morning, Sunday, October 28, at 9:00 A.M., and it was a letter. Since the United States had pledged not to invade Cuba, the Soviet government saw no need for missiles on the island. They would be promptly dismantled. There was no mention of the missiles in Turkey; those were removed by the United States several months later, with no reference to the Cuban missile crisis.

"This," the president told Bobby on October 28, "is the night I should go to the theater." It was a reference to Abraham Lincoln's visit to Ford's Theater after the Union victory in the Civil War. "If you go, I want to go with you," Bobby replied. The reference to Lincoln's assassination raised in his mind the specter of presidential succession. I would sooner die, Bobby implied, than endure a Johnson presidency. "I would go, too," Bobby explained later, "having witnessed the inability of Johnson to make any contribution of any kind during the [ExComm] conversations."

There was more to this than personal antipathy. Certainly, LBJ added little to the ExComm discussions. But he had, at times, pointed in thoughtful and helpful directions. Bobby remembered none of this. He recalled only that "after the meetings were finished, [LBJ] would circulate and whine and complain about our being weak."

White House tapes and transcripts often fail to record the moments that matter most: a whisper, an exchange of glances, a hushed conference in the hallway. These moments linger nonetheless in the memories of participants. LBJ's "whining" may be absent from the pages of the transcripts, but it was not forgotten by Bobby Kennedy. Nor were the events of Saturday night, October 27; and they go a long way toward explaining Bobby's disdain for LBJ.

That night, just hours after speaking so lucidly about the Turkish missiles, Johnson seemed to collapse under the weight of the crisis. The final ExComm meeting had dwelt upon invasion plans and contingencies. President Kennedy had been visibly exhausted and depressed. Johnson appeared haggard; they all did. But looking at him tonight, Sorensen wondered whether the vice president was "angry, or worried, or tense, or [if] he'd had something to drink." As the ExComm members filed out, LBJ took Bobby Kennedy and Ken O'Donnell aside and objected to the president's plan. "All I know," Johnson said pointedly, "is that when I was a boy in Texas, and walking along the road when a rattlesnake reared up, the only thing you could do was take a stick and chop its head off." The moderate man of hours earlier was gone. Johnson was clearly over the edge, and now, reversing himself again, was siding with the "warhawks."

More than anything LBJ had said or not said in the previous twelve days, his behavior in these few minutes seared itself into Robert Kennedy's consciousness. For the rest of his life, Bobby would carry the conviction that in a crisis, Johnson was unlike Bobby or John Kennedy or even Bob McNamara or Ted Sorensen. Johnson was a coward; he broke down; he went to pieces. Even worse, as Johnson collapsed, he lost control and lashed out; he sought to drag the world down with him.

Robert Kennedy rarely spoke of this view. That fellow showed very bad judgment in October '62, he would say, and leave it at that. He would say there had been thirteen men in the cabinet room, and if any one of seven of them had been president of the United States, the world would have been blown up; and Lyndon Johnson was one of those seven. Bobby only hinted at this belief in candid oral history interviews. He omitted it altogether from his memoir of the missile crisis, *Thirteen Days,* written in 1967 while Johnson was president. But Adam Walinsky, the legislative assistant who worked at Bobby's side during the writing of the book, later described its underlying message and intent: to contrast the cool, rational, deliberate decision-making of the Kennedy cabinet with the muddled, reactive nature of Johnson's Vietnam policy by 1967.

Thirteen Days was RFK's cautionary tale to the country and its policy-makers. And to President Johnson, it conveyed a special message: I remember.

Who was doing what to whom? Vice President Johnson eagerly awaited his daily call from Bobby Baker. Bored and isolated, Johnson hungered for gossip about his former colleagues in the Senate. Baker understood Johnson's nostalgia for the perquisites of office; pitying his former boss, Baker duly reported even the smallest stories and rumors from Capitol Hill.

It was a vicarious pleasure only. After his humiliating rejection by the Democratic Caucus, Johnson was skittish and ambivalent toward the Senate. Aside from his constitutional role as the Senate's presiding officer, which he regarded as an obligation but an indignity, Johnson remained aloof from the chamber. When Majority Leader Johnson had walked into the Senate cloakroom, pulses quickened; newspapers ceased rustling and were folded humbly in laps. Johnson's visits were never social—there was business to discuss, compliments to scatter, veiled threats to make. But when Vice President Johnson walked in, nothing happened. He was barely noticed. Senators took delight in the snub, and every raised, rustling newspaper was a banner proclaiming the impotence of Lyndon Johnson.

LBJ sat mute and humbled at weekly meetings with legislative leaders. Observers described him as "vacant and gray . . . discontented and tired." Beyond Texan issues, little aroused his personal interest. On occasion, Johnson was lucid and forthcoming on congressional relations, but his restraint was evident. "I never speak on legislative matters unless I'm asked," he said privately. And when Johnson *was* asked for his views, he usually demurred, saying, "Well, I don't know enough about that. . . ." Ted Sorensen perceived that as a jab at White House staff members who excluded Johnson from policy briefings.

When given assignments on the legislative front, Johnson completed them without complaint. Johnson seemed pleased to be included, thought Fred Dutton, the assistant secretary of state. On the administration's foreign aid bill, LBJ "couldn't have been better. He couldn't have been more helpful and generous and to the point" in his congressional work. The vice president was similarly supportive with international treaties and ambassadorial appointments. Mike Manatos, President Kennedy's Senate liaison, found Johnson eager to assist with even the most menial headcounts. But overall, as Johnson himself later admitted, "I didn't do what I should have done or could have done . . . to pass some of the measures." In his own defense he wondered whether "it would have made a bit of difference." Johnson knew that real legislative leadership could only be exercised from within the Senate chamber. He recognized, as did one political observer, that "Lyndon has no chits to call in anymore."

President Kennedy never understood Johnson's loss of influence on Capitol Hill. Kennedy was frustrated and angered by what he considered a deliberate abdication. Johnson, in his view, was still the Johnson of the 1950s, the master tactician, the force of coercion and conciliation. And as Kennedy tried, often in vain, to advance his own program on the Hill, "he thought that Lyndon ought to be up there really beating their heads in," as presidential aide Ralph Dungan recalled. Sorensen, who was responsible for JFK's legislative effort, said that "we expected him [LBJ] to be a major voice in not only shaping but delivering and selling the program, and he did very little, if any, of that." Johnson's tentative, halfhearted advice disappointed Kennedy. His respect for LBJ began to wane.

Yet the president seemed to want it both ways: he solicited Johnson's advice, cursed his reticence, and at the same time denied him major legislative responsibilities. As Mike Feldman explained, Kennedy "thought Lyndon had an ego that just was so great that it might handicap the Administration" in Congress. Johnson read JFK's mixed signals quite accurately. "President Kennedy," he said later, "didn't feel the vice president ought to be mixing in those things. He wanted to rely on the accepted procedures."

At heart, the issue was control. Accepted procedure was to keep the White House congressional operation firmly under the president's

thumb. Kennedy's congressional liaison was Larry O'Brien, a burly
member of Kennedy's Irish Mafia. O'Brien was amenable and unquestioningly loyal and responded well to orders. Few expected that Lyndon
Johnson would do the same. Johnson complained to Harry McPherson
that not once in two years did O'Brien so much as stop by his office for
advice. The Kennedys were running their own show.

By most accounts, it was run rather poorly. President Kennedy, weakened by a slim margin of victory in 1960 and equally thin standing on
Capitol Hill, was plagued throughout his tenure by poor congressional
relations. Confronted by stalled bills and complaining senators and congressmen, the president simply threw up his hands, handing all domestic
matters besides the economy and civil rights to Sorensen and Feldman,
the policy duo of his Senate days. And O'Brien, in the withering assessment of career professional Bobby Baker, was "out of his element" on
the Hill and "had no more idea than a small child" of its complexities
and Byzantine courtesies. By early 1963, the Kennedy agenda was moribund. The press was beginning to label JFK a political failure.

Lyndon Johnson was contemptuous of the whole operation. Presiding over the Senate in 1963, he sighed audibly as another young, liberal
senator rose to praise JFK's latest message to Congress. LBJ turned to
Harry McPherson, who sat behind him, and said, "We've got all the
minnows. We've got none of the whales." With Bobby Baker, LBJ
scorned "those kids . . . from the White House [who] start yelling 'frog'
at everybody and expect 'em to jump. They don't have any idea of how
to get along and they don't even know where the power is." In a telephone conversation with Sorensen in June 1963, LBJ marveled that in
six months it would be an election year, and "we haven't passed anything
yet!" Johnson scoffed at "this shooting from the hip business" that
doomed Kennedy's literacy bill. Sorensen muttered, "Well, I think we
could have done better"—a wan echo of campaign rhetoric. "Sure we
could have, sure we could have," replied Johnson. Yet he made it "abundantly clear that I'm on the team and you'll never hear a word out of me."

In retrospect, some Kennedy aides wished they had embraced Johnson more fully. Some blamed Johnson for holding back. Others, like
Sorensen, held the more balanced view that LBJ "did not have nearly as
much [of a role] as he should have had, as he could have had, as we wanted him to have." Sorensen's own relationship with the vice president was
instructive: when drawn out on a matter of utmost importance, Johnson
could be a valuable adviser. In June 1963, after racial violence in Birmingham awakened the administration to the moral urgency of the civil
rights struggle, JFK finally crafted a bold legislative response. It seemed
natural that he consult his vice president. Lyndon Johnson, after all, was

the architect of the 1957 and 1960 Civil Rights Acts; and during the Kennedy administration's civil rights meetings with groups of Southern leaders, Johnson spoke with what Arthur Schlesinger remembered as an "evangelical force" that impressed the entire gathering. JFK refused to advance his civil rights bill until his top advisers—Sorensen and Robert Kennedy—had consulted LBJ.

When the attorney general called, Johnson peppered him with questions: Have you done this? Have you done that? Have you talked to this person or that one? "Well, Bob," Johnson said, emboldened by his new relevance, "I think you've still got a lot of homework to do." It was a striking role reversal. Johnson's secretary, Juanita Roberts, listened to the conversation on the speakerphone and thought Bobby's resentment was palpable.

Johnson's talk with Sorensen was long and sprawling and covered much the same ground. Recorded on Edison Voicewriter disks, the conversation remains a vivid testament to the honest and thoughtful counsel of which Johnson was still capable. It provides an unfiltered glimpse of Johnson's legislative mastery and the moral passion he brought to the civil rights debate.

The vice president did not speak frankly without acknowledging the risks. "Now, I want to make it clear," Johnson told Sorensen, "I'm as strong for this program as you are, my friend. But you want my judgment now, and I don't want to debate these things around fifteen men and then have them all go out and talk about the vice president and [what he thinks], because I haven't talked to one Southerner about this. I haven't been able to talk to one executive man about it except the Attorney General and Ken [O'Donnell] very briefly this morning. I haven't sat in on any of the conferences they've had up here with the senators. I think it would have been good if I had," Johnson said, needling Sorensen for shutting him out. "I don't care. I'd just as soon be included out on all these things, but if at the last minute I'm supposed to give my judgments, I'm going to do it honestly . . . and I'm going to do it loyally."

Johnson did both, chiding Sorensen for poor preparation. "I don't think it's been thought through," Johnson said. "You haven't done your homework on public sentiment, on legislative leaders, on the opposition party, or on the legislation itself. I think it [the bill] can be more constructive and I think it can be better." But he expressed doubt about the bill itself: "I don't know who drafted it; I've never seen it," Johnson snapped, again betraying his wounded ego. "Hell, if the vice president doesn't know what's in it, how do you expect the others to know what's in it? I got it from the *New York Times*."

Sorensen defended the bill, insisting it was "the minimum we can ask for and [the] maximum we can stand behind. . . . The question is one of timing," he said, "and I think that this—"

Johnson cut him off. "I don't agree with that," he said, calling the bill, in its present form, a threat to the rest of the president's legislative agenda. "This Kennedy program oughtn't go down the drain, and I'm afraid that's what will happen if you send this up here. . . . I think he'll be cut to pieces with this and I think he'll be a sacrificial lamb." Other legislation had to be passed first, to clear the path. Johnson offered a homespun metaphor: "I'd move my children on through the line and get them down in the storm cellar . . . and then I'd make my attack."

With regard to the attack itself, LBJ issued a torrent of practical, detailed advice. He carefully listed the committees and members to target and identified likely coalitions. More important in Johnson's estimation was a public commitment to civil rights; JFK, he said, should employ the moral power of the presidency, "this aura, this thing, this halo around the president," to press the issue. At present, Johnson said, "we got a little pop gun and I want to pull out the cannon. The president is the cannon." What the vice president was suggesting echoed his own "Gettysburg speech" of several days earlier, in which LBJ honored the centenary of the Battle of Gettysburg by concluding, "One hundred years ago, the slave was freed; one hundred years later, the Negro remains in bondage to the color of his skin. The Negro, today, asks justice—we do not answer him—we do not answer those who lie beneath this soil when we reply to the Negro by asking, 'patience.' "

By traveling the country Johnson had learned "one thing—that the Negroes are tired of this patient stuff and tired of this piecemeal stuff and what they want more than anything else is not an executive order or legislation; they want a moral commitment that he's [JFK's] behind them." That, he told Sorensen, "will do more to satisfy them than your bill will. . . . I don't think that means that a legislative approach ought to be abandoned. I think it means that some specific proposals have to be weighed a lot more carefully."

As Sorensen listened patiently, interjecting an occasional word of agreement, the vice president assessed the costs of upping the moral ante. "I know these risks are great and it might cost us the South, but those sorts of states may be lost anyway," LBJ said, foreshadowing the sort of moral and political calculus he would himself employ as president. Court orders, he added, would only cause resentment; moral pressure would force an issue of conscience. It would also dispel doubts about the administration's intent, showing Negroes that the administration was on their side and convincing Southerners that it was not "just playing politics to carry New York."

LBJ followed up his legislative unburdening with a series of memos to Sorensen and a comprehensive strategy session with Assistant Attorney General Norbert Schlei, RFK's representative on the civil rights bill. Even Bobby had to concede that Johnson had contributed "some good ideas," which, according to Sorensen, were "heeded and respected." But the extent to which President Kennedy followed Johnson's counsel or the similar recommendations of other aides is unclear. He did not delay the bill's introduction until September, as Johnson advised, but did, at Johnson's urging, court Senate Minority Leader Everett Dirksen of Illinois, stressing the need for joint conciliation. Kennedy did not cross the Mason-Dixon line to confront Southern bigotry; instead, he spoke to the nation by television in the heated aftermath of Birmingham. JFK's address of June 11, 1963, did, however, evoke Johnson's Gettysburg speech. "We are confronted primarily with a moral issue," Kennedy declared. "It is as old as the Scriptures and is as clear as the American Constitution. . . . One hundred years of delay have passed since President Lincoln freed the slaves, yet their heirs, their grandsons, are not fully free." Kennedy's passionate closing remarks bore the direct stamp of Lyndon Johnson, as did the ultimate structure of the civil rights bill.

The civil rights bill offered Johnson a rare moment of relevance, and he savored it. But by June 1963, LBJ had been long stripped of his illusions of an active vice presidency. His inclusion on this issue could only be seen as an anomaly, and it did little to lighten the deepening gloom that afflicted him like a physical ailment. His body grew bloated, his face flushed by Cutty Sark, his features tugged downward in a perpetual hangdog expression. Harry McPherson, joining LBJ for an afternoon swim at the Elms, Johnson's mansion, thought the vice president looked "absolutely gross," like a man who was collapsing physically, spiritually, and intellectually.

In this chastened, vulnerable state, Johnson grew increasingly sensitive to slights. There were many, both real and imagined. LBJ grew indignant when the Secret Service forbade him from flying on the president's plane on a political trip to the West Coast in November 1961. He was enraged not to receive a hero's welcome upon returning from Berlin; he wanted to land at Hyannis Port, where the president was vacationing, but was sent instead to Washington. Press reports of his "disappearance" wounded him deeply.

More painful still were the jibes of the Kennedy circle. After eight years of the earnest, dowdy Eisenhowers, the press and public were enthralled by the charm and culture of the Kennedys, and even presidential aides jostled for space in the society columns. The superficial splendor of Camelot became, in Johnson's mind, an intimidating reality that aroused his deepest insecurities. The swing, the glamour, and the remote grace of the Kennedys alienated Johnson; at Kennedy parties he felt terribly out of place, an oafish, unschooled, ill-bred man from the Hill Country. As Eastern intellectuals (or would-be intellectuals) traded witticisms, Johnson kept his backwoods homilies to himself. He was a compelling storyteller and a marvelous and sophisticated mimic, but Johnson, encumbered by shame, hid his talents. And while even the self-admittedly clumsy Dick Goodwin worked his way onto the dance floor to attempt the Twist, Johnson, a surprisingly limber dancer, stood shyly to the side.

The heart of the Kennedy social circle was the "Hickory Hill gang," a frequent gathering at Robert Kennedy's estate in McLean, Virginia. These were small parties "by Kennedy people for other Kennedy people," remembered one participant. Johnson was rarely on the guest list; one of Ethel Kennedy's master lists of dinner-party invitations shows the Humphreys, the McNamaras, and a thin line drawn through the names of Vice President and Mrs. Johnson. When LBJ was invited, it was only at the last minute; and when he arrived, "nobody was terribly interested in him," sniffed JFK's Chief of Protocol Angier Biddle Duke.

The Hickory Hill gang may not have been interested in Johnson's company, but as an object of amusement and derision, Lyndon Johnson was always present. Johnson jokes and Johnson stories were as inexhaustible as they were merciless. Those that percolated during the campaign had been humorous, but this new material betrayed a real bitterness, a mean-spiritedness that was hard to explain. Apparently, the slights of the 1960 campaign had not been forgotten. Partygoers asked, "Whatever happened to Lyndon?" But no one could forget the galling fact that LBJ was in John Kennedy's administration. He was, in their eyes, a gatecrasher, an anomaly, an embarrassment to the president, and a blight on the bright New Frontier. *Time*'s Hugh Sidey, a frequent visitor to Hickory Hill, was appalled by the gang's ridicule of LBJ, which he described as "just awful . . . inexcusable, really." In October 1963, friends gave Bobby Kennedy an LBJ voodoo doll; "the merriment," Sidey later reported, "was overwhelming."

The mocking tone of the Hickory Hill gang became so routine, so reflexive, that it was difficult to drop even in Johnson's presence. In November 1963, at a stag party for a recent Kennedy appointee, two midlevel officials stood in animated conversation. Ron Linton, a Kennedy campaign hand now working at the Pentagon, was talking excitedly to John J. Riley, JFK's nominee to chair the Federal Trade Commission, when Linton sensed a third party hovering at his side, awaiting a break in the conversation. Perhaps thoughtlessly, the two men continued chatting. When Linton finally turned his head he saw the tall figure of Lyndon Johnson walking away dejectedly. "John," Linton said to Riley, "I think we just insulted the vice president of the United States."

"Fuck 'im," Riley blurted. And Lyndon Johnson, halfway across the room, froze in midstep and wheeled around to face the men. The vice president stood stiffly and stared, indignant and proud. But he said nothing, and quickly lost himself in the crowd.

Johnson's self-effacement was, perversely, one of his greatest achievements as vice president. He knew what was being said at Hickory Hill, and it was deeply hurtful. In the retelling, and there was always a retelling, the stories gained in cruelty. Watchful and overprotective Johnson men, playing to their boss's fears and prejudices, fed him the meanest gossip in a steady stream. "There were always people trying to make bad blood," lamented Joe Alsop, the columnist and friend of the Kennedys and Johnson. Alsop, taking it upon himself to create "a little bit of good blood," found the task impossible. Inevitably, someone had already told Johnson "some perfect lie about what Bobby Kennedy had said."

Beset by vicious rumors true and untrue, Johnson did his utmost to remain a loyal vice president. In this role, LBJ revealed a personal power few had ever seen: his rigorous self-discipline, his ability to suppress explosive emotions. In cabinet meetings, in smaller gatherings and discussions, and even among friendly reporters, Johnson was tight-lipped. In official letters to RFK, he was even warm: "Dear Bobby, I don't know when I have spent an evening so completely delightful," Johnson gushed after a spontaneous get-together in Texas in September 1963. For a man given to majestic displays of rage, to shouting and swearing and pounding on desktops, Johnson's restraint was uncanny. It was also unhealthy. Bobby Baker worried about the psychic—and physical—toll of LBJ's "brooding and bottling up his emotions day after day." The cost grew more profound the deeper Johnson sank into obscurity.

Among friends and aides, Johnson allowed himself an occasional release. To McPherson (still employed, until autumn 1963, on Capitol Hill), LBJ vented the "emotional fallout" of White House meetings and assorted indignities. At weekly vice presidential staff meetings at the Elms, Johnson groused about Bobby Kennedy's latest attacks while staff members sat quietly, eating bowls of fruit. Every day brought a new gripe, ranging from the serious to the absurd: one day Johnson fretted over his waning Texan power base, the next he bemoaned Ambassador Chester Bowles's halitosis.

Yet among these scattershot complaints there was one constant. Even in his most private harangues, LBJ never denounced John Kennedy. Johnson's words about the president were almost always touched by a strange affection and even admiration. "Johnson was a good actor," recalled Ron Linton skeptically, and this was undoubtedly so. But LBJ seemed honestly to appreciate the president's courtesies and to respect the burdens of the highest office. Thanking the president for a birthday cake, Johnson wrote, "I am constantly amazed, amid all you have to do, that you never overlook the extra kindnesses." The tone was fawning but genuine. When a guest at the LBJ Ranch spoke negatively of John Kennedy, Johnson nearly threw him out of the house, shouting that no one would denigrate the president in his presence. A more important measure of Johnson's gratitude was his scrupulous silence about disagreements.

Johnson and John Kennedy, despite their substantial differences in personality, established a bond that few could explain. Schlesinger observed that President Kennedy held a "certain fondness" for his vice president, seeing Johnson, "with perhaps the merest touch of condescension, as an American original, a figure out of Mark Twain, not as a threat but as a character." When JFK called Johnson "riverboat," it was only the mildest of epithets. Kennedy liked a rogue; he, too, had a taste for the more reckless perks of power.

But their relationship was doomed, perhaps inevitably, by the dynamics of executive office. Vice presidents make unpleasant company. They exist to remind presidents of their own mortality. "Every time I came into John Kennedy's presence," Johnson admitted, "I felt like a goddamn raven hovering over his shoulder." *Newsweek*'s Ben Bradlee noticed that, at times, "LBJ's simple presence seems to bug [Kennedy]." But more important, as Harry Truman once explained, "the president, by necessity, builds his own staff, and the vice president remains an outsider, no matter how friendly the two may be. . . . Neither can take the other completely into his confidence." No ticket, once elected, has in practice approached a true partnership; no president has given his vice president wide discretion in the major prerogatives of office. Vice President Johnson's arrogant and hopeful disregard of this truth vexed him at the start of his term and nearly broke him by its end. He built up deep frustrations, insecurities, and resentments, but remained almost incapable of blaming John Kennedy for anything. JFK, somehow, would always be the curious, affable, magnetic young protégé who made good and even taught his mentor a thing or two.

It was not John Kennedy, after all, who was tearing Johnson down. The president's Johnson stories—and he loved to tell them, with relish and affection—pointed at LBJ's sense of humor, not his liabilities. As president, Kennedy seemed not to forget Johnson's past greatness and generosity. He always gave Johnson a sympathetic hearing; he was always respectful, benevolent, and, within bounds, indulgent. "President Kennedy," Johnson said, years later, "was very good to me and tried his best to elevate the office [of the vice presidency] in any way he could."

Someone else, then, was responsible for Johnson's political ruin. In Johnson's eyes, that could only be Bobby Kennedy—a man so reckless and ruthless that even his own brother, the president, could not restrain him. Bobby, Johnson believed, had slipped the bonds of his brother's authority at Los Angeles and was still running amok, through the White House and around the whole of Washington, hell-bent on destroying Lyndon Johnson. Bobby could not be stopped.

Johnson's hatred and fear of RFK grew increasingly intense and obsessive. He complained about Bobby to reporters, advisers, and even the president himself. Friends endured tedious reenactments of Bobby's act of sabotage in July 1960. The loyal Baker worried that Johnson's complaints against Bobby Kennedy were "border[ing] on the paranoiac." Bobby, Johnson groused, was making a mockery of congressional relations. Bobby's elitist private parties, glamorized by the newspapermen who attended them, were alienating the middle class. Bobby was cutting LBJ out of meetings; Bobby was undermining him in Texas. Bobby was plotting to bounce Johnson from the ticket in 1964. Bobby was tapping his phone and bugging his office.

Johnson spoke bitterly and jealously about Bobby's access to the Oval Office. "Every time they have a conference," Johnson told AP writer Jack Bell, "don't tell me about who is the top adviser. It isn't McNamara, the chiefs of staff, or anybody else like that. Bobby is first in, last out. And Bobby is the boy he listens to." This was fodder for outrageous analogies. Speaking to reporters on October 16, 1963, LBJ compared America's leadership to South Vietnam's: a president with a "very strong" brother. The metaphor was lost on no one; Premier Diem's autocratic, repressive brother, Ngo Dinh Nhu, posed a grave threat to American interests. As reporter James Wechsler later commented, "The inescapable overtone was that . . . Bobby Kennedy was running things, and . . . [it] seemed to be an extremely bitter thrust."

LBJ's fixation on Bobby Kennedy was surprising only in its intensity. If Johnson was looking for a scapegoat or nemesis, Bobby was a natural fit. Bobby's famous brusqueness, observed Lee White, "would have offended anyone, especially a sensitive soul like Johnson." And Johnson, feeling acutely his own impotence and invisibility, was understandably pained when Bobby darted past him into the Oval Office without a word or nod; or when Johnson was asked to speak at the close of a meeting and Bobby stood up, muttered that the meeting had gone on too long, and left the room.

These stung, but there were greater indignities. Johnson's office condemned him to the margins of power; but as he groped for the few threads of authority he might reach, he found them snatched up, one by one, by Robert Kennedy. Bobby co-opted the two matters in which LBJ could claim some small stake: international relations and civil rights. Bobby's role as global ambassador eclipsed Johnson's foreign junkets both in profile and importance. And while the explosive summer of the Freedom Rides established Bobby as the administration's point man on civil rights, Johnson's CEEO toiled in the thankless obscurity of incremental administrative reform. Headlines did tell the whole story: in fewer than nine months, "No. 2 Man Lyndon Baines Johnson" was supplanted by "Robert Kennedy: No. 2 Man in Washington," the "Assistant President," leaving "LBJ in Search of His New Frontier" and prompting others to wonder "What Ever Happened to Lyndon Johnson?"

Bobby was less interested in that question than Johnson presumed. Socially, of course, Johnson was a favorite target of Bobby and his circle. But professionally, Bobby was less intent upon undercutting LBJ than on avoiding him altogether. Contacts between the two men during the Kennedy years were infrequent, brief, and, with rare exception, unmemorable. Like the White House staff, Bobby was mostly too busy to concern himself with the vice president. "I never heard Bob Kennedy . . . say anything unkind or political about the Vice President the whole time I was there" in the Justice Department, said Assistant Attorney General Ramsey Clark.

To Robert Kennedy, Johnson was at best a nagging reminder of the confusion and lingering bitterness of the 1960 convention, at worst a threat to the president's autonomy. "If your brother is president," Harry McPherson argued later, "and you've got this powerhouse accustomed to [being in] command as vice president, and you're in Bobby's shoes—his brother's political manager, his handler—it would make you as suspicious as anything. It would make you fight to establish your brother's primacy."

This apprehension, though, must have faded as Johnson sulked quietly through White House meetings. After LBJ's early, blundering attempts to consolidate power in the vice presidency, he could hardly have appeared a disloyal schemer. Bobby Kennedy did not appear to consider him one. Nicholas Katzenbach, Bobby's deputy at Justice, never heard him accuse Johnson of disloyalty to JFK. In retrospect, Bobby had to concede that "Johnson was very loyal and never spoke against the president." Both Kennedys were in fact delighted to have Johnson in the vice presidency and out of the Senate, where he could have caused real trouble. The president often told Bobby "how lucky he was to have Lyndon Johnson as vice president," because as majority leader, "Johnson would screw him all the time."

All the same, Bobby complained, Johnson "wasn't very helpful at times that he might have been helpful. . . . He never gave any suggestions or ideas on policy." From the Bay of Pigs to the Cuban missile crisis to a score of minor legislative skirmishes, this was a recurring refrain of Bobby Kennedy's; and though he never shared it with his staff, RFK was more candid in the Oval Office. He and the president frequently discussed how "exasperating" it was "that Lyndon Johnson wouldn't . . . make more of an effort in connection with a lot of legislation." Johnson's few efforts drew begrudging praise: "His ideas about how to proceed were helpful on occasion—for instance, on the civil rights bill—but as far as making any personal effort . . . he almost invariably refused to do so."

By 1963, according to Bobby, President Kennedy "was really irritated with him"; Bobby's own threshold, surely, had been crossed long before. JFK would test his vice president on occasion, telling Bobby before meetings, " 'I'm going to give him a chance . . . to go on the record as to how he stands.' And [LBJ] would never say how he stood on any matter! . . . And then he groused at people afterward." It was this "grousing" that infuriated Robert Kennedy—Johnson's mumbled critique, his insinuation of weakness—and then his retreat into silence.

Equivocation never sat well with Robert Kennedy. In an early profile, *Life* noted the attorney general's "genuine contempt for liars, complainers and those who reveal some lack of moral or physical courage." And if Johnson's complaints angered Bobby, Johnson's lies simply baffled him: cornering Bobby at a White House dinner dance, LBJ insisted he had never sought the presidency; Bobby recalled Johnson saying "he was just interested in helping John Kennedy." Johnson said his supporters had been beyond his control, but he himself never lifted a finger, and, well, he personally couldn't recall anything negative being said about JFK. Later, retelling the story, Bobby laughed in amazement. Johnson, he said, "lies all the time. I'm telling you, he just lies continually about everything. . . . He lies even when he doesn't have to lie."

In this case, Johnson may have felt he *did* have to lie. He could never undo the missteps of 1960 or take back the scathing attacks that earned him Bobby's enmity. But with LBJ, history was a malleable quantity; he was continually spinning and recasting events in the most useful light. Johnson had that trait of the best storytellers: the ability, amid the wildest, most implausible hyperbole, almost to believe it himself. His outrageous lies about 1960 seemed to carry a veiled plea for forgiveness: I meant no harm, he seemed to suggest. Can't we put all this behind us? Of course, Johnson nursed his own bitterness from those days, bitterness he was loath to relinquish, yet he seemed oddly desperate for Bobby's approval, asking him, "Why? Why don't you like me?" Bobby's obvious disdain was puzzling and hurtful; but now, given Bobby's new power, it was also politically dangerous.

On November 12, 1963, Robert Kennedy convened the first strategy session for his brother's 1964 reelection campaign. Larry O'Brien, Ken O'Donnell, and Ted Sorensen of the White House staff, John Bailey and Richard Maguire of the national committee, and Richard Scammon, a political scientist and director of the Census Bureau, gathered to analyze the South. Lyndon Johnson was not invited. His status was not discussed.

"What is the Vice President's standing now with the White House?" *U.S. News & World Report* asked earlier that year. "What are his chances of being on the Democratic ticket in 1964?" Was he, in fact, to be dumped? Rumors to that effect were circulating in Washington; they hardly required a leap of the imagination. LBJ was having a very bad year: in 1963 he clashed with the president's staff over civil rights legislation, the CEEO, the sale of wheat to the Soviet Union, and the coup against the Ngo brothers in South Vietnam. Johnson's presence in the White House, never very frequent, was on the wane: the president's personal secretary, Evelyn Lincoln, calculated that in 1961, Johnson had spent a total of ten hours and nineteen minutes in private meetings with JFK; in 1963, the two men met for a mere one hour and fifty-three minutes.

As time passed, those close to John Kennedy sensed his growing disappointment in the vice president and a gradual pulling away from LBJ. He grumbled about Johnson's uselessness. "I think [JFK] admired him, and [LBJ] rather amused the president . . . but he wasn't helpful," Bobby remembered. Yet "there was never any intention of dropping him," Bobby said later, speaking for himself and JFK. "And there was never even any discussion about dropping him." The brothers expressed unease about Johnson's mood and personality but knew him to be loyal, self-effacing, and capable. He was marvelous on the campaign trail. He was essential in the South. Johnson's place on the ticket was not discussed on November 12 because (barring illness or scandal) it was a given.

LBJ never sought assurances of his status, and later claimed that his status was understood between the president and himself. In fact Johnson was convinced he was to be abandoned in 1964. The decision, Johnson alleged to friends in a confidential whisper, was made at a secret meeting of the Kennedys' inner circle (curiously, with only Jackie dissenting). The tale was utterly groundless, but some of Johnson's friends fed his fears that Bobby wanted an "intellectual type" as vice president and might just get his way.

Racked by these fears and bitter in his stagnation, Johnson was no longer certain he even wanted the job. He hinted very strongly to Orville Freeman, Kennedy's secretary of agriculture, that he wanted off the ticket and was seriously considering a change in career, perhaps a college presidency. Johnson may have been cushioning his dignity against the expected blow. But he did remain obsessed about dying young, like his father. Some aides wondered if this fear, combined with his frustration at the incompetence of the Kennedys on Capitol Hill, might lead him to retire.

Vice presidential aide Jack Valenti expected Johnson to hang on and retire from politics in 1968, at age sixty. That, in the Johnson family, was not young; and Kennedy had made the presidency seem a young man's game. Johnson "felt that he had come to the end of the road," observed Tom Wicker, and felt in his last years he was simply wasting away, an embarrassment to the administration and to himself. If public life offered nothing but indignity, Johnson might as well retire.

There seemed little sense in holding out for a shot at the presidency. Johnson's political calculus of July 1960 seemed far-fetched now. President Kennedy, after eight years in office, would certainly handpick his own successor, and no one imagined that man would be Lyndon Johnson. In March 1963, writer Gore Vidal tried to handicap the race for the 1968 Democratic nomination. "The public . . . has already forgotten the dynamic Lyndon Johnson who was once master of the Senate," Vidal wrote in *Esquire*. "Eight years of Vice-Presidential greyness will have completed his obscurity." LBJ felt larger forces at work against him: he prophesied again and again that no Southerner would be nominated for president in his lifetime; 1960 had proved that.

"As the days passed," Bobby Kennedy said later, JFK "felt stronger and stronger that he [LBJ] shouldn't be president, and that we would have to move in some different direction." If not Johnson, then who? John Kennedy's preference was probably Robert McNamara. The defense secretary's confident, impressive service during the missile crisis had won him the president's, and the attorney general's, highest esteem. "He was head and shoulders above everybody else," said Bobby. The president considered "trying to move in the direction that would . . . get the nomination for Bob McNamara, because the president really didn't have much respect for Johnson, didn't think that he would do well" in the

Oval Office. Still, as Bobby hastened to point out, there were other contenders. "I suppose it was always a question what I was going to do."

The idea of a Kennedy dynasty was more than self-indulgence. With Bobby as a high-profile attorney general and emerging diplomat, and thirty-year-old Ted Kennedy elected senator from Massachusetts in 1962, starry-eyed fans and even some veteran observers predicted a succession of three Kennedy presidencies—a twenty-four-year reign. At Camp David during the winter of 1962–63, floating in the swimming pool, the president and Charles Bartlett discussed the race. Kennedy posed a surprising question: "Who do you think the nominee will be in 1968? Bobby or Lyndon?" The matter seemed to worry him, though he had once given Bobby a cigarette case inscribed, "When I'm Through, How About You?" But that was in the giddy days of 1960. The president no longer stated any preference or prediction; and after several conversations like this one Bartlett concluded that JFK was not "particularly thrilled by the fact that Bobby had decided that he would try to succeed him."

In fact the matter was far from settled in Bobby's mind. He was unclear about his role even in a second John Kennedy administration. If he toyed with the notion of succeeding his brother, no friends or insiders remember him mentioning it. From the vantage point of 1963 it is hard to imagine Bobby Kennedy seriously contending for the nomination—in 1968 or at any future point. He did, of course, inspire fierce, total loyalty among his Justice Department staff, and campaign devotees were legion and scattered throughout the government. RFK's popular image, boosted by *Life* and *Look* pictorials of sprawling family romps at Hickory Hill, was beginning to blossom. Still, there was little indication that Robert Kennedy was a beloved public figure or that, independent of his brother, he could sustain interest, affection, or power. He was vilified in the South, painted by many Southern Democrats as a "radical" in the camp of Martin Luther King, Jr. And for all his electoral mastery, Bobby was no favorite of party leaders or regulars, many of whose egos he had trampled in the march toward victory in 1960. When Bobby was insulting or brusque, one could always remember with relief that Bobby was not the candidate. How formidable was Robert Kennedy on his own—even if buoyed by his brother and the national committee?

Some observers scored the matter differently in 1963. So captivating was the family mystique, so remarkable was Robert Kennedy's rise, that anything seemed possible or even probable. Gore Vidal was bullish on Bobby's prospects: "It seems inevitable," he wrote, "that Robert Kennedy will be the candidate because by definition a major career in politics must set the White House as its goal, and Bobby's career is major. . . . In

1968 he will seem beautifully qualified—and from the point of view of experience he *will* be qualified." Vidal predicted a buildup of Bobby in the press as 1968 approached; and with the religious issue moot, Bobby faced none of the obstacles his brother had in 1960. Whatever Bobby's weaknesses in the public eye, "backed by the President and the machine, with an 'image' already floodlit by favorable publicity, one cannot imagine any Democrat seriously opposing Bobby at the '68 convention."

If Lyndon Johnson entertained any such thoughts, they were surely fleeting.

Ten days after the first campaign meeting for 1964, on November 21, 1963, John Kennedy, Lyndon Johnson, and their wives left for Texas. The trip was primarily a fund-raiser for the coming election. There was also the matter of a minor squall between factions of the Texas Democratic Party, between the populist Senator Ralph Yarborough and Governor John Connally, Johnson's man and the darling of conservative oil interests. Kennedy and Johnson would try to heal the widening rift. Later, Bobby would recall that on the eve of his departure, John Kennedy expressed "how irritated he was with Lyndon Johnson, who wouldn't help at all in trying to iron out the problems in Texas, and that he was an s.o.b. . . . [Johnson] just wouldn't lift a finger to try to assist."

The clash between Democratic factions lingered after the Texas trip; old quarrels were difficult to settle. And on November 22, the uneasy peace between Lyndon Johnson and Robert Kennedy was shattered, violently and irreparably, by the bullets in Dallas and Johnson's return to Washington as president of the United States.

CHAPTER 5

A Heavy
Reckoning

At 3:00 P.M. on November 22, 1963, the new president sat restlessly in the cabin of Air Force One in Dallas and placed a call to the brother of the dead president.

It was more than a condolence call. Lyndon Johnson had an important question: Am I truly president before I have taken the oath of office? No one on the funereal plane knew the answer. Dumbstruck by grief, few of them cared. But Lyndon Johnson cared very much; it was now his responsibility to care. He had been lobbying his bereaved cabinmates one by one, forcing a consensus that the plane should not leave the ground before the transition of power was properly—constitutionally— confirmed. Even so, LBJ was unsure what the U.S. Constitution actually said about presidential succession. He was desperately concerned that history judge his actions as prudent—and that the grieving Kennedy family consider them tactful and appropriate.

Only Robert Kennedy could answer both of these questions. Bobby was the head of the Kennedy clan, so very suddenly and cruelly, and was also the nation's chief legal adviser, as absurd as that seemed to Lyndon Johnson. The new president could not go forward without his sanction.

Bobby sat poolside at Hickory Hill when the telephone rang. He had learned of his brother's murder an hour earlier in a dispassionate call from J. Edgar Hoover. Now, shocked and numb, reeling from a flurry of frantic calls, Bobby understood little of Johnson's dark muttering about a "worldwide plot" that demanded swift action.

"A lot of people down here think I should be sworn in right away," Johnson insisted. "Do you have any objection to that?" Kennedy was taken aback, stunned into silence. "I didn't see what the rush was," he reflected. Jack had been dead only an hour. It would be a comfort to the family if he returned to Washington as President Kennedy—"But I suppose that was all personal."

Filling the void left by Bobby's silence, Johnson rattled off a list of questions: Who could swear him in? When? How? "I'll be glad to find out and call you back," Bobby replied numbly. He dialed Nicholas Katzenbach, his deputy attorney general. "Lyndon wants to be sworn in," Bobby said flatly, matter-of-factly, "and wants to know who can administer the oath."

Katzenbach was "absolutely stunned" by Johnson's request. "My recollection," Katzenbach told Kennedy, "is that anyone can administer the oath who administers oaths under federal or state laws. Do you want to hold on while I check?" While Bobby held the line, Katzenbach checked with the Office of Legal Counsel, which confirmed his thinking.

"Then any federal judge can do it?" Bobby asked. He was struggling to hold himself together.

"Anybody," Katzenbach said, "including a district court judge. I imagine he'll want Sarah Hughes." Hughes, a Dallas judge, owed her seat to Johnson's lobbying.

Bobby called the president to tell him so. Ed Guthman, who sat by Bobby's side at Hickory Hill, remembered him saying, "Anybody can swear you in. Maybe you'd like to have one of the judges down there whom you appointed. Any one of them can do it." After a brief exchange over the wording of the oath, the two men hung up.

President Johnson was impressed. Bobby, he said later, was "very businesslike, although I guess he must have been suffering more than almost anyone except Mrs. Kennedy."

The business, however, was superfluous. There was no need for a swearing-in; upon John Kennedy's death, the mantle of the presidency fell immediately to Johnson. Nonetheless, at 3:38 P.M., Judge Hughes arrived to swear him in. He raised his large hand, placed the other on John Kennedy's Bible, and repeated the oath in a sorrowful tone. And finally, after a seemingly interminable delay, Air Force One crept from its remote corner of the tarmac and took off for Andrews Field in Virginia.

As the stunned, grief-stricken group flew eastward, Bobby Kennedy steeled himself for their arrival. Head down, hands in his pockets, he paced the grounds of his estate, trailed by his dog Brumus. Later, in the half hour before the plane's arrival, Bobby shunned the developing crowds and television cameras at Andrews. He walked alone across the black runway in the dark and rested for a moment in the back of an army truck. When Air Force One touched down, Bobby leaped from the truck and waited, muscles coiled. It seemed he might at any moment bolt toward the plane in a full sprint. Attention focused on the rear entrance, where the coffin was to be unloaded. As the ground crew pushed a ramp toward the front of the plane, Bobby darted, unnoticed, up its steps as it rolled. He entered near the pilot's cabin. With elbows thrusting and eyes fixed straight ahead, he rushed and pushed toward the back of the plane, muttering, "I want to see Jackie."

In the stateroom, Lyndon Johnson stood impassively in the aisle. He was trapped by a large crowd, unable to move until the coffin was removed. Bobby burst in from the staff cabin. Their eyes did not meet; Bobby looked past Johnson, searching for Jackie. Then, as he had done so many times before in the Oval Office or the corridors of the West Wing, Bobby brushed past him without a word. Bobby did not stop before reaching Jackie, whom he hugged and then helped off the plane.

Johnson's expression was stoic, but the brush-off wounded him deeply. What can I do but turn the other cheek? the president shrugged to a cabinet member; I can't get into a fight with the family. Years later, asked about the incident, Johnson pretended not to remember it. Even if it had happened, he told Walter Cronkite in a television interview, "I would have thought that the natural thing to do was go as quickly as you could to the widow, Mrs. Kennedy, and to try to console her and give her strength. . . . I would have found nothing improper in it." Few would have. But Johnson was a deeply sensitive man, at the peak of his vulnerability, and he clearly thought "the natural thing to do" was at least to acknowledge the new president of the United States. He could only perceive Bobby's indifference as an intentional snub, a denial of his legitimacy. "[Bobby] ran," Johnson told a friend, "so that he would not have to pause and recognize the new president."

Other observers thought Bobby so dazed, so desperate to find Jackie, that he did not even see LBJ. Regardless, Johnson was onto something: the transition of power was nearly as painful for Bobby to accept as Jack's death.

In the fog and grief of the next few days, every interaction between Lyndon Johnson and Robert Kennedy left a bitter wake of recriminations. Tempers flashed at the slightest spark. Petty, perceived indignities loomed large, and Bobby was keeping a private tally. "There were four or five matters," he said later, "that arose during the period of November 22nd to November 27th or so . . . which made me bitterer, unhappy at least, with Lyndon Johnson." It began, in Bobby's view, with "the treatment of Jackie on the plane trip back and all of that business."

"All of that business" referred, first, to the delay on Love Field. No one, of course, wished to linger in Dallas. "What raced through my mind," Johnson remembered, "was that if they had shot our president driving down there, who would they shoot next? And what was going on in Washington? And when would the missiles be coming? I thought that it was a conspiracy." He was not the only one. "None of us had any idea whether this was a conspiracy, whether Johnson was the next victim," recalled Larry O'Brien. Jacqueline Kennedy, who huddled by her husband's casket with O'Brien, Ken O'Donnell, and Dave Powers, was thinking less of national security than of her children back in Washington.

All presidential attendants, new and old, were present on the plane; the widow had arrived and the body had been delivered. O'Donnell sent word to the pilot to leave Dallas immediately. But the plane was not moving. The late president's party grew confused and then agitated by the delay. When Brigadier General Godfrey McHugh, President Kennedy's Air Force aide, barked orders at the cockpit to lift off, he was rebuffed. Weakly, hoarsely, McHugh repeated his plea: "Mrs. Kennedy and Kenny O'Donnell want it."

"General," said Malcolm Kilduff, a Kennedy press aide, "they're not in charge anymore."

On Johnson's orders, Air Force One was not going anywhere until Judge Hughes arrived and delivered the oath of office. Or were these Bobby Kennedy's orders? "The attorney general wants me to be sworn in before we leave the ground," Johnson kept saying tersely and defensively, quelling an argument before it started. "I've talked to the attorney general, and it's his opinion that I should be sworn in here." In the confused crucible of the presidential plane, where even the simplest instructions were now open to misinterpretation, LBJ twisted Bobby's words, knowing that Bobby's opinion—or what passed for it—was unassailable. It was garbled further as it filtered through the airplane's cramped and humid cabins until, in a short time, the swearing-in became *Bobby's* idea: "We can't [leave], we have to take the oath," one aide explained to another. "Bobby requested it."

These misunderstandings (or mistruths) composed a good portion of "the business" that enraged Robert Kennedy in the following days. He remembered giving his official judgment and begrudging consent to LBJ, but nothing more. What room was there for confusion? One charitable Kennedy aide thought Johnson must have meant the attorney general of the state of Texas, not the United States, but O'Brien and O'Donnell were sure they heard Johnson say "Bobby," not "Waggoner Carr." Their bitterness grew on the long flight home.

To find that Johnson blamed *him* for the holdup was especially galling to RFK. In the months ahead he often repeated his brother's final judgment of Lyndon Johnson: the vice president, John Kennedy told Jackie on November 21, was simply "incapable of telling the truth."

Within hours of their return to Washington, O'Donnell, O'Brien, and others were inciting Bobby with accounts of Johnson's boorishness and insensitivity on Air Force One. The stories were legion and spread quickly in the charged atmosphere. Kennedy partisans—though, notably, not Jackie Kennedy herself—portrayed two enemy factions, one maligned and vulnerable in its grief, the other coarse and indifferent in its newfound power. Godfrey McHugh, for example, recounted for Bobby LBJ's behavior during the plane's delay. "McHugh said that Lyndon Johnson had been—and I remember the word that he used— . . . obscene," recalled RFK. "It was the worst performance he'd ever witnessed." It was hard to imagine worse circumstances under which to perform, but in his pain Bobby was unforgiving.

This version of events reflected Kennedy aides' contempt for Lyndon Johnson more than it did any actual indignities. "I didn't see any hostility on that airplane," said Jack Valenti, who sat with the new president. "I read about it later, but I didn't see it then." Neither did reporter Charles Bartlett, who had been friendly with JFK; he probed his memory of the flight for some example of Johnson's insensitivity, but found none. Charles Roberts, *Newsweek*'s White House correspondent, went so far as to call Johnson's conduct "perhaps his finest hour." Johnson was thoughtful, dignified, and self-effacing during the flight, and, like his aides, mostly sat in numbed silence. The feelings of shock and horror were universal.

Within twenty-four hours of their arrival, though, there was fresh fodder for contention. Bobby Kennedy went to the Oval Office at 9:00 in the morning to clear out his brother's desk and papers. Entering the outer office, Bobby found JFK's secretary, Evelyn Lincoln, weeping in obvious anguish. President Johnson, already in the Oval Office, had told her on his way in, "I have a meeting at 9:30 and would like you to clear your things out of your office by then so my own girls can come in."

As Lincoln wept, the new president beckoned Kennedy into the office. "I need you more than the President needed you," he implored Bobby, who did not want to discuss it. Bobby was more interested in discussing LBJ's callous haste. It was going to take some time to move John Kennedy's belongings out of the office, Bobby said. Couldn't Johnson wait a day or two?

President Johnson offered mild apologies: he didn't *want* to move in, of course, but Rusk and McNamara had insisted he must—in the interest of national security. Otherwise, in Bobby's caustic recollection, "the world would fall apart."

The president gave Evelyn Lincoln until noon to gather her belongings and leave the office. By 11:30, she was gone. This transition, so cruel and abrupt, was symbolic for Robert Kennedy. His brother's famous rocking chair sat in the hallway, indecorously overturned; it had been removed from the Oval Office to clean the carpet while the president was away. Now, as Bobby told a friend, the upside-down chair was a rude reminder: Austin was moving in on Boston before the body was cold.

Austin, though, had no choice but to forge ahead; Johnson had to jolt the government and the country out of shock and sorrow. Robert Kennedy, meanwhile, had to help plan a funeral, and to grieve. Each man labored under the weight of his unique burden, and neither showed the other much empathy. "During all of that period," Johnson said later, "I think [Bobby] seriously considered whether he would let me be president, whether he should really take the position [that] the vice president didn't automatically move in. I thought that was on his mind every time I saw him in the first few days." It was on Johnson's mind, at least. He could only view Bobby through the haze of his own monumental insecurity. He imagined that Bobby was plotting against him. "I think he was seriously considering what steps to take," Johnson insisted. "For several days he really kept me out of the President's office. I operated from the Executive Office Building because [the Oval Office] was not made available to me. It was quite a problem."

This was manifestly untrue, and just the sort of self-justifying fiction that emerged from and inspired bitterness on both sides. It was just the sort of willful blindness that drove these two men, in the midst of this great trial, farther apart rather than closer together.

But Johnson's story contained a certain element of truth: it revealed an obsession with *legitimacy* that plagued him acutely in those first weeks as president. It would haunt him the rest of his days—because no matter what Johnson achieved, his presidency would remain accidental, a cruel inheritance. Johnson felt it as acutely as Bobby did. "For millions of Americans," LBJ told his biographer Doris Kearns, "I was still illegitimate, a naked man with no Presidential covering, a pretender to the throne, an illegal usurper."

Johnson desperately needed affirmation, and in the hour of his greatest burden, it came from unlikely sources—from the Congress, which had spurned and mocked him for a thousand days; from the cabinet, appointed by his predecessor; and from the American people, who cherished John Kennedy in death as they had not in life. All rallied toward the new president. They gave him their patience and their trust.

Bobby Kennedy was not among them, and in Bobby's absence Johnson felt the suspicion and rejection he feared from the rest.

Johnson convened his cabinet at 2:30 on Saturday. He carried a list of six talking points. "1. The President is dead," it began, bluntly. "We must keep the business of this government moving. . . . None of us in this room can really express the sadness we all feel. Yet we have work to do. We must do it." As Johnson entered the cabinet room, Dean Rusk announced, "Gentlemen, the president of the United States!" Johnson walked to the vice president's chair, which had been moved to the center of the long table. He sat down. His cabinet members followed suit, their places marked by fresh yellow pads and sharpened pencils.

One chair, the attorney general's, remained empty. Mac Bundy, the national security adviser, was worried about Bobby, worried he "was reluctant to accept the new reality." "Reluctant" did not begin to describe RFK. "I was upset about what had happened on the plane and the fact that [Johnson] came into the [Oval] Office," Kennedy explained later. "So by this time I was rather fed up with him." After the morning's Mass, though, Bobby had drifted in from the living quarters and noticed that President Kennedy's cabinet chair had yet to be removed. Checking again that afternoon, he stumbled into the meeting, five minutes underway.

Bundy gestured to him, making clear his attendance was crucial. "Mac Bundy said it was very important that I come in. So I went," Bobby recalled. Bundy remembered having "virtually to drag Bobby" into the meeting. Bobby demanded that no pictures be taken and grudgingly entered the room. Several cabinet members jumped to their feet. President Johnson did not.

As Kennedy settled into his seat, Agriculture Secretary Orville Freeman looked at him and blanched. Bobby was leaning back, his eyes deadened by exhaustion and contempt. It was "quite clear," Freeman observed, "that he could hardly countenance Lyndon Johnson sitting in his brother's seat." This was hardly a wonder. Bobby's brother had yet to be buried and JFK's cabinet members were already offering paeans to the new president. Rusk stood and pledged his faith on behalf of the cabinet—"a nice little statement," Bobby recalled with scorn. Adlai Stevenson read a few paragraphs "on how nice Lyndon Johnson was. . . . It didn't offend me," Bobby insisted, "I felt it was fine. It just struck me that he had to read the damn thing. . . . Afterwards somebody told me . . . how impressed Lyndon was with Dean Rusk because he's the only one who spoke up at the Cabinet meeting. So I thought . . . what he wanted is declarations of loyalty, fidelity from all of us."

Johnson looked pleased, but only momentarily. There was little to be accomplished in the meeting. Cabinet members later called it "drab," "awful," "highly unsatisfactory," and "almost mechanical." After twenty-five minutes, as the dazed men rose from their chairs and filed out, LBJ turned to one of them and grumbled that the attorney general arrived late to ruin the meeting's effect. "We won't go in until he has already sat down," Johnson imagined Bobby scheming. Why, the president demanded, can't Bobby be as graceful as Jackie? When aides repeated this outburst to Bobby, he was astonished and, much later, amused.

The petty quarrels continued. The next flashpoint was Johnson's address to Congress. LBJ wanted to speak on Tuesday—but hedged a bit, claiming that "the leadership of the government" was pushing him to speak "as soon as possible." It was crucial to assert right away the continuity of American power, to assure Americans and their allies that there was no crisis of leadership.

No one questioned that fact, but the timing of the speech was another matter, and Bobby "didn't like [it]. I thought we should wait one day—at least one [more] day after the funeral." Bundy, once again the awkward intermediary, repeated that the president wanted Tuesday. "Well, the hell with it," Bobby snapped. He did not like being patronized. "Why do you ask me about it? Don't ask me about what you want done—you'll tell me what it's going to be anyway. So go ahead and do it." Johnson tried again, this time using Kennedy's brother-in-law Sargent Shriver. These indirect attempts at diplomacy only angered Bobby further. "Why does he tell you to ask me?" Bobby asked Shriver impatiently. "Now he's hacking at you. He knows I want him to wait until Wednesday."

Back in the Oval Office, Shriver relayed what Johnson had heard before: "Bob prefers you wait a day, unless there are overriding reasons for having the address earlier." The last, conciliatory note was Shriver's; he was concerned about the "condition which was exacerbating" between Kennedy and Johnson. Impatiently, the president picked up his phone and rang his staff, one after the other. "It will be on Wednesday," he said sharply, stabbing one telephone button after another.

At 12:30 on Wednesday afternoon, November 27, Johnson delivered a masterful address, forceful, eloquent, and reassuring. "All I have," he began solemnly, "I would have given gladly not to be standing here today." He spoke slowly in a deep voice that dropped at times to a near-whisper; at other moments he called out, urging swift passage of a civil rights bill. The substance of the speech mattered little. Rather, as Tom Wicker of the *New York Times* observed the next morning, "it was the way the President spoke . . . , the seemingly sure grasp of the mood and the moment, that impressed a city long accustomed to thinking of Mr. Johnson as flamboyant."

The eyes of many spectators darted back and forth from the president to the front row, where Bobby Kennedy sat with other members of the cabinet. Watching from Mrs. Johnson's box, Arthur Schlesinger noted that the attorney general "was pale, somber and inscrutable, applauding faithfully, but face set and his lips compressed." *Times* reporter Anthony Lewis considered the slight, hunched figure of RFK to be "the most moving sight in the House chamber. . . . He was white with fatigue and grief, and he stared glassily ahead without a flicker of emotion." Johnson's ringing exhortation—"Let us continue!" he shouted, one of five times he intoned the word "continue"—was cold comfort to Kennedy. "People just don't realize how conservative Lyndon really is," Bobby had told Ed Guthman just hours after the assassination. "There are going to be a lot of changes."

Infused with confidence and purpose for the first moment in his presidency, Johnson finally felt secure enough to confront Robert Kennedy, and invited him to the Oval Office that afternoon. In the spirit of his address to Congress, Johnson sought consensus for the difficult days ahead. It would not be easily won, and he knew it. As Bobby made his way to the White House, a presidential aide (probably Bill Moyers) hastily drafted a memo:

> 3:30 p.m., Wednesday, November 27
> *Memorandum of Conversation*
>
> There are several points of misunderstanding that should be cleared up between the Attorney General and the President. Everyone's interest is involved—the President's and Bobby's, the Party's, the country's.
>
> Here are the points about which there is misunderstanding, rumor, [and] gossip, all of which has reached Bobby and the family.
>
> (1) The question of the plane's departure. Is it true that LBJ said the plane couldn't take off until he was sworn in? Did Johnson hold up the departure? Why?
>
> (2) What was the cause for the argument with [Air Force aide] Godfrey McHugh? Did the President curse him?
>
> (3) There is supposed to be something the President said about wanting to move into the White House office right away. Is it true that the President or someone on his staff had [JFK's] furniture moved?
>
> (4) The Attorney General has heard the rumor that the President has said he is going to move into the White House right away.
>
> (5) The question of the National Cultural Center. Steve Smith called Bobby and said the President would not send up a bill which also asked for money. The family feels that it is kind of an empty gesture to change the name [to the Kennedy Center] without asking for the money to make it tangible. . . .
>
> (6) The Attorney General has the feeling that the President doesn't deal directly. [The] only way to deal with Bobby is directly. The arts of the Hill are not his arts. They are not his strength. You have to be straightforward, matter-of-factly [sic], tough, determined, open.

"The arts of the Hill," of course, were Johnson's arts, Johnson's strength, and he would have been better advised to use them—just as he had that afternoon, filling the ranks of his Warren Commission with reluctant senators and congressmen. But now that he was alone with Bobby, Johnson's finesse escaped him. Their meeting began awkwardly. "Your people are talking about me," Johnson said. His attempt at directness sounded more like an accusation. "You can't let your people talk about me and I won't talk about you." Clumsily the president plodded down his bill of particulars, offering explanations and justifications for all charges. Again Johnson pled that Rusk and McNamara had urged him to move into the Oval Office right away. This much was true. But then Johnson insisted that Air Force One "took off as soon as Jackie got there."

This was not true. In fact, the assertion was absurd—anyone aboard could testify to that—and it is hard to fathom Johnson's thinking. With explanations like this he would convince Bobby of nothing but his duplicity. In Bobby's view, Johnson had used and mistreated Jackie Kennedy and there was no point in debating it. The meeting ended in twelve minutes and the two men did not see each other again for nearly two months.

There was something both earnest and perfunctory about Johnson's attempt at unity, a heartfelt desire for peace that was devoid of real warmth. It betrayed his deep ambivalence. On the one hand Johnson understood Bobby's pain and shared it: both of their worlds were shattered irrevocably. On the other hand Bobby's carping left Johnson cold and indignant. Surely, the new president had made missteps, but never recklessly or callously. Despite his own pain, bewilderment, and enormous responsibilities, LBJ was impeccable in his treatment of the Kennedy family and its entire, extended circle—many of whom, he knew, had mocked him at Hickory Hill. Johnson felt at his best in moments like these, moments of crisis (and more likely to "blow it" on matters of little importance). Years later, looking back at his own behavior, Johnson would change nothing. "I took his program and his family after he was fallen and I did everything that I would want a man to do for my program or my family if the same thing happened to me."

Bobby Kennedy's complaints were not only unfair; they were distracting and possibly destructive. Bobby's approval—or at least his acquiescence—was important to Johnson's ability to govern. First, there was the public fixation on the heir apparent: as early as November 23, television networks began predicting Bobby's resignation. "Will Bobby stay?" was a question on countless lips. Then there was the administration itself. Bobby would help determine whether it would be Johnson's in fact or in name alone. "In a sense," wrote Stewart Alsop several months later, RFK was "*the* key figure in the great transition. Almost without speaking a word, he might have made the transition immensely difficult for the new President." Bobby's bitterness might feed others' bitterness. Bobby's departure might spark a wave of resignations. "Instead," Alsop continued, "he did what he could to make the transition period as easy as possible for his brother's successor, even during the first weeks when he was sick with grief." Surely, this was giving credit where it was undue. Bobby never actively sought to undermine Johnson and would not have thought of doing so. But at the same time he did little to ease the president's troubles.

Would Bobby stay? The question gripped Johnson in his first week as president. Having failed in his own attempt at personal diplomacy, LBJ dispatched Clark Clifford to hear Bobby's concerns. On the evening of December 4, Clifford called the Oval Office. "I've just finished a two-hour session with Bobby," Clifford said. "He's going to stay."

"Yes," Johnson replied.

"I had better report in some detail about it so you get the feel and all. We really had it out. And we covered it all. I think there are some arguments that he found unanswerable . . . and I'm just authorized to say now that he's going to stay. . . . He's going to have a talk with you and I ought to have a talk with you first. It is a relationship that I think is exceedingly important and it is one that we ought to look at together."

"All right," agreed Johnson. He flipped through his schedule and penciled in Clifford at 12:30 the next afternoon.

Kennedy had agreed to remain, indefinitely, in the administration. His friend Dean Markham had warned him a decision to resign could "boomerang," benefiting Johnson at Kennedy's expense: "Public sentiment will be on his side," Markham cautioned Bobby, "and the feeling will be that he tried to cooperate and work with you, but you didn't want to." In his grief, Bobby could have eased gracefully out of the administration. But he could see no place else to go.

RFK and the president never had the talk Clifford promised. Johnson soon sent another invitation, but Bobby "didn't feel like seeing him in December, so I never went to see him." To Richard Goodwin, a friend and presidential adviser, Bobby admitted, "I'm not mentally equipped for it, or physically."

Through Christmas, as Johnson and Kennedy took a holiday from each other's company, there was little healing. The wounds of the past month instead formed ugly scars. The conflicts that divided the two men were petty and, in many cases, ill-founded; they were products of a traumatic period, but also symptoms of a deeper, irreparable division.

Before the assassination, there had been cause but no need for reconciliation. What did it matter if the vice president and attorney general
did not get along? But now that Johnson was president and Bobby was
heir to the Kennedy legacy, it did matter, very much. And while there
had once been no point in reconciliation, there was now no hope for it.
The Johnson-Kennedy antagonism was wrapped up with the murder of
a president—a murder in which each man held the other accountable.

The assassination of John F. Kennedy, in the cold reckoning of Malcolm
X, was a case of "chickens coming home to roost." Malcolm's was a typically ringing indictment of a systemic, peculiarly American brand of
violence—violence within its borders, directed against black Americans—which, Malcolm argued, had come full circle and claimed the
country's leader.

The journalist I. F. Stone, in a column published shortly after the
assassination, drew his circle of condemnation more widely. "How many
Americans," he asked readers of his *Weekly*, "have not assumed—with
approval—that the CIA was probably trying to find a way to assassinate
Castro? . . . Where the right to kill is so universally accepted, we should
not be surprised if our young president was slain. It is not just the ease
in obtaining guns, it is the ease of obtaining excuses, that fosters assassination." Stone, like Malcolm X, was decrying the climate of political
violence within the United States; but Stone's sweeping indictment
extended outward, impugning American foreign policy and the geopolitics of the bullet.

Stone drew the link between Cuba and Kennedy's killing obliquely,
almost arbitrarily. For his moral parable Stone might well have chosen
South Vietnam, where Premier Ngo Dinh Diem had been assassinated
in a U.S.-sanctioned coup only weeks earlier, or the Dominican Republic, where the United States had encouraged (though not directed) the
killers of dictator Rafael Trujillo in May 1961. The question of Castro's
involvement in John Kennedy's death did not particularly interest I. F.
Stone, but it did interest other men—America's foreign-policy makers,
members of Stone's culpable class. These men drew the link to Castro
more directly and explicitly. They wondered whether America's covert
and public provocation of the Cuban regime had reaped its reward in the
blood of John Kennedy. And if so, did it not follow that American policy-makers were to blame for the death of their president? "I hope this
has nothing to do with the Cubans," one CIA officer said to another on
November 22.

It was a chilling thought. In the months and years that followed John
Kennedy's assassination, it was on the lips and in the minds of the men

most profoundly affected by the assassination. Most prominent among them were Robert Kennedy and Lyndon Johnson.

In the hours of panic that followed the assassination of John Kennedy, conspiracy theories were as rife and outrageous as in the decades to come. Kennedy aides, thinking first of the reactionary politics endemic to Texas, suspected a right-wing cabal. Officials with national security credentials saw a more ominous specter—the Soviet Union or, perhaps, China or Cuba. But "hindsight began early," as the writer William Manchester observed. "Most of those who had considered the possibility began trying to forget it. They felt that they had been absurd." There had been no second strike or suspicious activity, and the assassination of American presidents was not the *modus operandi* of the USSR.

Still, the arrest of Lee Harvey Oswald and the discovery of pro-Communist propaganda among his meager possessions prompted a new wave of dread. FBI, CIA, and State Department records detailed Oswald's shadowy past: defection to the USSR, contacts with the Soviet embassy in Mexico, and pro-Castro activity in New Orleans. Had this erratic young man been duped by Castro or the KGB into killing the president? Was this "silly little Communist," as Jackie Kennedy dubbed him, an agent of vengeance?

The Soviet card was quickly forsaken. The USSR, obviously discomfited by its ties to the assassin, offered its intelligence on Oswald's activities in Russia. But for those Americans who had plotted to overthrow Fidel Castro, the possibility of Cuban involvement could not be easily dismissed. Only two months earlier, on September 7, Castro had given a marathon impromptu interview to an AP reporter. In an outpouring of vitriol against the United States, Castro warned against assassination plots targeting his regime. "We are prepared to . . . answer in kind," he said. "United States leaders should think that if they assist in terrorist plans to eliminate Cuban leaders, they themselves will not be safe."

Clearly, three years of subversion had begun to rattle Castro and his followers. American activities were hardly covert, after all; they were widely reported in the sort of left-wing periodicals read by sympathizers like Oswald, and Castro well understood what the United States was up to. By Castro's own tally, eight of the twelve plots on his life were linked to the CIA. The campaign of harassment and sabotage that began after the Bay of Pigs waxed and waned during the Kennedy years, but it never ceased.

Though Washington took note of Castro's dramatic posturing, there was no reconsideration of American policy. Five days after Castro's AP interview, administration officials met to weigh the threat of retaliation. All agreed Castro was likely—almost certain—to strike back at the

United States. Still, the possibility of an attack against Americans on American soil was quickly dismissed; this was too foolhardy for even the impetuous Castro. Plans for other contingencies, though, were clearly inadequate, and various agencies were ordered to devise better plans.

As early as November 24, American analysts rejected the notion of Castro as conspirator. A French journalist had spent the day of November 22 with the Cuban leader and recorded every nuance of his reactions. Upon hearing of the assassination, Castro panicked; he was terrified LBJ would blame Cuba and send in the Marines. If there was a mastermind behind the assassination, it did not appear to be Fidel Castro.

Yet the question remained: had American belligerence toward Cuba driven Oswald to kill Kennedy? Castro need not have pulled the strings; American policy toward Cuba appeared to have embittered Oswald deeply. The stranglehold of the U.S. trade embargo and the expulsion of Cuba from the Organization of American States (OAS) in 1962, both common knowledge, must have jarred the man who marched the streets of New Orleans demanding "Hands off" and "Fair Play for Cuba," the same man who tracked Radio Havana and devoured leftist screeds like the *Militant,* which chronicled the activities of Operation Mongoose. However murky Oswald's politics, Cuba was his singular passion.

Likewise for Robert Kennedy. Bobby's strong grip left an imprint on the administration's Cuba policy as surely as Oswald's fingerprints appeared on the murder weapon. If Oswald's Cuba connections gave anyone cause for painful self-reflection, it was Bobby. He had been entangled in the unsavory web of Cuban affairs since the first months of his brother's presidency. After the Bay of Pigs disaster, RFK and General Maxwell Taylor advised the president bluntly that "there can be no long-term living with Castro as a neighbor. . . . His continued presence within the hemispheric community as a dangerously effective exponent of Communism and anti-Americanism constitutes a real menace capable of eventually overthrowing the elected governments in any one or more of weak Latin American republics." The two men recommended a new covert program of "political, military, economic and propaganda action against Castro."

When talk turned in the fall of 1961 to contingency plans for a post-Castro Cuba—not the means to remove him, but what to do if Castro was "in some way or other removed from the Cuban scene," as a presidential adviser put it optimistically—the CIA argued that the regime would outlive the man. The notion of "removal," in any case, troubled John Kennedy. "We can't get into that kind of thing," he told his assistant Dick Goodwin in October 1961. "Or we would all be targets."

Still, Castro's presence rankled. "Welcome to the Site of the First

Defeat of Imperialism in the Western Hemisphere," proclaimed an official sign on the shore of the Bay of Pigs. In November 1961, the president installed RFK at the head of a pyramid of plotting. In Bobby's purview was the Special Group (Augmented), as well as the CIA's Directorate of Plans, its covert policy shop.

Bobby was watchdog, strategist, and catalyst, and Cuba quickly became his obsession. "Bobby is a wild man on this," Richard Bissell of the CIA concluded privately. White House aide Harris Wofford later identified Bobby as "the driving force behind the clandestine effort to overthrow Castro. From inside accounts of the pressure he was putting on the CIA to 'get Castro,' he seemed like a wild man who was out-CIAing the CIA." At a January 19, 1962, meeting at the Justice Department, the attorney general declared the Cuban problem to be America's greatest. "No time, money, effort or manpower is to be spared," he said, renewing his call for action and impressing the others with his vehemence. He visited Mongoose facilities in Florida. He clamored for the specifics of sabotage raids—"in nauseating, excruciating detail," said a CIA operative. The weather, the boats, the munitions, the terrain—every tidbit of information fascinated him. Richard Helms, director of covert activity for the CIA, was a bit exasperated by the attorney general's enthusiasm. Almost daily, Bobby was on the phone to Helms, Helms's executive assistant, or his assistant's staff, pressing for tangible results.

Helms needed no prodding. "The CIA," as Arthur Schlesinger recalled, "was a rogue elephant from way back." Since the 1950s the Agency had been plotting, in concert with Cuban exiles and the American Mafia, to assassinate Castro. Neither President Eisenhower nor President Kennedy was informed. The doctrine of "plausible deniability"—protecting a president from the most unsavory activities of his own operatives—provided convenient cover for dark, secret agendas. (Even the CIA's director, Allen Dulles, was told of its Mafia contacts only after the fact.) The plots continued during the Kennedy years, and the CIA felt little obligation to inform its elected superiors. They were "transient." They did not need to know.

On May 7, 1962, however, Robert Kennedy found out. CIA representatives briefed him on the assassination attempts against Castro—not to seek authorization but to stop the administration's prosecution of a CIA associate in a wiretapping case—and Kennedy was visibly unsettled by the news. "If you have seen Mr. Kennedy's eyes get steely and his jaw set and his voice get low and precise," a CIA representative later testified, "you get a definite feeling of unhappiness." Bobby was particularly incensed by the use of mafiosi like Sam Giancana in such schemes. "I want you to let me know about these things," he said curtly as the briefing concluded.

The CIA men assured Bobby the plots had been terminated. And on May 9 the attorney general ordered that the CIA "never again in the future take such steps without first checking with the Department of Justice."

The CIA felt no such obligation. Years later, as its schemes came to light, the question whether the Kennedys knew of or even endorsed the plots inflamed the passions of participants: in 1977, Arthur Schlesinger and Bill Moyers waged a public dispute and "interrupted" a long friendship over the matter (Schlesinger argued that the Kennedys did not know; Moyers believed that they did). Richard Helms testified before Senator Frank Church's investigative committee in 1975 that he had received no direct order to kill Castro; nor, Helms admitted, had he sought one.

In Helms's view, none was needed. Bobby Kennedy's "intense" pressure generated the "kind of atmosphere" in which assassination was authorized implicitly. "It was made abundantly clear to everyone involved in the operation that the desire was to get rid of the Castro regime and to get rid of Castro," Helms told the Church Committee. "No limitations were put on this injunction." Bobby, according to Helms, "would not have been unhappy if [Castro] had disappeared off the scene by whatever means." Assassination appeared to be well within the bounds of the administration's efforts to overthrow Castro.

The point is arguable. Kennedy administration officials, at those same Senate hearings, insisted that assassination was beyond the pale, that a direct order was required for such action and none was given. Still, there was something to Helms's logic, however self-serving his testimony. The Kennedys' Cuba policy was marked by a moral and operational ambiguity in which the line between acceptable and unacceptable means was never clearly drawn. Neither JFK nor RFK ever explicitly endorsed the plotting. It was an immoral policy, the sort Bobby opposed during the Cuban missile crisis, and it was unwise, too, by the administration's own analysis—Cuba experts were quite certain the Communist regime would outlive its dictator. Yet Bobby never ruled out assassination; he only required his stamp of approval.

Thus, a central, crippling irony: by his eager antagonism toward the Castro regime, his relentless, "white heat" pressure on the CIA and other agencies, and his tacit endorsement of any means necessary, Bobby Kennedy helped create what the Church Committee called a "conspiratorial atmosphere of violence." And if the baiting of Castro incited Oswald to retaliate, did Bobby Kennedy not share the blame?

Few men dared ask the question. Only with the distance and clarity of a dozen years could the Church Committee conclude, "The conspiratorial atmosphere of violence which developed over the course of three years of CIA and exile group operations should have led CIA investigators to ask whether Lee Harvey Oswald . . . who [was] known to have at least touched the fringes of the Cuban community [was] influenced by that atmosphere."

Robert Kennedy, too, should have known enough to ask, and it appears that he did—privately. Judging by his demeanor he seems to have believed the worst. In the months after the assassination, while his siblings limped toward recovery, Bobby remained nearly paralyzed. Manchester called it a "brooding Celtic agony." Much of this, of course, was the pain of separation and loss. Bobby had been closer to Jack than the rest of the family had been; closer, in many ways, than the president's widow. But what seized Bobby may also have been guilt—or fear that his own adventurism had cost his brother's life.

Several accounts suggest this. On the evening of December 9, Arthur Schlesinger asked Bobby about John Kennedy's killer (and instantly regretted the lapse in tact). Schlesinger recorded Bobby's response: "that there could be no serious doubt that Oswald was guilty, but there was still argument if he had done it by himself or as part of a larger plot, whether organized by Castro or by gangsters." Only days earlier, Bobby had wondered whether CIA-connected men were behind the assassination; he asked Director of Central Intelligence John McCone "in a way that he couldn't lie to me, and [McCone replied] they hadn't." There was something burdening Bobby, something he could not share; McCone later concluded that it was guilt. What Bobby could not explain was that, whether directly or indirectly, he had condoned the plans that might have incited his brother's killer.

RFK was not committed to any particular conspiracy theory, or even to the notion of a conspiracy. A Cuba connection made sense, but Bobby, as Schlesinger points out, "perceived so much hatred about, so many enemies," that it was foolish to single out the Cubans. After the assassination, Bobby asked about Jimmy Hoffa's reaction and wondered aloud whether the Chicago Mafia was behind the killing. But this notion offered Bobby little solace. His brother was still dead. And the Teamsters and organized crime, like Cuba, were Bobby's domain. "There's so much bitterness I thought they'd get one of us," he told Ed Guthman, not specifying or even guessing who "they" were. "I thought it would be me."

None of this is to say that Robert Kennedy consciously or solely blamed himself for his brother's death. At times Bobby flirted with existentialism, recognizing if not accepting the random brutality of life. But Bobby was no agnostic; his universe was not arbitrary. More than the rest of the Kennedys, Bobby dwelt in a world "infused by the Almighty with pattern and purpose," as Schlesinger observed. Bobby grasped for divine order and reason. He immersed himself in Greek tragedies, searching for solace, underlining passages with an aggressive curiosity he had not shown as a student. In a work by Aeschylus, he underlined this passage:

"All arrogance will reap a harvest rich in tears. God calls men to a heavy reckoning for overweening pride."

If there was poetic justice, a morality play, to be found in the tragic events of November, Lyndon Johnson, too, searched for it.

In 1975, when Richard Helms testified before another investigatory body, the CIA officer was asked pointedly: Had it occurred to him in 1963 that Oswald might have shot the president on Castro's behalf, if not by his direct orders? "No, I don't recall the thought ever occurring to me at the time," Helms told the panel guilelessly. "The very first time I heard such a theory as that enunciated was in a very peculiar way by President Johnson."

Johnson was in fact full of such theories. The day after John Kennedy's funeral, LBJ stood in the hallway of his house and pointed at a portrait of Diem. "We had a hand in killing him," Johnson said to Hubert Humphrey. "Now it's happening here." Was Johnson merely pointing out a cruel irony, or suggesting some darker connection? Days later, LBJ told Pierre Salinger a story. Like so many other Johnson stories, it was almost certainly apocryphal, but made its point bluntly. This one told of a childhood friend who had misbehaved—and then crashed his sled into a tree and gone cross-eyed. It was divine retribution, Johnson told Salinger, gravely. And perhaps John Kennedy's assassination was, too.

On November 29, 1963, Lyndon Johnson displayed less interest in divine ordinance than in Oswald's possible ties to Cuba. On the phone that afternoon with Hoover, the president wanted to know "whether [Oswald] was connected with the Cuban operation [Mongoose] with money."

"That's what we're trying to nail down now," Hoover told him, but judged the connection unlikely. Oswald, it was already clear, "was strongly pro-Castro, he was strongly anti-American, and he had been in correspondence—which we have—with the Soviet embassy here in Washington . . . and with this committee we call Fair Play to Cuba [sic]." If Oswald was entangled in Cuban affairs, Hoover implied, it was not on our side. That notion was reinforced several hours later by Senator Richard Russell. "I wouldn't be surprised if Castro had something [to do with it]," he told Johnson.

The theory found a ready subscriber in Lyndon Johnson, and he clung to it. Even years later, LBJ's "inner political instinct," Jack Valenti recalled, was that Castro was behind the killing. Yes, Johnson conceded, the FBI had no evidence to prove it or even to suggest it; neither did the CIA or the State Department or anybody else. But the equation had a concise, appealing logic: "President Kennedy tried to get Castro, but Castro got Kennedy first," Johnson told his aide Joseph Califano. Johnson said "President Kennedy" but he knew it was Bobby who tried to "get" Castro. Ever since the Bay of Pigs, LBJ had blamed Bobby for the excesses of American policy in Cuba.

Several years later, in January 1967, the hornet's nest of allegations was stirred again, to Johnson's great interest. *Washington Post* columnist Drew Pearson met with Chief Justice Earl Warren to pass along a curious rumor: a client of Edwin Morgan, a prominent Washington lawyer, was insisting that the United States tried to kill Castro during the Kennedy years and that Castro killed Kennedy in retaliation. Warren considered the charge serious enough to pass along to the Secret Service, which then forwarded it to the FBI. The FBI called it old news and buried it. Uncharacteristically, Hoover did not even inform the president. "Consideration was given to furnishing this information to the White House," read an internal FBI memo, "but since this matter does not concern, nor is it pertinent to, the present administration, no letter was . . . sent."

But the rumor was in the air, in Washington and elsewhere. In New Orleans, District Attorney Jim Garrison pressed ahead with a sensational case, charging several CIA- and Cuba-connected men with a conspiracy to kill President Kennedy. And Pearson, having been rebuffed by the FBI, now took his story to the Oval Office. Lyndon Johnson was tantalized. On February 18, 1967, speaking on the phone with Acting Attorney General Ramsey Clark, his excitement was evident:

"You know this story going around about the CIA sendin' in the folks to try and get Castro?" the president asked Clark.

"To assassinate Castro?"

"Right. You got that full story laid out in front of you, you know what it is and has anybody ever told you all the story?"

"No," Clark replied.

"I think you oughta have that," Johnson went on. "It's incredible. I don't believe there's a thing in the world to it and I don't think we ought to seriously consider it, but I think you oughta know about it."

As Johnson told it, Pearson had spoken of "a man that was involved [in the JFK assassination], that was brought into the CIA with a number of others, and instructed by the CIA and the attorney general"—Bobby Kennedy—"to assassinate Castro after the Bay of Pigs."

"I've heard that much," Clark said, "I just haven't heard names and places."

"I think it would look bad on us if we'd had it reported to us a number of times and we just didn't [investigate]," the president told him. He instructed Clark to develop "a file that protects you, [so] that you don't just look like they report these things to us and we just throw 'em overboard and say, well, we don't like 'em, and they're not what we want to hear, so we're not gonna do anything about it.

"But anyway," Johnson continued, the American-sponsored assassins "had these [cyanide] pills and they were supposed to take 'em when [Castro] caught 'em. And they didn't get to take their pills, so he tortured 'em, and they told him all about [the plot]—who was present and why they did it. So he said, Okay, we'll just take care of that. So then he called Oswald and a group in . . . and [Castro said] go set it up and get the job done."

The president was certain he'd heard the story two or three times before, from sources other than Pearson, but their names escaped him. "They were reputable people," he insisted, "or they wouldn't have gotten in here." Still, Johnson cautioned, "I credit it 99.99 percent untrue, but . . . y'all oughta do what you think oughta be done to protect yourselves."

Why Ramsey Clark and the Justice Department needed to protect themselves was not entirely clear; if any official body would be held accountable for not pursuing the story, it was not Justice but the FBI. Johnson seemed less interested in providing cover for Clark than in passing along a salacious rumor. He was particularly titillated by Robert Kennedy's role in the alleged caper-gone-awry. On the evening of March 2, LBJ took a call from his old lieutenant, Texas Governor John Connally, and the two men traded confidences on the subject.

Connally passed along a secret report from a man claiming to have seen Garrison's files in New Orleans—files "proving" Castro had sent four separate teams of assassins to kill JFK. One or two teams had been picked up in New York and grilled by the FBI and Secret Service; but another, consisting of Oswald and three accomplices, had skirted the trap and made it to Dallas.

In this scenario, a slight variation on the one Johnson told Clark, Robert Kennedy's role was especially damning. Connally's source claimed that after the missile crisis JFK and Khrushchev cut a deal to leave Castro in power. About six months later "the CIA was instructed to assassinate Castro, and sent people into Cuba. Some of them were captured and tortured," Connally reported. "And Castro and his people . . . heard the whole story . . . that President Kennedy did not give the order to the CIA, but that some other person extremely close to President Kennedy did.

"They did not name names, but the inference was very clear," Connally said. "The inference was that it was his brother."

LBJ's interest was piqued. "This is confidential, too," Johnson told the governor, belying the fact that it was, indeed, confidential. "We have had that story, on about three occasions. The people here say that there's no basis for it. . . . I've given a lot of thought to it. . . . I talked to another one of our good lawyers [who] evaluated it pretty carefully and said that it was ridiculous." Hoover, too, deemed the Garrison story "a phony."

What LBJ found hard to swallow was not Bobby Kennedy's culpability—that seemed likely enough; it was that anyone really knew what Castro was thinking.

"But," Johnson added, "we can't ever be sure."

In fact, Johnson was so reluctant to concede that "there's no basis" to the story that he continued to badger the FBI for a full investigation. On March 17, presidential assistant Marvin Watson told Cartha "Deke" DeLoach, the FBI's White House liaison, that "the president had instructed that the FBI interview Morgan [the lawyer] concerning any knowledge he might have concerning the assassination of President Kennedy." DeLoach demurred, arguing that Morgan did not want to be interviewed, and the FBI certainly did not want to do business with the "publicity seeker" Garrison. But the president's wishes were clear. "Under the circumstances," DeLoach reported glumly to his seniors at the Bureau, "it appears that we have no alternative but to interview Morgan and then furnish the results to Watson in blind memorandum form."

The interviews yielded no great insight into JFK's murder. But the renewed allegations of the attorney general's plots against Castro only further convinced LBJ of Bobby's complicity. Bobby "had been operating a damned Murder Incorporated in the Caribbean," Johnson told Leo Janos of *Time*. The plots remained classified information—they were never mentioned to the Warren Commission—but the president began dropping hints to friendly reporters. And however strongly Johnson professed not to believe them, he was fascinated by and took delight in repeating rumors of Bobby's role in this circle of conspirators. If these stories made it to Hickory Hill, Bobby would have to wonder how much Johnson knew.

By 1967, Lyndon Johnson was not alone in questioning the Warren Commission's account of events. But the president's attachment to this particular conspiracy theory was rooted less in its merits than its trail of blame—back through layers of CIA agents and Cuban exiles, through obscure schemes and counterschemes, to the desk of Robert F. Kennedy.

As vice president, Johnson had sat through those cabinet meetings and listened as Bobby browbeat yet another beleaguered bureaucrat. The RFK that Johnson remembered was not the cautious consensus-builder

of the missile crisis but the hotheaded advocate of sabotage and skul-
duggery. Johnson was convinced: Bobby reaped what he had sown. The
killing of John Kennedy was savage, unjust, a tragedy unparalleled; but it
was divine retribution, and, in this way, it found its place in the moral
universe of Lyndon Johnson.

The blame-game was infectious. Fingers pointed in both directions.
Johnson could not forget that the murder had happened in Texas: "Texas,
my home, the home of both the murder and the murder of the murderer." Whatever else would be called into question about the official
account of the assassination, this much was never in doubt. Though the
killer was an enigma and his motives a muddle, everyone knew that the
killing had happened there—in plain daylight, on film, in front of a
crowd, in front of the world—at Dealey Plaza, Dallas, Texas. In Lyndon
Johnson's home.

The association was as inescapable as it was unfair. It was also instan-
taneous. The moment they heard news of the assassination, a half-dozen
officials rushed to the near-vacant White House and gathered in Ralph
Dungan's office, just a few feet from the Oval Office. They sat in silence.
Minutes later, Hubert Humphrey burst into the room in tears. Clutching Dungan, he cried out, "What have they done to us?"

" 'They,' of course, were the Texans," writes Daniel Patrick Moynihan,
witness to the outburst. "It was that bad." On the helicopter ride to
Andrews to meet the presidential plane, Ted Sorensen turned to Johnson's aides Walter Jenkins and George Reedy and said, "I'll help as best I
can. But I hope you don't mind if I don't think too much of the State
of Texas." Reedy (a Chicagoan) quietly agreed. McGeorge Bundy was
more forgiving, pointing out that "one madman doesn't make a mad-
house," but he was alone in his generosity.

In the coming weeks, it seemed that the president's men showed as
much bitterness toward Texas as they did toward Lee Harvey Oswald.
Oswald was not even a native Texan, but it mattered little. "I'll never visit
Dallas again," Kennedy men repeated among themselves. It was as if they
remained frozen in the first, confused hours after the assassination, before
Oswald's arrest, when they filled the vacuum of information with a
"general revulsion" toward the whole state of Texas. There was something wrong with "that city," with "those people."

This judgment betrayed more than misplaced grief; it articulated
deeply held antagonisms that lingered for years. In 1966, Arthur
Schlesinger cautioned William Manchester that his manuscript for *The
Death of a President* contained an "unconscious argument . . . that Johnson killed Kennedy (that is, that Johnson is an expression of the forces of

violence and irrationality which ran rampant through his native state and
were responsible for the tragedy of Dallas)." Few others were so indiscreet as to personalize their hatred. But one need not mention Johnson
to condemn him: to most of these men—and most of the country—
Lyndon Johnson *was* Texas. He was its first president. He peppered his
talk with the idioms and clichés of the Hill Country. He had been
brought onto the Kennedy ticket not as majority leader but as a Texan;
rarely was a regional alliance touted as relentlessly as "the Boston–Austin
axis." Now, Boston was dead, killed in Austin's backyard. The bitter irony
escaped no one.

Texans felt an irrational shame and dishonor. Lady Bird Johnson,
doing her best to console Jackie Kennedy during the long wait at Love
Field, acknowledged as much: "What wounds me most of all," she said,
regretting her words even as they tumbled from her tongue, "is that this
should happen in my beloved state of Texas." "Was Dallas to blame?"
asked the *New York Times*. As citizens searched for an answer, "the defensiveness was massive. It verged sometimes on combativeness." Dallas civic
leaders began a wrenching public debate over the city's responsibility to
subdue, somehow, its "forces of hatred."

LBJ, of course, could not reasonably be expected to restrain the forces
of hatred that raged in his state as in so many others, south and north.
Yet he could, perhaps, be expected to referee its political squabbles, and
in this he was a failure. Back at home, Vice President Johnson aroused
some reflexive Texan pride but little loyalty. Frustrated by both Connally and Yarborough, as well as by Bobby Kennedy and others in the
administration, Johnson had little federal patronage to dispense and he
receded further in the memory of Texas Democrats. His emerging moderation, too, cost him dearly at home. At last a national figure, Johnson
had slipped free of the narrow regionalism that constrained most of his
career—and found himself at odds with both wings of his state party.

Still, in the eyes of "Harvards" and the Eastern establishment, Johnson
was indelibly Texan, a representative and product of the state that had
killed a president. The damning charge was leveled on the first page of
Manchester's book:

> In the tranquil autumn of 1963 a political issue was about to take the
> President and his Vice President a thousand miles from Washington, into
> deepest Texas. They had to go, because the state's Democratic party was
> riven by factionalism. Governor John Connally and Senator Ralph
> Yarborough were stalking one another with shivs. . . . If the Governor and
> the Senator didn't agree to a truce soon, the national ticket wouldn't stand
> a chance there next fall. No party writes off twenty-five electoral votes,
> so both Kennedy and Johnson were going down to patch things up.

The trip, Manchester continued, was born of Lyndon Johnson's neglect.

> The Lone Star State was, after all, the Vice President's fief. . . . As a professional Kennedy coolly assessed the present crisis and concluded that he must go after all. But he reached the decision grudgingly. It appeared to him that Johnson ought to be able to resolve this petty dispute himself.

Among the late president's inner circle, this was the conventional wisdom: the Dallas trip was nothing but a political errand for LBJ. "Absolutely, absolutely," said JFK aide Ralph Dungan. "Kennedy made that trip, I can say for all history and posterity, without a doubt, as a favor to Lyndon Johnson," as a party-building exercise at "Lyndon's strong urging." So persuasive was Johnson, by this account, that his influence outweighed the reservations of the White House staff. Noting the rise of the right wing in Texas and recalling the ugly reception to Adlai Stevenson's recent visit to Dallas, staffers sparred over the merits of a trip. This was hostile territory, protested Ken O'Donnell. But to each objection Kennedy's response was reportedly the same: "Lyndon Johnson really wants me to do it, and I've got to do it."

This was a convenient excuse, one that played to the bias of the White House staff, and it stalled further argument. But it really made little sense. What had suddenly rendered the president so pliable, so responsive to Johnson's whim? Surely this trip was beyond the call of political etiquette. And as for Johnson's famous skills of persuasion, well, most agreed he had left them on the Hill.

Looking back, even Dungan had to concede the element of self-interest in the president's calculus. A favor for Johnson "was also a favor for John F. Kennedy, because it was [in] his interest that the party in Texas be united" by 1964. And in Arthur Schlesinger's view, it was JFK who was "quite worried over the divisions in the Democratic Party in Texas and thought he ought to go down there for that reason."

This concern, too, may have been a political conceit. There was little doubt that the governor and senator were "incompatible personalities"; or, more important, that Connally viewed Yarborough's liberal-labor coalition with utter distaste. These tensions were no help to Democratic fortunes in an increasingly reactionary state.

Neither did they constitute a "crisis," as Manchester asserts. In the context of Texas politics the feud was nothing new or unusual. "We always have a split of some kind," said Jake Jacobsen, a Connally aide. The party organization remained sound nonetheless. And President Kennedy's liabilities in Texas had less to do with Connally or Yarborough than, say, with his own brother Bobby. According to Connally aide Larry Temple, Robert Kennedy was "substantially less popular in Texas" than

the president. In Texan Democratic circles, there were distressed whispers: "If he would get rid of Bobby, he'd be a whole lot better off. I'd like
him if he'd get rid of Bobby." It wasn't any one issue, like desegregation,
that nettled Texas Democrats—"it was just that [Bobby] was an irritant."

The president, determined to regain ground in the South, continued
to insist upon a fund-raising trip to Texas. Connally acquiesced, reluctantly, cringing at the thought of an unsuccessful visit. Lyndon Johnson
was even less enthusiastic. In fact, he was downright resentful, having
learned of the trip secondhand. The president already had his hands full
with Connally and made no effort to inform LBJ. Shut out of plans concerning his own "fief," Johnson was livid—and wounded. He also considered the trip a certain embarrassment to himself, Kennedy, Connally,
and the state of Texas.

In the aftermath of the assassination, Johnson exploded with rage at the
fiction—so often repeated—that the trip was his idea, that he had
dragged a reluctant president to Dallas and to his death. "That's a great
myth," Johnson complained privately. "I didn't force him to come to
Texas. Hell, he wanted to come out there himself!" But LBJ was not
about to interrupt Kennedy's long wake by protesting his own inno-
cence. He was powerless to silence Dungan, O'Donnell, Schlesinger,
Sorensen, or any of the other agents of his humiliation. And behind
every one of them he saw Robert Kennedy.

Bobby was no puppet master, but among friends he was not shy about
assigning blame. "Just before the president went to Texas," he said later,
"just that week, he spoke to me about the fact that Johnson wouldn't
help in the dispute in Texas." President Kennedy didn't understand it. He
"always thought those things could be worked out. . . . He said how irritated he was with Lyndon Johnson who wouldn't help at all in trying to
iron out any of the problems in Texas, and that he was an s.o.b. . . .
because this was his state and he just wasn't available to help out or just
wouldn't lift a finger to try to assist." This explained the visit to Texas—
an otherwise useless trip, "a strain on busy people," Bobby told Ramsey
Clark.

RFK had his own cross to bear, and perhaps such explanations eased
the burden, or shared it. But to Bobby Kennedy, Johnson's role in the assassination was more than metaphorical. John Kennedy had gone to Dallas
to clean up Johnson's mess and returned to Washington in a casket.

CHAPTER 6

Uneasy Alliance

The new year, 1964, began with displays of unity. On January 1, President Johnson wired Robert Kennedy from the LBJ Ranch.

I KNOW HOW HARD THE PAST SIX WEEKS HAVE BEEN FOR YOU. UNDER THE MOST TRYING CIRCUMSTANCES YOUR FIRST THOUGHTS HAVE BEEN OF YOUR COUNTRY. YOUR BROTHER WOULD HAVE BEEN VERY PROUD OF THE STRENGTH YOU HAVE SHOWN. AS THE NEW YEAR BEGINS, I RESOLVE TO DO MY BEST TO FULFILL HIS TRUST IN ME. I WILL NEED YOUR COUNSEL AND SUPPORT.

LYNDON B. JOHNSON

Robert Kennedy responded from Aspen, Colorado, on January 4:

GREATLY APPRECIATE THE THOUGHTFULNESS OF YOUR TELEGRAM. I AM LOOKING FORWARD TO VISITING WITH YOU IN WASHINGTON AT YOUR CONVENIENCE. RESPECTFULLY,

ROBERT F. KENNEDY

Johnson's telegram was thoughtful indeed. It typified his efforts to treat the Kennedys—even Bobby—with compassion. Sharing their grief and recognizing how much their approval meant to his presidency, Johnson embraced the late president's extended family. "He went out of his way . . . to be sympathetic," recalled Ralph Dungan, "not only to the family but to all of us." Arthur Schlesinger thought "Johnson behaved, . . . under great difficulties of a personal and political sort, with grace and dignity."

LBJ's concern for Jacqueline Kennedy was so achingly earnest as to be almost desperate. He denied her nothing, no favor or small kindness. A few days after John Kennedy's funeral, Jackie had dinner at the White

House with Charles Bartlett. "Of course, I've always liked Lyndon Johnson," she told him. "He has been very generous with me. Bobby gets me
to put on my widow's weeds and go down to his office and ask for
tremendous things, like renaming Cape Canaveral after Jack, and [John-
son] has come through on everything." President Johnson was so attentive to Jackie that Harry McPherson supposed he would have renamed
the country as "the United States of Kennedy" if she so desired. LBJ and
Jackie exchanged heartfelt, handwritten notes for months, each consoling the other, each acknowledging and sharing the other's burdens.

Johnson's gestures to Jackie made little impression on RFK. Despite
LBJ's "thoughtful" telegram, Bobby rebuffed or misinterpreted most of
the president's overtures. Reconciliation was far from Bobby's mind; it
was hard enough simply to cope with the loss of his brother. At Hobe
Sound, Florida, during Thanksgiving, the attorney general was "the most
shattered man I had ever seen in my life," observed Pierre Salinger.
Bobby had almost ceased to function. He walked alone for hours. Occasionally he rallied to organize the family's traditional touch football
games, but these were different from the competitive but carefree matches of years past. These were "really vicious games," Salinger remembered.
Bobby seemed to be venting his feelings by knocking people down.

Over Christmas, Bobby's grief lightened imperceptibly if at all; his
bitterness toward Johnson did not diminish. Secondhand reports, each
alleging some new offense by LBJ, continued to filter to him. "The
atmosphere," said Bobby's friend Milton Gwirtzman, "was beginning to
be poisoned." But the poisoning had begun long before, and the air was
now heavy with charges and countercharges.

Back in Washington after the holidays, Pierre Salinger wondered aloud
whether he should remain as Johnson's press secretary. Robert Kennedy
told Salinger that he had no choice; everyone owed LBJ his best effort
during the transition. While others struggled with the decision, Bobby
seemed resigned about staying on. He made no attempts to draw others,
whether cabinet or staff members, out of the White House. "Stay, for
God's sakes, this is where you belong," Bobby told congressional liaison
Larry O'Brien.

In asking them to stay, Johnson showed similar pragmatism and an
appreciation of history. On November 30, Clark Clifford, who had
served in Harry Truman's White House, recounted for Johnson the
experiences of 1945: "the rapid departure of the FDR loyalists, the con-
descending attitude of some of the Roosevelt holdovers, [and] the
unfortunate decision to make James Byrnes Secretary of State . . . I urged
President Johnson to proceed slowly, allowing the Kennedy people to

leave at their own pace, and retain as long as possible those whose services would be most valuable."

Political instinct told Johnson to retain them. As early as the plane flight from Dallas, Johnson had developed the Pitch, and over the following weeks he perfected it. "I need you more than President Kennedy needed you," he told everyone from Robert Kennedy to Robert McNamara to Lee White. And if some considered this Johnson hyperbole, it was not. He *did* need them, all of them, more than President Kennedy did. Any reshuffling of the cabinet would smack of disrespect for the dead. As Johnson put it, "I needed that White House staff. Without them I would have lost my link to John Kennedy, and without that I would have had absolutely no chance of gaining the support of the media or the Easterners or the intellectuals. And without that support I would have had absolutely no chance of governing the country." Kennedy loyalists cast adrift could easily coalesce into a government-in-exile, one with brains, money, experience, a vast network of contacts—and with Bobby Kennedy as its head of state.

Holding on to the Kennedy staff, though, was risky and unpleasant; it required, as Harry McPherson judged, "tremendous guts." Kennedy men were distraught and grieving. Some were offended by Johnson's manner, some by his very presence. And some had been gleefully cruel to LBJ at Hickory Hill parties or in West Wing corridors. With agendas and ambitions cut short by the assassination, "the potential for internecine warfare was very high," McPherson remembered. It took a large measure of political courage and wisdom to keep Kennedy loyalists in the White House, to trust them, even to rely on them. And for Johnson, it demonstrated an uncommon ability to swallow his pride in pursuit of a larger goal, in this case the stability of his administration.

Johnson understood the swift cruelty of their reversal of fortune. It reminded him of his own. "Suddenly they were outsiders just as I had been for almost three years, outsiders on the inside. . . . So I determined to keep them informed. I determined to keep them busy. I constantly requested their advice and asked for their help." For the sake of his own political legitimacy, Johnson assumed the role of supplicant. Another reason to cling to the Kennedy men was that there were so few Johnson men. "I don't know anybody," Johnson moaned to Ralph Dungan in December.

"Mr. President," corrected Dungan, "you know a hundred thousand more people than I'll ever know, across the length and breadth of this country."

So strong in recent days, Johnson's confidence seemed now to ebb. "No," he said, "you don't understand . . . I don't know the kinds of people that we're going to need." Johnson often feigned weakness to command sympathy or loyalty, but this concern struck Dungan as genuine. After all, it was true: Johnson's camp was sadly depleted by three years of political obscurity. He had no Johnson government-in-exile ready to spring into service. Unlike John or Bobby Kennedy, LBJ aroused little personal affection, and many lieutenants had long deserted him for those with real, not ceremonial, power. Now, although they rushed back into Johnson's open arms, he worried that his own men lacked the magic gloss of the Kennedy team that had licked them all in 1960.

Thankfully, then, the Johnson Pitch worked. Almost every important Kennedy man stayed at his post. "Hell," recalled Lee White, "I don't think there [was] any kind of alternative." Fred Dutton cited "public responsibility . . . [and] ongoing work" as reasons for remaining at the State Department. It never occurred to him or to White, who had worked for John Kennedy even in his Senate days, that staying on conveyed any measure of disloyalty to the memory of JFK, or to RFK. Men like White and Dutton felt they had invested their loyalty in the institution of the presidency, not just the president himself.

Predictably, some staff members had a hard time seeing it that way. There was something intensely personal about the loyalty John Kennedy—and now his memory—commanded. "We came down to be with Kennedy, and he [is] no longer president, so perhaps we ought to leave," shrugged Senate liaison Mike Manatos. Arthur Schlesinger, who did leave, felt strongly that every president deserved his own team, that "the White House staff was a personal extension of the president." And who among John Kennedy's men wanted to be a personal extension of Lyndon Johnson? LBJ, in 1963, appeared a shabby relic to the New Frontiersmen. In the view of the "loyalists," as Schlesinger termed them (including himself), the 1960 Kennedy-Johnson ticket had been a self-contradiction. Kennedy was wry, urbane, chic; Johnson was crass, expansive, "cornpone." JFK offered vision and direction; LBJ offered tactical concessions and half measures. How could the legislative mechanic of the 1950s be the standard-bearer of a new age? As the antithesis of everything Kennedy, Johnson could not have been a more perverse reminder of their loss.

It was unclear how long this tenuous marriage of interests and ambitions could hold. Absent a clear alternative to LBJ, these New Frontiersmen might have scattered like seeds across a barren landscape, some settling with Scoop Jackson, others with Hubert Humphrey, others, perhaps, with George McGovern. But it was immediately clear that all had not been lost. There, out in front, leading the funeral procession, was Bobby Kennedy. And in the depths of their despair the very *idea* of Bobby provided comfort. After all, as William Manchester writes, "Here was a cabinet member who looked like, sounded like, and thought like the slain leader; who had been his second self; who was one of his two chief mourners; and who, at times, had . . . exercised executive power in his brother's name. It was as though Edwin Stanton had been Abraham Lincoln's twin."

The loyalty of Kennedy men accrued—reflexively, wholeheartedly—to Robert Kennedy. Only twenty-four hours after the assassination, a handful of White House aides and their wives responded to Arthur Schlesinger's summons and gathered in a private upstairs room at the Occidental Grill, blocks from the White House. Over lunch—"the Harvard lunch," as it became known, on account of the diners' predominant affiliation—the group brooded over what they agreed was a national crisis. Looking forward into the void, their course of action seemed obscured. John Kenneth Galbraith later recorded in his journal that Schlesinger "was reacting far too quickly to the chemistry of the moment and was dwelling on the possibility of a ticket in 1964 headed by Bob Kennedy and Hubert Humphrey. This of course is fantasy, unless of course Johnson stumbles unbelievably."

But all the men at this Harvard roundtable shared Schlesinger's impulse. After Dallas, aides hastily chose sides between Bobby and Lyndon, widening a breach that Ted Sorensen later described as "unfortunate, unnecessary, and highly emotional." Few chose LBJ. Even the pragmatists yearned for restoration: Galbraith, by Schlesinger's telling, "is a realist. He would infinitely have preferred Kennedy, but he is ready to face facts and make the best of them. Like Kenny and Bobby, I am a sentimentalist. My heart is not in it."

Johnson asked not for their hearts but for their labor. It came at a price. In its first days, LBJ's White House was filled by men whose discomfort was palpable. They bridled at the new president's manic pattern of work—some "thought he was nuts!" blurted Lee White. Many retreated into shells of one sort or another. Pierre Salinger found it hard to survive the day without a bottle of Scotch. Ken O'Donnell seemed a hollow man, drained of blood and spirit; Sorensen was simply aloof. LBJ's longtime secretary, Juanita Roberts, read contempt in their eyes. It was evident to her which ones "utterly despised not only [Johnson] but all of us. They made it very obvious."

Yet as the Kennedy staff watched the new president work, some were awed by Johnson's incredible, undiminished capacities and strove to match them. The transition marked one of Johnson's finest hours. He radiated confidence, competence, and resolution. He stoked the dying coals of the New Frontier, breathing new life into what had been, in John Kennedy's last days, a stagnant program. There was little question that Johnson was worthy of the presidency. To Hugh Sidey, he seemed "a totally new man," more imposing than the majority leader of old. Even before the sensational string of legislative successes of the next two years, Lyndon Johnson's performance, in the words of Fred Dutton, was simply "magnificent."

The amalgam of Kennedy loyalists, political pragmatists, and Johnson men worked in surprising harmony as "sort of a dual staff." Even the staunchest Kennedy partisans had nothing but respect for the Johnson staff, which, recalled Larry O'Brien, "moved heaven and earth to make themselves available and as helpful as possible." Schlesinger rated them "first-class," likable fellows. Dungan called Jenkins "the Rock of Gibraltar," the foundation of a competent group functioning brilliantly in a foreign environment. Jenkins, LBJ's principal adviser, had to be forced to take an office on the main floor of the White House. "I didn't want to disrupt things," Jenkins said. Lyndon Johnson's men were so overcourteous that Lee White suspected Johnson had bullied them into it.

Still, staff relations were correct but not close. There were occasional moments of tension. Wherever he walked, O'Donnell left a trail of ill will, which Dungan judged "90 percent O'Donnell's fault," the product of a prickly personality. (In fairness to O'Donnell, the president's death had shattered him like no one but a family member.) Ted Sorensen, JFK's erstwhile wordsmith, refused to let Jack Valenti even hold the printed text of Johnson's State of the Union address in the limousine to Capitol Hill. During the following weeks, Sorensen guarded his prerogatives zealously and gave Valenti "a rather bad time" before regaining his collegiality.

Johnson, meanwhile, bared a politician's forced smile, peacefully coexisting with Kennedy aides while feeling the sharpness of their glares. Even Jackie, in his view, had let him down by refusing to attend White House ceremonies. Johnson dared not let slip his facade of goodwill, but insiders saw his painful resentment. "In private," recalled columnist Arthur Krock, "he revealed it plenty." "They still don't believe that President Kennedy is dead," Johnson "sneered" to Hugh Sidey. "Those touch football boys who used to make these decisions aren't making them anymore." Years later, Johnson openly rued having kept so many of John Kennedy's men—not only JFK's staff but his cabinet, which contained loyal Kennedyites like Stewart Udall, Orville Freeman, and Abraham Ribicoff. If he could go back and do it again, Johnson said sourly, he would replace the whole lot of them.

Bobby Kennedy, in these early, anxious days of the Johnson administration, was a remote figure. Conspicuously absent from cabinet meetings, the attorney general hid somewhere within the safe haven of the Justice Department. But he was never far from Johnson's thoughts. Bobby Kennedy dominated LBJ's attention and concern like nothing else in his first months as president.

In every real or imagined word of reproach, LBJ heard Bobby's voice; in every misdeed he saw Bobby's hand. Where O'Donnell, Sorensen, and the rest were once extensions of John Kennedy, they were now extensions of Bobby. Placating O'Donnell was like kissing up to the Soviet ambassador: it helped ease tensions, perhaps, but only went so far with the man behind the Kremlin Wall. From the inner chamber came a stony silence that conveyed disapproval.

More to the point, neither O'Donnell nor Sorensen attracted much media speculation; neither laid claim to a political dynasty. Bobby Kennedy did. He also held the power to frustrate any decision on domestic or foreign policy or even personnel. Johnson was president but at the moment he enjoyed little autonomy. He was doubly yoked—by the Kennedy legacy and by Robert Kennedy. Were they the same thing? And if not, if the two forces pulled in different directions, which way was Johnson to go?

These were questions for later days, and could not have been more than inchoate in Johnson's mind as the election year dawned. But it was clear that trouble—and a torturous reckoning with RFK—lay ahead. Anyone could have predicted it, and many did. After the assassination, Tommy Corcoran called Lady Bird and warned, "You're going to have trouble with Bobby. We all know how an attorney general can screw everything up. He can indict anybody, he can investigate anybody." Corcoran suggested the creation of a White House post, staffed by a Harvard man, with a simple job description: "handle Bobby."

Johnson made no such appointment, but he plumbed the Kennedy staff for goodwill ambassadors. The affable O'Brien, who was as accommodating as anyone during the transition, seemed a natural choice. Johnson never directly asked O'Brien to act as intermediary; LBJ was too coy—and proud—for that. But "it was obvious," O'Brien said later, that Johnson was looking for a liaison to smooth things over with Bobby, to slip him a few unsolicited kind words from the president, to find out once again what was eating at him. Johnson inched closer to Edward Kennedy, whom he regarded as infinitely more collegial than the dour Bobby. But Ted was only the means to an end, and that end was RFK.

Just as President Kennedy had instructed his staff to mind the prerogatives (and ego) of his vice president, Johnson demanded that Bobby be apprised of every development. LBJ was not about to invite charges that he was easing the Kennedy heir into early retirement. After the assassination, LBJ called presidential counsel Lee White into the Oval Office. "I want you," Johnson said, pointing his big finger at and looming over White, "to keep the attorney general informed on everything. You hear that?"

"Yes, sir," White replied.

"I'm not kidding. . . . I don't want anybody ever to say that we didn't keep him well informed. And that especially means you," Johnson said, referring to White's leading role on civil rights. "Don't make any moves in any of these fields where there's any doubt without checking with him."

Otherwise the president took a hands-off approach—it was better to ignore Bobby than disagree with him. In January the president released a review of the Justice Department's crackdown on organized crime and racketeering, using the occasion to praise Bobby's leadership. But in all other respects Johnson kept a wary distance. He had been eyeing the Justice Department suspiciously for months. Since the summer of 1963, LBJ had feared a departmental conspiracy, directed by Bobby Kennedy and intended to knock Johnson off the 1964 ticket. Kennedy's secret weapon: Bobby Baker.

Johnson was extremely fond of Baker, the Senate secretary and longtime devotee. "I have two daughters," Johnson once mused. "If I had a son, this would be the boy." Most senators regarded Baker with similar fondness. Like LBJ and the majority leadership, Baker had endowed his position with unprecedented reach and power. He was cunning and driven, a shrewd, no-nonsense master of the head count. By this service and many others—building support for bills or campaigns, offering wise counsel, and even, on occasion, procuring "dates" for lonely senators—Baker rendered himself invaluable to members on both sides of the aisle. They called him the 101st senator. He was more powerful than the rest, they joked—but their laughter was shrill and nervous, for Baker "had the goods" on his hundred colleagues and the tenacity to use them.

Johnson was not Baker's only powerful patron. According to George Reedy, Baker viewed the whole Senate as "a mechanism that cranked out good things for Bobby Baker if he played it right." Baker played it right for many years, buoyed first by Lyndon Johnson and then thriving under the permissive rule of Mike Mansfield. By 1963, Baker had amassed an impressive array of professional perks: he co-owned motels, vending machine companies, housing developments, insurance companies, and twenty-two corporations. He was feeling invincible.

That autumn, however, Baker's tight coil of personal debts and favors unraveled when Senator John Williams of Delaware began to probe

Baker's finances. On October 7, Baker downed four martinis, marched stiffly into the Senate, and resigned in an attempt to defuse the matter. But the case and its implications were too far-reaching to go away. Investigators alleged, provocatively, that Vice President Johnson was entangled in the mess: in separate transactions, Baker had given the Johnsons an expensive hi-fi and had taken a commission for acquiring two life insurance policies for LBJ. These were tenuous links, but strong enough to terrify the vulnerable vice president. Johnson desperately denied any knowledge of Baker's unsavory dealings. He called a press conference to confess accepting the stereo. Beyond the occasional gift, though, Johnson could not remember ever having had much contact with—what was his name? Bakey? Bakerly? Beggerly? Johnson could not keep it straight.

In fact, Johnson knew little of Baker's business affairs. "No doubt [Johnson] should have tried to know; politicians are willfully obtuse about such things where a valuable friend is involved," observed Harry McPherson, and there was something to the argument that Baker's most flagrant violations occurred under Mansfield's watch, not LBJ's. "They said [Baker] deceived me!" Johnson fulminated later. "He didn't deceive me a damned bit! He just didn't do it while I was there!"

Johnson's desperate wriggling exposed his political insecurity as 1964 approached. Disavowing Baker was "one of the most inept things that he ever did," in Reedy's view. "Just trying to sell that line that he 'hardly knew Bobby Baker.' Oh, my God, that was incredible." But it was not uncommon. "Whatever Johnson tells you at any given moment, he thinks is the truth," Reedy reflected. "The first victim of the Johnson whopper is always Lyndon Baines Johnson. In his own mind I don't think the man has ever told a whopper in his life."

There was little doubt, then, that "the boss," as Walter Jenkins cautioned Baker, "would hate to see this thing blown up." The case subsequently blew up in Baker's face, not Johnson's, but reporters had begun to pester the vice presidential staff with questions. Allegations were leaking from the Senate to the press, but behind them Johnson saw a familiar specter. "He's afraid Bobby Kennedy's putting them up to hanging something on you so as to embarrass him," Jenkins told Baker. Baker didn't think so, but LBJ and his intimates were convinced. On a Connecticut highway, in a car bound for an appreciation dinner for Senator Thomas Dodd, the vice president barked at Senate aides that Bobby Kennedy had "cooked up" the Baker case to make LBJ appear a "crook." Kennedy was conducting covert daily press briefings, Johnson was sure of that. No one knew where Johnson got this idea. He prodded George Reedy to investigate the matter, and when Reedy returned to his boss empty-handed and skeptical, LBJ scoffed at Reedy's naiveté. Johnson tried to settle the question himself by laying a trap for complicit reporters. Rambling amiably, Johnson stopped and abruptly revealed his "knowledge" of the secret Kennedy briefings. Some reporters wondered about the vice president's "mental stability."

Kennedy was in fact loath to touch the case, however incredible his later claim that "I didn't really follow it particularly." Like most Washington insiders, RFK had heard tell of Baker's free hand with money, but it was only "after a good number of newspaper stories had appeared about" the case that Kennedy felt "there really wasn't any choice but to look into some of the allegations." Special agents at the Internal Revenue Service, needing no prodding by Kennedy or Justice, were doing the same thing. They, too, read the papers.

RFK explored the Johnson connection with little enthusiasm, for any taint of corruption on the vice president was a blight on the Kennedy administration. Nor was he anxious to tangle with LBJ, who would surely perceive a vendetta. But Baker's abuses appalled Kennedy, and he pursued the case with typical thoroughness. By early November 1963, the attorney general had concluded that Johnson, if not lily-white, was innocent of any crime. And though Kennedy knew Baker to be guilty of everything from sketchy loans to shady investments, Kennedy hardly seemed eager to destroy Johnson's protégé. As if to prove his goodwill, RFK made a surprising phone call to Baker: "I want you to know," Kennedy told him, "that we have nothing of any consequence about you in our files—except for newspaper clippings which I'm certain you've read. My brother and I extend our sympathies to you," Kennedy continued. "I know that you'll come through this."

Baker, stammering, did not know what to say. "I'm grateful, Mr. Attorney General," he managed. "What you've just done required a lot of courage." Baker was not sure he meant this; in fact, he had no idea what to make of Kennedy's call, since the Justice Department had far more than a clipping file on Bobby Baker, and some of Kennedy's aides were telling reporters just that. Perhaps the administration feared Baker would drag Senate Democrats into a widening, swirling morass; perhaps this was a sign that the Justice Department intended to "drag its feet." Or was Bobby Kennedy simply more forgiving than Baker had imagined? "I just wanted to assure him that he'd get a fair shake," Kennedy later explained, "and if there was any problem that he could send his lawyer to the Department of Justice and he would be fairly treated." This conciliatory message may have been intended for Johnson's ears. After all, as Kennedy later judged, the idea of an anti-Johnson conspiracy simply "didn't make any sense. . . . There were a lot of stories then, after November 22, that the Bobby Baker case was stimulated by me, and that this was part of my plan to get something on Lyndon Johnson. That wasn't correct."

After November 22, and throughout Johnson's presidency, the scandal hounded him intermittently. He never ceased to blame Bobby Kennedy. In March 1964, *U.S. News & World Report* reported "a feeling . . . among Johnson friends that the information was being leaked from the Justice Department—headed by Robert Kennedy—to keep the Baker story alive . . . to cause trouble for Mr. Johnson." For years President Johnson continued to regard Justice as the enemy within. As the prosecution of Baker proceeded, Johnson saw the department as Kennedy's den of con-spirators—even after RFK had long departed for the U.S. Senate. In 1966, when Johnson appointed Mitchell Rogovin, former chief counsel to the IRS, to the Justice Department, the president spoke bitterly of Rogovin's new colleagues—from the assistant attorneys general all the way to the top, Attorney General Nicholas Katzenbach. I don't care that they're all still loyal to Bobby, the president told Rogovin, but they have no right to be disloyal to me. By January 1967, Johnson had replaced the suspect Katzenbach with Ramsey Clark, a Texan. The president contin-ued to fume about the case and the department. "There's a double stan-dard," Johnson bellowed to Clark on the telephone. "I'll take justice. I [was] willing to let them investigate, and investigate anything they could. . . . But I knew it was politically motivated the whole time. I know it now. I feel deeply about it, and I damned sure want to do something about it. I just know it is."

Johnson's anxiety was typically overworked. The charges were not sticking to the presidency; though Baker privately called the stereo "a kickback pure and simple," the inept Goldwater forces were unable to make much of it in the 1964 presidential campaign. "LBJ for LBJ . . . and Bobby Baker, too!" made a clever-sounding bumper sticker, but it was unclear what it meant to say or even who was saying it. As Johnson suc-cessfully skirted the issue, Baker spiraled downward. On January 5, 1966, a federal grand jury indicted him on nine counts, including theft, tax evasion, conspiracy to defraud the federal government, and the misap-propriation of $100,000 in campaign money; he was convicted on most of those charges a year later in a U.S. district court. In January 1971, Baker was locked up in Lewisburg Federal Prison, where he spent the next year and a half.

Yet throughout Baker's long, wretched undoing, President Johnson cursed not Baker's fate but his own. Johnson could not help feeling that Baker had overplayed his hand, that he had been a gluttonous, careless fool, and Johnson would be damned if he would jeopardize his own credibility for the sake of Baker's millions. At the same time, said Harry

McPherson, LBJ felt Baker had been wronged, and wanted to find his friend the best legal representation. "Johnson felt defensive and protective about Bobby [Baker]," McPherson recalled, but it seemed more the former than the latter. To those who later charged Johnson with white-washing the case, Baker offered a bitter rebuke: "Lyndon Johnson's Justice Department investigated me, indicted me, tried me, and convicted me. If he did me any favors, or in any way attempted to protect me, I am unaware of it."

Johnson shrugged his shoulders, professing helplessness. In his eyes it was still Robert Kennedy's Justice Department, even as late as 1967, and the Bobby Baker scandal had less to do with Bobby Baker than with Bobby Kennedy. To LBJ, several years' worth of evidence and testimony attested less to Baker's guilt than to the extent of Kennedy's vindictiveness.

If Johnson intended to pacify Bobby Kennedy he would have to stomach his own festering spite. Mere civility required supreme tact and self-control. In early 1964 it was not clear Johnson was steeled to the task. During those first months of Johnson's tenure, Pierre Salinger remained as press secretary and, unexpectedly, as presidential confidant. In the afternoons LBJ would summon Salinger to the White House pool, where these two large men, one full-framed and imposing, the other short and famously portly, would bob in the water "and talk and talk and talk," Salinger recalled. Startling Salinger by his candor, LBJ conducted long and involved harangues about Bobby, Jackie, and the snubs of O'Donnell and Sorensen. "Right from the beginning came the message that he hated Bob Kennedy. . . . It all went back to 1960."

Johnson paddled closer, bearing down upon Salinger in an aquatic version of the Treatment. He railed on, recounting every detail of Bobby's act of sabotage at the 1960 convention. "He spent all his time trying to prevent me from becoming the vice presidential candidate," Johnson alleged.

"Wait a minute, Mr. President," Salinger interrupted, and described for LBJ Bobby's words from the bathtub on the early morning of the vice presidential nomination. Bobby had argued in favor of his candidacy, Salinger explained. But every time he and Johnson had this discussion—"five, six, seven, eight times" in those early months, according to Salinger—the president was not to be dissuaded. He returned again and again to the act of betrayal he was certain Bobby had perpetrated. Salinger had the distinct and unsettling impression Johnson intended him to convey these feelings to RFK.

The depth of Johnson's bitterness showed the strength of will required for him to build a correct, if not cordial, relationship with Robert

Kennedy. Yet LBJ strove to do so, remembering the stakes and offering whatever was required to keep Bobby from resigning. The president made gestures of inclusion. In mid-January 1964, he dispatched RFK to East Asia, where Indonesian President Achmed Sukarno had announced his intention to "crush" the new Federation of Malaysia; the two countries shared a border on the island of Borneo. Averell Harriman, under secretary of state and a friend of Bobby's, had proposed the trip partly on its merits, partly to revitalize the depleted attorney general. Advisers reminded the president of Bobby's rapport with Sukarno. Johnson disliked the idea, but before he made a decision, news of the trip was leaked to the *Washington Post*. Johnson was irritated. The publicity had forced his hand; now, canceling the trip would be read as a repudiation of RFK. Staff members, LBJ complained, had subverted him, pushing him into approving the trip in thoughtless disregard of the "Johnson interest." "Where did the *Post* get its story on Bobby?" Johnson barked at Mac Bundy. Bundy explained that a staff member at the State Department had accidentally let it slip. "Damned if I don't wish they'd let *me* announce something," Johnson groused. "I thought it came from Justice."

"No, I don't think so, Mr. President," Bundy replied. "But I will say that you should know that the attorney general's children knew about it and people's children hear from other people's children—so it was not as tightly held as certainly all of us hoped it would be."

"Well . . . we just got to watch that," Johnson warned. Still, he found some pleasure in the fact that the trip was probably a fool's errand. "I'm going to send Bobby Kennedy to Indonesia and just put it right in his lap," he crowed to Richard Russell. "Let him go out there and have whatever row it is with Sukarno."

By some accounts, Bobby was unenthusiastic about the trip, though Larry O'Brien remembered him being "excited about the opportunity and the challenge" and appreciative of what he considered a meaningful gesture by the president. In either case, Kennedy was glad to get out of the country. Accompanied by Ethel and several aides, he responded to condolence cards on the long, somber flight to Tokyo, where he met Sukarno on January 16. "Did you come here to threaten me?" Sukarno asked him. "No, I've come to help get you out of trouble," Bobby replied, smiling.

Over the next thirteen days, Kennedy shuttled back and forth among six countries, cobbling together a difficult and "shaky" cease-fire and negotiations on the border dispute. Kennedy "was very, very frank with Sukarno," an American aide said later, "told him things that nobody else would have dared to say to him. . . . He never told a lie; he never misquoted anybody; he never concealed. . . . He was always absolutely impersonal, spoke with great directness softened by humor."

This candid approach to the Indonesian president seemed to pay dividends, and when RFK returned to Washington on January 28, he expected a private audience with the president. For three years that had been the norm, but this was a different president. Bobby entered a room crowded with ranking members of the Senate Foreign Relations Committee and Armed Services Committee. Johnson never spoke to him again about the matter. The State Department, meanwhile, sniffed at Bobby's report with vague contempt; Secretary Rusk thought his plan a "policy of accommodation" of Sukarno. "Sukarno was a crook, and the attempt to play ball with Sukarno was bound to fail because he was a crook," Rusk said later. "This did lead to some division between Bobby Kennedy and Lyndon Johnson because Lyndon Johnson was not inclined to cater to this strange individual [Sukarno]." It was an odd time to raise these concerns about Sukarno; what was shuttle diplomacy if not "playing ball"? Rusk, anyway, had approved the trip at its inception. Now he dismissed Bobby as an interloper. After a thousand days of taking second seat to Robert Kennedy in foreign policy, Rusk now basked in a measure of autonomy.

The Indonesian-Malaysian talks took place as Kennedy had arranged, but the two parties failed to agree to terms for a cease-fire. Kennedy labored to follow up on the simmering conflict, but without support from LBJ or the State Department his efforts flagged. If Johnson was sincere in helping lift the attorney general out of despair, "Bob," Ed Guthman writes, "concluded otherwise." The incident left Kennedy with a "bitter taste." It set him drifting, slowly but inexorably, away from the center of power.

The center of power was the Oval Office—more so than at any time since the New Deal. Energy surged outward from the White House, generated and propelled by Lyndon Johnson, whose political mastery had never been more apparent. The presidency reawakened within him a fervor dormant since his days as majority leader. "There were tasks to perform that only I had the authority to perform," Johnson wrote in his memoirs. "A nation stunned, shaken to its very heart, had to be reassured that the government was not in a state of paralysis." Years later on the ranch, LBJ put it more colloquially: "We were like a bunch of cattle caught in the swamp, unable to move in either direction, simply circling 'round and 'round. I understood that; I knew what had to be done. . . . The man on the horse [had] to take the lead, to assume command, to provide direction. In the period of confusion after the assassination, I was that man."

In that first, heady year, Johnson's grip on the reins was essentially unbreakable. Where John Kennedy's legislative program had sputtered early (to be revived only late in his presidency), Lyndon Johnson determined right away—during his first week in office—not only to woo Congress but to tame it. He arrived unannounced at weekly luncheon meetings, paid surprise visits to leaders like Speaker John McCormack, and ran a virtual shuttle service along Pennsylvania Avenue, back and forth between the White House and the Hill. Legislators who had never dreamed of invitations to meet JFK found themselves with open and easy access to the new president. For unlike Kennedy's, Johnson's social life *was* his political life, and to LBJ a late-night session with a group of Democratic backbenchers was something other than a political chore—it was entertainment.

Johnson reattached himself to the telephone. As vice president, he had never been far from the receiver, but now his calls were answered with alacrity. When his chief domestic adviser Joseph Califano failed to pick up his POTUS (President of the United States) line, Johnson was told Califano was away from his desk. "Well, where the hell is he?" the president barked at Califano's secretary. "He's in the bathroom, Mr. President," she answered, mortified. LBJ paused a moment. "Isn't there a phone in there?" After a second presidential outburst, a red POTUS phone was hurriedly installed in the lavatory.

Assistants like Califano rapidly accustomed themselves to Johnson's "two-shift day": the president awoke at 6:30, worked relentlessly until 2:00, and then took a brisk walk or swim. Donning his pajamas, LBJ stretched out for a spell; by 4:00, he had showered and dressed and was primed for the "new day's work" that lasted until midnight, at least. Aides were not granted naptime.

Johnson reconciled with old enemies, his magnanimity born of political necessity and a newly expansive spirit. He overwhelmed his opponents with the sheer force of his personality. "LBJ has been hurling himself about Washington like an elemental force," observed columnist Richard Strout in *The New Republic*. In mere months, all officialdom seemed to bend under his will, and Johnson reaped his rewards in legislative accomplishments. In his first significant victory, LBJ tested the patience of Congress, demanding an unprecedented Christmas Eve vote—on sending wheat to Russia, no less. But an impromptu party that night drew two hundred congressmen to the White House and replaced their resentment with cheer.

The president seemed incapable of making a misstep. When an aide cautioned him against expending all his political capital on John Kennedy's legislative program, LBJ paused, bemused. Eyebrows arched,

Johnson replied, "Well, then what the hell's the presidency for?" As he marched toward the 1964 election, Johnson showed exactly what the office was for: tallying up victories. From a once recalcitrant Congress LBJ extracted a tax cut, a trimmer budget, a wilderness act, aid to mass transit, aid to college students, price supports for wheat, and—most significant—the civil rights act and a massive antipoverty program, the foundation of Johnson's war on poverty.

"It was the damndest performance the first few months," extolled Harry McPherson. "It was a spectacular performance." In March a somewhat more neutral observer, James Reston of the *New York Times,* declared an end to "the period of mourning for Kennedy and of experimentation for Johnson. . . . Washington is now a little girl settling down with the old boyfriend. The mad and wonderful infatuation with the handsome young stranger from Boston is over—something she always knew wouldn't last—so she is adjusting to reality," Reston wrote. "The lovers of style are not too happy, but the lovers of substance are not complaining."

Johnson's achievement demanded a postscript to Grover Cleveland's description of Theodore Roosevelt as "the most perfectly equipped and most efficient politician thus far seen in the Presidency." Roosevelt, who had also inherited the presidency after an assassination, was hardly considered a caretaker for a "William McKinley agenda." Yet Johnson could not escape the obligation to his predecessor or to the public sense of promise unfulfilled. At the passage of every bill, LBJ invoked the name of John Kennedy and pandered to the pride of the "Kennedy wing" of his party. He had to: any deviation from the late president's program would undermine Johnson's store of public trust and political legitimacy, crippling his hopes for reelection. He projected both strength and humility, leadership and deference. It truly was, as McPherson put it, a spectacular performance.

It was not, however, entirely heartfelt. While fighting a crusade in the name of the martyred president, Johnson privately—and rightly—claimed any victories as his own. Meanwhile, Johnson was marking time and building momentum for the Johnson agenda. "After I finished writing and completing and enacting and inaugurating . . . the dreams that he had, I started on my own. And I had some, too."

One dream was to become president in his own right. Yet as long as he remained beholden to the Kennedy name—and thus to Robert Kennedy—he could not do so. Increasingly, Johnson found himself in a political trap of his own making. He could not strike out on his own until he had been elected on his own. But by swearing fealty to the memory of John Kennedy, Johnson only strengthened the legacy to which RFK held the greater claim. LBJ, after all, would never be mistaken as the heir apparent.

Moving from success to success at a furious pace, Lyndon Johnson could not outrun his dilemma: to rid himself of Bobby was to forfeit his own legitimacy; to cling to Bobby was to forfeit his own identity.

In mid-December 1963, RFK assured Dick Goodwin, "We're very important to Johnson now. After November third . . . we won't matter a damn. But between now and then he needs us." Despite the signs, Bobby clung to the hope. But when crisis brewed over the Panama Canal Zone, Bobby was not consulted. "It's really the worst matter involving an international problem that I have not been in," he said, and judged it "very badly handled" by the new president. Johnson's lack of interest in Bobby's Indonesian trip dashed any further hopes of an active role.

In February, though, Bobby reentered the foreign policy fray when the Coast Guard seized four Cuban fishing vessels in U.S. waters. Cuba had been Bobby's charge, and he could not be tactfully bypassed here. He was invited to the emergency NSC meeting. Thomas Mann, Johnson's new Latin American adviser, promoted the view that Fidel Castro had sent the ships, that they, like the missiles of October 1962, were a Soviet "test." Kennedy was incredulous. "A traffic violation," he shot back. "If you wanted to fine them a couple of hundred bucks, fine them," Bobby said later, "but the idea of locking them up and creating a major crisis about it was foolish." The premise of American policy was that Castro was behind the incident. When Kennedy asked for proof, for some kind of intelligence on the matter, none was forthcoming. He and Robert McNamara waged a "rather violent argument" with Mann at the next NSC meeting, forcing its adjournment.

Later that afternoon, CIA Director John McCone agreed with Bobby and sent the unfortunate fishermen back to Cuba. But the president, feeling perhaps doubly tested, was determined to show some backbone. In response to the boats' seizure, Castro had shut off the water supply to the American naval base at Guantánamo. Mann now claimed that the two thousand Cuban employees on the base were security risks and should be fired; their wages, he reasoned, were fueling the Cuban economy. Latins were different from North Americans, Mann continued. The only thing they understood was money.

"I said I thought he sounded like Barry Goldwater making a speech at the Economic Club and that this policy of the United States had gone fifty years before," Kennedy griped later. Why were workers who had caused no problems during the missile crisis a sudden threat to American security? No answer was sought. To Bobby, the cabinet meeting felt like a setup. "It was my feeling that they'd all arranged it beforehand and that they were going to be fired." Indeed, the Cubans were dismissed, and so was Bobby Kennedy. It was his last invitation to a substantive meeting on foreign policy.

There was more to this quarrel than the shape of Johnson's Cuba policy. It was Mann—and what he represented—that rankled some Kennedy men. To Arthur Schlesinger, the appointment marked a return to the "Tex-Mex policy of condescension and manipulation" toward Latin America and a defeat of JFK's Alliance for Progress. Mann's appointment was also, as Schlesinger wrote Bobby on December 15, LBJ's "declaration of independence." "It is necessary," Schlesinger continued,

> to face a hard fact: Johnson has won the first round. He has shown his power to move in a field of special concern to the Kennedys without consulting the Kennedys. This will lead people all over the government to feel that their future lies with Johnson. Having succeeded here, he will be all the more free to act without consultation and impunity in the future. If he wishes, he will be able to pick off the Kennedy people, one by one, and either sidetrack them or drive them out of government. . . . He has shown, I believe, that we are weaker—a good deal weaker—than we had supposed. He has understood that the only sanctions we have are resignation and/or revolt—and that both sanctions are meaningless, and will seem sour grapes, unless they are provoked by a readily understandable issue—and this LBJ will do his best to deny us.

"They're tryin' to run [Mann] off," Johnson complained to Richard Russell, "because he believes in free enterprise." But this was not Kennedy's complaint, and though he deemed the appointment "a disaster, in my judgment," he did not share Schlesinger's pessimism. Johnson was bound to the Kennedy people at least until the 1964 election—which gave them influence over his choice of vice president and secretary of state (should Johnson, like JFK, wish to replace Rusk). Schlesinger wondered how much leverage the Kennedy forces had left: could they possibly impose a deal on the president? "It is not so hard," Bobby assured him. "I will be perfectly willing to ask President Johnson what his plans are for the State Department before we decide the role we are going to play in the campaign."

Schlesinger was unconvinced. He had long discarded any fleeting fantasies of capturing the nomination for RFK. "We will all have to play a role in the campaign, or we will be finished forever in the party," he said.

"Yes," Bobby replied, "but there is a considerable difference between a nominal role and a real role. We can go through the motions or we can go all out."

But Bobby was not intent on playing the spoiler. In the first months of 1964, he was determined to play a positive role in the Johnson administration. First there was the Department of Justice, where his control remained unfettered. "I don't think Lyndon Johnson paid one iota of attention to the Justice Department," recalled Nicholas Katzenbach. "Bobby Kennedy had license to do what he wanted to do."

What Bobby wanted to do was much of the same. There was unfinished business and some small comfort in continuity. As he sat in the familiar shambles of his office, Kennedy loosened his tie and breathed more freely. "I have this feeling that I can go on doing the same old things I always did," he said hopefully. "A month can go by before I need to take a problem to the White House. After all even my brother never asked me about the Lands Division."

In reality Kennedy was enervated and withdrawn. There were fine lawyers in the Lands Division, to be sure, but little of interest. Even the string of guilty verdicts that felled his old nemesis Jimmy Hoffa filled RFK with a strange melancholy. At a Justice Department party celebrating Hoffa's conviction, Bobby was disconsolate, commenting sourly that there was "nothing to celebrate." He seemed almost unhappy that Hoffa was prison-bound. "Bobby had enough tragedy of his own now," observed Ken O'Donnell. The attorney general spoke worriedly of Hoffa's fate at Lewisburg. "How's Hoffa doing?" he asked puzzled aides periodically.

Robert Kennedy was tired of chasing people. For three years he had stalked Hoffa and the mob and kept the pressure on Castro. These had been his professional passions. Now Hoffa was in prison. The mob was on the defensive and in the docket. And while Castro remained in power, Bobby had lost his zeal for that fight.

There remained the struggle for civil rights. By November 22, 1963, John Kennedy's bill had narrowly escaped the Judiciary Committee and neared introduction to the full House. Bobby was optimistic. But as he and his brother looked toward the Senate they wondered aloud, "Where are we going to get the votes?"

They had not answered the question by the time of the assassination. But to Bobby it was now even more relevant than before: the bill carried great weight as a matter of policy and morality and as a symbol. It was the capstone of the Kennedy presidency. "I felt not only did I want to get a civil rights bill by," Bobby said later, "but I wanted to get it by for personal reasons, you know, because I thought that it was so important for President Kennedy." There were other reasons. The civil rights bill was the culmination of Robert Kennedy's efforts as attorney general. The watershed crises of the past three years had been his to manage; and in the process he had learned a great deal about being black in the United States of America.

There had been no civil rights platform in the Kennedy campaign of 1960. "Those running for office in the Democratic party looked to just three or four people who would then deliver the Negro vote," Bobby explained. "And you never had to say you were going to do anything." For civil rights activists, then, RFK's appointment as attorney general must have seemed doubly unfortunate. "I did not lie awake at night worrying about the problems of Negroes," Bobby conceded. "I never even thought or suggested or even had a very serious conversation—or any conversation that I can remember about sending civil rights legislation up." His main objective was to contain the civil rights struggle—not to encourage civil disobedience and thereby antagonize Southern Democrats. Bobby reserved his greatest contempt not for segregationists but for liberals who were "not dealing with facts but . . . from emotion" and who failed to look out for "the best interests of President Kennedy." Under Bobby's active stewardship the Justice Department filed a series of voting rights suits in the South, but this was largely an effort to keep the matter in the courts and out of the news.

In the summer of 1961, when voter registration efforts sparked violence in Southern rural districts, Bobby's instinct was to obfuscate. He blocked an inquiry by the Civil Rights Commission (a creation of LBJ's Civil Rights Act of 1957) into white violence, arguing that hearings would create "an emotional demand" for federal action. Mostly he was infuriated at the commission's intrusion into his domain. Staff director Berl Bernhard "had never seen anyone so angry at the commission as Robert Kennedy—not even [Alabama governors] John Patterson or George Wallace." As Southern whites continued to brutalize civil rights workers, the attorney general retreated behind the shield of states' rights, the last refuge of segregationists. RFK was a federalist, not a racist, but to bloodied and terrified activists the difference was one of degree.

Soon Bobby was involved in the struggle "up to his eyeballs," as Ken O'Donnell put it. Beginning in the spring of 1961, a series of civil rights crises jolted the administration out of its indifference. The Kennedys spent the rest of their one thousand days reacting to events rather than leading them, siding mostly with the movement but resenting activists who were stirring up trouble. In May, when the Freedom Riders encountered savage Southern mobs armed with clubs, knives, bricks, iron pipes, and firebombs, Bobby Kennedy resisted the commitment of federal troops. In the politically powerful South, intervention was akin to occupation; and with the president due to meet Khrushchev in Vienna, Bobby dared not exacerbate an embarrassing spectacle.

Instead, he improvised. When local officials proved unwilling to guarantee the Freedom Riders safe passage, Kennedy deployed five hundred U.S. marshals. He withdrew them as the caravan reached Mississippi, allowing the Riders to be arrested and imprisoned rather than beaten up. As the disturbances continued, Kennedy harrumphed that the activists had "made their point." Meanwhile. he asked the Interstate Commerce Commission to draft regulations prohibiting discrimination in interstate travel.

Several years later, Kennedy defended his "selling out" of the Freedom Riders on familiar grounds of federalism. "You can say that it would be much better if we could send people—large numbers, perhaps, down to Mississippi and been able to protect that group down there," he told Anthony Lewis. "But I think it comes back to haunt you at a later time. I think that matters should be decided over a long range of history, not . . . under the stress of a particular crisis." As he continued, though, Bobby displayed a disturbing callousness: "Mississippi is going to work itself out, and Alabama is," he stated blithely. "Now, maybe it's going to take a decade and maybe a lot of people are going to be killed in the meantime. And that's unfortunate. But in the long run I think it's for the health of the country and the stability of the system. It's the best way to proceed."

In practice, Kennedy was less reluctant to call in the troops the next time violence erupted—at Ole Miss in autumn 1962. The following spring, in Birmingham, Police Commissioner Bull Connor's attack dogs and firehoses dealt another shock to Robert Kennedy's consciousness on civil rights. So did a long breakfast meeting with writer James Baldwin and thirteen other black artists and activists on May 24, 1963. (Later, John Seigenthaler called it Kennedy's worst day of the year before November 22.) From the moment the group filed into RFK's Manhattan apartment, the attorney general found himself under attack. Putting up a feeble but angry defense, offering percentages and legislative proposals, Bobby finally surrendered, red-faced, to a three-hour harangue on black survival in a racist society.

The intensity of the outburst—what an observer called "one of the most violent, emotional verbal assaults . . . that I had ever witnessed before or since"—shattered Kennedy. He resented it, did not understand it, and took it personally. But it was his first real exposure to the depths of black frustration and rage. He grappled with it and seemed to absorb the lesson. In time he reestablished ties to most of his antagonists and pushed harder than almost anyone in the administration for a civil rights bill. RFK, along with Ted Sorensen, was the chief architect and steward of John Kennedy's legislation of 1963. Bobby now had something to prove—to himself if not to Baldwin and company—though his moral zeal remained tempered by pragmatism. For the "selfish" liberals who clamored for more, finding nobility in losing, Bobby had nothing but disdain. They were "sons of bitches . . . in love with death."

Like Bobby, Lyndon Johnson had "personal reasons" for pushing the civil rights bill. "I knew," he said later, "that if I didn't get out in front on this issue, they [the liberals] would get me. They'd throw up my background against me, they'd use it to prove that I was incapable of bringing unity to the land I loved so much. . . . I couldn't let that happen. I had to pro- duce a civil rights bill that was even stronger than the one they'd have gotten if Kennedy had lived. Without this, I'd be dead before I could even begin."

Johnson's background on civil rights was inconsistent. Growing up on the banks of the Pedernales he had not seen many blacks—but he had seen many Mexican immigrants and much poverty. His brief teaching career drew him closer to the disenfranchised. "I never had any bigotry in me," he explained later. "My daddy wouldn't let me. He was a strong anti-Klansman. . . . The Klan controlled the state when I was a boy. They threatened to kill him several times." In the mid-1930s, when Johnson directed the National Youth Administration in Texas, black leaders did not know him at first. Then, said a Negro leader of the time, "we began to get word up here that there was one NYA director who wasn't like the others. He was looking after Negroes and poor folks and most NYA people weren't doing that." Nor were most NYA people secretly divert- ing funds from other programs to create projects for black youths. On trips to Houston, Johnson stayed overnight in the Negro dorms, ate with young blacks, asked how they were doing. When Johnson announced for Congress, they backed him enthusiastically.

As senator, Johnson had a wider and more conservative constituency. "I'm not prejudiced nor ever was, but I will say that civil rights was not one of my priorities in those days. I had other concerns," he said later. So did most senators: civil rights was hardly a national issue in the late 1940s and early 1950s. There were occasional battles (over the poll tax or antilynching laws) but no fundamental debates. Never a segregationist, Johnson was one of only three Southern senators to shun the Manifesto of 1954. But he did not "rediscover" civil rights until he began striving for national stature in the late 1950s. Johnson's rhetoric as vice president was strong on the issue, even radical, but that and the quiet accomplish- ments of his CEEO were hardly enough to quash old stereotypes.

Johnson, then, seemed an unlikely shepherd for the most sweeping civil rights reform since the Emancipation Proclamation. He clearly had something to prove. "No compromises on civil rights," Johnson assured Dick Goodwin in early 1964, and he told Congress and the public the same thing: "no deals." Goodwin betrayed no hint of skepticism, but others—civil rights leaders, administration officials—remembered Johnson's bargained bill of 1957 and worried this one, too, would be diluted to appease Republicans and Southern Democrats.

This time Johnson was resolute. "I'm not going to bend an inch, this year or next," he told Goodwin. "Those civil rightsers are going to have to wear sneakers to keep up with me. . . . Those Harvards think that a politician from Texas doesn't care about Negroes. In the Senate I did the best I could. But I had to be careful. I couldn't get too far ahead of my voters. Now I represent the whole country, and I have the power. I always vowed that if I ever had the power I'd make sure every Negro had the same chance as every white man. Now I have it. And I'm going to use it."

Johnson's public posture was one of humble but steely determination. Yet his voice bespoke defensiveness. The liberals, the "Harvards," all the Johnson-haters, were primed to attack at the slightest betrayal of the Kennedy legacy. And to go forward without Bobby Kennedy was the quickest route to invite suspicion. Swallowing months of bitterness, Johnson reached out to his attorney general. In January he told Bobby, "I'll do on the bill just what you think is best to do on the bill. . . . We won't do anything that you don't want to do." On the Hill, the president cautioned Senators Mansfield and Humphrey: make no move without Bobby's approval. "Make damned sure the attorney general agrees to the procedures they follow," Johnson told Larry O'Brien. If the civil rights bill was to succeed, Johnson and Kennedy would have to work in concert. There was no avoiding it.

Johnson's sudden embrace left Bobby uneasy. He suspected that Johnson—like so many others—feared Southerners would filibuster the bill to death or dilution. And "if we were not going to obtain the passage of the bill," Kennedy reflected later that year, "[Johnson] didn't want to be the reason, to have the sole responsibility. If I worked out the strategy, if he did what the Department of Justice recommended, suggested—and particularly me—then . . . he could always say that he did what we suggested and didn't go off on his own."

For Johnson to forfeit control was, in Kennedy's view, a dangerous ploy. "[Johnson] had a particular problem, being a Southerner," Bobby said, echoing Johnson's own concern. "If we decided that he should follow a particular line of strategy and then it didn't work, it could be very, very damaging to him." But the high cost of failure demanded cooperation, and even LBJ could not have feared Robert Kennedy would sabotage the civil rights battle waged in his brother's name.

An uncomfortable union was forged. "For political reasons it made a great deal of sense," Kennedy admitted. And there was another, more personal element: "Our relationship was so sensitive at the time that I think that he probably did it to pacify me. It was the best way to proceed." In Johnson's view it was the only way to proceed. The president's exact motives remain unclear, but a manipulator of men as adept as LBJ surely spotted the opportunity to co-opt—in one sweeping, generous embrace—Kennedy, Kennedy's partisans, and the Department of Justice in support of the civil rights bill. To do otherwise was to invite sniping now and recriminations later.

Having strengthened and broadened the original Kennedy bill, Johnson released his own civil rights legislation to the House on January 31. It passed shortly with little opposition. As House members voted on February 10, the president and attorney general kept in touch by telephone. That evening Johnson offered praise for a job well done. "Congratulations," he said with rare warmth.

"Yeah, it was very nice, wasn't it?" Bobby replied.

"I thought it was wonderful—290 to 130, you can't do better than that."

"I would think that would put a lot of pressure on them in the Senate, wouldn't you?" Bobby asked.

"Yeah," Johnson agreed, savoring the victory for only a moment before looking ahead. "Now, you get together with Larry and Mike Mansfield in the morning and work out procedure," he instructed. A few hours earlier Johnson had reminded Kennedy of the need to work together: "We're going up against a more difficult task. I've never been able to see my way through it and I want to do everything I possibly can, but I don't want anybody to think there's any disagreement among us or that there is any sabotaging taking place. . . . You touch whatever bases your wisdom indicates and then get back to me with your ideas."

Johnson referred to disagreement among Democratic leaders, not just that between Kennedy and himself. He was right, in any case, that the real fight awaited in the Senate, where arcane rules of conduct allowed for unlimited debate—the filibuster, with which Southerners had turned back hundreds of past attempts to end debate (to "invoke cloture") and vote on civil rights bills. It was the filibuster that drove Majority Leader Johnson to barter away the heart of his civil rights bill in 1957. "No compromise" likely meant no bill.

For all his uncompromising talk, though, Johnson was unsure he had the sixty-seven votes—two-thirds of the chamber—to invoke cloture and free the bill to pass by simple majority. In meetings with the attorney general and the White House staff throughout February and March, Senators Mansfield and Humphrey were discouraged. They had dodged the delay tactics of Senator Richard Russell and driven the issue to the floor, but the segregationists, hunched in a familiar defensive crouch, began the endless drone of the filibuster. Could it possibly be broken? Mansfield and Humphrey pressed for a cloture vote in March or April. "They'd lose it substantially," explained Kennedy's assistant Burke Marshall, "and then they'd give away the employment title and try again." And if they lost a second time, at least they could go to the voters in November having given it their best. Then, scoffed Bobby, the administration would shrug its shoulders and say, "We've done everything that people can do."

The equal employment provision was both the heart and the soft underbelly of the civil rights bill. Even optimists thought Johnson might be overreaching here. Why not trade it away in hopes of salvaging another controversial clause, the one guaranteeing equal access to public accommodations? This compromise, to Bobby Kennedy, smacked of Adlai Stevenson and his inability—or unwillingness—to prevail. Kennedy urged Mansfield to wait. The votes would come. "We just made such a fuss about it," Bobby said later, that Johnson had to stand his ground on equal employment. "I had some conversations with him," Bobby remembered, but Johnson was not an active participant in the discussions, leaving Bobby to wonder about the president's commitment. Kennedy seemed to believe that LBJ, by delegating strategy to the Justice Department (as well as Mansfield and Humphrey), had divested himself of the bill's leadership. Kennedy and his aides perceived the president as puzzled and discouraged. "[Johnson] didn't see *how* we'd get a bill" passed, Marshall said later, and Kennedy agreed, conceding that "it was damned difficult" to find the votes.

It *was* difficult, but Bobby was wrong to imagine that LBJ was overwhelmed by anxiety. If Johnson admitted to doubts—and he did, privately—his resolve had not weakened. The president had his own strategy and was vigorously pursuing it. He demoralized the weary Southerners by vowing to outlast them: with Humphrey's help, LBJ would suspend all Senate business until the filibuster was broken. And the president was every bit as aware as Bobby or anyone else where to get the votes for cloture: "I knew right away that without Republican support we'd have absolutely no chance of securing the two-thirds vote to defeat the filibuster," Johnson recalled. "And I knew there was but one man who could secure us that support, the Senator from Illinois, Everett Dirksen," the Republican leader.

"We all knew that," Bobby retorted several months later. But how to extract the votes from a reluctant Republican? Dirksen was inclined toward integration but loath to regulate the behavior of private industry; he regarded equal employment regulations as the first step on a treacherous slope toward hiring quotas. Acting on Johnson's instructions, Hubert Humphrey spoke passionately on the Senate floor against discrimination and quotas alike. Privately he agreed to accommodate some of Dirksen's more minor concerns. Frequent telephone calls from RFK kept the president up-to-date on Dirksen's shifting state of mind.

Johnson, meanwhile, bore down upon his old colleague with full force. Such breathless courting would surely have embarrassed a man of lesser ego than Everett Dirksen. From the White House issued forth a flood of photographs and personal notes for Dirksen, judgeships for his cronies and federal projects for his state. The president sought unlikely allies in his crusade for Dirksen's votes, prevailing upon civil rights leaders Roy Wilkins and Whitney Young to "get down here and start civil-righting. . . . I think you are all going to have to sit down and persuade Dirksen this is in the interest of the Republican Party and I think that he must know that if he helps you then you're going to go along and help him." Other Republicans, too, got their first taste of the Treatment since 1960: Johnson called them late at night and their wives during the day, flattering them all and appealing to patriotism, morality, and common sense.

On June 10, 1964, Dirksen relented and called for cloture. "No one knew why," contends Arthur Schlesinger, but in the White House, Johnson staffers were quick to credit the president. Robert Kennedy saw a different, and familiar, inspiration. "Everett Dirksen liked President Kennedy a great deal," Bobby said later, "and much, much, much more than he liked Lyndon Johnson. And I think that he made an effort—at least, part of his motivation, in the last analysis, was because of President Kennedy." And when the Senate passed the Civil Rights Act, the first unadulterated piece of civil rights protection in its history, RFK was thrilled but equally dismissive of Johnson's role. If President Kennedy had lived, Bobby insisted, the bill "wouldn't have been any different. I think that a lot of this legislation would have perhaps come later . . . a month later, maybe."

Others strongly disagreed. In the midst of the Johnson legislative whirlwind, the myth developed that LBJ had saved JFK's civil rights bill from slow but certain death. "We could have beaten Kennedy on civil rights," Richard Russell lamented to Orville Freeman, "but we can't [beat] Lyndon."

Robert Kennedy's blood boiled at comments like this. And he was right to protest: JFK had not been destined for defeat, and LBJ was not the first president to woo members of Congress. In late November 1963, after weeks of lobbying and only days before the assassination, President Kennedy persuaded House Minority Leader Charlie Halleck to support the bill. This was the crucial advance. The Senate remained an obstacle, but with Halleck's sanction the bill would sail smoothly through the House. And since the brutality of Birmingham and other Southern cities had imbued the issue with moral urgency, it was safe to assume that if John Kennedy had lived, months of struggle and compromise would have produced some sort of civil rights act.

Johnson's singular achievement was to pass a bill, as he pledged in January, without compromise. He refused to trade away the equal employment clause (which JFK might well have been forced to abandon), and it was more than Bobby's "fuss" that saved it. Whatever the recommendations of Humphrey and Mansfield, Johnson would cut no deals. As a Southerner, he could not afford to; lacking his predecessor's credibility as a civil rights president, LBJ knew he had to out-Kennedy Kennedy. The new climate of opinion permitted it: in a nation not yet numb to violence, the murder of JFK and racist riots in the South generated a wave of sympathy for civil rights reform and sapped the strength of its opponents. LBJ forcefully seized the moment, outgunning and outmaneuvering his fellow Southerners. As he struck a blow for civil rights he laid claim to its political sponsorship in the 1960s.

On July 2, Lyndon Johnson signed the 1964 Civil Rights Act in a White House ceremony. Victor and Roy Reuther, both labor leaders, saw Bobby Kennedy in the back of the room, staring at the floor. "Surely no one had contributed more to this moment than he," Victor later commented with sadness. Grabbing Kennedy's arm, Roy led him to Lyndon Johnson. "Mr. President," Roy said, "I know you have reserved a pen for your Attorney General." Johnson perfunctorily handed Bobby a series of pens. "Give this one to Burke Marshall. Give this one to John Doar," Johnson said, rattling off a list of Bobby's top civil rights aides and passing the pens back one by one. "You got any more, now?" he asked, and for good measure tucked another pen into Kennedy's hand. Bobby, mumbling inaudibly and wearing a weak, forced grin, nodded and faded backward into the crowd.

Reverend Walter Fauntroy—attending with Martin Luther King, Jr.—watched the encounter glumly: "Our enthusiasm—that of Dr. King and myself—was sort of dampened by the sadness that we saw in Bobby's eyes and the coldness with which the President obviously treated him. We commented afterwards at the coldness on the part of Johnson toward Kennedy on that important day." The moment was symbolic on many levels. Despite his private deference to Robert Kennedy and his public deference to the memory of John Kennedy, this was one victory Johnson was claiming as his own. Neither John nor Robert Kennedy had passed the Civil Rights Act; Lyndon Johnson had. By out-Kennedying the Kennedys, Johnson achieved a new measure of autonomy as president. And as LBJ moved closer to election in his own right he pulled farther away from his past and farther away from Bobby Kennedy.

"Give this one to John Doar," Johnson had said, and before Bobby Kennedy sent the pen to his assistant he framed it along with a photograph of the bill-signing ceremony. In the photograph Bobby sits in the front row of the audience and stares vacantly ahead. The inscription below the pen read, "Pen used to sign President Kennedy's civil rights bill."

Yet the thousand days had never seemed more distant. The civil rights bill had offered rare cause for cooperation between Bobby Kennedy and Lyndon Johnson, but the signing ceremony showed quite clearly that the moment had passed. There was no longer any disguising the fact: where the Justice Department had once been the most powerful arm of the White House, with Bobby's chambers an extension of the Oval Office, it was now a remote outpost virtually cut off from central command. And while Bobby clung to administrative autonomy, he was slowly being squeezed out of other concerns.

Poverty was one of those concerns. In the last days of November 1963, Robert Kennedy found a sheet of paper on which his brother had repeatedly scrawled and circled the word "poverty" during the final cabinet meeting of his life. Bobby framed the paper and hung it in his office at the Justice Department. Poverty was on both Kennedys' minds that fall; earlier in 1963 they had begun to consider an antipoverty program—not a war but an "offensive" of uncertain magnitude. At the time of the assassination, Walter Heller, chairman of the President's Council of Economic Advisers, was preparing a comprehensive picture of the poverty problem. By the time Heller placed the memo on President Johnson's desk the morning of November 23, the fight against poverty had attained the solemnity of a dead man's last wish.

Lyndon Johnson immediately saw its importance—both symbolic and material. "Push ahead full-tilt," Johnson told Heller that evening without a moment's reflection. "That's my kind of program. It will help people." On January 8, 1964, in his first State of the Union Address, Johnson declared "unconditional war on poverty in America." It was a characteristically bold claim—especially bold at a time when 83 percent of Americans believed poverty would never be eradicated. It was bolder still given that Johnson's kind of program was not really a program at all, yet—it was only a loose collection of ideas, and most of them belonged to Bobby Kennedy.

In 1961, at Robert Kennedy's first press conference as attorney general, he spoke of an "alarming increase" in juvenile delinquency. Juvenile delinquents intrigued Kennedy; he identified with outsiders, "young toughs," underdogs. Bobby once said that if he had not been born a Kennedy he would have become "perhaps a juvenile delinquent or a revolutionary." The issue of juvenile delinquency was something of a vogue among social scientists in the early 1960s, though on its face delinquency was a law enforcement issue. In May 1961, John Kennedy installed his attorney general as chairman of the President's Committee on Juvenile Delinquency (PCJD); Bobby appointed a lifelong friend, David Hackett, as director. The square-jawed Hackett was a former Olympic hockey player and, though not exactly the administration's best or brightest, possessed a shrewd intelligence. He knew nothing, however, about juvenile delinquency.

Neither did Bobby Kennedy. The committee was his education and his gateway to the ghetto. After visits to Harlem and other troubled areas, Kennedy and Hackett very quickly learned to equate delinquency with poverty and poverty with racial discrimination. "Bobby best understood things by feeling and touching them," said Richard Boone, Hackett's deputy. Bobby was not a social scientist; this was an emotional, visceral connection, and it broadened his horizons considerably. In later years it was common to say that John Kennedy's assassination opened Bobby's eyes to the world's pain, but Bobby had seen it years earlier, in these first, tentative trips to the ghetto.

Here at the new frontier of urban policy the chairman and his committee were in harmony: PCJD staff members were not timid bureaucrats but lively, self-styled "guerrillas." Bobby matched their social science credentials with his zeal. Together they developed contrarian, almost radical, views. Two, as it turned out, were crucial: first, that insufficient opportunity was the root cause of poverty; and second, that the problem required "community action"—a vague notion but clearly something other than bureaucratic, top-down, federal largess. "We felt that you could spend $30 million in one city and not have any impact whatsoever," Hackett explained later. The committee held that government must not impose solutions but empower the poor to develop their own. The PCJD financed and coordinated a dozen local initiatives on an experimental basis in cities like Cleveland, New Haven, and New York. The programs provided comprehensive services (education, employment, and job training) that encouraged self-sufficiency.

When Johnson assumed the presidency, most of the PCJD projects were barely a year old; it was too early to assess their effectiveness. Johnson, in any case, was not waiting for the reviews. He was calling out the big guns in his fight against poverty—and wanted something grand, something worthy of the New Deal, not tiny or tentative like community action. "He had this sort of *concrete* idea," recalled Walter Heller. "Bulldozers. Tractors. People operating heavy machinery." When Heller visited the LBJ Ranch over Christmas 1963 to sell Johnson on community action, Johnson told him to forget it. Community action was social work, not government policy; it did not educate children or put people to work. The limited demonstration programs Heller (and the PCJD) proposed were certain to incite local political opposition by bypassing city machines, and any program that failed to pump federal dollars into congressional districts was a loser on Capitol Hill. Community action was soft policy and bad politics.

Perhaps worst of all, community action was Bobby Kennedy's idea. "Few things that Robert Kennedy had touched were not . . . viewed with suspicion, fear, and distaste by the staff of the Johnson White House, and . . . most of all by the President himself," recalled Pat Moynihan, who as assistant labor secretary helped craft the antipoverty program.

Johnson's suspicion, fear, and distaste for Kennedy were strong, but his instinct for self-preservation was stronger. Johnson had pledged to "continue"—to fight the Kennedys' battles. This implied that Johnson would fight them on the Kennedys' terms. Community action was Bobby's pet project. "If [Johnson had] said no to it," grumbled presidential aide Horace Busby, "people would've said, 'Oh, he's not really sincere, he's just a Southern racist.' " Some people would say that in any event, but Johnson saw no political sense in flouting the Kennedy legacy. And who was LBJ to doubt the Kennedy economists? "Harvards" and intellectuals awed Johnson as much as ever, and now his accidental presidency left him doubly insecure. "The forces of learning and light said it's the way to go," Busby bitterly recalled. "If *they* thought it up, that was it." Heller returned the next day to Johnson's ranch house and convinced the president to change his mind.

But under Johnson, community action began to take a very different shape from what Kennedy, Heller, or Hackett intended. "What we said," Hackett recalled, "was, 'Go stage by stage, don't rush into legislation.' But Johnson just said 'Go.' " And so they went, all the president's men, from the Council of Economic Advisers to the Budget Bureau, from the Department of Labor to Health, Education, and Welfare—rushing into a mad scramble for control of the poverty bill. Kennedy's influence was cut short by the assassination, but he weighed in with a memo to LBJ. The problem, Kennedy explained on January 16, was that "most federal programs are directed at only a single aspect of the problem. They are sometimes competitive and frequently aimed at only a temporary solution or provide for only a minimum level of subsistence. These programs are always planned for the poor—not *with* the poor." Kennedy's solution was a new cabinet-level committee to coordinate comprehensive, local programs that "[involve] the cooperation of the poor." Kennedy listed six cities where local "coordinating mechanisms" were strong enough that pilot programs might be operational by fall. "In my judgment," he added prophetically, "the anti-poverty program could actually retard the solution of these problems, unless we use the basic approach outlined above."

If there was such a thing as a "classical" vision of community action, Kennedy's memo was its epitaph. On February 1, while Kennedy was in East Asia, Johnson appointed Sargent Shriver to head the war on poverty. It was an important signal that the president would be running the program his way, not Bobby's. It was also a canny personal slap at RFK—who, according to Ted Sorensen, had "seriously consider[ed] heading" the antipoverty effort. Viewed in this light, Johnson's choice of Shriver was particularly shrewd. Not only was Shriver hardworking and dynamic—a great salesman—but he was a Kennedy in-law, married to Bobby's sister Eunice. In Kennedy family photos Shriver stood barrel-chested and beaming, a member of the inner circle, every bit as vigorous, handsome, Catholic, and aristocratic as the rest. By placing Shriver at the helm of the war on poverty, Johnson demonstrated his fealty to the dead president.

But LBJ and Bobby both understood that Shriver was very much his own man. After the assassination Shriver signaled his independence from the Kennedys by slipping the new president a note card delineating "What Bobby Thinks." In 1964, Shriver's status as a quasi-Kennedy made him Bobby's rival for the vice presidency, but even before then their relationship was hardly fraternal. Within the Kennedy family Shriver was gently mocked. His liberalism on civil rights earned him the monikers "Boy Scout," "house Communist," and "too-liberal in-law." Bobby's unease was returned in kind. "Believe me," RFK's Senate aide Adam Walinsky observed, "Sarge was no close pal brother-in-law and he wasn't giving Robert Kennedy any extra breaks." If Shriver's loyalty was divided, it was split between Johnson and himself, not Johnson and Kennedy.

Shriver shared Johnson's skepticism toward community action. "It'll never fly," Shriver told an assistant early in the drafting process, and was reluctant to include the PCJD's small-scale demonstration projects in the poverty bill. Demonstration projects hardly constituted "unconditional war" on poverty; and by the time they bore fruit the patience of Congress and the public might well have expired. Some task force members wondered how much Shriver's fetish for quick results had to do with his contention for the vice presidency, but Shriver's concerns were valid. The PCJD wanted studies, diagnoses, analyses, and experiments. But

LBJ's poverty program had to show progress quickly—before its reau-
thorization, when Congress considered its second year of funding. "I'm
sure politically [Shriver] was right," conceded Kermit Gordon of the
Budget Bureau. "Having sold the program as a matter of the highest
urgency, it would have then been very difficult to say we needed a year
for planning."

Some participants credited Robert Kennedy with saving community
action by forcing it upon Sargent Shriver. "Bob won every argument,"
said David Hackett, but it is difficult to conceive when those arguments
took place. Virtually paralyzed by grief and indecision, Kennedy stayed
well clear of the happy tumult of Shriver's planning sessions. Bobby was
also loath to join in what was now obviously a Johnson enterprise, and
Shriver's leadership was one more reason not to get involved. Kennedy's
input was limited to the occasional phone call. When Shriver led a mission to Hickory Hill to solicit Bobby's opinion, the hollow-eyed attorney general asked his advisers only one question: was the bill what
President Kennedy had in mind? They assured him it was. "Fine," Bobby
said, and that was all. Though Bobby's support for community action was
already well established, Shriver vehemently denied his influence, insisting it was LBJ who demanded that community action be included in the
bill. "The only thing [Johnson] gave me was community action," Shriver argued later. Shriver's resistance faded as nearly every one of his
experts (with the strong exception of Pat Moynihan) gave community
action an unreserved endorsement. There was little agreement, though,
on the meaning of community action itself.

As the drafting process continued, Shriver seemed determined to
prove how far he had departed from RFK's conception. Kennedy's six-
city list of community action programs ballooned to fifty during Shriver's sessions—and to 250 during the program's first year in operation.
When an assistant drew up a $30 million budget for community action,
Shriver told him to add another zero. Meanwhile, the president conveyed his general approval while taking little interest in the particulars.
Johnson's impatience was clear—and helped propel Shriver's group
toward a hasty compromise between community action, job creation,
and a host of other programs designed to impress and entice the Congress. The PCJD's guerrillas, mostly marginalized by their association
with Bobby Kennedy, watched with unease as drafters took the fuzzy,
experimental notion of community action and transformed it into a
grotesque, gargantuan self-parody—an unworkable amalgam of Bobby
Kennedy's New Frontier progressivism and Lyndon Johnson's New Deal
grandiosity.

"Technically, the bill was a mishmash," recalled Tip O'Neill, who helped rush Johnson's Economic Opportunity Act through Congress before the fall elections. After intensive lobbying by Johnson and skillful salesmanship by Shriver, the bill passed by a surprisingly wide margin. On August 20, 1964, President Johnson signed the act creating an Office of Economic Opportunity (OEO), and he promptly installed Shriver as its director. Johnson had won the first important battle of his war on poverty. His debt to RFK went unacknowledged, though in the years ahead, when one community action agency after another erupted in spectacular public controversy, Johnson would credit Robert Kennedy with every failure.

"Johnson needs us," Bobby had assured Dick Goodwin, but by summer 1964 a grim realization was setting in. Perhaps Johnson did not need them. Perhaps Schlesinger had been right that "we are . . . a good deal weaker than we had supposed." Each contact with Johnson—at meetings on Indonesia and Cuba, and at the civil rights bill signing—brought the point home, dispelling Kennedy's illusions. The balance of power between Johnson and Kennedy had been completely inverted.

Sensing the diminution of his own role, Bobby attended fewer and fewer cabinet meetings, sitting in sullen silence when he did appear. He still could not bear to acknowledge the new president's authority. Johnson men treaded carefully around the attorney general, who was prone to flashes of pique. But LBJ's men aroused Bobby's sympathy and pity more often than his resentment. "I haven't had many personal dealings with them," Bobby said in 1964, but "they've all treated me very well." Valenti was a "nice fellow," and George Reedy was "fine." Bobby was especially fond of Bill Moyers, "a smart fellow and an honorable man" and the rarest of Johnson protégés—one who had shone in the Kennedy administration, as Sargent Shriver's brilliant deputy at the Peace Corps. These men were professionals, dedicated and generous men, loyal to Johnson but not disrespectful to Kennedy. They were as delicate in their treatment of Bobby and Ethel as they were in their relations with the Kennedy White House staff, and consequently they won the sympathy of RFK. "They're all scared, of course, of Lyndon," Bobby observed. "Lyndon talks about everybody, you see, *with* everybody. And of course that's dangerous. . . . He doesn't think anything of a lot of people. And he yells at his staff. He treats them just terribly. Very mean. He's a very mean, mean figure."

The problem, as Bobby perceived it, was Johnson's need for absolute submission. There was a "side of him in his relationship with human beings which makes it very difficult [to get along] unless you want to kiss his behind all the time." Robert McNamara, Bobby's closest friend in the cabinet, suggested that he do just that—"kiss his behind," essentially—for the sake of harmony. "I can't do that," Bobby concluded, "and so, therefore, I think it's probably difficult to get along."

McNamara, anyway, was getting along a little too comfortably for Bobby's liking. So were many others. The Johnson men were going to be loyal to LBJ; that was easy to accept. But it was the Kennedy men that really galled Bobby. "I thought that they felt: 'the king was dead, and long live the king,' " he complained in 1964. "I thought that an awful lot of things were going on that President Kennedy did that [Johnson] was getting the credit for," he went on, unwilling to recognize LBJ's plans as ambitious or progressive in their own right. Bobby blamed New Frontiersmen who forgot too quickly the source of their power and mission. "Some of the people who were closely involved with President Kennedy—like Bob McNamara and Mac Bundy—I didn't think stood up enough on some of these matters."

The A-11 plane, for example, was a project of Eisenhower's that "was really pushed [by] and was a favorite of the president [JFK]." But John Kennedy's name was never invoked. Bobby, upset, appealed to McNamara; and though the secretary promised to redress it he did not. Bundy even had the nerve to question JFK's interest in the plane. "That made me upset," said Kennedy. "I had heard the president discuss it so much. I'd known he was responsible for it." And in April 1964, when LBJ announced the destruction of fissionable nuclear materials, JFK was forgotten by all but his brother—a lone, bitter voice pointing out for the record that the plan "was all worked out in August 1963."

Complicit in this revisionism were veteran Washington insiders. "That's what makes me so bitter about people like Scotty Reston now," Bobby griped, referring to the *Times'* establishment columnist. "I just don't think they understand it anymore, in their buildup of Lyndon Johnson comparing him to the President. . . . They miss the whole point of what went on for three years and miss the whole feeling of the country."

Case after case of misplaced or forgotten loyalty was "important to what my relationship has been with [Johnson]." Even more important was Bobby's scathing view of Johnson as a leader and as a man. In Bobby's uncritical eulogies of the Kennedy administration, each virtue of JFK marked another Johnson vice. "Our president," Bobby said, pointedly articulating the prejudice of the Hickory Hill gang, "was a gentleman and a human being, and . . . this man is not. He's mean, bitter, vicious—an animal in many ways.

"I think his reaction on a lot of things is correct," Bobby continued, but expressed scornful disbelief at Johnson's management of the presidency. Bobby portrayed LBJ paradoxically as a remote, deferential weakling and a domineering, devouring bully. He marveled at Johnson's ability "to eat people up, even people who are considered strong figures," like Mac Bundy or Bob McNamara. "There's nothing left of them." But at the same time Bobby considered Johnson an ineffectual leader, easily cowed. Where "Jack was his own Secretary of State," Lyndon deferred to the rudderless Rusk; and "with the kind of president you have now, [State] can't function so well." Bobby was "shocked" that LBJ either missed ExComm meetings or showed up "for five minutes." As a result McNamara was now "more effective and stronger" than he had been under JFK "because there's not the balancing force that the President [JFK] was for [McNamara's] very, very strong personality." Since Johnson, in Bobby's view, lacked John Kennedy's foreign policy expertise, "[McNamara's] position carries."

McNamara the conqueror, McNamara the conquered: if these two notions were not contradictory, it was because Bobby saw Johnson's pernicious influence as circular. LBJ's overbearing manner first meant that McNamara "gets influenced by what President Johnson wants," and then McNamara, freed of constraints and eager to please, could convince Johnson of anything. McNamara thus "adapts himself to somebody who is not that effective," Kennedy concluded, intent on having it both ways, "and that can be dangerous."

So was following the polls. And that, declared Kennedy, was the major difference between "the President" and Lyndon Johnson. Both men "were affected by what was written in the newspaper . . . you wouldn't be a political figure if you weren't." But LBJ's tracking of public opinion was inhibiting; he was losing the big picture in his alertness to the day-to-day. "What the present President reads in the papers or what people are going to think is what is fundamentally important. . . . In the last couple of months," Bobby said that spring, "I've heard policy decisions discussed on the basis of what it would do to the vote. . . . And that, in any major matter, was never a factor with President Kennedy."

Relatedly, Johnson's grasping need for approval led him to stretch the tightly woven Democratic quilt to the point of tearing; Bobby did not like the direction the new president was taking the party. "Lyndon Johnson has explained quite clearly that it's not the Democratic party anymore, it's an all-American party, and the businessmen like it. All the people who were opposed to the President [JFK] like it. I don't like it much."

It was clear, in mid-1964, that Bobby did not like much of anything having to do with LBJ. He felt passionately that President Kennedy had left America a vastly better country. It had not been easy, overcoming eight years' worth of problems put off by Eisenhower, but Bobby wistfully extolled the Kennedy years as a thousand days of relentless, irresistible progress—from the balance of payments and economic growth to Berlin and Soviet-American relations. "It's just fantastic, the difference in the world," Bobby enthused. And now, watching from the sidelines as Johnson rushed past him, building on and besting the Kennedy legacy, it was perverse but really no wonder that Bobby felt the country "going flatter, going down."

"It was a curious attitude," judged Clark Clifford, "completely illogical, wholly emotional." Clifford, an intimate of both John Kennedy and Lyndon Johnson, had never held Bobby in particularly high esteem, but he was partly right. Bobby was acting illogically and emotionally, though it was obvious (even to Clifford) that the traumas of the assassination and the transition had left Bobby an uncharitable man.

Even Johnson's desire to temper the growing feud earned Bobby's scorn. O'Donnell and O'Brien described for Bobby the president's constant imploring. Why, Johnson moaned, does Bobby hate me? Why do the rest of the Kennedys like me when Bobby does not? He fretted again and again that perhaps he should invite Bobby to the White House for a drink and a heart-to-heart. Hearing this, Bobby scoffed that Johnson "always wants somebody to come with him and have a drink at night and swim, do something." But Bobby "didn't have any interest in becoming involved with him."

O'Donnell's heart was with RFK; he would soon take flight from the Johnson administration and join Kennedy's shadow cabinet. But for those like O'Brien, the "realists" who stayed with the president, Kennedy's vehemence was troublesome. "There [were] a number of people who were trapped in that situation," reflected Bobby's friend Milton Gwirtzman. "I think they made a mistake if they offered themselves as a bridge."

Gwirtzman, unlike O'Brien, was in no position to do so; he was not a White House staffer. But as Gwirtzman listened to Bobby's litany of complaints he saw the futility of the "broker's role":

> I don't think that Robert Kennedy at that time could appreciate the fact that other people could make the same claim of loyalty on subordinates that his family could. He felt that if McGeorge Bundy [had] worked for John Kennedy he had to continue to give his loyalty to the Kennedys. . . . He thought that anything Bundy did out of loyalty to Johnson, or at Johnson's orders, or even any suggestions Bundy made to Johnson to heal the wounds caused by the rejection, was a disloyal act to the Kennedys.

As the bruises of the transition faded, Bobby grew no more receptive to reconciliation; if anything, he hardened against it. Like Johnson during his vice presidency, Kennedy on the periphery of power felt increasingly like an alien, a victim, a forgotten man. "Bobby was absolutely convinced that Lyndon Johnson was out to destroy him in public life," said Charles Bartlett. "There was really no way to bridge it." And for every friend who tried to narrow the growing chasm, another widened it. Bobby's intimates—or, more accurately, his would-be intimates—did him the disservice of inciting him, filling him with spiteful rumors and tall tales about LBJ. Bobby was told that at cabinet meetings the president was continually complaining, "Why is the press always comparing me with John Kennedy? I had a lot more experience than he did"—a comment LBJ might well have uttered alone with Reedy or Jenkins but never in a room full of Kennedy appointees. Then there was the famous incident, almost certainly apocryphal, in which LBJ was alleged to have spotted a PT-Boat 109 tie clasp—JFK's trademark souvenir—on a Secret Service agent. LBJ was purported to have torn the clasp from his tie, thrown it in the trash, and reassigned the agent. Surely Johnson would not have spent months cultivating Kennedy aides to blow it all in one rash moment, but Bobby heard the story and believed it. And like any story that contrasted the old and the new, it enraged him.

Lyndon Johnson had the same sort of friends. They painted for him a grand, dynastic conspiracy by the Kennedy clan to recapture the Oval Office and they updated LBJ on all its alleged doings. "Some [were] within the government and some outside," recalled Bobby's press aide Ed Guthman. "Some meant well. Some were malicious, and some sought to curry favor from the President or Bob."

By the summer of 1964, rumor and reason were drawing both men to the same conclusion: that Robert Kennedy had no proper place in a Johnson administration and he would be leaving it shortly. Johnson naturally preferred to see Bobby vanish from the political map altogether, but that was unlikely. Bobby wanted to remain in public service. But where? Was there an office large enough to contain his capacities, his ambitions, and his brother's legacy? The question gnawed at Kennedy and Johnson both. It was unclear who was more troubled by the answer.

CHAPTER 7

The Bobby Problem

Robert Kennedy's only plan in early 1964 was not to make plans. That and to remain, somehow, in public life. Friends urged him to take some time out while he was still young (not yet forty in 1964): travel around the world, they told him; broaden and deepen your understanding, take the edge off your image. High office—*which* office was unclear—would await his return.

Pulling Bobby back, though, was a single-minded dedication to his brother's legacy—and fear and distrust of Lyndon Johnson. In December 1963, Rowland Evans joined Bobby in his big office at the Department of Justice. The attorney general ate lunch off a tray on a small table. "It's too early for me to even think about '64," he told Evans, "because I don't know whether I want to have any part of these people." Bobby cast a wary eye down Pennsylvania Avenue, toward the White House. "I don't want to tie my future to somebody who isn't going to really do his job."

Yet somebody had to mind the New Frontier. "What does [Johnson] know about people who've got no jobs, or are undereducated?" Bobby asked Dick Goodwin. "He's got no feeling for people who are hungry. It's up to us." For this reason, Bobby was almost pleased to see Kennedy appointees remain in senior posts in the Johnson administration. If the new president's commitment flagged, Kennedy men could pick up the slack or, at least, sound the alarm. Still, sharing his friends with "these people" pained him. In March, when Johnson asked Dick Goodwin to become his chief speechwriter, Goodwin turned to Bobby for approval. If a solid offer were to come (it did, the next day), Goodwin asked Bobby that night, should I take it? Bobby thought for a moment and said, "Well, from the selfish point of view—you can think selfishly once in a while—I wish you wouldn't. But I guess you have to. After all, if any one of us is in a position to keep him from blowing up Costa Rica or something like that," he continued, his choice of country somewhat arbitrary, "then we ought to do it. So I guess you should do it. If you do, you have to do the best job you can, and with complete loyalty. There's no other way."

Goodwin would never devote "complete loyalty" to LBJ, and Bobby knew it. Goodwin's allegiance to the Kennedys was beyond reproach. And whatever Bobby's "selfish" impulse, by encouraging LBJ's dependence on Kennedy men like Goodwin, Bobby gained a bit of leverage over the administration.

This was some kind of role, but not much, and it was precarious. How long before Kennedy men in a Johnson administration became Johnson men? Back in December, Arthur Schlesinger had warned that Johnson was already "picking off" Kennedy forces, and though Bobby downplayed that threat he had his own worries about Johnson absorbing, or devouring, Kennedy holdovers. Still, Bobby clung to the notion of collective action. "The important thing is to do something for the country," he told his friend William vanden Heuvel. "Collective action . . . that's the secret—but how to do it?"

"I haven't thought it through yet," Kennedy admitted that winter, but he was beginning to do so. On Monday, December 16, just two days after the Thomas Mann appointment, Schlesinger and Goodwin (Latin American specialists, both) sought out Bobby to commiserate. Clutching glasses of bourbon, the three men sat and talked listlessly about politics, plans for oral histories, and the creation of a Kennedy presidential library. Their mood was bleak as Bobby sketched out his vision of collective action: "There are hundreds of guys around here in positions of influence. We're important to Johnson," Goodwin recalled him saying. "I'm the most important because my name happens to be Kennedy. But we're all important, if we act together."

As Bobby reassured them he reassured himself, but barely. Goodwin watched, heartsick, as Bobby stood stiffly by his desk, fighting to suppress the grief that seized and contorted his features. "I've lost a brother. Other people lose wives," he said, and was silent for a moment. Bobby lurched between past and future. "I've lost a brother, but that's not what's important. What's important is what we were trying to do for this country. We got a good start; we had a committee working on poverty, a juvenile delinquency study. You can't do a lot in three years, but we'd gotten started. We could have done a lot in five or more years. There's a lot of people in this town. They didn't come here just to work for John Kennedy—an individual. But for ideas, things we wanted to do. I don't want people running off. . . . What's important is what we can get done."

It was a wistful, nostalgic notion. Only a month after the assassination, it was hard for Bobby (or Goodwin or Schlesinger) to imagine, but it was inevitable: these men, or most of them, would adjust to the presidency of Lyndon Baines Johnson, finding new outlets for old ideals, abilities, and ambitions. Absent the magnetic pull of John Kennedy, men of different ideals, motives, and personalities were bound to disperse, their collective power ebbing. Bobby, to these men, would remain in many real and important ways a surrogate Jack. But he was only partly their leader and certainly not their president. Johnson's liberal course ensured that many Kennedy men would eagerly follow.

Robert Kennedy could not build his own future on others' loyalty to the past. If collective action was to have any viability in LBJ's Washington, Bobby would have to find himself a prominent, independent niche. And as the months passed and blind grief succumbed to reason, Bobby began his search.

"Power is where power goes." With these words Lyndon Johnson had reconciled himself to the vice presidency in 1960, and now, in 1964, Robert Kennedy grasped at the same vain hope. His idea of serving as Johnson's vice president seems absurd in retrospect. To most observers it seemed absurd at the time. Even RFK had occasional moments of clarity: "It would be an unpleasant relationship, number one," he said that spring. "Number two, I would lose all ability to ever take any independent positions on matters." If Bobby became his vice president, "[Johnson is] not going to have to pay any attention to me whatsoever anymore." Bobby looked at the brewing crises in Southeast Asia and South Africa and imagined the psychic toll of silence. Then he imagined speaking out against the president: one critical speech and he would be forever muzzled. As for internal, clandestine opposition—"Boy," he reflected, "that's a pretty . . . disloyal operation."

Kennedy's common sense was fleeting, however. "I think it's possible to be vice president," he declared. There were echoes of LBJ in his self-assurance: yes, Bobby argued, I would only be vice president, but I would be Vice President *Kennedy*, and by definition more active and effective than my predecessors. Kennedy's independent national constituency would grant him powers unprecedented in the vice presidency. Though Bobby would never enjoy the autonomy he had had as his brother's attorney general, his responsibilities would surely remain interesting and wide-ranging. And Johnson's vice president was the obvious choice to become Johnson's successor.

Throughout this period, Kennedy's thinking was incoherent and often downright irrational. His flirtation with the vice presidency showed that he had yet to own up to the extent of his break with Johnson. Bobby knew that Johnson did not want him, but thought that Johnson might need him. He seemed to believe his ties to LBJ were no weaker than his brother's had been. And in a most ironic twist, Bobby took Johnson as his model. Having little understanding of how LBJ operated (or did not) under JFK, Bobby presumed that a Vice President Kennedy would function in the Johnson White House much as Vice President Johnson had functioned in the Kennedy White House.

However tortured his logic, Bobby's Johnsonian notions of "a different kind of vice presidency" were reinforced by many of those closest to him. If they could not put a Kennedy back in the Oval Office—yet— they could at least put one down the hall. Pressing for collective action, advisers implored Bobby to claim the vice presidency or at least to keep open the possibility—giving them, in the meantime, greater leverage over the emerging Johnson program. Ken O'Donnell, while refusing to believe that Johnson would ever concede the vice presidency, urged Bobby to contend for it anyway. "I'll stay in," Bobby replied, grudgingly. "I wouldn't take it if he gave it to me on a silver platter, but I'll stay in there if you feel [it's] that important and [labor leader] Walter Reuther and all those guys feel it's that important. Okay." O'Donnell considered Bobby's contention for the vice presidency almost a personal favor. The office itself did not, could not, enthrall Bobby; it was the feeling of obligation to his brother's—and now his own—men that compelled him. "He just felt the weight of all those people," recalled Burke Marshall, who was one of them.

"If there is some way I can avoid serving under Lyndon and maintain some political base and strength," he told Ed Guthman in April, "I think I'd do it." In search of a way out of the dilemma, Bobby called on Milton Gwirtzman to write a memo comparing two offices: governor of Massachusetts and senator from New York. Gwirtzman asked and set out to answer the following questions:

1. Which [office] would engage your abilities to the fullest?
2. Which would be the easiest to win?
3. Which would be a better place from which to carry on the responsibilities you have assumed as a result of the President's death?
4. Which will be a more comfortable place to be during a Johnson administration?
5. Which would be a better place from which to make a run for the Presidency in future years?

Massachusetts, Gwirtzman concluded, was Kennedy's in a walk. His brother Teddy was already senator. But the job of governor was loaded

with "frustrations." Massachusetts was hobbled by debt, an unruly legislature, and a weak statehouse. "The Governor of Massachusetts is as
restricted an executive as any Governor in the nation," Gwirtzman
wrote Bobby. But the office on Beacon Hill offered one important
advantage: isolation from Lyndon Johnson. As governor, Gwirtzman told
Bobby, "you could separate yourself from the operations of the Johnson
administration. If you are in Washington, even as a Senator, you will not
be able to get away from the problems of the Kennedy men in the
Johnson administration. Segments of the press will picture you continually peering over Lyndon's shoulder. Any criticism you make of the
administration will be magnified. . . . The press will always look for trouble here."

On that count, Massachusetts was a far safer base than the U.S. Senate.
But could the governorship contain a man of RFK's stature and ambition? "You are going to receive invitations to attend dedications and to
speak around the country and abroad and to undertake other activities
in connection with President Kennedy," Gwirtzman reminded him. "It
would seem easier to do this as a Senator based in Washington than as a
Governor based in Boston." As a Kennedy, a former cabinet member, and
the representative of an important state, Bobby would command instant
power in the U.S. Senate, quickly claiming prestigious committee assignments and exercising unusual influence on his more senior colleagues.

Of course, Washington was Lyndon Johnson's town. Conflict between
the two men was inevitable, prompted by clashing ambitions and ideals
and provoked by a leering press. And New York itself was no safe haven:
the state could not be expected to welcome "a newcomer" like
Kennedy; the carpetbagger issue was certain to nag his run for Senate. If
elected regardless (and Gwirtzman predicted he would be, by 53 percent
of the vote), Senator Kennedy would be freer of his constituency than
any governor could ever be, though within certain bounds. Gwirtzman
(an upstate New Yorker) cautioned that New York's articulate Negro,
Jewish, and labor communities, in addition to its liberal *Post,* conspired
"to force a Democratic Senator from New York to the left of the general position from which a presidential candidate is chosen."

These, then, were the issues to be weighed, and Gwirtzman did not
attempt to do so himself. He merely offered his own bias: that Bobby
run for the Senate from New York now and for governor of New York
in 1970. Ted Kennedy and Steve Smith agreed with the first half of
Gwirtzman's proposition. The presidency, presumably, would wait. In
1976, Bobby would only be fifty-one, younger than Lyndon Johnson
was when he inherited the Oval Office.

Bobby ruled out a run for Massachusetts governor rather quickly, but he was deeply ambivalent about the New York Senate race. It was sure to be a difficult one, and Bobby was not feeling particularly spirited about anything in the spring of 1964. He had never been a backslapping, handshaking political type, an LBJ; he held that sort in disregard. As his brother's political lieutenant, Bobby had escaped the unsavory public side of electioneering. He looked upon a campaign of his own with something akin to horror.

And was it worth it? Was the job of senator worth emerging from his shell of solitude and grief? In his dealings with Congress as attorney general, Bobby had often found it difficult to hold his temper. The Senate's incremental pace and the necessity of compromise infuriated him when he believed right was on his side. Why can't they do this quickly? Bobby railed at Larry O'Brien, his brother's congressional liaison.

But Bobby was running out of options. "If Lyndon Johnson hadn't been such an s.o.b. about everything," he told Ed Guthman in April, "things might have been different. Being his vice president could be a real dead end. He could put me in cold storage and I'd suffocate. But if I were elected to the Senate, I'd have some impact along with the other younger senators—Teddy [Kennedy], Birch Bayh and Joe Tydings and Pierre [Salinger], if they're elected. As a group, we could have some effect. He would have to listen to us."

And in the Senate Bobby could speak out. "If I was in the United States Senate, I would have raised a fuss about Panama," he said that spring, referring to the January riots in the Canal Zone that ruptured diplomatic relations between the U.S. and Panama. Kennedy's words, carefully measured, parroted by "the other younger senators" and reported prominently in the press, would have to influence LBJ: "I'd not just be a senator. I'd be the Senator from New York. And I'm the leader of the Kennedy wing of the Democratic party." Here, too, Bobby felt the weight of responsibility. "It's damned important," he said, "that the Kennedy wing . . . continue to be a very important force in the party."

Was there in fact a "Kennedy wing" of the party? Kennedy had no doubt, but he was hardly a disinterested observer. If there had ever been such a thing as Kennedy Democrats, their continued vitality depended in large part on the November election and Bobby's role in it. In early 1964, Robert Kennedy leaned toward the Senate but refused to foreclose on the vice presidency. For now he surveyed his options spiritlessly, remaining inscrutable, confused, and conflicted.

Despite his dejection, though, one could detect in RFK a touch of schadenfreude. For however difficult his own decision, Lyndon Johnson's was even more torturous. "I don't think that Bobby was so perfect that he didn't enjoy nettling Johnson a bit," judged Bobby's old friend

Charles Spalding. "The idea of Johnson and Bobby on the same ticket .
. . in those sick days was almost too much. You couldn't help but consider that with a certain . . . relish."

"The one thing Lyndon Johnson doesn't want is me as vice president," Bobby said matter-of-factly. Then, with evident delight: "I think
he's hysterical about how he's going to try to avoid having me or having to ask me. And that's what he spends most of his time on, from what
I understand: figuring out how he's going to avoid me."

Kennedy hardly overstated the situation. President Johnson was obsessed
with what aides dubbed, simply, "the Bobby problem." Ever since the
convention of 1960 Johnson had fussed over one Bobby problem or
another, but this one gripped him with a single-minded intensity. For six
long months, according to Ken O'Donnell, the president spent "90 percent of his time" on keeping Bobby off the 1964 Democratic ticket. An
exaggeration, surely, but even years later, Johnson could not forget the
chokehold of panic and self-pity. "Every day," LBJ reflected,

> as soon as I opened the papers or turned on the television, there was
> something about Bobby Kennedy; . . . about what a great Vice President
> he'd make. Somehow it just didn't seem fair. I'd given three years of loyal
> service to Jack Kennedy. During all that time I'd willingly stayed in the
> background; I knew that it was *his* Presidency, not mine. . . . And then
> Kennedy was killed and I became the custodian of his will. . . . But none
> of this seemed to register with Bobby Kennedy, who acted like *he* was the
> custodian of the Kennedy dream, some kind of rightful heir to the throne.
> It just didn't seem fair. I'd waited for my turn. Bobby should've waited for
> his. But he and the Kennedy people wanted it now.

The issue permeated the White House. There was no eluding it. Jack
Valenti remembered "the pulling and tugging of the Kennedy partisans,
the tiptoeing around the subject that was the staff ballet in the West
Wing, the grim unsettling political climate it was creating. . . . Something
was sure to give."

What gave was the president's poise. At the peak of his power, having
settled into the presidency and having mastered Congress for the second
time in his career, Johnson began to lose his sense of control. Could
Bobby force his way onto the ticket? Or did he merely want the right
of refusal? The questions had a familiar, discomforting ring.

Certainly, Johnson despised Bobby; no one imagined the two men
might work well, or even peaceably, together. But this was more than
personal enmity. It was a matter of political legitimacy: "I don't want to
go down in history as the guy to have the dog wagged by the tail and

have the Vice President elect me, because that's what they're going to write," LBJ told O'Donnell. "With Bobby on the ticket, I'd never know if I could be elected on my own." John Kennedy's murder put Johnson in the Oval Office; his legacy nourished Johnson through the difficult transition. To think now that Bobby Kennedy, the "little shitass" who had never run for anything, would carry Johnson into a full term as president—it was too much. It was public emasculation. It would render LBJ a virtual lame duck for the rest of his presidency. "I'll quit it first!" he barked at O'Donnell in the Oval Office. "I don't want it that much!"

But he did want it that much, or more. Later, in a more reflective mood, Johnson told O'Donnell, "Look, if I need Robert Kennedy I'll take him. I'll take anybody. I want to get elected. I'm a pragmatic fellow." Perhaps the president was merely keeping the peace by bowing to O'Donnell's master; Johnson knew that O'Donnell was a direct pipeline to RFK. But Johnson most likely meant what he said: he was a political realist. As *The Nation* quipped in February, "If the election hinged on it, Mr. Johnson would run with Beelzebub, and so would any Democrat, Republican, or Prohibitionist."

Mr. Johnson would determine whether the election did hinge on it before signing on his personal demon. With the Republicans likely to nominate Senator Barry Goldwater, a right-wing Arizonan, as Johnson's opponent, the president was free (in O'Donnell's estimation) to "nominate Mickey Mouse if he wanted to." The president would wait for the summer and the polls.

While LBJ and RFK played their respective waiting games, a band of Kennedy supporters forced their hands.

The trouble started with Paul Corbin. Corbin was Bobby Kennedy's watchdog on the Democratic National Committee, and a deeply, widely unpopular man—even among John Kennedy's aides, who loudly protested Corbin's appointment to the DNC. Corbin was abrasive and intemperate. He was a constant liability and frequent embarrassment to RFK. He was "the Rasputin of our administration," sputtered Ken O'Donnell. "The dark side of Bobby Kennedy," declared Joe Dolan. "An ass," denounced Rowland Evans. But one did not say these things around Bobby Kennedy. "You ought to drop Paul Corbin," Evans once warned him. "He's really hurting you."

"Listen, Rowlie, when I want your advice I'll ask for it," Bobby snapped back. Though occasionally irritated by Corbin's scrapes, Bobby valued him as a dogged, no-nonsense political infighter, a man much like himself. "If you have a job and you want to get it done, and you don't care *how* it's done, send Paul Corbin out to do it," explained Helen

Keyes, a campaign aide to JFK, "but understand you can never send him back to the same district." In 1960, Corbin came through for Jack during the crucial Wisconsin primary and Bobby did not forget it. Ensconced at the DNC, Corbin revealed his plan to "stay in Washington for 16 years, eight years with Jack and eight years with Bobby. And if Jack doesn't do better, we'll run Bobby in '64."

Corbin was surely listening when the drumbeat for Bobby began in January. By sending his attorney general to Indonesia, Johnson returned RFK to visibility and unwittingly sparked a "small Vice Presidential boomlet," according to the *New York Times*. Excitement centered in the Northeast, the region where Johnson might need Kennedy most. Here, *U.S. News & World Report* declared, "the buildup begins for Robert Kennedy." On March 10, New Hampshire would hold the first Democratic primary; an impressive showing by RFK might portend a Kennedy renewal.

While Bobby was in Indonesia, Joseph R. Myers, the Democratic city chairman of Manchester, New Hampshire, decided to wage a massive write-in campaign on his behalf. ("We didn't do this to embarrass Johnson," Myers protested in March. "The Kennedy name is just magic up here.") Naturally, Myers called Corbin, who struck Charles Bartlett as uncharacteristically loath "to stage a big Kennedy show up there," especially without Bobby's sanction. But it was not difficult to convince Corbin that the campaign was in Kennedy's interest, and he quickly launched a vigorous effort in New Hampshire. Corbin's contacts in the state were minimal, but his very presence struck some as impertinent at best. By beginning every sentence with "Bobby says . . ." Corbin's message to potential supporters was plain: ignore me at your peril.

Corbin's ham-fisted tactics incensed John W. King, the state's Democratic governor, but King promptly bowed to the strength of the Kennedy forces. As King caved, the state's national committeeman, Hugh Bownes of Laconia, placed an agitated call to the White House. He reminded the president's men that Johnson, too, was a write-in candidate (facing no opposition, LBJ had not filed for the New Hampshire ballot) and might receive fewer votes for president than RFK for vice president. Bownes's warning echoed portentously through the West Wing. This was it, aides muttered, the Bobby problem had come to a head; Bobby was making his move.

Cliff Carter, Johnson's key man at the DNC, ordered Bownes to stop the Bobby-for-veep movement dead in its tracks. But one cannot order a state chairman to do anything, especially something contrary to the wishes of his rank and file. In any case it was never clear where Bownes stood on the issue. Bownes seemed less distressed by the prospect of a

Johnson-Kennedy ticket than by outsiders like Corbin usurping authority in Bownes's own state.

Kennedy, too, was losing control. But events were already pushing him
to assert himself—to throw his hat in or bow out. At the very least he
had to comment on Corbin's rogue effort. With little to gain by embarrassing the president, Bobby sent word to the White House that he
would disown the New Hampshire movement. Yet Johnson demurred;
the president was terribly afraid of being blamed for pushing Kennedy
out of the ring. Nor was Bobby ready to forfeit his growing political
momentum. The result was a tepid disclaimer. His spokesman Ed
Guthman explained that

> the Attorney General has said that the choice of the Democratic nomi-
> nee for Vice President will be made and it should be made by the
> Democratic Convention in August, guided by the wishes of President
> Johnson, and that President Johnson should be free to select his own run-
> ning mate. The Attorney General therefore wishes to discourage any
> efforts in his behalf in New Hampshire or elsewhere.

A statement like this, of course, was unlikely to deflate the expanding
Kennedy balloon. Nor was it probably intended to: then and thereafter,
Bobby issued his disclaimers in the evenings, after the important morn-
ing papers had shut down. Bobby pointedly refrained from asking
Corbin to "cease and desist," his usual order to wayward lieutenants.

Johnson knew well enough to mistrust even the most unequivocal
political disavowal—he had issued many himself—and Bobby's was
hardly unequivocal. Fearing a primary-day debacle, Johnson dispatched
his political foot soldiers to New Hampshire to convert a Kennedy
write-in movement into a Johnson-Kennedy write-in movement. It
risked creating an alliance that Johnson could not break come the July
convention but for the time being it averted embarrassment.

Still, a joint effort, or the appearance thereof, was impossible with Paul
Corbin antagonizing Johnson supporters in New Hampshire and in
Washington. President Johnson was determined: Bobby's boy Corbin
had to go. "We either make him desist or get rid of him," Johnson
ordered Cliff Carter. But rather than risk an untimely confrontation
with RFK, the president again leaned on intermediaries. Johnson told
Ken O'Donnell that Corbin was effectively fired—but that Bobby
Kennedy would have to do the firing. O'Donnell carried this presidential edict to Kennedy, who had a short reply: "Tell him to go to hell."

As much as he might have liked to, O'Donnell was not going to stand
in the Oval Office and tell the president of the United States to go to
hell. Tell him yourself, O'Donnell said to Bobby. But when LBJ called

Bobby into the Oval Office after a cabinet meeting in early February, Bobby let the opportunity pass. Their brief and brutal exchange lasted no more than five minutes. "It was a bitter, mean conversation," Kennedy later recalled. "It was the meanest tone I'd ever heard. . . . The substance wasn't that drastic, but the tone was so . . ." Kennedy did not finish the thought, but later, piecing the conversation together, Charles Bartlett did it for him: "so . . . *savage.*"

Johnson's message was simple: he wanted Corbin out of New Hampshire and off the national committee. "He was loyal to President Kennedy; he'll be loyal to you," Johnson barked. "Get him out of there. Do you understand? I want you to get rid of him."

"I don't want to have this kind of conversation with you," Bobby replied. He wasn't sure Corbin actually *was* in New Hampshire, though he didn't doubt it. He suggested gamely that Johnson find out himself, betraying a trace of amusement at Johnson's rage. Paul's not my responsibility, Bobby said. "He was appointed by President Kennedy, who thought he was good."

This was stretching the truth, but to Johnson it was beside the point. "Do it," he demanded. "President Kennedy isn't president anymore. I am."

In its naked bitterness, Johnson's comment was shocking. Never had he been so openly brutal to Robert Kennedy, who struggled to maintain his dignity: "I know you're president," he said flatly, "and don't you ever talk to me like that again." He stormed out of the White House in a cold rage.

Johnson was momentarily unnerved. He did not wish to cross RFK until absolutely certain that Corbin was guilty as charged. Like an attorney he began to amass evidence against the accused. "How much does Corbin make?" he asked Cliff Carter. "What's he supposed to do?" Who were his allies and enemies? "Is Dick [Maguire of the DNC] against him? Is Ken [O'Donnell] against him?" Johnson ordered National Committee chairman John Bailey to "come over here tomorrow and bring this fellow Corbin's record with you. . . . Everything you have on him. . . . I want his travel records—and just see where he's been goin', what he's been doin'." But Johnson could not contain himself another day. That evening, February 11, he called Kennedy at the Justice Department to demand Corbin's resignation. Kennedy protested, repeatedly and vainly calling Corbin "harmless." The president replied that Corbin's relentless boosterism was "quite a problem." As a member of the DNC, Corbin should not be taking sides in a vice presidential contest that had to remain fair and competitive. That, after all, was why LBJ had sent Bobby to Indonesia: "to keep things equal" among the leading candidates. "I did you a favor sending you to the Far East," Johnson offered.

"A favor!" Bobby exploded. "Don't ever do me a favor again!" He slammed down the phone. Standing by the window, Bobby stared into the darkness, silent and still for four or five minutes. Then, suddenly shuffling papers into his briefcase, Bobby turned to Ed Guthman. "I'll tell you one thing," Bobby said. "This relationship can't last much longer."

Privately, Kennedy allowed that Corbin had been "very indiscreet about the fact that I should be vice president." But the clash with Johnson, he thought, had little to do with Paul Corbin or the New Hampshire ballot. It instead represented LBJ's "conscious effort to separate himself, to establish his own identity—and not to be involved with President Kennedy and therefore, to some extent, me."

Johnson, meanwhile, vented his anger at Kennedy surrogates. While O'Donnell and Maguire sat silently at the other end of the telephone line, Johnson launched into a relentless monologue (recorded by ever-whirring Dictabelts). Line by line he reconstructed recent conversations with Bobby. "He said . . . the president [JFK] liked the work [Corbin] did. I said, I know it, Bobby, but *I'm* president, and I *don't* like what he's doing. . . . We're not gonna have him goin' around operatin' independently and not a part of the team." Johnson felt genuinely betrayed. His generosity to Bobby and the Kennedy men had gotten him nowhere, he complained. "You said that we ought to tell Bailey to stay on, I said OK," he thundered at O'Donnell the next morning, this time at the Oval Office (and again recorded by speakerphone). "You said Bobby ought to go to Indonesia, I said OK. I'm not draggin' my feet on anything. Pierre Salinger has got more freedom and more knowledge—and you have, too—than you'd have if [John] Kennedy was here. And you've got more *power*, if you want to exercise it, because I give my people power and let 'em use it! And [Bobby] has [more power]—but I just don't want him to feel that Corbin [does, too]."

Johnson and Kennedy were both right: Corbin's firing carried greater portent. LBJ was less concerned by New Hampshire than by his own entanglement with Robert Kennedy and all he represented. The Corbin affair was also significant in a way that Bobby, at this point, only dimly perceived. The episode revealed Johnson's growing appetite for the sort of political intelligence served up by the FBI. It further showed that in his war with RFK, Johnson had a powerful ally: J. Edgar Hoover.

The Federal Bureau of Investigation showed an interest in the Corbin affair from its beginning. As early as January 1964, Johnson brought the FBI into his confidence on the matter, and the agency quickly made itself indispensable. "Walter Jenkins told me last night," wrote Cartha "Deke" DeLoach, the FBI's White House liaison, in a January 15 memo to Hoover, "that he was seriously concerned about the continued employment of Paul Corbin at Democratic National Committee Headquarters. He indicated that the President had also expressed some concern about Corbin. Jenkins told me," DeLoach continued, "that Corbin was strictly Bobby Kennedy's boy and that Kennedy had been protecting him all along. He further added, as a matter of strict confidence, that the President was not yet quite ready to take on Bobby, however, Corbin would definitely be eased out in the near future when the time was right."

As the events of March would show, this was no hollow threat. At Johnson's behest, the Bureau had in fact already done some digging on Corbin. What it found only further incited LBJ: FBI documents referred to Corbin suspiciously as "Paul Corbin also known as Paul Kobrinsky" and, more ominously, to his "former association with the Communist movement." Cliff Carter at the DNC bragged of access to "a file seven inches thick" on Corbin's "completely un-American activities background." As DeLoach reminded Hoover in a memo, in 1961 the House Un-American Activities Committee had aroused RFK's ire by threatening hearings to expose Corbin. Kennedy had accused the FBI of leaking confidential materials to the House committee; DeLoach assured Hoover the Bureau had not done so.

If not, it was more an oversight than a statement of principle. The head of the FBI had never liked Bobby or any of the Kennedys; moreover, he had never paid any mind to the attorneys general who came and went while he, in office since the 1920s, sat firmly lodged in his director's chair. But Robert Kennedy was different; he was an activist and the president's brother. He demanded attention. And unlike his predecessors, who honored Hoover with something greater than reverence (fear, to be sure), Bobby thought Hoover "rather a psycho" and "senile and rather frightening." Bobby entered office determined, with typical zealousness, to retire Hoover—certainly by 1965, when Hoover would reach the federal mandatory retirement age of seventy.

Until then, Bobby would simultaneously court the aging director, "mak[ing] a fuss over him," and agitate him by pushing for progress against organized crime ("He'd always denied that it existed," scoffed Bobby) and on civil rights ("the second area where the FBI hadn't done a hell of a lot. They'd jealously guarded their relationship with the police officers in the South and with the Southern congressmen and senators, and suddenly they were thrust into this struggle"). And with Bobby's brother in the White House, the attorney general knew that Hoover "couldn't complain about it and there wasn't any place to go."

Now, with Johnson in the Oval Office, Hoover once again had someplace to go. The two men had been friends—neighbors, even—since the 1940s, when they thundered happily around the suburbs of northwest Washington searching for Johnson's wayward dog, "Little Beagle Johnson." During Vice President Johnson's painful exile, Hoover was a rare source of comfort, and LBJ was open in his admiration. "J. Edgar Hoover has Jack Kennedy by the balls," the vice president chortled over cocktails with friendly reporters.

Within hours of the assassination, Hoover moved quickly to cultivate his connection to Johnson and, as Guthman recalled, "to really stick it in [Bobby], and hard." At first Hoover simply refused to have anything to do with RFK. He reported directly to LBJ, completely bypassing the attorney general and the Department of Justice. Courtney Evans, Hoover's White House liaison, had long been suspected of fraternization with the enemy. The long-term G-man had grown too close to Bobby and was removed from duty—all duty. Six months later his assignment book was still empty. At the White House, Evans's place was taken by Deke DeLoach, a Georgian and old friend of Johnson's. Hoover was back in good graces.

Taking nothing for granted, though, the FBI director worked intently to consolidate his position with LBJ and to edge Bobby farther toward the sidelines. On November 29, just four days after the presidential funeral, Hoover was already widening the breach, manipulating LBJ with insinuation and mortal terror. "We've gotten a lot of letters and phone calls over the last three or four, five days," Hoover told the president. "We got one about this parade the other day [the funeral procession] . . . that they were going to try to kill you then. And I talked with the attorney general about it. I was very much opposed to that marching."

"The Secret Service [said] not to," Johnson explained, "but the family felt otherwise."

"That's what Bobby told me, but when I heard of it, I talked with the Secret Service, and they were very much opposed to it. . . . It was even worse than down there in Dallas."

"Yes, yes," replied Johnson, duly concerned.

"You were walking down the center of the street."

"Yes, I think that's right."

"And if somebody on the sidewalk would dash out . . ." Hoover left the image to dangle in the new president's mind.

Johnson needed no one to spell it out for him. He believed that selfishly, Bobby had made him march, contrary to Johnson's own wishes and the advice of the FBI and the Secret Service. Johnson was lucky to be alive, lucky to have escaped a second funeral procession, one led (more gingerly, no doubt) by a President John McCormack.

Hoover's protectiveness earned Johnson's gushing gratitude. "You're more than the head of the Federal Bureau as far as I'm concerned," he told Hoover, "you're my brother and personal friend, and you have been for 25, 30 years." Johnson was laying it on thick; he well understood the power (and vanity) of the FBI director. But in his vulnerability the new president was desperate for an ally, and there was a touching earnestness to his remarks. Hoover, at least, was touched. "I certainly appreciate your confidence, I do," he replied. Later that day Hoover boasted to his colleagues that the new president "ha[s] more confidence in me than anybody in town." Not since the Roosevelt years had Hoover been so appreciated—or so useful. Overnight he discarded the loose-fitting shackles of the Kennedy years and resumed his role as chief political intelligence adviser to the president of the United States.

"Intelligence," as ever, was a misnomer. Under the guise of national security, the thinnest rumors made their way to Johnson's desk, and they often concerned Robert Kennedy. "Hoover used to send over all this material on me," said Bobby, "and Lyndon Johnson would read it to [Robert McNamara]," who, completing the loop of misinformation, would repeat it to RFK. In reports hand-delivered by DeLoach, Hoover alerted the president every few days to Bobby's "activities," "contacts," and so on. Hoover did not just repeat rumors, he created them. When McNamara had dinner at Nick Katzenbach's house to discuss their children's upcoming biking trip on Martha's Vineyard, it was reported to LBJ as a meeting, led by Bobby, of a secret cabal to overthrow the president. Ethel Kennedy was said to have complained of secret FBI wiretaps installed in her phone "so Lyndon Johnson can listen in."

"Now, Lyndon Johnson told me that he never received an adverse report from J. Edgar Hoover on me," said Bobby, incredulous. If so, and if Johnson believed this particular "whopper," it was only because Hoover's reports had less to do with Bobby than with Bobby's devotees. And in 1964, as Bobby-for-veep movements were springing up across the nation, Hoover easily stoked Johnson's suspicions, relaying every sinister rumor of a far-flung Kennedy conspiracy: Bobby's boys were out there somewhere, everywhere, plotting Johnson's downfall. "There was always somebody who was saying something and making some move on behalf of Bobby, and this would drift back," recalled Charles Bartlett. "So it was possible to depict the thing as sort of a coordinated conspiracy."

In this atmosphere it was easy for a small social event to explode into a raging, if closely kept, political scandal. On February 6, 1964, friends gathered in Washington to celebrate John R. Reilly's appointment to the

Federal Trade Commission. Reilly's nomination had been pending in the Senate in November 1963, and President Johnson, as a small gesture to the attorney general and Ken O'Donnell, had not withdrawn it. Reilly had served in Bobby's Justice Department, and his colleagues there were throwing him a small party. Miles Lord, the U.S. attorney in Minneapolis, was at the department on business and stopped by the gathering.

Late the next afternoon, a Friday, Lord was back in Minneapolis and sitting, agitated, in the office of Richard Held. Held was the FBI's special agent in charge (SAC) of the Minneapolis office. After a short exchange of pleasantries, Lord revealed that he had a matter of great concern to share with the FBI. He began to describe yesterday's encounter with "the Kennedy crowd." As Held dutifully reported to Hoover, Lord "stated that these individuals openly discussed how they were doing everything they could to stir up the 'Bobby Baker mess,' with the avowed purpose of trying to embarrass the President in every way possible." Lord recalled standing aghast as department officials gleefully described their second objective, which had once been to "freeze Mr. Johnson out as Vice President" but was now to lock Mr. Kennedy in as vice president–designate.

When Held pushed Lord for details—specific schemes, slanders, or identities—Lord backed off skittishly. He refused to name names, referring only to "that wide-eyed bunch around the Attorney General." These were "hard-nosed politicians," Lord said; they could cause him trouble. He was also loath to tie Bobby directly to the group's plans (whatever those were), but noted that its members were all close to Bobby and might very well be speaking for him, even repeating his views.

The SAC was unsure whether to make much of the story. Lord was a devoted Humphrey man, a close social and political confidant of the Minnesota senator, and owed Humphrey his job. Perhaps, Held suggested to Hoover, this had "slanted" Lord's remarks, since Humphrey was Bobby Kennedy's chief competitor for the vice presidency. Hoover was less circumspect. He passed the Held memo to a host of top lieutenants without even the most cursory investigation. Under Held's signature Hoover scribbled one comment: "I believe the President is alert to this."

If Johnson had not been alert to the gossip, he was now; Hoover saw to that. DeLoach handed a report to the president, who griped about it bitterly to Ken O'Donnell, Bobby's closest remaining friend in the White House. O'Donnell's protestations carried little weight with the president, whose worst fears about Bobby and "Bobby's Justice Department" had been confirmed.

When Ed Guthman confronted DeLoach about the rumors, DeLoach angrily dismissed his concerns as "petty jealousy and distorted gossip." Then he informed Hoover that

> there has been a bad leak either in the White House or FBI Headquarters. With your permission, I showed Jenkins, and he showed the President, the letter from the SAC in Minneapolis [Held]. . . . Jenkins told me that the President was shocked over this matter. [Guthman's] second allegation specifically concerns the two memoranda we furnished the President regarding Paul Corbin and Carmine Bellino, after which both men were fired. *These memoranda were specifically furnished at the direction of the President.* Jenkins told me later . . . that the Attorney General was extremely shaken by the dismissals of Corbin and Bellino. [Kennedy] obviously expected to use these men in the campaign for the Vice Presidency.

The next day, March 7, Jenkins told DeLoach that the president had identified the "bad leak": O'Donnell, to no one's surprise. Yet Jenkins professed that "both he [Jenkins] and the President were deeply hurt by this matter," as DeLoach informed Hoover. "Obviously O'Donnell had more loyalty to the attorney general than he had to the President."

The next day DeLoach reported more suspicious activity to the FBI director: in the halls of the Justice Department, Nick Katzenbach had been "needling" the Bureau's black sheep, Courtney Evans, asking him about the president's dispute with Bobby Kennedy. Hoover sounded a final, ominous note in response: "If Guthman, Katzenbach or anyone else brings this up again they should be told . . . to take it up with me as I am fed up on [sic] the malicious lies & calumnies they have circulated."

There was little point in further discussion. Bobby's friends were bitterly defensive, the FBI tight-lipped, and the president momentarily appeased. But Johnson's relief was fleeting: on March 10 in New Hampshire, he received 29,317 write-in votes for president, Kennedy 25,094 for vice president. "The 4,223-vote difference was not much, but it drew a sigh of relief that could be heard right in the White House Oval Office," commented *Time.* Both sides claimed vindication, a clear sign that the political picture was even more muddled than before. While LBJ avoided significant embarrassment, Kennedy and his backers gained all the confirmation they needed.

Corbin or no Corbin, Kennedy-for-vice-president movements sprang up in New York, New Jersey, California, and elsewhere. Just as New Hampshire volunteers took down the bunting, the attorney general of Wisconsin filed papers to establish a "Draft RFK for Vice President of the United States Grass Roots, Groundswell Committee." Political callers and visitors sought Bobby's affirmation that he would take the vice presidency if it was offered. Family members urged him not to abandon power or the ideals of his brother, though Edward Kennedy and brother-in-law Stephen Smith wanted him in the Senate. An ailing General Douglas MacArthur advised Bobby to focus on the vice presidency. "Take it! Take it," MacArthur rasped, reading hesitation in Kennedy's eyes. "He won't live. He gambled on your brother and won. You gamble on him and you'll win!"

RFK was increasingly in a gambling mood. His soft, perfunctory disavowals were "couched in terms likely to discourage only the most naive voter," observed the *Wall Street Journal*. Few voters, apparently, were so naive: a Gallup poll of April 12 showed Kennedy's support for the vice presidential nomination rising among rank-and-file Democrats from 34 percent in January to 47 percent; Adlai Stevenson's numbers dropped from 26 to 18 percent and Hubert Humphrey's from 14 to 10 percent. If January saw a boomlet, April brought a full-fledged boom.

Buoyed by poll numbers and the growing cult of JFK, burdened by nagging reservations, Bobby threw himself into pursuit of the vice presidency after New Hampshire. For the first time since the assassination, Bobby made widespread appearances; at a United Auto Workers convention, the *Journal* spotted Kennedy "acting more and more like a candidate." Delegates to the annual convention of the NAACP cheered his arrival. In June, Kennedy spoke to a crowd of fifty thousand in Berlin, at the dedication of John F. Kennedy Platz. "Under President Johnson, as under President Kennedy, we are committed to your freedom," Bobby assured the Berliners (and LBJ) before moving onward to Poland.

The European trip, from its inception, had been a battle of wills between Kennedy and Johnson, a conflict not about geopolitics but the vice presidency. "The attorney general's callin' me," LBJ grumbled to Bill Moyers on the evening of April 23. "You know what that's about?"

"I suspect it's this, Mr. President," Moyers replied, his words recorded by Dictabelts. "Bundy came by to see me a while ago . . . said, 'I've just had a very frustrating session with the attorney general, and he was very *angry* when it was all over, because he wants to go to Berlin and feels that he's going on behalf of his dead brother, and that if we want to stop him, then we just are not being faithful to the memory of his brother.' " According to Moyers, Bundy had told RFK, "if you really want to go because it's a tribute to John Kennedy, then you're the one who ought to tell that to the president."

"Well," Johnson asked Moyers, "what do you think I ought to say to him?"

"Well, I think you ought to say to him that the civil rights [bill] is in progress and that . . . you don't want that to be upset. . . . If he wants to wait until after that, as you indicated to Bundy this afternoon, that is another question."

Two weeks later, when Thomas Mann called to report that Kennedy had been invited to speak in Panama, Johnson growled in exasperation: "I'm tryin' to keep him in town. They're givin' him to Berlin, and they're movin' him every place in the damned country. I'd like for him to pass this civil rights bill, if he would," Johnson said sarcastically.

Kennedy delayed the Berlin trip until the civil rights bill passed the Senate. (He did not travel to Panama.) By then, however, new tensions had erupted over the addition of Poland to his itinerary. Poland's Communist government was not eager for the unscripted fanfare of a Kennedy visit and granted him "nonofficial" status only. After weeks of Polish interference with his visa, Bobby turned in frustration to his friend Fred Dutton, whose jurisdiction at the State Department included congressional travel. Dutton was a busy man; Johnson had just asked him to begin the basic research and planning for the fall campaign. By the time Bobby called to say that "the Polish trip has come unstuck," Dutton was on his way out of State, preparing to resign in July. In fact, Bobby's request reached Dutton at the Paramount Hotel in San Francisco, where Dutton was accompanying the president and his staff on a political trip.

Yet here was an opportunity to do a favor for a friend. Dutton made a few calls, some to Bill Moyers, and within days his efforts had come to the attention of the president and the press corps. Evans and Novak soon reported that, as Dutton painfully recalled, "while I'm traveling with Johnson, I'm setting up Kennedy's trip to Poland to pressure Johnson to nominate him vice president." Thereafter, Dutton explained, "my [relations] with Johnson . . . were not of the best." Dutton was still asked to assemble the Democratic platform but he was now suspect, held at arm's length.

Kennedy had been foolish to imagine he could arrange a controversial, high-profile foray into the Communist bloc by relying solely on his personal network; he had failed to recognize that Kennedy men were also beholden to President Johnson. On June 18, hoping to contain the damage, Kennedy placed an awkward call to LBJ. "I had thought that the State Department talked—I guess they had talked to the White House, but I don't know if it got to you—"

"Who?" Johnson feigned ignorance.

"The State Department, on this trip. I, you know, was going to Berlin. Then there was some discussion about going to either Cracow or Warsaw for a day and speaking to the university there. But I didn't—

from what I understand, it hadn't been brought up with you, so I didn't want to go or even contemplate going unless you thought it was advisable, or helpful, or—"

"I don't know anything about it," Johnson lied. "If you think you ought to, go ahead."

"Well, I don't know that I *ought to*. I don't think it's one of those things. You know, I think it's—"

"I wouldn't say *not* to do something," the president interrupted, "but I don't know anything about the *wisdom* of it. This is the first I heard of it. But I'd be guided by your judgment."

Kennedy, looking for guidance himself, was growing flustered: "Well, I think that they—uh—no, I—I—I don't know whether it's helpful or not, Mr. President. I had had some conversations with the people at the State Department, and they thought that it might be, but I don't know that it wouldn't, you know, so I don't—"

"You just use your own judgment and I'll ride with it," Johnson said impatiently.

"All right. OK. Fine."

Hanging up the phone, Johnson turned to Mac Bundy and said, "I don't want him sayin' that the president's sendin' him to Warsaw or directin' him to go or approvin' him to go. . . . And I don't want to say . . . I'm not gonna let you go."

"You can't," Bundy agreed.

Exercising his own judgment, Kennedy went to both Cracow and Warsaw. He envisioned himself an ambassador—an ambassador not, as before, for the United States government, but for the late President Kennedy. Bobby felt a heavy but proud responsibility to bring the "Kennedy message" to those without liberty or justice. But there was little question that the trip was also a message to LBJ. If Bobby could draw crowds in Poland (and he did, clambering atop a car and being hoisted on the shoulders of students to address the throngs in Cracow), he could draw Polish-American votes at home—in solid, Northern, Democratic ethnic communities where Johnson doubted his own strength. And in the unlikely event that his message failed to register with LBJ, Bobby trumpeted it to the cheering students of Warsaw University: "I am not running for President," he told the boisterous crowd, "but if I were, I wish you could all come to the United States and vote."

Kennedy returned home to a near frenzy of press excitement that had been building for months. Each week brought more insider gossip and breathless speculation. With the Democrats' choice for president a closed case and the Republicans' increasingly obvious, only one question captured headlines: "What's Bobby Going to Do?" asked *Newsweek*. *U.S.*

News devoted pages of analysis to "Bobby Kennedy's Future." The pot-
boiler of "Bobby Kennedy's Dilemma" captivated even the staid *Wall
Street Journal*.

In six hours of extensive, exclusive conversation with *Newsweek*'s Ben
Bradlee, RFK assessed his chances. "I should think I'd be the last man in
the world [Johnson] would want," Bobby told Bradlee, "because my
name is Kennedy, because he wants a Johnson administration with no
Kennedys in it, because we travel different paths, because I suppose some
businessmen would object, and because I'd cost them a few votes in the
South. . . . I don't think as many as some say, but some." Still, Kennedy
held some important cards: "Most of the major political leaders in the
North want me," he said. "All of them, really. And that's about all I've got
going for me."

Bradlee believed that Kennedy had more going for him. *Newsweek*'s
Washington bureau chief had clearly been spun by Johnson staffers who
attested guilelessly to the president's "new opinion" of Bobby—a stature
conferred by RFK's "contributions" to resolving crises in civil rights and
Southeast Asia. Dampening talk of a feud that could only reflect poorly
on LBJ, White House aides told Bradlee of a "significant improvement"
in relations between Johnson and Kennedy.

But relations were not so improved as to let the *Newsweek* interview
pass without rebuttal. Administration insiders were clearly irked by
Kennedy's earnest statement of purpose:

> I'd like to harness all the energy and effort and incentive and imagination
> that was attracted to government by President Kennedy. I don't want any
> of that to die. It's important that the striving for excellence continue, that
> there be an end to mediocrity. The torch really has passed to a new gen-
> eration. People are still looking for all that idealism. It permeated young
> people all over the globe. And I became sort of a symbol, not just as an
> individual.
>
> If I could figure out some course for me that would keep all that alive
> and utilize it for the country, that's what I'd do.

Close Johnson aides fumed to *U.S. News* a week later that "the
Attorney General seemed to feel that a 'striving for excellence' might
not continue under President Johnson unless Bobby Kennedy was next
in line for the Presidency . . . that the 'torch' of idealism, so important to
young people, could best be carried by him. The feeling was that somehow President Johnson was left out of it all."

This bitter retort made Kennedy's optimism appear naive. "These
things have a way of solving themselves," Kennedy had told Bradlee. "All
of a sudden everything is obvious and right." But in dealing with LBJ,

things were not necessarily going to work out right; Bobby would have to do his best to ensure they did, and his blithe fatalism belied the intensity of his campaign for the vice presidency. Kennedy issued no direct orders; he remained wilfully ignorant of specifics. But Corbin had been right: RFK approved the spirit of the campaign. "He let it be known that he would like to get the nod," Milton Gwirtzman recalled, and with legions of supporters as skilled and devoted as Kennedy's, that was enough.

Yet suspicions lingered. The campaign seemed too widespread to be self-generated, and everyone remembered Bobby's logistical genius in 1960. "To what extent," mused the *Journal's* Alan Otten, "is [Kennedy] himself participating in current efforts to stir grassroots support for his nomination?" President Johnson, for one, found it impossible to believe that Bobby Kennedy was not personally stoking his supporters. In the creation of the Wisconsin grassroots committee, Johnson perceived the controlling hand of RFK, and he exploded with rage. "Rightly or wrongly," wrote Otten, the president "appears to think Mr. Kennedy is behind the sudden rash of vice presidential endorsements and write-ins." At least Johnson could turn this perception to his own advantage. Presidential friends revived the stereotype of "ruthless Bobby": "Lyndon always thought that Bobby had a knife out for him," one muttered to *U.S. News.*

Daggers were being unsheathed on both sides. While Johnson aides offered careful, calculated praise of Bobby's "contributions" (intended to highlight the president's generosity of spirit), their attacks on his vice presidential campaign were unrestrained. And the political press, prodded by Johnson and Kennedy partisans, was catching on to the feud. For the first time, the press reported the expectant rumblings of a clash that had been roiling since 1960. Still, by the summer of 1964, even the keenest Washington observers had only a dim sense of the antagonism. Reporters began to note that it all dated back to Bobby's act of "sabotage" at the 1960 convention—an event chronicled minutely in Theodore White's 1961 best-seller and Pulitzer Prize winner, *The Making of the President 1960,* but seemingly forgotten until now. James Reston noted only "the odd silence between Johnson and Kennedy" and added that "important divisions" within the administration might be widened by the write-in campaigns. "Some aides of President Johnson," added *U.S. News,* "are reported to feel that the organization built by Robert Kennedy tends to be more loyal to the Attorney General than to the President," who "sees Robert Kennedy as the one potential rival right now in sight." The magazine surmised that the pressure had caused the president "some irritation."

Bobby, by contrast, appeared comfortable with his direction if not his chances. On June 23, he even counted himself out of the New York Senate race. In reality he was having second thoughts. There was from the beginning a forced quality to Bobby's run for the vice presidency; a deep ambivalence stalked his every footstep along the *de facto* campaign trail. He had never quite convinced himself he wanted the job. Nor did he really believe Johnson would offer it to him. Kennedy's optimism, offered up to reporters and friends, was a bit of a hoax. With the Democratic Convention only two months away, Kennedy was looking for another way out of his dilemma.

In June, Bobby mentioned offhandedly to John Seigenthaler that he was thinking about going to Saigon. "For how long?" Seigenthaler asked, imagining another Kennedy "mission."

"Well, I might go indefinitely," Bobby replied. "I thought I'd be Lyndon's ambassador."

Seigenthaler had not heard this one before. "Bobby wouldn't do that," Ethel told him dismissively when he raised the subject. But late in the afternoon of June 11, Kennedy stopped by Clark Clifford's law office to report that he had just sent a letter to LBJ. "Dear Mr. President," Bobby's letter began,

> I just wanted to make sure you understood that if you wished me to go to Viet Nam in any capacity I would be glad to do so. It is obviously the most important problem facing the United States and if you felt that I could help I am at your service.
>
> I have talked to both Bob [McNamara] and Mac [Bundy] about this and I believe they know my feelings. I realize some of the complications but I am sure that if you reached the conclusion that this was the right thing to do then between us both or us all we could work it out satisfactorily.
>
> In any case I wished you to know my feelings on this matter.
>
> Respectfully, Bob.

By "any capacity," Bobby clearly meant the ambassadorship, about to be vacated by Henry Cabot Lodge. Lodge, Nixon's running mate in 1960, had been appointed to the post by JFK to inoculate his administration against partisan sniping on Southeast Asia. Now Lodge was returning to help bolster the GOP's moderate wing in an election year. Lodge's tenure in Saigon had been troublesome; he helped instigate the coup (to which the Kennedy administration had uneasily acquiesced) against Diem in November 1963. Lodge's departure amid growing instability in South Vietnam gave LBJ an opportunity to strengthen his embassy staff.

At Clark Clifford's office, Bobby repeated that Vietnam was America's most pressing problem. This was not idle chatter. Bobby was hardly in the habit of seeking Clifford's advice. When Bobby told Clifford his offer was not a political ploy, he obviously meant the message for President Johnson. Clifford, with surprising charity, later judged Bobby's "remarkable offer" to be "an utterly sincere act from a man still deeply depressed by his brother's death." Perhaps, he and others surmised, Bobby felt responsible for the perilous path his brother had laid. Perhaps he sought to head off disaster. Or perhaps, as Ted Sorensen later suggested, Bobby had simply found a way to remain in public life but escape the painful memories and harsh new realities of life in Washington.

In any event, Johnson's rejection came swiftly, on the evening of June 11. "I just wanted you to know that the nicest thing that ever happened to me since I've been here was your note," Johnson told Kennedy after reaching him on the phone.

"Well, thank you."

"And I appreciate it *so* very, very much—and I can't think of lettin' you do that, but you've gotta help me with who we do get, and we gotta get it pretty soon, and we'll talk about it in the next few hours. . . ."

"Thank you very much, Mr. President," Kennedy replied, sounding a bit confused. Johnson had not offered him a reason for the rejection, just an effluence of flattery.

"I appreciate it more than you'll ever know," the president repeated.

"Oh, well, that's very nice."

"You're a great guy or you wouldn't write that kind of letter."

In Johnson's view, Bobby's offer did have its merits: sending Bobby to Saigon might be preferable to having him in Washington. The post would also give him a share of political responsibility for American policy in the region. Still, Vietnam was a war zone. RFK would make a prized target for any vengeful Diem supporter; and as ambassador he could hardly be expected to sit behind the embassy gates and keep a low profile. "I would be accusing myself for the rest of my life if something happened to him out there," the president told Jack Valenti. "He could do the job. He could do it damn well, but I can't trust the security there and someone or some group might want to do him in. I couldn't live with that."

The prospect of two martyred Kennedys was indeed too horrible to contemplate, but Johnson's claim that RFK could do the job "damn well" was a cheap bit of praise probably intended for Valenti's memoir (which is where it landed). In fact, for a host of reasons, Johnson considered Kennedy a terrible choice for the post. When Mac Bundy called the Oval Office on June 17 and read aloud a draft of Scotty Reston's column on the subject, LBJ took strong exception to one point: "No, no. No, no, I don't want to say that at all. . . . I don't want to say that I consider him the best qualified man for the post, 'cause I frankly don't."

"Oh, I thought you'd said that to me one time—I—I'm the source of that," Bundy stammered. "The other thing [Reston's] hanging it on is your unwillingness to put a man whose family had been in such danger in danger himself."

"Not at all, I don't want to say that at all, that hasn't got anything to do with it," Johnson said impatiently. "I just told him when I got his letter that it was a fine thing, that I appreciated it very much, but I couldn't under any circumstances consider it. . . . I just wish that, by God, a responsible guy like Scotty, before we go sayin' things . . ." He trailed off. "I don't want Bobby or anybody else to get a lot of feeling in the country that I'm tryin' to banish him to the isle!"

"Yeah," Bundy replied. "What is your reason for not considering him, then? What shall I say to Reston on that?"

"My reason for not considerin' him is that I want him to stay right where he is."

"Nothing else."

"I think it'd just be controversial as hell on the Hill, that's another good reason. But I don't want to say that, I don't want to cut the guy."

"No. No, no. You can't say that," Bundy agreed.

"Same problem we have on the vice presidency. Bobby's a very, very controversial character in this country. And I don't want this [ambassadorship] to be a Democratic campaign manager's, [former president's] brother's thing, but I don't want to say that to Reston," Johnson repeated.

"No, no, no—"

"I want the best man to be above political matters of any kind, and not to have been in any wars with the Democrats *or* Republicans."

Johnson called Reston himself and squelched the rumors. Off the record, the president scoffed at the notion that family or safety were concerns. "If he was single I wouldn't send him. If his name was Brown I wouldn't. We've got all these problems here with civil rights, he's been headin' this division; there's talk of his runnin' for office for other things; there's a good deal of speculation about our relationship; and they're not gonna catch me banishing someone to the isle," he said, suddenly laughing at his own shrewdness.

"I got the impression that lately you have been talking to him more," Reston replied.

"I've been talkin' to him ever since I came here. All the time. There's never been a month since I've been [president] that I haven't seen more of him than I have of almost any cabinet officer. . . . There's never been anything to the [idea] we didn't see each other."

"I'll do a little story and straighten it out," Reston promised, restoring his status as "responsible" in Lyndon Johnson's eyes.

Like Kennedy, Bundy and Robert McNamara volunteered for the post, but Johnson wanted them to stay right where they were as well. Instead he selected General Maxwell Taylor, chairman of the Joint Chiefs of Staff. But the vice presidential post remained open, and with it the question of Bobby Kennedy's future. Johnson and Kennedy remained caught on the horns of the same dilemma.

For President Johnson, the nature of the dilemma had changed by the summer of 1964. The time for pulse-taking and painful weighing had passed. The question now was not whether to eliminate RFK from contention for the vice presidency. The question was how, and when.

Lyndon Johnson did not need a Kennedy on the ticket after all; the tail would not wag *this* dog. In June 1964, LBJ stood astride the political landscape like a behemoth, his every new bill a giant step toward reelection. Unions, liberals, the NAACP—all the traditional Democratic powers lined up behind a president who promised them great things, almost unimaginable things, and seemed uniquely able to deliver. Johnson's approval ratings hovered near 75 percent. John Kennedy, in his first year as president, faced embarrassment on the Hill and humiliation at the Bay of Pigs. Lyndon Johnson earned accolades and collected accomplishments—a flawless performance that rivaled FDR's Hundred Days. Early polls showed Johnson crushing any Republican challenger by margins that would have impressed Roosevelt at his zenith. "We've got 'em worried now, Mr. Speaker," Johnson gloated to John McCormack.

"If they try to push Bobby Kennedy down my throat for Vice President," Johnson threatened, increasingly strident, "I'll tell them to nominate him for the Presidency and leave me out of it." To another friend, more bitterly: "We'll let Bobby and them take over and let 'em run against the Republicans and let a Republican beat 'em." Most establishment Democrats considered the notion of adding Bobby to the ticket preposterous or even offensive. Though rank-and-file Democrats liked Kennedy for the nomination by a wide margin, 41 percent to Hubert Humphrey's 11 (Stevenson polled second with 26 percent), Democratic county chairmen preferred Humphrey to Kennedy by 29 to 15 percent.

Governors, senators, congressmen, state chairmen, and national committeemen, almost seventy-five of them a day, spoke to party headquarters in Washington and inveighed against Bobby's presence on the ticket.

After a White House meeting with LBJ, Wisconsin's Democratic Governor John W. Reynolds stepped outside and denounced his state's grassroots campaign as "asinine and premature." Even among the JFK holdovers in Johnson's immediate circle—Sorensen, O'Donnell, O'Brien, Salinger, and Bundy—none pushed for a Johnson-Kennedy ticket. Most, in fact, seemed to agree that Bobby should not be on the ticket—though surely for different reasons from LBJ's.

Even more comforting, in Johnson's current state of mind, were polls indicating that Bobby's presence on the Democratic ticket meant little to its success. Bobby was not only irrelevant to the ticket, he was harmful to it—in Southern and border states and among businessmen, Democratic and Republican moderates, conservative Democrats, and independents. A Louis Harris survey showed that 33 percent of Southern Democrats would bolt a ticket with Bobby's name on it. The results filled Johnson with glee; his relief was expansive. Bobby could be safely ruled out. In fact, by Johnson's calculus, he *had* to be ruled out.

But how to do it? The question plagued Johnson. He had not solved the Bobby problem after all; it had merely changed shape. Here the possibility of a misstep seemed great, even inevitable. Knowing now that he would not choose Kennedy, LBJ grappled for a means of cutting him out without alienating the party's "Kennedy wing" or offending the public. There was no way to finesse the situation or to resolve it quietly. In this way Johnson's political prowess was a curse: his lack of a Democratic challenger and the anemic Republican field left only his vice presidential choice to fill the void of a very dull election year. There was simply nothing else worth discussing. The pressure for Bobby, emitted at constant but low frequencies, was being amplified by the press. Johnson's biggest headache in the summer of 1964 was the media, which in his view set the Kennedy bandwagon rolling.

As "inside sources" chattered and the convention crept closer, Johnson stalled. Anticipating Bobby's exit—or elimination—from the pack, the president toyed distractedly with potential running mates. In June, he quietly offered the spot to Secretary McNamara. After the assassination, LBJ had asked McNamara to be his "number one executive vice president in charge of the Cabinet"—a seemingly meaningless bit of Johnsonian puffery. It was typical for LBJ to fatten his men with praise, rendering them sluggish and agreeable. But in this case the president seemed to mean it; his respect for McNamara bordered on awe.

Yet a Johnson-McNamara ticket had an uncomfortable ring. Despite the cult of competence that hallowed his name, Robert Strange McNamara was a registered Republican and an avatar of big business, the former "whiz kid" of Ford Motor. For traditional Democrats, a cabinet seat was one thing, the vice presidency another. Perhaps sensing this, McNamara declined. "I lacked political skills and I knew it," he added later. He also knew Johnson well enough to imagine accepting the offer and having it yanked away.

What LBJ really wanted, Robert Kennedy supposed, was to have "a Kennedy without . . . having a bad Kennedy." But were there any good Kennedys left, in Johnson's eyes? Ted was unobjectionable but green; only thirty-two, he was not even old enough to serve as president. A few years older and he might have been a serious contender for the second spot on a Johnson ticket. "Of all the Kennedy brothers, the most qualified man to be President is Teddy Kennedy, because he has the greatest knowledge of government of any of the three," Johnson reflected several years later. What Johnson probably meant was knowledge of the *Senate,* for that was what he liked about Ted—the youngest Kennedy had dedicated himself to becoming a first-class senator. Jack Kennedy, in Johnson's view, had never really had any respect for the institution. Additionally, Johnson found Ted's rambling manner in private meetings a bit endearing. Perhaps it was because Ted was the least imposing Kennedy, young and fresh-faced and respectful. "I had the Senators all down here, we briefed them, we got by pretty good," Johnson told Nicholas Katzenbach in 1967. "Teddy was there. Bobby never accepts. He won't show up, but Teddy was there and asked good questions. He was smiling, in a good humor, and was reasonable."

Still, constitutionally speaking, an LBJ-EMK ticket was an impossibility. And a Kennedy—even a good one—on the ticket could only undercut Johnson's autonomy. What Johnson wanted was someone with Bobby's appeal, his glamour, his religion, his family ties—but without his personality or family name. Johnson settled, briefly, on Sargent Shriver. As a Kennedy in-law, Shriver seemed the perfect compromise. Bill Moyers, Shriver's former deputy at the Peace Corps, pled his case to the president. But Moyers got the discouraging message from "the family" that "if you are going to take a Kennedy, it's got to be a *real* Kennedy, which Shriver isn't." The Shriver balloon "doesn't make a hell of a lot of sense," Bobby scoffed that summer, and he was sure most Democrats agreed. Bobby was half right: Shriver drew only single-digit support among the party rank and file, and county chairmen liked Shriver no more than they liked RFK.

The Shriver balloon quickly deflated. Johnson was less interested in putting a Kennedy "clone" on his ticket than in making it known he was considering one—and in driving a deliberate wedge between Bobby and Sarge. Actually, Johnson considered Shriver too close to the Kennedys for comfort. "Just remember, Bill," Johnson told Moyers.

"Blood is thicker than water." Of course, Shriver was no blood relative, but Moyers well understood the president's views on loyalty.

While Johnson dithered, seeking constant counsel on the Bobby problem, more Bobby-for-veep movements sprang up in important states. On July 22, the Democratic National Committee's Cliff Carter insisted that the president throw a blanket on these small but scattered brushfires lest they continue to spread. In fact the final blow to Bobby's hopes had fallen a week earlier, on July 15, when the GOP gathered in San Francisco and nominated Arizona Senator Barry Goldwater for president. On the convention floor of the Cow Palace, Republican delegates hissed, stomped, booed, and even spit when the moderate governor of New York, Nelson Rockefeller, tried to address them. (Actor Ronald Reagan, speaking on Goldwater's behalf, got a warmer welcome.) The mood befit the ticket. Liberals, unions, and minorities now needed little if any coaxing to fall straight into the Johnson column. Even moderate conservatives were likely to go Johnson's way—that is, if his vice presidential choice did not scare them off. It was time to end the speculation and remove Bobby from the running.

On July 22, Johnson asked Clark Clifford to draft a talking paper to use with RFK. "The Goldwater nomination and the resulting situation in the South and in the border states makes it clear that the President cannot choose the Attorney General for this job," Clifford stated bluntly in a memo submitted the next day. "On the other hand," he continued,

> the Party has the greatest possible need for the Attorney General's help, on three grounds:
> a. Only his help can sustain the full effectiveness of the original [John] Kennedy/Johnson partnership.
> b. The Attorney General's support will be decisive with very large numbers of American Catholics, and with younger people of all faiths too.
> c. The Attorney General has an unequalled talent for the management of a campaign.

Therefore, Clifford concluded, the president should designate Kennedy as campaign chairman and appoint him to a senior post in the new administration.

With Clifford's memo on his desk, LBJ phoned Kennedy on Monday, July 27, and asked him to come to the White House the next day. The attorney general had some meetings scheduled in New York on Tuesday but offered to cancel them. No, Johnson said, Wednesday afternoon would be all right; it was nothing urgent.

Bobby hung up the phone and turned to Ed Guthman. "He's going to tell me I'm not going to be Vice President," Bobby said. "I wondered when he'd get around to it."

This was the endgame. At 1:09 P.M. on Wednesday, Kennedy arrived at the Oval Office and took a seat to the president's right. Lyndon Johnson, sitting stiffly behind his desk, looked at the wall, then at the floor.

There are two accounts of the meeting that followed, and predictably, they diverge. Johnson remembered saying that someday, all of it—the Oval Office, the White House, the country—would be Bobby's, and that would be just fine with Lyndon Johnson. Every man had his moment. But this, Johnson said to Bobby, is not your moment. He looked at Bobby for a reaction and heard him gulp. Otherwise "the kid" took it rather well. Generously, Johnson offered to let him run the campaign, since Bobby had done such an outstanding job for his brother back in '60. Bobby said he would think about it if Johnson would consider replacing him as attorney general with Nick Katzenbach. Johnson said he would think about that, and then the two men worked out a mutu-ally satisfactory spin for the newspapers. They parted peaceably.

The perspective from Bobby's chair was very different. By his recol-lection, Johnson clutched the "official" version of Clifford's talking points and read them aloud, graceless and deliberate. "I have asked you to come over to discuss with you a subject that is an important one to you and me," the president began. And after several paragraphs of niceties, Johnson got to the point: he had been thinking about the best vice presidential candidate for the country, the party, and himself, and it was not Bobby Kennedy. "I have concluded," Johnson said, with consid-erable understatement, ". . . that it would be inadvisable for you to be the Democratic candidate for Vice President in this year's election."

"Inadvisable." With one sober, bureaucratic word, uttered three min-utes into the meeting, Lyndon Johnson dispatched seven months of angst. What followed was less important, and Bobby listened with mild, detached curiosity. Glancing at the president's speakerphone, Bobby saw that its "record" buttons were depressed and he thought better of speak-ing his mind. Johnson rambled on, blaming his decision on Goldwater's nomination and supposed strength in Southern and border states. "I am sure that you will understand the basis of my decision," Johnson read from the memo, ". . . because President Kennedy had to make a similar type of decision in 1960"—a statement Clifford knew would "evoke bit-ter memories" for RFK.

Whether Johnson knew it too was unclear, for he spent most of the meeting burying Bobby with praise. With your name and your record, Johnson said, "you have a unique and promising future." When Bobby took his own shot at the presidency someday, Johnson would be there to help. Until then, he hoped he could rely on Bobby's "great talents." ("He wanted me to know that if I wished to go around the country and speak he would never be jealous of me," Bobby wrote in a memo the next week.) The president offered Bobby his choice of jobs—ambassador to Britain, France, the Soviet Union, or the United Nations, where JFK had put Adlai Stevenson out to pasture. There was no mention of the party chairmanship, which Bobby had offered as a consolation prize to LBJ in 1960.

Kennedy preferred to stay put as attorney general, and for a moment the two men seemed to agree: "I said," Bobby recalled,

> that I wasn't interested in any other position. He said that if he were me he would stay over in the Department of Justice. He said I had an outstanding staff. He thought I should remain there.
>
> He said in comparison to the staff he had at the White House the group I had selected were unusually competent. The people that contributed in the White House, he said, were the group that was selected by President Kennedy. He said he really could not count on his own people—Jenkins, Valenti, Reedy. He said Bill Moyers was good but his most useful function was rewriting what other people did. I was shocked to hear him being so critical to me of people who had been so loyal to him. Just as much as anything else, it convinced me that I could not have worked closely with him.

If Johnson read aloud the last sentence of his memo—clumsily citing this talk as "a basis upon which you and I can build a lasting relationship that would prove valuable to both of us and to our country"—it must have rung hollow. But the two men made tentative steps in that direction by putting aside the vice presidency and discussing, for the better part of their hour together, the incipient campaign. Johnson asked Bobby to run it from the Justice Department. "I was reluctant," Bobby said later, "to take on both of these jobs." An attorney general, he felt, should be above politics; and to drop his cabinet seat for the campaign chair would leave him nowhere to go after November.

In a strange, seemingly hazardous twist, Kennedy brought up the Bobby Baker affair: "I said that we had an active case and we had to make a judgment how to proceed." Bobby suggested bringing in an outside adviser, someone like Jim Rowe. Johnson preferred Abe Fortas or Clark Clifford, even though Fortas had been Baker's lawyer; Kennedy voiced concern about a conflict of interest but let it pass. Johnson, anyway, was more interested in expressing his low opinion of the man: Baker, he said, latched on to power and money and led himself into the quicksand. I don't suppose the Republicans are eager to expose themselves to similar scrutiny, Johnson smiled. With that, at 2:10, the conversation ended and Kennedy stood to leave.

Here again the two versions of the story coincide—in part. Both men recalled Bobby's parting words:"I could have helped you, Mr. President." As Johnson later told it, Kennedy sounded melancholy. As Bobby's friends told it, he sounded sardonic.

When Kennedy emerged from the Oval Office, he looked to one passerby as if he had taken a punch to the mouth. Shortly he joined O'Brien and O'Donnell for lunch. At the restaurant Bobby was wry and fatalistic, chuckling to himself as he described the meeting with LBJ. It was stilted, he said, probably staged, and definitely suspicious. Kennedy found the speakerphone more unsettling than the conversation. "I'm just persuaded it was taped," Bobby said, adding, "I would absolutely resent it" if it was so. "If the president had said to me, 'I'd like to have this conversation on the record. Do you mind?' " Bobby would surely have agreed. But this was just the sort of off-putting, underhanded tactic Bobby expected from LBJ. (Johnson, fearful that Kennedy would later distort the conversation, did, in fact, record it on his speakerphone. "In a conversation with Kenny and Larry he inadvertently and virtually admitted as much," Kennedy wrote the next week.)

Ed Guthman, greeting RFK on his return to the Justice Department, sized him up as at once "miffed, disappointed and relieved." The collective air of melancholy was shattered by Mac Bundy's call, another awkward errand for LBJ: the president wanted to know if Kennedy would publicly bow out of the race before news of the meeting leaked. "The fact that I had not volunteered to say that I would withdraw was obviously going to cause [Johnson] some difficulty," Kennedy later observed. "How he could say that he had gotten rid of me was his biggest problem." Indeed it was; and Bobby was not about to relieve him of it. Kennedy told Bundy he wouldn't fight Johnson's decision but wouldn't make it easier for him, either. Kennedy could accept that Johnson did not want him on the ticket; why could Johnson not accept the consequences?

Now Bobby was not miffed but mad—mad at Johnson for using Bundy as a political messenger and mad at Bundy for allowing it. In the pages of *Newsweek* one Kennedy intimate branded Bundy "a Machiavellian turncoat." This was Bundy's reward for trying to help. Torn by conflicting loyalties, drawn into a broker's role, he felt his ties to Bobby slacken. Several of Bobby's friends were in a similar bind, and if they offered themselves as a bridge they soon regretted it. When Bundy called the next day for Bobby's input on the presidential statement, he again drew an angry refusal.

Johnson, for his part, believed he had acted magnanimously in a difficult situation and was deeply annoyed by Kennedy's unwillingness to acknowledge it. Kennedy's tone of wounded disapproval—as if *he* had been wronged—was doubly infuriating. By Thursday afternoon, July 30, the president could barely contain his mounting rage. Lee White walked into the Oval Office to discuss a project and stepped back abruptly as he spotted George Reedy "catching unshirted hell." The president, remembered White, "was pounding the goddamned table, and he was jumping up and down and really yelling, and old George, with that shaggy head of his, was standing there like a solid old St. Bernard."

"Jesus Christ!" Johnson shouted. "Staff work, staff work, staff work! Goddamn it, George, the Kennedys always had perfect staff work and we can't do the simplest little damned thing!"

By afternoon, LBJ had collected himself. At a midday press conference he bantered with reporters about the vice presidency, even painting a picture of his eventual running mate: "well-received in all the states of the Union among all of our people . . . experienced in foreign relations and domestic affairs . . . attractive, prudent and progressive." Tom Wicker of the *Times* quipped that Johnson's "list of qualifications [was] so exacting that few statesmen since George Washington could meet them." If John Kennedy had held to such a list in 1960, LBJ would still be a senator.

In the White House that afternoon, reporters and presidential aides passed around the latest Associated Press poll of Democratic delegates: Humphrey 341, Kennedy 230. The poll revealed no serious challengers, but the pressmen bandied about other names—Shriver, McNamara, Orville Freeman—as they anticipated the president's pick. Back in the Oval Office, Johnson and Clark Clifford shared "amusement at these journalistic fantasies." Clifford made a more serious suggestion. "Let's grab on to that," he told the president. "Why don't you reach a policy decision that after careful consideration, you've decided that you're not going to select anybody from your cabinet?"

Johnson paused. "That's pretty thin, isn't it?"

"Well," Clifford conceded, "it is pretty thin, but it's a lot better than nothing." And the president, warming to the idea, sent Clifford into another office to draft a short statement. Clifford wrote it longhand and delivered it to Juanita Roberts, the president's secretary.

It was another "masterstroke." As 6:00 approached, LBJ hastily convened reporters and newsreel cameras in the Fish Room beside the Oval Office. Again he recited Clifford's words verbatim: "In reference to the selection of a candidate for Vice President on the Democratic ticket, I have reached the conclusion that it would be inadvisable for me to recommend to the Convention any member of the Cabinet or any of those who meet regularly with the Cabinet in this regard. . . . In this manner, the race has been considerably narrowed."

As Johnson retired to the Oval Office, George Reedy and his flacks did their best to spin the story: each cabinet member was essential to his job, they told the press; continued speculation might impair relations with Congress; Johnson acted to "keep his official team on the job and running efficiently." Reporters knew better. The next morning's headlines said it all: PRESIDENT BARS KENNEDY, FIVE OTHERS FROM TICKET, proclaimed the *New York Times.* "The President's surprise move," reported *U.S. News,* ". . . . seemed to be aimed at one target: Attorney General Robert F. Kennedy. . . . Few doubted that Mr. Johnson moved to cut these [Kennedy-for-vice president] movements off before they built up a national drive."

The import of Johnson's move was equally obvious. "Mr. Johnson's decision not to ask Mr. Kennedy to run with him was one of the major political steps of his administration," commented Tom Wicker. "Mr. Kennedy is regarded as the inheritor of much of President Kennedy's political strength and, in addition, evokes strong political loyalties in his own behalf." Thus, as Democratic luminaries made clear, "the President is eager to win this fall in his own right, with no hint of having relied upon the Kennedy name to put him into office." With no small satisfaction, a presidential confidant described the sea change: "It was still a Johnson-Kennedy party until yesterday. Now Johnson has cleared the air."

White House staffers, feeling generous, claimed that Kennedy took the news with "good grace." Publicly, it seemed so. "As I have always said," Bobby declared, "it is the President's responsibility to make known his choice for Vice President. . . . It is in the interest of all of us who were associated with President Kennedy to continue to advance the programs and ideals to which he devoted his life and which President Johnson is carrying forward." Privately, though, Bobby's friends were incensed. Bobby himself felt a little guilty: "Sorry I took so many of you nice fellows over the side with me," he joked in telegrams to Shriver, McNamara, Freeman, Rusk, and UN Ambassador Adlai Stevenson.

LBJ was exultant. "Now that damn albatross is off my neck," he told an aide. On Friday, in a surprisingly unrestrained display of gloating, he summoned three prominent reporters—Wicker of the *Times,* Douglas Kiker of the *New York Herald-Tribune,* and Edward Folliard of the *Washington Post*—to the White House, treating them to an exquisite lunch and thrusting forth fistfuls of supportive telegrams. You see, Johnson grinned, the party doesn't want Bobby after all. "It was as if a coup had been accomplished," wrote Theodore White, "as if a tenuous control had been reinforced and confirmed by a stroke of action."

Then, with great relish, Lyndon Johnson spun a Texas tale. It was his *pièce de résistance,* the crescendo of an expansive, four-hour performance. "When I got [Kennedy] in the Oval Office," Johnson began, "and told him it would be 'inadvisable' for him to be on the ticket as the Vice President–nominee, his face changed, and he started to swallow. He looked sick. His adam's apple bounded up and down like a yo-yo."

For effect, the president gulped, audibly, at the reporters. He mimicked Bobby's "funny voice" and proceeded to tell, in lavish detail and with evident delight, his version of the meeting. Finally, LBJ ran down a list of possible running mates and explained the ways each would hurt his chances. "In other words," recalled Folliard, "he would do better in the November election if he had no running mate. This left Wicker, Kiker and me baffled—and that is just what the man evidently wanted us to be."

Within days Johnson's story was the talk of Washington. His portrait of RFK as a "stunned semi-idiot" left columnist Joseph Alsop and other Washington insiders feeling rather stunned themselves. It was not long before the gossip found its way to Bobby Kennedy, who stormed back to the White House and accused the president of mistruths and a violation of trust. I knew the meeting was taped, he said, but I never expected this. Wasn't our talk a matter of confidence? Aren't we honorable men?

LBJ was unrepentant: I've revealed nothing, he assured Kennedy, gesturing wanly at an empty page in his appointment book. He promised to check his notes for any conversations that might have slipped his mind. Bobby stalked out, seething, and caught a plane to Hyannis Port. "He tells so many lies," Kennedy said of Johnson the next week, echoing the words of George Reedy, "that he convinces himself after a while he's telling the truth. He just doesn't recognize truth or falsehood."

Bobby spent the first weekend in August on Cape Cod with Arthur Schlesinger, concocting possible public statements about LBJ's ruling: "I swear to the best of my knowledge I am not now nor ever have been a member of the cabinet on the ground that it might tend to eliminate me." He struck Schlesinger as good-humored and "matter-of-fact." But Bobby's wit could not disguise the fact that after seven months spent convincing himself that the vice presidency was worth pursuing, the disappointment was bitter—and made worse by Johnson's duplicity.

Still, it equaled liberation. In Dallas, Bobby had been cut adrift from JFK; now he was freed by LBJ. In casting Bobby aside, Johnson inadvertently charged him with a new sense of self-determination—and drove him toward the first office truly his own. "Now I have to decide what to do," Kennedy said to Ed Guthman bleakly. "Either run for the Senate in New York or work for Lyndon." But the latter was no longer an option. Nor was the one Bobby offered his top assistants: "Ah, what the hell," he laughed, "let's go form our own country."

CHAPTER 8

Get on the Johnson-Kennedy Team

As Lyndon Johnson savored a moment of peace after a vicious political squall, Robert Kennedy's strategists were gearing up for a different sort of combat. Even before LBJ's ruling on the vice presidency, their focus snapped from Washington to New York, where Kennedy's Senate prospects were very much alive. At the time of the Kennedy-Johnson meeting the New York State party convention was only a month away—"27 days of hard politicking," wrote the *New York Times'* R. W. Apple, Jr., at the end of it of all—and RFK had much lost ground to cover.

The Senate seat was not open for Kennedy to claim. It would have to be taken from Kenneth B. Keating, the popular, silver-maned six-year incumbent and the first Republican senator to reject the Goldwater ticket. In Nelson Rockefeller's New York, this was hardly a controversial position, and Keating's moderate politics put him in good stead. Democrats were not exactly leaping forth to challenge him.

Kennedy's men labored in this vacuum. His strategists leaned hard on key New York Democrats, trying to create an impression of inevitability, stressing—as a Quayle poll of July had shown—that RFK was the only Democrat with the wherewithal to beat Keating. Saddled by the carpet-bag issue that Keating was sure to exploit, Kennedy was nonetheless buoyed by a team of seasoned and aggressive New York pols ("the most discredited of machine hacks," complained the *Times,* a bit unfairly).

Kennedy's chief aide was Stephen E. Smith, son of wealthy Brooklyn Irish Catholics and husband of Bobby's sister Jean. Only thirty-six, Smith was called "the Kennedy clansman no one knows" and, by those few who did know him, "the eyes and ears of the Kennedy family" in New

York. Thin and athletic, boyish and almost shy, he was a background figure—and a powerful one. In 1958, at age thirty, Smith had been office manager of JFK's last Senate race. In 1962 he ran Teddy's first. Meanwhile, he controlled the purse strings—as a key fund-raiser in 1960 and, after Joseph Kennedy's stroke the following year, as manager of the family's investment portfolio. His attention to detail was the stuff of political legend: in 1964, he decided the number of buttons and balloons to order before Bobby had even decided to run. Of Smith's intuition, JFK once said, "Anyone can talk to him and feel he's talking to the candidate himself."

With the help of men like Smith, Charles Buckley, the codgerly old Bronx leader, and John F. "Jack" English, an ambitious upstart from Nassau County, Kennedy's drive for the nomination gathered momentum. He had not yet declared but was automatically the presumptive nominee. "If this was a steamroller," one observer noted, "it was . . . sitting on a steep hill. All they had to do was release the brake, because there was almost nothing standing in their way."

Almost nothing. Despite the intervention of Bill Haddad, a JFK campaign aide and former Reform candidate, Bobby was having trouble with New York's zealous Reform Democrats. On the eve of the state convention, twenty-seven of them refused to back RFK, saying he had "evidenced no comprehension of the aims of our group" and accusing him of cozying up to old-line power brokers like Buckley and Peter Crotty of Buffalo. They expressed unease about Bobby's former ties to Joe McCarthy and his prosecution of Jimmy Hoffa. "We will never board the Kennedy bandwagon," they vowed publicly. As Kennedy's nomination became a certainty, some Reformers threatened to sit out the fall campaign; some formed a Keating-Johnson committee; and some agreed to do the minimum work while others pledged to "campaign like hell" for Kennedy though they had opposed his nomination.

Then there was the *New York Times*. With caustic resignation the editorial board waited for "Bobby-come-lately"

> to fly here, symbolically purge himself of Massachusetts residence by announcing his withdrawal as a delegate from that state at [the] Democratic National Convention and then wait for a supine New York State convention to hand him the toga September 1. . . .
>
> Mr. Kennedy, in frantic need of a new launching pad for his political fortunes after President Johnson blackballed him as the Democratic Vice Presidential nominee, simply moved into a vacuum. . . . In characteristic fashion, he did not wait to be asked. With the aid of his political field marshal, brother-in-law Stephen Smith, he set in motion a steamroller that flattened the party's bemused state leadership into a doormat bearing the legend, "Welcome, Bobby."

There was more hostility—within the Liberal Party, which Arthur Schlesinger sought to soothe, and among rank-and-file precinct workers, who felt Bobby was not playing by the rules. But the key to the nomination was the mayor of New York City, Robert F. Wagner. He met twice with RFK, on August 7 and 17, but held back his support, fearing eclipse by Kennedy's swiftly rising sun. Former New York governor Averell Harriman, surveying the political landscape for LBJ, reported that "Mayor Wagner doesn't like any 'other stars in the orbit' but . . . will accept the President's wishes."

What were the president's wishes? President Johnson was of two minds about Kennedy's Senate candidacy: he certainly wanted Bobby out of the cabinet room, but considered his presence up north more than a little menacing. Like Wagner, Johnson was loath to help build a Kennedy machine in New York. "LBJ has very special feelings about New York," *Newsweek* reported, "valuing it second only to Texas as his personal power base. He can hardly relish the prospect of a Kennedy bloc taking hold there." Nor, however, did the president relish Kennedy lingering in Washington, keeping hold of the Justice Department. The thought of Bobby on his own was a relief and a terror at the same time.

"Harriman wants you very much to give a nod to Bobby to run," press aide Liz Carpenter informed the president. "Bobby can carry [New York] by 500,000 and is the only person sure of beating Keating." Johnson had seen the polls and needed little convincing. He was a pragmatist; in the final analysis he saw no choice but to support RFK. After denying him the vice presidency, undercutting his Senate race would rightly be seen as petty and vindictive. Backing him instead might ensure the sympathy of Kennedy loyalists. And if Bobby won, he became another liberal vote in the Senate. Another Johnson Democrat.

Then there was the tantalizing possibility that Bobby would not win: he led the early polls, 52 percent to Keating's 35, but the incumbent was genial and popular, and he would exploit the carpetbagger issue. (RFK had in fact lived in New York from 1925 until 1942, far longer than JFK had lived in Massachusetts. Still, his accent and family history made the claim seem absurd; when Bobby declared for the Senate, Keating welcomed him to New York with a road map and guidebook.) Having supported a losing Kennedy bid, Johnson would escape with honor intact and a pliable Republican in New York. Keating, after all, was not so bad. He was voting for LBJ in November.

In late August, Johnson gave Wagner the Treatment. Playing the host at the White House, the president urged Wagner to back Kennedy and promised him a continuing say in patronage in New York. On Thursday, August 20, Wagner was present as Johnson signed his omnibus antipoverty bill in a Rose Garden ceremony. The spotlight was on the president and the nation's poor, but *New York Times* reporter Marjorie Hunter sensed "political currents" crackling in the heavy summer air: Wagner and Kennedy stood behind the president, side by side, softly chatting. That Saturday, Wagner threw his support to Kennedy. Or, as the *Times* put it, "[threw] in the towel."

With Wagner's blessing thus extracted, Kennedy was free to announce. "I think I shall respond to the spontaneous draft of my brother-in-law," he scribbled in a note to a reporter, as if it had just occurred to him. Kennedy took up residence in New York—in a suite at Manhattan's Carlyle Hotel and a twenty-five-room mansion in Glen Cove, Long Island. On August 25, he entered the race formally. Standing on the lawn of Gracie Mansion, the mayor's residence along the East River, flanked by Wagner and Ethel and dressed in the black pin-striped suit and black tie he had worn almost exclusively since President Kennedy's death, Robert Kennedy declared his candidacy for the Senate.

"The search for enduring peace and for enduring prosperity begun by President Kennedy and continued by President Johnson" was under Republican attack, Bobby warned, his hands trembling slightly. "No one associated with President Kennedy and with President Johnson—no one committed to participating in public life—can sit on the sidelines with so much at stake." It was a deft nod to his benefactors, past and present, and at the same time a declaration of independence. Kennedy added that President Johnson would campaign for him in New York.

Meanwhile, in Atlantic City, the Democratic National Convention had already begun.

Lyndon Johnson must have welcomed Bobby's temporary absence. For weeks, thoughts of Bobby's role—or his very presence—at the convention consumed Johnson, filling him with dread. Aides could see it in his eyes but were at a loss to explain it. Larry O'Brien recalled,

> It was going to be a routine convention without any basic problems. The President was high in the polls. It was well understood that he would be elected. . . . The selection of a vice presidential candidate would be widely accepted; no difficulties there. Thus you could put on a show for public consumption and go about your business.
>
> The only area that emerged as a difficulty was the role of Bobby [and] the film.

The film was a brief tribute to JFK. It was scheduled to run on the convention's first day—before the nomination of a vice president. "What if the memorial movie inspires a floor demonstration for the late President?" wondered the *New York Daily News* in July. "And what if that turns into a 'spontaneous' demonstration for Bobby-for-Veep?" Johnson asked himself the same question. He was terrified by rumors, broadcast by NBC radio, of a supposed secret meeting at Hyannis Port where Jacqueline Kennedy resolved to attend the screening and give a boost to Bobby's drive for the vice presidency. "Jackie and Bobby really are behind the build-up," Johnson reportedly remarked.

This betrayal, whether real or imagined, hurt. Jackie had been so understanding during the difficult transition, a gentle counterpoint to Bobby's slow-burning bitterness; now, it seemed, Bobby had turned her. Frustrated, wounded, and indignant, LBJ struggled to safeguard what was by rights *his* convention, *his* political beatification. White House aides gave Wolper Productions a stern warning: leave Bobby on the cutting room floor. The final version of *A Thousand Days* contained two fuzzy, fleeting images of RFK and no more. In July the film was mysteriously shuffled to the end of the convention schedule—after the selection of a vice president. In the press, presidential aides explained sheepishly that an opening-night tribute would have cast a pall over the proceedings. But now, tacked to the end of an exhausting schedule, the film seemed less a poignant reminder than a macabre afterthought.

"You might as well have taken out an ad in the paper on the attitude of the Johnson people toward the Kennedy people," said Larry O'Brien, amazed at the extent of LBJ's "absolute paranoia" toward anything Kennedy. O'Brien was a realist, not a loyalist (in Schlesinger's lexicon), but the rescheduling struck him like a slap. In his view, it was as if Johnson had said outright: "We're suspicious of you people; we know that if [we give] an inch, you're going to pull something." What surprised O'Brien most about the film's postponement was that it was so completely gratuitous. LBJ had pulled the curtains and exposed his own anxiety and desperate machinations.

The convention that began on August 24 was a Lyndon Johnson production, a masterpiece of political staging. "Let Us Continue," banners proclaimed. Enormous portraits above the dais placed LBJ in the pantheon of great Democratic presidents: Roosevelt, Truman, Kennedy, Johnson. LBJ's script of events was meticulous and his grip on security was white-knuckled and tight. "The reason," explained Ken O'Donnell,

> . . . was he was afraid that there were going to be busloads of people coming in from Philadelphia and New Jersey and they were going to stampede the convention for Bobby Kennedy for Vice President. . . . [Johnson] just lived in mortal fear of what was going to happen to him at that convention, so he orchestrated the whole [thing] and that was his total consumption.

Not all security personnel were recognizable as such. Aside from the usual discreet Secret Service contingent, Johnson had Hoover's FBI men at his disposal, and they were certainly not identifying themselves with badges or floor passes. Instead, they flashed bogus NBC press credentials and other forms of false identification. The undercover G-men were part of a special squad, the first ever sent to a party convention.

The request had come from the Oval Office. The president was concerned about potential "disturbances" at the convention—primarily by the Mississippi Freedom Democratic Party (MFDP), which planned a noisy challenge to the traditional (all-white, Jim Crow) Mississippi delegation, but also by Kennedy supporters. At the president's direction, Walter Jenkins called Deke DeLoach and asked the FBI to send a team to Atlantic City.

The agents swept into Atlantic City with a simple, broad directive: prevent any "embarrassment to the President." During the week, they provided Jenkins with forty-four pages of "intelligence data" while DeLoach "kept Jenkins and Moyers constantly advised by telephone of minute by minute developments," as he reported on August 29. A September 10 letter from DeLoach to Moyers revealed the coziness of the relationship between the FBI and the Johnson White House. "Dear 'Bishop,' " it began, a reference to Moyers's "ministerial background,"

> Thank you for your very thoughtful and generous note concerning our operation in Atlantic City. Please be assured that it was a pleasure and privilege to be able to be of assistance to the President. . . . I think that everything worked out well, and I'm certainly glad that we were able to come through with vital tidbits from time to time which were of assistance to you and Walter.

The tidbits were turned up by a variety of means, from infiltrating groups to wiretapping phones. Taps on the phone of Martin Luther King, Jr., helped the White House to anticipate the MFDP's every move. "The Agents," DeLoach reported, "were constantly alert to exploit opportunities for penetration of key dissident groups in Atlantic City and to suggest counter measures for any plans to disrupt the Convention."

It was hardly a stretch, given the overheated rhetoric of the past eight months, for the FBI or LBJ to consider Bobby-for-veep movements "dissident groups." A decade later, when a Senate subcommittee investigated the political abuses of and by the FBI, agents denied that Robert Kennedy had been a target of the squad's investigation in Atlantic City. Documents released to the subcommittee contained no mention of RFK. According to the Bureau, "allegations in the press that the coverage of the FBI was used to follow the activities of Attorney General Robert F. Kennedy were not substantiated in any way by file reviews." But the FBI's William Sullivan later testified that the special squad's hidden agenda was to collect information that might be helpful "particularly in bottling up Robert Kennedy—that is, in reporting on the activities of Bobby Kennedy."

Against the wishes of his aides, the irrepressible LBJ made an early appearance at the convention hall. On August 26 he personally announced his selection of Hubert Humphrey as a running mate. Urging delegates to second the nomination, Johnson told a cheering crowd, "This is not a sectional choice. This is not just merely the way to balance the ticket. This is simply the best man in America for this job." Soaking up the delegates' wild approval, LBJ returned to Washington.

Earlier that day, though, the president had been in the throes of depression. On the eve of his greatest triumph—his nomination by acclamation of the Democratic Convention—Lyndon Johnson sat alone in the Oval Office and drafted an announcement of his political retirement. The party, he said, could pick a different nominee, one it really wanted. "I assumed it would be Bobby Kennedy or Hubert Humphrey. They were the two most outstanding ones," Johnson recalled. His note made no reference to a particular successor but was shocking in its self-doubt:

> The times require leadership about which there is no doubt and a voice that men of all parties and men of all sections and men of all color can and will follow. I have learned after trying very hard that I am not that voice, or that leader. Therefore I shall carry forward with your help until the new President is sworn in next January, and then I will go back home as I've wanted to since the day I took this job.

There was some truth to the latter claim. A month into his presidency, Johnson and Pierre Salinger were floating in the White House pool when Johnson said suddenly, "You know, I'm not sure I want this job. Maybe I shouldn't be President." Salinger was stunned. After all, Johnson had seemed to want the job quite badly in 1956 and 1960. At this early stage, so soon after the assassination, Salinger was inclined to write off the president's misgivings. Johnson was in a terrible, unenviable position, but Salinger expected his doubts to pass.

Several months later, after hearing Johnson say "at least fifteen times how much he hated the White House, how much he'd rather be down on his ranch," Salinger finally came to believe it. Neither a seemingly endless succession of legislative victories nor astronomical approval ratings seemed enough to buoy the president's spirits for long. Every private conversation left Salinger more "convinced that if [Johnson] could have figured out a way not to run for president in 1964 without giving the nomination to Bob Kennedy . . . he would not have run."

The night before the convention it certainly seemed so. For two hours, LBJ paced the south lawn of the White House, trailed by the bushy-haired and beleaguered George Reedy, insisting he was going to quit the presidency. "He actually had me believing it for a while," Reedy recalled. He knew he was supposed to talk Johnson out of it; and though he made all the obvious points, they hardly seemed to register with LBJ. The president subjected Reedy to his standard monologue: "The whole world was against him; he was a Southerner. These Ivy League intellectuals were always going to consider him a cornball. Why should he mess around with all this bullshit, which is the way he put it in his milder moments. And then he'd go back to the ranch in Texas and say, 'Fuck 'em all.' "

In these moods—and they were frequent enough to be identified as moods, not momentary crises of faith—LBJ was terribly convincing. Reedy went home that night "in a nervous funk, thinking, 'My God, he's going up there tomorrow [to] resign; the convention will be thrown into chaos; Goldwater will be the next President.' . . . But I should have known better because ever since I knew him he was always quitting something; [yet] he would never quit." Later Reedy wondered about the point of the whole exercise, and decided it was a means of controlling other people—of making men (in this case, a crowd of anxious aides) beg for his leadership. Managing Johnson's personality, Reedy reflected, required "an incredible amount of service. Unbelievable."

At that job none was more experienced than Lady Bird Johnson. In response to Johnson's sorrowful note, she scribbled one of her own: "Beloved," she began ("And I knew the way she started off she didn't agree with me," LBJ said later),

> To step out now would be wrong for your country, and I can see nothing but a lonely wasteland for your future. Your friends would be frozen in embarrassed silence and your enemies would be jeering. I am not afraid of time or lies or defeat. In the final analysis I can't carry any of the burdens that you have talked of, so I know it's only your choice, but I know you're as brave as any of the thirty-five Presidents. I love you always. Bird.

"I took that and wrestled with it a great deal," Johnson later claimed. "As I often have, I took her judgment instead of mine." The flight back to Atlantic City was businesslike but celebratory; Dick Goodwin had never seen Johnson in a better mood. That night, August 27, LBJ exuberantly accepted the nomination of his party for a full term as president.

Before Lyndon Johnson's speech came Robert Kennedy's. The afternoon prior to his introduction of the film, Bobby drew cheers and dodged grasping hands as he went from hotel to hotel greeting Democrats who had worked for his brother in 1960. Standing on a chair in a hotel lobby and in the courtyard by the pool, he spoke to groups of two hundred and three hundred delegates. When asked repeatedly about Johnson's choice of Humphrey, Bobby gamely replied, "I think this is the strongest possible ticket—the best we could get." But mostly he seemed solemn and sad, even at a reception in his own honor. Bobby had little heart for the spotlight and even less for the much-feared "stampede" for the vice presidential nomination. He restrained John Seigenthaler, who was anxious to agitate on his behalf. It was pointless, Bobby told Seigenthaler, Johnson didn't want him. A demonstration, spontaneous or otherwise, would only mislead supporters about Kennedy's chances. "If something had happened, that would have been fine [with Kennedy]," judged Seigenthaler, "but it had to happen in the heart of Lyndon Johnson."

That was unlikely. Despite the watchfulness of the FBI and Bobby's absorption in the Senate race, Johnson was taking every precaution. The *New York Times* listed Larry O'Brien and Ken O'Donnell along with Johnson's key White House advisers—Jenkins, Moyers, Reedy, and Valenti—as residents of the Pageant Motel, just across the street from Convention Hall. O'Brien remembered it differently: he and O'Donnell were "in some motel somewhere as far removed [as possible] from what was transpiring in the convention [hall]." Whether this distance was literal or figurative, O'Brien and O'Donnell felt "absolutely isolated at that convention" because of their ties to Bobby and Johnson's fears of disruption. The last two remaining JFK advisers on LBJ's team sat laughing in their suite at the absurdity of it all—laughing because if they took it seriously, this questioning of their loyalty, "that would bother you." Their good humor vanished when O'Donnell—still a special assistant to the president of the United States—was temporarily and inexplicably denied entry to the convention floor.

Bobby's speech marked the first appearance by a Kennedy at LBJ's convention. Backstage, Bobby and John Seigenthaler sat in a small, dark dressing room. A friend stepped into the room to shake Bobby's hand. "Would you check on the program?" Bobby asked. "We can't hear anything back here. . . . I think Lyndon may just have put us back here with orders to forget us. They'll probably let us out the day after tomorrow," he joked. "We'll go out to find . . . that they announced I didn't show up to introduce the film." He sat back and reached into his pocket, producing a quote from *Romeo and Juliet,* something Jackie had recommended. He glanced at his brief address and scribbled a few changes.

On the platform, Scoop Jackson read a brief introduction: ". . . And now, it is my privilege and honor to introduce a man who stood closer to him"—President Kennedy—"in times of crisis and in times of fun, than anyone else—his brother, Robert Kennedy."

Then, recalled Seigenthaler, "it hit." As Bobby stepped timidly onto the dais, appearing a slight, black-clad figure amid a bombast of colored placards, delegates erupted in thundering, deafening applause. There was no cheering or parading, no one leaning on the background organ to manufacture a swell of support. There was only clapping: clapping from the galleries and on the floor, clapping everywhere in the cavernous hall. Bobby stood tentatively as it cascaded over him; he smiled wistfully, almost wincing, as if he were in physical pain. Tears welled in his eyes and he signaled repeatedly for the demonstration to end. "Mr. . . . Mr. Chairman . . ." he said meekly, and at every word applause erupted anew from another corner of the hall. Bobby, obviously touched, broke into an embarrassed grin and looked helplessly at Jackson, who put an arm around his shoulder. "Just let it go for a little bit, Bobby," Jackson told him. "Just let it go." Speaker John McCormack, the convention chairman, banged his gavel for silence.

For sixteen cathartic minutes the delegates applauded, sounding a terrific outpouring of grief, a desperate last gasp of the New Frontier. Finally, when the ovation subsided, Bobby thanked the delegates for their support of President Kennedy. Discarding most of his text, he spoke extemporaneously of his brother's accomplishments and urged, "the same efforts and the same energy and the same dedication that was given to President John F. Kennedy must be given to President Lyndon Johnson and Hubert Humphrey."

But the words that lingered longest in the public imagination were those from *Romeo and Juliet*. "When I think of President Kennedy," Bobby said, "I think of what Shakespeare said . . .

> " 'When he shall die
> Take him and cut him out in little stars
> And he will make the face of heaven so fine
> That all the world will be in love with night,
> And pay no worship to the garish sun.' "

The hall burst again into applause. In a hotel room off the boardwalk, O'Brien, O'Donnell, Salinger, and Dave Powers watched the proceedings on television and wept. Elsewhere, Johnson men chafed at Bobby's reference to the "garish sun." An obvious, petty jab, they said. It was just like Bobby.

After the twenty-minute film, as the lights in the hall were raised, Lyndon and Lady Bird Johnson entered the presidential box in which

Bobby and Ethel had watched the tribute. Delegates began to cheer; the organ began a rousing reprise of "Hello, Lyndon!" The president shook Bobby's hand. As Bobby and Ethel stepped to the back of the box, Johnson generously beckoned them forward. They sat at Lady Bird's side while the president, moments later, gave his acceptance speech. "Let us now turn to our task!" Johnson charged the convention hall crowd in a fervent thirty-five-minute speech. "Let us be on our way!"

As the red, white, and blue balloons fell on himself and Humphrey, LBJ should have felt both validated and relieved: as *Newsweek* observed, "the emotional storm loosed by the Attorney General's appearance— and by the film itself—vindicated Lyndon Johnson's canniness in having the documentary rescheduled. . . . Had the original schedule held fast, the impact on the convention might well have posed an unbeatable challenge." Instead, the Democrats in Atlantic City—*Johnson's* Democrats— displayed no discord, only a party at ease in power, with itself, and with its new leader.

Still, the applause for Bobby Kennedy must have echoed in Johnson's ears—sounding the opening fusillade in the battle for the soul of their party.

On September 3, 1964, Robert Kennedy resigned the post to which his brother had appointed him. "I leave with great pride in what has been accomplished by the dedicated and able staff of the Department of Justice," Bobby wrote the president. He praised "the effective continuity of leadership" under LBJ, noting that

> the Civil Rights Act, originally proposed by President Kennedy, was signed into law by you. . . .
> What has been true in the Department of Justice has been true of the whole of your Administration. Under your leadership, accomplishments of the last few years have already been consolidated and the Nation continues to move forward with confidence.
> I hope that by election to the Senate I can continue to be of service— to the State of New York, to the Nation and to the ideals and purposes to which President Kennedy was, and you are, so dedicated.

The president's candid reaction to Bobby's letter was not recorded. One cannot imagine he was pleased. The Civil Rights Act was doubtless an important example of "continuity," but Bobby's comment seems almost a dig at LBJ. Johnson, after all, had done far more than sign the bill into law; he had gone far beyond "consolidating" John Kennedy's gains. As flattery, Bobby's letter was thin and begrudging.

In response, LBJ took the high ground. His reply, written by Dick

Goodwin and Bill Moyers, was effusive, almost warm, addressing Kennedy not as "Mr. Attorney General" but as "Bob."

> It is with regret that I have received your resignation. You have played a very vital role in the conduct of public affairs.
>
> Both President Kennedy and I sought your counsel on a wide range of matters going far beyond the usual concerns of the Department of Justice. For four years you have shared in deliberations on major matters of national security, and your contributions have been significant. . . .
>
> My regret at your leaving is tempered by satisfaction in the knowledge that you intend to continue your service to your country. You will soon be back in Washington where I can again call upon your judgment and counsel.

Robert Kennedy's reaction is similarly lost. But after the past nine months he could not have put much stock in appeals to his future "counsel." His fate was still bound to Johnson's, but starting to diverge.

"He was in trouble from the beginning," said New York pol Jack English. Hounded by the carpetbagging charge, abandoned by many Reformers, and uneasy on the stump, Robert Kennedy faced a series of hurdles before the November election. His electoral experience had been as manager, not candidate, and aides thought him emotionally unprepared for the role. Among friends, Bobby had to admit he was not totally familiar with New York State. He radiated uncertainty; he lost his edge in the polls. Kennedy's strongest qualification, his government experience, seemed at times less a help than a hindrance. Having worked at the federal level for the past decade, Bobby was inclined to consider problems broadly, not parochially. Nor did he have much success conveying the scope or depth of his service as attorney general: his role during the Freedom Rides and the Cuban missile crisis, for example, went largely unacknowledged. Even university audiences just wanted to see a flesh-and-blood Kennedy.

The resulting campaign was confusing, a blur of nostalgia and caricature that was largely devoid of concrete issues. Yet Kennedy quickly gained back ground and confidence. For a novice candidate and newcomer to New York, he sparked an unprecedented emotional response, especially among the young. Lyndon Johnson might own John Kennedy's job, but Bobby claimed his emotional and political legacy. "They're for him," Bobby told Ed Guthman as they surveyed the yearning crowds, "they're for him." Critics accused Bobby of exploiting the Kennedy name. Even friends like Paul Corbin urged him to be something other than John Kennedy's brother. "Get out of this mysticism. Get out of your daze," Corbin scolded. "God damn, Bob, be yourself. . . . You're real. Your brother's dead." But Bobby *was* being himself—a man teetering uncertainly between past and present. And of his future, one thing was clear. If he wanted to become a United States senator he was going to need the help of LBJ.

Kennedy had to acknowledge what all political observers already knew: in 1964 the state of New York belonged to Lyndon Johnson. It had been ceded him early by Barry Goldwater, who made only one token appearance in the state that election year. "One wishes all campaigns could be that easy," sighed Edwin Weisl, Jr., director of the Democratic effort in New York. Johnson's deft handling of the transition and his aggressively liberal program had won him the universal acclaim of the state party hierarchy. In New York (as in most states), LBJ expected a big victory in November.

In the fall, while Johnson cruised toward a landslide win, Kennedy's poll numbers dipped beneath Keating's for the first time. Kennedy had been voicing support for Johnson at nearly every campaign stop, but more to tweak Keating than to display any real enthusiasm. "I know where I stand," Bobby would say. "I'm for Lyndon Johnson and I'm against Barry Goldwater and no other candidate can make that claim." But soon, as Republicans and even some Democrats reconciled themselves to voting Johnson-Keating, RFK found himself on the defensive. In the higher councils of his campaign the question became urgent: should Kennedy tie his fate more closely to Johnson's? "Winning as a part of a landslide victory by Lyndon Johnson . . . was the least desirable of all possible ways for him to win," recalled John Nolan of the Justice Department. Arthur Schlesinger did not doubt this, but frankness compelled him to warn Kennedy that "it is essential that you do everything you can to take advantage of the fact that Johnson will probably carry the state by 1.5 million votes."

Kennedy yielded to the inevitable. By September he began to clutch hesitantly for Johnson's coattails. References to Johnson and Humphrey crept into Kennedy campaign literature. Kennedy's old posters, featuring him in shirtsleeves and reading, "Let's Put Bob Kennedy to Work for New York," were scrapped for pictures of Kennedy in a business suit. The new slogan: "Get on the Johnson, Humphrey, Kennedy Team." One pamphlet showed a smiling Bobby receiving a pen from President Johnson after the signing of the poverty bill. "Remember how he worked with President Johnson to get justice for the poor and underprivileged?" it reminded voters. "That's how he'll work for New York."

It was just as well that there were no promises of working *together* for New York; the Johnson-Humphrey-Kennedy team was an uneasy alliance. "We were really ready . . . to run a coordinated campaign," insist-ed Jack English. "It didn't turn out that way." The best to be hoped for was mutual accommodation, a détente of sorts. Hubert Humphrey made three trips to New York to campaign for Bobby, praising his "great con-tributions to the Kennedy-Johnson Administration" and giving him a much-needed boost in liberal and Jewish circles. But the vice presiden-tial candidate did so in defiance of the White House staff. "Humphrey," judged Walter Mondale, also a Minnesota Democrat, "is pathologically opposed to personal hostilities."

The two men who bracketed Humphrey's name on the New York slate were not. Neither were their campaign workers. At Kennedy's headquarters the sign remained "Kennedy for Senate"; at Johnson's it read "Johnson-Humphrey." "People beat on the two of them sufficient-ly," recalled a Kennedy aide, "that finally . . . the signs went down and came up 'Johnson-Humphrey-Kennedy.' " Local congressmen were less pliable: wary of associating with a controversial newcomer, they stumped for Johnson and made no mention of Kennedy. RFK's campaign aide Bill Haddad implored him to find his own speakers.

Of course, some of Kennedy's strongest advocates were still in Johnson's employ. Schlesinger, out of the White House but still in Washington, wrote Bobby on October 9, "Dick Goodwin and Mike Feldman both want very much to help but are somewhat stymied by LBJ; LBJ called Feldman while he was at my office and, when Feldman advanced the thought of [Feldman] spending several days in New York, LBJ was most negative. Even when Mike suggested going there for sev-eral evenings, LBJ said he would have to think about it." Assistant Secretary of Labor Daniel Patrick Moynihan also "wants to do every-thing he possibly can," Schlesinger reported, and "will go to New York in the evenings, etc., regardless of what the White House thinks." The president granted Adlai Stevenson special dispensation to campaign for Bobby—but only, as Bill Moyers instructed, in a manner "consistent with your current duties and responsibilities."

Finances, like endorsements, raised tensions. Ed Weisl pushed for joint financing and made detailed arrangements with Steve Smith, but there was bickering between the two camps over campaign debts. Kennedy insisted that half the money raised by New York Democrats go to the state party, not to the national committee. "That made President Johnson very sore," recalled Nicholas Katzenbach. The DNC was saddled by debts from 1960, and if Johnson gave in to New York he would have to do so elsewhere. Yet he gave in. Backed by the state organization, Kennedy prevailed.

Despite these tentative steps, Bobby had made little progress in chang-ing public perceptions by mid-October. Bill Haddad told him a joke making the rounds in Brooklyn: "One kid said to another, 'I'm for Keating because he's for Johnson, but you don't know who Kennedy's for.' " Haddad recommended that Kennedy appeal directly to the president for joint television spots; Schlesinger pressed for the same.

No call was forthcoming. Kennedy refused to admit that LBJ was a critical factor in his election. Joint appearances, Bobby conceded, could only help, but he was not going to go begging for them.

As Lyndon Johnson planned a campaign trip to New York, aides tried to divine his intentions. In Larry O'Brien's view, the president was eager to widen his popular mandate—while establishing a record of being helpful to Kennedy. Ken O'Donnell saw it differently from his vantage point in the White House. Johnson, he said, "tried to shaft Bobby in every way" and "wanted Bobby dumped." Convinced of Johnson's secret agenda, O'Donnell installed a group of old Kennedy advance men as Johnson-Kennedy advance men in New York. Shrewdly, he also persuaded the president to schedule a second trip to New York:

> The President called me and said, "I don't want to go to Brooklyn again." I said, "I don't think you should go to Brooklyn again . . . because I think Bobby's much better off now alone. Did you see the latest *Daily News* poll?" "No, what?" I said, "It shows Bobby winning 56-57 per cent, and I think he's better off alone without you because people think you're drawing the crowd when it's really him." Silence at the other end of the phone. He said, "I think I'd better go through to Brooklyn." You bet your life he showed up at Brooklyn.

Whether or not Johnson was trying to "shaft Bobby" (and no evidence suggests that he was), there was an emerging rivalry between them that O'Donnell was quick to exploit. Even as allies Johnson and Kennedy were competitors. Kennedy needed Johnson as badly as he wished to prove he did not. Johnson agreed to help Kennedy, at the same time enjoying an opportunity to "rub it in" (as Harry McPherson put it) by reminding Bobby where the real power lay.

President Johnson made his triumphant appearance in New York on Wednesday, October 14. Unable to bear the ride from the airport alone with LBJ, Bobby beseeched the heavily pregnant Ethel to come along. Hoarse and exhausted from days of campaigning, a nonetheless ebullient LBJ stepped off the plane at 1:32 and grabbed Bobby's hand, patted him on the shoulder, and kissed Ethel. Johnson whisked the couple into a waiting limousine along with Mayor Wagner and Edwin Weisl, Sr., New York's national committeeman. Johnson talked animatedly to Bobby as the motorcade entered New York City.

Together they roared through Harlem behind a fleet of thirty police motorcycles. Though this was Johnson's first visit to a Northern ghetto, it hardly counted as a visit; the crowd of 2,500, packed onto the sidewalks between 123rd and 125th streets, was lucky to catch a glimpse of the waving president as he and his camp hurtled toward downtown. The *New York Times* declared Kennedy, "who stood the most to gain from being seen with the President, [as] the principal loser in the relatively poor exposure to the crowds."

Still, the message was cooperation, not competition. "President Johnson . . . threw his arm, literally and figuratively, around the Democratic candidate for the Senate, Robert F. Kennedy," reported the *Times*. Ensconced in the president's thirty-fifth floor suite at the Waldorf-Astoria, Johnson and Kennedy met privately for an hour—while aides touted the meeting as proof of their great friendship. Later, at a solo press conference at the Carlyle, Bobby denied that a rift had developed since his elimination as a vice presidential candidate. In response to a question, Bobby described his relationship with the president as "very close, very warm." Of newspaper reports that indicated otherwise, Bobby said, "maybe they were written in the hope it would come true."

That evening, LBJ called Bobby at the Carlyle and asked for his company on a surprise visit to Jacqueline Kennedy. Bobby walked the half block to the corner of Park Avenue and 76th Street, where the president's limousine picked him up with little fanfare. Their ride to Jackie's was as discreet as their Harlem motorcade had been flashy. LBJ could not be seen as crassly capitalizing on the company of John Kennedy's widow; and Bobby, surely, would not permit it. After the short drive they spent a quiet, pleasant half hour with Jackie in her new Fifth Avenue apartment before departing for the Alfred E. Smith Memorial Dinner. The president spoke briefly about Soviet-American relations until his voice and strength gave out around midnight. He cut his speech short and referred reporters to his written statement.

The Johnson-Kennedy blitzkrieg began the next morning at 9:00 at La Guardia Field, from which the two men, joined by Ethel, Wagner, Averell Harriman, and state Democratic chairman William H. McKeon flew to Rochester and Buffalo. All day, said the *Times*, LBJ and Bobby were "as close as twins." They seemed comfortable, even content, in each other's company as they rode, flew, and stumped together from morning until midnight. The two men seemed determined to quell rumors of a feud. At one rally, Johnson announced in a voice raw and husky, "You don't often find a man who has the understanding, the heart and the compassion that Bobby Kennedy has." Bobby, in Rochester, went so far as to declare Johnson "already one of the great Presidents of the United States. . . . I think of President Johnson with affection and admiration."

In Buffalo that afternoon, Johnson impulsively grabbed Bobby's right arm and thrust it upward in a victory gesture, drawing an appreciative roar from the Niagara Square crowd of more than fifty thousand.

Later they drove through Brooklyn to Albee Square, where the president conducted an exuberant street-corner rally. "The United States needs a young, dynamic, compassionate, fighting liberal representing New York in the United States Senate: Bob Kennedy," he told the crowd. "His knowledge of housing, his knowledge of slum clearance, his knowledge in fighting crime, his knowledge in education, his knowledge in bringing peace to the world is what Brooklyn needs voting in the United States Senate."

"What about the Brooklyn Navy Yard?" someone shouted.

"That's another reason you need him," said Johnson, laughing and gesturing. "He's already been down there talking about this Navy Yard so much that I'm going to have to get an earphone!"

The press remained skeptical; reporters distilled a bitter elixir from this great gushing of goodwill. "Mr. Kennedy," noted Layhmond Robinson of the *Times*, "signed at least as many autographs and shook as many hands as the President" and drew just as much applause. But "sometimes," Robinson added, "the surging mobs seemed to be more excited by the 38-year-old former Attorney General . . . than by the President." At the Rochester and New York City airports and along the thirty-mile parade route in Brooklyn, chants of " 'We Want Bobby' . . . almost drowned out the fervid cries of 'We Want Johnson' and 'All the Way with LBJ.' " And while the president drew "mature men and women" in swarms around him, Kennedy seemed to attract mostly "teenage girls" and women in their twenties.

Johnson returned to New York on October 31, the last Sunday before the election. Just after 3:00 he bounded down the ramp of Air Force One to the tarmac at the Republic Aircraft Corporation airport. He was greeted by Bobby and Ethel, for whom he had another vigorous handshake and kiss on the cheek, respectively, and by Averell Harriman and Eugene Nickerson, the Nassau County executive. LBJ and Lady Bird ushered the group into the presidential bubbletop limousine, which sped through Suffolk and Nassau counties. As many as 150,000 people lined the sixteen-mile route. President Johnson, waving perfunctorily out the window with his right hand, held in his left the latest poll results and read them aloud to his companions. He expressed alarm at any state poll awarding him less than a sixteen-point lead. Johnson also voiced concern, as they sped toward New York City, that Goldwater was going to "pull something" at the last minute—something like the Jenkins affair.

Only two weeks earlier, during LBJ's first visit to New York, the Republican National Committee had tipped off reporters to the October 7 arrest of Walter Jenkins—LBJ's most trusted aide for a quarter century—for "indecent gestures" in a Washington YMCA locker room. After a brief tempest the scandal had passed, but LBJ had not forgotten. Now, under the safe shield of his bubbletop, LBJ wielded a statement linking Jenkins to the opposition: Barry Goldwater had been Jenkins's commanding officer in the Air Force Reserve. Johnson, with an arched eyebrow, left the rest to the imagination. His insinuation—though totally unfounded—was clear enough.

The FBI, which had tried (at Johnson's request) and failed to contain the Jenkins affair, was apparently proving useful in other regards. Johnson sat up the night of October 30 reading stacks of "raw" FBI files on prominent Republicans; he had also requested background checks on Goldwater's campaign staff. In the limo the next day he excitedly described his discoveries, each one explosive (and probably suspect). The former attorney general did not share in Johnson's wonderment. "It was the *same* material that I had had a year or 14 months ago," Bobby said later. Johnson was eager to leak it to the press. "I said that I didn't think that he should do that," Kennedy recalled. It reminded him of the Baker case: "Every time I have any conversation in which there's any attack on Bobby Baker, the response always is, 'We should bring this out about such-and-such a senator.' . . . Lyndon talks about that information and material so freely."

This time, though, Johnson's indiscretion invited not disdain but "some joshing," as Nickerson recalled. The president, fixated on his sheaf of innuendo, repeated Hoover's adage that one could spot a homosexual by the way he walked. "Well," Bobby asked Johnson, "does that mean you'll watch the cabinet carefully as they walk into cabinet meetings?" Everyone laughed, including the president. The ride was remarkably free of tension. "One thing I can assure you of, Mr. President," Bobby said, grinning, "it isn't me."

Johnson deposited Kennedy in Belmont Park that afternoon for the first of three rallies in which he substituted for the president. The surging crowds were slowing both candidates' progress; LBJ was waylaid further by news of a Vietcong strike on an American airbase outside Saigon. After a series of urgent conferences at the Waldorf-Astoria, Johnson rejoined Kennedy for an enormous nighttime rally at Madison Square Garden. To Johnson, already favored to win New York by more than 1.5 million votes, the rally might have seemed overkill. Still, it was an important favor to RFK, who had inched back above Keating in the polls but needed the boost only Johnson could give him. After being entertained by Gregory Peck, Tony Bennett, Connie Francis, and a group called the LBJ Chorale, the crowd of eighteen thousand in the Garden heard the president praise Bobby Kennedy's patriotism, energy, and talents—demonstrated in "ways and actions that are far beyond my inadequate descriptions."

The mere mention of Bobby's name brought bursts of applause and showers of confetti from the Garden floor. And Bobby, matching their enthusiasm, told the crowd that "New York State is going to give President Johnson the largest majority any President has ever received from any state in the history of the United States!"

Kennedy surely hoped so. It might be his only route to victory. As James Farley, Democratic national chairman during FDR's first two presidential campaigns, predicted earlier that day, the bigger Johnson's margin, the more likely "Kennedy will win on the Johnson slide."

Election day, November 3, 1964. Watching the returns in hotel suites thousands of miles apart, Lyndon Johnson and Robert Kennedy saw both predictions come true.

President Johnson captured New York by a margin of 2.5 million—the greatest majority in any state, in any election. It was only part, though, of his crushing, debilitating defeat of Barry Goldwater. The president collected 486 electoral votes to Goldwater's 52 and won all but six states, a popular mandate of which even LBJ had dared not dream.

Robert Kennedy ran far behind Johnson—few did not—but won the Senate race handily, by 719,693 votes. Kennedy's margin of victory was almost twice what he and his advisers had expected. Like Johnson's, it was a landmark, if less profound: Kennedy's was the greatest victory by a Democratic senator or governor in New York since 1938, and this despite a million split tickets for Johnson-Keating.

On the penultimate day of the campaign, on his last trip upstate, Bobby had slumped in the tan leather seat of his family plane, the *Caroline,* and mused about campaign tactics with a reporter. Kennedy was relaxed and uncommonly talkative. The two biggest boosts to his campaign, he said, were his own television ads and Keating's debate blunders. "The TV spots showed that I was something more than a Beatle," Kennedy said. Thinking twice about his candor, Bobby asked that the interview be published only *after* the election.

There were other factors, of course, in the victory that followed—Kennedy's tight campaign organization, his relentless drubbing of Keating's record, and the strong black vote. But there were more important debts that Bobby failed to acknowledge. To many observers, the most crucial element in the Kennedy victory was Lyndon Baines

Johnson. In its first reference to Kennedy on election day, the *New York Times* portrayed Bobby "riding Mr. Johnson's long coattails."

It was unclear whether Kennedy could have won without them, and the question mattered little now. At New York's Statler Hilton Hotel on election night, fifteen hundred Kennedy campaign workers were more interested in catching a glimpse of the senator-elect. The mood in the ballroom was jubilant, even raucous, as eager young volunteers pressed up against the platform, nearly smothering a small girl. Color portraits of RFK flashed on giant screens across the room. ("Repeatedly it seemed as though a halo surrounded his head," observed a reporter, "rays streaming dashed lines of light down upon him and again out from his brow." Democratic officials insisted it was an accidental by-product of high magnification and television floodlights.) Behind the podium loomed an enormous photograph of Bobby shaking hands with LBJ—the relic of a brief but productive partnership.

In the midst of the madness, the "screaming, triumphant adulation," as one reporter put it, the object of all this affection seemed oddly untouched by it. "If my brother was alive," Bobby told a friend, "I wouldn't be here. I'd rather have it that way." And when he stepped onto the dais at 1:22 A.M., flanked by his family and aides, Kennedy declared his victory an "overwhelming mandate" of his brother's policies. But this was not a moment for looking only backward. The senator-elect was braced for the tasks "of education, of housing, of helping our elderly people, of bringing up our young people in the right kind of society." He quoted Tennyson, as he had so often during the campaign:

> "Come, my friends,
> 'Tis not too late to seek a newer world."

And then, a brief nod—and perhaps a veiled warning—to the president. The resounding Democratic victory, said Bobby, "was a mandate to continue what we started four years ago and it was a great vote of confidence for President Johnson and Hubert Humphrey."

Bobby thanked his family and supporters. He thanked Averell and Marie Harriman, Mayor Robert Wagner of New York, and Mayor John Burns of Binghamton. He thanked state party chairman Billy McKeon, campaign director R. Peter Strauss and his wife Ellen, and thanked Stephen Smith for labor "far beyond the effort one brother-in-law gives to another brother-in-law." Bobby thanked his volunteers, waved good night, and retreated to his suite. He did not thank Lyndon Johnson.

At Austin's Driskill Hotel, where the president watched Bobby's televised speech, it seemed a pointed omission. "Bobby thanked the postmasters, he thanked the precinct captains, he thanked every two-bit person who helped in the campaign," recalled Liz Carpenter, who sat beside LBJ. "But he didn't thank the President of the United States. He just couldn't choke it out of himself." Jack Valenti kept his eye on the president as Bobby recited his litany of thank-yous. Johnson's facial expression never changed, but there was a "vacancy"; to a close observer like Valenti, LBJ's silence spoke volumes. A landslide victory had made him "legitimate" at last, his own man; but he would never, it seemed, win Bobby Kennedy's approval.

"This is more than a victory of party or person," Johnson told the crowd at Austin Municipal Stadium later that night. "It is a tribute to the program that was begun by our beloved President John F. Kennedy." The Democrats' triumph, he said, was "a mandate for unity, for a Government that serves no special interest. . . . Our nation should forget our petty differences and stand united before all the world."

For Johnson and Bobby Kennedy, a shared victory offered the same opportunity. Yet as the two men settled into their distant suites for an hour of sleep, one could not but feel that a very small window had been slammed shut.

A week later, back in a White House he could begin finally to call his own, Lyndon Johnson had not forgotten petty differences. He was settling scores. The smear campaign against Republicans, a brief flight of fantasy, had never materialized; RFK was right to laugh it off. But Kennedy might have laughed less heartily had he known that in the first week after the election, President Johnson would direct the FBI's attention toward Bobby's top aides—not for suspicion of homosexuality, but for disloyalty.

Only a month earlier, Joe Dolan was still in Washington. The assistant deputy attorney general was waiting impatiently for Bobby's invitation to campaign in New York. "I was very mad at him," recalled Dolan, whose offers to help had gone unanswered. He sat and stewed at the Justice Department until the last few weeks of the campaign. Then, late one night, Bobby returned from four rallies in Brooklyn, where he had not seen a single Kennedy leaflet. "Call Joe Dolan and see if he'll come up here," Bobby ordered Ed Guthman.

Guthman called Dolan at 6:00 the next morning; at 7:30, Dolan was on the first flight to New York. From a pay telephone at La Guardia, Dolan called Acting Attorney General Nicholas Katzenbach. "I'm in New York, Nick, and I'm not coming back until after the election." But Dolan did hope to come back; Kennedy had not offered him a permanent job, and Dolan had no reason to expect one was imminent.

Thinking of his two children, thinking of his mortgage, Dolan asked Katzenbach not to replace him. "I'll try," promised Katzenbach.

Like Dolan, a handful of senior assistants left posts at the Justice Department to work for Kennedy's Senate campaign. These were not cabinet members; their departures did not make the papers, and they too hoped to return quietly. But only a week after his stunning vindication at the polls, LBJ closed down the revolving door and changed the locks. He ordered J. Edgar Hoover to find and blacklist any defectors. On November 13, after a conversation with LBJ, Deke DeLoach wrote the director:

> The President stated that he had previously talked with the Director about the fact that the Department of Justice was re-employing a number of individuals who had worked on the Bobby Kennedy campaign. The President asked how many of this number had been re-employed. I told him I knew of only a few; however, a discreet check would be made. . . . He stated he would like to know as soon as possible. He then asked if these people had been reinvestigated. I told him no such requests for reinvestigations had been made. . . . He stated that the re-employment of these people could prove very embarrassing to the Administration and that after he gets the facts from the FBI he plans to raise hell with Katzenbach regarding this matter.

DeLoach had assured the president that the Bureau would look into the career plans of "these people" and "pass this information on to Moyers or Valenti so that nothing will be written in this regard." Under normal circumstances, "discreet checks" like this were handled by a White House assistant and a departmental personnel office. These were not normal circumstances. The Justice Department was tainted irredeemably; anyone who had worked for, or even with, Bobby Kennedy was not to be trusted. Only Hoover could be expected to place the president's best interests above RFK's. Hoover quickly engaged the IRS in a probe of Dolan and the others and sent the results to Johnson's desk.

It was already too late. Dolan had outmaneuvered LBJ by returning the day of the November election and slipping his name back onto the payroll. It was an auspicious move: Dolan's quick thinking saved his job (though Bobby soon hired him as administrative assistant). The others, less fleet-footed, were out of luck. On November 20, LBJ called Katzenbach and told him that Dolan could remain but, as an FBI memo explained, "none of the other individuals who had left the Department to assist Robert F. Kennedy . . . should be re-employed."

Now that Johnson's tenure was secure, he could begin purging his administration of Bobby's influence. The task would never be complete, in Johnson's view, but he could at least begin.

CHAPTER 9

"Little Potshots"

When Robert Kennedy entered the United States Senate in January 1965 he was already impatient. He had little love for the Senate; it was, he said, a hell of a place to get anything done. It was a deliberative body, and though Bobby Kennedy was a deliberative man he was always rather quick about it: target the problem, consult this man and read that report, craft a solution, get it done. He had been spoiled by the rapidly deployed power of the executive branch, by its speed and autonomy. The Senate Foreign Relations Committee was not the ExComm, that much was certain. The slowly churning machinery of the Congress frustrated him and filled him with dread.

Then there were the unwritten rules of etiquette and deference that govern behavior in the Senate. In a system built on seniority, freshmen do not assert themselves; they sit quietly in the back of the chamber, doomed to irrelevance and reluctant silence as the thrill of their recent victories rapidly wanes. Impotence or impudence: those were Bobby Kennedy's options in his first months as senator, and if he was inclined by nature to choose the latter, political prudence held him back. From the beginning, RFK was "conscious of the fact that people were watching him, and that he shouldn't be tagged as unduly brash," observed Peter Edelman, Kennedy's young and somewhat brash legislative assistant. Kennedy was intent upon starting quietly in the Senate; he was in no hurry to make a maiden speech. Dissent was an even dicier prospect: one hint of dissatisfaction and reporters would be calling the Senate a new arena in the Kennedy-Johnson feud.

"He was feeling his way in the Senate," said Edelman, and Kennedy's ever-present black tie revealed a man still in mourning, a man still "in that post–November-'63 funk." Kennedy was not given to introspective musings, but Adam Walinsky, Kennedy's other young assistant (more cocky and combative than Edelman and equally brilliant and hardworking) sensed immediately his sadness and loss—"that streak of fatalism, acceptance . . . and that curious detachment about his own career and his own future." In a shrug or sad smile he let Walinsky know that "whatever [Kennedy] attained for himself, whether he got to be president or not, it was the most fun and the [most right] before, when John Kennedy had been president; and that he would never be that young again, that he would never have that kind of joy again." How bleak it all seemed in the twilight of the New Frontier.

Yet there were few fears, and little pretense, that Bobby Kennedy was going to be a quiet or even an ordinary freshman senator. As the self-proclaimed head of "the Kennedy wing of the Democratic party," Bobby was anxious to assume a position of substantive leadership. Walinsky expressed the same expectation in a memo of November 7, 1964—four days after Kennedy's election. In crafting a legislative strategy for the new senator, Walinsky foresaw the challenge inherent in LBJ's own package of programs: "Since last January," Walinsky informed Kennedy,

> the President has had high-level confidential study groups drawing blueprints for his "Great Society." . . . Early reports I saw in Washington indicated that the programs to be proposed by the groups would be comprehensive, forward-looking, and highly imaginative.
>
> If the President incorporates these recommendations into proposed bills, it will be relatively difficult for you to establish a reputation as an individual leader for progressive legislation.

Walinsky sketched out several lines of approach. First, Kennedy could support Johnson's program unequivocally, taking a backseat to Senate powers and committee chairmen but traveling around the country as the Great Society's greatest exponent. "You might thus gain both considerable national exposure and solidify your relations with the President," Walinsky suggested, a bit naively. Kennedy's alternative was to present his own legislative solutions and fight to incorporate them into LBJ's final program. Successful amendments—particularly those meeting the needs of New York State—"would be a significant accomplishment," wrote Walinsky. Relatedly, he thought it crucial that RFK be a catalyst in implementing programs, since poor local and private coordination meant that "much federal assistance now goes to waste." In these ways Kennedy could make Johnson's Great Society partly his own. "A possible drawback," cautioned Walinsky, ". . . is that failure to achieve incorporation might be seized upon by others as evidence of rejection by the President." And there was danger in overreaching: "Your more forward-looking programs would then be taken as a challenge to the President's leadership," Walinsky warned Kennedy. "I assume that such a challenge would now be premature."

Clearly, the parameters of Bobby Kennedy's legislative game were being defined by President Johnson. In this Kennedy was not alone: LBJ in 1965 dominated Congress like no one since—well, since LBJ in the 1950s. The congressional agenda was entirely his own—Johnson's Great Society, a vision he laid out in a speech at Ann Arbor, Michigan, on May 22, 1964. "The Great Society," Johnson explained,

> rests on abundance and liberty for all. It demands an end to poverty and racial injustice. . . . The Great Society is a place where every child can find knowledge to enrich his mind and to enlarge his talents . . . where the city of man serves not only the needs of the body and the demands of commerce but the desire for beauty and the hunger for community. . . . It is a place where men are more concerned with the quality of their goals than the quantity of their goods.

It was almost utopian, this vision, even if it did not seem so in 1965; the Great Society was not only a manifestation of the personality of Lyndon Johnson but an expression of the national will, a collective hubris mutually reinforced. "Lyndon," observed Lady Bird, "believes that anything can be solved, and quickly." And the public, milk-fed on the postwar liberal ideology of plenty and still buoyed by an economic boom and skyrocketing sales, profits, and wages, did not doubt it. In 1964, voters had given Johnson an unprecedented mandate and an enormous congressional majority (295 Democrats in the 435-member House). The result was the most incredible profusion of legislation in the history of the republic. The breadth of Johnson's agenda was staggering, as was his ambition—to fulfill the legacy of the New Deal and then to outdo it, to do more good for more people than Roosevelt or any other president ever had. The Great Society codified Johnson's grandiose compassion, promising something for everyone: by Doris Kearns's count, there was

> Medicare for the old, educational assistance for the young, tax rebates for business, a higher minimum wage for labor, subsidies for farmers, vocational training for the unskilled, food for the hungry, housing for the homeless, poverty grants for the poor, clean highways for commuters, legal protection for blacks, improved schooling for the Indians, rehabilitation for the lame, higher benefits for the unemployed, reduced quotas for the immigrants, auto safety for drivers, pensions for the retired, fair labeling for consumers, conservation for the hikers and the campers, and more and more and more.

The columnist James Reston quipped that Johnson was "getting every-thing through the Congress but the abolition of the Republican party, and he hasn't tried that yet."

Members of Congress were so overwhelmed Johnson might well have slipped it past them. In a typical year the White House transmits one or two dozen presidential messages to Congress; between January and August 1965, LBJ delivered sixty-five expansive requests for action. "If you're not doing it to them, they're doing it to you," he told an aide, and this was the heart of Johnson's congressional strategy: keep them busy. Two or three big proposals were not enough to occupy potential trou-blemakers (and they were all potential troublemakers); Johnson con-sumed the agendas of even the smallest subcommittees. The president knew his political capital would not last and he acted quickly and relent-lessly to spend it. "You've got to give it all you can, that first year," he lectured Harry McPherson. "Doesn't matter what kind of majority you come in with. You've got just one year when they treat you right, and before they start worrying about themselves."

It was as if, in the 1950s, Majority Leader Johnson had staged a coup, deposed President Eisenhower, and ruled both branches of government. LBJ was more prime minister than president, and many observers made reference to the parliamentary system in which both branches—execu-tive and legislative—propose, and both dispose. "There is but one way for a President to deal with the Congress," Johnson later explained, "and that is continuously, incessantly, and without interruption. If it's really going to work, the relationship between the President and the Congress has got to be almost incestuous. He's got to know them even better than they know themselves."

As always, this knowledge came instinctively to Johnson. He was, after all, only five years removed from his Senate leadership; most of the major players remained the same, and freshmen were automatically loyal to a president who had swept them so generously into office on his long coattails. Johnson kept the rest in line by his constant, attentive presence on the Hill—both by telephone and in person, at weekly working breakfasts where congressional leaders munched on eggs, homemade bread, and deer sausage from the LBJ Ranch and watched, stupefied, as President Johnson pointed at charts and plotted a bill's progress from "cradle to grave."

Johnson had done well completing the Kennedy agenda in 1964, gaining approval for 58 percent of his proposals. In 1965, Johnson did even better passing his own: a stunning 69 percent. (Eisenhower, after a landslide reelection, achieved only 37 percent in 1957.) White House aides began to wonder whether they were running out of laws. But with every achievement, Johnson grew more anxious his consensus would erode. The rapid succession of Johnson's "Big Four" measures—aid to education, Medicare and Medicaid, immigration reform, and voting rights—left Congress exhausted, but Johnson, determined to extract every last concession, only pushed harder. If his margins of victory were not razor-thin, then Johnson had not pushed hard enough, had not demanded enough.

Maximum output in minimum time was the White House strategy. Doris Kearns called it the "politics of haste," and its measure of success was passing a law, not solving a problem. Johnson's endless task forces—135 of them, by 1968—could not even agree on what those problems were, and the administration dodged fundamental questions that could take years to answer or even to frame. Thus the core strategy of the Great Society became its central flaw. Johnson, denying this, described himself as a farmer madly sowing seeds; later, he argued, there would be time to cultivate and time to reap.

Johnson's real anxiety was political. He had done more for the liberal cause than any other president had—far more, certainly, than John Kennedy. But Johnson felt unappreciated, unloved by the people. Liberals and Northeasterners still scorned him, mocked his accent, and questioned his sincerity—or so Johnson imagined. "I always knew that the greatest bigots in the world lived in the East, not the South," he said later. "Economic bigots, social bigots, society bigots. Whatever I did, they were bound to think it was some kind of trick. How could some politician from Johnson City do what was right for the country?"

Johnson was one of the few who doubted it. Throughout the country there was, in that first year or two, what Dick Goodwin called "an almost universal suspension of disbelief," and even LBJ had to pause occasionally and revel in the praise. He showered himself in glowing newspaper and magazine articles, reading them aloud to his aides: "Now just listen to this," he would say, picking up one clipping after another. But this, too, reflected the president's monumental insecurity. He allowed the imagined jibes of "bigots" to sully his impossibly massive accomplishments. "It didn't really seem to matter to Johnson that he had won his place in the pantheon of successful presidents by mid-1965, when you would have thought he'd have been so self-confident," reflected Harry McPherson. "It was a sensational performance for more than two years, but always dogged by Vietnam, and always dogged by a fear and loathing of Bobby Kennedy."

Johnson's loathing was easy to explain, but for once his fear seemed misplaced. Bobby Kennedy, in 1965, was a freshman senator just scrambling to keep pace with LBJ, to catch up with the presidential messages that seemed, to Peter Edelman, to arrive daily. "What a crazy time that was!" recalled Adam Walinsky. "I mean, we were going to reshape American society, all of us! There was a new bill every day." Kennedy had his own legislative agenda, one he set for himself in the 1964 campaign—"left-overs . . . good-government, liberal-type amendments," Walinsky called them. But RFK's was an amendments-only strategy; no junior senator, not even a Kennedy, expects in his first months in office to propose any-thing huge or historic. The Great Society was like a speeding train, and rather than build, foolishly, an alternate engine, Kennedy hoped to tack his own car onto Johnson's. It was not in Kennedy's nature to be a rider, but "what could he do?" shrugged Walinsky.

The Johnson-Kennedy policy relationship was defined early, in Bobby's first week as senator. The administration's Appalachian regional development bill was pending, and there was no time for Kennedy to ask fundamental questions. There was barely time to ask the more pressing question, "What can we do for New York?" Building on old contacts and relationships, Kennedy amended the bill to include the thirteen south-ern-tier counties of New York State which had the same geographic and economic conditions as the Appalachian counties Johnson was targeting for assistance. By that point, Edelman recalled, the deal was being cut on the Hill, so "it didn't matter what the administration said." Kennedy was always fearful that Johnson would undercut him simply because of their past relationship, but in this case Johnson did not. It was Robert Kennedy's first legislative success.

"The president proposes, the Congress disposes"—even though Johnson had blurred the distinction, Kennedy seemed destined to be a bit player in the Great Society. Kennedy cosponsored the important Immigration Act, which he had drafted as attorney general and which abolished the invidious system of ethnic quotas dating back to the 1920s. When Johnson delivered his stirring "We Shall Overcome" speech to Congress in March and called for a voting rights act, an admiring Kennedy told a friend, "He's got some guts." But as Johnson shepherd-ed his historic bill through the Senate he neglected Kennedy, leaving him hurt and, said Walinsky, "somewhat miffed." Kennedy passed an amendment to abolish literacy tests in Puerto Rico, but this was hardly earthshaking legislation.

Kennedy made a more significant contribution to LBJ's landmark Elementary and Secondary Education Act. Johnson cleverly framed his education bill as an antipoverty program, allocating $1 billion to improv-ing the lot of poor students. It was a deep honey pot, with a little some-thing for almost everyone—90 percent of the nation's school districts

and 95 percent of its counties. The ESEA, unsurprisingly, passed with
minimal debate. On April 11, 1965, a triumphant LBJ traveled to his old
one-room schoolhouse in Stonewall, Texas, and signed the bill with his
first teacher, "Miss Kate" Deadrich, by his side. "No law I have signed or
will sign means more to the future of America," Johnson declared.

This legislative strategy, Walinsky recalled with scorn, was classic
Johnson: "You started with a base of support and then you bought everybody else. You just kept adding the dollars into the programs until you
convinced people it was in their interest to buy in." With $1 billion, LBJ
"bought all the educators, and bought all the teachers' unions, and
bought all the businessmen who hoped to sell fortunes in equipment to
the schools." But Walinsky's judgment was the product of hindsight. At
the time, Kennedy's first question was—as it had to be—what to do for
New York. During that spring of 1965, as the bill sailed through
Congress, RFK was besieged by state school administrators eager for
federal cash. "Well, what are you going to do with it?" Bobby asked
them. He was deeply concerned by their inability to answer. He worried
they would ignore the interests of the poor when spending ESEA appropriations.

Soon there was creeping doubt of a more fundamental kind: Kennedy
began to question Johnson's premise that more money meant better
education. As administrators and experts paraded before his committee,
testifying to the benefits of federal largess, Kennedy questioned them
about standards—for students and teachers, for schools and progress.
"Nobody," recalled Walinsky, "had any answers."

"What is an educationally deprived child?" Bobby asked Education
Commissioner Francis Keppel, a former Harvard dean, at the hearings.
What, moreover, was the wisdom of giving local districts primary
responsibility for conceiving and conducting the programs? Were local
school districts themselves not part of the problem? "I am sorry to say
that is true," Keppel conceded. Kennedy pressed him: if Congress poured
funds "into a school system which itself creates this problem, or helps
create it, or does nothing, very little to alleviate it, are we not just in fact
wasting the money of the Federal Government . . . ?" Keppel assured him
educators were evincing "a rapid change in attitude." He did not explain
that program control was the price of local districts' support; without it,
they would never allow the bill to pass.

Kennedy's substantive badgering was an affront to Lyndon Johnson's
legislative strategy: pass now, ask questions later. And when Johnson
demanded that the Senate pass his bill without amendment, Kennedy
called Keppel, a rare, friendly voice in the administration. Together they
crafted an evaluation procedure—providing for the comprehensive test-

ing of disadvantaged students before and after the program to see whether the money had made a difference. "That," said Walinsky, "was as much as we could hope for." Rather than bog down the bill in the Senate, Keppel's staff fed Kennedy's amendments to members of the House, where they passed easily.

On Medicare, three months later, the picture was the same: again, an urgent need exacerbated by decades of inaction, a ringing presidential challenge, and a rush of well-funded legislation. And again, Kennedy was caught between nebulous doubts and very clear responsibilities to New York State. As the bill passed through Congress it was rewritten and expanded dramatically. Medicaid—coverage for the poor, by an enormous extension of the welfare system—was tacked on almost as an afterthought. Its premise, like ESEA's, was "classic Johnson": more money equals more, or better, health. There were no real controls on the new entitlements. The projected cost of Medicare alone in its first year was $6.5 billion.

Bobby Kennedy did nothing to impede the bill's march through the Senate; it was hard enough, amid the clamor for more and bigger benefits, simply to ask questions. Friendly doctors in New York fed his suspicion that federal expenditures of this magnitude would unbalance the whole health care system. Kennedy called John Gardner, Johnson's secretary of health, education, and welfare, and set up a meeting with Gardner, Assistant Secretary Wilbur Cohen, and several public health care providers from New York. They gathered in a conference room at HEW. According to Walinsky, who accompanied RFK to the meeting, Cohen chided the doctors: "No, no, you don't understand. This year you just get the *program*. Next year you get controls."

Walinsky left the meeting feeling vaguely unsettled. "Of course," he said later, "I was too naive and too young and stupid at the time to understand that if there had been controls, there never would have been a Medicare program." It was in fact this unregulated, "direct transfusion from the taxpayers' aorta that was going to get that program through." Kennedy, meanwhile, tapped right into that aorta, diverting as much of the flow as possible to New York. And in doing so, Walinsky concluded sadly, "we helped to generate the insanity of New York's Medicare and Medicaid policy, which is to offer more lavish services than any other state." Kennedy was hewing to Johnson's standards.

Later that year RFK inched toward independence, but again the direction was not really his own. At Peter Edelman's initiative, Kennedy and his colleague from New York, Jacob Javits, rushed to introduce narcotics legislation before the administration did the same. "That was why we were in such a hurry," said Edelman. "We were very much under the gun to beat the Administration." But it was still an amendments-only game: Kennedy hoped to amend Johnson's bill, not to pass his own, and by a preemptive strike Bobby sought greater leverage and greater credit. In seeking to fund treatment facilities for drug addicts, Kennedy's politics of haste led instead to a petty turf war with the Department of Justice. "His pals were still in there," said Edelman, who also had a few pals left in the department, and they had given Kennedy's staff a peek at the administration's bill; now they accused Edelman of legislative thievery. (In fact, both bills were based in part on an earlier bill of Kenneth Keating's.) Kennedy testified for the narcotics addiction rehabilitation bill in 1965 and early 1966, but it was snared by internal jurisdictional battles in Congress until October 1966. By then Kennedy was busy on the hustings, stumping for fellow Democrats.

Robert Kennedy's greatest contribution to the Great Society was not an amendment but the concept of community action. Unfortunately, the Community Action Program—the centerpiece of LBJ's war on poverty—was a failure from the beginning. The heart of the problem was a clause inserted into the poverty bill by Dick Boone, one of Kennedy's "guerrillas" on the President's Committee on Juvenile Delinquency, requiring the "maximum feasible participation" of the poor in local community action agencies (CAAs). In the mad melee of drafting the bill, Boone's clause drew little debate or attention. Some considered it a mere rhetorical roulade, others a vital commitment to "local programs, locally conceived." Either way, it embodied RFK's political concept of poverty—the notion that enlisting the poor in the program's implementation would give them work, money, and a sense of self-determination.

Yet no one intended the poor to run the programs. Budget Director Kermit Gordon was certain "all of us at that time thought of community action as organized, controlled and managed . . . by elite groups—by the city government, by business groups, by churches, by labor unions, by non-profit social organizations, welfare bodies, et cetera." Sargent Shriver's deputy Adam Yarmolinsky later insisted that maximum feasible participation "was not thought of as the way to fight city hall . . . not at all."

But the fighting—for resources and control of the CAAs—broke out immediately across the nation and reduced much of the war on poverty to an ugly series of local brawls. The poverty program coincided with the first great outbreak of urban unrest in the 1960s; local militants, newly energized, were determined to seize the federal funds. Local politicians sputtered with rage as the flow of federal money and patronage bypassed city hall. Where urban officials denied the poor maximum feasible participation, the OEO withheld funds entirely. One of the first angry calls to the White House came from Chicago Mayor Richard J. Daley. "What in the hell are you people doing?" Daley shouted at Moyers. "Does the President know he's putting M-O-N-E-Y in the hands of subversives? To poor people that aren't part of the organization? Didn't the President know they'd take that money to bring him down?" Johnson returned the call immediately and took more of Daley's abuse. "That," Moyers recalled, "began to form a dark cloud in Johnson's mind."

Reports by other big-city mayors, political lieutenants, and the press confirmed Johnson's growing fears. In September 1965, Johnson's new budget director, Charles L. Schultze, relayed to him the mayors' belief that "*we ought not to be in the business of organizing the poor politically.*" Meanwhile the embattled OEO hastened to define "maximum feasible participation." The agency decreed that no less than one-third of representatives on local boards must be poor people elected by the poor. It was a helpful, if controversial, clarification, but months later the *New York Times* was still moved to conclude that "little real guidance has come from Washington on how balance can be achieved in setting up community programs." The *Times* deemed maximum feasible participation "the most confused element in the war against poverty."

The problems inched closer to home, closer to the White House. In June 1965, Johnson's friend Jim Rowe told the president, "Something quite odd is going on!" in the District of Columbia. Rowe warned LBJ that "the national headquarters of the Office of Economic Opportunity (Sarge Shriver's own headquarters) is giving instructions and grants to local private groups for the purpose of training the Negro poor on how to conduct sit-ins and protest meetings against government agencies, federal, state and local." Atop Rowe's memo, Johnson scrawled a note to Moyers: "Bill—for God's sake get on top of this & put a stop to it at once—L." Rowe added ominously that U.S. senators were advising a D.C. antipoverty activist that "protest was the only way to get things done. One of the Senators [the activist] mentions is Robert Kennedy. (Personally, I would doubt that Kennedy knows anything about this other than to say that protest marches are the only thing that have helped the Negroes in the past. With this I agree and I am sure you do too.)"

Whether Johnson agreed with Rowe on the efficacy of past protests was incidental. Any mention of Robert Kennedy was a warning shot, and Johnson was already concerned about Bobby's inroads into the OEO. The conflagration of the CAPs was troubling enough; now Johnson began to worry that the whole program was, as Joseph Califano recalled, "the nucleus of a political force the Kennedys would use against him." That fall, when Shriver backed away from community action by proposing, among other things, a guaranteed minimum wage, Johnson saw Shriver's proposal as a Kennedy manifesto—written not to implement but to leak to the press as proof that Shriver and RFK wanted to invest more in the war on poverty than Johnson did. "Is the OEO being run by a bunch of kooks, communists and queers?" Johnson demanded of Shriver. Meanwhile, Johnson loyalists were amassing a litany of complaints against the OEO director; prominent among them was his Kennedy connection. A New York tabloid reported that "many in the [poverty] program believe Shriver is every day and always working for Bobby Kennedy. The family clan permits nothing—absolutely nothing—short of that and . . . Johnson grows steadily more aware that he has a whale by the tail." Perhaps Shriver was not so independent after all.

In late 1966, when presidential assistant Marvin Watson sent Johnson a newspaper article on Kennedy and Shriver, Johnson fired back, "Marvin: Start keeping me a file on these two." Thereafter aides kept a watchful eye on Shriver's public support of the president: how "forceful" was it? "Johnson couldn't look at Shriver without trying to see whether Robert Kennedy was in the shadows behind his brother-in-law," recalled Califano. As Shriver and Johnson parted ways on policy, Johnson imagined it had all been a setup from the start: that Shriver's OEO was, in truth, Bobby Kennedy's 1968 campaign organization. "They're not against poverty, they're for Kennedy," Johnson grumbled at Bill Moyers.

Feeding off Johnson's distrust, administrators at the departments of Labor, Agriculture, and HEW competed for pieces of the OEO pie. In December, LBJ asked Califano "in the strictest confidence" to draw up a plan dismembering OEO and transferring its programs to other agencies. Johnson sought to dismantle his once proud creation by stealth, keeping the issue off Capitol Hill, where Bobby Kennedy could accuse him of selling out the poor. In the end, Johnson rejected a wholesale reorganization as politically inexpedient and sullenly considered himself the prisoner of Kennedy's program. Community action, maximum feasible participation, the OEO, Shriver—in Johnson's view they all belonged to RFK.

In fact, Kennedy had few friends in OEO. And though community action was a "Kennedy idea," Bobby joined LBJ in the general retreat from the program. There was more to this than political expedience. The president's CAP looked nothing like what RFK had envisioned or endorsed only a year earlier: LBJ had bastardized, bloated, and Johnsonized Kennedy's original conception beyond recognition. Kennedy had never supported community action on such a colossal scale or to the exclusion of anything else. "Community action was part of a strategy," recalled Edelman, "but always of lesser priority" than education, for example. And unlike Shriver's team, Kennedy always understood that community action meant confrontation. Confrontation rarely troubled Kennedy, but he knew that big-city mayors felt differently. Many times in 1964 and 1965 he told Edelman, "It's not going to be popular to have the Federal Government financing people to come down and tell City Hall that it's doing the wrong thing."

Publicly Kennedy had no comment on the collapse of community action. No politician was about to ally himself with the madness the program seemed to have unleashed in the ghetto. Instead, Kennedy ignored the CAP battle and pushed repeatedly for greater funding of the larger crusade—to little avail and to Johnson's perpetual irritation. Johnson was extracting all he could from Congress; he would not compete in Kennedy's game of one-upmanship. Johnson's aides encouraged this view. In May 1966, Harry McPherson wrote LBJ that Kennedy, New York City Mayor John Lindsay, "and some of the far-out Negro leaders . . . are talking the same game—as Lindsay put it last night, 'Viet Nam or Brownsville.' They are using the money-for-the-ghetto argument to capitalize on our Viet Nam problem without explicitly condemning our policy there, for which they have no viable alternative. In doing this they are playing a devisive [sic] role."

The following January, Johnson complained to Nick Katzenbach that Kennedy was recklessly endangering the entire war on poverty. "We've got Bobby . . . and this crowd hitting us every day from the inside so our party's just split wide open," Johnson said, as Dictabelts recorded his words. "And I don't know what the hell they think they can do. . . . I've got in all the Congress would authorize. . . . I got it all in my budget, but I'm gonna lose every damned dime of it because of the way they do it. Same thing with poverty. I am going to lose my [war on] poverty" because of "what Bobby, [Wayne] Morse and [Joe] Clark and these wild men put in there." Johnson saw no principle behind Bobby's request; it was nothing but a "little potshot."

Johnson was no longer interested in saving community action. The program he truly feared losing was Model Cities, a five-to-ten-year multibillion-dollar infusion of federal funds into the ghetto—not to empower residents to leave but to improve the quality of life of those who remained. Johnson hoped it was the salvation of his war on poverty. In late 1965, he positively delighted in Califano's bill to transform "the slum core [of several cities] into a modern area with a total approach—new homes, schools, parks, community centers and open spaces," in addition to health care, police protection, and transportation.

Model Cities was managed not by OEO but by the politically pliable Department of Housing and Urban Development, a recent Johnson creation; also, the program's focus on public housing gave it a tangible goal that the CAP lacked. Model Cities was lastly a gesture of reconciliation to urban politicians, who would now have their hands on plenty of federal funds.

When the administration introduced the plan in spring 1966, Robert Kennedy was underwhelmed. "It's too little, it's nothing, we have to do twenty times as much," he pronounced at a small dinner of administration officials. It was a small taste of what was to follow that summer, when Kennedy and Abraham Ribicoff held extensive hearings on the Model Cities bill. The proceedings began on August 15 with Kennedy's long and detailed indictment of federal efforts. "Our present policies," he said, "have been directed to particular aspects of our problems—and have often ignored or even harmed our larger purposes." Declaring himself a strong supporter of the Model Cities program, he then dismissed it as "a drop in the bucket." He urged adoption of "a Marshall Plan approach," far broader and better-funded than Model Cities. At the close of Kennedy's exhaustive list of proposals, Ribicoff praised his "challenging, provocative, realistic, and deep statements," adding that "Congress should not and need not always wait on the executive branch to take the initiative."

The high-minded, well-intentioned hearings quickly became a sustained blast at the administration for shortchanging the poverty program. One after another, Johnson's top officials—Robert Weaver of HUD, John Gardner of HEW, Sargent Shriver, Nicholas Katzenbach, Willard Wirtz—sat before the Subcommittee on Government Reorganization in the nervous crouch of criminal defendants. Kennedy was mostly sparing in his treatment of his brother-in-law, Shriver, and his former deputy, Katzenbach, but regarded other witnesses much as he had Dave Beck and Jimmy Hoffa nearly a decade earlier. After a tense and extended back-and-forth over figures on substandard housing, Kennedy exploded at Bob Weaver: "I don't know whether we delude ourselves, Mr. Secretary, just by spending so much time going over what we have [achieved]. . . . We wouldn't be holding these hearings and you wouldn't be as concerned as you are if it was not a fact that we are not doing enough." Following a similar exchange, Mayor Samuel Yorty of Los Angeles snapped back, "I do not need a lecture from you on how to run my city. I think you should confine your questions to things that are possible for me to answer without bringing a computer."

Kennedy argued with increasing fervor during the next two weeks that the administration had neither a comprehensive understanding of the problem nor a comprehensive approach to solve it. "We have done more of that than has ever been done," Shriver insisted. "Like you, everybody in the executive branch would like to do more. . . . It is a question of whether it is technically possible to do more."

"I understand," Kennedy replied, obviously frustrated, and getting to the heart of the matter. "I just am not going—cannot be satisfied. . . . I think the United States, with a gross national product of over $700 billion, spending $24 billion in Vietnam, $600 million for economic aid to Vietnam, that we can't appropriate $200 million more for children in HeadStart in the United States . . . I don't think as a civilized nation we can be proud or satisfied. I think it is an outrage."

President Johnson thought the hearings were an outrage. Even when Ribicoff led the attack, Johnson thought he was fronting for RFK— because "Abe wants to be America's first Jewish Vice President." Johnson worried that his own budget for Model Cities was too big to pass congressional muster, and now Kennedy and Ribicoff were asking for more. "Johnson felt he went as far as he could go," Hubert Humphrey recalled; the president wanted to know "why the devil Bobby Kennedy and Abe Ribicoff [were] raising hell and stirring up trouble and giving the administration really no credit." Johnson refused to talk with either senator and promptly left for a tour of the Northeast—to plug his existing programs, lobby for Model Cities, and divert public attention from the Kennedy-Ribicoff hearings.

Henry Hall Wilson, a legislative aide to LBJ, judged that Kennedy's "entire play in the Ribicoff hearings was to prove that the President was doing nothing about these problems." ("They know better," added McPherson in a memo to the president.) Wilson lamented that Bobby's "ignorance" had "not yet been properly exploited by us" and suggested the discreet planting of stories in the press. Yet it is unlikely that any plant, however well-placed, could have sparked the outrage shown by the editors of the *Washington Star* two days later:

> In the last two weeks Senator Robert F. Kennedy has treated the country to a kind of senatorial entertainment which adds nothing to his stature. The junior senator from New York, assisted by the junior senator from Connecticut, has summoned cabinet members and the mayors of large cities before him as if they were errant schoolboys and he their properly indignant teacher.
>
> He has, unfortunately, very little to teach anyone on the subject in hand except the extent of his animosity in several directions and the lengths to which he will go to vent it. The ostensible subject of the hearings is not the ineptness of the Johnson administration nor the alleged negligence of mayors nor even the new and different charm of Bobby in anger. . . .

Free-wheeling assaults upon public officials trying to deal with the problem contribute nothing to understanding or action in a field in need of both.

Kennedy backpedaled rapidly from confrontation with Johnson. In late 1966, at another hearing on urban problems, Kennedy refuted charges that LBJ was insensitive to the needs of the poor. Bobby's about-face followed a round of attacks against the administration's poverty program. On the morning of December 12, Senator Joe Clark accused Johnson of having "starved" the program. Later, an antipoverty activist named Katie Ripley testified before the Senate panel. Ripley was short, boxy, uncompromising—and agitated by reports that LBJ would seek only a slight increase in antipoverty appropriations in 1968. "From all the speeches I've heard from Senator Kennedy—and, I will say, kind of quietly from Mr. Johnson—Mr. Kennedy is one of the poor man's friends. And I cannot say this for our President," Ripley declared. The crowd of two hundred that packed the Senate Caucus Room erupted in effusive support. When the cheers subsided, Kennedy paused a moment, then replied, "All of us feel we have a responsibility to those who are less well off. President Johnson needs no defense from me. The poverty program originated under him. He has immense responsibilities, great problems over defense costs and the budget. Also a very serious struggle in Southeast Asia.

"I understand the problems you face," Kennedy continued. "But the President is a man of great compassion."

"I'm not knocking the Vietnam War," Ripley replied, undeterred. "[But] the war on poverty is also a great war. If you're going to fight two wars, why don't you fight them equally?" Another great roar of support erupted behind her.

Yes, Kennedy agreed, Congress and the White House had "made a past commitment, and unless we do more than we have in the past, I don't think we will keep that commitment." Kennedy spent the rest of the afternoon dodging suggestions that he was the savior of Johnson's war on poverty. That was a political burden Kennedy was loath to assume.

Kennedy's energies were elsewhere in December 1966. He had essentially given up on Johnson's war on poverty and was starting his own. It was a strategy born partly of necessity: Kennedy was not going to get an alternate program passed by Congress or signed by LBJ. But experience, in any case, had taught Kennedy that the federal government was not up to the task of community development. Model Cities looked to be no different. In Kennedy's view the program smacked of bureaucratic social engineering. Bobby believed Johnson was playing a very complicated game in the cities that was bound to backfire—putting federal funds in the hands of the mayors might preclude the problems of the CAP, but the premise of community action from the beginning had been that local government was unable or unwilling to consider the needs of the poor. Kennedy saw no reason to believe that had changed.

Bobby's thinking evolved gradually from community action to community development. As early as August 1965 his aides pointed out the growing gap between the president's soaring rhetoric and the harsh realities of life in places like Harlem and the Bedford-Stuyvesant section of Brooklyn. "When in two or three years this gap becomes apparent," Dave Hackett and Tom Johnston warned Kennedy, "when the residents are convinced that the promises have in fact been broken, these areas may well experience a form of lawlessness quite unlike anything in the past." Kennedy's aides recommended an immediate plan of economic development—"tailored to the specific needs of each area and mobilizing the full resources of both the public and private sectors." This embrace of the private sector required something of a shift for Bobby Kennedy. He had inherited his father's reflexive distaste for the business community; the successful businessman Joseph Kennedy had taught that businessmen were selfish "sons of bitches," political conservatives, friends of the status quo. Bobby Kennedy was no friend of the status quo or of big business. (LBJ in fact blamed Bobby for the administration's "anti-business reputation.") He certainly did not cultivate its support in the fawning, venal way Lyndon Johnson had cozied up to oil and gas interests in Texas. But then, a Kennedy did not need to.

But now he needed business to help solve the problems that government could not. In February 1966, Dick Goodwin wrote Bobby that "I share . . . many hostilities to the business and conservative community. But it is also true that in some confused way [America has] turned natural instincts of greed into a force which has raised the standard of living in this country more effectively than in any other. Perhaps we might think through some ideas to involve the most progressive corporations— IBM, Xerox, etc., in public problems." Goodwin recommended that Bobby convene a business advisory council in New York. "Maybe you have already done so," Goodwin added.

Indeed, Kennedy was already in the process of enlisting the private sector in an ambitious community development project. On December 10, 1966, Kennedy announced the creation of two nonprofit corporations—one of community leaders (political, religious, labor, and civil rights) and the other of business leaders—to revitalize the black and

Puerto Rican ghetto in Bedford-Stuyvesant. At a press conference in a school auditorium, Kennedy argued that current programs "don't have their origin in the community, but are imposed from the outside." This was the sad legacy of the CAP; by bureaucratic incompetence, previous federal grants had been "frittered away." Kennedy admitted that he "sounded like a Republican" in appealing to the private sector, but its involvement was crucial. So were block grants and tax credits from federal and state governments.

Kennedy's Bedford-Stuyvesant program subscribed to the basic tenet of Johnson's Model Cities—that poor neighborhoods must be transformed into safe, stable, middle-class ones. Larry Levinson, Califano's assistant, disparaged Bedford-Stuyvesant as Model Cities "with a twist," a parallel program driven by politics. White House "intellectual-in-residence" John Roche mocked Bobby as "a real-estate developer." But Bedford-Stuyvesant represented a greater departure than all that. As Pat Moynihan wrote Bobby the following July, the project was about "get[ting] the market to do what the bureaucracy cannot." Kennedy's corporate embrace rendered Bedford-Stuyvesant distinct from LBJ's Great Society: it was not that Kennedy placed greater faith in business than Johnson did; it was that Kennedy had less faith in government on a grand scale. Where Model Cities was vast and disparate, Bedford-Stuyvesant was tightly focused. Where Johnson hyped Model Cities as a uniform panacea, Kennedy sold Bedford-Stuyvesant as a singular experiment. With typical bluster, Johnson predicted that the Model Cities Act "will be regarded as one of the major breakthroughs of the 1960s." More modestly, Kennedy expressed hope that Bedford-Stuyvesant "could become a prototype for corporations in other cities."

Model Cities did not last long enough to be considered a breakthrough. Poor people who received government jobs used their government paychecks to move out of bad neighborhoods that grew steadily worse. The program was a greater boon to the upwardly mobile than the poor. In other cities the chief beneficiaries were urban political machines. Kennedy's venture was even less successful than Model Cities in creating jobs; tax incentives lured few corporations to locate in Bedford-Stuyvesant. Only IBM—with two former Kennedy aides on its board and a Democrat, Thomas J. Watson, Jr., as its chairman—built a significant plant in the ghetto. (IBM had already considered the move independently.) Johnson offered little federal support. In 1966, Kennedy and Jacob Javits had amended the Economic Opportunity Act to allow funding for "special impact" programs like Bedford-Stuyvesant. Though Congress funded the amendment for two years, LBJ consistently opposed it. Kennedy complained in 1968 that the administration "has

spent most of the funds appropriated on other manpower activities"—
namely, its own.

In the long run, however, RFK's Bedford-Stuyvesant project was one
of the few antipoverty efforts to bear fruit. Its greatest success was in creating and managing housing for the poor. An influx of outside
resources—grants, loans, and subsidies from government and private
foundations—helped stabilize the neighborhood. In later years the
Bedford-Stuyvesant Corporation was indeed a prototype for community development corporations that sprang up across the country. By 1974
there were thirty-four federally funded and seventy-five privately funded corporations. Twenty years later there was one in every major
American city. Kennedy and Johnson shared authorship of the concept
of community development, but Kennedy claimed its most important
legacy.

CHAPTER 10

A Wider War

Robert Kennedy had been a United States senator for four weeks when the bombs began to rain upon North Vietnam.

During the night of February 6, 1965, the Vietcong attacked an American air base at Pleiku. The insurgents killed nine Americans and wounded more than a hundred; they destroyed five American planes and damaged fifteen. The cursory two-hour debate that followed among the president's national security advisers was hardly deliberative. The Joint Chiefs of Staff had drawn up plans for reprisal long before the attack. "We have kept our gun over the mantel and our shells in the cupboard for a long time now," the president said impatiently. "I can't ask our American soldiers out there to fight with one hand tied behind their back." Within forty-eight hours the series of retaliatory bombings that constituted Operation Flaming Dart gave way, with the imperceptible ease of a foot on an accelerator, to the sustained pounding of Rolling Thunder that, but for an occasional and ephemeral clearing of North Vietnamese skies, would not ease until 1968. It was the largest aerial bombing campaign in the history of warfare. Officially, the administration marked this watershed with another assurance that "we seek no wider war. Whether or not this course can be maintained lies with the North Vietnamese aggressors."

Three weeks later, Bobby Kennedy received a letter from his new colleague Senator William Proxmire of Wisconsin. Proxmire planned to voice full support of the administration's Vietnam policy on March 1 and would be "delighted and flattered" if Kennedy followed the speech with a "colloquy" of his own. In fact, Bobby was already considering a speech of his own, and if delivered it would make a poor complement to Proxmire's. "We must understand," Kennedy's draft read, "that while bombing targets in North Viet Nam may induce more caution in Hanoi, they will not bring peace to South Viet Nam. In the last analysis, the way to defeat the terrorists is to increase our capability to fight their kind of war."

This was hardly a vote of confidence in the administration's policy. Nor was it an antiwar speech; despite the bombing campaign, there was not yet much of a war to oppose. That would come soon, as would the real doubts and deeper questions. Kennedy's speech draft was weeks old and already out-of-date. Earlier that year, sources within the administration had told him, in error, that Johnson intended to withdraw from Vietnam—a costly, dangerous disengagement, in Bobby's view. His own travels revealed the symbolic and strategic importance of an American presence in the region. Without that presence, anti-Communists would lose heart; fragile governments would fall like Joseph Alsop's prophesied dominoes. The effects would ripple outward beyond Southeast Asia, undermining faith in American commitments and the fight against Communism. Bobby's undelivered speech was an entreaty to stand firm.

Still, the bombing of North Vietnam unsettled him. Kennedy was as firmly opposed to escalation as he was to withdrawal, and if he failed to recognize this dilemma, it was because events had not yet forced him to do so. In January and February 1965 it still seemed feasible to steer a middle course, to fight the Vietcong on their own terms—in "their kind of war."

In 1965 this view was common if rarely articulated. Kennedy balked at articulating it himself. Though the joint campaign effort of autumn 1964 had mostly silenced speculation about the Johnson-Kennedy feud, Bobby understood that the press would portray his public qualms on Vietnam—however tentative—as a hasty grab for the limelight, as playing politics with national security, as the "first break" with LBJ. Reporters would call him ruthless and opportunistic and anything but an honest (if timid) critic.

Abandoning the speech, Kennedy sourly accepted the political constraints of his new job and his old feud with Lyndon Johnson. The Senate floor was not the cabinet room, where he had once spoken freely and without reproach. Now Kennedy chose silence over sincerity, accommodation over antagonism. Rather quickly, he found it not at all to his liking.

No one, in February 1965, really expected Bobby Kennedy to define a clear position on Vietnam. During the fall campaign it had hardly been an issue. When a Columbia student asked his "exact position" on Vietnam, Bobby let loose some convoluted platitudes about the French in

1951, the need to persist, the lack of an easy solution, and his belief that "we're not going to win that war unless the [South Vietnamese] government has the support of the people. That, in my judgment, is the key to success." At the time, that sort of judgment was enough.

Publicly, Kennedy had said nothing of significance on the subject since February 18, 1962, when he paused in South Vietnam long enough for an impromptu press conference. En route from Djakarta to Bangkok, the attorney general stopped in Saigon for two hours, never leaving the heavily guarded airport. "We are going to win in Vietnam," he told the small gathered group of journalists. "We will remain here until we do win."

Asked whether the United States was involved in a war, Bobby answered, "We are involved in a struggle."

"What is the semantics of war and struggle?" a reporter interjected.

"It is a legal difference. Perhaps it adds up to the same thing. It is a struggle short of war."

"American boys are dying out here," said a British correspondent. "Do the American people understand and approve of what is going on?"

"I think the American people understand and fully support this struggle," Bobby replied. "Americans have great affection for the people of Vietnam. I think the U.S. will do what is necessary to help a country that is trying to repel aggression with its own blood, tears and sweat. . . . This is a new kind of war . . . fought not by massive divisions but secretly by terror, assassination, ambush and infiltration."

It was an adequate statement of President Kennedy's Vietnam policy, ambiguities and all: the pledge of support, ill-defined; the nod toward self-determination; the rejection of the term "war" for the deliberately vague "struggle." In Saigon the attorney general appeared the picture of confidence, but neither he nor his brother had a clear plan of action in Southeast Asia. The Kennedy policy, if it could be called such, was a policy of neglect, of equivocal gestures and uncertain, yet creeping, commitment. With the exception of Bobby's recommendation of a "sharp step-up" of advisers in 1961, the two brothers had rarely discussed the virtues or liabilities of intervention in Vietnam. But they had discussed the sort of war it would be, if it was to be a war, or struggle, or whatever. Bobby Kennedy's picture of a war fought "secretly by terror, assassination, ambush and infiltration" showed him gripped firmly by the latest Washington fad in foreign policy thinking. He and JFK were fairly infatuated by counterinsurgency and saw in the developing theory a model for Vietnam.

New challenges, after all, demanded new thinking. Counterinsurgency emerged as a response to the threat of Communist wars of liberation in the third world and, accordingly, to the outdated Dulles doctrine of massive retaliation. The tough intellectuals of the New Frontier had little patience for the enervated establishment generals of the Eisenhower years. David Halberstam of the *New York Times* remembered the growing cult of counterinsurgency in the Kennedy years, the romantic, premature celebration of "these brilliant, young, great physical specimens in their green berets, swinging through the trees . . . arm over arm, and speaking six languages, including Chinese and Russian, and who had Ph.D.'s in history and literature, and ate snake meat at night." This was military strategy as Beltway fad, or vice versa, and it infected a good portion of the Kennedy administration, particularly Bobby Kennedy.

In 1961, as Walt Rostow put it (somewhat approvingly), Bobby Kennedy "got into the guerrilla war business." As the chief gadfly in the Special Group CI, Bobby viewed most of the Kennedy administration's foreign policy concerns, from Latin America to Southeast Asia, through the lens of counterinsurgency. But Bobby's understanding of counterinsurgency was more nuanced than his critics allowed: America's interests, he believed, were best served not by engaging the enemy itself but by training and supplying a cadre of counterinsurgents. The intervention of U.S. Special Forces was best kept to a minimum; operations were to be small-scale, covert, and often civilian, and tactics flexible, gradual, tough, and tireless. Counterinsurgency meant knife thrusts, not tank blasts. It eschewed "the big things"—saturation bombings, invasions, massive troop deployments—in favor of smaller, sharper, smarter strikes. Of course, it remained a particularly virile strain of adventurism that only fed America's appetite for intervention. It would take more than a decade of bloodshed to dispense with that.

As a theory, counterinsurgency placed equal emphasis upon strength through social reform—"winning the hearts and minds" of the people, as a later slogan had it. But in practice, as one member of the CI Group complained, it "only fully addresses itself to the equipment and training aspects." Teetering third-world regimes were hardly inclined toward radical, populist reform; usually it was neglect or repression of their own people that had set them teetering in the first place. Neither were Green Berets much given to nation-building. "When you've got 'em by the balls, their hearts and minds will follow," went their cruel retort to well-meaning democrats in Washington. The U.S. Army, meanwhile, had about as much taste for social revolution as it did for the unfettered forces of the Green Berets. The Army was geared toward high-technology, set-piece combat and did not need Bobby Kennedy or even General Maxwell Taylor to teach it any new tricks.

By the summer of 1963, Bobby Kennedy knew that his pet strategy was pretty well doomed. Hardly tested, counterinsurgency was falling out of vogue and into the hands of the Army and the Special Forces, which preferred coercion to cooperation. Dispirited, Bobby lost interest in the workings of the CI Group; but he had not shaken free of the untested assumptions of the new thinking. Perhaps, Bobby thought, counterinsurgency could force a political settlement in Vietnam, as it had (he believed) in Laos in 1962. John Kennedy, too, continued to see Vietnam as a proving ground for his new brand of warrior.

What that meant in practice neither man knew. And by the summer of 1963, there was precious little time to sort it all out. South Vietnam tumbled swiftly downward into disorder, falling finally into the Kennedys' sights and displacing Latin America as their foreign fixation. The Buddhist protest movement, fired upon by government troops in the city of Hue in May 1963, erupted in a surreal and literal manner the next month when a monk immolated himself in front of a screeching streetside crowd in Saigon. Premier Ngo Dinh Diem, a devout Catholic, had never been popular among the nation's Buddhists. And now Madame Nhu, the wife of Diem's brother and partner Ngo Dinh Nhu, reveled in her reputation as the forked-tongued "Dragon Lady" by offering the monks gasoline and matches for further "barbecues." In August her husband's American-trained forces ransacked pagodas in major cities and arrested more than fourteen hundred Buddhists. This bonfire of the bonzes seared the government of South Vietnam irrevocably; the entire society—and its anti-Communist effort—seemed on the verge of collapse.

The Kennedy administration, propelled by events toward an early reckoning in Vietnam, was racked by confusion and division. In the summer of 1963, Bobby began privately to express grave doubts about the whole enterprise. He peppered presidential assistant for Far Eastern affairs Mike Forrestal with the hard, pragmatic questions no one wanted to ask:

> Was the United States capable of achieving even the limited objectives that we then had in Vietnam? Did the United States have the resources, the men and the philosophy and the thinking to have anything useful to contribute or say in a country as politically unstable as South Vietnam? Was it not possible that we had overestimated our own resources and underestimated the problem in South Vietnam?

Bobby himself bristled at these questions, at least when posed by others. On August 31, Paul Kattenburg, staff director of the Interdepartmental Task Force on Vietnam, returned from Saigon to brief the NSC. Kattenburg called Vietnam policy "a garden path to tragedy" and recommended that the United States "get out honorably." The attorney general fixed him with an icy glare. But Bobby did not, as Secretary McNamara did, blurt out in self-defense, "We are winning this war!" Of that Bobby was less sure.

A related but more immediate concern was the fate of Diem. At the Saigon airport in 1962, Bobby had read an official statement praising the premier as "brave and patriotic" and expressing "full confidence" in him. In fact, Diem was a stubborn and unreliable partner to the United States. By September 1963 even public expressions of goodwill were hard to muster. "In my opinion," President Kennedy told Walter Cronkite in a televised interview on September 2, "in the last two months the [Diem] government has gotten out of touch with the people." Its brutal repression of the Buddhists that summer had laid bare the moral and political bankruptcy of the regime, and neither Kennedy brother held much hope that Diem could be counted on in the mounting crisis. But where was an alternative? Diem's brother Nhu was even more autocratic, secretive, and sinister. And any change in the South Vietnamese government might propel the country into chaos.

Absent any serious analysis, events assumed their own deadly momentum. In late August, just days after the pagoda raids, a cabal of South Vietnamese generals contacted U.S. Ambassador Henry Cabot Lodge to solicit support for a coup. The news reached the State Department during the weekend of August 24; the president was on the Cape, trying to relax. Back in Washington an anti-Diem group of advisers—Averell Harriman, Roger Hilsman, and Mike Forrestal—drafted an ambiguous but blunt cable to Lodge: Diem must be given an opportunity to rid himself of Nhu, they allowed, but if Diem refuses, "then we must face the possibility that Diem himself cannot be preserved." The cable instructed Lodge to "urgently examine all possible alternative leadership and make detailed plans as to how we might bring about Diem's replacement if this should become necessary." Inattentive and ill-informed, President Kennedy approved the cable. And in light of what followed, even Bobby had to agree: "He passed it off too quickly."

Within days it was manifestly clear that the coup was on. Lodge had not even talked to Diem to resolve American differences with the regime. The ambassador's behavior baffled Bobby Kennedy, and, galvanized by the August 24 cable, the attorney general immersed himself in the particulars of Vietnam policy. At a September 6 meeting of the NSC, Bobby wondered aloud whether South Vietnam could win the war with Diem and Nhu. No, Dean Rusk told him frankly, it could not.

"Then why not grasp the nettle now?" Bobby wondered aloud, frustrated. "We have to be tough. . . . We have to tell Diem that he must do the things we demand or we will have to cut down our effort as forced by the American public."

Rusk was in favor of pressuring Diem but he was upset by Bobby's suggestion. "It is very serious to threaten to pull out of Vietnam," he said sternly, as if curbing an impulsive child. "If the Viet Cong takes over in Vietnam we are in real trouble."

Robert Kennedy did not need Rusk to tell him this was "real trouble"; nothing caught Bobby's eye like danger to the president. But this was the end of his exchange with Rusk, and for the time being the end of the larger debate. Bobby's comments provoked no serious discussion of either a negotiated settlement or withdrawal, and as the weeks passed, the administration remained paralyzed by ambivalence.

Though Bobby was not exactly a detractor from this nonpolicy, he continued to question the inexorable drift toward a coup. In the late afternoon of October 29, William Colby of the CIA briefed the president's Vietnam group on the status of coup forces in Saigon. In Bobby's view, Colby's flurry of maps and pointers was rather beside the point. Bobby listened as his colleagues compared a quick success to a protracted success. He said nothing as they debated the effect of the American position on the larger war effort and bandied about numbers of pro- and anti-Diem forces, which they judged to be about equal.

When the president spoke up, pointing out hopefully that more troops would join a successful coup in progress, Bobby disagreed. Allowing that he had not seen all the reports, the attorney general declared that the present situation in Vietnam made no sense to him at all. Vietnam was not a South American country where a coup could be brought off promptly. Nor was the situation today any different from July and August, when these same generals had been unable to orchestrate a coup. To support one now was to put the fate of not just Vietnam but all Southeast Asia in the hands of one man unknown to them all. And, Bobby warned, "a failure risks so much. . . . We can't go halfway. If the coup fails, Diem will throw us out."

He added, "I know my view is the minority view."

As if to prove the point, Rusk leaped forward to disagree, saying that if the United States did not support a coup it would harm the war effort, which rested in the hands of the scheming generals. Maxwell Taylor and CIA Director John McCone rallied to Bobby's defense, arguing that in fact a successful coup would hurt the war effort by ushering in a cadre of untested leaders. A failed coup, they added, would be disastrous. The president, seeming at first uncertain, sided in the end with his brother: "If we miscalculate," JFK concluded, "we could lose our entire position in Southeast Asia overnight."

Despite the charged atmosphere, this was no repeat of the Cuban missile crisis, when Bobby Kennedy led a divided group toward consensus and a more rational, enlightened policy. In the days that followed, President Kennedy did nothing to discourage the generals. He did nothing to encourage them, either, but in Saigon, Lodge was giving them all the moral support they needed. On November 1, while Diem sat talking with Lodge, the generals seized control of communications and military installations in the South Vietnamese capital. Later, after a harrowing escape from the palace through an underground passage, Diem and Nhu offered their surrender to the generals, who promised the brothers safe passage and promptly shot them in the back of the head. Their bodies were dumped in an unmarked grave next to the home of Ambassador Lodge after being mutilated by bayonets.

At 9:00 the next morning, news of the deaths (suicides, said a cable from Saigon) hit John Kennedy like a body blow. Pale and visibly sickened, he rushed from the briefing room without saying a word. "What did he expect?" whispered General Taylor under his breath. Robert Kennedy said nothing. Shaken by the assassination of Diem, Bobby and Jack—but principally Bobby—began to consider withdrawal. They did so vaguely, wistfully, and only halfheartedly.

This, then, was Robert Kennedy on Vietnam in November 1963: opposed to escalation, opposed to a pullout, skeptical of South Vietnamese democracy, and hopeful of counterinsurgency. It was not much different from Robert Kennedy on Vietnam in February 1965, despite a succession of ineffectual regimes in South Vietnam and an intensification of the military effort there. Throughout, Kennedy wished to shake free of the commitment, to abandon the struggle, but he could not countenance the cost to American credibility. Like his colleagues, Kennedy was caught on what the Pentagon's John McNaughton called "the horns of a trilemma," and with every twist and turn he found his predicament more painful and harder to escape.

It was unclear how Lyndon Johnson felt about counterinsurgency. Prior to November 22 it was unlikely that anybody asked or cared. If Bobby Kennedy was inattentive toward Vietnam (before autumn 1963), LBJ was downright indifferent. When Roger Hilsman returned from a fact-finding mission to Vietnam in early 1963 and submitted a report to President Kennedy, JFK asked Hilsman to deliver the same report to a number of his advisers. One was Bobby Kennedy. Another was Vice President Johnson, who brought Hilsman into his office and proceeded to make a series of phone calls, offering Hilsman a curt "Excuse me" before dialing another number or dictating something else to his secretary. "What were you saying?" Johnson would ask, and before Hilsman had completed a sentence Johnson would be on the phone again, trying to settle a political tempest in a Texan teapot—another one of the petty flare-ups with which Johnson entertained himself as vice president. "You know, he just couldn't care *less,*" Hilsman complained later.

Johnson had never shown much interest in Southeast Asia or foreign policy in general. As minority leader in spring 1954, while the French struggled to stave off defeat against the Communist Vietminh at Dien Bien Phu, Johnson saw Vietnam less as an American strategic interest than as a political weapon against President Eisenhower. Johnson refused to lend bipartisan support to intervention. The Democratic leader promised Secretary of State John Foster Dulles support for military action only if it was backed by America's allies and if the French granted independence to Vietnam. The conditions were seemingly honorable but obviously impossible. And as Dien Bien Phu fell in May, LBJ chalked up more political points against the administration by mocking the "*new dynamic foreign policy* . . . New York advertising hucksters and TV experts have merchandised." He asked a group of Democrats at a party dinner, "What *is* American policy in Indo-China? It is apparent only that American foreign policy has never in all its history suffered such a stunning reversal. . . . This picture of our country needlessly weakened in the world today is so painful," Johnson concluded, "that we should turn our eyes from abroad and look homeward."

Which Johnson did, in large part, until vice presidential duties carried him abroad in 1961. In May of that year, when President Kennedy sent him to Saigon to show support for the Diem regime, LBJ returned to deliver a frank assessment of the costs and challenges of American leadership in the region, to which Johnson saw "no alternative." In October, JFK asked General Taylor and Walt Rostow to review their own, more important report with the vice president. Unlike Hilsman, Taylor found LBJ actively interested and evincing "a rather unusual understanding of the seriousness of what we were recommending"—a significant boost in American involvement, ranging from equipment to advisers to a small "logistical task force" of engineers and infantry (JFK rejected the latter). Taylor left LBJ's office on the Hill with the impression that the vice president saw the uncertainties ahead but agreed rather reluctantly that the Rostow-Taylor plan was about the only choice America had.

As vice president, LBJ had little more to say about Vietnam and no real perspective to add. John Kennedy fashioned himself a global pundit in his days as a Harvard undergraduate; Lyndon Johnson developed no such ambition in a quarter century of public service. Johnson voiced no challenge to the Kennedy administration's policy in Indochina. "I don't recall any substantial difference that I expressed to the President on Vietnam," Johnson told an adviser later. Then he corrected himself: "I know that I felt that the wire that Hilsman sent out"—the August 24 cable to Lodge that precipitated the coup—"was a very unwise thing."

Johnson would have been best advised to keep this opinion to himself. His opposition to the cable deeply embittered Bobby Kennedy. "Lyndon Johnson was against, strongly against the coup," Bobby grumbled in 1964—a surprising complaint given his own qualms and regrets. But Bobby could give LBJ no credit for strategic thinking. Johnson objected to the coup only "because he liked President Diem and he liked his brother and his wife." Even worse, Johnson had proposed no alternative means of coping with Diem. Of course, neither had Bobby Kennedy or anybody else, and it was unfair to fault the vice president for not offering a "minority view" in an open meeting of the NSC. Insecure in foreign affairs, Johnson was following Bobby's lead; usually he followed Jack's. After November 22, when the mantle of Vietnam policy crashed down upon his shoulders, LBJ followed Jack's advisers to their collective doom.

Lyndon Johnson had been president for only two days when Ambassador Lodge told him that Vietnam was going to hell in a handbasket, that the coup had killed Diem and his country's will to fight. The wretched new leadership in Saigon left LBJ feeling like a catfish that had "grabbed a big juicy worm with a right sharp hook in the middle of it." Lodge urged that the United States boost morale in the South by bombing the North. LBJ refused, but he did order Lodge to "go back and tell those generals in Saigon that Lyndon Johnson intends to stand by our word."

"Our word": uttered repeatedly by John Kennedy and previous presidents, the American commitment had attained the authority of holy writ. Lyndon Johnson, his legs shaky on the global stage, could not conceive of another direction. He would "continue" in Vietnam just as he would "continue" at home. Kennedy's key advisers—Rusk, McNamara, Rostow, Bundy—would tell Johnson what Kennedy would have done, and Johnson would do it.

For some time, surely, Kennedy would have stalled, watching Southeast Asia's beacon of democracy grow dimmer and dimmer: Communists were deepening their penetration of the South, where Diem's murder had left a yawning political void; the ruling junta was plagued by division and shortly overthrown by another that, in turn, collapsed; and the Vietcong had made a mess of American plans to secure the countryside through ill-conceived "strategic hamlets." So Johnson stalled. "From November '63 until July '65," he said later, "I did everything I could to avoid the commitment that ultimately I had to make—either run or stand."

But at no point did LBJ seriously think of running: almost every one of Johnson's top advisers insisted that Vietnam remained a vital security interest, the front line against Communist aggression, a crucial test of American power and resolve. And who was LBJ to question the collective wisdom of Truman, Eisenhower, Kennedy, McNamara, Rusk, and the Joint Chiefs? This was a "solid phalanx" for intervention, as Clark Clifford put it. Johnson, moreover, was an ardent nationalist and believer in peace through military strength. "Everything I knew about history," Johnson reflected, "told me that if I got out of Vietnam . . . then I'd be doing exactly what Chamberlain did in World War II. I'd be giving a big fat reward to aggression."

Vietnam itself meant virtually nothing; it was a "little piss-ant country," Johnson scoffed. What truly hung in the balance was American credibility in the larger war against Communist expansion. "Knowing what I did of the policies of Moscow and Peking," Johnson recalled, "I was as sure as a man could be that if we did not live up to our commitment in Southeast Asia and elsewhere, they would move to exploit the disarray in the United States and in the alliances of the Free World." Johnson in fact knew little of Moscow, Peking, or geopolitics. What he understood was domestic politics. He knew intuitively that "losing" Vietnam would provoke a right-wing backlash—"a mean and destructive debate"—that would destroy his Great Society and his entire presidency. "I knew that Harry Truman and Dean Acheson had lost their effectiveness from the day that the Communists took over in China," Johnson said years later. "The loss of China had played a large role in the rise of Joe McCarthy. And I knew that all these problems, taken together, were chickenshit compared with what might happen if we lost Vietnam." And McCarthy, presumably, was chickenshit compared to LBJ's adversary: "This time there would be Robert Kennedy out in front leading the fight against me, telling everyone that I had betrayed John Kennedy's commitment to South Vietnam. That I had let a democracy fall into the hands of the Communists. That I was a coward. An unmanly man. A man without a spine. Oh, I could see it coming, all right."

This, however, was hindsight of a typically self-serving kind: LBJ wanted history to record that Bobby had boxed him in politically, had forced him to make war in Vietnam. In reality, Johnson well understood that Kennedy was no hawk. The two men had spoken at length about Vietnam in May and June 1964, in surprisingly straightforward conversations that the president surreptitiously recorded, and though Kennedy did not shy from a military presence in Vietnam, he was increasingly doubtful of a military solution.

"Being quite frank about it," he told the president on May 28, "based on my two meetings [with] the National Security Council, I thought that . . . there was too much emphasis, really, on the military aspects of it. I would think that that war will never be won militarily, that where it's gonna be won, really, is the political war. And the best talent, of course, is over at the Pentagon, because you have Bob McNamara. But that same kind of talent really has to be applied to doing what needs to be done *politically* in that country, and whether it's setting up an organization for each one of those countries *politically*. . . . They're dropping a bomb someplace, or sending more planes there, but [the Vietnamese] people themselves aren't interested—as you point out frequently—but I'm not sure that they [the Pentagon] concentrate on that sufficiently.

"I think that a real major effort [must be made] in the political field, as is being made in the military field, because the military action obviously will have to be taken, but unless the political action is taken concurrently, in my judgment, I just don't think it can be successful."

"I think that that's good thinking," Johnson replied, "and that's not any different from the way I have felt about it." He professed to prefer a political settlement: "We're not ready to have a declaration of war," he argued, "or war by executive order. We are trying, every way we can, to soup up what we've got, to stabilize it, and to . . . have some diplomatic programs and political programs instead of just sending out twenty extra planes." The conflict, after all, was not about military domination of the North but political self-determination in the South. "We don't want to be the power in that part of the world," Johnson reminded Kennedy, ". . . all we want to do is get 'em to leave these other folks alone."

Johnson appeared to agree with Kennedy on everything, even his suggestion that the president appoint an ExComm, an emergency council, on Vietnam. Whatever form it took, Johnson wanted Kennedy on the team. "We'd like to have you," he said, "if you—"

"I'd be glad to," Kennedy interrupted. "I'd be glad to."

"I just think it's the hottest thing we've got on our hands, and the most potentially dangerous."

"Yes," Kennedy replied, sounding suddenly uneasy. "I didn't want to—uh—I, I, you know—uh, put myself in there—"

"You put yourself into everything that you've ever been doing," LBJ said paternally. "Just forget that stuff, now, I've told you that about three times. You are wanted, and needed, and we care, and we must have all the capacity we have and all the experience. You just go and do it like you did it last August, this August. And wear the same hats. You're even needed more than you were. . . . Now, I wouldn't say that if I didn't mean that, and I don't *need* to say it, and I'd just say, 'Much obliged and thank you' if I didn't want it. I sincerely want it, and genuinely want it. They're never gonna separate us as far as I'm concerned."

"Thank you," Bobby said softly.

"And if any of my people ever contribute to it, why, I'll get rid of any one of 'em if we can put the finger on it."

Nearly every one of his people had contributed to it, of course, and LBJ had no real intention of cleaning house. Kennedy understood that. Yet he did step cautiously into Johnson's inner circle of foreign policy advisers, and emerged unimpressed. "We went through the plan for Vietnam," Bobby told the president on June 9, "and I had some serious questions about it. . . . For instance, the congressional part of it—getting a congressional resolution. I think it poses all kinds of problems."

Johnson agreed. Ever since he entered the executive branch he had considered Congress more hindrance than help in a foreign policy crisis. "I am fearful," he admitted, "that if we move without any authority of the Congress, that the resentment would be pretty widespread and would involve a lot of people who'd normally be with us if we asked for the authority. On the other hand, I would shudder to think if they debated it for a long period of time, and they're likely to do that. So neither choice is very good."

"No," Kennedy replied. "It seems likely that they'll start asking somebody to spell out exactly what's going to happen—if you—we—drop bombs there, and then they retaliate, will we eventually bomb Hanoi and all that kind of business. And the answers to those questions are *so* difficult to give, particularly if you're giving them to a lot of people that are antagonistic." Kennedy was still a cabinet member, not a senator, and he was still thinking like a cabinet member. He was also acknowledging, by implication, that there would be no political settlement without a sufficient flexing of military muscle. He and Johnson were both now talking about war.

"By what authority, by what executive order, do you declare war?" the president asked. He was tempted to bypass Congress altogether.

"I haven't looked into it," the attorney general cautioned, "but it's not essential, it's not necessary constitutionally" to seek congressional approval. "The alternative, of course, is for you and Secretary McNamara and Secretary Rusk, at the appropriate time, to start bringing in the labor leaders and the business leaders and the congressional leaders and talk with them, you know, sort of as if it was a National Security Council meeting . . . briefing them that this is what we have to do at this time, and that if you have to take any further steps that . . . you'll keep them advised. And rally—and bring in some of the newspapers and bring in some of the television people—"

"And I think probably talk to the country," Johnson interjected.
"Yes."

"About why we're there and how we're there and what we're confronting there, and what we may do, *before* you submit a resolution, because I have doubts about what would happen to it right now."

"Well, that's what I think," Kennedy replied. ". . . And some people will say we're not doing enough, the others will say it's too much. . . . All you need is fifteen of them up there that are doing that, and unless the ground's laid, it's really gonna be unpleasant."

Neither man had any notion how unpleasant it would become, or that Robert Kennedy's would be the loudest voice in a cacophony of many more than fifteen dissenters. For now, these two conversations seemed to herald broad agreement between LBJ and RFK: on the proper balance of diplomatic and military pressure, on the subordinate role of Congress, on a wartime coalition built on candor.

Yet Lyndon Johnson was an agreeable man in the months before his reelection and in the year that preceded his significant buildup in Vietnam. He accepted every argument and counterargument; he seemed to hold all positions on Vietnam simultaneously. Among "war hawks" he decried the costs of withdrawal; among doves he lamented the pointlessness of the whole exercise. To Bobby Kennedy, LBJ spoke excitedly of "political thinking, political programs"; to Robert McNamara, he derisively described "Bobby's reaction—a political job, not a military job." Johnson was convinced by every adviser; he was convinced by none of them.

Most likely, Johnson meant what he said when he was saying it. Shrewdly, he was also buying time, forestalling controversy until the November election had passed. Until then he would play the cool-headed contrast to the "war candidate," Barry Goldwater. But mostly Johnson was confused and terribly afraid: afraid of standing, afraid of running, afraid of crusading anti-Communists and neo-isolationists. He was afraid of betraying John Kennedy and inciting Bobby. He was afraid, as Hugh Sidey observed, "that the historians might say he was not a brave leader." All these fears were entwined, forming a powerful snare that, in the end, trapped Johnson in Vietnam. "If I ran out," Johnson explained later, "I'd be the first American President to ignore our commitments, turn tail and run, and leave our allies in the lurch—after all the commitments Eisenhower had made, and all that SEATO had made, and all that the Congress had made . . . and all the statements that [John] Kennedy had made, and Bobby Kennedy had made, and that everybody made." Withdrawal was unthinkable. "I chose to stand."

A purported North Vietnamese attack on an American destroyer in the Gulf of Tonkin in August 1964 prompted only a limited retaliatory air strike and no further escalation; though at the same time, it prompted congressional authorization of "all necessary measures to repel any armed attacks against the forces of the United States and to prevent further aggression." The Tonkin Gulf Resolution granted Johnson a free hand to expand the war, but for the time being he hoped to succeed with limited means. The first casualty of a wider war would surely be his beloved Great Society. "I was determined to keep the war from shattering that dream," he reflected.

In February 1965, when American B-52s began to darken the skies of North Vietnam, Johnson still believed he was steering a middle course between escalation and withdrawal. Most of the Congress and the American people agreed with that course. Johnson did not now or later seek the unconditional surrender of the North; only the most staunchly anti-Communist of his military advisers pressed for that, and he disregarded them. The rest of the establishment believed that the tightening vise of military pressure would cause Ho Chi Minh to abandon his claim on South Vietnam—that gradually, the United States would push Ho over and above his threshold for pain. In meetings with congressional leaders, Johnson stressed the incremental nature of the conflict, and meant it when he told Senator George McGovern, "I'm going up old Ho Chi Minh's leg an inch at a time."

But to Bobby Kennedy—who had little faith in the Joint Chiefs and even less in Lyndon Johnson—the sound of Rolling Thunder was portentous. And one thing was clear: the wider war was coming.

In late April 1965, Robert Kennedy visited the White House to urge a bombing halt. He was not the only one, said LBJ, as the two men sat in the small private study next to the Oval Office. An "interagency working group" was giving the idea careful study. Bobby suggested a pause of a day or two or three; it could do no harm, he said, and might even do some good. The president repeated that Kennedy could "rest assured" the idea was receiving serious attention. Bobby, the president said later, "did influence" his decision. "I was anxious to have his cooperation, his support. [But] I didn't do it just for that. [Kennedy's] was one of many voices."

Personally, Johnson was concerned that a bombing pause sent the wrong message to Hanoi. It might give Ho Chi Minh "the impression we were so eager for a settlement we would do anything," Johnson wrote in his memoirs. The president's military advisers assured him that a short pause was probably meaningless but, they supposed, worth the minimal risk. The air attacks ceased on Wednesday, May 12. This was a message not to Hanoi but to Johnson's critics, and was begrudgingly delivered. "I never was convinced," he told an interviewer, showing his contempt by calling it "Bobby Kennedy's pause." Hanoi, in a defiant guarantee of its brevity, scoffed at the gesture. The United States resumed bombing on May 18.

Bobby Kennedy, too, scoffed at the gesture, for it had been rendered moot on May 4 by the president's request for a supplemental $700 million for military operations in Vietnam. Kennedy, outraged, was inclined to vote against it. He complained to Arthur Schlesinger that ample funds were available. What Johnson obviously wanted was congressional endorsement of his decision to escalate. It was a naked ploy, but a skillful one: a vote against the request was bound to be seen as a vote against "our boys" in uniform. Kennedy's advisers urged him to vote for the resolution but to articulate clearly what he was voting for and what he was not. As he had in February, Kennedy again bowed to politics, though this time he delivered rather than stifled a speech.

The past week had also brought crisis in the Dominican Republic, which Kennedy viewed in a light similar to Vietnam. Latin America had been a sore spot between Bobby and LBJ since the president's appointment of Thomas Mann. Johnson obviously disdained the Alliance for Progress; now he seemed to flout the entire Organization of American States. On April 24, 1965, an ideological jumble of leftist insurgents revolted against the Dominican Republic's authoritarian regime. Overcome by panic, the American ambassador in Santo Domingo relayed an increasingly absurd series of cables to the State Department: the Communists, he said, had taken control of the uprising; they were publicly decapitating rightists; the streets were running with blood. Without any attempt at verification by the CIA, Johnson used this information as pretext for an invasion by 22,000 American troops to restore order and, Johnson insisted, to prevent takeover of the island by "Castroite" elements. The president bypassed the OAS, a body he dismissed as impotent and incompetent.

The invasion "outraged" Robert Kennedy. Taken together with the bombing campaign in North Vietnam and the request for $700 million, it seemed to confirm Bobby's fear of October 1962: in a crisis, Lyndon Johnson would lash out, overreact, explode. On May 5, as Kennedy's aides crafted a measured, politic response, Adam Walinsky sent a reflective memo to RFK that gave some measure of the anxiety in the office: "[Peter Edelman,] Wendell [Pigman] and I are all concerned about the implications of the vote on the $700 million for Vietnam," Walinsky explained. "The 'irrevocable commitment of our people and nation' which the President wants is—in our not-very-informed judgment—

close to a declaration of war, a declaration that covers North Vietnam and China by implication. . . . A silent vote in favor is a flat endorsement of every major aspect of his policy—commitment of ground troops, continued bombings, and whatever else may be used to increase pressure in future."

To Walinsky the issue was the same in Vietnam and the Dominican Republic: "for at the heart of both is a foreign policy based on force, a reliance on military pressure almost to the complete exclusion of political solutions, and a simplistic equation of revolution with communist conspiracy. Almost without serious debate, the foreign policy of the United States has shifted radically in the last year. The Congress is now being asked to confirm that shift, and to surrender any right of stopping the present course. Though all of us feel somewhat silly trying to tell you what to do in this area, we do feel that the debate is necessary. And it will be a more constructive and meaningful one if you take part."

Two full months before Johnson's dispatch of fifty thousand troops to Vietnam, Walinsky identified the central confusion of American policy—the equation of indigenous revolution with communist conspiracy—and the key faultline dividing Johnson and Kennedy, the line between a military and a political solution in Vietnam. Coming so early in the war, Walinsky's memo was uncannily perceptive and prescient and profoundly affected the senator's evolving thought on Vietnam.

The next day, May 6, Robert Kennedy rose in the Senate chamber and declared his support for an appropriation meant for "our fighting forces." He denied that Congress was issuing Johnson a "blank check" for further commitment. Then, as Schlesinger had suggested, Bobby explained himself for the record. He was not for withdrawal. "Such a course would involve a repudiation of commitments undertaken and confirmed by three administrations," he said. Nor was he for escalation. "Let us not deceive ourselves: this would be a deep and terrible decision."

Kennedy favored a third course: negotiations. "This, I take it, is the policy of the administration, the policy we are endorsing today," Bobby stated hopefully and a bit insincerely. Like Walinsky, he saw the handwriting on the wall. But at this early hour, there might be something gained by conciliating LBJ. Kennedy thanked the president for his "cordial invitation to discuss these matters with him" and for the "courtesy and interest" with which he had received Kennedy's concerns. This was perhaps a bit much to be believed, but it was the best Bobby could do to keep the "Kennedy Blasts Johnson" headlines out of the evening editions.

Bobby then turned to the heart of the matter. "We have erred for some time in regarding Vietnam as purely a military problem," he said, stating it plainly, "when in its essential aspects it is also a political and diplomatic problem. I would wish, for example, that the request for appropriations today had made provision for programs to better the lives of the people of South Vietnam. For success will depend not only on protecting the people from aggression but on giving them the hope of a better life which alone can fortify them for the labor and sacrifice ahead."

Describing American policy as, "I trust, a seamless web," Kennedy inched into the western hemisphere and spoke of the Dominican Republic—the "tragic events of the last few days." Kennedy warned his colleagues that America's determination to stop the spread of Communism in this hemisphere "must not be construed as opposition to popular uprisings against injustice and oppression just because the targets of such popular uprisings say they are Communist-inspired." Such "blanket characterizations" would only drive genuine democrats into the arms of the Communists. Moreover, Bobby could not imagine a case in which Americans should "act on our own without regard to our friends and allies in the Organization of American States." He reiterated the call for democracy in the region, evoking the name and spirit of the Alliance for Progress and expressing confidence that the United States would surmount the crises in both hemispheres. "My only concern," Kennedy concluded, "is that we emerge from these crises in an honorable position to continue our leadership in the world at large."

The more immediate danger was to Lyndon Johnson's political consensus, impaired by an outburst of criticism about Latin America and suspicious murmurs about Vietnam. "When I consider what the administration did in the Dominican Republic," Adlai Stevenson told Schlesinger ominously, "I begin to wonder if we know what we are doing in Vietnam." But despite the growing hue and cry, or even the bitter public break between Johnson and Senator J. William Fulbright of Arkansas, chairman of the Senate Foreign Relations Committee, over the Dominican intervention, Kennedy's cautious remarks had not been eclipsed. The Kennedy-Johnson feud burst forth from its dormancy and back onto the pages of the political press. The fallacy of the fall campaign was laid bare. The two men were at it again and the stakes, reporters wrote gleefully, were only getting higher.

On the basis of this one speech and a failed attempt (more Ted Kennedy's than Bobby's) to ban the poll tax, *U.S. News & World Report* was ready to declare Bobby the leader of a "liberal break" with LBJ—the instigator of urban Democrats "who are turning on their fellow Democrat in the White House." Given that Johnson won his $700 million appropriation by a vote of 88 to 3, with Kennedy in the majority, it was unclear where this Pied Piper was leading his followers. But

observers like the *New York Times'* Tom Wicker saw portent in the simple *potential* for mischief. In the widespread unease that followed Johnson's appropriation request, Kennedy "could have sparked a serious
Senate uprising." A leading Democrat had reportedly told Kennedy outright that "if the brother and heir of President Kennedy threw his name,
prestige and political power against Mr. Johnson's Vietnamese policy, others would be emboldened to stand up in the protecting shadow of a
Kennedy." The crusade would have failed, but Wicker judged that
Bobby could have amassed "an impressive total" against LBJ on this vote
of confidence.

At what cost to his own credibility? Senators Ernest Gruening, Wayne
Morse, and Gaylord Nelson, who voted against the appropriation,
earned by their dissent a certain moral cachet that doves-come-lately
would never attain. But while Kennedy's moral (and policy) instincts
matched those of Gruening, Morse, and Nelson, his political calculus had
to be different. No one ever accused Ernest Gruening of scheming for
the presidency. RFK faced the charge constantly—and an arsenal of
adjectives like "ambitious," "ruthless," and "Machiavellian." Bobby's well-
known history with Johnson weakened rather than strengthened his
credibility. Common sense bred caution.

Bobby also understood that bickering with Johnson would squander
whatever authority he held as his brother's heir. Bobby had no taste for
the martyrdom of the moral purist or the perpetual dissenter; men of
that sort were outsiders, ineffectual, impotent. And while questioning
the war effort or the Dominican invasion was one thing, condemning
them was another. "I am awfully glad you didn't make that proposed
floor speech on the Dominican conflict," Joe Dolan wrote Bobby on
May 27. "I think there is a big difference between what should be said
and what you should say. Further, if and when you feel [compelled] to
speak about this situation, I feel very strongly that you should avoid such
strident and biting remarks as 'a Western Budapest' which was in the
draft of the speech." Bobby was walking a fine line between moral credibility and political viability. As time passed it would become harder and
harder to tread.

In retrospect it is easy to assign more moral urgency to the situation in
Vietnam than policy-makers perceived in early 1965. Until LBJ's July
decision to send fifty thousand troops into the jungle (with more to follow), no one outside the administration could be sure that Johnson was
approaching the Rubicon—or would cross it. As Kennedy saw it in
June, "the most vital issue now facing this nation and the world" was not
Vietnam or the Dominican Republic. It was the spread of nuclear

weapons, which had greatly occupied JFK during his presidency. Fred
Dutton, an informal adviser and until recently an assistant secretary of
state, suggested that Kennedy make "a major, thoughtful talk on nuclear
arms control" to "provide a striking, hopeful contrast" to an administration "preoccupied with Southeast Asia."

However striking the contrast of policies, Kennedy's political challenge was tentative. He restrained his more ardent speechwriters, soften-
ing some of their sentences and excising others. He had "an inordinate
faith in fine shadings," remembered Walinsky. "God, we could spend a lot
of time . . . shading the tone just slightly this way and that way." Kennedy
still hoped to influence rather than antagonize Johnson. Walinsky was less
concerned about that. Before Dallas, he had watched Vice President
Johnson give a rare interview, and it "scared the hell out of me," Walinsky recalled. Even before Vietnam, the young Justice Department lawyer
recoiled at Johnson's nationalism and "terrible chauvinism." By 1965,
Walinsky's unease was brewing into a heady disgust. Seeing his boss as
the only conceivable opposition to LBJ, Walinsky stuffed Kennedy's
briefcase full of facts, figures, liberal columns and commentary on Vietnam. If Walinsky deepened Kennedy's doubts, he was less successful in
spurring the senator to speak against the war. "Adam fought a very lonely battle for a long time," remembered Milton Gwirtzman.

Walinsky's differences with RFK were more strategic than substantive. Walinsky played the voice of conscience; he was Bobby's own
Bobby, but without the eye toward (or for) politics. That was what the
other advisers were for—the Dolans, Duttons, Smiths, and Sorensens.
Kennedy and Walinsky clashed amicably that first year about tactics,
agreeing all the while that the war was a bad idea and going badly. But
Walinsky had to acknowledge that Kennedy was far more conflicted
about the war than he. Bobby felt there had been a major shift in the
basis of Vietnam policy since his brother was in the White House but,
said Walinsky, "he was not all that sure that he was right and the others
were wrong." These were his brother's men, after all, good men—McNamara and Taylor and even Rusk—and Bobby was not about to condemn
them and their policy as villainous. He had to admit that this was not
just Lyndon Johnson's war.

Knowing this and fearing the press, Bobby went to extreme lengths
to finesse his differences with Johnson. It rendered the Kennedy speech-
writing operation a difficult process of collaboration and compromise
even when dealing with subjects other than the war. Kennedy sent
Walinsky to Mac Bundy's basement office at the White House with a
detailed draft of the nonproliferation speech in hand. On June 23, this
caution seemed at first to pay dividends: Vice President Humphrey, hav-

ing read an advance copy of the speech, told Bobby in the moments before its delivery that his forthcoming comments were "thoughtful and constructive."

But in the end, Kennedy's diplomacy was to little avail. His speech was not strident but it was strong; and, provocatively, it was laden with quotes from JFK. When Bobby rose in the Senate chamber he spoke first of the threat of nuclear holocaust. "President Kennedy saw this clearly," Bobby said, implying—perhaps unintentionally—that President Johnson did not. Bobby called for an extension of President Kennedy's 1963 Nuclear Test Ban Treaty, the initial step toward nonproliferation. "We have not yet taken the second step," he declared, calling for a formal treaty with the Soviet Union and the "vigorous pursuit" of negotiations with a truculent China. Beyond these specific proposals, Kennedy stressed that "we can and must continue to reexamine our own attitudes, to ensure that we do not lapse back into the fatalistic and defeatist belief that war is inevitable, or that our course is too fixed to be affected by what we do." He might well have been speaking of Vietnam.

Clinton Anderson, Democratic senator from New Mexico and a member of the Joint Committee on Atomic Energy, followed Kennedy's speech with a complaint that the White House was being unhelpful on nuclear matters. Three months earlier, Roswell Gilpatric had prepared—at Johnson's behest—a top-secret report on nuclear proliferation; but the White House refused to release it to Anderson's committee or the Armed Services Committee. At a news conference after the speech, Kennedy was asked why the Gilpatric report had been suppressed. "You better ask the executive department," Bobby snapped, a bit impertinently. He implied that the report—which, one suspects, he had seen or discussed in his recent meetings with Gilpatric—had sown dissension in the White House. Was Johnson abandoning President Kennedy's policies? someone asked. "No," Bobby said, "but I think we need a fresh initiative. There are disputes within the executive departments on how some of these matters should be handled. We should make a decision on how far we want to go and then proceed. We should not let the matter drag on."

Sixteen senators commended Kennedy's maiden speech, but the comment from the White House, as the *Times* observed, "was short and chilly." Johnson's press secretary George Reedy cited the Gilpatric report as evidence of the president's commitment to nonproliferation and explained that the highly classified report was being studied by the appropriate agencies. "Of course," Reedy added, "we are glad Senator Kennedy is also interested in this field."

Privately, President Johnson was less than glad. Since May, he had been looking forward to unveiling a substantial package of arms control proposals at the anniversary of the United Nations. Johnson had been "delighted" by Dick Goodwin's draft of the speech. That was before Kennedy's speech—"a somewhat academic utterance," in Goodwin's judgment, but Johnson saw it differently. "I want you to take out anything about the atom in that speech," the president barked at Goodwin in the Oval Office. "I don't want one word in there that looks like I'm copying Bobby Kennedy."

"But Mr. President," Goodwin objected, "the Kennedy speech is very different from yours. . . . These are formal proposals from the president of the United States. The entire world will be listening."

At the moment, Johnson was not listening. He thrust a newspaper at Goodwin. "Here's Reston's column on Kennedy's speech. You make sure we don't say anything that he says Bobby says. I'm not going to do it," Johnson added stubbornly. Goodwin grudgingly obliged, excising everything of importance—every arms control proposal—from the speech and rendering it little more than "a banal birthday felicitation." The initiatives were gone and forgotten; this president would not be taking any "second steps" toward disarmament.

Goodwin was right to be disappointed. Later, Johnson told Moyers proudly, "I read the whole draft of that speech to some editors of the *Manchester* [England] *Guardian* who came to visit. They said it was great, one of the best speeches they ever heard. You know what I told them? I said I was glad they liked it, because they were the only ones that were ever going to hear it. I wasn't going to give one word of it."

Like Johnson, Kennedy awaited the morning papers warily the day after his arms-control speech. Moments after the *Washington Post* hit his doorstep at Hickory Hill he made a peevish wake-up call to Walinsky: the *Post* had buried his speech midsection, calling it a rehash of administration proposals. Well, Walinsky asked Kennedy nervously, had he seen the *New York Times*? Neither man had; Kennedy's had not even arrived. Walinsky dashed to retrieve his own copy, and to his profound relief the story was spread across the front page, complete with a picture and the text of the speech—unusual treatment for a senator. Walinsky rushed back to the phone. "All right," Bobby said. "Well, that's okay. So that's just the *Washington Post*. They're just screwing around with Johnson. The hell with them." Still, the *Times* was hardly a pushover: on page 16 Kennedy would find Tom Wicker's update of the Johnson-Kennedy feud and his unhelpful (if valid) observation that Bobby "left the strong implication that Mr. Johnson was not doing as much as he might in this field—or as much as President Kennedy had planned to do." A *Times* editorial saw things in tactical terms: Bobby was "edging . . . slightly to the left of President Johnson and squarely within the image of new-generation idealism bequeathed [him] by John F. Kennedy."

In Saigon, political leadership was like a small, furtive flame, greedily snatched by one faction, snuffed out, and fumblingly relit by another. After a brief lull under the civilian rule of Phan Huy Quat, crisis again erupted in May 1965 when the government was overthrown by the Young Turks—Air Marshal Nguyen Cao Ky and General Nguyen Van Thieu. The Ky-Thieu partnership would endure far longer than any government since Diem's, but it never inspired much confidence among American policy-makers. Thieu, who assumed the helm of the South's armed forces, was a credible military leader, but Prime Minister Ky was a drinking, gambling, scheming self-caricature. A State Department official likened him to "a sax player in a second-rate Manila night club." Regularly decked out in a black flying suit and bright purple scarf, Ky posed absurdly with ivory-handled pistols hanging at his hips. "Absolutely the bottom of the barrel," groaned an American analyst.

Once again, the manifest weakness of the Saigon regime renewed calls among Johnson's advisers for intensification of the American effort. Chafing under the constraints the president placed on the air war, Rostow, the Joint Chiefs, and General William Westmoreland called for a step-up in the bombing. In June, LBJ's military advisers requested an additional 150,000 American troops; the enclave strategy, never a sincere effort, was being abandoned for a more aggressive strategy of direct engagement and attrition of enemy forces. "No one ever won a battle sitting on his ass," proclaimed General Earle Wheeler, chairman of the JCS. Over the next month Johnson was careful to hear out all his advisers, but only George Ball and Clark Clifford opposed the large-scale commitment of ground forces. Even General Taylor parted with his reservations.

"We know, ourselves, in our own conscience," Johnson told Robert McNamara on the night of July 14, "that when we asked for this Tonkin Gulf Resolution, we had no intention of committing this many . . . ground troops."

"Right," said McNamara.

"And we're doin' so now and we know it's goin' to be bad," Johnson prophesied. McNamara agreed with this, too. Yet it was McNamara who clinched the argument for escalation, just days after another hurried visit to Saigon. In a memo signed by Bundy, Rusk, Taylor, Westmoreland, and Wheeler, McNamara spelled out three courses of action with characteristic clarity. First, the United States could "cut our losses and withdraw," a decision he judged "humiliating . . . and very damaging to our future effectiveness on the world scene." Second, American involvement could "continue at the present level," with troop numbers limited to about 75,000, thereby forestalling escalation until it was "perhaps too late to do any good." And third, LBJ could (and should, his advisers agreed) "expand promptly and substantially the U.S. military pressure" against the regime in the North and the insurgents in the South, concurrently increasing political pressure for a "favorable outcome." Again, the objective was not unconditional surrender but to "stave off defeat in the short run" and to produce a settlement in the long run. McNamara cautioned that this last alternative committed the United States "to see a fighting war through at considerable cost in casualties and matériel and would make any later decision to withdraw even more difficult and even more costly."

McNamara's memo did not alter Johnson's course but clarified and justified a conclusion preordained; as Johnson implied ruefully on July 14, the ground troops were as good as committed. And Johnson rejected McNamara's most salient piece of advice: like Robert Kennedy a year earlier, McNamara urged the president to declare a national emergency, summon the reserves, request a tax increase, and mobilize the public for war. "Well, that makes sense," Johnson told McNamara, who argued that an open debate would ensure the support and understanding of Congress and the American people. But the president, fearing a "right-wing stampede" toward total war and a military response from China or the Soviet Union, protective of pending legislation, and unwilling to arouse any "undue excitement," elected instead to lead the United States into war in Vietnam by duplicity and dissimulation. On July 28, Lyndon Johnson announced the swift deployment of fifty thousand men to Vietnam and a boost in draft calls. By year's end, American troops in Vietnam would number 200,000. Johnson had made the war his own, and America's.

In July, while Lyndon Johnson weighed the costs of war in Vietnam, Robert Kennedy weighed the costs of keeping silent. Reporters' responses to Kennedy's speeches discouraged him; Bobby's looming "Lyndon problem" was overshadowing his ideas, blocking the light of reasoned debate. His public delicacy in dealing with LBJ was halfhearted, transparent, and largely unrewarded. But the drift of Johnson's policy in Vietnam left Kennedy even more apprehensive and less conciliatory. As the commencement speaker at the International Police Academy—the fresh-faced counterinsurgents of the U.S. Agency for International Development (AID)—Kennedy would argue that the war had far exceeded the bounds of counterinsurgency. The draft of the July 9 speech was Walinsky's, but Walinsky was not yet the radical of later years; the initiative and the anger here were mostly Kennedy's own.

Ironically, the desperate attempts to split the difference between Kennedy and Johnson came this time from the White House. On July 8, the day before Kennedy's address, Sherwin Markman, assistant to presidential appointments secretary Marvin Watson, was at AID offices when a friendly reporter called and read him the text of Bobby's speech. Kennedy's office had already released it to the press. Markman, hearing its more incendiary passages, was overcome by anxiety. "If all a government can promise its people in response to insurgent activity is ten years of napalm and heavy artillery," quoted the reporter, "it would not be a government for long. . . . Victory in a revolutionary war is won not by escalation but by de-escalation." Markman imagined the embarrassment to AID's administrator, David Bell, who was to introduce RFK and share the platform with him at the academy.

Markman called Watson in a panic. "Do you think there's anything you can do to stop it?" Watson asked.

"Well, I'm going to try."

"Do what you can and keep us out of it," Watson ordered stiffly, before warning the president that Vietnam "will be another Kennedy vs. Johnson issue." He advised that a Johnson staffer have a "talk with various agencies" so that the White House might keep abreast of "who they intend to invite to make speeches."

Markman jumped in a taxi and raced to Kennedy's Senate office. A Stevenson man in 1960, Markman had no real connection to the Kennedys. So it was with a certain humility that he introduced himself to RFK and Walinsky and asked to see the speech, which they willingly provided him. They waited as he read it. Markman looked up. "Dave Bell is going to be on this platform, and Bell was an old and dear friend of President Kennedy's," he told them. "I just think that it would be very bad form for you, Senator, to do this. I wonder if there is any possibility of trying to modify this speech?"

They debated it awhile, the three of them, until Bobby relented. "Adam here writes a pretty fire-branding speech," he said, putting the onus on his assistant. "Maybe it does go a little too far." Kennedy's office phones, after all, had been ringing non-stop since the release of the speech; journalists wanted to know if this was the first fusillade in a sustained attack on LBJ. The senator left Walinsky and Markman to hammer out a compromise draft, which was not easy work; they argued over the text through most of the evening. When Bobby returned from Hickory Hill later that night, the three men read it over and agreed upon a final revision. Markman, though, was still full of anxiety. Despite all this teamwork, he wasn't sure he trusted Kennedy, and wanted assurances his own participation would be kept secret. "The possibilities of disaster were just endless," Markman explained later. Bobby might accuse LBJ of trying to censor his speech. Markman returned to the White House and handed the changes to Watson, who was "just ecstatic."

The next day Bobby delivered the modified speech, though many newspapers printed the original version. And even in its diluted form the speech was pretty strong stuff, sharpening the contrast between the Kennedy and Johnson approaches to Vietnam: "The essence of successful counterinsurgency is not to kill," Kennedy told academy graduates, "but to bring the insurgent back into the national life." Though he did not say so explicitly, it was obvious that Bobby saw the emerging Johnson policy as wrongheaded. Reading a paragraph that the White House had tried to excise, Kennedy declared that "our approach to revolutionary war must be political—political first, political last, political always. Where the needs and grievances of the people begin to be met by the political process," he said, with an eye to the bereft program of pacification, "insurgency loses its popular character and becomes a police problem."

Later, bumping into Sherwin Markman, Bobby called him "the man who kept me out of trouble." Indeed the administration, perhaps chary of revealing its hand in the speech, was muted in its response. But to LBJ there was no mistaking it: the speech was another personal strike by Bobby Kennedy, another step toward reclaiming the White House in the name of his slain brother. When a speech began with the words "President Kennedy said," Johnson knew what was coming: another comparison to JFK, another implication that Johnson was not, as promised, *continuing*. When it was not being said on the Senate floor it was being uttered in Georgetown salons, where Kennedy men rubbed shoulders a bit too comfortably with leading journalists. In late July, Horace Busby informed LBJ that "Bobby, Schlesinger, Teddy White, et al. (but mainly Bobby)" were inflating JFK's legacy so obscenely that even friendly reporters were taken aback. Reportedly, one columnist considered Bobby's accounts of the 1960 convention and the Bay of Pigs fiasco "made up." "So do I," concluded Busby. When Busby wrote LBJ that Tony Day of the *Philadelphia Inquirer* "now believes [John] Kennedy would have taken the same decisions in Viet Nam that you made," one might well have asked what it mattered to the president of the United States; but to this president it mattered very much, and in the battle for the hearts and minds of the Tony Days of the world, LBJ savored each and every victory.

CHAPTER 11

Hawk, Dove, or Chicken?

In the fall of 1965, Robert Kennedy invited Dick Goodwin to join him in South America. "You won't be expected to do any work, just come along," Kennedy said. Goodwin was hooked, for he was not expected to pay, either. Kennedy had not visited the subcontinent since an overnight stay in 1962, but it remained a preoccupation (had JFK lived, he might well have placed Bobby formally in charge of Latin American affairs) and, since Johnson's ascendancy, a serious concern. Jack Hood Vaughn had replaced Thomas Mann as LBJ's top Latin American official, but the Mann Doctrine—private investment before social reform, military stability over chaotic constitutional government—still shaped U.S. policy in the region. John Kennedy's Alliance for Progress was moribund. Democratic nation-building, it appeared, was off Johnson's agenda permanently. Of course, the Alliance for Progress had never performed to JFK's hopeful expectations; economic growth rates in South America languished somewhere below zero in 1963. But it was Johnson's wholesale, almost flippant, abandonment of the ideals of the Alliance for Progress that enraged Bobby Kennedy. One expected more from a president who hailed from Texas, larded his speeches with romantic references to his Latin American brothers, and considered himself something of an expert on hemispheric affairs.

When Bobby Kennedy accepted an invitation to speak in Brazil during the Senate's November recess, he hoped to show the Latins another face of the United States. His sense of his brother's legacy impelled him. Bobby hoped not to undercut Johnson's foreign policy but to humanize it, to redirect it toward reform and development and away from a reflexive anti-Communism. "His hope," wrote Arthur Schlesinger, Bobby's frequent counsel on hemispheric affairs, "was to remind the Latin Amer-

icans that there was more to the United States than the International
Petroleum Company." And, relatedly, that there was more to American
foreign policy than Lyndon Baines Johnson.

Therein lay the political audacity of Kennedy's mission. He was not
just a senator on a fact-finding mission; he was a Kennedy, and his electric presence—the windswept coif, the slightly hunched posture, the
clipped gestures and Yankee twang—would render his visit something
closer to a spiritual revival. As heir to the revered John Kennedy he
would, simply by turning up, renew the promise of the Alliance for
Progress and possibly unleash democratic forces he had no official
responsibility—or ability—to contain. That would be Johnson's problem. Bobby's problem was political: whatever his message, the press was
sure to castigate him for running an independent foreign policy, bound
not to American security interests but to his own political interests.
These were all important concerns in the weeks before the trip. But
short of staying home or, miraculously, ending the feud with Johnson,
there was little Bobby could do about them.

Another concern was the Dominican Republic: Bobby could not
very well travel to Latin America and speak in support of Johnson's invasion. If he had not already spoken against it—in May, on the Senate
floor—he would have been ill-advised to go at all. But while Kennedy
would—cautiously—dispute American foreign policy on the floor of
the Senate, he was appropriately loath to do so before a crowd of thousands in Lima, Peru. Perhaps foolishly, Kennedy sought guidance from
the State Department. Vaughn, who was to conduct the briefing, asked
Jack Valenti whether he should simply discourage Kennedy from going
to Argentina, Chile, and Venezuela. Valenti raised the matter with LBJ,
asking, "What kind of briefing should he give Kennedy?"

Judging by Vaughn's performance, Frank Mankiewicz—the Peace
Corps' regional director in Latin America, and its representative at the
meeting—could only conclude that "someone had given him orders to
be just as hostile and bitter as he could be." Mankiewicz was surprised;
usually he found Vaughn an affable man. On the other hand, Walinsky,
who accompanied RFK to Foggy Bottom, considered Vaughn "a Johnson crony who . . . was proceeding to clean out as many as he could of
the Kennedy people" and was "one of the prime apologists for that
insane policy" in the Dominican Republic. As if to sharpen the con-
frontational tone of the briefing, officials from the State Department,
AID, and the U.S. Information Agency lined up on one side of a long
table; Kennedy and Walinsky were seated on the other. It was like a conference between two warring nations, one large, one laughably small.
Bobby asked what he should say in Latin America about the Dominican

invasion. "In the first place," Vaughn replied, twitching his disturbingly crooked mustache, "nobody will ask you about it because they don't care about that issue. No one asks about that any more."

"Well, you and I don't talk to the same Latins," Kennedy said, "because that's all they ever ask me." Kennedy bet Vaughn it would be one of the first three questions he faced in Latin America. (Kennedy won.) Taking the bet, Vaughn added, "If they *do* ask you, you can always tell them what your brother said about Cuba."

Bobby's eyes went dead cold. It was a look, said Walinsky, who received it only rarely, that could "wither tree branches a hundred miles away." Slowly and icily, Kennedy asked, "Which comment of *President Kennedy's* was that, Mr. Vaughn?" Vaughn continued referring to JFK as "your brother" either out of obliviousness or spite. He mumbled something about JFK's statement that the United States would not tolerate Communism in this hemisphere. Bobby, obviously annoyed, said in a level tone, "I hope you are not quoting President Kennedy to justify what you did in the Dominican Republic."

Kennedy expressed further concern about Peru, where a dispute over drilling rights with an American oil company was stalling U.S. aid; and Brazil, where a military cabal had overthrown the country's constitutional government and gained American recognition in twelve hours. "Well, Mr. Vaughn," Kennedy concluded, "let me get this straight. You're saying that what the Alliance for Progress has come down to is that you can lock up your political opposition and outlaw political parties and dissolve the congress, and you'll get all the American aid you want. But if you mess around with an American oil company, we'll cut you off without a penny. Is that right? Is that what the Alliance for Progress has come down to?"

Vaughn looked at him and said, "Well, that's about the size of it, Senator."

What had begun as an effort to placate LBJ, to differ from American policy without undercutting it, had only succeeded in raising tensions. While the foreign policy breach widened, Kennedy would not stop trying to narrow the political breach between himself and Johnson. Just after boarding the plane in Miami on November 10, Kennedy told reporters, "I am not thinking of running for the presidency. I have a high feeling for President Johnson. He has been very kind to me. I would support his bid for reelection in 1968, and I strongly wish to campaign for him."

A bit over the top, this disclaimer, but for the moment it forestalled inevitable questions. It was not, after all, so unbelievable. Bobby's pretense of warmth toward LBJ fooled no reporter, but few imagined

Bobby so reckless or ambitious as to challenge Johnson in 1968. Kennedy's political horizons stretched outward toward 1972 or beyond. Still, Bobby wondered whether he ought to have raised the issue. "Why should I deny something everyone knows isn't going to happen?" he asked Dick Goodwin. "It just encourages speculation. But I didn't want them to write this like some kind of a campaign trip."

The problem, as they landed in Lima, was that it looked like a campaign trip. Kennedy did not just draw a crowd, he *was* a crowd—accompanied by Ethel, Walinsky, Goodwin, John Seigenthaler, Angie Novello, Tom Johnston of Kennedy's New York office, and an entourage of other friends, photographers, film crews, and reporters. William and Jean van-den Heuvel joined them in Peru. And so did thousands of cheering Peruvians, who waved American flags as they trailed Kennedy's green-paneled truck through the ancient Inca capital of Cuzco, tearing his pant leg and pushing him against a barbed-wire fence in their enthusiasm. Poor, malnourished children with bloated bellies leaped on spindly legs and cried "Viva Kennedy!" in the *barriadas* of Cuzco and Lima. When Bobby plunged into a maze of wretched tar-paper hovels, stepping over open sewage to kick a soccer ball with a group of giggling children, it reminded Goodwin of campaigning in a working-class neighborhood of New York. But this was not a pat political performance, and later, in the car, Kennedy's outrage burst forth: "These people are living like animals," he told Goodwin, "and the children—the children don't have a chance. What happened to all our AID money? Where is it going?" He sat back, disgusted with Johnson's negligence; the AID money was still in the United States, awaiting settlement of the oil dispute. "Wouldn't you be a communist if you had to live there?" Kennedy asked Goodwin, or himself. "I think I would."

Television cameras, recording conditions in the South American slums, posed the same question—and the same challenge to administration policy. In the White House, surely, it did not matter how often Kennedy repeated that his trip was "an unofficial, privately financed fact-finding mission" when his other stated purpose—to assure the Latins that the Alliance for Progress was, despite appearances, "still as alive and important as it was under President Kennedy"—was threatening enough to LBJ. Even Frank Mankiewicz thought Bobby's trip "quite reckless." And despite Bobby's defense of American policy ("You are not going to solve your problems by blaming the United States and avoiding your own personal responsibility to do something about them," he lectured students in Lima), his calls for peaceful revolution were an unmistakable affront to U.S. policy.

On November 20, in Brazil, Kennedy's entourage celebrated his fortieth birthday with silly poems and skits; Ethel, producing a toy airplane, said Lyndon Johnson had sent a tiny U-2 to spy on Bobby's activities. In fact, an unnamed source was tracking Bobby's travels and sending scornful "impressions" to the president. The sum of those impressions was that Bobby Kennedy had gone to Latin America to launch a calculated bid for the 1972 Democratic nomination. "Bobbie," as Johnson's source referred to him, sought to boost his international standing by telling Latins what they wanted to hear. In doing so he was "obviously well tutored by Richard Goodwin, his new South American advisor." This was a gesture to Johnson's prejudices, for Goodwin was preparing to leave the administration permanently in January, and the president smarted over the impending betrayal. Goodwin, Johnson said scornfully, had decided his "future was with those Kennedys." Apparently so: poring over wire reports of Kennedy's statements, LBJ marked sentences he was sure "could only have been written by Goodwin." (In reality, they were all written by Walinsky.) When Bobby gestured to Goodwin as the author of the Alliance for Progress, Johnson's Latin American source reported, "Goodwin stood in the back of the room with his arms folded and a wise smile on his face. He badly needed a haircut and, of course, so did Bobbie."

But Johnson's source did not doubt that both men would look fine on television, noting ominously that the ABC camera crew in Argentina was the same crew RFK had employed in his New York Senate race; they had exchanged warm welcomes at the press conference in Buenos Aires. "Someone suggested privately . . . that perhaps the documentary was an early Christmas present from a Kennedy friend," wrote the source. The real problem, he hastened to add, was that Kennedy had in effect

> disassociated himself from the Johnson Administration. He portrays himself as the complete liberal. His inference was that Johnson is an old-guard imperialist whose administration is unaware of South American problems.
>
> Bobbie apparently sees himself as the new champion of Latin America, filling a vacuum in the Senate. It is expected that he will emphasize Latin America in his Senate speeches and overall publicity. . . .
>
> Embassy aides in the countries he visited shuddered at some of the things he said and did. Nevertheless they waited on him hand and foot. . . . The newsmen traveling with him from the New York Times, Herald-Tribune, etc. appeared to be under his spell. Most others saw Machiavellian motives. . . .
>
> He cashed in heavily on the popularity of JFK in South America. The similarity in voice and in some mannerisms seemed to hypnotize the people and obviously for many, he was Jack reincarnated. Bobbie does nothing to divorce himself from this image.

Americans closest to the scene . . . resented the way he and the group acted. They were cocky and overbearing and made themselves as much at home as if they were in Massachusetts.

As one Yank put it, "he made Republicans out of a lot of loyal Democrats down here."

So bitter were Johnson's men that any journalist not openly critical of Kennedy was "under his spell." The *Times,* in fact, was quite even-handed in its reporting, and even *The Nation* was no pushover for RFK: Bobby, its editors wrote, was inching leftward "perhaps less from personal preference than as the only means available to distinguish himself from President Johnson." By opening a dialogue with students and other critics of the United States, Bobby drew an implicit contrast between the FDR/JFK "Good Neighbor Policy" and the LBJ "Bad Neighbor Policy," with "far-reaching political implications." More caustically, *The Saturday Evening Post* chronicled Bobby's travels under the heading "The Compulsive Candidate: Robert Kennedy Runs for President Every Day."

The press also charged Bobby with a sort of running assault on Lyndon Johnson's Alliance for Progress (not John Kennedy's Alliance, which Johnson had betrayed). Bobby's ground troops, the story went, were the young Peace Corps volunteers who crowded him at every stop, unburdening themselves of frustration and despair; Bobby, exercising family prerogative, was obviously using Shriver's people to smite LBJ. Even prior to Kennedy's trip, Bill Moyers had called Frank Mankiewicz and asked him kindly to shut up his volunteers or the president would yank them out. Mankiewicz flew to the problem area, the Dominican Republic, to urge his team to keep quiet about American policy and stop complaining to the press about the intervention. Personally, though, Mankiewicz thought they were right: "Jesus, Bill," Mankiewicz said upon his return, "there's three wars going on there in the Dominican Republic—social, political and religious—and we're on the wrong side of all three." It was candid comments like this that got Mankiewicz called back to Washington while Kennedy stirred up the volunteers down south; Shriver wanted his deputy far away from his troublesome brother-in-law.

A week after his return, Kennedy blasted administration policy on *Meet the Press.* Latin Americans, he said, had the unfortunate impression that "business determined the internal policy of the United States," and the administration's indiscriminate anti-Communism did nothing to counter the notion. "If all we do . . . [is] associate ourselves with those forces which are against subversion and against Communism," Kennedy warned, in an obvious reference to the Dominican Republic, " . . . then I think it is self-defeating and will be catastrophic."

This was not, however, the first mortar in a round of attacks; Bobby did not fulfill the prediction of Johnson's source in South America by becoming the Senate's champion of Latin America. (Nor did he attempt to learn Spanish.) In the end, Kennedy's hopes for Latin America were engulfed by his fears in Vietnam. Kennedy continued to meet with Latin American officials and dissidents, and in a twenty-thousand-word Senate speech of May 9 and 10, 1966 (the longest of his career), pressed for "revolutionary change" in the subcontinent. He urged the Johnson administration to identify itself with those who sought economic and social reform; by backing dictators the United States only strengthened the Communist cause. "Counter-insurgency," he warned, "might best be described as social reform under pressure.... Any effort which disregards the base of social reform and becomes preoccupied with gadgets and techniques and force is doomed to failure."

Despite the obvious allusion to Vietnam, this was not the dramatic break that Kennedy's supporters had hoped for. He had circulated the speech widely among academics, experts, and former advisers to President Kennedy—mostly critics of the Johnson administration—but it hardly seemed to bear their imprint. "The speech is reflective rather than polemic in tone," commented the *New York Times.* "It selectively praises President Johnson . . . but it questions the way the President's purposes are carried out, and the caliber of the men involved." Kennedy's own associates expressed disappointment at his unwillingness to deliver a ringing indictment of U.S. policy in the region.

Awkwardly, Kennedy was contorting his views to avoid a break with Johnson, and was pleasing no one. Neither his travels nor his speech had any impact on the administration's policy in Latin America. Kennedy turned again to Vietnam.

A few months behind the curve, *Time* heralded "The Turning Point in Viet Nam" in a cover story of October 29, 1965. President Johnson's July decisions had left the press scrambling to catch up, and Robert Kennedy was no different. Through 1965, Kennedy's public statements on the war were confused and contradictory. His comment of August 25 was typical:

> I support the effort that's being made in Vietnam by President Johnson. I believe this to be most important. If the effort in Vietnam becomes merely a military effort, we shall win some of the battles, but we will lose the overall struggle. . . . Social, political, economic, educational [and] agricultural progress has to be made for the peasants of that tragic land. And we need to do much in this field.

The administration had largely abandoned "this field"; Bobby was supporting a war he knew did not exist. He was stumbling haltingly but inexorably toward open dissent. When Walinsky typed out a memo to LBJ on the indiscriminate bombing of villages, maltreatment of prisoners, Americanization of the war, and neglect of a political solution, the draft languished in Kennedy's in-basket. It was never sent. But when college students set alight the first batch of draft cards, Kennedy flirted with defending their behavior: "If a person feels that strongly and wants to . . . burn his draft card . . . I don't agree with it personally but I think that obviously [is] a way [chosen by] somebody that feels very strongly about this matter." In the same interview, he recklessly declared giving blood to North Vietnamese POWs "a good idea . . . in the oldest traditions of this country." In the fury that followed in the nation's papers (the *New York Daily News* suggested that Kennedy "light out for the enemy country and join its armed forces"), Bobby's tepid defense of LBJ was overlooked entirely.

Privately, Bobby was just as conflicted and ambiguous about the war—and about Lyndon Johnson, whose intentions were hard to divine. Did Johnson want war or peace? That April, in an important speech at Johns Hopkins, he had declared himself open to "unconditional discussions" (a move which Arthur Schlesinger, in January 1966, publicly attributed to the influence of intellectuals and senators like RFK and Frank Church). Now, in November 1965, a special Italian mission to Hanoi seemed to offer an opportunity. "I am prepared to go anywhere; to meet anyone," Ho Chi Minh had told his visitors, and Italian Foreign Minister Amintore Fanfani forwarded the news to President Johnson along with Ho's terms of negotiation, his "four points." (In essence, all four urged the United States to abide by the General Agreements of 1954.) Rusk described himself as "far from persuaded" by the gesture. After a two-week delay that killed any momentum, Rusk asked Fanfani to clarify a few matters. Meanwhile, word had come that American bombing of Hanoi or Haiphong would stifle negotiations in their cradle, and the Italians passed this warning along to a handful of influential Americans, including RFK. If it reached the Oval Office it was disregarded: on December 15, Johnson ordered the first bombing of a major industrial target in North Vietnam, a power plant on the outskirts of Haiphong.

Several days later, RFK threw an early Christmas party at Hickory Hill. Unburdening himself in a rambling monologue, he appeared weary and perplexed:

> Why didn't we accept the Fanfani message positively, agreeing to the four points and offering our own interpretation of what the four points meant—plus some points of our own . . . Then the onus would be on

Hanoi to refuse. This would make us look good whether the offer was real or not. But to dismiss it out of hand is disastrous. We lose all credibility. How could the State Department wait for two weeks? How could they? . . . If we had acted that way in the Cuban crisis we might have had war. If, on Friday night, we had asked the Soviet government for an explanation of their message instead of just agreeing to our own interpretation of it, it might have been chaos.

I don't believe in pulling out the troops. We've got to show China we mean to stop them. . . . I'm upset over our policy in Vietnam, I don't think we've shown an open approach. I really think Johnson wants negotiations. Ball, Harriman, McNamara, too. But Rusk is against them. Fifty percent of the government is probably for them; fifty percent against them. We're in a stalemate.

I'd like to speak out more on Vietnam. I have talked again and again on my desire for negotiations. But if I broke with the administration it might be disastrous for the country.

Bobby's surprisingly charitable assessment of LBJ (if not his policy) was probably a product of the president's Christmas bombing halt of 1965. The halt was Johnson's reluctant gift to McNamara, who had been lobbying since early November for a temporary cessation in the bombing. "We have been too optimistic," McNamara told Johnson at a December 18 White House meeting. The secretary was increasingly doubtful of winning the generals' war of attrition. A bombing halt was a gesture of goodwill that might just bring Ho Chi Minh to the table. Overcoming his own skepticism, the hostility of the Joint Chiefs, and the opposition of most of his advisers, Johnson conceded the Christmas truce. It tantalized the hopeful as it stretched improbably through the month of January.

Still, the pause was precarious. The growing din from the Joint Chiefs promised an imminent return to the old policy. Hoping to steel Johnson against the pressure and to soften, a bit, their personal antagonism, Bobby Kennedy sent Johnson a handwritten note and a copy of Bruce Catton's *Never Call Retreat,* a book on Lincoln's solitary agony during the Civil War. The book, Bobby explained, made him "[think] of you and your responsibilities." In his cramped handwriting Bobby acknowledged,

Reading the newspapers and their columnists and listening to my colleagues in Congress (including myself) on what to do and what not to do in Viet Nam must become somewhat discouraging at times. . . .

I thought it might give you some comfort to look again at another President, Abraham Lincoln, and some of the identical problems and situations that he faced that you are now meeting. . . .

In closing let me say how impressed I have been with the most recent

efforts to find a peaceful solution to Viet Nam. Our position within the
United States and around the world has improved immeasurably as we
face the difficult decisions of this year.

Johnson's words of January 27, grandiose in their self-pity, were scripted by Jack Valenti:

Your warm letter arrived at an appropriate time. It was one of those hours
when I felt alone, prayerfully alone.

I remembered so well how President Kennedy had to face, by himself,
the agony of the Cuba[n] missile crisis. I read the paragraph in Catton's
book that you had marked, and then I went to a meeting in the Cabinet
Room with the Congressional leaders of both parties. I read them that
passage where Lincoln told a friend that all of the responsibilities of the
administration "belong to that unhappy wretch called Abraham Lincoln."
I knew exactly how Lincoln felt.

You know better than most the gloom that crowds in on a President,
for you lived close to your brother. Thus, your letter meant a great deal to
me and I tell you how grateful I am for your thoughtfulness.

As a peace feeler Bobby's letter seemed to have done wonders. But in
terms of policy it had no impact. Thirty-seven days of waiting for Ho
had brought him no closer to the table, and President Johnson bowed to
the generals. On January 31 he resumed the bombing.

The end of the bombing halt, and the accelerated wave of sorties that
followed, spelled the swift and bitter end of Bobby Kennedy's own truce
with LBJ. Rising on the Senate floor on January 31, Kennedy sharply
condemned the renewed air war: "If we regard bombing as the answer
in Vietnam," he declared, "we are headed straight for disaster. In the past,
bombing has not proved a decisive weapon against a rural economy—or
against a guerrilla army. And the temptation will now be to argue that
if limited bombing does not produce a solution, that further bombing,
more extended military action, is the answer. The danger is that the decision to resume may become the first in a series of steps on a road from
which there is no turning back—a road which leads to catastrophe for
all mankind."

Though counterinsurgency now seemed hopelessly outdated, almost
quaint in its redemptive faith, Kennedy continued to perceive Vietnam
primarily in political terms—political first, last and always, as he told
graduates of the International Police Academy. That had been his instinct
from the start. In 1965, a diplomatic attempt to free an AID official kid-
napped by the Vietcong confirmed it. Enlisted in the effort by columnist
Joseph Kraft, Bobby pursued the matter with typical determination and

found the process instructive: the Vietcong, he learned, had a legitimate political structure, the National Liberation Front, and the NLF was far from the terrorist gang of American caricature. When the Johnson administration rejected Bobby's attempt to broker a prisoner exchange between the NLF and South Vietnam (the arrangement, said Maxwell Taylor, would upset Saigon), Bobby emerged bitter at Johnson but hopeful of broader negotiations. Kennedy was now convinced that the NLF, if granted a place at the table, might not be entirely disruptive. In any case, the NLF was essential to the legitimacy of any negotiated settlement. Its inclusion, however distasteful, was the price of peace.

This belief left Kennedy isolated: no one, not even Senator Fulbright, whose Foreign Relations Committee began public hearings on Vietnam on February 4, was making the argument for including the NLF in negotiations. Nor had Rusk, when summoned by the committee, revealed the administration's terms for talks with Hanoi. President Johnson, meanwhile, tried to outshine Fulbright with a spontaneous, flashy trip to Honolulu to meet with Ky and Thieu. On February 8 the three leaders proclaimed their joint dedication to crushing the Vietcong and eradicating social injustice in Vietnam. Kennedy was outraged by what he considered a public relations stunt.

But as others led the debate, Kennedy—standing at the back of the hearing room, watching Fulbright's proceedings with undivided, almost unnerving, intensity—was at risk of being marginalized. Two months earlier, he had considered traveling with Burke Marshall to South Vietnam, but Johnson had forbidden it. Now Bobby entertained the idea again, this time at the invitation of Bob McNamara, Maxwell Taylor, and Averell Harriman, whose motives did not necessarily agree with his own. On February 8, Fred Dutton advised Bobby that more foreign travel, so soon after his trip to Latin America, would appear "too much junketing . . . rash, presumptuous and opportunistic." And following the Honolulu conference, it would look like " 'me-tooing' LBJ." Dutton thought a Kennedy trip would detract from the Fulbright hearings and distract Bobby himself from "racking up some tangible legislative accomplishments now," at the beginning of the session. Most important, Dutton advised that Kennedy keep his distance from Johnson policies reeking of "growing self-righteousness and simplistic Texas nationalism." Kennedy was successfully building a political base to Johnson's left. "Why louse all that up," Dutton asked him, "on a trip which . . . appears to me to be an unconscious effort by McNamara, Taylor and Harriman to have you help pull their and President Johnson's badly charred chestnuts out of [the] fire?"

Kennedy took heed and stayed home. But Dutton was not suggesting

he keep a low profile on the issue. Almost two weeks later, Bobby dialed
Dick Goodwin's number in Connecticut; it was 7:00 A.M. and Goodwin
let the phone ring until he could stand it no longer. "Have you been following the Fulbright hearings?" Bobby asked.

Goodwin had been tracking the committee's daily revelations in the
press. "I think he's done a pretty good job," he replied drowsily.

"Do you think there's anything constructive I can add?"

An hour later, after thinking about it, Goodwin called back and told
him that "everyone, even the administration, claims that the only solution is a negotiated settlement, but nobody's been willing to spell out
what it would look like, what terms would be acceptable. That's something you could do."

Later that afternoon, Goodwin read a draft statement to Kennedy,
who liked it. Both men saw the "unanswerable logic" in inviting the
NLF to the negotiating table and even in going a step further: giving the
Communists "a share of power and responsibility" in the future government of South Vietnam. With one foot poised on the slippery slope of
"coalition," Goodwin refrained from using the word itself, tainted by its
association with Communist coups in the Eastern bloc.

"Please protect me absolutely on this," Goodwin pleaded on February 17 in an accompanying note to Kennedy. "Even from your notoriously discreet associates. Say you wrote it yourself," he added with irony.
But when Goodwin cautioned that the draft "reaches to the edge of
political danger," he was referring not to himself but to RFK. It was
Bobby who would bear the public brunt of suggesting that the administration do business with Communists. Kennedy needed no such warning: if he was mindful of Goodwin's reputation he was even more
protective of his own. By the time Goodwin's draft arrived on his desk,
Kennedy had consulted with Walinsky, Edelman, McNamara, and Taylor
on the NLF's possible role in a postwar Vietnam. All agreed: power-sharing (by any name) was essential.

This gave Bobby some measure of comfort. Cavalierly, he even drew
an "X" through a paragraph praising "President Johnson's increased
emphasis on the process of pacification . . . [as] the most important and
hopeful development in the recent history of the war." But Bobby
remained fearful that by speaking too boldly he made *himself* the issue.
On February 18, the day before its release to the press, Bobby sent a copy
of the speech to McNamara with a handwritten note: "If you have any
thoughts, you might call me at home. I told Bill Moyers I was going to
make it [the speech]—and what I was going to say. I don't believe it
causes problems—but then I've been wrong about that before."

He was wrong again. Kennedy's careful hedges against offending the administration seemed clever at first: on Saturday, February 19, a half hour before Kennedy's press conference, Moyers told reporters that the people of South Vietnam "can choose any form of government that they want—and we will accept that decision." This was a hopeful, conciliatory beginning to the exchange of views—so conciliatory that Kennedy naively feared his own statement would go unnoticed. "Do you think there's any news in it?" he asked Wes Barthelmes, his press secretary.

Bobby read his statement to the press before leaving for a ski trip to Vermont. "There are three routes before us: military victory, a peaceful settlement, or withdrawal," he declared, echoing his speech of the previous May, and again dismissing victory as costly and uncertain and withdrawal as "impossible for this country." President Johnson had suggested no different at Johns Hopkins when he committed himself to "unconditional negotiations." But Kennedy questioned whether the administration was truly ready to drop its preconditions, particularly its refusal to negotiate with the NLF. "A negotiated settlement means that each side must concede matters that are important in order to preserve positions that are essential," like the independence of South Vietnam. He continued,

> Whatever the exact status of the National Liberation Front—puppet or partly independent—any negotiated settlement must accept that fact that there are discontented elements in South Vietnam, Communist and non-Communist, who desire to change the existing political and economic system of the country. There are three things you can do with such groups: kill or repress them, turn the country over to them, or admit them to a share of power or responsibility.

The last, Kennedy concluded, "is at the heart of the hope for a negotiated settlement," though "it may mean a compromise government fully acceptable to neither side."

"It *may* mean a *compromise* government"—here was the nuance for which Kennedy and his speechwriters had labored. Substantively, the statement was hardly different from his speech at the International Police Academy, where he urged that "insurgents . . . be returned to the political process." But now Kennedy had gone a step further: "compromise" obviously meant "coalition," which most understood to mean "Communist." Kennedy was suggesting only that the NLF be guaranteed a place in negotiations, not necessarily in a postwar government, but the calculated ambiguity of the statement was sure to cause controversy. And moments later, in the question-and-answer session, Kennedy seemed to ask for trouble. Rather pedantically, he listed the lessons of the Cuban missile crisis: first, that the United States use no more force than neces-

sary to reach its objectives, and second, that "it is always necessary to realize what an opponent can accept and what he cannot retreat from." As
if to taunt Johnson further, Bobby pointed out that he had discussed his
position with the presidential press secretary and found "no disagreement between what Mr. Moyers said and what I have said."

"Do you speak for the White House?" asked a naive newsman.

Kennedy flashed a grin. "I don't think anyone has ever suggested that
I was speaking for the White House."

The frenzy that followed proved this point and obliterated any other
he might have made. VIET COALITION RULE, INCLUDING VIETCONG,
URGED BY KENNEDY, shouted the *Washington Post*. BREAKS WITH JOHN-
SON, read the *New York Times*. A *Chicago Tribune* editorial labeled him
"Ho Chi Kennedy." The White House reaction was hardly more forgiving. "Coming from any other senator," *Newsweek* reported, "the suggestion might have stirred a ripple of controversy; coming from a
Kennedy, it jolted the Administration with the force of a Claymore mine
planted in Dean Rusk's in-basket." Typically, Johnson and his advisers
perceived Bobby's proposal as the culmination of a growing congressional conspiracy. "Most feel Senator B. Kennedy is the motivating force
behind the Senate [Fulbright] hearings and the Saturday statement was
only his climax," an aide informed the president. LBJ and Rusk thought
Bobby's "switch" on Vietnam was cynical, hypocritical, and dangerous. It
was part and parcel of a "new" liberalism that Rusk deemed "a political
maneuver . . . rooted in his own personal ambition." To George Reedy,
Kennedy was not a cynic but a fanatic, and his "antiwar" zealotry nothing more than his anti-Johnson animus, displaced.

Johnson ordered his marshals to attack. From New Zealand, where he
was promoting the war, Vice President Humphrey assailed Kennedy's
plan as "a prescription for the ills of South Vietnam which includes a
dose of arsenic." He was full of metaphors: NLF participation was like
putting "a fox in a chicken coop" or "an arsonist in the fire department."
Even George Ball, the administration's senior skeptic, was dispatched to
ABC's *Issues and Answers* to argue that a coalition government equaled a
Communist government. On NBC's *Meet the Press,* Bobby's friend
McGeorge Bundy quoted John Kennedy, out of context, from a 1963
speech in Berlin: "I am not impressed by the opportunities open to popular fronts throughout the world. I do not believe that any democrat can
successfully ride that tiger." And Moyers, who had been so helpful to
Kennedy a day earlier, now coolly disavowed him. He refused to comment on Kennedy's NLF proposal except to say that "if Hanoi changes
its mind about aggression and the subjugation of South Vietnam by force
and agrees to discussions and negotiations on the question of peace, the

...Vietcong will have no problem in having their views represented at such a conference."

Stunned and beleaguered, Kennedy returned from Vermont and hunkered down in what Edelman called their "little fortress" on the Hill. He conferred with Edelman and Walinsky late into Monday night and waited for the next bomb to drop. "There was kind of a command-post feeling about it," recalled Edelman. Bobby's young aides marveled at LBJ's persuasive powers: "God! Look at who's come out against us now! Can you believe he said that? Boy, Lyndon must've had to twist his arm all the way around his back!" Kennedy wondered who would speak in his own defense—Vietnam experts, friendly columnists—and tossed names back and forth. "Can Dick Goodwin get somebody?" Bobby asked plaintively. "Who can we get?" They felt the entire federal government was against them.

The next morning, February 22, Bobby went on NBC's *Today* to defend himself. In closing, he clumsily admitted that his evolving position was "a little confusing." Later that day he called a press conference to "clarify" his statements and, in the moments beforehand, took a phone call from Moyers. Moyers was working hard—again—to narrow the differences between Johnson and Kennedy, to take the edge off the confrontation. In the bathroom near the conference room, Kennedy and Walinsky puzzled over the meaning of Moyers's call. Moyers had promised that Johnson would pursue Kennedy's ideas. Kennedy and Walinsky were deciding whether to believe him.

At the 5:00-P.M. conference, Kennedy again spoke haltingly, almost apologetically. He was still shell-shocked. "It was not that I thought . . . that there would be any difference between my position and their position. I didn't see that there would be any," he insisted. "What I was suggesting was just a further step" in the same direction. The administration had been "confused" in its response.

"Senator," a reporter interjected, "when you talked to Bill Moyers this afternoon—"

Kennedy cut him off. "I don't want to speak for him. I don't want to get him in trouble." And then he contradicted himself by confessing that he did, in fact, disagree with the administration's position that "we can't have a coalition government and, secondly, that we frown on that and we can't let the Communists in this kind of operation." Those, he argued, were preconditions that precluded truly free elections.

Johnson let this slide. He had made his point. He worried, in fact, that he had made it too severely, and held his men back from further attacks. But there was still the troubling matter of General Maxwell Taylor, a close friend of Bobby's, who had kindly suggested on Monday that if the

South Vietnamese voted for Communists, the United States would abide by those results. Now, in another surprising turn, Moyers worried that the administration was moving too far toward accommodating RFK. "There is enormous confusion on the Kennedy-Taylor coalition question and the Administration is going to be the one most suffering from it" unless it is cleared up, Moyers advised LBJ. Journalists were getting the impression that the administration was split between a Taylor (Kennedy) faction and a Ball-Bundy-Rusk faction. "In effect," Moyers explained, demonstrating the ease with which he slid back into the president's pocket, "Kennedy has managed to create the image of division among us, thus escaping the necessity of clarifying his own position." Moyers neglected to mention his own role—now a matter of public record—in sketching out that position, instead putting the onus on Taylor to distance himself from RFK. Taylor did so dutifully in a White House statement.

The waters had been hopelessly muddied; it was increasingly unclear where anyone stood. At a press briefing that day, Moyers offered the diplomatic assurance that "if Senator Kennedy did not propose a coalition government with Communist participation before elections are held, there is no disagreement." In a pointed reference to Bobby's comment on *Today*, Moyers added, "I don't think it is the administration that is confused." The *Washington Star*, noting that Moyers had approved Kennedy's statement in advance, commented wryly that "the Kennedy-Moyers pact did not appear to rest on entirely solid ground."

Tensions had diminished enough by February 23 that Kennedy, joining the rest of New York's congressional delegation on Air Force One, accompanied Johnson to the Freedom House dinner at the Waldorf-Astoria. The president, dressed in black tie, received the National Freedom Award and a bronze sculptured bust of himself (the second that week). But as LBJ stood at the podium and answered his critics on Vietnam, he seemed to be delivering a particular rebuke to Kennedy, who sat a few feet away on the dais. Johnson denied that the United States was trapped in "mindless escalation" that would provoke a wider war. "Our purpose in Vietnam," he lectured the audience of fifteen hundred, "is to prevent the success of aggression. It is not conquest, it is not empire, it is not foreign bases, it is not domination."

Bobby, who had never suggested it was any of these things, sat chewing a cigar, applauding perfunctorily. He stared vacantly but sullenly ahead even as the intellectuals booed, even as Johnson quoted JFK's inaugural address in strident self-justification. An old New Dealer in the audience read the expression on his face: "I have heard all this hokum a thousand times." It meant little to Kennedy that Johnson had just committed himself to abide by the wishes of Vietnamese voters—however objectionable the results. "We stand," Johnson repeated, "for self-determination."

By blurring the lines of debate, both men seemed reluctant to concede that this was, in fact, a debate. The press knew better. According to the *New York Times,* "the Kennedy-Johnson controversy" was "the first serious public debate by responsible men on the Vietnam issue" and had "brought a significant step forward in Administration policy by defining sharper limits to American war aims . . . [and] removing taboos on what can be negotiated." Most encouraging for RFK, the editors described his statement as "less a criticism of the President's policies than an invaluable contribution to the decision-making process." But the hawkish *Washington Post* mocked Kennedy's "clarifications" and captioned its editorial not "Kennedy vs. Johnson" but "Kennedy vs. Kennedy."

Neither Kennedy nor Johnson could have been pleased that the *Times* called Bobby's speech a "major gain" for a new breed of Democrat willing to split the party over Vietnam. A leading party member deemed Kennedy "the only one with the strength and independence to stand up to Johnson." On February 19, actor Robert Vaughn (star of *The Man from U.N.C.L.E.*) stood before a gathering of the California Democratic Council and shouted, "Is there any doubt in your mind that if the Vietnam war is going on in 1968 . . . [Kennedy] can win the Democratic nomination and the Presidential election?" Delegates cheered wildly. Bobby, hearing of the spectacle, was hardly flattered. "Those are the people with picket signs and beards, aren't they?" he asked. He told intimates scornfully, "I'm not their Wayne Morse."

In a *U.S. News* interview, Kennedy denied that he was trying to outflank the president to the left. "I know there has been such talk," Bobby replied. "It probably is based on the assumption some people make on their own that I expect to run for the Presidency. . . . My own experience in the past in these matters is that it is empty to speculate about what one is going to be doing five or six years from now—or even whether one is going to be here then." Kennedy stressed he had no plans to challenge Johnson and no plans for either 1968 or 1972.

This was part of a general retreat. "Keep stating your position in terms of its being the logical extension of, not opposition to, the Administration's stand," Fred Dutton counseled RFK. In a draft statement of February 26, Bobby omitted a stronger, more direct challenge to the bitter thrusts of Humphrey and Rusk—citing instead the words of Bill Moyers. And lastly, Bobby made a sheepish return to the Sunday talk show circuit, appearing on CBS's *Face the Nation* on February 27. He attempted to narrow the gap between himself and the administration, portraying himself as helpful and responsible rather than disloyal or confused.

Kennedy "had a great capability for provoking [Johnson]," Walinsky remembered. "And he had a great capability to hurt his friends inside the administration." If Bobby pushed too hard, Johnson might cut the McNamaras and Taylors out of his circle—with dire consequences in Vietnam. So he stopped pushing.

Before Bobby's appearance on CBS, Arthur Schlesinger and Fred Dutton ran him through potential questions. Schlesinger quizzed him on JFK's responsibility for the trouble in Vietnam, and Kennedy paused a moment, thinking. "Well," he replied, "I don't know what would be best: to say that he didn't spend much time thinking about Vietnam; or to say that he did and messed it up." Suddenly, Bobby thrust his hand upward and said, "Which, brother, which?"

The question, thankfully, was not raised on the air, but Walinsky was right to declare Kennedy's performance "appropriately tortured." His tone was moderate, calm, reasonable; but his logic was contorted: was he insisting that Communists be included in a coalition, or just that they be granted the right to vote? One position was incendiary, the other was hardly news. Bobby seemed to hold them both. But he did land a solid blow for pragmatism and against the rhetoric of his critics: "Statements that are made that we will never deal with assassins and . . . murderers make it difficult for [the Vietcong] to believe that they are being asked to come to the negotiating table other than to surrender."

An hour later, Vice President Humphrey appeared on *Issues and Answers* and proved the point. He had obviously seen the Kennedy interview, and his defense of Johnson's policy was coarse and harsh. The Vietcong, he said, "engage in assassination, murder, pillage, conquest, and I can't for the life of me see why the United States of America would want to propose that such an outfit be made part of any government." The door had swung back and slammed shut on the NLF, which Humphrey derided as a "stooge" of Hanoi, certainly not "a sovereign entity." And as for Kennedy, the vice president professed amazement that "a person of liberal persuasion . . . should spend his time trying to find out how he can accommodate himself, or someone else, with the Communist thrust for power." Kennedy, watching the broadcast with Schlesinger, was so irritated after a few minutes that he drifted away silently. Humphrey's outburst was a fitting crescendo to the ugliest and most hysterical confrontation yet between Johnson and Kennedy.

The behavior of Humphrey, Rusk, Ball, and Bundy upset Bobby Kennedy but could not have surprised him. The behavior of Bill Moyers was more puzzling. During the "power-sharing" affair, Moyers was at first helpful to Kennedy—without incurring Johnson's wrath. In the end

Moyers held Kennedy at arm's length and even gently mocked him in the press—without losing Kennedy's trust. It was a daring tightrope walk across the chasm that separated Johnson and Kennedy. It required skill, shrewd diplomacy, and no small measure of duplicity.

Billy Don Moyers was Kennedy's most important link to the White House—and after Dick Goodwin's retreat to Middletown, Connecticut, in January 1966, Kennedy's only link. Pierre Salinger and Ted Sorensen had once been go-betweens, but were long gone by 1966. Now there was only Moyers. He seemed, at first glance, an unlikely ally. The young Texan had been tucked so closely under Johnson's wing for so long he seemed an appendage. As a student at North Texas State in the summer of 1954, Moyers wrote a letter to Senator Johnson—a rather audacious letter, Moyers thought in retrospect—instructing Johnson how to win the youth vote in his campaign for reelection. The letter earned Moyers a summer internship in the majority leader's office. By 1960, Moyers had completed his studies, been ordained a Baptist minister, and returned to LBJ's office. The sight of the earnest young preacher in his thick-rimmed glasses opening mail inspired giggles among Johnson's secretaries, but Moyers was not their fodder for long: within months he leapfrogged from the back to the front office and right to Johnson's side. At the 1960 convention he slept in the bathroom of Johnson's suite and raced through the halls of the Biltmore as "a combination valet-messenger-administrative assistant," in Evans and Novak's words. In 1961, Moyers became a key assistant to Vice President Johnson.

But the best favor Johnson could do for Moyers in those stultifying years as vice president was get the young man out of his employ. On the strength of LBJ's recommendation and his own performance during the 1960 campaign, Moyers became Sargent Shriver's deputy at the Peace Corps. A skillful shuttle diplomat, Moyers slid easily back and forth between the Kennedy and Johnson camps, cultivating "the family's" respect and affection while somehow escaping the distrust Johnson felt toward other "traitors." On November 22, 1963, Moyers scribbled a note to the new president: "I'm here if you need me," it said, and Johnson did. "That boy's like a son to me, even if he did go work for those Kennedys," Johnson told Dick Goodwin a few months later.

On July 8, 1965, when Moyers replaced George Reedy as press secretary, his influence was already widely felt within the executive branch. Since the assassination Moyers had overseen key task force meetings that spawned the Great Society. His mastery of budget issues and his receptiveness toward innovation impressed the old Kennedy brain trust as he channeled their grief into progress. In early 1966, Johnson brought him into his shrinking circle of foreign-policy makers. Johnson's premium was now on loyalty as much as insight, and Moyers offered both.

To keep the president supplied with fresh ideas, Moyers developed his own network of contacts throughout the intelligence community, the executive branch, and the Congress. George Christian, Moyers's successor in the press office, called the operation a "staff-within-a-staff," a "little White House." Meanwhile Moyers continued to manage Johnson's press relations. It was hardly hyperbole when the *Times* described Moyers as "one of the most remarkable collectors of hats ever worn by a White House staff member" or, more simply, as "one of the most influential and active staff aides in Presidential history."

"Anybody that understands the relationship between Bill Moyers and the President," reflected Reedy, "will have the real key to the personality of Lyndon Baines Johnson." Moyers's relationship with Johnson was more complicated than father-son or patron-protégé. In Reedy's (admittedly jaded) view, an "unfortunate predilection to flattery" explained LBJ's excessive fondness for Moyers. Johnson was also "a little bit overawed by self-confident people." And when bold, ambitious young men—like Moyers or Bobby Baker—bestowed their loyalty upon him, Johnson could be fawning in his gratitude.

Still, Johnson's treatment of Moyers was terribly, typically uneven. Some days Moyers was like a son to him; on others, Johnson barely acknowledged his existence. Moyers spent more time in Johnson's company than most aides and bore the brunt of his moods. "This affected [Moyers] very, very deeply," recalled Christian. McPherson called it the "Valenti Syndrome"—judging yourself as Johnson judged you at any given moment—though this was a little unfair to the long-suffering Valenti. By McPherson's own admission, the whole staff was vulnerable to Johnson's whims. "When I was in favor, I was on top of the world; when I was out of favor, I was in the dumps," said McPherson, who eventually pulled back from Johnson to "save my sanity." But Moyers was unable to break away, and as Johnson surged from the depths to the heights and spiraled back down again he dragged Moyers along for the ride. It was an emotional roller coaster, "a distressing thing" to watch, said Christian.

Bobby Kennedy's regard for Moyers was more consistent than Johnson's. There was something about Moyers—his youth, drive, vigor—that distinguished him from the rest of Johnson's staff. "A smart fellow and an honorable man," Bobby judged in 1964. Kennedy's admiration was deeper than he let on. In fact, when Bobby visited the Oval Office to urge a bombing halt in April 1965, he made an astounding proposition: that Johnson replace Secretary of State Dean Rusk with the thirty-one-year-old Moyers.

Of course, Kennedy was probably less interested in promoting Moyers than in removing Rusk. Rusk was "a rather weak figure" in Bobby's view, a captive of tired, lockstep career diplomats—a British civil servant with a Georgia twang. Rusk had fared poorly in the rough-and-tumble of President Kennedy's roundtables; by 1963 his reticence had begun to "irritate" both Kennedys. "It was terrifically frustrating for the President," Bobby recalled. "[Rusk] would never follow anything up. He'd never initiate ideas." Bobby argued that Rusk had let the State Department slip from his control—"virtually gave up its operation, delivered himself of it and the responsibility"—ceding it to the master manager McNamara. The Kennedys considered making the arrangement official. They spoke frequently about removing Rusk—perhaps shuffling him over to the United Nations and making McNamara secretary of state.

After the assassination, Bobby foolishly continued to press for Rusk's dismissal. It was a lost cause. If President Johnson ever purged the remaining Kennedy cabinet members, Rusk would be the one survivor. "I love that Dean," Johnson told friends, and the feeling was mutual. "LBJ never used the 'treatment' on me," recalled Rusk. "He never had to!" George Ball thought Johnson "in awe" of his secretary of state, who mirrored his own simplistic cold war assumptions. In return, Johnson trusted Rusk completely. They were close professionally and personally—two Southerners with a grudge against the Eastern establishment and Bobby Kennedy. Bobby's hostility only drove them closer together: as Joe Califano observed, "No testament to Rusk's loyalty could be more persuasive to Johnson than Kennedy's desire to see the Secretary fired."

Years later, Johnson recounted Bobby's proposal with considerable amusement:

> Bobby Kennedy came down to my little room and proposed . . . that I make Bill Moyers Secretary of State to succeed Dean Rusk. . . .
>
> He was very anxious for me to remove Rusk in '63 and '64, and his whole life was dedicated to removing Rusk, and electing himself President. . . . He recommended Bill Moyers for Secretary of State and I just couldn't believe he was serious and I wondered if there was something wrong with his thinking processes, and I looked at him and asked him if he was really serious. Oh, yes, he was serious. He went ahead to tell me not so much Moyers' qualifications, but all of Rusk's disqualifications, and what a terrible State Department, how terrible everybody over there was. And I said: but these are people President Kennedy selected and . . . [JFK] had confidence in them. And I said I can't understand your feeling this way. Well, [Bobby] said, [JFK] was going to get rid of all of them. And I said, well . . . I like Bill Moyers, but I'm not about to remove Rusk.

Kennedy continued to cultivate Bill Moyers, and vice versa. They spoke often—to review a speech draft or just sound out views. "God . . . he was on the phone every day with Moyers!" Joe Dolan exclaimed. This was no surprise to Frank Mankiewicz, a close comrade of Moyers from their Peace Corps days. Mankiewicz considered Moyers "the best presidential press secretary that ever was" and a role model of sorts. Dolan, however, didn't like the connection. He didn't trust Moyers, didn't understand how he could "serve two masters." Nor did Dolan consider the dialogue "a proud moment in Robert Kennedy's life. . . . How does he defend talking to the president's press secretary when he's supposed to be at war with the president?"

Dolan might have put the same question to Moyers: how did the president's closest adviser defend talking to the president's nemesis? At times Moyers needed no defense—particularly when he called Kennedy at Johnson's behest. "[Johnson] had assigned me to the task of trying to moderate Bobby Kennedy's opposition to the war," Moyers later explained. But as time passed, according to Rowland Evans, Moyers was prodding Kennedy to speak out on Vietnam. "If that's so," argued George Christian, "the president knew about it. No question in my mind. . . . He kept tabs on everything through the Secret Service or the Signal Corps or somebody. . . . If there were a lot of contacts between Bill and Bobby Kennedy, then he knew about it."

And if that was so, he did not like it. Johnson was never sure just how close Moyers and Kennedy had grown. He became constantly suspicious, fearful that Moyers would betray his trust and hurt his presidency. "That's the trouble with all you fellows," Johnson shouted at Moyers after McGeorge Bundy had appeared on television without permission. "You're in bed with the Kennedys." By mid-1966, this feeling intensified Johnson's other concerns about his press secretary—that Moyers was building his own fiefdom within the West Wing, aggrandizing himself at the president's expense, leaking freely, and widening the credibility gap by telling reporters too much or what they wanted to hear.

Among his colleagues in the press office, Moyers fretted openly about the president's growing suspicions. The strain between them was becoming obvious and Moyers labored to prove his loyalty to LBJ. Though he continued making visits to Hickory Hill and calls to Kennedy's office, Moyers played increasingly to Johnson's prejudices. He forwarded a clipping from the London *Daily Telegraph* to LBJ with the message "Mr. President: This anti-Kennedy piece was done by one of the most distinguished writers in Britain." Moyers added, as if relishing a victory over the Georgetown crowd, that the writer "recently came to this country and was wined and dined at one dinner party after another by the Kay

Grahams, Joe Alsops, etc." Of course, Johnson well knew that Moyers was being wined and dined by Graham and Alsop; in such memos Moyers seemed to scramble for critical distance. Similarly, Moyers used inside knowledge of Kennedy's plans to prod Johnson to action. In September 1966 he wrote Walt Rostow, "I think it is important for the President to speak thoughtfully about Europe and East-West relations. It will go a long way to counter the charges that he is exclusively obsessed with Vietnam and Asia. In addition we have known for some time that Bobby Kennedy is planning a major speech on this subject." Understanding that his own credibility had slipped, Moyers urged Rostow to take up the matter with LBJ.

"Moyers was reaching out in every direction," judged Charles Bartlett. But as his ties to LBJ slackened, Moyers reached more and more toward Bobby Kennedy. Whether or not Johnson was reelected in 1968, Kennedy was the future. Perhaps he was Bill Moyers's future. But in the meantime, Moyers would continue to offer the president his tattered and divided loyalty, and the president would continue to accept it—at least for the time being. As Johnson often said, it was better to have a man in the tent pissing out than out of the tent pissing in.

Throughout 1966, Bobby Kennedy labored to maintain the fiction that he had not broken with LBJ. On March 1, when Wayne Morse moved to reexamine the Vietnam War, Kennedy joined ninety-one other senators in voting to table the amendment. Peter Edelman noted with regret that Kennedy had become "quite reticent" to speak out about the war, fearing that "Lyndon Johnson was so insane that he would literally prolong the war simply because Bobby Kennedy was against it." The February clash over the NLF had been a watershed for the whole Kennedy circle: afterward, its members began to pull their punches. In speeches and interviews, Kennedy men like Galbraith, Goodwin, Schlesinger, and Sorensen criticized the war but never the president who waged it.

But Kennedy was more volatile than the rest and in a position of greater responsibility. He chafed at his self-imposed restraint. On April 27, after four days of clashes between U.S. Phantoms and MiG-21s (of uncertain origin) over North Vietnamese skies, Kennedy broke his silence in a brief speech on the Senate floor. He blasted the administration's policy of allowing "no sanctuary" in China or elsewhere for enemy planes; the practice of sending American fighters over North Vietnam, inviting attack, and darting across the Chinese border in "hot pursuit" was achieving little but the risk of Chinese intervention. While the policy inspired much hand-wringing on the Hill, Kennedy was the only senator to express his "grave concern" publicly. Again he urged the administration to turn from the North to the South and from the military to the political.

That night, Kennedy made the rounds on the network news. Presidential assistant Robert Kintner was watching, and later informed LBJ that "Senator Kennedy was quite effective on both Huntley-Brinkley and Cronkite. . . . In a summary of his Senate speech, which in effect accused you of unwisely escalating the Vietnamese war, his statement was so uncomplicated as to have an appeal to a great many people, as well as to the New York Times, etc. *The picture he is painting of you as President, without mentioning you, is the opposite of what I think is the right public posture—namely, a President being very careful of the use of the Armed Forces in Viet Nam.*" Kintner advised LBJ and the White House staff to remain above the fray this time. But perhaps Rusk might lean on New York Senator Jacob Javits, a liberal Republican, to answer RFK. Kintner suggested that Moyers—"on a confidential basis"—arrange a *Today* appearance for Javits. That Sunday, May 1, Javits appeared instead on *Issues and Answers* and defended Johnson's course in Vietnam. As the show ended and the senator walked off the set, the studio phone rang; it was LBJ. Javits later expressed public "gratitude" for the brief call, but he and Johnson played coy about the nature of their discussion.

Stymied on Vietnam, Kennedy turned his attention elsewhere, and the White House tracked his moves carefully. In early March 1966, White House watchdog Marvin Watson notified LBJ that "Senator Robert F. Kennedy has applied to the South Africa[n] Embassy for a visa. . . . He plans to address three groups in South Africa." At the invitation of the anti-apartheid National Union of South African Students (NUSAS), Bobby was indeed bound for South Africa, to speak at the students' annual Day of Affirmation in June. Months would pass, however, before South Africa agreed to admit him; it denied the visas of forty American journalists assigned to cover the trip. The Ministry of Information declared that South Africa would not allow Kennedy to transform his visit "into a publicity stunt . . . as a buildup for a future presidential election."

On this matter, the White House shared South Africa's concern: Bill Moyers, with help from the State Department, was keeping tabs on Kennedy's itinerary. A week before Kennedy's departure for Johannesburg, Johnson decided "it was time to look at the area as a whole." No doubt he was prompted by Moyers, who saw several reasons to take that look now: to "lay the foundation for a Johnson Doctrine for Africa," to "splash big headlines" in African newspapers, and as a sop to the American civil rights community—"a cheap way to keep them quiet on at least one issue," Moyers wrote to Johnson on May 26, just after 3:00 A.M.

"There is also another reason," Moyers continued.

> Bobby Kennedy goes to South Africa next week. He will try to get ahead
> of you on the question of political liberty for Negro Africans. Your
> speech prempts [sic] the stage. I think it would be wrong for us simply to
> offer economic assistance and material aid while Kennedy trots off mak-
> ing hay on the intangible issue of the rights of man. The attached speech
> is reasonable and restrained, but it will nonetheless make it difficult for
> Bobby to get far ahead of you on this issue.

Later that day, Lyndon Johnson made his only presidential speech on
Africa, addressing the ambassadors of the Organization of African Unity
and three hundred guests in the East Room of the White House. "I
spoke directly of enforced inequality and racial prejudice," Johnson stated proudly in his memoirs, and he trumpeted the "unity of purpose that
transcends two continents." The bulk of his speech concerned economic challenges facing the region, but, copping a page from Kennedy's
book, Johnson gave special attention to African self-determination: "The
United States," Johnson said, "has learned from lamentable personal
experience the waste and injustice that result from the domination of
one race by another. Just as we are determined to remove the remnants
of inequality from our own midst, we are also with you—heart and
soul—as you try to do the same." The occasion marked the third
anniversary of the OAU, but there was clearly something else behind the
president's timing. "Cynics will wonder," smirked the *New York Times*, "if
the attention given to Senator Kennedy's forthcoming visit" did not illu-
minate the "dark continent" for LBJ.

Minutes before midnight on June 4, Bobby, Ethel, Adam Walinsky, and
executive secretary Angie Novello landed at Johannesburg's Jan Smuts
Airport. Kennedy had been an advocate of African independence movements since his days as attorney general, when he frequently served as a
back channel for African dissent. Kennedy had looked forward to this
visit, but not without trepidation. As an assistant reported to Bill Moyers, "[Kennedy] arrives in Johannesburg at a time of increasing friction
between the government and the universities and trouble could occur."
But the screaming fans, who grasped and tugged at Kennedy as they had
in Peru, Poland, and elsewhere, overwhelmed the hecklers. On June 6,
the Day of Affirmation, Kennedy spoke—in words more dramatic than
LBJ's—of oppression and the "shared determination to wipe away the
unnecessary sufferings of our fellow human beings." At the University of
Cape Town, Kennedy uttered the words that resonated through his public life:

Few will have the greatness to bend history itself; but each of us can work to change a small portion of events, and in the total of all those acts will be written the history of this generation. . . . Each time a man stands up for an ideal, or acts to improve the lot of others, or strikes out against injustice, he sends forth a tiny ripple of hope, and crossing each other from a million different centers of energy and daring those ripples build a current which can sweep down the mightiest walls of oppression and resistance.

The journey (which carried Kennedy to Kenya, Ethiopia, and Tanzania) was an international success. Even white South Africans praised Kennedy for his sincerity and tact, and American reviews were overwhelmingly positive. *The Nation* credited RFK with a new "political élan" that would strengthen his hand against LBJ: "Kennedy's voice is already strong enough so that he cannot be ignored. His African trip made him an international figure. Now, with a continuation of nerve and verve, he is in a position to capitalize on it in U.S. politics." Kennedy returned to the United States brimming with boosted confidence.

As a matter of protocol and personal diplomacy, Bobby reported his findings to LBJ in an Oval Office meeting on Wednesday, June 22. Weeks earlier, an aide to Walt Rostow expressed the naive hope that Bobby's trip to South Africa offered the administration a "unique, if difficult, opportunity . . . to encourage the development of liberal sentiment in South Africa." Rostow, by June 21, was skeptical. In an extensive memo on Bobby's travels, he began ominously: "[Bobby] made few points without quoting President Kennedy." Rostow's memo offered more political than substantive analysis, though he did show some concern about Kennedy's effect on American policy in Africa. With evident relief, Rostow reported that "Kennedy carefully avoided any hint of a threat of external pressure against apartheid." Bobby avoided the subject of sanctions while in South Africa but spoke against them after his return to Washington. "He adds that the blacks would suffer most in the event of a trade embargo. He advises a freer dialogue with South Africa rather than reduction in contact," Rostow told the president. "He has not yet put this in any document or formal speech . . . [but] I think we can expect it on the Senate floor soon." A more pressing—and constant—concern was Vietnam. Bobby had not volunteered any remarks while in Africa, but when questioned "made several strong defenses of U.S. policy." This was what Johnson wanted to hear. His meeting with Bobby passed without incident.

In July 1966, Dick Goodwin sipped a late-night whiskey at Bobby Kennedy's New York apartment. As the conversation stretched into early morning, the two men grew more wistful and pessimistic. "The worst thing about the war," Bobby said, rotating his glass in tight, small circles, "is not the war itself, although that's bad enough, but all the great opportunities that are going down the drain. We have a real chance to do something about poverty, to get blacks out of the ghettos, but we're paralyzed. I don't like Johnson, but he was doing some good things. Now there's no direction."

"Well, Senator," Goodwin asked, prodding him, "what are you going to do about it? What's your plan of action?"

"Why, I'm going to make speeches," Bobby said. "That's what a senator does. I might even write a book. That'll show them," he grinned ironically.

Robert Kennedy had not given a single speech on the war itself since his brief comments of April 27. And he would not speak on Vietnam again for many months. In part, Kennedy was rebuilding his political capital after the heavy losses of February 1966. "Don't engage in a running attack every day or so," Fred Dutton urged Bobby in the midst of that controversy—advice that conformed to Bobby's notion of statesmanship. The former hothead had emerged from his years as "assistant president" with a heightened sense of responsibility and restraint. As senator he continued to conduct himself, particularly in matters of foreign policy, as if he were *president*. He focused on the fundamentals. And though prone to an occasional outburst (in October, while Johnson was meeting Ky in Manila, Bobby said that the South Vietnamese wanted Ky about as much as they wanted the Communists), Kennedy carefully crafted his positions to endure. "Those weren't potshots," said Walinsky.

Yet by late 1966, Bobby's silence bespoke a certain timidity. He began to draw criticism for evading the issue. In October, I. F. Stone charged that "while others dodge the draft, Bobby dodges the war." College students taunted him with hand-scrawled signs—"Kennedy: Hawk, Dove, or Chicken?" Jack Newfield of the *Village Voice* beseeched Kennedy to say *something* about the war. "You haven't said anything for a year," Newfield blurted that fall. "When will you talk again?"

"If I become convinced that by making another speech that I could do some good, I would make it tomorrow," Newfield recalled him saying. "But the last time I spoke I didn't have any influence on policy, and I was hurt politically. I'm afraid that by speaking out I make Lyndon do the opposite, out of spite. He hates me so much that if I asked for snow, he would make rain, just because it was me. But, maybe I will have to say something. The bombing is getting worse all the time now."

He did not say anything. Silence, though, was not paralysis, and during these quiet months Kennedy was exhausting every means of influencing policy—everything short of a public break with LBJ. "Time and again Kennedy tried to influence that fellow," Walinsky recalled, "but he never had any great expectations." Edelman described the senator's restless, almost frantic, attempts:

> He tried talking privately to the President, to members of the Cabinet, to members of the White House staff . . . backgrounding the press, not for attribution, talking on the record on television and in the press, talking to other Senators to urge them to do things, working with people on the outside. . . . He tried every way he knew how through 1966 and '67.

It was not enough. I. F. Stone was not the only one who expected more of Bobby Kennedy—especially after Kennedy had flirted so daringly with assuming the leadership of antiwar Democrats. On January 23, 1967, from his office at the City University of New York, Arthur Schlesinger wrote Kennedy that it was time to speak out again on Vietnam. True, it risked accusations of "ruthless political ambition." Even worse, it might antagonize Johnson into expanding the war. But Schlesinger alerted the senator to widespread feelings of

> despair and fatalism—i.e., that our country is embarked on a mistaken and possibly disastrous course but that there is very little, given the nature of our political system and the character of our President, that anyone can do about it. I do not think that any of us can acquiesce in this and live easily with ourselves for the rest of our lives. I do not want to say that the future of the republic rests with you, which of course it doesn't; but, if someone doesn't do something to arrest this madness, we deserve our fate.

CHAPTER 12

All-Out Loyalty

In the last week of July 1965, Fred Dutton sent Bobby Kennedy a lengthy memo about the senator's public image. "What," Dutton asked Kennedy to consider, "are the basic impressions people have of you, not merely in your past roles but now and prospectively?" There was no simple answer—except to say that Kennedy was the object of intense (and growing) fascination and speculation, and that impressions varied widely. The *New York Times* asked, "Will the Real Robert Kennedy Stand Up?" Was he a brash, clumsy upstart, a shrewd Machiavellian, or an anointed idealist? An extensive Gallup poll that fall revealed confusion on all counts. To Kennedy's fans he was intelligent, aggressive, sincere, and, of course, a *Kennedy*. To his detractors he was "pushy" and power-hungry and had capitalized on his family name. Every strength was a weakness. Forty-four percent of those polled rated him less capable a senator than John Kennedy had been, but 40 percent (and 56 percent of Democrats) hoped to see him elected president someday. There was overwhelming agreement on one point alone: his ambition. Seventy-four percent believed that Robert Kennedy wanted the White House.

Whatever the polls said, political tabloids and serious newspapers both were obsessed with RFK, giving him more coverage (usually positive) than anyone but the president. Bobby Kennedy "receives more mail and speaking invitations" than any other member of Congress, reported *U.S. News and World Report*. It was telling enough that anyone was keeping count. RFK was the principal tourist attraction on Capitol Hill, far outranking his younger brother, Ted; long lines of excited teenagers snaked from Bobby's door into the cavernous hallway of the Senate Office Building. "He's packing 'em in like that every day," a staff member bragged. "And they'll nearly all be voting by the next time he runs for whatever it is he's going to run for."

The buildup, observers declared, had begun; and the giggling teens were an ominous portent—if not for Johnson, then for "Johnson's man" Hubert Humphrey, Bobby's likely opponent in the race for the 1972 Democratic nomination. Johnson was obviously ensconced in the White House for the next seven years; he was a colossus. But Kennedy could surely foil his plans for the succession. According to the press, Bobby was already "buckling down," carefully plotting each step to the Oval Office. "It took Jack four years of unrelenting effort," said a political aide, feeding the speculation. "Bobby has almost twice that much time. People who would like to see him in the White House feel that not a minute of it should be wasted." There was meaning, then, in every movement, however slight. The science of Bobby-watching became as elaborate and arcane as Kremlinology: instead of scanning the lineup on the Lenin mausoleum, Bobby-watchers read meaning into 50-cent fan mags (*Bobby Kennedy—Next President of the United States*) or obscure documentaries on the Kennedy administration. When Bobby climbed a mountain in Canada named for his brother, a cartoon pictured him gazing into the distance toward a higher, more daunting peak, labeled "White House."

Prematurely, the press hailed Bobby's emergence as a "powerfully independent figure" in the Democratic Party. "There is no doubt that the Kennedy brothers, in promoting themselves as national leaders, have a tendency to stir up the 'liberal' community," declared *U.S. News.* "The Kennedys aren't playing second fiddle to anyone and they are expanding their power base to include as many 'liberals' as they can. This has given the 'liberal' cause more steam than many people are aware of." In the less excitable *New York Times,* James Reston offered a more nuanced assessment of Bobby's growth as a public figure, giving him

> good marks for his first half-session in the Senate. . . . He has supported the administration just enough to avoid the wrath of the White House, yet has opposed it just enough to establish a political base a little left of Lyndon. . . . He has not been wildly successful but he has learned much and suffered much and come a long way in the last year.

Reston credited Kennedy with highlighting central issues—nuclear proliferation, racial injustice, poverty, and the struggles of developing nations. But Reston, too, saw the inexorable political trajectory of Bobby's "intellectual game": "Bobby . . . is doing nothing to discourage the thought that he would like to be president."

Most congressional press secretaries were charged with creating pub-

At the Democratic Convention in Los Angeles,
July 1960, after the affront.
(AP/Wide World Photos)

Outside his convention suite, LBJ signs on to the Kennedy ticket. To one friend,
LBJ looked like he "had just survived an airplane crash." July 14, 1960.
(Library of Congress, *U.S. News & World Report* Collection)

The "assistant president" briefs JFK as Secretary of State Dean Rusk and
Vice President Johnson listen. February 28, 1962.
(Library of Congress, *U.S. News & World Report* Collection)

RFK receives his brother's posthumous Medal of Freedom from President Johnson,
December 6, 1963. Defense Secretary Robert McNamara looks on.
(Yoichi R. Okamoto/ LBJ Library Collection)

Kenneth O'Donnell, 1960. After
the assassination of JFK, the FBI
labeled him a "bad leak" who was
"more [loyal] to the attorney general than . . . to the president."
(Library of Congress, *U.S. News
& World Report* Collection)

Arthur M. Schlesinger, Jr., 1961.
In December 1963, he urged
RFK to "face a hard fact: Johnson
has won the first round."
(Library of Congress, *U.S. News &
World Report* Collection)

Kennedy briefs Johnson on a diplomatic dispute, January 28, 1964.
(Yoichi R. Okamoto/ LBJ Library Collection)

LBJ gives Kennedy many pens but little credit at the signing of the
Civil Rights Act, July 2, 1964.
(Cecil Stoughton/ LBJ Library Collection)

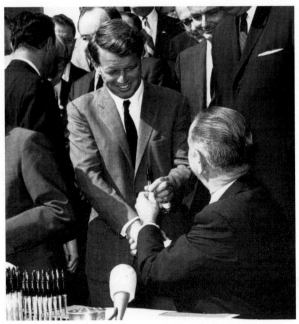

Signing the antipoverty bill, August 20, 1964. A Kennedy
campaign pamphlet featured this photo and the caption:
"Remember how he worked with President Johnson
to get justice for the poor and underprivileged?"
(National Archives, Abbie Rowe Collection)

On the campaign plane, October 14, 1964.
(Cecil Stoughton/ LBJ Library Collection)

The Johnson-Kennedy Team: "as close as twins" in New York, observed reporters.
October 14, 1964.

(Cecil Stoughton/ LBJ Library Collection)

A dime-store magazine read by the president, 1965.

(Library of Congress, *U.S. News & World Report* Collection)

Press Secretary Bill Moyers gets the Johnson Treatment, 1965.
"You're in bed with those Kennedys," LBJ later charged.
(Yoichi R. Okamoto/ LBJ Library Collection)

Aides Harry McPherson, Joseph Califano, and Bill Moyers in the Oval Office, 1966.
In the background, LBJ scrutinizes the news ticker.
(Yoichi R. Okamoto/ LBJ Library Collection)

RFK and Connecticut Senator Abraham Ribicoff attack Johnson's war on poverty, December 1966. "It's too little, it's nothing, we have to do twenty times as much," Kennedy complained.
(Library of Congress, *U.S. News & World Report* Collection)

The feud, and Kennedy's ambitions, were fodder for cartoonists.
(©Ed Valtman/ LBJ Library Cartoon Collection)

Enduring a Johnson stump speech, autumn 1966.
(Bill Eppridge/*LIFE* Magazine ©TIME Inc.)

Fred Dutton, 1962. As the 1968 election approached he warned RFK against another "slugging match" with the president. (Library of Congress, *U.S. News & World Report* Collection)

Richard Goodwin, 1961. The speechwriter decided his "future was with those Kennedys," Johnson complained in 1965. (Library of Congress, *U.S. News & World Report* Collection)

Joe Dolan, 1963.
To Kennedy's top aide,
LBJ was simply "that
son-of-a-bitch."
(Library of Congress,
*U.S. News & World
Report* Collection)

Johnson aide George
Reedy blows smoke,
1968.
(Yoichi R. Okamoto/
LBJ Library Collection)

Marvin Watson, 1968.
LBJ's political watchdog
labeled Vietnam
"another Kennedy vs.
Johnson issue."
(Mike Geissinger/ LBJ
Library Collection)

Kennedy, with aides
Peter Edelman and
Adam Walinsky, heads
for the Senate Caucus
Room to launch his
campaign against LBJ.
March 16, 1968.
(©George Tames/*New
York Times* Pictures)

March 31, 1968:
Fifteen days after
Kennedy's entry,
Johnson withdraws
from the race.
(Yoichi R. Okamoto/
LBJ Library Collection)

Kennedy and Johnson at the "unity meeting," April 3, 1968.
(Yoichi R. Okamoto/ LBJ Library Collection)

RFK, Ted Sorensen, and LBJ review a map of Vietnam, April 3, 1968.
(Yoichi R. Okamoto/ LBJ Library Collection)

Press Secretary Frank Mankiewicz at the
Good Samaritan Hospital, Los Angeles.
"Senator Robert Francis Kennedy died
at 1:44 A.M. today, June 6, 1968.
. . . He was 42 years old."
(Julian Wasser; courtesy
of Frank Mankiewicz)

Lady Bird and LBJ react to Robert Kennedy's death, June 6, 1968.
(Yoichi R. Okamoto/ LBJ Library Collection)

Watching assassination bulletins, June 6, 1968. "He must have been filled with a hundred competing emotions," reflected Harry McPherson.
(Yoichi R. Okamoto/ LBJ Library Collection)

The Johnsons at Arlington National Cemetery, June 8, 1968, trailed by Ethel and Ted Kennedy, Bobby's son Joe (behind Ted), and Stephen Smith (upper left). Two days earlier, Johnson had tried to prevent RFK's burial here. (©*Washington Post*; Reprinted by permission of D.C. Public Library)

licity, but Kennedy's press secretaries had essentially the opposite function—to keep the media at bay, fend off interviews, stem the tide of requests. "The volume . . . was so intense," gasped Kennedy's first press secretary, Wes Barthelmes, who quickly found himself overwhelmed (and, by year's end, out of a job). "There was just too much, just too many to handle." Frank Mankiewicz, who succeeded Barthelmes, fielded up to a hundred phone calls a day from reporters asking for a brief statement by the senator or just a brief moment of his time. "They were all over us," Mankiewicz recalled. Of course, Kennedy himself stimulated much of this interest by issuing what newsman Arthur Krock called "a Niagara of Kennedy statements and speeches"—the largest spate of official handouts and press releases from any quarter outside the White House, a continuous Kennedy torrent. It helped land him on the front page more than any other senator.

Kennedy pored over those front pages, read the magazines, watched the TV news every morning and night—and jumped to correct any errors. Still, like his brother before him, Bobby was mostly candid with the press. He believed that attempts to manage the news were bound to backfire. The best way to defeat the "ruthless" stereotype was not by photo ops (though they were frequent and well orchestrated) but solid achievements. Dutton, comfortably ensconced at a Washington law firm, might spend pages crafting strategies to highlight Kennedy's "human qualities," but Kennedy and Mankiewicz were too busy, impatient, and fatalistic for canned attempts at image enhancement. Bobby's image would grow organically or not at all. "There really isn't much you can do about it," Bobby shrugged on occasion.

He was less dismissive of his other persistent image problem—the widespread perception of a vendetta against Lyndon Johnson. LBJ was the great, looming, inhibiting presence in the Kennedy press office. "The press," complained Peter Edelman, "did not convey an adequate picture of his development. . . . Everything had to be cast in political terms—was this or was this not a break with Lyndon Johnson or a fight with Lyndon Johnson or were we trying to screw Lyndon Johnson." Press coverage reached new levels of absurdity. When Ted Kennedy's dinner-dance in honor of Bobby's fortieth birthday conflicted with hostess Perle Mesta's party for Johnson's successor, Senate Majority Leader Mike Mansfield, newspaper society scribes eagerly canvassed invited guests. Whom to snub, Kennedy or Johnson? became the question in Washington. Humorist Art Buchwald described the conflict in the overheated prose of a war correspondent: "Perle Mesta and Teddy Kennedy were highball to highball and neither one would clink." In the end, Mansfield gracefully arranged for Mesta's party to begin much earlier than Kennedy's and thus, in Buchwald's words, "a tragic social holocaust was avoided and President Johnson was advised it was safe to return to Washington."

More damagingly, journalists sharpened the conflict between Johnson and Kennedy by facilitating a war of words: eager reporters carried Bobby's advance press releases to the White House and demanded a response. Often the White House aired its rebuttal before Kennedy had even delivered his speech. It was impossible, it seemed, for Kennedy to get a fair hearing or to argue an issue on the merits. This black-and-white breakdown of what was often a subtle, perhaps semantic, disagreement left Kennedy's press secretaries feeling powerless and filled Bobby with resentment—less toward the press than toward LBJ, whose surrogates accused Bobby of promoting himself at the president's expense.

According to Walinsky, Kennedy grew "immensely concerned" with suppressing his true opinion of LBJ: even in his own office, RFK was "very, very careful to conceal it from us." Kennedy understood that public restraint required private restraint, and a staffer accustomed to disparaging LBJ in the office might just disparage him in an on-the-record interview. It was a constant struggle. Feelings about Johnson ran strong in the Kennedy office: Joe Dolan was given to calling LBJ "that son-of-a-bitch" and took pleasure in needling him. One comment drew a curt correction from the White House press office. "Dear Mr. Dolan," it read, ". . . The President at one time had a pair of beagles named Him and Her. The President has had the dog Him for several years and he has always been referred to as 'Him,' never 'Ho Chi Him.' "

More savagely, Adam Walinsky took a pencil to the cover of his 1966 Democratic Campaign Handbook, endowing a photo of the president with a Hitler mustache and Nazi armband. (Admittedly, Johnson's outstretched arm, saluting to the crowd as he stood in the backseat of a convertible limousine, invited the embellishment.) Mankiewicz, in the weeks between being hired and starting work as Kennedy's press secretary, delivered a commencement address in which he "ripped the shit out of Johnson," according to Dolan. In fact it was U.S. foreign policy, not Johnson, that Mankiewicz blasted for "unbelievable smugness and blandness." But the speech made the papers, and upon Kennedy's return from a foreign trip, he was asked for comment at Washington National Airport. "I didn't know about that. No, I don't agree with that," Kennedy said of Mankiewicz's charge. He added pointedly, "He doesn't work for me yet, you know." Walking past Dolan on the tarmac, Kennedy delivered a two-word verdict: "Fire him." The next morning Dolan persuaded the senator to give Mankiewicz a second chance. Kennedy did so, reluctantly.

Respect for Johnson did not come easily to Kennedy, either. He was having enough trouble simply calling Johnson "the president," a term Bobby reserved for his late brother. Usually, Johnson remained nameless, referred to by a simple "he" or "him" —as in "Can you believe what he just did?" In the sanctuary of Hickory Hill, among friends, Bobby could work himself into a cold rage over Johnson's lies, his disloyalty, his greed. "I can't stand the bastard," Kennedy told Dick Goodwin after a private meeting with the president. But at his Senate office Kennedy admitted only that he hated the term "Great Society." Occasionally he made wry reference to "that wonderful man who is President of the United States." But when Walinsky made a sneering mention of "Lyndon," Kennedy cut him off. "Okay, Adam, that's enough. That'll be enough of that." Kennedy evinced no rage, bitterness, or frustration; just wry regret and a determination to persevere. Only later did aides learn the depths of Kennedy's dislike and distrust of LBJ, and, in retrospect, they marveled at Kennedy's self-restraint.

By 1966 there was enough harsh talk about LBJ in Kennedy's circle; Kennedy would not contribute to it. A clash of personalities would undermine the senator's policy arguments and cheapen his public stature. And it would weaken the presidency, an office Kennedy expected, someday, to occupy.

Lyndon Johnson, too, expected Kennedy to occupy the Oval Office, or at least to pursue it. He believed Kennedy was already pursuing it—and was aiming for 1968, not 1972. If LBJ overreacted to the Bobby Kennedy phenomenon (and surely he did), it was because history had taught him something. In the late 1950s and well into 1960, Johnson (and the rest of the Washington establishment) had consistently, grossly underestimated the strengths of John F. Kennedy. Johnson would not make the same mistake about Bobby. Whatever the polls said, Bobby was not a lesser senator than Jack had been. Bobby's achievements and public profile, enshrouded by the glow of his martyred brother, rendered him a far more formidable figure in the mid-sixties than John Kennedy in the fifties.

During the Eisenhower era, the Democratic arena had been too cluttered for a one-on-one rivalry; Johnson and JFK were joined by Humphrey, Stevenson, Kefauver, Symington, and others. Each jockeyed for attention and prestige and a following of his own. But after 1963 there was no one left but Lyndon Johnson and Robert Kennedy. Johnson knew this, and it frightened him. The press knew it too: "Next to LBJ," U.S. News observed, ". . . RFK is turning out to be the most attention-gaining public figure in the nation. . . . His presence has tended to overshadow every public official in Washington other than the President himself." In this political vacuum, LBJ and RFK were competing centers of gravity; and in orbit around them were crowded fields of lesser bodies. It was a galaxy with two suns, and as one shone more brightly the other dimmed.

President Johnson, even at the peak of his power and public approval, never felt himself the brightest star. The Great Society kindled no passion, just respect; there was no emerging Johnson legend, just a Johnson record. On the second anniversary of the assassination—after Medicare, Medicaid, voting rights, and all the rest—two-thirds of Americans still considered John Kennedy a "better president" than Lyndon Johnson. *Time* cut to the heart of the problem: "Johnson's mythogenic capacity is limited. . . . His creased face, with its oddly forced smile, cannot displace the memory of Kennedy's youthful radiance, and his unctuous prosiness cannot match Kennedy's eloquence. Compared with Kennedy's graceful dignity, Johnson's homely touch can be embarrassing. . . . Often the contest seems downright unfair." And it was a two-front contest, LBJ against the Kennedy legend and its living heir.

Robert Kennedy, more slight and awkward than JFK and hardly as eloquent, faced challenges of his own as he grasped the fallen standard. But Bobby's problems seemed paltry as LBJ considered his own public image—something he did constantly, obsessively, gazing at his custom three-television panel like Narcissus at the reflecting pool. Still, Johnson, though vain, was hardly lovestruck by what he saw. On radio or television, at a press conference or college commencement, LBJ knew he sounded canned, nothing like the mellifluous and forceful man of private encounters. Senator Paul Douglas said famously that he never saw Johnson win a debate on the Senate floor and never heard him lose one in the cloakroom. LBJ's freewheeling oratory, exaggerated gestures, and homespun homilies translated poorly to television—a medium still smitten by Johnson's predecessor, and far more receptive to Bobby Kennedy's laconic wit.

Advisers encouraged Johnson simply to be himself—"that," McPherson counseled, "is what the country wants to see and hear"—and dreamed of bugging the cabinet room and leaking recordings of Johnson at his best. But LBJ, fearing his monologues "unpresidential," held back in public. Even McPherson had to acknowledge the danger in letting Johnson cut loose. "There are times," McPherson confessed, "when I frankly would not like to see Lyndon Johnson being Lyndon Johnson." One week Johnson might charm the public. The next he might spook it with a profane, conspiratorial rant.

When Lyndon Johnson did allow himself to be Lyndon Johnson, the results were mixed. Stumping for his antipoverty bill in the South, LBJ put on his Texan hat and thickened his accent; *Time* called him "corny as a johnny-cake" but "efficient and effective." Yet when he invited reporters on a presidential tour of his ranch, it was high and hair-raising comedy: careening over yucca plants at eighty-five miles an hour, cowboy hat over the dashboard display of his Lincoln Continental, LBJ narrowly avoided a head-on collision. Reporters noted slyly that the president kept a cup of beer "within easy sipping distance." Two weeks later, on the White House lawn, Johnson proudly lifted his two pet beagles by their ears and, regrettably, landed the picture in a thousand newspapers. His aides complained that all hunters treated their dogs ruggedly; all ranchers kept a cold beer handy. Johnson griped that the press would never have reported the incidents had they been committed by John Kennedy.

But the point, of course, was that no Kennedy would ever raise a beagle by its ears. Knowing this, White House press aides contrived to present Lyndon Johnson as a "closet" Kennedy—a Texan Kennedy, if there could be such a thing. The Lyndon Johnson one saw in *Life* was an athlete, toting a golf bag or surrounded by young Olympians; a charismatic family man, proud father of two lovely daughters; and a fashion trend-setter (even if the trend was a modified cowboy hat). Much of this was stock political imagery, but there were deliberate echoes of the Kennedy "era." In a memo to LBJ, presidential aide Horace Busby recommended "shots of you among the young people," adding, "I wouldn't want a notably less demonstrative showing vis-à-vis the Kennedy image." The March 1966 cover of *GQ* featured President Johnson on the front porch of his Texas homestead wearing not ranch clothing (as the magazine had wished) but a "Kennedyesque" two-button suit (as Johnson had insisted).

Johnson might fill an Ivy League suit, but he was no "Harvard." This aspect of the Kennedy image was much harder to mimic. Awestruck aides bragged of Johnson's intellect, sophistication, and rich vocabulary; yet Johnson himself bemoaned his "poor" education. Intimidated by "men of ideas," LBJ mocked them as "overbred smart alecks" who knew nothing of politics and therefore scorned his artistry—"just like a pack of nuns who've convinced themselves that sex is dirty and ugly and lowdown and forced because *they* can never have it." Intellectuals, scoffed a national Democratic leader, "are types who serve as handmaidens to men of power and influence"; and though Johnson agreed, he desperately wanted them as *his* handmaidens. He had a weakness for the academic credential, and George Reedy was often infuriated by Johnson's deference to his intellectual inferiors, by his "blank amazement" at a Harvard degree or Phi Beta Kappa key. But intellectuals were important to the

Johnson image and the Johnson program: they were the idea men, the opinion-makers. They had been John Kennedy's bedfellows, had given the New Frontier a certain *frisson,* and if Johnson did not court them aggressively they would flit to Bobby like moths to a flame.

Johnson set out to co-opt the Kennedys' cult of high culture. He signed the Kennedy Arts Center Bill in January 1964, appeared at museums and art exhibits, created the Presidential Scholars and White House Fellows programs, curried favor with countless writers and artists, and appointed Princeton historian Eric Goldman as the White House "intellectual-in-residence," an ambassador of sorts. The president dispatched Douglass Cater, Joe Califano, and Harry McPherson to college campuses to cultivate contacts and "size up" prospective task force members. But mutual suspicion tainted Johnson's relationship with the intellectual community from the beginning. As NBC anchorman Chet Huntley put it, intellectuals had regarded the Kennedy White House as "the Palace of Fine Arts of the United States." And no calendar of cultural events would disguise the fact that the Johnson White House was primarily a political institution and its inhabitant a political animal. Johnson cared for nothing but politics—it was his art, his culture, his sport, and his entertainment. Even the political intellectuals (or intellectual politicians) of the Americans for Democratic Action (ADA) sensed this. They had known and disdained LBJ since the 1950s. No amount of cultural window dressing was going to alter their view of LBJ as a philistine. He was not even convincing as a dilettante. Goldman detected an undertone—or overtone—of social snobbery to the intellectuals' growing disenchantment with LBJ. With equal fervor, they felt betrayed by Johnson on Vietnam and bemoaned his widening credibility gap. "More perhaps than other people," sniffed *The Nation* in September 1966, "intellectuals are trained to compare script with performance; more perhaps than others, they resent deception."

Admitting failure, Goldman resigned in 1966. Johnson replaced him with Brandeis University's John Roche, who regarded his fellow academics with a bitterness that surpassed even LBJ's. Roche was Johnson's kind of intellectual: self-hating. The Roche appointment was a signal that the mission had failed; Roche was in the White House not to reach out to intellectuals but to reinforce LBJ's political prejudices. The only thing Roche hated more than literary critics was Bobby Kennedy, whom Roche considered a "demonic little shit," and said so as he chewed on a black cigar and typed up another incendiary memo to the president.

Meanwhile, at home in Virginia, Bobby was hosting "Hickory Hill seminars." Senators and college professors gathered there for informal discussions. Administration officials were enthusiastic participants; friendly newsmen guarded their identities, Life reported, "lest they be mistaken by LBJ for Trojan horses." Here, as elsewhere, Johnson was competing on Bobby's terms and losing. By mimicking Kennedy's strengths—his cultural roots, his athleticism, his glamour—Johnson highlighted his own weaknesses. Bobby Kennedy played parlor games with artists and poets; when Johnson visited a museum he looked uncomfortable, like a misplaced exhibit. Bobby played touch football, shot the rapids, climbed mountains, and went on fifty-mile hikes; Johnson, contriving to appear in "graceful, in-motion Presidential form," threw around his six-foot-three-inch, 225-pound frame in a most ungraceful fashion. (Fred Dutton advised Bobby to undertake "at least one major, exciting personal adventure" every six months specifically to contrast his "verve and vitality" with "the dull middle-aged tone that President Johnson and Hubert have [hung] like a pall over the country.") When the Kennedy brothers (in a staged attempt to make Jack look healthful) strode from the surf in swimming trunks, Jack sucked in his stomach; Bobby did not need to. After a Life pictorial of a Johnson boating trip on Granite Shoals Lake in Texas, one reader wrote the editors that, having seen "the picture of President Johnson in a bathing suit, I feel he should be advised [to find] . . . a better one . . . preferably one that wasn't topless." Even Johnson's boat invited unflattering comparisons: Bobby sailed, elegantly, like his brother; LBJ drove a powerboat, loud and crass.

Johnson was a man of appetites: he drank, overate, and chain-smoked. No degree of manipulation of man or image could make him into a Kennedy. And no measure of coaching could prevent Johnson from lifting his shirt and showing photographers the scar from his gall bladder operation. At such moments Johnson advertised his differences from Bobby Kennedy. And when he tried to finesse those differences by imitating the Kennedy style, Johnson became something less than Bobby, and something less than himself. As a public relations strategy it was ill-conceived. And whatever one's feelings about Lyndon Johnson, it was excruciating to behold.

The reviews were poor. They grew poorer as the war and the riots dealt a double blow to Johnson's stature. Johnson expected it, but took it poorly. Since the beginning of his career, LBJ had been hypersensitive to criticism and "scrutinized the daily papers," said Dick Goodwin, "like a playwright for whom each night of his life was a new opening." Reading an otherwise glowing magazine profile, Johnson would fixate upon one neutral adjective with an eagle eye for criticism that others could not perceive. In the early days of his presidency, Johnson confronted his staff with "negative" articles. Aides scratched their heads and tried in

vain to find an unfavorable sentence. When the press *did* grow more negative, an aide recalled, "you could never convince President Johnson that
a sentence or two of critical comment about him really meant nothing."
Conversely, you could never convince LBJ that a word of praise about
Bobby Kennedy meant nothing.

In Johnson's view it was all connected, Bobby's good press and his
own lousy press. It was all part of a coordinated conspiracy. As early as
1960, Johnson was railing against "Kennedy press zealots." Now, five
years later, Johnson ordered the FBI to investigate Bobby's ties to the
Washington Star. The *Star*, Johnson said, had been attacking him ever
since Kennedy bought "considerable stock" in the paper. When *Star*
reporters John Barron and Paul Hope wrote a detailed report on LBJ's
financial dealings in Texas, LBJ told George Reedy that "unquestionably
these opponents of ours for the [1964 Democratic] nomination" were
behind it.

"No doubt," Reedy replied.

"I think that there's no question but what Bobby and this group have
got the *Star* and they're usin' it, and the play they give [the Barron story]
is most unusual for the *Star*," Johnson complained.

"Yes," Reedy agreed. "And they've spent a lot of dough on this.
They've obviously done an awful lot of work and research for a story
that just as a news story isn't quite worth it for them."

". . . Now, the *Star* is not a Goldwater paper," Johnson mused, "not a
mean Republican paper, and always been friendly to me, 'til the last three
or four months. 'Til, I guess, 'til I became president. . . . Now, they came
in and told Pierre [Salinger] that they were gonna write this story, and
Pierre knew all about it. That's why I think Bobby Kennedy owns it."

"That is unusual," concluded Reedy.

A cursory FBI investigation revealed that Bobby had made no investment in the *Star*, which had long been hostile to Democratic administrations. Undeterred, LBJ put the Bureau on the trail of Peter Lisagor, a
Chicago Daily News reporter rumored to be a "particularly close friend"
of Bobby Kennedy. Hoover was a willing accomplice, for he was convinced that "Bob Kennedy has been able to plant stories with the *New
York Times* and the *Saturday Evening Post* where he has contacts."

Kennedy's influence seemed more pervasive than that. At private dinners with Chet Huntley, Johnson thundered about "the Georgetown
press," rattling down a long list of reporters and columnists who were out
to get him and to make Bobby president. Huntley did not imagine there
really was a Georgetown press, but he understood what Johnson meant:
the nebulous circle of liberal academics, government officials, and journalists who gathered at Georgetown dinner parties, men like Charles

Bartlett, David Brinkley, Art Buchwald, Rowland Evans, Anthony Lewis, Arthur Schlesinger, William vanden Heuvel, Sander Vanocur, and numerous others. These were Washington's "beautiful people," said Hugh Sidey, and they "thought they were terribly brilliant and smart and knowledgeable, and what they were doing was right and correct."

With John Kennedy's death, the group's focus had shifted naturally to Bobby. But the group, in a way, had always been Bobby's: the social headquarters of the New Frontier was Hickory Hill, not the White House, and the "Georgetown dinner circuit" of the mid-1960s was Bobby's Hickory Hill gang, redux. Bobby gave the group its energy, élan, and political purpose: restoration. And if Lyndon Johnson, in the early sixties, had been its foil, he was now its nemesis. After the assassination, the mockery of LBJ had grown more bitter, hardening by 1966 into a reflexive intolerance. "They thought they had a buffoon at the head of the country," Sidey said of the Georgetown group, "and [that] it would ultimately prove disastrous."

The venomous talk trickled back to the White House, carried by the few aides—Joe Califano, Harry McPherson, and Bill Moyers—who won invitations to Georgetown dinner parties. Johnson arched an eyebrow at their social calendars (he suspected McPherson was "in bed with all those bomb-throwing, ass-kissing, fuzzy-headed Georgetown liberals") but valued the pipeline of gossip. Johnson's interest was part prurience, part paranoia, but no one doubted that the gossip mattered: McPherson reported back that vanden Heuvel was poisoning New York society against LBJ. The friendly columnist Joe Alsop believed the bitterness of the Kennedy crowd was stoking anti-Johnson feelings across the country. Chet Huntley noted the defection of one or two of his colleagues to Bobby's side and caught some on-air "inferences" or telling turns of phrase. "Very frequently I could see in a given piece that . . . all the Kennedy attitudes were very thoroughly aired," he said later, ". . . while something that Mr. Johnson might have had to say about the subject had been rather glossed over and dismissed."

Here was the real danger to LBJ. The Georgetown circle was the journalistic elite. "They spread the doubt," the president complained to a small crowd of aides in the Oval Office during the summer of 1965. "Every morning I wake up and see another column attacking me, or some professor on television. Naturally people get confused with all these voices shouting and hollering about how awful I am." An unflattering Evans and Novak column galled—and unnerved—Johnson more than a low popularity rating. He was convinced that the former propelled the latter, that the press steered the people away from Lyndon Johnson and toward Bobby Kennedy.

In a memo of April 1966, Liz Carpenter urged the president, "Let's start working to soften up the Kennedy columnist set . . . subvert them from 'buying' everything Bobby does. We ought to be able to move in [on] them when Bobby makes an error as he did on Viet Nam. . . . I hope we can include some of this jet set, even though they are personally obnoxious, at the next glamorous White House evening. I believe it's a gamble that would pay off." Johnson scrawled his response in thick pencil at the bottom of Carpenter's memo: "*Tear this up and flush it down the toilet.*"

Johnson had already tried to "soften up" the Kennedy press, and by 1966 his failure left him indignant. In a clumsy attempt to shield himself from RFK's pervasive influence, Johnson had once banned press pools from Air Force One and ordered reporters to fly separately. They were "spies," anyway, Johnson told aides; their only purpose was to root out embarrassing secrets. He insisted that Pierre Salinger had concocted the press pools "at Bobby Kennedy's instigation." Johnson's appointment of Bill Moyers as press secretary was partly an attempt at reconciliation. Moyers was popular with the press and accepted by the Georgetown crowd. Reporters responded positively. But as Johnson's image continued to tumble and stories of his mood swings, hypersensitivity, and humorlessness crept into the nation's newspapers, Johnson blamed Moyers for creating the "credibility gap." Within the press office, Moyers's assistant expressed a different view: Johnson's problem, argued Hayes Redmon, went beyond Vietnam, civil disorder, and inflation. "His regionalism, accent and his press reputation for cantankerousness . . . are creating an atmosphere of unpopularity for him," Redmon wrote Moyers in June 1966. "I believe there is a serious need to freshen his image."

This much was obvious. But instead of turning inward, LBJ lashed outward. Increasingly on the defensive about his policies at home and abroad, Johnson blamed every attack on Bobby Kennedy. "Not a sparrow fell from a tree but what he was convinced that it was the intervention of a Kennedy," said John Roche. Bobby's pernicious influence was everywhere, even in Johnson's own administration. "Some of the people who served did not share either the desire or the hopes that I had for the country and for the government," Johnson told Walter Cronkite in later years, "and . . . [they] undermined the Administration and bored from within to create problems for us and leaked information that was slanted and things of that nature. A good many of them resigned . . . and left the impression that the government was not in keeping with their views." These were the Kennedy men: once Jack's, now Bobby's, and Johnson believed that anybody associated with either of them was against him.

In 1963 and 1964 it had troubled Johnson that half his staff and most of his cabinet remained loyal to John Kennedy. But by 1965 and 1966, Bobby posed a far greater threat. The dead president remained a powerful force but an intangible, inaccessible one. Bobby, on the other hand, was very much alive and only sixteen blocks away down Pennsylvania Avenue. And with Bobby so close, Johnson could never trust the Kennedy men who remained in the administration, even after the 1964 election. What did they really want? Who were they really working for? This constant, if silent, scrutiny "used to frustrate the hell out of us," said Fred Dutton, who remained, for a time, in Johnson's State Department. Dutton left the administration in 1965 and became an informal adviser to RFK. During the next year many others left, too, creating the impression of a liberal exodus. "You see, Kennedy took them out," judged Roche, reflecting the president's suspicions. It was not Vietnam or simple exhaustion that sent men packing. It was Bobby. He lured them, like a Pied Piper.

Yet those who quit concerned Johnson less than those who remained. Like the Justice Department, the State Department was "Kennedy's," despite Rusk's impeccable allegiance to Johnson. In April 1965, the leaders of India and Pakistan canceled visits to the White House. A week later, on an Air Force One flight to Texas, the president leaned over and almost whispered into Dick Goodwin's ear. "Do you know there are some disloyal Kennedy people over at the State Department who are trying to get me; that's why they stirred things up?" Johnson asked knowingly. "I didn't know that," Goodwin replied. "Well, there are," Johnson said, "and we can expect to hear from them again. They didn't get me this time, but they'll keep trying." When American diplomats suggested that Humphrey undertake a goodwill tour of Asia, Johnson inexplicably exploded at Moyers. "It's those damned Kennedy ambassadors trying to get me and discredit me," the president fumed.

Johnson could never really believe his administration was his own— even after winning reelection in his own right and installing his own men at all levels. He inserted a hardcore Johnson loyalist into every cabinet department, especially those in which the secretary himself might bear more allegiance to Bobby Kennedy than to the president. In doing so, LBJ stoked a subterranean conflict; one official observed that some of the new, ardent Johnson appointees were "quite outspoken about cleansing the government of the stigma of Kennedy."

In general, the Johnson and Kennedy circles were not warring camps so much as overlapping spheres of influence. This made it especially difficult for Johnson to find anyone in Washington with a "clean" résumé untainted by association with RFK. In August 1966, after McPherson

and Watson recommended the appointment of Berl Bernhard as counsel to the Democratic National Committee, Johnson wrote back, "O.K.
if you are satisfied with all-out loyalty." McPherson had already warned
LBJ that Bobby Kennedy had tried three times to recruit Bernhard for
"various chores. . . . Kennedy recognizes talent and is obviously after it
in Berl." Bernhard was finding Kennedy increasingly difficult to refuse,
so "it would be wise to get him on our team now," McPherson concluded. From his office at the ranch, Johnson marked this passage in
McPherson's memo with a pencil and added, "I agree with that."

The competition for talent was growing fierce, and so was Johnson's
fixation on "all-out loyalty." By 1965, loyalty had become virtually the
sole criterion of the presidential appointments process, and not just for
political jobs. Johnson's growing obsession with loyalty bogged down
government commissions and task forces alike: he refused to approve any
commission until he had a thorough breakdown of not only the ideolo-
gies but the affiliations of every proposed member. "The process," said
Wilbur Cohen of HEW, "became so cumbersome and so involved that
. . . it took an inordinate amount of time" and consumed a great deal of
energy on the part of Johnson, Cohen, and the department. When David
Black left one federal power commission for another in 1965, LBJ summoned him to the White House and quizzed him about energy policy
and personnel. It was a relatively minor appointment, and though Black
was thrilled to meet the president in the Oval Office, he was surprised
Johnson would lavish a half hour's attention on a midlevel administrator.
At the meeting's end, Johnson explained that he expected three things
of any appointee. "First, of course, skill and capability. And second,
absolute loyalty." Third, Johnson wanted to know "that you are not
going to work for Bobby Kennedy down the line." Black had never even
met Bobby Kennedy. He pledged Johnson his undivided loyalty.

The experiences of Pat Moynihan and Roger Wilkins are illustrative.
Both were talented men who deserved a place in any Democratic
administration. Both had loose ties to Bobby Kennedy. And in Lyndon
Johnson's Washington, that was an untenable combination.

Daniel Patrick Moynihan had lifted himself by raw intellect and
ambition from a working-class New York neighborhood into a succession of prestigious universities and scholarships and, by 1962, into the
Kennedy administration. As assistant secretary of labor, Moynihan
helped to lay the foundations for what became Johnson's war on poverty. Moynihan was temperamental, a bit pedantic, and unerringly brilliant.
He fell hard for JFK's adventurous liberalism; the president made Moynihan swell with Irish pride. The attorney general, on the other hand, was

more irritant than inspiration. In 1962, Bobby pushed Moynihan to leave Labor and help direct Robert Morgenthau's ill-advised campaign for governor of New York. Dutifully but reluctantly, Moynihan left for New York, where Morgenthau lost decisively to the incumbent, Nelson Rockefeller.

This experience left Moynihan something less than a devout "Bobby Kennedy man." Still, in 1964, when Kennedy sought his expertise on New York's racial politics, Moynihan began spending weekends in New York writing speeches for RFK's Senate campaign. Moynihan's disaffected boss at Labor, Willard Wirtz, grumbled to the president that Moynihan had quit Labor and joined Kennedy. Wirtz knew better, but Johnson did not; the president declared Moynihan an ingrate and a traitor and henceforth barred him from aiding Kennedy. Johnson never forgave Moynihan the affront, and, the following spring, cast him adrift.

Harry McPherson, a close friend of Moynihan's, bridled at this waste of intellect. In May 1965, when McPherson left his post as secretary of state for educational and cultural affairs and became White House counsel, he wanted Moynihan as his replacement. "Nobody in the country would do it better.... [Yet] there is the 'loyalty problem,' more fanciful than real," McPherson confided to Bill Moyers. "How would you recommend I proceed to overcome it?" Judging from McPherson's next move, Moyers must have advised him to confront the problem directly. On June 14, McPherson wrote the president that Moynihan "is the most imaginative man in Washington. I know you have raised questions about his loyalty, but I honestly believe there is no basis for them. He was intensely pro–Jack Kennedy but did not even know Bobby until the latter asked Moynihan to write speeches for him.... He would do a brilliant, probably controversial job at State."

This was just what Johnson did not need: another "controversial" Kennedy man in a department already crawling with potential subversives. To make matters worse, the *New York Times* had just reported, erroneously, that "Kennedy Administration holdovers" were pushing Moynihan to run for mayor of New York City. For once Johnson's suspicion was justified: RFK's Senate aides, eager for an ally at Gracie Mansion, had planted the story without consulting Moynihan or the White House.

None of this aided Moynihan's case in the Oval Office. Neither did a remarkable pair of memoranda that McPherson wrote to Johnson on June 24. The first was a lengthy apologia for Moynihan's entanglement with RFK. If Moynihan had flirted with Bobby, McPherson maintained, it was because any good Democrat was "excited by the idea of beating Keating." McPherson implored,

Pat can develop the kind of loyalty to you that you must have. I believe he can understand and abide by the necessity to keep things within the family here. I don't believe his relationship to Bobby Kennedy is deep enough to make him disloyal to you. This is not to say he would instantly, or perhaps even in time, become the man you need to keep Bobby in line—directly. But I believe that Pat's imagination and liberalism would be at your service and not Bobby Kennedy's and that it is just that imagination and liberalism that is required for meeting and surpassing the "Kennedy image." . . .

The burden of this memorandum is then to urge you, instead of Bobby Kennedy, to make use of a truly remarkable young man.

Later that evening McPherson produced another lengthy memo to LBJ. Under the heading "Thoughts on Bobby Kennedy and Loyalty," McPherson considered the impact of the Bobby Kennedy phenomenon on the Johnson administration. Assessing the Kennedy challenge as it took shape in June 1965, McPherson wrote that Bobby

is trying to put himself into a position of leadership among liberal Senators, newspapermen, foundation executives, and the like. Most of these people mistrusted him in the past, believing him (rightly) to be a man of narrow sensibilities and totalitarian instincts. A number of brave votes for pure liberalism, and a number of internationalist, "open" speeches such as the one on nuclear proliferation, and he will seem to them like St. George slaying the conservative dragon. . . .

He will pick his issues for both immediate and cumulative effect. He will not care whether he ever becomes *of* the Senate. It will be enough for him that he is *in* the Senate and can use it as a platform in his search for power. . . .

He will become a voice of reason and enlightenment—powerless within the Senate, so far as majorities are concerned, but well-regarded in the country.

McPherson played masterfully (and sincerely) to Johnson's prejudices. But at the same time he confronted, rather than pandered to, Johnson's insecurities. McPherson argued sternly that LBJ must not "weed out of government every man who came down here in 1961." These were able, valuable men, dedicated less to the Kennedys than to the fulfillment of the Kennedys' ideals—and Johnson's programs. "We can not afford to lose them," McPherson warned. "Neither, in my opinion, can we afford to give them a polygraph-loyalty test." Loyalty tests only forced men to choose sides, and that was a contest Johnson would lose. "It is possible," McPherson contended,

. . . for people to work hard for you, maintain confidences, and still find the Kennedys (including Bobby) attractive and adventurous. The

Kennedys are handsome and dashing, they support fashionable artists, and they can pay for almost anything. . . . To some people even their rudeness and ruthlessness is exciting. . . . There is an air of tragic loss about them now. They are still rich and powerful and liberal. People who knew them and admired them when Jack Kennedy, their most winning member, was alive, no doubt still feel attracted to them. But this does not imply disloyalty or real danger to you. . . .

In the long run there is an even greater danger in applying a test requiring fealty to you alone. You run the risk of limiting your choices severly [sic]. Most men of intellect and independent spirit do not want to start out swearing never to talk to a popular Senator, particularly to one who espouses liberal causes. If the word gets around that one has to put on horse-blinders to work for you, you will probably come out with a bunch of clipped yes-men who are afraid of their own shadows and terrified of yours.

None of this suggested surrender: according to McPherson, the administration must meet Bobby's progressive policies with its own. "There is no reason why we have to let Bobby have the role of prophet, always goading the Administration to get off its chair and make a real effort toward peace," McPherson added. "You have the office, the policies, the personal magnetism, the power to lead and inspire, and above all the power to put good ideas into effect. An obsession with Bobby and with the relationship of your best people to him may, I believe, distort policy and offend the very men you need to attract."

No one had ever put it to Johnson so bluntly. McPherson's memo was a bold, almost brazen, attempt to confront Johnson's insecurities, break them down rationally, and dispel them. It was a heartfelt plea to judge individuals by their contributions to the Johnson administration and not by their feelings toward Bobby Kennedy. The memo achieved none of these things. Instead it killed Moynihan's chances and imperiled McPherson's own place in the president's inner circle. If McPherson could not find a suitable candidate for his old job at State, then he could have his old job back, Johnson declared. And when McPherson made one last, foolhardy plug for Moynihan, Johnson considered banishing McPherson into the bowels of the federal bureaucracy.

LBJ's appointment of Roger Wilkins as head of the Community Relations Service in January 1966 showed that he had learned little, if anything, from McPherson's memos. Wilkins's ties to Bobby Kennedy were even weaker than Moynihan's. When the Kennedy Justice Department briefly considered Wilkins, the nephew of civil rights leader Roy Wilkins, for a senior post, RFK dismissed him as "too brash." Wilkins, for his part, considered Bobby's Justice Department "lily-white" and too slow-moving on civil rights, and in 1962 said as much in an incendiary memo. But after November 1963, Wilkins sensed a change in Bobby Kennedy. "With the death of the President, he became connected to the world's pain," Wilkins said later. "And he became a deeper and wiser person. And I began to like him." Wilkins liked him from afar—he and Kennedy had no personal relationship—but by 1966 they had developed a mutual professional respect.

In late 1965, Attorney General Nicholas Katzenbach called Wilkins to convey his appointment as director of the Community Relations Service, a civil rights agency within the Commerce Department. "How do you want your commission to read?" Katzenbach asked. It was a minor matter of protocol, that was all. Wilkins wanted it to read "from New York," where he was licensed to practice law. It followed that Robert Kennedy, the junior senator from New York, would introduce Wilkins at his Senate confirmation hearings.

As the hearings approached, Wilkins began to get "these cryptic messages" from Katzenbach: "You're not from New York. We've got too many people from New York. You're from the District of Columbia." This was odd, Wilkins thought to himself. What did the White House care how his commission read? "I was just arrogant and stupid, young," Wilkins said later about his confusion. "Johnson just didn't want Bob Kennedy up there getting the credit." Wilkins ignored the messages that continued to accumulate—until January 25, 1966, the morning of his confirmation, when an "urgent" White House call drew Wilkins from his seat before the Senate Commerce Committee. "Remember, Roger," a presidential aide told him, "you're from the District of Columbia!"

"Right," Wilkins replied. Then he returned to his seat and asked RFK to proceed with his introduction. After a cursory hearing Wilkins received the committee's unanimous approval.

Wilkins now had the Senate's consent—but he seemed to have lost the president's. Before the hearing, Johnson had promised him an elaborate swearing-in, in the East Room of the White House. Wilkins cringed at the suggestion. It was an obvious, shameless gesture to his uncle Roy and the civil rights movement. Housing Secretary Robert Weaver had taken the oath in the East Room, but Weaver was the first black cabinet member; Wilkins was only an assistant secretary of commerce. Soon, though, it began to seem that Wilkins would not be sworn in at all. Days passed with no word from the White House. Finally, after some prodding by Secretary of Commerce John T. Connor, the White House asked for a list of invited guests. Wilkins's list included Bobby Kennedy. A presidential aide sent it back, claiming the crowd would never fit in the White House Theater (to which the ceremony had been shifted). The list went back and forth and back again. It was becoming a war of wills between Wilkins and Johnson, and Johnson rarely lost wars of will. When Wilkins finally struck RFK's name from the guest list, the White House instantly approved it.

On February 4, 1966, LBJ stood before the guests assembled in the White House Theater and praised Roger Wilkins's "poise and . . . calm judgment." And as the two men stepped off the dais, Wilkins recalled, "*the son of a bitch did not speak to me!* He spoke to my mother, my stepfather, my wife, my kids, my mother-in-law, to my uncle, to my aunt. . . . *But he did not speak to me!*" When Johnson darted his eyes in Wilkins's direction it was only to show that "he was really pissed at me. He just looked at me furiously! I mean, he was conveying *profound* displeasure." As official White House photographers snapped an image for public consumption, Wilkins cast an embarrassed grin downward at his six-year-old daughter. The president smiled paternally but looked away.

A few days later, LBJ ordered Solicitor General Thurgood Marshall, Wilkins's mentor, to the Oval Office. "My car is outside," Johnson said ominously. "Go downstairs, it's waiting. I want you here right now." As the car sped him to the White House, Marshall shuddered to think what sort of scandal was breaking. He was whisked into the Oval Office for a conversation that was short and to the point:

"Do you know Roger Wilkins?" Johnson asked.

"Yes, sir."

"Well, goose him in the ass, then!" Johnson exploded, thrusting his hand at Marshall and jutting his middle finger upward.

This was the president's message for Roger Wilkins. Years later, Wilkins remained astonished that President Johnson would brood for weeks over the loyalties of a lowly assistant secretary. Wilkins could conceive of only one explanation: "pure hatred of Robert Kennedy."

It was not so much hatred as *fear*. Johnson's spasm of panic at the mere mention of Bobby Kennedy underscored his growing political vulnerability as well as his deep-seated personal insecurity. But the president's behavior was by any measure completely out of proportion to the Kennedy challenge. "Johnson's paranoia used to get on my nerves," said John Roche, whose own tales of "Kennedy spies" only fed Johnson's fears. LBJ had always been eccentric and conspiratorial, but it was not until 1965 that aides began to utter the term "paranoia"—some flippantly, like Roche, others ominously, like Dick Goodwin and Bill Moyers. Goodwin noticed the change in Johnson during the first phase of escalation in Vietnam. "The president's always large eccentricities had taken a huge leap into unreason, [though] not on every subject, and certainly not all the time," Goodwin recalled. In these irrational moments Johnson's manner was quiet, intense, confidential. Yet his comments were wildly outlandish—and it struck observers that (at those moments) Johnson believed every word.

Typical was a presidential outburst in summer 1965, provoked by nothing in particular but encompassing everything. "Bobby saw his chance," Johnson told a few staff members, according to Goodwin. "He saw I was in trouble, so he put [Martin Luther] King on the Kennedy payroll to rile up the Negroes. That's why we had the riots. After all I've done for the Negroes. They never would have *attacked me* if they hadn't been put up to it.

"Bobby gave the communists the idea," Johnson went on. "Now, I'm not saying he's a communist, mind you. But they saw they might be able to divide the country against me. They already control the three major networks. So they began to complain that we were killing civilians, that we ought to stop the bombing. That got back here, and my critics took it up. Not just in the press. I was always getting advice from someone in the communist world. Hell, you can always find [Soviet Ambassador Anatoly] Dobrynin's car in front of a columnist's house the night before he blasts me on Vietnam. . . ."

Riots in the ghettos, criticism of the war, opposition in Congress, and the constant threat of Bobby Kennedy were dealing Johnson's psyche a heavy, steady drubbing. Johnson's bizarre outbursts grew more frequent—so constant, according to Goodwin, that they began "infecting the entire process of presidential decision." After enduring another maniacal monologue, Bill Moyers made a midnight phone call to Goodwin and expressed profound concern. Moyers said that as he listened to Johnson he felt strange, as if Johnson were something other than a human being.

In the months that followed, Moyers and Goodwin met often to discuss the president's behavior. Separately, the two aides flipped through medical textbooks and consulted psychiatrists. The diagnosis was always the same: paranoia. At the very least, Johnson exhibited excessive secrecy, an obsession with hidden motives, and an elaborate denial of reality. To Goodwin, LBJ resembled Freud's paranoid "official who has been passed over for promotion [and thus] needs to believe that persecutors are plotting against him and that he is being spied upon." Goodwin turned to the writings of social psychologist Elias Canetti, who described the paranoiac's "gift of seeing through appearances and know[ing] exactly what is behind them. He tears the mask from every face and what he then finds is essentially the same enemy."

Whatever Johnson's clinical condition, it certainly did infect his White House. Bobby Kennedy—and the conventional wisdom—held that LBJ had bullied his aides into cowering yes-men. One friend of Bobby's who had worked for LBJ likened the president to a vampire, feeding off his staff members' lifeblood. After Moyers left the White House in January 1967, the *Wall Street Journal* lamented the loss of "brilliant and independent-minded advisors." Johnson's sorry lot was "not quite as sharp or as willing to argue" as it once had been. But the real picture was more complicated. Johnson's advisers were not sycophants; they were almost universally capable, perceptive, and blunt. Their memos to LBJ were often shocking in their candor. Even after the departures of Jenkins, Moyers, and McPherson, men like Califano, Christian, and even Watson disagreed openly with Johnson.

Yet none could completely resist the force of Johnson's personality. As Harry McPherson, one of Johnson's most independent-minded aides, put it, LBJ was "all-absorptive," suffocating, overpowering. "His preoccupations become yours." Charlie Boatner, a member of LBJ's vice presidential staff, recalled the way Johnson swept up an aide's entire life. "When you were working for Johnson," Boatner said, "you were caught up in the Johnson scheme of things." And as Johnson's general scheme became more unreasonable, so did his staff's. They parroted Johnson's prejudices, feeding them back to him in a steady stream of rumor, gossip, and innuendo. Standing at Johnson's bedside at 7:00 A.M., White House aides would begin the day's business and, inevitably, recount thirdhand stories of RFK: "Last night, somebody told me that Bobby Kennedy said. . ." It was an easy means of currying favor, of affirming one's loyalty to a president obsessed with loyalty. But the hostility toward Kennedy was genuine and mutually reinforced.

An average day in the Johnson White House began with a round of phone calls. The president started with McNamara and Rusk and then swept through the West Wing, calling his top aides one by one and asking, "What do you know?" His appetite for information was insatiable. Press aides struggled to keep pace as Johnson scoured newspapers and night memos, listened to the radio and watched all three television networks simultaneously, and tore reports from the teletype machine that clattered constantly beside his desk. The president, recalled McPherson, demanded it all: "Rumor, speculation, opinion, fact. Reports of vendettas and alliances. 'Pure politics' and [issues] 'on the merits.'" Johnson consumed every morsel of information. Or perhaps it consumed him. Unable to filter bad material from good, or to distinguish dubious sources from credible ones, Johnson was awash in minutia. At some point, nearly every one of his top aides urged him to ignore the news

reports and tickers and broadcasts. When a poll showed LBJ more popular than Bobby Kennedy, the president could not resist: he read the
results aloud to reporters. McPherson counseled Johnson that "it is valuable and encouraging information, but in my opinion it should not be
delivered to you."

But aides could not stop themselves. Qualms aside, they stuffed the
president full of the most incendiary and irrelevant details on every subject—especially Bobby Kennedy. "I don't know why he wanted all that
junk," said George Christian, who had neither time nor inclination to
feed the president's Kennedy obsession. That was Marvin Watson's job.
Marvin J. Watson was a Texas businessman, a real provincial. Johnson
named him appointments secretary in spring 1965 and charged him
with controlling access to the Oval Office. A man of little sophistication
or intelligence, Watson was Johnson's most literal-minded adviser. "He
really didn't have a hell of a lot of imagination," observed Lee White. "If
the President said, 'Marvin, damn it, I want you to go out on Pennsylvania Avenue and urinate at twelve o'clock every day' . . . he would do
it." Watson asked few questions, offered fewer answers, and subscribed to
no ideology. As Johnson's watchdog, he kept one eye on the political
landscape, the other on senior government officials. Watson watched
unflinchingly for the slightest encroachment by Bobby Kennedy.

If Johnson was a Kennedy news addict, Watson was his dealer. He was
a one-man clearing house for erroneous reports. Sent by IRS officials or
state supreme court justices, scissored from obscure newspapers like the
Long Island Star-Journal or *Portland Press Herald,* clippings told of
Kennedy plots to "use students to cut down LBJ," to use Harvard's Insti-
tute of Politics as a springboard to the White House, or to enlist civil
rights militants in his campaign for the presidency. Watson highlighted
passages and sent them all, dutifully, to President Johnson. Watson sent
Johnson a "Robert F. Kennedy for President Club" business card "that
seems to be circulating in Denver." He passed along invitations to unofficial "Kennedy in '68" cocktail parties ("Help us," one invitation read,
"to recover for Robert F. Kennedy that political football which LBJ has
fumbled"). He sent Johnson a tabloid magazine that revealed "What the
Stars Say About Bobby's Presidential Hopes" (what they said: "Kennedy's
horoscope . . . adds up to a very complex melding of his destiny with
that of the nation"). Watson was a conduit to every small-town pol with
a grudge against RFK: within twenty-four hours, wild rumors made
their way from local committeemen to state party chairmen to the
Democratic National Committee to Marvin Watson and, inevitably, to
the president of the United States. It was no wonder that Johnson per-

ceived a nationwide Kennedy conspiracy. Every day, Marvin Watson handed him a new piece of evidence.

Johnson needed a filter and hired a sieve. But Marvin Watson cannot shoulder all the blame. Most of Johnson's staff—including McPherson and Moyers—were complicit in his undoing. Even after Moyers left the White House he was still passing along rumors and sending anti-Kennedy clippings to LBJ. McPherson wrote Johnson snide memos about RFK's "credibility problem." After all, Johnson was the shrewdest judge of character either man had ever met. McPherson and Moyers marveled at Johnson's ability to be right "about ninety-five percent of the time." Who were they to say he was wrong about Bobby Kennedy?

As a White House aide, McPherson explained later, "you tend to view everything in terms of whether it hurts your Administration [and] your President . . . or helps. You look at almost nothing from the point of view of whether it's true or not." Few doubted that Bobby Kennedy had the ability—or the inclination—to hurt Lyndon Johnson. But the White House staff, by feeding, justifying, and echoing the president's most irrational fears, inflicted a deeper wound. In the end, LBJ had no one left to protect him from himself.

CHAPTER 13

Shadowboxing

On January 12, 1966, in his State of the Union Address, Lyndon Johnson declared that America was to have both guns and butter. "This nation is mighty enough, its society is healthy enough, its people are strong enough, to pursue our goals in the rest of the world while still building a Great Society here at home," Johnson proclaimed. He unleashed a flurry of new legislative proposals and upbraided those who preached moderation. "There are men who cry out that we must sacrifice. Well, let us rather ask them: Who will they sacrifice? Are they going to sacrifice the children who seek the learning, or the sick who need medical care, or the families who dwell in squalor . . . ? Will they sacrifice opportunity for the distressed, the beauty of our land, the hope of our poor?"

Robert Kennedy, who watched Johnson's address from the floor of the House, pursued the same paradox: guns and butter. Defense expenditures were essentially nonnegotiable—Kennedy uneasily approved every appropriation targeted toward "our boys over there" in Vietnam. At the same time he pushed Johnson harder at home. In mid-October, Kennedy brazenly pressed for a $750 million addition to Johnson's $1.75 billion authorization for the war on poverty. It was Kennedy's first major antipoverty bill. But even as Bobby spoke on the Senate floor ("a bravura performance," judged *Newsweek*), Johnson was covertly taking his proposal to pieces. The president summoned the Senate majority and minority leaders, Mike Mansfield and Everett Dirksen, to the Oval Office and shouted, "I don't want my budget shot to hell." Dirksen gleefully carried the message to the Hill. "You should have heard him on the budget," the Republican leader told his colleagues. "He fulminated like Hurricane Inez." With this bipartisan blessing, the original appropriation easily withstood Bobby's last-minute scrambling on the Senate floor. "The administration just cut out the ground from under him," said Peter Edelman. Bobby weakly told the press that "the Administration made a mistake. . . . We turned our backs . . . on those who need help so desperately."

To be sure, Bobby had baited LBJ by quoting his State of the Union Address ("Who will they sacrifice?") while undercutting him. A $750 million grab, moreover, was especially audacious for a senator seen by his colleagues as a "hit-and-run" legislator. "Look," snapped a veteran senator, "if [Kennedy] really wanted to win that poverty fight, he'd have stayed right here in town for the past six weeks nailing down votes and coordinating pressure groups all over the country. . . . If you're running for president, you don't have time to do anything solid on the legislative front." The judgment was unfair, if partly true. Edelman and Adam Walinsky were competent and inventive legislative draftsmen, despite a reputation for arrogance ("nasty and brilliant, in that order," another Capitol Hill staffer said of Walinsky). Emboldened by the partial success of their "amendments-only" strategy in 1965, Kennedy and his staff aimed higher in 1966 and 1967. But they quickly learned that the administration, as Frank Mankiewicz complained, was "dedicated to the proposition that nothing Robert Kennedy advanced was going to get anywhere." It was the beginning of LBJ's legislative blockade.

In the spring of 1967, Bobby Kennedy shone a spotlight on rural hunger—and Lyndon Johnson tried furtively to avert the glare. That March, Kennedy listened as a twenty-seven-year-old civil rights lawyer, Marian Wright, sat before the Senate Subcommittee on Poverty, Manpower, and Employment and testified that disaster had struck the Mississippi Delta. Mechanization had torn a wide swath of hunger. Cotton fields lay fallow in accordance with guidelines for federal subsidies. Clothing, housing, health care, and food were inadequate; the region was on the brink of crisis.

Kennedy was a member of the committee, which investigated the effectiveness of Johnson's antipoverty programs. Here, apparently, was an area the programs had failed to reach. On April 9, 1967, Kennedy, Jacob Javits, George Murphy, and committee chairman Joseph Clark followed LBJ's entreaty to "[go] into the field" to fight poverty at its roots: they traveled to Jackson to investigate the problem and hold hearings. The local poor echoed Wright's testimony, but for Kennedy this secondhand contact was not enough: "I want to see it," he said. The next day he and Clark stepped into what an observer called "one of the worst places I've ever seen." The windowless shack was dark and smelled of mildew and urine. A small child, his stomach bloated by malnutrition, rubbed grains of rice in circles on the ground. Kennedy picked him up, sat on a filthy bed, and caressed the child's belly. "I'm going back to Washington to do something about this," Kennedy said tearfully as the child stared, trance-like, at the floor. Marian Wright had suspected the senators came for publicity. Later she exclaimed that Kennedy "did things that I wouldn't do. He went into the dirtiest, filthiest, poorest black homes . . . and he would sit with a baby who had open sores. . . . I wouldn't do that! I didn't do that! That's why I'm for him."

When Kennedy did go back to Washington, he and Clark paid an immediate visit to Orville Freeman, Johnson's secretary of agriculture. Freeman listened warily to their stories of "starvation conditions" in the Delta. He was not the only skeptic: "We thought they were exaggerating," recalled Joseph Califano, Johnson's domestic policy chief. LBJ, who otherwise felt the pangs of rural hunger as if they were his own, could only perceive Kennedy's interest as political, not humanitarian. But the president had read the wire stories and on April 17 demanded a "quick report" from Califano. "Freeman does not want to upset the entire [food stamp] program," Califano wrote Johnson twenty minutes later, "by either giving free food to these negroes in the delta or by lowering the amount of money they have to pay for food stamps until he has the food stamp program through Congress."

Johnson already had reservations about food stamps. "I just don't know about these programs," he had told Freeman. "Food comes and food goes. You don't get anything for it. Education and job training get more for the money." The point was arguable, though in the short term, education meant little to starving blacks in Mississippi. In any case, Johnson had already given food stamps to "these negroes in the delta" and that was all they were going to get. When Johnson's aides unanimously endorsed a generous food package, the president flatly refused. The White House swung wildly back and forth on the issue, alternately denying that the problem existed, denying that the money existed to solve it, and then leaking ambitious and expensive schemes to do just that. Ultimately, this was Kennedy's problem. Kennedy had stirred up these Negroes—and continued to do so, appealing directly to LBJ for free food stamps to the poor, cheaper food stamps to the slightly less poor, and emergency food rations to the forty to sixty thousand neediest inhabitants of the region. Johnson did not reject the proposal—he simply ignored it. *The Nation* asked the obvious question and gave the obvious answer:

> Why would he respond so coldly when he knows thousands of desperate people are depending on him for relief? Because, simply, he is incapable of rising above personal politics. Look at the subcommittee that made the

request: one man he hates (Robert F. Kennedy); one man he thoroughly dislikes (Edward M. Kennedy); one man has been a constant nettle to Johnson since the late '50s (Joseph Clark); and all the others . . . have often opposed him.

Kennedy agreed with Pat Moynihan that the president viewed the whole affair "as an attack by Kennedy on Johnson." Johnson's sudden souring on food aid demonstrated to *The Nation's* editors that while "Robert Kennedy could put aside personal politics for mercy's sake . . . President Johnson could not." In May, seemingly for the same reason, LBJ opposed a bill by the Kennedys, Javits, and Clark to add $137.5 million to the antipoverty budget. Johnson refused even to discuss the bill— and shortly undercut it with his own $75 million bill, designed to cover the summer rather than the full year. There was no emergency food aid until April 1968. And when Freeman planned to spend $145 million more than the 1968 budget had allocated to food programs, an enraged Johnson said, "I never authorized you to do that." As the Vietnam War consumed more and more of the budget, federal dollars were harder to find. Kennedy understood this. He also understood that LBJ was able to find funds when their expenditure was his own idea (or claimed as such).

The president's double standard was bitterly frustrating. Tensions broke to the surface in the summer of 1967, when RFK introduced the two most sweeping, ambitious bills his staff had ever drafted. The companion bills—one on employment, the other on housing—took six months to assemble. Kennedy's staff consulted nearly one hundred economists, lawyers, businessmen, and bureaucrats in the process. "The two bills were incredibly intricate," recalled Jeff Greenfield, a young aide. "They involved almost a total rewriting of the tax codes and, at the same time, safeguards ensuring real community control." The tax incentives built into the program marked an important change in Kennedy's thinking. "I've learned you can't rely on altruism or morality," Kennedy said at the time. "People just aren't built that way." Neither were corporations. Bobby's moral exhortations alone were not enough to bring private industry into the ghettos: if America was to have more Bedford-Stuyvesants, investors needed incentives. The premise of Kennedy's two bills was that government tax credits were catalysts to community development.

Kennedy introduced his employment measure on July 12, 1967, declaring its purpose to be "the creation of new jobs in poverty areas, to be filled by the residents of those areas." Kennedy promised tax deductions to companies that opened plants in the ghetto and hired previously unemployed workers. The housing bill followed on July 13. In order to construct or rehabilitate 300,000 to 400,000 low-cost housing units in the slums, Kennedy pledged more tax credits, low-interest loans to renters, and $3.3 billion from the government over seven years. Kennedy knew that his bills stood little chance in their original form, that the Treasury Department, the IRS, and the new Department of Housing and Urban Development (HUD) would oppose them automatically on the grounds that the tax code was a cumbersome tool, prone to exploitation. "But he thought [the bills] were worth putting in," said an adviser, to "start that ball rolling."

The ball stopped short abruptly. After a summer of deadly riots in the cities, President Johnson was not going to let Kennedy claim credit for an innovative urban program. "Johnson put a whole task force of Treasury and HUD officials on refuting . . . and discrediting those bills just because they were Kennedy bills," complained Peter Edelman. This was not just youthful paranoia: the *Wall Street Journal, The New Republic,* and the *New York Times* each referred to a Johnson "task force" bent on "discrediting" Kennedy's bills. In mid-September, when the Senate Finance Committee held three days of public hearings on the housing bill, the *Times* observed that "the Johnson Administration mounted a concerted attack." Predictably, HUD Secretary Robert Weaver labeled the Kennedy proposal "superfluous." He insisted that a bit of tinkering with LBJ's rent subsidy program would accomplish just as much. Joseph Barr, under secretary of the treasury, said Kennedy's plan imperiled the tax code: "We have consistently opposed the use of the tax code for narrow and specialized purposes"—like social problems, Barr said.

Bobby marshaled some former JFK advisers in defense of the bills, but the fight was over. Three weeks later, LBJ announced his own ghetto development plan—similar to Kennedy's but smaller in scale. Johnson also hastily convened a group of insurance companies to pledge their resources to community development. The following March, when Kennedy was scheduled to testify before the Senate Banking Committee on housing legislation, an aide informed Johnson that "HUD and Treasury are primed to take Kennedy on. Mayor [Carl] Stokes of Cleveland will testify after Kennedy and is prepared to support fully and endorse the new housing program [you] submitted." By this time, though, Johnson had usurped Kennedy's notion of tax incentives, once regarded by Johnson's policy aides as "anathema." In its own bill the administration mimicked Kennedy's down to its details—like its "pass-through" of early-year operating losses—but hardly matched its ambition. Baffled, the *Wall Street Journal* asked LBJ how "you turn right around and propose as your own the very tomfoolery you were opposing" last year. The paper mocked Johnson's game as "follow the leader."

Bobby was less amused. "How can they be so petty?" he asked reporter Jack Newfield the day after Johnson introduced his own program. "I worked on my plan for six months, and we talked to everyone in the Administration in all the relevant agencies. We accepted many of their ideas and put them in our bill. Now they came out with this thing, and the first I hear about it is on television. They didn't even try to work something out together. To them it's all politics."

Later in the summer of 1967, Kennedy proposed a refinancing of Social Security—adding federal revenues to the trust fund to cover a projected shortfall in payroll taxes. When the Social Security Administration (SSA) lent him technical assistance in drafting the bill, Kennedy and his aides were rightly shocked. "That was almost the only incident where we ever got major cooperation out of the government agencies," recalled Edelman. But even here that cooperation was dilatory. "It took a long time to get anything out of them," said Edelman, who at first suspected institutional inertia. "They're just bureaucrats and they're busy," he remembered thinking. And it was partly a problem of high expectations: "We were terribly demanding. . . . We expected agencies, really, to fall over dead at our feet," confessed another Kennedy aide. But the interference was so endemic that Edelman began to suspect LBJ was behind it. Finally a friendly bureaucrat leaked Edelman an intra-agency memo by the assistant commissioner of the SSA that said, in Edelman's words, "We really have to respond to Edelman on this. Pretty soon they're going to notice we're dragging our feet. And they're likely to criticize us publicly."

Other leaks confirmed that the SSA was in no way a rogue agency. The word was out: administration officials were to refuse Kennedy the most basic technical assistance until doing so became politically untenable. Sometimes, of course, Kennedy's proposals were too insignificant to command attention. Most amendments were like that. But progressive bills drew public attention—and utter administrative intransigence. More often than not, agencies refused to answer Kennedy's basic questions or offer him the informal assistance accorded to Democratic senators as a matter of courtesy. Kennedy's advance man Jerry Bruno canvassed his contacts in the administration and stewed about the fact that RFK never got the "inside dope." Even Jacob Javits, a Republican, had easier access than Kennedy.

Still, government agencies could never be politically airtight. "When you have a hundred thousand employees," reflected HEW Secretary John Gardner, "you just can't follow everybody." A staff member might quietly serve his own purpose—or somebody else's. This was Kennedy's lifeline and Johnson's worst fear: throughout the government, scores of

Kennedy supporters aided Bobby surreptitiously. Some had once worked for President Kennedy, others for Bobby. Some, like Under Secretary of Agriculture John Schnittker, were eager to help, if quietly. Others were more cagey, watching their backs or playing both sides. The Kennedy staff nurtured covert contacts in the departments of Agriculture, HUD, HEW, Labor, and especially Justice, Bobby's old domain. But "you had to be careful not to expose the Kennedy partisans," said Ron Linton, a former adviser to JFK.

There was nothing glamorous or exhilarating about this legislative subterfuge. It was draining and, in the end, often frustrating—especially when Johnson steamrolled or supplanted a carefully crafted bill or had his friends strangle it in committee. Nevertheless, Edelman described the Kennedy office as "really upbeat" and energetic. Aside from an occasional flash of anger, Kennedy was unmoved by Johnson's interference, and the staff followed his example. "We were going flat-out every day," Edelman recalled, "and getting a lot done." This enduring optimism highlighted the contrast between RFK and LBJ as legislators. Whether majority leader or president, Johnson saw output—the number of bills passed, period—as the gauge of success. Bobby viewed it much the same way in 1964, scoring grandstanding liberals as "selfish . . . sons of bitches . . . in love with death." There was nothing romantic about losing; achievement was essential. For this reason, in April 1966, Fred Dutton advised Kennedy to introduce by year's end "at least one or two bills with your name on them concerning basic, mainstream subjects." And Kennedy did so (though not until July 1967 and not for reasons as narrowly political as Dutton's). But by that time Kennedy understood there was more to legislating than writing (or even passing) bills. Legislating meant alerting the public to hunger in its midst, opening hearings on migrant farm workers or auto safety, and creating public-private partnerships for ghetto development. Bills and amendments were only one aspect of what Edelman called "three-dimensional activity."

In the end, Bobby described Johnson's legislative blockade as more liberating than inhibiting. It infused Kennedy's idealistic staff with pragmatism as they collected small-scale, tangible accomplishments and charted a more ambitious course for the future. "We were laying the groundwork," said Edelman. But the groundwork for what? Kennedy's dedication to the Senate was always uncertain; he showed little interest in becoming a baron of Capitol Hill. Nor did he express open interest in the presidency—however safe it might be to assume. By 1967, Kennedy's proposed legislation comprised "the guts of a presidential campaign, at least in domestic policy," Edelman said in retrospect. "Anything that could be put into legislation, Kennedy had a bill that he could

point to and use as a political device . . . though we hadn't done it for
that reason."

It was true: Kennedy was too impulsive and too great a fatalist for
master plans. "Long range planning," confessed one adviser, "is thinking
about next Saturday." Kennedy covered his legislative bases haphazardly.
But by late 1967 he had laid—however unintentionally—the groundwork for a Kennedy presidency. And Johnson had unwittingly given
him an incentive to run: as Frank Mankiewicz explained, "the more
political of us—Joe Dolan and I, among others—responded [to the
blockade] by saying how important it was that Kennedy ran for president. Nothing was going to get accomplished if that didn't happen."

Lyndon Johnson had little patience for position-striking. If Bobby
Kennedy was not passing bills, he was accomplishing nothing—except
the persecution of the president of the United States. Johnson considered Bobby a needler, a spoiler, a cynical crank. Bobby obviously had no
commitment to the Great Society or even the Democratic Party. Joe
Califano reflected that LBJ "[bit] his lip" as Kennedy found fault with
one program after another. Privately, though, Johnson ranted about
Bobby's "little potshots," seeing them even where they did not exist:
when a group of Catholic bishops attacked the administration's family
planning policy in November 1966, LBJ said that the Kennedys, "probably Bobby," had orchestrated it.

Robert Kennedy was not a team player, and Johnson's policy team
resented it. The most charitable among them believed Kennedy was
often right but always overzealous and unrealistic. The rest of the staff
reflected LBJ's outright hostility. "Our office had a line open" to
Kennedy's office, said Matthew Nimetz, a young assistant to Califano.
Califano himself was a bridge of sorts: "Our relations with him were at
least cordial and probably better than that," judged Peter Edelman. Califano, a former assistant to Secretary McNamara, was an occasional guest
at Hickory Hill and seemed even to like Bobby Kennedy. Yet Frank
Mankiewicz, who later grumbled that Califano was a "Johnson bitter-
ender," typified the distrust that lingered. Contacts between the two
staffs were infrequent and uneasy. Califano's staff regarded Kennedy's staff
skittishly, fearful that Bobby would betray their trust and use inside
information for his own political gain—or simply to embarrass the
administration.

The fear was never realized. It was as ill-founded as LBJ's perception
of "potshots." Though Kennedy did prod the White House to "do better" (as he implored the nation), to build more low-cost housing, to educate more children, and to assist more unemployed workers, he did not

snipe incessantly at administration proposals. For political reasons, Kennedy was more inclined to support Johnson than oppose him. "He thought very carefully about any decision which would put him . . . in opposition to President Johnson," recalled Senator Joe Tydings of Maryland. By 1967, Kennedy's opposition to the war was such that the press characterized minor steps as great strides to Johnson's left. And major disagreements—for example, Kennedy's rejection of Johnson's proposed 10 percent income tax surcharge that autumn—drew headlines like "Bobby Kennedy: New Thoughts About Tackling LBJ in '68?"

Despite Johnson's caricature of Bobby as "spoiler," Kennedy was in fact a reliable ally in Congress. "Contrary to what may be a public impression," U.S. News reported in 1966, "Robert Kennedy's voting record shows he has been a consistent supporter of the Johnson Administration's 'Great Society' program." Kennedy supported every major program and most of the minor ones. He voted to raise the federal debt ceiling and supported every foreign aid authorization. Two years later, with his own legislation under constant fire, Kennedy's support of the administration had not diminished. In a March 1968 review of Kennedy's legislative record, a Johnson staffer concluded (a bit sadly) that "one has to look into the amendments to find his disagreements." By Kennedy's count he had supported LBJ in 73 percent of roll-call votes in 1965, 60 percent in 1966, and 62 percent in 1967. According to a private White House study, Kennedy's support of the administration was even higher on "select Senate votes" in 1967: 75 percent.

Kennedy was choosing his battles carefully. "Don Quixote may have been a likeable fellow," Joe Dolan wrote him in November 1967, "but husbanding of strength and careful selection of targets makes for greater effectiveness. . . . If you push too far up the path, you *lessen*, not *increase*, your ability to accomplish things." Fred Dutton echoed this advice. "Taking occasional digs at the Johnson administration for its real deficiencies will win the cheers of those . . . already for you," he counseled Kennedy, but it was sure to "feed the latent suspicions" about his character.

Lyndon Johnson's suspicions were hardly latent and they needed no confirmation. Numbers could not reveal the real Kennedy challenge, which cut far deeper than any piece of legislation. "It is the speeches, travels and attention-getting stunts of Senator Robert Kennedy—not his votes—which give the appearance of a smoldering political feud" between Kennedy and Johnson, U.S. News noted perceptively. And while Johnson did much to contain Kennedy on Capitol Hill, he could do little to contain Kennedy elsewhere. It was off the Hill that Kennedy appeared most effective—and most threatening.

In the state of New York, Robert Kennedy was something of a victim of high expectations—journalists' and Lyndon Johnson's. Within a day of Kennedy's election as senator the *New York Times* portrayed him "looming as a new center of power" in the state Democratic Party organization. New York Democrats fully expected Bobby "to play an immediately expanding role in party affairs in the state, in an effort to build a strong political base for possible future use." The only uncertainty, Democrats told the press, was the attitude of President Johnson. Would LBJ step quietly aside while Bobby took control?

These were high expectations indeed for Bobby Kennedy, who, only months earlier, had to receive a textbook primer on the history and government of his adopted state. Yet when he assumed office in January 1965 he inspired more fear among the ranks of New York politicians than any state leader since Governor Thomas E. Dewey. And while Dewey had been a skilled organizer and disciplined executive, he had the personal charisma of a thin-lipped bank manager. Bobby Kennedy had all Dewey's attributes plus a winning smile and a family fortune. In 1965, Kennedy was the only statewide Democratic official (besides the comptroller) in a state controlled by Republican Governor Nelson Rockefeller. Kennedy's own party was full of tired hacks and angry reformers and surprisingly little talent. Mayor Robert Wagner was Kennedy's only local rival for party leadership. LBJ lurked along the sidelines.

Yet Joe Kennedy had taught his sons that city politics was an "endless morass," and Bobby was inclined to agree. "You know, there aren't ten politicians in the whole state I like and trust," he told a reporter, off the record. "They all want me to become the boss of the state until the time comes to make the first decision. Then they go at each other's throat. And meanwhile they can't carry their own district." To a new arrival like RFK, New York's political landscape was baffling terrain—a maze of geographical and factional disputes, of ideological and personal feuds, of reformers and regulars. Kennedy was a United States senator with a national following; New York had little to offer him but headaches. Looking back in 1967, Bobby reflected that "it didn't make a great deal of sense to get into all those . . . fights in a state, because after a period of time it sucked away all your strength." His own election had been exhausting enough. It left him bored with politics.

Moreover, any takeover of the state party organization would have to be a hostile one: as a freshman senator in perpetual conflict with the president, RFK had little patronage to dispense to soothe embattled egos. Unlike his brother Teddy in Massachusetts, Bobby inherited no county-by-county organization. Building a machine required patience and energy; and, given the demands he faced in Washington and across the country, Bobby had little of either. His choice seemed clear: national leadership or local leadership. Fight Johnson or fight Tammany Hall. "It would have been almost impossible for him to do both," said a friend.

At the same time, Kennedy had certain obligations. The state party was a shambles: Lyndon Johnson's 1964 sweep had caught Democrats unprepared, giving them control of the state legislature for the first time in thirty years but leaving them without leadership. Kennedy was hardly a crusader for local reform, but the high expectations of his party and the press thrust the mantle of leadership uncomfortably upon him. Kennedy owed something, surely, to the party rank and file who had put themselves out for him in a rancorous campaign. Albert Blumenthal, a West Side reform leader, reminded him of that and told Kennedy to "exercise the power that everybody thought he had." Bobby faced constant appeals for endorsements; even in upstate counties, Democrats coveted the magic of the Kennedy name. Abdication invited resentment. As an ambitious national leader, Kennedy could ill afford the self-inflicted wound. New York was his political base. And if Kennedy failed to secure it, New York would be prime for plundering by Lyndon Johnson.

Inauspiciously, in January 1965, Kennedy stumbled into a battle for leadership of the state legislature. By backing a pair of progressives against the men from the machine, Kennedy delivered a challenge to two powerful Democrats: Mayor Wagner and Tammany leader J. Raymond Jones. Wagner had long filled the vacuum atop the state party. Jones, in 1960, had bucked the trend among his state's delegation and backed LBJ at the Democratic Convention. Jones hated Robert Kennedy. Kennedy called Jones a "thorn in my side." Their clash surprised no one, and the press eagerly reported a "Kennedy-led revolt."

In truth, Kennedy's intervention was so covert that his own candidates were never really sure of his support. On February 3 he was deftly outmaneuvered by Wagner, who cut a deal with Governor Rockefeller and cleared the path for his machine hacks. It was an embarrassment for Kennedy and a triumph for Jones and Wagner. The mayor, argued *The Nation,* had won "a substantial, if slightly tainted victory over the forces . . . that were grouped around U.S. Senator Robert F. Kennedy, despite Mr. Kennedy's fulsome, and at times too plaintive, denials that he was in any way involved." Some Democrats said Kennedy had stepped too deeply into the quicksand of local politics. Others believed he meant to crush Wagner and collect the pieces of power for himself.

A defeat for Kennedy was a victory for Lyndon Johnson, and the White House followed the internecine battles in Albany with interest. Within months, Johnson's aide Marvin Watson began discussions with

Mike Prendergast, a New Yorker Bobby had ousted from the state party chairmanship in 1961. Shortly, Watson reported to LBJ on "ways in which your Administration can properly recognize the Democratic Party machinery there and therefore take away the separate organization which Senator Kennedy is planning."

In the summer of 1964, while Robert Kennedy ran for the Senate, President Johnson took out a political insurance policy in New York by installing Edwin Weisl, Sr., as his new Democratic national committeeman. Weisl was an old New York lawyer. And though he claimed to be his own man, dedicated only to promoting "unity and harmony" in the state party, Weisl had been close to LBJ for a quarter century. Associates called him the president's "eyes and ears" in New York—LBJ's Stephen Smith. "He was an original Johnson man," said William vanden Heuvel, an original Kennedy man.

As committeeman, Weisl wielded very little real power in New York. But his appointment was a sign of Johnson's growing concern. Since November 1963, LBJ had been doting on New York like a kindly uncle. As senator and vice president, Johnson had had little time for New York. But in the first months after the assassination, Johnson was hyperattentive to the state's needs, calling Democratic leaders about any minor matter, "things you couldn't care about," said Jack English. "It was really kind of silly." Johnson wooed the state party establishment with the same eager intensity he displayed in Texas or Washington, D.C. He showered "Kennedy people" with flattery. And when New York elected Bobby Kennedy its junior senator, Johnson took an even greater interest in the state's affairs. The president called Bobby and, at great length, held forth about specific veterans' hospitals in New York. They *concerned* him, Johnson said earnestly.

But Johnson's main concern in New York was shutting down the "Kennedy machine." Of course, there was no Kennedy machine. But Johnson's men kept telling him there was, and Kennedy's sponsorship of antiestablishment candidates in January was proof enough for Johnson. "Mr. Johnson may not want to see Bobby 'flying so high' in so important a state," predicted one reporter in November 1964. "Mr. Johnson could keep a restraining finger on him . . . by presidential decisions on the flow of federal patronage in New York." And so he did. Very early in Robert Kennedy's term, Johnson froze him out of the patronage process.

Johnson savored sweet vengeance: during the Kennedy administration, he had blamed the attorney general for "double-crossing" him on similar matters. According to Bobby Baker, Johnson complained that RFK and Texas Senator Ralph Yarborough usurped his right to appoint judges, border guards, and customs officials, conspiring "to reduce him to a cut-dog impotency in Texas and to drive him from the national ticket." Though it was Yarborough who confounded Johnson's patronage prerogatives, Kennedy made an inviting target. It was Kennedy, after all, who scrutinized Johnson's choices for judgeships. When the Justice Department momentarily balked at appointing a controversial Johnson nominee (Sarah T. Hughes, who later administered the oath of office on Air Force One, was labeled "unqualified" by the American Bar Association), Johnson blamed RFK. This attitude, recalled Ralph Dungan, "caused all sorts of pain and sweat."

As president, LBJ relished every opportunity for retribution. From 1965 onward, in almost every case, he denied Kennedy standard Democratic courtesies. He ignored Kennedy on federal judgeships. He went behind Kennedy's back to Weisl or even friendly Republicans like Jacob Javits. And for any given vacancy, Johnson selected someone Kennedy did not want but could not oppose.

A typically shrewd maneuver followed Johnson's appointment of Thurgood Marshall as solicitor general. Marshall's departure from New York's Second Circuit Court of Appeals left an important vacancy, and Bobby Kennedy had a choice to fill it: District Court Judge Edward Weinfeld. Kennedy phoned Attorney General Katzenbach to remind him of the obvious: Weinfeld was widely considered the finest trial judge in the country. The ABA would certainly rate Weinfeld "exceptionally well-qualified." His elevation to the court of appeals would please liberals, Jews, and the New York bar. On July 14, 1965, in a memo to LBJ, Katzenbach reported that Kennedy believed a Weinfeld nomination "to be preferable from your viewpoint as well as his own." But Kennedy had emphasized, as a matter of courtesy, that "he wanted to do whatever you would like to do in New York."

What Johnson wanted to do was stick it to Kennedy. The president elevated a different district court judge, Wilfred Feinberg, a man of merit but hardly considered to be Weinfeld's caliber. Yet Bobby could not oppose Feinberg: Feinberg's older brother, Abe, had been a big financial supporter of both John and Robert Kennedy in New York. Bobby was infuriated, but the real loser in the affair was Weinfeld. "It really was a very mean thing that Johnson did," reflected Katzenbach. (Judge Feinberg, as it turned out, found few equals on the federal bench; he emerged as one of the great jurists of his day.)

Johnson continued to bypass Kennedy, dealing him one deliberate slight after another. In 1966, Bobby asked LBJ to fulfill a promise of President Kennedy's—to finance New York Democratic campaigns through the DNC, since New York added so much to national coffers.

According to Bobby, Johnson replied, "You don't seem to understand. That was a different president." In October 1966, Ed Weisl in New York and Ramsey Clark of the Justice Department seconded Kennedy's endorsement of Jack Weinstein, a well-respected Columbia law professor, for a New York judgeship. But LBJ shot down the nomination, denying angrily that he had (as Joe Dolan claimed) reached an agreement with Bobby Kennedy. "Never discussed this," Johnson added curtly to a memo on Weinstein. He dashed the professor's hopes with a simple check mark by the word "No." "President Johnson," said Katzenbach, "was putting the squeeze on."

The White House accused Kennedy of the same, retributive tactics. When a mysterious leak in August 1967 killed the nomination of "one of the few pro-Administration figures in New York State" to a high federal post, Johnson advisers charged Bobby with a "clever, cunning Machiavellian ploy." Kennedy's staff denied making the leak. Still, it was increasingly clear that Bobby had nowhere to turn but the press: appealing to his allies in the administration for backdoor patronage achieved little. Larry O'Brien, now Johnson's postmaster general, did allow Kennedy to pick the new regional postal director, an important position with patronage power of its own. Kennedy's choice was Jerry McDougal, a wealthy businessman who had helped Steve Smith during the 1964 campaign. But when O'Brien's Postal Department cleared the appointment, Johnson refused to approve it. The post remained vacant for the rest of his presidency. "Kennedy was very, very disturbed about that," remembered Jack English. "It caused very bad blood between Kennedy and Johnson."

Johnson's policy in New York State was a policy of containment. Its premise, of course, was that RFK was consolidating power in his home base. "We have few . . . barriers," a nervous Humphrey aide wrote Marvin Watson, "to [RFK's] total political control of a state with 43 electoral votes." Bobby was boss. Every month the press trembled with a new prediction: Bobby Kennedy was about to "shake up" the Democratic Party in New York; he was scheming to wipe out the Liberal Party; he was tightening control over the 1968 delegation to the Democratic National Convention; he was going to name the next mayor, governor, or senator. And each successful gambit would move Kennedy one step closer to the White House.

It was a farcical notion, a shadow conjured by an insecure president and an excitable press. In reality Kennedy dodged, or botched, every power play but one. Typical was the New York City mayoral race of 1965, in which Kennedy dabbled ineffectually and provided no real leadership. Kennedy's only real victory came in June 1966, when he turned the primary contest over an obscure (but prestigious) judgeship—Manhattan surrogate—into a major coup over Johnson's man Ray Jones. Again Kennedy staked his own reformer against Jones's hack. But this time Bobby joined the public fight, putting his own prestige on the line and winning a dazzling victory against Tammany Hall. "He [is] now the ruler of the Democratic Party in New York," declared Pete Hamill of the *New York Post*. And with typical hyperbole, the *Washington Star* let the word go forth to "friend and foe alike that—just possibly—Chapter I of 'The Making of the President, 1972' was written" in the surrogate primary.

The easy triumph fed expectations Kennedy was loath to fulfill. His interest in New York politics was sporadic, his rule remote. Bobby was too impatient for local intrigues, too distracted and impulsive to craft a master plan for domination. He outshone his rivals but rarely challenged them. In an epithet of the time, he was an "absentee prince." At the same time, Kennedy worked hard for New York. He brought home the dividends of the Great Society. He recruited local talent for his pet projects and took great pride in his accomplishments. "How am I doing?" he asked his staff. "What do New Yorkers think about this?" He tracked statewide polls with interest. But even his New York City office was a national political center, fielding questions on Vietnam as often as questions on Bedford-Stuyvesant. An aide called Kennedy's operation "schizophrenic." As senator, Kennedy straddled two worlds—local and national—but no one doubted he was first and foremost a national leader.

Johnson did not doubt that Kennedy wanted to be president of the United States, not governor of New York. One way or another, Johnson supposed, Kennedy would use the state house as a stepping stone to the White House. And in early 1966, as Kennedy dabbled in gubernatorial politics, Johnson's anxiety was palpable.

By March, several Democrats had emerged as contenders for their party's nomination and the unenviable right to challenge Governor Rockefeller. The Johnson/Humphrey candidate was Frank D. O'Connor, president of the New York City Council. Backed by the organization, O'Connor was the Democratic favorite. Bobby's man was Eugene Nickerson, the Nassau County executive. As early as autumn 1964, Bobby had urged Nickerson to travel abroad and thereby heighten his profile. On March 9, 1966, Kennedy called the State Department and suggested it send Nickerson overseas as a lecturer under the American Specialists exchange program. An American Specialist crossed the globe and talked about politics, foreign affairs, or whatever he liked. Kennedy pressed the State Department to send Nickerson on a month-long trip—at taxpayer expense—to lecture on local government, politics, the judicial system, and public welfare.

Sponsored by powerful Democrats, most officials of Nickerson's stature were sent without question. On March 31, Harry McPherson acknowledged as much in a memo to LBJ: "Under ordinary circumstances we would consider him a find. . . . Frequently members of Congress suggest people for American Specialist grants. Generally they are not much good. Nickerson is much better quality than most." But McPherson's caveat—"under ordinary circumstances"—and Johnson's attention to this trifling matter meant the circumstances were decidedly *un*ordinary. Nickerson, McPherson hastened to add, was "quite obviously running for Governor in 1966. . . . A trip to Israel and Africa for the State Department will benefit him a good deal." McPherson recommended that Johnson send Nickerson on a scaled-down trip. Anything less and "Kennedy will probably raise hell."

Johnson turned Kennedy down coolly but secretly. On April 14, a State Department official told RFK that there was a surplus of Specialists. Furthermore, the exchange program was nonpartisan; candidates for high office were ineligible. "How do you know Nickerson's a candidate?" Kennedy fired back. And if he was a candidate, well, why not send Rockefeller, too? "There must be more behind this than there appears to be," Kennedy mumbled angrily.

Later that day, McPherson informed LBJ that "we may hear more [of] this, one way or the other. At no time was my name or yours mentioned, but my deputy came away with the feeling that Kennedy's suspicions were sharply aroused." A week later, Bobby sent Dick Goodwin to the White House on a rescue mission. "I am still playing dumb and bureaucratic," McPherson wrote Moyers on April 21. "Let me know what you tell [Goodwin] so we can have our stories straight." But McPherson's amusement belied Johnson's fear. According to a presidential aide, "the Kennedy organization . . . is working vigorously at the local level." Another aide described Kennedy's purported strategy:

1) Deny the Democratic governorship to anyone with the slightest shred of independence, even at the risk of losing the general election to Rockefeller.
2) If Nickerson wins, he is in RFK's pocket; if not, RFK runs for governor in 1970, and has the delegation in 1972, if he can win.

By this calculus, Kennedy could not lose. But the truth, as usual, was hardly so byzantine. Rockefeller was no threat to Kennedy's hold on the

New York Democratic delegation—in 1972 or 1968. Nor was Nickerson in RFK's pocket. Kennedy was typically reluctant to state his preference, worrying that the "Kennedy candidate" tag would hang like an albatross on Nickerson's neck. "It's not going to help," Bobby stated flatly. But mostly, Kennedy feared embarrassment. Nickerson was bright enough but wooden on the stump, and would probably make a better governor than candidate for governor. Reluctant to wage a losing fight against the organization, Kennedy drifted away from Nickerson and cast about for alternatives. "Party leaders are waiting for direction and guidance from you," an adviser implored Kennedy in April, but in the end the senator declared neutrality. O'Connor sailed toward the Democratic nomination and defeat by Rockefeller.

By late 1966, Kennedy had established himself as a focal point and a brilliant fund-raiser in New York, but hardly a leader. He was aimless and equivocal, inaccessible and easily frustrated. Yet as Kennedy stumbled in and out of New York's political arena, the Johnson White House and the press invested every step with great purpose. They displayed a seemingly willful blindness to Kennedy's weaknesses. With O'Connor gone, declared Richard Reeves of the *New York Times,* Bobby was finally poised to "take over the state Democratic party and wait for the right year to run for President." Johnson surely agreed. Ignorant of New York politics, ill informed by his associates, and far too credulous toward Kennedy's good press, Johnson looked at Bobby Kennedy and saw Richard Daley: "the boss."

In the autumn of 1966 the Kennedy challenge seemed to spread from New York and Washington to every state in the country. "Robert Francis Kennedy," *Newsweek* declared, "is the phenomenon of a campaign autumn in which he is running for nothing—except the Presidency of the United States." While Lyndon Johnson's popularity sagged under the weight of the war, inflation, and racial strife, Bobby's shot skyward. In mid-August, Harris and Gallup polls placed Kennedy ahead of Johnson in pursuit of the 1968 Democratic nomination for president—by a slight margin (2 percent) among Democrats and a wide margin (14 percent) among independents. A month later, Johnson's popularity rating skidded to 50 percent. Public approval of his handling of Vietnam had plummeted 23 points since October 1965 (from 65 to 42 percent) and his handling of the economy 20 points (from 69 to 49). It was no wonder, then, that Democratic candidates wanted Bobby by their side on the dais. As Governor Edmund G. "Pat" Brown toured California with Lady Bird in September, a reporter asked whether LBJ might join them later. "We need help wherever we can get it," Brown said ungenerously, "but the guy I'd really like to see come to California is Bobby Kennedy."

California was one of many states in which the rivalry between Kennedy and Johnson threatened to eclipse the fight between Democrats and Republicans. As Democrats faced Democrats in the primaries, candidates eagerly chose sides between LBJ and RFK. Johnson and Kennedy themselves backed off, disavowing any political battles waged in their names, but the press knew a Johnson-Kennedy contest when it saw one (or suspected it did). Obscure local races became contests for "ultimate control of the party, even in 1968." Twice-removed Kennedy associates were "Kennedy mafia." Magazine exposés listed candidates' "old lines of association" and provided handy reference charts of "Johnson men" and "Kennedy men." In Tennessee, where a longtime Johnson friend, former governor Buford Ellington, ran against a former assistant to Attorney General Kennedy, John Jay Hooker, Jr., the *Memphis Commercial Appeal* argued that "the real contest in the Democratic race for governor of Tennessee is Johnson . . . vs. Kennedy" and the real prize was the Tennessee delegation to the 1968 Democratic Convention. An editorial cartoon pictured Ellington and Hooker as faceless boxers dwarfed by their shadows: LBJ and RFK. (Ellington won.)

Johnson and Kennedy had little to gain and much face to lose in these intraparty squabbles. A year earlier, the DNC's Cliff Carter had warned Watson of a coming contest in Wisconsin, noting, "I rather doubt we will be able to show any preference or take any part in this primary . . . despite what Bobby Kennedy does." Kennedy in fact did nothing in the Wisconsin primary. But once the primary ballots were counted, he and Johnson both stormed onto the hustings, crisscrossing each other's path across the nation, collecting political IOUs. Fred Dutton counseled RFK that a "vigorous" effort "can demonstrate your service to the Democratic party on a nation-wide basis and build firm local friends. It is the kind of work that President Kennedy did so extensively in the 1956–60 period." As Bobby barnstormed across the Mid-Atlantic and Midwest, fifty newsman tailed his entourage of a dozen cars and limousines and a fleet of police escorts. It was positively presidential—"everything but 'Hail to the Chief,' " observed one reporter. In Columbus, Ohio, as elsewhere, young, screaming supporters surged toward his plane and flattened a restraining fence. As Bobby stepped from the Boeing 727 he waved cheerfully if almost shyly, brushing his bronze hair aside and hunching his shoulders as if in embarrassment. On the platform he was wooden but forceful. "We can do better!" he shouted, jabbing his finger like JFK. "We can keep this country moving." Drowned out by screams of "Bobby!" his speeches were as inaudible as Beatles concerts. It hardly mattered. "I can't hear what he said," swooned a woman on the town green of Marion, Iowa, "but whatever it was, was right."

Meanwhile, Johnson's large, vibrant crowds belied his dismal poll numbers, and the president relished the public's roars of reassurance. As he bounded toward the fence to pat a baby, Johnson's eyes wrinkled appreciatively. As he reached out, one long arm over the other, he appeared energized, replenished, relieved. Everything, Johnson proclaimed, was "great": this great city, this great state, great candidates, great Democrats, the "great 89th Congress," and, of course, the Great Society. And Johnson himself, according to *Newsweek,* "seemed more like his old tub-thumping, hand-grabbing, partisan self than at any time since the campaign of 1964."

They were two men triumphant. But whenever Kennedy and Johnson campaigned together in New York, the contrast was striking. On August 21, Johnson's speech drew solid, respectful applause from a Catskills crowd. Johnson introduced half a dozen congressmen. Then, as he gestured toward "a young man for whom I have the deepest respect," the audience erupted in shrieks of anticipation: "Bobby!" Kennedy was chary of scene-stealing. He gestured quietly. But the electricity that surged through the crowd was, in the words of one reporter, a "deeper response. . . . Some incalculable button had been touched." The next day's headline in the *Christian Science Monitor* read, NEW YORKERS APPLAUD JOHNSON, SQUEAL AT KENNEDY. And despite these joint appearances, "pro-Kennedy" was coming to mean "anti-Johnson": placards like "Kennedy in '68," "Keep Harassing LBJ," and "RFK Minus LBJ in 1972" greeted Kennedy at every stop.

A Herblock cartoon of August 25 pictured Johnson chasing Kennedy across the country, competing for the allegiance of Democratic candidates. The caption: "See Bobby run. See Lyndon run. They are running to help their fellow party members, of course. They seem to be running very hard." Yet in October, Lyndon stopped running. Mysteriously, he withdrew into the solitude of the Oval Office. "Why," wondered Max Frankel of the *Times,* "has the candid partisanship of spring become a striving for statesmanship in autumn? Why has the plan to row hard for his Congressional team turned into sideline coaching duty with only an occasional dip of the oar?" Partly because Johnson and his desegregation policies were unwelcome in the South. In the North (as elsewhere), Vietnam and inflation stoked growing discontent. Quite naturally, as Frankel reported, "candidates would prefer a Kennedy or a Mansfield or a Humphrey who could draw the crowds and impress the press without arousing suspicion and fears and hostility."

As election day approached, the president did not, as Frankel predicted, "retreat for the duration." But when Johnson left the White House on October 17 he departed for—of all places—Asia. Asked about his shifting campaign plans, Johnson told a reporter, "We don't have any more plans at this moment." This was not entirely so: while in Asia, LBJ planned a campaign swing for the last four days before the election. He made detailed arrangements and notified candidates. And then he canceled, abruptly, afraid that Democrats would blame him for their losses. Again Johnson growled at an inquisitive reporter that "we don't have any plans, so when you don't have plans, you don't cancel plans. . . . The people of this country ought to know that all these canceled plans primarily involve the imagination of people who phrase sentences and write columns, and have to report what they hope or what they imagine."

On November 8, 1966, voters wiped out LBJ's liberal majority. Republicans picked up forty-seven House seats and three Senate seats and elected eight governors. "We've beaten hell out of them," crowed Richard Nixon, who had campaigned as vigorously as Bobby Kennedy. "And we're going to kill them in '68."

Kennedy men in general met a mixed reaction. According to *Congressional Quarterly*, Kennedy "batted in" a mere 39 percent of candidates for whom he campaigned. Trumped again by high expectations, Kennedy and his staff were reduced to publicly contesting the statistics. *CQ*, they insisted, had omitted a few winners and Kennedy's real record was 51 percent. Even so, Bobby was no kingmaker. Richard Nixon, on the heels of two devastating electoral defeats, batted in 69 percent (he claimed 71).

Johnson refrained from bragging, though the White House staff calculated his winning percentage at 66. His silence was politic; Democratic tempers were high. In December, at a private three-hour meeting in White Sulphur Springs, West Virginia, angry Democratic governors complained that the president was to blame. Johnson, they said, had pushed his Great Society too fast, too far, and without respect to local conditions. From top to bottom, party professionals echoed their complaints: LBJ had confused the issues, made limp endorsements (or none at all), failed to arrive where he was needed, and widened the Democrats' credibility gap. He had also emasculated the Democratic National Committee, slashing its budget because its director, John Bailey, was a "Kennedy man."

As a referendum on Lyndon Johnson's record, the 1966 elections were a debacle. As a referendum on Kennedy's future, they said little—though Frank Mankiewicz understood their real portent. "It is, I think, a brand-new ball game," he wrote in an exultant memo to the senator. "In every contested election the young, attractive, more non-political candidate won. And the oldest, least attractive, most political candidate is LBJ." Mankiewicz predicted that Johnson could win in 1968 only if he ended the war or if the GOP nominated Richard Nixon. Both possibilities struck Mankiewicz as less likely than Johnson's withdrawal from politics. The presidential field was opening up—to a progressive Republican or to RFK. "A move to opposition and availability—openly—has to wait," Mankiewicz advised Kennedy. "You can't kick a man when he's down, but why not your own State of the Nation address, at least?"

Kennedy refused to join in his staff's gloating. A grandiose speech was the surest way to invite charges of opportunism. And though the pendulum of popularity had swung Kennedy's way, typically, he waited for the inevitable correction. "In the politics of the country at this moment, this is a fad," Bobby said of "the Bobby phenomenon." He estimated that voters agreed with LBJ on 80 percent of the issues between them. It was simply that no one believed Johnson anymore. "[Kennedy] is rueful about his own vogue, which he regarded as transient," Arthur Schlesinger noted in his journal. And during the next few months, Kennedy seemed determined to prove the point.

CHAPTER 14

Malapropaganda

Bobby Kennedy believed Lyndon Johnson was tapping his telephone. Kennedy asked Joe Dolan if he agreed. "No," Dolan replied. "Johnson would be afraid he'd get caught. But you should act on the phone as if you thought Johnson was tapping it." Kennedy's suspicions lingered. But in December 1966, it was he and not Johnson at the center of a public controversy over electronic eavesdropping. The bitter dispute erased some of Kennedy's great gains in popularity. And a gleeful President Johnson, acting in concert with J. Edgar Hoover's FBI, exploited Kennedy's record to emerge the defender of Americans' right to privacy.

The practice of wiretapping telephone lines, which had been common for decades, required written authorization by the attorney general. Bobby Kennedy, during his brother's administration, authorized a number of taps—mostly to investigate leaks of classified information. Kennedy also permitted the FBI to wiretap Martin Luther King, Jr., for evidence of Communist or subversive connections. In addition, the FBI bugged King—without checking with Kennedy. "Bugs"—small microphones—were a more invasive form of surveillance than taps. Hidden in a room, they recorded all conversation and usually required illegal trespass to install. Kennedy, like previous attorneys general, was probably willfully ignorant of the practice. "In retrospect," testified Nicholas Katzenbach in 1975, "we probably should have inferred its existence from memoranda we received, and Mr. Hoover may have believed we did in fact know."

Senator Edward Long of Missouri also believed Kennedy knew. A friend of Roy Cohn and the Teamsters, Long was unabashedly eager to tie RFK to illegal eavesdropping. In December 1965, Long began investigating surveillance practices by the Department of Justice. "[Long] is out to get Bobby," Bill Moyers told Dick Goodwin. "Johnson is egging him on." So was the FBI: Deke DeLoach recommended the Bureau supply information to Long "on a completely confidential basis," since "Long thoroughly dislikes former Attorney General Kennedy and will use such information against Kennedy."

This left Katzenbach, who succeeded Kennedy as attorney general, torn between his predecessor and his president. "While his heart and guts were with Kennedy, his mind was with Johnson and he maintained a consistent loyalty," judged John W. Macy, who vetted Johnson's potential appointees for loyalty. LBJ did not agree: believing Katzenbach a Kennedy man, the president let him dangle as *acting* attorney general for six months before promoting him. Kennedy had recommended Katzenbach strongly for the post. "I don't think that helped," Katzenbach recalled.

And now, as Long probed department records, Katzenbach envisioned a shooting match with RFK on one side, LBJ and Hoover on the other, and himself in the middle. In a phone call to DeLoach on December 20, 1965, Katzenbach expressed fear that Kennedy would make one claim and Hoover would make another. "Well," Hoover replied in a note to DeLoach, "I will if Attorney General [Katzenbach] and Kennedy continue to feed out untrue information." A month later, Katzenbach lay awake at night, full of regret for mailing a letter to Long—a letter by Hoover charging RFK with having approved FBI bugs. "Upon giving the matter second thought," DeLoach recorded after another Katzenbach confessional, "he felt that there was one provision in the letter that would infuriate Bobby Kennedy. [Katzenbach] then told me that he needed Bobby's support for two bills in the Senate" and feared Bobby would turn his anger on the Justice Department.

DeLoach feigned sympathy but shared Katzenbach's confidences with LBJ and Marvin Watson. At an American Legion banquet on March 2, 1966, Watson took DeLoach aside and asked, "How does your boss feel about Katzenbach?" Not warmly, said DeLoach. Hoover believed Katzenbach "had tried in every manner to defend Bobby Kennedy, to the detriment of the FBI." He considered Katzenbach's handwringing over the bugging controversy annoyingly typical. Together, DeLoach said, Katzenbach and Kennedy were conspiring to leave the Bureau "to the wolves." Watson replied that he suspected as much. LBJ was growing more and more distrustful of Katzenbach; when LBJ had a request for the Justice Department he referred it not to Katzenbach but to Ramsey Clark, a Texan. Watson expressed doubt that Katzenbach would be around much longer.

Katzenbach was still around that summer when the Justice Department made a disturbing discovery: it was an illegal FBI bug that had led to the successful prosecution of Fred R. Black, Jr., a public relations man and an associate of Bobby Baker, for income tax evasion. The department was obliged to inform the Supreme Court, which had just denied Black's appeal. Yet this invited controversy: the FBI would claim authorization by Kennedy and Kennedy would vehemently deny it. In a round of anguished conferences, Katzenbach and Solicitor General Thurgood Marshall drafted a blurry compromise memo to the Court. Kennedy asked Katzenbach to insert a statement that Kennedy, as attorney general, had had no knowledge of the Black bug or bugging in general. Katzenbach said the draft memo was so vague it could not hurt Kennedy; Kennedy disagreed and accused Katzenbach of betrayal. On July 13 he wrote Katzenbach:

> As you know this is a damn important matter for me. I just don't want to receive a shaft—it's not deserved—and anyway I don't like them deserved or not. I'm getting too old I guess. I can't write you as many memos as J. Edgar Hoover. And there is no sense in talking about it by phone, I feel strongly about it—and I write you just that as there's not much else to say.

Four days later Kennedy called his old friend with an earnest apology: "All right, Nick. You were right and I was wrong." Kennedy admitted having listened to recordings made by bugs. But he insisted that at the time he had assumed the bugs were installed by state law enforcement officials outside his jurisdiction. Was this belief born of expediency? "I am absolutely persuaded that Bobby Kennedy did not know about the FBI buggings," Katzenbach said later. "I am also absolutely persuaded that any objective observer would believe that he did." In this case Katzenbach believed Kennedy because "Kennedy did not lie"—at least not privately with such conviction.

Kennedy's first instinct was right: he *was* about to "receive a shaft." Senator Long seized upon the Katzenbach memo (published as a footnote to a Supreme Court opinion) as evidence of Kennedy's criminality. And then, on December 10, Hoover exploded the issue by charging that Kennedy had directly and enthusiastically approved all electronic surveillance during his tenure as attorney general. "Mr. Kennedy," Hoover asserted, ". . . not only listened to the results of microphone surveillances but raised questions relative to obtaining better equipment." Any abuse by the Bureau was therefore Kennedy's fault. To obscure the issue further, Hoover enclosed an August 1961 document in which RFK authorized not a bug but a wiretap—a different matter entirely.

At PS 305 in Bedford-Stuyvesant, a reporter confronted Kennedy with the Hoover letter. "You can get a comment from my Washington office. I have nothing to say now," Bobby snapped. Later, his office issued a terse statement—"Apparently Mr. Hoover has been misinformed"— and a letter from Courtney Evans, the former FBI liaison to President Kennedy, which said that bugging was Hoover's domain and that RFK received wiretap requests only in "serious national security cases." Unfortunately, the distinction between bugs and taps eluded even the *New York Times,* which referred to the matter alternately as the "bugging feud" and "wiretap controversy."

Katzenbach tried to be helpful by arguing that both sides were right: Kennedy had not authorized the bugs, but Hoover believed that Kennedy had. "This explanation made Hoover absolutely furious and made Bobby absolutely furious," Katzenbach recalled. And Hoover's case against Kennedy, however circumstantial and incomplete, was sticking. "There is little doubt," said news commentator Robert Spivack, "that J. Edgar Hoover has severely damaged the image of Senator Robert F. Kennedy, particularly among young people to whose idealism Kennedy has appealed. By portraying him as party to what is essentially the dirty business of snooping, Hoover is saying that Kennedy is no innocent, but a hard and ruthless young man on the make."

At the Justice Department, sources sympathetic to Kennedy tried to allay the damage. They leaked to *Washington Post* reporter Richard Harwood a Kennedy memo from 1962 banning "improper, illegal and unethical" surveillance. Though the attorney general's directive had not specifically limited wiretapping or banned bugging, Harwood argued in the *Post* that it implied as much and that Hoover had obviously ignored it. LBJ fulminated against "little Harwood at the *Post*" but directed most of his anger at Jack Rosenthal, Ramsey Clark's special assistant for public affairs. Johnson was convinced Rosenthal had leaked the memo—"to help Bobby." Call Rosenthal and "ream his ass," LBJ ordered Joe Califano. (Califano did not.) "They're not only tappin' wires," Johnson shouted at Supreme Court Justice Abe Fortas on the telephone, "they're riflin' their goddamn files! . . . And Ramsey's standing there lettin' 'em do it!"

Publicly, Johnson was more circumspect. The president, observed James Reston, "is managing to restrain his grief over seeing the Senator in an embarrassing situation with Mr. Kennedy's new-found liberal supporters." Press secretary George Christian took obvious delight in pointing out that the "incidents referred to in the present ruckus did not take place" during the Johnson administration, so LBJ felt no obligation to resolve the dispute. Privately, Johnson sided with Hoover. "I have heard that Bobby listened to these [bugged] conversations," Johnson told Califano. "Hoover called Bobby, asked him to stop it."

Johnson's sanctimony was tainted by hypocrisy. On the one hand, Hoover's eager eavesdropping filled the president with disgust. Invasions of privacy made him genuinely edgy—wiretapping, bugging, and spying were "anathema to him," said Harry McPherson. "He just hates it." In June 1965, long before the Kennedy-Hoover blowup, LBJ prohibited wiretapping except in cases of national security. By February 1966, Johnson was considering a complete ban on all taps, even in national security cases, and scribbled a note to Joe Califano about electronic bugs: "Urge legislation to stop this." Johnson's fervor was evident in May when IRS Commissioner Sheldon Cohen, under attack by Senator Long, defended electronic eavesdropping. "Sheldon—" Johnson wrote him, "Stop it all at once—and this is final—no microphones—taps or any other hidden devices, legal or illegal if you are going to work for me—L—."

Yet at the same time, Johnson was surreptitiously recording telephone conversations at his desk and bedside at the White House and the LBJ Ranch. Yes, he confessed, there was something "weird" about Hoover's obsession with people's personal lives. And the old G-man probably had a fat file on LBJ under lock and key. Johnson wrinkled his nose at FBI files on the peccadilloes of powerful men, but he read them voraciously. He delighted in secret reports on the unsavory activities of JFK. And in 1964, LBJ had considered using Hoover's material in a campaign of innuendo against Goldwater. "Lyndon talks about that [FBI] information and material so freely," Bobby Kennedy complained.

Still, it was Bobby and not LBJ who was charged with snooping. Johnson now made a great production of correcting earlier abuses. On January 10, 1967, in his State of the Union Address, LBJ argued ardently for a ban on all taps and bugs except in cases of national security. The appeal drew hearty applause—except from Bobby Kennedy, who folded his arms and pursed his lips tightly. "A more limp attempt at applause has not been registered on TV in years," observed *The Nation*. A congressman watching Kennedy thought he looked "rather embarrassed." The same congressman later charged that LBJ's strong stand against wiretapping was little more than "a rather blunt rebuke" to RFK. Ramsey Clark denied it angrily, but Joe Califano later confessed that the president "took delight" in drafting the privacy portion of his crime message. When Johnson passed his Right to Privacy Act, Kennedy's staff suspected there was more on the president's mind than wiretapping and bugging. The bill, said Frank Mankiewicz, was part of the administration's "major objective": destroying Bobby Kennedy.

At the same time, a battle over a book was doing more damage to RFK than any bill of Johnson's ever could. "It was a mistake from the beginning," said Ed Guthman of the Manchester affair, which began unremarkably—as an authorized history of the assassination of John F. Kennedy. In the relatively few months before the Warren Commission report and the deluge of conspiratorial accounts that flooded bookstores in its wake, Jacqueline and Robert Kennedy believed, naively in retrospect, that they could stem the tide. By granting interviews and privileged materials to one writer and one writer alone, they hoped to fend off an onslaught of interview requests and sensationalist accounts of the events in Dallas and afterward. They wanted one account—dignified and complete—an imposing tome that would scare the hacks into silence. There was also a political imperative: on the flight back to Washington and in the weeks afterward, John Kennedy's shocked and embittered aides had been quite forthcoming with their impressions of the new president; many cruel, cutting comments were made, and many reached LBJ. An authorized account could help keep this nastiness under wraps.

Most reporters would surely have recoiled at the conditions the Kennedys imposed on their historian-for-hire. William Manchester, a mildly accomplished writer, did not. His 1961 book on John Kennedy, *Portrait of a President,* was so adoring it might well have been commissioned, or written, by the image-obsessed Kennedy press office (it was in fact approved by the White House, at Manchester's insistence). On March 26, 1964, Manchester sat in the attorney general's wood-paneled office and affixed his signature to seven copies of a memorandum of understanding. "The final text," it read, "shall be approved by Mrs. John F. Kennedy and Robert F. Kennedy." RFK had marked out the clause and scratched a more restrictive one in the margin: "The final text shall not be published unless and until approved by them." Manchester, already supine, offered up no resistance; before the meeting he had written Bobby that "if you had not suggested this, I would have." Without the Kennedys' explicit consent, the book could not be published before November 22, 1968—five years after the assassination and, perhaps more to the point, weeks after the 1968 election. In 1964 it was already clear that Bobby had little to gain by stirring up unpleasant memories for LBJ in the midst of a campaign. In a public statement, the Kennedys defended the arrangement "in the interest of historical accuracy and to prevent distortion and sensationalism."

By early 1966, Manchester had already failed on one count—preventing distortion. President Johnson had some hand in this by repeatedly denying Manchester an interview. "I'm not under any obligation to Manchester," Johnson wrote Jack Valenti in response to another series of requests for notes and documents, though Johnson did proffer some written replies. Twice Johnson agreed to receive Manchester, and twice he rescinded the offer. "He could not bear to do it," Manchester wrote in his foreword, acknowledging the freshness of Johnson's wounds, but in reality Johnson thought Manchester "a fraud." The feeling was mutual. "Though I tried desperately to suppress my bias against a certain eminent statesman who always reminded me of somebody in a Grade D movie on the late show, the prejudice showed through," Manchester confessed that summer in a letter to Jackie. That much was certain. The manuscript of *The Death of a President* —"long, deeply felt, greatly overwritten," in Arthur Schlesinger's view—circulated among Bobby's advisers like a piece of bad news. Manchester's Johnson did not walk, he "heavily lumbered"; he "sprawl[ed]" rather than reclined; and he behaved in general like a boorish, callous wretch, not a great man, and hardly even a good man.

Even worse—far, far worse than these loaded verbs and adverbs—was the book's opening scene, which became known among its first readers as the "deer-hunting incident." Manchester vividly recounted John Kennedy's visit to the LBJ Ranch eight days after the 1960 election. When LBJ suggested a deer hunt at dawn, Kennedy—according to Manchester—was appalled. But the president-elect was Johnson's guest; and at 6:00 A.M., JFK dutifully donned a checked sports jacket and slacks and climbed into his vice president's white Cadillac. After a wild ride through the fields, Johnson shot a couple of deer and forced Kennedy to make his own kill. The vision of the helpless animal caught in his sights haunted Kennedy, Manchester wrote; it left an "inner scar." Later LBJ had the head mounted and he clamored insistently until it was hung in the White House.

This was an inauspicious way to begin a book about a man hunted down and shot dead in the state of Texas. As history it was questionable, and as literary foreshadowing it was cruelly irresponsible. It had the effect, Schlesinger cautioned Manchester, "of defining the book as a conflict between New England and Texas, decency and vulgarity, Kennedy and Johnson." Schlesinger thought the portrait of LBJ

> fine when it sticks to the facts, but it too often acquires an exaggerated symbolism—so much that some critics may write that the unconscious argument of the book is that Johnson killed Kennedy (that is, that Johnson is an expression of the forces of violence and irrationality which ran rampant through his native state and were responsible for the tragedy of Dallas).

Evan Thomas, Manchester's editor at Harper & Row, feared his author had been so carried away that his "tragic narrative" had become a "fairy tale" in which "the Texans in their polka dot dresses and bow ties are seen as newly arrived scum—plucked from the dung heap by magical Jack."

There was an obvious injustice here, and not only to the historical record. Still, Thomas's sympathies were not really with the Texans. "Frankly, gentlemen," he wrote to Bobby's arbitrators Ed Guthman and John Seigenthaler, "I am deeply disturbed by some of this. It's in part, I guess, an ambition to make sure that Bob Kennedy is not hurt by association (an association which he cannot escape) with the book which is, in part, gratuitously and tastelessly insulting to Johnson." Bobby himself was willing to concede the book's historical claims. One chapter, he told Manchester, "will injure both Johnson and me, but apparently it's factually correct and a contribution to history. I'd like you to change it, but I guess you won't." What Bobby feared was not injuring or inciting Johnson—how much more hostile could Johnson become, after February 1966?—but the implication that the Kennedys had never given LBJ an honest chance, that they had stacked the deck against him from the beginning.

In subsequent drafts, Manchester toned down what Schlesinger called the "mythodrama"; the author censored his account of the deer hunt and buried it elsewhere in the text (though JFK still "looked into the face of the life he was about to take" before somberly squeezing the trigger). Publication was even bumped ahead, to the fall of 1966, to head off a competing (and unauthorized) account. But as *Look* magazine prepared to serialize Manchester's book, the controversy ignited again, in a sordid public spectacle that left Bobby wishing he had taken his chances with the hacks. At issue was Jackie's control over the interviews she had granted Manchester at the peak of her grief; she now claimed the right to destroy every page of the transcripts and threatened Manchester with legal action. Increasingly hysterical, she offered Gardner Cowles of *Look* $1 million to kill the serialization. When he declined, she filed suit against Harper & Row. "My God," Mankiewicz said to Bobby, "I think that's a terrible mistake."

"Yes, it's a terrible mistake," Bobby replied, "but nothing can be done about it." Out of loyalty to Jackie he joined the fray, and though he agreed that Manchester had been dishonorable in ignoring her wishes, Bobby thought it all a "damned nuisance," recalled Evan Thomas.

Regardless, the book was widely perceived as a Kennedy-sponsored attack on LBJ, and Bobby, not Jackie, was the one with something to gain by it. Jackie tightened Bobby's bind by painting her actions as a defense not only of her right to privacy but of Lyndon Johnson. The Manchester book, she said publicly, was "generous" to the Kennedys but con-

tained "inaccurate and unfair references to other individuals." The press
helpfully elaborated: according to one columnist (and friend of the president's), the book was Bobby's weapon to "gut Johnson." And though the
fight against Manchester's bias had been waged (and largely won) privately, in months past, the "anti-Johnson" passages now circulated widely and seized center stage. After all, the book's treatment of President
Johnson was far juicier fare than the arcane legal debate over control of
the interviews and the Kennedys' contract with Manchester. High-
minded editorials on the freedom of information segued seamlessly into
political gossip about the Kennedy-Johnson feud. *U.S. News* provided a
helpful guide to the points of controversy: the trip to Texas; the transfer
of power; the flight to Washington; the funeral; and competing claims to
the Kennedy legacy. "The President, his family and his associates are
indignant about this [portrayal]," the magazine reported, "feeling that he
has no recourse, no proper forum, no legitimate way to clear the air and
set the record straight in connection with derogatory reports that have
gained wide credence."

Leaks like this were part of Johnson's most powerful self-defense: a
posture of defenselessness. In the White House there was some ambivalence about this approach. Johnson at first demanded a point-by-point
refutation of the Manchester book. On December 5, in a telephone conversation with Nick Katzenbach, the president listed a few of the "forty-
six mean, vicious errors" in *The Death of a President* and worried that "it's
just gonna be really raucous when it comes out. I just want to talk to
you about it sometime to see if there's anything we can do to at least
moderate the charges." Johnson marveled at Manchester's account of the
swearing-in on Air Force One: "All of it makes Bobby look like a great
hero and makes me look like a son-of-a-bitch and 95 percent of it is
completely fabricated. Visionary. [Manchester] doesn't even remember
that I talked to Bobby." Johnson laughed bitterly. "Yet he's got you callin' at Bobby's instructions and readin' the oath. Just all kinds of stuff.
And that thing is gonna require a look or two [before] answer[ing] it,
you see, and they're gonna hit back the other way. And it's not gonna do
the country any good."

Steeling himself for this distasteful tit-for-tat, Johnson sought the
counsel of his crony Abe Fortas. "Somebody really ought to be put on
this full-time, day and night," said Fortas. Johnson suggested he "bor-
row" Harold "Barefoot" Sanders, quietly, from the Justice Department. "I
don't know about the propriety of gettin' a Justice lawyer to do it, but I
guess you have to," the president said. Fortas proposed that Johnson's secretary, Juanita Roberts, gather up the assassination-related materials the
White House had furnished to Manchester and mark them for further

review. "She has to," Johnson shouted in response, "because we have so damn many spies around us!"

Over the next few weeks it was presidential aide Jake Jacobsen, not Roberts or Sanders, who solicited the president's detailed recollections in a memo full of questions ("Describe the hunting trip. . . . Bear in mind that the contention is made that the President [JFK] did not want to shoot a deer and that he was forced into doing this") and prepared a page-by-page, often line-by-line response to the book's charges. Press aide Hayes Redmon did the same for Bill Moyers—and so did Johnson, on the phone, in a running rebuttal to anyone who would listen. Dictabelt recordings of Johnson's conversations capture a president alternately terrified, outraged, sanguine, paranoid, and fatalistic about Manchester's claims. Here was Johnson on the deer hunt:

> It is just a manufactured lie. . . . [sarcastically] Poor little deer, [JFK] saw it in his eye, and he just couldn't shoot it. Well, hell. . . . He shot it and he jumped up and hoorahed; and it went right on the fender of the car so he could kill another one. And we had to stay out there an hour or two later until he killed the second one. Most [ranchers] got a rule, they won't let you kill but one, but he was the president and the law says you can kill two, and we wanted him to have whatever he wanted; but didn't nobody force this man to do a damned thing. . . .
>
> I think it is the greatest desecration of his memory that an impotent vice president could force this strong man to do a goddamned thing.

On his swearing-in:

> [Reading Manchester] "He said, 'I hate to bother you at a time like this' to Bobby." Now, I [never said] anything like this. . . . I felt the most important thing in the world was to decide who was president of this country at that moment. I was fearful that the Communists were trying to take us over.
>
> " 'I think you should be sworn in there,' Bobby said." I don't think Bobby said that at all. I don't think Bobby took any initiative or any direction. I think that Bobby agreed that it would be all right to be sworn in and said he wanted to look into it and he would get back to me, which he did. I think that after they found out there was no recording [of the conversation]—and there may be one— . . . they leaked some of this.

On the flight from Dallas to Washington:

> [Manchester says] I slumped, had a vapor inhaler and wouldn't take any leadership—and the next day I was so arrogant I was bossing everything. And the thought that I would go to a plane that didn't have the [nuclear control] "bag" . . . by God, after this terrible thing had happened, is just inconceivable to me!

"He sprawled out on the bunk." I didn't sprawl, I sat and talked on the phone....And "he lumbered out of the room as she came in." Well, now, lumberin'—I don't know, I guess that's [Manchester's] way of sayin' I *walked* out. But he didn't see me walk out, and he didn't know whether I lumbered or trotted or walked or anything else!

On his treatment of Brigadier General Godfrey McHugh and Jacqueline Kennedy:

I [never said] a son-of-a-bitchin' word to McHugh! . . . I never said to anybody that I called [Jackie] "honey" because "that was the Texas way"! I don't b'lieve that's the Texas way! I think I would call people "honey" if I thought they were honey! And I might very well have said that to Mrs. Kennedy, although I never felt that way about her and never believed it! I have held her kinda up on a pedestal and been very reserved with her as her letters to me will indicate—very proper. Very appropriate. Very dignified. Very reserved—[just] as I don't think I called Mrs. [Rose] Kennedy senior "honey." I think that is the creature of someone's imagination!

With Jacobsen's memos in hand and his own recollections refreshed (or revised), the president was chafing to respond—not personally, of course, but via the usual surrogates. "Kennedy is trying to destroy Johnson, and that's what Manchester's book is all about," said Governor John J. McKeithen of Louisiana. John Connally, who did not come off too favorably in the book himself, blasted it as "filled with editorial comment, based on unfounded rumor, distortion and inconsistency . . . an astonishing propaganda instrument." Others described the political stakes: "If the Kennedys allow this manuscript to be published in 1967," a friend of Johnson told *U.S. News,* "it will be a clear signal that Robert Kennedy intends to challenge Lyndon Johnson for the 1968 Democratic presidential nomination."

Publicly, Johnson maintained a dignified but nervous silence as the battle of the book descended into farce. "The Kennedy 'corporation' is in fantastic disarray," John Roche reported gleefully to LBJ. "My spies tell me that Jacqueline is already blaming Bobby for her troubles....As more and more of the deleted passages are leaked to the press, this squabbling will increase." This, Roche continued, could only hurt the Kennedys, not LBJ. Thus the president should "issue absolute orders that the Administration policy is *silence*. Let the Kennedy stockholders fight this one out among themselves."

Roche was right: while Bobby's and Jacqueline's poll ratings plummeted, the president's remained stable. Johnson, quite literally, could not believe his own luck; he still seemed to regard Kennedy as invincible.

Johnson was certain that, in time, the Kennedy machine would right itself and exact its revenge. Roche saw silence as a weapon; Johnson considered it a measure of his own, sorry impotence. "I do not believe," LBJ confessed to Moyers,

> that we are equipped by experience, by tradition, by personality or financially to cope with this. I just do not believe we know how to handle public relations and how to handle advertising agencies and how to handle manuscripts and how to handle book writers. . . . So I think they're gonna write history as they want it written and as they can buy it written. And I think the best way we can write it is to try to refrain from gettin' in an argument or a fight or a knock-down, and go on and do our job every day as best we can.

Partly, this was a jab at Moyers, whose job was handling public relations and whose allegiance, Johnson increasingly suspected, was with RFK. And Moyers's betrayal was only one of many; Johnson, under siege by antiwar forces and the press, felt abandoned by friends and advisers. "We've had a bunch of traitors and kids . . . that just brought it about," Johnson complained pointedly to Moyers. Johnson demanded to know who had sold him out to Manchester. "Who," he asked Fortas, "is the perpetrator of the fraud on us—Kenny O'Donnell or General McHugh or who?"

"Both. Those two," Fortas replied. "It's pretty obviously those two fellas."

"Now, what about [JFK press aide Mac] Kilduff? Is he against us?"

"I think Kilduff, by and large, comes down on their side. . . ."

"What about Larry O'Brien?" Johnson asked.

"There's very little about Larry O'Brien in there," Fortas said of the Manchester book, "and I would not say that it was hostile."

"Could we find out . . . if O'Brien thought that we did anything improper?" Johnson seemed desperate for affirmation. And when Fortas attributed a leak to Nick Katzenbach, Johnson seemed indignant. "You want to talk to Katzenbach about that pretty quick? 'Cause I'm convinced he's on that other side every day."

"Yeah," Fortas agreed.

"But maybe he'll be fair," the president replied, and issued a long sigh of self-pity.

Johnson feared that Bobby Kennedy had lured White House aides into collusion with the press and the Georgetown circle and all the forces that sought his downfall. It was a massive web, a Washington-wide conspiracy. "For instance," Johnson explained to Fortas, anything known to Moyers "becomes known to Schlesinger immediately." And what became known to Schlesinger became known to Manchester and Teddy

White and Scotty Reston and Art Buchwald and Charlie Bartlett and Peter Lisagor and Kay Graham—"agents of the people who want to destroy me"—agents, of course, of Bobby Kennedy.

"Ask Kay," Johnson pleaded with Moyers on December 26. "Just say this is just murder to us, and you've got headlines [like] 'LBJ Differs on Kennedy Friction.' That's eight columns! That's like a war story! . . . 'LBJ Version Clashes with Book Detail.' They're tryin' to build up the story, you see." In phone call after phone call, as Moyers patiently crafted a response to an account in *Newsweek,* Johnson sat at his communications post at the ranch and spun conspiracy theories, each more paranoid than the last. "We've got to be very careful," he warned Moyers. "They have deliberately built this credibility [problem]. By picking up the Communist line on it. So that any difference I have with Bobby, Bill—I think this has been carefully constructed through the months to prove that I cannot be believed. So I'm disarmed."

The press was complicit, but Johnson had no doubt who was pulling the strings. "I believe," he told Fortas,

> that Bobby is having his governors jump on me, and he's having his mayors, and he's having his nigras, and he's having his Catholics. And he's having them just systematically, one after the other, each day. And I think this [Manchester] book—he got rid of [released] the Evans book last month and he's got this book and I believe that each one of these things are timed—he got rid of Schlesinger and he got rid of Sorensen and he told somebody that he had ten books coming out in a period of ten months and it'd be ten good ones and ten bad ones—ten good ones on Kennedy and ten bad ones on Johnson. I don't know whether that's true or not, I haven't counted. There are six or eight of 'em.

It was not Lyndon Johnson's finest hour. But in the end his paranoia—and the policy of silence it engendered—served him well. At Moyers's insistence, the president uttered one dignified disavowal only: "I will not discuss the various attributions credited to so-called friends and alleged intimates, except to say that I believe them to be inaccurate and untrue." Privately, Johnson confessed to Moyers, "I don't want to debate with them. I don't think the president of this country, at this time, ought to. It's just unthinkable that my whole morning would not be spent on Vietnam or anything else but be spent on this kinda stuff."

Johnson needed not dignify the Manchester book with further comment. It was RFK, after all, who was on the defensive. On February 3, Mankiewicz wrote the senator that "in general the matter is dying down," though the *New York Post* was "running a series of much hoopla on page one and a thin gruel of innuendo inside." The next two installments in *Look,* Mankiewicz predicted, would surely keep the storm waters roiling. A month later, Kennedy asked Harper & Row to halt publication of a collection of his speeches called *New Problems, New Proposals.* Mankiewicz claimed it was merely a postponement—to allow RFK to revise the manuscript and add the texts of his recent speeches on Vietnam. Observers blamed the Manchester dispute. And if not bitterness, then ambition: "Some sources in the publishing trade," reported the *New York Times,* "did not rule out the possibility that Senator Kennedy may have decided to postpone the publication of his book to avert a more obvious rift with the Johnson Administration." (In the end, the book was reworked by Walinsky, retitled *To Seek a Newer World,* and published by Doubleday.)

MANCHESTER BOOK DULLS RFK STAR, declared the *Washington Post* on March 26, 1967, and Johnson's star, accordingly, shone a bit brighter that spring. Joe Frantz, director of the Texas State Historical Association (and later director of the oral history program at the LBJ Library), wrote the president that "you are steadily gaining admiration by your refusal to be drawn into the controversy. I am very proud of you." Governor Connally called to congratulate LBJ on his skillful statement and "gentlemanly attitude" and urged continued silence on the affair. Presidential aides slipped dozens of letters of support and book reviews (including the TV commentary of Raleigh-Durham's rising voice of the right wing, Jesse Helms) into LBJ's night reading. Even the left-wing *Nation* considered the book "malapropaganda . . . a political weapon in a factional feud." In *Book Week,* Gore Vidal argued that *The Death of a President* offered a glimpse behind the curtain at "a preternaturally ambitious family" furiously working the gears, "manipulating history in order that they might rise."

But the Kennedys had fallen, and mightily. The president delighted most of all in a new Harris survey that inverted the Johnson vs. Kennedy rating (now a staple in opinion polls). "As a result of this Manchester crap . . . instead of his leading us, we're leading him," a triumphant Johnson explained to Ramsey Clark before subjecting him to a lengthy recital of every cross-tabulation by race, region, and religion. Overall, as the Democrats' choice for 1968, Johnson rocketed from 47 to 61 percent while Kennedy fell from 53 to 39. Gallup, too, recorded a swift reversal of Kennedy's poll ratings, which had risen steadily through 1966 and now plummeted: in January, voters of all affiliations had preferred RFK to LBJ by 48 to 39 percent; now, Johnson led Kennedy 45 to 41. Kennedy was not invincible after all, it appeared, and the president was staggered by the extent of the damage: "God, it just murders Bobby and Jackie both," he told Katzenbach. "It just murders them on this thing."

The most telling statistic: 20 percent of Americans thought less of Robert Kennedy as a result of the Manchester affair. "They ought to," Johnson crowed to Clark. "That's the damnedest lowest blow I ever saw."

"It's amazing how the truth comes out, though, isn't it?" Clark replied. "I mean, of all ways. By their own hand."

On January 28, 1967, Kennedy and friend William vanden Heuvel fled to Europe to escape the Manchester mess. "I never saw such an arrogant fella," Johnson griped to Ramsey Clark. "[Kennedy] calls up the State Department, [says] he wants to call on de Gaulle. He's going to see de Gaulle, he's taking foreign relations completely in his hands. He's going to see the Prime Ministers of Germany, France, Italy. . . ." Shortly thereafter, a "high" White House source told *Newsweek* that Kennedy would return from Paris with a French-sponsored three-point peace plan—a devious bit of deflation, for if Kennedy was indeed carrying such a plan he would not be at liberty to discuss it. Empty-handed, Kennedy would appear to have chased nothing but headlines in his haphazard dash across the continent.

Kennedy's ten days in Europe had the air of an official visit, but was as much a vacation as a fact-finding tour. His itinerary was loaded with social and political engagements. In London, Kennedy met with Harold Wilson and pressured him on Vietnam: you know the United States is wrong on Vietnam, he told the prime minister. I understand the pressures you're under to support American policy, Kennedy said, but if you're a true friend of America you'll tell Johnson how you feel. As Kennedy stepped out onto Downing Street, he offered vanden Heuvel his appraisal: "Wilson has an ambition to be Lyndon Johnson but he's a very pale imitation." Not manipulative enough, Bobby said. At the Oxford Union, Kennedy admitted only to "grave reservations" about the bombing. His discretion was partly patriotic, partly politic. Before entering the chamber, he had received a surprising telegram from Ethel:

> SUNDAY GALLUP POLL WILL SHOW . . . DEMOCRATS REPUBLICANS AND INDEPENDENTS COMBINED KENNEDY 48 JOHNSON 39 NEITHER 13. IF THIS KEEPS UP YOU JUST MAY HAVE TO DUMP OLD HUCKLEBERRY CAPONE [LBJ] LOVE AND KISSES AND GOOD WORK.

As it turned out, Kennedy's subsequent meeting with de Gaulle was less fated to cause commotion than his meeting on February 1 with an obscure career civil servant, Étienne Manac'h, the director of Far Eastern affairs in the French Foreign Office. Manac'h was the French expert on Indochina; he had spent the better part of a decade immersed in its byzantine politics. John Gunther Dean, the American embassy's man on Vietnam, had been in frequent contact with Manac'h and accompanied Kennedy to the meeting. Fluent in French, Dean translated for the senator. Manac'h revealed what he believed was an "important" message from the North Vietnamese representative in Paris, a crucial shift in Hanoi's stance: talks "could" follow an unconditional bombing halt. He proceeded to outline his own three-stage plan for peace negotiations.

Kennedy had difficulty following the conversation, despite Dean's best efforts to translate, and though Manac'h offered some sensible ideas there did not seem to be anything new in what he said. Kennedy moved on to Germany and Italy, where he met with Pope Paul and Foreign Minister Amintore Fanfani and, again, learned little more than the depth of foreign dismay at American policy in Vietnam. Thus when he returned home on February 4, the senator was surprised to find, upon clearing customs at New York's Kennedy International, a crowd of agitated newsmen asking whether his talks "had upset the delicate balance of international relations." Kennedy climbed atop a chair at the airport terminal to reject the notion. "All I was interested in was in doing all I can toward a peaceful solution in Southeast Asia. . . . I think we are all interested in learning the facts."

That night Frank Mankiewicz called him and asked if he had heard about the *Newsweek* story. What *Newsweek* story? Kennedy asked. The new issue reported that Kennedy, while in Paris, had received a "feeler" from Hanoi—"a significant peace signal . . . unveiled for the benefit of Robert F. Kennedy for reasons best known to the enemy." The *New York Times* had picked it up; it would be Monday's lead story. This was powerful, explosive news—another collision of war, peace, and the Kennedy-Johnson feud. And though the story was unfounded, Kennedy and Mankiewicz understood immediately that LBJ would blame the leak on Kennedy. Unfortunately, there was no way to suppress the story. Mankiewicz could merely offer the *Times* a nervous "no comment" until the senator had a chance to confer "with the Executive Branch of the government."

The executive branch, in the person of Lyndon Baines Johnson, was outraged. These private peace feelers—red herrings all—had been keeping his State Department busy for months, chasing down each and every half-promise of "movement" by Hanoi. Scores of foreign do-gooders were streaming in and out of Hanoi, hearing things they deemed, either out of ignorance or good intentions, important. Rusk, scornful of these Nobel Prize seekers who arrived at his door "eight months pregnant with peace," understood the political cost of rejecting these endless dead ends. He also believed that one of these secret contacts might carry a genuine prospect for peace. Pursuing peace feelers was an exhausting and unrewarding business, and it was a testament to Rusk's diplomatic skills that he had avoided more than the occasional public relations disaster to this point.

To this point. It was impossible for Johnson or Rusk to respond to Robert Kennedy with subtlety or tact, and their hysteria at evidently being blindsided by Bobby threw them off balance. For there could be no doubt, in Johnson's mind, that this "feeler" was not a feeler at all—it was a seditious plan by Kennedy to embarrass the White House. Rusk agreed that Bobby had heard nothing new but "let the press play with it a bit," just to cause trouble. If so, Bobby was looking to soften the administration's diplomatic stance at a time of renewed official optimism: on January 8, Ambassador Henry Cabot Lodge, back at the Saigon embassy, had predicted "sensational military gains." General William Westmoreland and Walt Rostow were praising the strategy of attrition (despite more sober estimates by the CIA). The State Department looked for a cable from Paris—for some evidence that the leak had not gone straight from Kennedy to *Newsweek*—and found nothing.

Yet there *was* a cable from Paris, from John Gunther Dean, and it escaped notice because it was stamped "Confidential" only—not "Top Secret" or "Eyes Only" or anything to alert a reader to its alleged importance. Digging through secret memos "right and left," Nick Katzenbach and his aides never found the Dean cable "because it was down with 100,000 other confidential cables!" Still, the elusive Paris cable was the source of the trouble. After Kennedy's meeting with Manac'h, Dean—who was far better versed than Kennedy in the semantics of Hanoi's conditions—saw potential importance in Manac'h's message that the senator did not. Dean had drafted a memo of the conversation and, before cabling it to the State Department, submitted it for Kennedy's approval. The memo was essentially a transcript of the conversation and struck Kennedy as accurate enough, though he still did not see what the fuss was about; he had not been party to any great diplomatic breakthrough. Dean cabled the memo to Washington that night, February 1, and Kennedy had gone ahead to Bonn. Before Kennedy's return, Edward Weintal, *Newsweek*'s diplomatic correspondent, was wandering the halls of the State Department and looking for news. Someone handed him the Dean cable—ubiquitous enough, given its low level of classification; three or four hundred people had a copy. The damage, then, was done in Washington, not Paris. Manac'h's message was now Kennedy's "peace feeler."

Monday morning, February 6, Kennedy called Marvin Watson to arrange an appointment with LBJ. Watson agreed that a meeting would be helpful and said he would see what he could do. But it was Nick Katzenbach who called the senator back; he seemed to be doing so at Johnson's behest, perhaps in place of an Oval Office meeting. The two friends met for lunch in Kennedy's Senate office. LBJ had put Katzenbach in an awful position, and Katzenbach was visibly unsettled. "I'm working for President Johnson," he reminded Kennedy, trying to keep his old friend at arm's length, "and I treat him just as you would have had me treat President Kennedy."

"Of course," Bobby replied. He stated that he had no problems with President Johnson's domestic policy, and whatever their differences on Vietnam, Kennedy insisted he would never have fabricated a story like the one in *Newsweek*. Katzenbach urged him to deny it publicly and categorically. Then the phone rang, interrupting their talk; it was Watson, and the president wanted to see Kennedy and Katzenbach at 4:00 P.M.

According to Katzenbach, the Oval Office meeting that followed was "Johnson at his absolute worst." Johnson and Kennedy shook hands but could not disguise their hostility. Johnson accused Kennedy of the leak and Kennedy denied it. Walt Rostow, who was also present, eyed Kennedy suspiciously; even years later, after the Dean cable became common knowledge, Rostow still believed Bobby was somehow behind the leak. As yet, though, the group remained unaware of *Newsweek*'s source. Kennedy supposed it had come "from your State Department."

"It's not *my* State Department, goddamnit," Johnson spat, heavy with sarcasm. "It's *your* State Department."

Growing quiet but obviously enraged, the president lectured Kennedy on the progress of the war, which was going so well, Johnson said, it would be over by summer. If Bobby kept up his talk of bombing halts and unconditional negotiations, he would be finished. "I'll destroy you and every one of your dove friends," Johnson threatened. "You'll be dead politically in six months."

Ignoring the remark, Kennedy advised that Johnson stop the bombing if he wanted a peaceful settlement—*that* was what the Europeans had told him. The senator recommended expanding the International Control Commission and extending the four-day pause the United States had already announced for Tet, the Vietnamese New Year. It would shift the onus for intransigence to Hanoi, Bobby suggested.

"There just isn't a chance in hell I will do that," Johnson muttered. "Not the slightest chance." He announced that he never wanted to hear Bobby's views on Vietnam again. Bobby and his friends, as far as Johnson was concerned, were giving succor to the enemy, encouraging Hanoi to keep on fighting and keep on killing American boys. Bobby, he said, had blood on his hands.

"Look, I don't have to take that from you," Bobby snapped. He stood to leave. Suddenly nervous, Johnson urged Kennedy to leave through the West Wing lobby and tell waiting reporters that there had been no peace feeler. "I didn't know what the hell had been said to me," Bobby said unhelpfully. Johnson turned to Katzenbach and Rostow for affirmation. "We never received any peace feelers at all," the president said. "Isn't that right? They agreed that it was.

Finally, after an hour and twenty minutes of this brutality, Bobby emerged from the office just before 6:00 P.M. to tell reporters, "I did not bring home any feelers. . . . I never felt that I was the recipient of any peace feelers." Asked about his contacts with foreign leaders, Bobby replied, "I think that the person who really has to deal with these matters is the President of the United States." Then, to defy all credibility: "I think not only from his public statements but from my conversation he is dedicated to finding a peaceful solution . . . in Vietnam."

Kennedy, brought low by the encounter, returned to his office. "You know . . . what I've been through is just unbelievable," he told Edelman, who had seldom seen Kennedy so shaken. "What does he mean, *my* State Department?" the senator asked Mankiewicz. Later, in his private office, Kennedy's composure returned along with his anger and disbelief: "Do you know what that fellow said? That marvelous human being who's President of the United States?" he said to Walinsky before repeating one of Johnson's choicer phrases. Though Kennedy expected this from Johnson, he was even more infuriated by what he saw as Katzenbach's and Rostow's servility. It was apparent to Walinsky that the senator had now lost all hope of influencing Johnson and moderating his course in Vietnam. The president had appeared confident—defiantly so—of the prospects not for peace but for victory. That weekend Johnson had even hardened his terms—demanding that Hanoi stop reinforcing its troops in the South as a precondition for a bombing halt. Genuine peace talks had never seemed further from Johnson's mind; days later, he scrapped a conciliatory letter to Ho Chi Minh and substituted a more demanding proposal.

Perceiving this new intransigence and still smarting from his man-handling in the Oval Office, Kennedy felt he no longer owed Johnson a thing. The embellished portrayals of their meeting that circulated in the press added more poison to the well: Rostow summoned Kay Graham, publisher of *Newsweek* and the *Washington Post,* to the White House and tried to persuade her that the president had showered Kennedy with "sweetness and light." *Time,* meanwhile, printed rumors that Kennedy had called Johnson a "sonofabitch." Evans and Novak chided Bobby for carelessly undermining "Mr. Johnson's status as the spokesman of U.S.

foreign policy . . . in the eyes of the world." Now Kennedy had nothing to lose; and in an ironic twist, he leaked his own version of the story to *Newsweek,* omitting none of Johnson's anger and profanity. Again Johnson exploded with rage and sent Rostow to "lean on" the magazine's editor. Rostow did so, "as instructed," but the story was out. Some reporters were beginning to wonder if Johnson's war with Kennedy was precluding peace in Vietnam.

In fact, peace in Vietnam had never been more remote. Despite Johnson's repeated insistence that he was ready to negotiate, his position had ossified; the more lives and weapons and hopes the United States invested in the fight, the less willing it was to grant the concessions Hanoi demanded. The administration was stalling, "rejuggling words" (as George Ball admitted) until it could impose its terms. The same was true of North Vietnam, unrelenting in its view that the "unity of our country is no more a matter for negotiations than our independence." Both sides had settled into a diplomatic stalemate.

Meanwhile, the war itself underwent a drastic escalation. By 1967 the United States had dropped more bombs on Vietnam than all combatants had dropped in all theaters during World War II. Nearly half a million American combat troops were on the ground, and each new deployment was quickly absorbed by Westmoreland's aggressive "search and destroy" missions. The influx of man and machine staved off what had seemed certain defeat in 1965, but at a heavy cost: by the end of 1966, American casualties (dead, wounded, or missing) numbered 33,000, surpassing those of the South Vietnamese military for the first time. And though the U.S. military notoriously inflated its "body count" of enemy dead, American forces were indeed inflicting a punishing blow against the Vietcong, North Vietnamese, and civilians. Still, preventing defeat did not equal victory. The North matched each infusion of American troops with evasive guerrilla tactics and a seemingly bottomless reservoir of conscripts. The theoretical "crossover point" at which the Communists would no longer be able to replenish their losses proved as elusive as the enemy. Fighting intensified and cost the United States more than $2 billion monthly by 1967.

Nonetheless, growing public concern about the war had yet to crystallize into outright, widespread opposition. Antiwar sentiment in late 1966 was still concentrated in liberal circles and on college campuses and was confined mostly to leaflets and petitions; even radicals had not shifted from protest to active resistance, though the change was imminent. Public opinion pollsters were calling 1967 "the year of the hawk"—that spring, one in four Americans favored a nuclear attack on North Vietnam if it would bring victory. The frustration feeding this new militancy was also feeding a backlash against the antiwar opposition.

Politically, then, Kennedy would have been better off staying out of the Vietnam morass. The tide of public opinion deeply distressed him— as did his belief that only he, and not any of the other antiwar senators, could lead the public back toward a sane policy in Vietnam. Kennedy's staff reinforced the notion that he had a singular responsibility and urged him to speak out in the wake of the "peace feeler" fiasco. Only you can make a difference, Mankiewicz wrote Kennedy on February 27. "Not Morse, who is querulous and a bore and mistrusted for his switching and his bombasts, not Fulbright who lacks the follow-through and who talks of . . . irrelevancies, not the [Vance] Hartkes and the [Eugene] McCarthys who have other fish to fry. If not today," Mankiewicz insisted, "you know the White House will turn the screws tighter until the day you must."

By this time Kennedy had already decided that he must speak out, and had begun to do so. On February 8, two days after LBJ had promised to "destroy" him by year's end, Kennedy called for a new American policy in China. "We have striven to isolate China from the world and treated it with unremitting hostility. That, however, is not a policy," he told his audience at the University of Chicago. "It is an attitude founded upon fear and passion and wishful hopes." He called for "contacts" in China and an end to "wildly exaggerated" fears of the Asian behemoth. But at heart the speech was about the war and the administration's "attempts to portray Viet Nam as a Chinese inspired conflict." Blasting the Johnson administration for operating in a policy vacuum in Asia, Kennedy came closer than ever to questioning the fundamental premises of the war. "We do not know . . . about our goals, our own policies, our own conception of the national interest in Asia," he concluded.

This was unusually harsh language, particularly for Kennedy, and the White House was indignant in its self-defense. "Sources close to" LBJ said Bobby was seeking to claim credit in advance for everything from peace in Vietnam to the rise of moderates in China. And in case of failure, Bobby could then say he had told them so; it was a no-lose situation. The administration huffily defended its Asia policy. But Johnson, once again, would have been better served by silence, by leaving his defense to a press that saw political calculation in Kennedy's every move. The headlines of *U.S. News* portrayed Kennedy's China speech as simply a "New Move to Stand Apart from LBJ." The magazine noted Kennedy's "accelerating . . . effort to propel himself into a position on the world stage clearly identifiable as contrary to that of President Johnson."

Kennedy was damned either way. If silence was moral abdication, every word was a political bombshell.

CHAPTER 15

Praising Brutus

Only days after his brutal Oval Office encounter with LBJ, Robert Kennedy clicked on the tiny television set in his bathroom and watched Soviet Premier Aleksei Kosygin deliver a peace feeler identical to Étienne Manac'h's: Hanoi would come to the table when the United States stopped the bombing. Even before Kosygin had finished, Kennedy was on the phone with Adam Walinsky, asking him to draft a response to the administration's paltry efforts to secure peace. The skies over North Vietnam were quiet at the moment—the brief annual Tet respite—but Kennedy had no doubt that the pause would be short-lived. By February 13 it was over, and Kennedy already had Peter Edelman, Dick Goodwin, Burke Marshall, Arthur Schlesinger and others at work revising Walinsky's first draft. A year earlier, when Kennedy had spoken on the NLF, he had taken great pains to obscure differences with Johnson. Now he appeared eager to highlight them.

On February 17, the *New York Times* told the president what to expect: RFK SETS MAJOR SPEECH ON BOMBING. Church, Fulbright, Gruening, Javits, McCarthy, McGovern, Morse, and more than a dozen senators had already called for a bombing halt, but it was Kennedy who stirred Johnson to action. The president was already predisposed against another pause in the bombing; he felt Robert McNamara had duped him into the thirty-seven-day Christmas pause of 1965. Johnson recalled angrily that it had been counterproductive, giving the North Vietnamese a chance to rebuild roads and bridges. "When it flopped," observed Clark Clifford, "[it] was quite a long time before anyone came up with that suggestion again."

The original objective of the bombing campaign had been to boost Southern morale and to check Northern infiltration. On these matters

Johnson bowed to his Joint Chiefs, repeating Sam Rayburn's dictum that if politicians didn't accept military advice then they were wasting a hell of a lot of money at West Point. Yet Johnson also commented that these generals, left to their own devices, would only bomb and escalate, bomb and escalate. Growing public and congressional scrutiny of the bombing campaign left Johnson deeply unsettled by a policy he had distrusted from the start. The bombing was by now a visceral issue in the Johnson White House: "There are dangerously strong feelings in your official family which tend to overwhelm the strictly military factors," Walt Rostow informed the president. McNamara's fears of inciting the Chinese and his moral aversion to bombing had to be weighed against Dean Rusk's diplomatic concerns and General Earle Wheeler's flat admonishment that "a withdrawal from Hanoi-Haiphong bombing would stir deep resentment at home, among our troops, and be regarded by the Communists as an aerial Dien Bien Phu"—as surrender.

Johnson continued to regard bombs as "carrots for the South" and "sticks against the North." Still, as the futility of the air war became more and more apparent (the United States began bombing power plants because, Mac Bundy told the president, "we have 'run out' of other targets"), Johnson's policy became increasingly contradictory. Mindful of antagonizing either his domestic critics or China, LBJ refused to unleash the unrestricted campaign the Joint Chiefs demanded. At the same time, he would not stop the bombing even briefly, except to show America's "good faith" during Tet. Steering a middle course between withdrawal and all-out war, Johnson stumbled, inexorably, into a bloody limbo.

Now, with Kennedy's challenge imminent, Johnson dug in his heels. He ordered General William Westmoreland to denounce a bombing halt. He also persuaded the aging Averell Harriman to talk some sense into young Bobby, to insist that he lay off the embattled president "in the national interest." Harriman called RFK on the evening of February 27. "I hope you are postponing your speech on the famous subject," Harriman said.

"Why?" Bobby asked.

Harriman, insisting that negotiations were increasingly possible, made a pitch to Kennedy's self-interest: "I think you are going to regret it," he said. "You would do yourself more good to keep quiet at the moment. People know you are against certain aspects of the policies and they respect you for it."

Still reeling from the Manchester affair, Kennedy might have been receptive to Harriman's appeals. But the second blow—the "peace feeler" fiasco—had somehow steadied Bobby, clearing his head and renewing his determination to challenge Johnson's policies. Kennedy had few hopes his speech would receive a fair hearing. "It's going to hurt me, isn't it?" he asked his friend John Burns, who agreed that it would, but assured Bobby he would be vindicated in the end. "That's the way I feel about it," Bobby replied.

Younger staff members prodded Kennedy toward provocation. Older advisers encouraged him to "fudge it." The latter option—never very likely—was ruled out four days before the speech, when Johnson announced new military tactics intended to speed the war toward its conclusion. "Horrible though the thought might be," Frank Mankiewicz wrote Kennedy, "this was done at least in part to head you off." Mankiewicz now worried that "the speech in its present posture offends the administration and will lead the press to talk of a 'break' with Johnson anyway, but it does not give enough hard leadership to those who want an honorable solution. . . . Even with a restricted urging of a suspension in bombing, and not much more, you will be listed by the press (and the White House) as Number One Dove, even though many have said more without talk of a 'final break.' Since that seems inevitable, you might as well say what really needs to be said." On March 1, the night before its delivery, the speech was rewritten by Mankiewicz, Walinsky, and Goodwin in a marathon session that lasted until 4:00 A.M. Kennedy, before heading off to sleep, seemed at ease with the final draft. At the office the next morning, he peeked in as Edelman, who had been bedridden with strep throat for days, read the speech. "Well," Kennedy said, grinning, "am I dove enough for you?"

"No," Edelman croaked.

"That's good."

At 4:00 P.M. Kennedy rose in the Senate chamber and began on a conciliatory note, becoming the first public figure to accept blame for the unfolding tragedy. "Three Presidents have taken action in Vietnam," Kennedy told the half-filled Senate galleries and twenty-one of his colleagues. "As one who was involved in many of those decisions, I can testify that if fault is to be found or responsibility assessed, there is enough to go 'round for all—including myself." It was an important admission, historically and personally, but neither this nor his condemnation of an "unyielding" adversary in Hanoi provided much tactical cover for a blistering attack on U.S. policy. "If our enemy will not accept peace, it will not come," Kennedy conceded. "Yet we must also look to ourselves. We must have no doubt that it is not our acts or failures which bar the way." One such failure was the bombardment of North Vietnam. "We are not in Vietnam to play the part of an avenging angel pouring death and destruction on the roads and factories and homes of a guilty land." The bombing, Kennedy charged, was not going to end the war and might well prolong it.

Keeping in mind the administration's "limited war objectives," Kennedy proposed a three-stage plan to end the war: first, test Kosygin's—and Hanoi's—sincerity by extending an unconditional bombing halt and calling for negotiations; second, secure international assistance in preventing further escalation by either side; and third, begin a phased replacement of American and Communist combatants in the South by international forces. Only these steps could ensure the self-determination of the South Vietnamese people. Anticipating charges of meddling, Kennedy vainly stressed the Senate's "ancient, eminent, and cherished obligation" to stimulate debate.

A volatile discussion erupted on the Senate floor. Questioned intently by Ohio Senator Frank Lausche, a Democrat, Kennedy conceded he was not seeking a *permanent* bombing halt: "We can't do that. We can't bind ourselves." In light of five previous pauses and five previous failures, what did Kennedy hope to gain? "Whether you're a hawk or a dove or a dawk or a hove," Bobby quipped a bit feebly, "I don't see what we lose." After all, North Vietnam had dropped its absurd insistence that the United States withdraw from Vietnam and accept Ho Chi Minh's four points as precursors to talks. "They came all the way 'round and said we'll talk if you stop the bombing," Kennedy pointed out. What, again, did the U.S. have to lose?

The answer came swiftly: Lyndon Johnson had much to lose, at least in his contest with Kennedy. "He talked today to end the bombing, had a pretty good crowd," Johnson told John Connally that evening on the telephone, shifting gears abruptly from another subject. There was no need to explain who "he" was. "Mansfield complimented him and Fulbright did and a good many [others did]. And you've got a very persuasive speech to the public that wants peace and all that kinda stuff. And he said if we just stopped for a week, and set a day certain, and tell 'em; and then if it didn't [work], go on. Well, we've done that three times and we just finished Tet period, we gave 'em a week and they didn't stop, they just floated 50,000 tons of cargo down there."

Publicly, Johnson's retort was delivered by Scoop Jackson—once Bobby's man for vice president but now quite evidently Lyndon's man. By prolonging debate until after 6:00 P.M., Jackson and Senator Gale McGee of Wyoming kept Bobby off the network news. Jackson called RFK neither hawk nor dove but a defenseless "pigeon." He read aloud a March 1 letter from the president explaining, "We are bombing North Vietnam because it is violating two solemn international agreements." In the letter, LBJ denied the bombing was ever intended to end the war or mete out punishment; rather, it was meant to raise the cost of infiltration, and it had done so. It was "an integral part of our total policy which aims not to destroy North Vietnam but to force Hanoi to end its aggression" against South Vietnam.

The words were Johnson's, but again they were articulated by surrogates. "While Senator Kennedy has . . . a popular idea in designating a term of peace," Robert Kintner wrote the president that evening, "I do not think the President, personally, should answer this suggestion. It should be answered . . . by Secretary Rusk." And it was—in the same weary tones with which Rusk greeted every Kennedy proposal, public or private. In a statement that night, Rusk recalled "substantially similar" proposals pursued "without result." Pauses of five days in 1965, thirty-seven days during the winter of 1965–66, and six days in 1967 brought nothing but "hostile actions" by Hanoi. "There is, therefore, no reason to believe at this time that Hanoi is interested in proposals for mutual de-escalation such as those put forward by Senator Kennedy," concluded Rusk. Nonetheless, he repeated Johnson's bland assurance that "the door to peace is and will remain open."

That is, if Bobby Kennedy, in his stampede for the presidency, did not bump it shut. A White House "insider" told *Newsweek* that "nothing will come of [American diplomacy] if the hang-on spirit in Hanoi is encouraged. The Bobby speech is bound to give it a shot in the arm." With Bobby as pretender to the presidency, Ho might well wait for "restoration" before coming to the table. Other Johnson men argued that "dovish" pressure on the president would, perversely, render him more "hawkish"—not to spite Bobby, of course, but to correct any resulting miscalculations in Hanoi or Moscow. More cruelly, White House aides wondered aloud whether Bobby was more interested in establishing political independence for himself than for South Vietnam.

While Johnson kept mum on the Kennedy speech, he was anything but silent on March 2. Through the evening LBJ was a traveling, free-wheeling sideshow spectacle. He held a surprise press conference at the White House and spoke unannounced at the Office of Education. He made another unscheduled speech, this one on civil rights, at a stunned but pleased Howard University. He invited the nation's governors to the White House for a meeting later that month. He confirmed the rumors that his daughter, Luci, was pregnant. As a *coup de grâce,* Johnson trotted out a letter—two months old—from Kosygin agreeing to discuss nuclear arms reductions. Was this a "bravura performance," wondered the *New York Times,* or "propaganda overkill"? Mankiewicz mocked the president as "a whirling dervish," but Kintner, Johnson's media adviser, blushed with pride. "I thought you timed the Kosygin memorandum admirably in relation to other events in Washington, and I also thought you handled it with restraint [and] decorum."

If this equaled restraint, it was hard to imagine the havoc of Johnson unbound. And by day's end he was finding it rather difficult to contain himself on the matter of RFK and Vietnam. "The American people should know that this is a question between their President, their country, their troops and Mr. Ho Chi Minh and [his] troops," Johnson announced after unveiling the Kosygin letter. "Everyone can take whatever side of the matter he wants to." Yet LBJ saw a right side and a wrong side; and it was clearly wrong to place much faith in the North Vietnamese. "If they are going to bomb Pleiku as they did and kill our men in the middle of the night, if they are going to bomb Danang as they did just a few days ago, if they are going to lob their mortar shells into the backs of our soldiers as they did last night, you must, if you are at all fair to those men who are defending you over there, permit them to respond." By this logic, a bombing pause was an act of betrayal.

In a March 4 interview, Kennedy shot back that the administration "wants a signal from the North before they go to the negotiating table. I don't know what that means." The previous night on CBS, Bobby had denied a "split" with LBJ; now he greeted the suggestion with a smile. "I just have some different ideas," he said, adding a bit petulantly that "this has not been tried before." For if it had, if there was nothing new or different in his proposal—as Rusk and the White House charged—then his speech had been driven by ambition or spite. "The suspension of the bombing is what I asked to be done, and that's exactly what was not done," Kennedy repeated for emphasis.

Though he had won the battle for the spotlight, its glare was largely unflattering. Praise for Kennedy's proposal was tempered with familiar qualifiers like "carefully calculated" and "opportunistic." The substance of the speech, too, was very nearly eclipsed by excitement over Kennedy's "open combat" with LBJ. Reporters raided their arsenals of hackneyed military metaphors: Kennedy was escalating hostilities; Kennedy "threw down the gauntlet"; Kennedy had "crossed the Rubicon" and refused to retreat. Kennedy and Johnson, declared *Newsweek,* were "men at war." The *New York Times,* however, perceived that if Kennedy was running into battle against Johnson, he did so with his shield, not his sword, held high, and uttered not war cries but cloudy language and disclaimers." Still, the paper's James Reston congratulated Kennedy for exposing America's crisis of conscience: "Politically and diplomatically, it was a fuzzy and maybe even an opportunistic speech, but more than any other Presidential figure he at least dealt with the human agony of the war. That is something." Kennedy, argued Reston, also penetrated a fog of obscuring issues by asking the president a simple question: why not? Why not stop the bombing and put Kosygin's word to the test?

Remarkably, the question was being asked in the White House. In later years it became conventional wisdom on both sides of the feud that the administration, in the words of Bobby's assistant Ed Guthman, "ignored his policy suggestions." Recently declassified documents indicate quite the opposite. Despite all the public bluster, Johnson did not dismiss Kennedy's proposal out of hand. Rather, he ordered a secret policy review. In the days after Bobby's speech, Rostow, Rusk, Taylor, and McNamara provided Johnson with comprehensive analyses on the merits of Kennedy's approach. Perhaps there was something here worth appropriating. "The president took [the proposal] very seriously," recalled Rostow.

Even so, presidential aide Bill Jorden had difficulty doing the same. To Rostow, Jorden confessed, "I cannot read this speech as a serious and responsible effort to grasp the real problems of Viet-Nam or to move in the direction of a realistic settlement. I read it as a clever move to keep the Senator in the forefront of foreign affairs." The proposal, Jorden argued, was nothing new, and its tone reminded him

> of Marc Antony's funeral oration—in which he praised Brutus but thoroughly damned him. The speech pays lip service to the Administration's policy, but undermines that policy in obvious ways. I am also reminded of the Nixon technique—constantly raising old issues as new issues, and raising as issues things which are not in dispute at all.

Rostow displayed the same bias in his memo to the president. Still, as instructed, he dissected Kennedy's "ambigu[ous]" proposal piece by piece. Rostow pointed out that a temporary bombing halt had been tried five times before and Kosygin had offered no real incentive to try again; he was only backing the position of Hanoi's foreign minister, Nguyen Duy Trinh, who on January 28 had demanded that the United States "halt unconditionally the bombing raids and all other acts of war." Moreover, Hanoi's refusal to recognize the legitimacy of the United Nations doomed Kennedy's hopes for international inspection. Rostow considered Kennedy's proposal overall as "part of the same family of proposals we have made since the first bombing pause in May 1965." Kennedy departed from Johnson by being "fuzzy," that was all. There was nothing of substance here, Rostow concluded; it was just politics.

Rusk's memo was shorter, terser, and equally dismissive. "The main difficulty with the Kennedy proposals," he argued, "is that Hanoi has made it clear that they would strongly oppose every essential point in them. The Senator's problem, therefore, is not with us but with Hanoi." If secret diplomatic channels ever yielded a genuine promise for peace, then a suspension of the bombing might be in order. Until then, Kennedy's proposals were premature. "I do not recommend that we accept them as a basis for action," Rusk declared, his flat prose betraying none of his profound irritation. Rusk was a diplomat. General Maxwell Taylor, a close friend of RFK's, agreed with Rusk. "The critics of the bombing think it is ineffective and unimportant," Taylor argued. "That is not the view of the North Vietnamese, the South Vietnamese or the American servicemen in Viet-Nam. They know better."

To this point, the conclusions of Johnson's advisers could have been predicted. Robert McNamara, however, was not playing along. Since a disheartening trip to Vietnam in October 1966, he had placed little faith in a military solution. "The prognosis is bad," he wrote LBJ upon his return; Hanoi was "attriting our national will." McNamara recommended stabilizing troop levels and the bombing campaign. "Ho Chi Minh is a tough old S.O.B.," he told his staff. "And he won't quit no matter how much bombing we do." By spring 1967, McNamara's qualms were turning to torment and skepticism had crept into his military prescriptions. Meanwhile, he was growing closer to RFK.

Johnson, then, could hardly have been surprised by McNamara's March 9 memo. Contrary to his peers, the defense secretary saw "signs" of a favorable shift in Hanoi, describing the leadership of North Vietnam as divided between two groups: one favoring war and the other favoring an immediate negotiated settlement. The latter group, McNamara argued, "was in the ascendancy" in late 1966 but had been dealt a blow by American bombing attacks on December 13 and 14. "We should soon make another effort to initiate negotiations," he insisted. "We have often said that a primary objective of the bombing was to assist in persuading the North to cease its aggression. Therefore, I would be prepared to terminate the bombing if negotiations, either public or private, were under way." Without saying so explicitly, McNamara was advising the president to adopt Bobby Kennedy's proposal. "I suggest you ask Messrs. Rusk, Katzenbach, Bunker, W. Rostow and McNamara to meet together to develop such an approach . . . by March 15."

On policy grounds McNamara was out of step, and politically he was stumbling badly. Advice like this had already earned him the president's deep distrust. For months Johnson had been edging McNamara out of his inner circle, disregarding his counsel and questioning his loyalty. Having "suckered" Johnson into the 1965 Christmas pause, McNamara was now recommending another, based on some weak and conflicting signals from Hanoi and a tacit alliance with Bobby Kennedy. Socially McNamara had always been a Kennedy man, no matter how ardently Johnson had courted him. And as McNamara inched toward RFK on matters of substance, Johnson shoved him aside. In mid-1967, when McNamara submitted a Kennedyesque proposal to reduce the bombing, Johnson turned it over to an aide and said, "You've never seen such a lot of shit."

The Vietnam debate was becoming a hopeless tangle of personalities, policies, and politics, inextricably bound to the Johnson-Kennedy feud. "Their war with each other," James Reston worried in his column, "has managed to dominate Washington thought about the Vietnam war itself." The press now perceived two divergent paths to peace: the Johnson path of careful, calibrated escalation, to wear down Ho Chi Minh; and the Kennedy path of de-escalation, to entice Ho to the table. The search for peace, it now appeared, was a competition—for credit, the Nobel Prize, or the presidency. Kennedy struggled in vain against this perception. Interviewed on the *Today* show on March 7, the senator told Hugh Downs and Sander Vanocur, "I don't think really the question of personalities should enter into this matter. . . . I know that President Johnson is a man of peace. I know that he wants to find an end to this struggle in Vietnam. I have perhaps some different ideas as to what should be done." He stressed his right—and responsibility—to dissent. "It's far more important [than] and transcends any loyalty to one's own political party. I remained quiet on this matter for over a year," breaking his silence only when "I thought we were at a critical and crucial time."

If moral integrity was to trump party loyalty, how could Kennedy so blithely assert that "I'm going to support President Johnson" in 1968? "If they feel it would help, I'll be glad to campaign," Kennedy added, making his proposition even more absurd. If his differences with LBJ were indeed fundamental, then an alliance was both politically untenable and morally irresponsible.

In fact the real question was not whether Bobby would support Johnson but whether Bobby would challenge him. The press was full of eager speculation; politics, after all, was easier to handicap than international diplomacy. "Will Bobby's friends trip up LBJ in '68?" *U.S. News* asked breathlessly. The *New York Times* wondered, "Could Senator Kennedy's demarche from the Administration lead away a sizable band of Democrats?"

For a host of reasons it appeared unlikely. Kennedy was out in front on an unpopular issue with no national peace movement to fall in line behind him. Kennedy was leading the charge, but had failed to rally the troops. As Fred Dutton had warned him a year earlier, speaking out proved little more than Kennedy's ability to "aggravate your Senate colleagues and the Administration." Kennedy's popularity continued to slide: in recent polls he managed only to tie Richard Nixon and Michigan Governor George Romney, the Republican front-runners. Meanwhile, on Capitol Hill, House members rejected Kennedy's position on the bombing by a vote of 372 to 18. In the Senate, Kennedy's speech exposed—even widened—a growing rift over Vietnam. GOP leader Everett Dirksen declared himself "entirely with" the president on the war, but upstart Charles Percy of Illinois, a contender for the 1968 Republican nomination, praised Bobby's proposal as more "useful" than the administration's "vague" offerings. Frequent critics of the war— William Fulbright, Joseph Clark, Albert Gore, John Sherman Cooper— rushed to Bobby's defense, while Majority Leader Mike Mansfield tried feebly to bridge the gap by praising both sides.

This hardly constituted a "peace bloc." While the American press remained tantalized by the prospect, the Communist Party organ *Izvestia* rightly judged Kennedy's equivocations as "characteristic of the Senate opposition on Vietnam. It is irresolute and its numbers are small. It does not influence the course of the White House." To be sure, the Senate contained a solid—and growing—body of dissenters, but it lacked the discipline and organization of a bloc. "The dissent was erratic [and] . . . unorganized," lamented George McGovern, a would-be leader. The two or three meetings of Senate doves proved a disappointment; senators were too independent, too bound to individual electorates, to act together with any consistency. If Fulbright, McGovern, or Gore, for example, could be counted on to join hands, Gruening and Morse were mavericks who bolted upon seeing a crowd. The strongest display of unity the Senate opposition could muster was an occasional joint letter.

Bobby Kennedy, meanwhile, could not even be counted on to sign his name. When Frank Church solicited signatures for a statement on the war, Bobby—though he agreed with Church—chose to make an independent statement on the Senate floor. Bobby was simply happier on his own. He was not naturally a joiner or a congenial, glad-handing member of the club; he was no Lyndon Johnson. "He didn't want to be part of a bloc," Frank Mankiewicz recalled. "He was never comfortable in that kind of situation." Kennedy was loath to join forces with Fulbright, the self-important gentleman-scholar ("really the antithesis of Robert Kennedy," judged Walinsky), or Mansfield, who was a good man but unerringly, unconscionably loyal to LBJ. *The Nation,* in its roundup of "Senate rebels," was disappointed that Robert Kennedy "has notably *not* tried to lead." At most he overlapped, temporarily, with others of his per-

suasion; sometimes he even nudged a colleague, like Maryland's Joe Tydings, in the right direction. But in the end Bobby paid little mind to his
fellow senators, least of all on Vietnam. "He knew the game was between
him and Lyndon," recalled Walinsky, "and that was the level at which it
was played. He didn't give a damn what Henry Jackson thought."

Lyndon Johnson knew more than anyone about the fragile nature of a
Senate coalition, having crafted many himself. He knew that Bobby
Kennedy had neither the experience nor the patience to sustain a coordinated Senate campaign against the war. Both houses of Congress, after
all, were complicit in its escalation; on both sides of the aisle, supporters
far outnumbered critics. Most members shared Johnson's assumptions
about the rightness of American intervention. Even skeptics agreed with
Richard Russell that "we are there now" and that the United States,
whatever the wisdom of its initial commitment, could never simply cut
and run. Also, foreign policy was a presidential prerogative; that was what
the Gulf of Tonkin Resolution had established. Members of Congress
slept easier believing Johnson alone would pay for Johnson's mistakes.

This, too, Johnson understood. The war was his. Congress supported
it, the public supported it, but Johnson had invested his presidency and
his very being in Vietnam. To criticize the war was to criticize Johnson;
to doubt the cause was to doubt the man and his place in history.
"They're up there on the sidelines kicking and crying and mouthing,"
Johnson complained of his few congressional critics, and at the other end
of Pennsylvania Avenue he kicked and cried and mouthed in response.
Any criticism—however tentative—sent him into a tailspin of rage and
self-doubt. LBJ took politics personally. As James Reston noted in January 1966, Johnson had transferred "to the White House the personal attitudes and political techniques he used as majority leader in the Senate
cloakroom. He operated on Capitol Hill through a system of punish-
ments and rewards and highly personal arrangements, and his system
worked."

By 1967, it worked no longer. Though Johnson's carrot and stick had
driven most Great Society programs through Congress, neither rewards
nor retribution had much effect on foreign policy. Once Vietnam had
paralyzed the Senate, the "war was everything!" exclaimed Harry
McPherson. "What you felt about the war was more important than
what you felt about anything else. I think you could even dislike Lyndon Johnson and support the war and that would be fine. You'd be on
his 'A' list."

Senators who opposed the war were not on his "B" list—they were
off the list, period. Beginning in the spring of 1967, Johnson cut off his
critics, terminating communications almost entirely. "However difficult

it was to pacify Vietnam," said McGovern, "it was probably less difficult than trying to pacify . . . the doves." When they refused to acknowledge the president's restraint in handling the war, Johnson took it as a personal betrayal. "How the hell could you do this to me?" he beseeched Tip O'Neill when the congressman broke with the administration. For LBJ, doubts about the war were not a matter of conscience; they were an act of malice.

While O'Neill wounded Johnson, and Fulbright infuriated him, only Robert Kennedy frightened him; only Bobby had the potential to fracture the party and disrupt the war effort and at times seemed intent on doing both. Blinded by his terror of Kennedy, Johnson lost sight of the rifts and schisms within Congress, complaining that they were all the same, all foot soldiers in Kennedy's crusade. After Johnson's clash with Bobby over the peace feeler in February, McNamara noticed a significant cooling in the administration's relations with the entire Congress. "Why is it they never find anything that the Communists have done that's wrong?" Johnson asked. His political world was ridden with conspiracies, false fronts, and secret pacts and agendas. Everywhere he turned, he saw a Communist or a Kennedy or, in his most hallucinatory moments, a Communist Kennedy: "Bobby's" bombing halt of May 1965, Johnson now charged, was one of many "jags which pretty much originated in the Communist world." LBJ's loyalists crudely suggested to reporters that Bobby was in bed with Ho Chi Minh. At a White House meeting the president confided to aides that Soviet agents were in "constant touch with anti-war senators . . . think[ing] up things for the senators to say."

At times Johnson seemed to know this was all nonsense; his fantasies, as Doris Kearns surmised, might have been a bizarre form of release or recreation. But when Johnson slipped into these self-hypnotic states it became harder, as the months passed and his opposition stiffened, to pull him out. Few of his advisers tried, lest the president label them "traitors." In many cases, he already had.

The gears of Johnson's public relations campaign were in constant motion. On March 21, he released a month-old exchange of letters between himself and Ho Chi Minh. In his own note Johnson had proposed direct talks to begin once Hanoi had ceased the flow of men and arms into the South. Ho, a week later, rejected the offer since the United States had not stopped the bombing or "all other acts of war." The Communist leader demanded an "unconditional" bombing halt as a precondition to talks. The administration pointed out, with evident satisfaction, that "unconditional" implied "permanent," which rendered Ho's concession moot.

The president's public airing of this inconsequential exchange had little purpose but to discredit RFK, for Ho Chi Minh's obstinacy made
Kennedy's bombing halt proposal seem pointless. But if Johnson intended the letters to quiet Kennedy, they only incited him. He charged now
that Johnson was raising the price of peace. According to Johnson's letter to Ho, the U.S. was demanding evidence that Hanoi had already
ceased infiltration—a "further condition," Bobby complained. "I can
only wish that we had seized the initiative publicly advanced by Premier
Kosygin . . . and halted the bombing in exchange for a beginning of
negotiations."

KENNEDY CRITICAL OF JOHNSON AGAIN, read the headline in the *New
York Times,* making no reference to the nature of the dispute. As usual
the feud was the news. Administrative Assistant Joe Dolan gently chided
Bobby for his intemperance. Attacks on the administration, Dolan wrote
the next day, "should have been, and still could be, made by others, with
you just chiming in that you thought there was a lot of truth in what
they said. This slides by and avoids the 'New RFK-LBJ Clash Erupts'
headlines. Your muted agreement in the background is needed to bring
the remarks to the fore, and . . . will sustain the argument without over-
heating the whole thing." The danger, in Dolan's view, was the administration's power to spin the story: "Despite the rebuff," NBC reported
that night, "the President pledges continued efforts." Credibility gap or
not, Johnson had transformed a diplomatic impasse into a testament to
his perseverance. Kennedy now looked like a bitter interloper.

Neither Kennedy nor Dolan, however, predicted the lengths—15,200
miles—which Johnson would travel to recapture the headlines. In February 1966, Johnson had left for Honolulu to draw attention away from
the Fulbright hearings. Now, as the LBJ–Ho Chi Minh exchange hit the
papers, the president dragged a weary and perplexed team of advisers to
and from Guam—across a dozen time zones and the international date
line—for a stay of barely thirty hours and a conference they privately
dismissed as "hasty and threadbare." Shuffled onto Air Force One with
no agenda and little explanation, even the best-informed officials and
journalists were baffled by the trip. "The most plausible explanation,"
ventured *The Nation,* "is that the motivation was political." Johnson, the
editors wrote,

> apparently came to the conclusion that Robert Kennedy is out to unseat
> him in 1968. The remedy? A big show across the sea, with the usual amal-
> gam of peace talk and military intensification. Coming just before Easter,
> it would serve as a launching platform for a spring peace offensive, cou-
> pled with further violence on the grand scale.

In Guam, jet lag drained the faces of Rusk and McNamara and the spirit of the working conferences. Even the indefatigable president seemed exhausted. Upon his return, Johnson hailed a "constructive two days" but could not seem to pinpoint any real achievements. He confessed he had made no major military decisions and no progress toward peace; the war remained a "difficult, serious, long-drawn-out, agonizing problem that we do not yet have answers for."

Easter came and went, and President Johnson's peace offensive looked more like a public relations offensive against Bobby Kennedy. On April 24, after the United States bombed airbases in North Vietnam, General Westmoreland blasted those who encouraged the enemy to believe "he can win politically that which he cannot win militarily." This time, Bobby took Joe Dolan's advice and merely "chimed in," letting his colleagues take the lead. "I know in a war a country is under strain and stress," Bobby said, interrupting George McGovern, who led the brief debate, "and that once our countrymen [are] being shot at it is appealing to automatically support that effort and not criticize." Members of four administrations, he repeated, shared the blame, "including myself." But Johnson's latest escalation invited a response from North Vietnam, China, and the Soviet Union—and risked "the destruction of mankind." Kennedy quoted the Roman general Tacitus: "We made a desert and called it peace."

By August 1967 the politics of 1968 cast a long shadow over Robert Kennedy's every move, but his more immediate concern was the elections in South Vietnam. Prodded by the United States, the Saigon government produced a slick new constitution and committed itself to elections that American officials hoped would endow the status quo with "a certain legitimacy." Yet the ruling Ky-Thieu junta had excluded two presidential candidates from running and banned slates of a Buddhist sect and a trade union faction from senate races. It disqualified Communists and "neutralist sympathizers"—two-thirds of all candidates—from holding office. Despite some unease in the State Department, the Johnson administration agreed with Ambassador Lodge that the government of South Vietnam "should not be discouraged from taking moderate measures to prevent elections from being used as a vehicle for a Communist takeover." American support of the current regime was an open secret.

As an exercise in democracy, the September 3 ballot struck Kennedy as a farce. But as 1968 approached, Bobby's motives appeared increasingly suspect. Again he grew "obsessed" with avoiding a direct attack on LBJ. "He felt so strongly that every word he said would be viewed through the prism of a potential presidential candidate," remembered Jeff Greenfield, a young aide who helped draft a speech on the elections. On August 11, however, Kennedy and Jacob Javits touched off ninety minutes of spirited debate in the Senate chamber by denouncing the plebiscite as a "fraud." The Saigon junta, observed Kennedy, was exploiting America's commitment, acting as if "we are trapped in there." "If there is no free election," Kennedy asked, "if somebody asks 'what are you doing in South Vietnam?' what can one possibly argue?" He urged the administration to affirm free and honest elections and thus restore "our moral position" in Vietnam.

Since 1965, Bobby Kennedy had been insisting the political was paramount. He had never denied that self-determination required security, but his continued lip service to American military efforts in Vietnam had a strained quality. There was a certain awkwardness, to say the least, in fighting for an unrepresentative government. A related worry was the pacification (Revolutionary Development) program: the United States had subdued only one-sixth of South Vietnamese hamlets, and RD cadres were crippled by desertion rates beyond 25 percent. Bobby knew that the president had a soft spot for the pacification program. Education, immunization, heartier hogs, and healthier crops: it was Johnson's Great Society for Vietnam. "Dammit," LBJ shouted at his aides, "we need to exhibit more compassion for these Vietnamese plain people." They were not all that different from Texan plain people, Johnson's plain people. "Crops and hearts and caring" were his heartfelt prescription. But the president's enthusiasm was not enough to overcome a sclerotic Saigon bureaucracy, poor coordination between American and Vietnamese administrators, and a lack of security in a countryside seething with Vietcong. LBJ had not forgotten the primacy of politics. But pacification—like so much else—proved a bitter disappointment.

The political landscape in Saigon was easier to control than the "hearts and minds" of the people, and an hour after the Senate debate the administration disclosed the regime's "invitation" to a team of congressional election observers. Meanwhile, American officials sought to cool tempers on the Hill by assuring that Vietnamese news reports had overstated the problem. The United States, according to Assistant Secretary of State William Bundy, was encouraging all parties to ensure "free, honest and effective" elections.

On September 3, Johnson's team of twenty-two prominent American observers, failing to find any false-bottomed ballot boxes, sang paeans to the new South Vietnamese democracy. The large turnout was indeed a healthy sign, but last-minute fraud was rampant—"Chicago politics, but with circumspection," declared one official. Thieu and Ky won a surprisingly narrow victory, a plurality of 35 percent, while Truong Dinh Dzu, an unknown lawyer who favored negotiations with the NLF, won 17 percent and exposed the rot at the regime's popular base. Johnson somehow found personal encouragement in the results: "No matter what the polls show, we are still leading every Republican," he told his Cabinet on September 6. "We have got to speak up and not tuck tail."

It was his own party Johnson had to worry about. In a Gallup poll taken the following week, Democrats favored RFK to LBJ as the party's 1968 nominee by a slim margin, 39 to 37 percent. But that was in an open field. If the choice narrowed to Johnson and Kennedy, Bobby picked up almost all the disaffected Democrats and trumped the president 51 to 39. By mid-October, Johnson had even lost his lead over Republican contenders: Kennedy was a far stronger candidate against either Nixon or Rockefeller (though both edged him out, too). Whatever the case in South Vietnam, electoral politics in the United States were healthy and vigorous.

In October 1967, Kennedy met Daniel Ellsberg, a young Defense Department analyst, at a meeting of CBS executives. Kennedy and Ellsberg each addressed the group on Vietnam, and each impressed the other. Bobby seemed to Ellsberg a different person from when they had last met, in the summer of 1964, when Bobby appeared fragile and uncertain. This guy wants to be a senator? Ellsberg had thought to himself. Now, more than three years later, Bobby appeared more confident, more substantial. His speech to the executives resonated with Ellsberg, who had spent most of the past two years studying pacification in Vietnam for an interagency team. Ellsberg had visited thirty-eight of forty-three provinces, but Kennedy, who got no farther than the Saigon airport, conveyed a "sense of personal involvement, concern and engagement" Ellsberg had not seen in Washington.

Kennedy invited Ellsberg to come back to his Senate office to talk more about Vietnam. As the car sped toward Capitol Hill, Bobby agreed that the war was now a stalemate, "which was *the* heretical position to Johnson," recalled Ellsberg. "The worst word you could use was 'stalemate.' " Its use was forbidden in official speeches. As Ellsberg and Kennedy talked about JFK's 1961 decisions, which the analyst was reviewing for inclusion in the Pentagon Papers (a secret and comprehensive history of American involvement in Vietnam), Bobby imagined the road not taken. "Of course, no one can know what my brother would have done in 1964 or 1965," he conceded. "But I do know he was determined not to send ground troops. He would rather do anything than that." Sending ground troops meant taking charge—and assuming responsibility. President Kennedy had not been ready for that. He had also feared that white troops would arouse Vietnamese nationalism, as the French did during the 1950s.

"But was he prepared to see Saigon go Communist?" Ellsberg asked. This, to him, was the crucial test.

"We would have fuzzed it up," Bobby replied. "The way we did in Laos." In 1961, facing the overthrow of the American-sponsored government in Laos, the Kennedys opted for a negotiated settlement rather than war. But Vietnam was not Laos; Bobby did not, in his conversation with Ellsberg, acknowledge that the administration's reticence in Laos had only increased the stakes in Vietnam—where, American officials then concluded, a stronger stand was essential. President Kennedy had in fact rejected a Laos-like settlement in Vietnam, fearing right-wing accusations of "losing" Southeast Asia.

Ellsberg did not challenge the claim. "What made your brother so smart?" he asked earnestly.

Bobby's manner changed; he stiffened visibly in the car's leather seat. "Because we were there!" he shouted, slapping his hand on his knee angrily to punctuate the point. "We were there! We saw what happened to the French!"

Bobby's raw emotion struck a chord within Ellsberg: in his own experience, those who were the most knowledgeable about the French experience in Indochina were also the most prescient about the American debacle. On the other hand, those who were the most contemptuous of the French ("Ah, the French. They're colonialists. They lost the Second World War. They don't have helicopters") were the optimists in Vietnam. The Kennedy brothers were not optimists. They were impressed, while visiting Vietnam in 1951, by the toughness of the French soldiers who were later chased from the country. Now, Bobby told Ellsberg that he and Jack "saw the position the French were in and saw what they were trying to do to the Indochinese. And my brother was determined early that we would never get into that position."

The thought preoccupied Robert Kennedy. And on November 26, on CBS's *Face the Nation,* he asserted that LBJ had departed from John Kennedy's policy in Vietnam. "We['ve] turned, we've switched," Bobby said. He had implied it many times, as early as 1965, but now he had said it. And he kept on talking, sharpening the distinction between his brother's policy and Johnson's: "First, we were making the effort there so that people would have their own right to decide their own future. . . . Now we turned, when we found that the South Vietnamese haven't given the support and are not making the effort." Again Bobby confessed to his share of responsibility, but blamed Johnson for Americanizing the war:

"Why, for instance, in the battle of Dakto, hasn't it been the South Vietnamese Army that has gone up the hill? Why hasn't it been the South Vietnamese Army that has been on the demilitarized zone and stayed there? Why does it always have to be the Americans?" Bobby answered his own question: Once the United States had waged war because the South Vietnamese wanted war; "Now, we've changed . . . maybe they don't want it, but we want it. We're killing South Vietnamese, we're killing women, we're killing innocent people because we don't want to have the war fought on American soil, or because they're 12,000 miles away and they might get 11,000 miles away."

He had opened the breach and come closer than ever to challenging the basis—rather than the conduct—of the war. RFK knocked out the pillars of American foreign policy—the strategy of containment, the morality of intervention, the domino theory—and sent the whole edifice crashing down on LBJ. "Do we have that right," Bobby asked,

> here in the United States, to perform those acts because we want to protect ourselves? This is our responsibility—we must feel it when we use napalm, when a village is destroyed and civilians are killed. When we switched from one point of view to another, I think that we've forgotten about it. . . . What this country stands for . . . is being seriously undermined in Vietnam.
>
> Now we're saying we're going to fight there so that we don't have to fight in Thailand, so that we don't have to fight on the West Coast of the United States, so that they won't move across the Rockies. Our whole moral position, it seems to me, changes tremendously.

So had Robert Kennedy's. It was one thing for him to question the morality of American policy in 1967, after years of fighting; after years of bombing and razing and burning; after years of corrupt and ineffectual rule in Saigon; after years of false starts and diplomatic retrenchment had won no more than a bloody stalemate. And it was about time that someone of his stature challenged, at long last, the domino theory. But on *Face the Nation* he got carried away; four years and one day after his brother's burial at Arlington, RFK was indulging in a romantic sort of revisionism. His ringing condemnation had a simple premise: President Kennedy's support of Vietnamese self-determination had become President Johnson's war against Communist expansion. "We switched," Bobby said, "from one point of view"—honorable, moral, moderate— "to another"—paranoid, reactionary, savage.

One need not descend into what the *New York Times* called "the never-never land of what might have been" to see that whatever President Kennedy might have done in Vietnam—and even Bobby had to

admit ignorance on that point—self-determination was low on JFK's list
of concerns. Like Eisenhower before him and Johnson thereafter, John
Kennedy pledged to support a small nation's fight for freedom. Vietnam's
fight, not America's. In *To Seek a Newer World,* Bobby quoted his brother's sensible statement of September 2, 1963: "It is their war. They are the
only ones who have to win it or lose it. We can help them, we can give
them equipment, we can send our men out there as advisers, but they
have to win it, the people of Vietnam, against the Communists." Bobby
did not quote President Kennedy's renewed endorsement of the domino theory, uttered only a week later:

> I believe it. I believe it. . . . China is so large, looms so high just beyond
> the frontiers, that if South Vietnam went, it would not only give them an
> improved geographic position for guerrilla assault on Malaya, but would
> also give the impression that the wave of the future in Southeast Asia was
> China and the Communists. So I believe it.

The loss of South Vietnam would also give Khrushchev the impression that the JFK of Laos and the Bay of Pigs—not the JFK of the missile crisis—was the real JFK, a man cowed by confrontation. A man to be
pushed, tested; perhaps in Berlin. It would give Americans the impression
that John Kennedy had "lost" Southeast Asia, and give Republicans political fodder for the remainder of Kennedy's once promising presidency.
John Kennedy had many concerns in Vietnam—domestic politics, containment of Communism, America's international credibility—and his
assumptions and aims were not all that different from Lyndon Johnson's.

President Johnson stood above the fray, watching *Meet the Press* as
Hubert Humphrey cheerfully defended the fighting spirit of the South
Vietnamese Army. But this was rather beside the point. Bobby's statements on *Face the Nation*—and the debate they sparked on the front
pages of the nation's papers—stirred Johnson's deepest insecurities about
the war. Bobby had lunged for Johnson's weak spot, his claim to the
Kennedy legacy. Bobby was openly asserting his ownership.

Surrounded by Kennedys, Communists, critics, and traitors, Johnson
was now charged with betrayal of JFK. Johnson believed—and often
stated in self-defense—that *he* was the one with Kennedy advisers and a
Kennedy policy and it was *Bobby* who had gone astray. The president
asked his aides to compile John Kennedy's statements on Vietnam as if
to prove this to himself. Former Kennedy men like Rusk and Rostow
comforted Johnson that his predecessor "would have made the same
decisions . . . and quite possibly made them earlier."

In a literal sense it was true: the war had not changed direction. From
Eisenhower to Kennedy to Johnson, the level of American engagement

was an unbroken line, ever upward. The objective had always been to prevent the Communist seizure of South Vietnam. Still, the war had changed *character* significantly, even if Johnson would not acknowledge it. He was not, in any case, going to debate the "Kennedy course" in Vietnam with a flesh-and-blood Kennedy.

Johnson was spared that fight. A banner headline crowded the Kennedy controversy off the front page of the *New York Times*: M'NAMARA IS NAMED BY U.S. TO HEAD THE WORLD BANK; JOHNSON MOVE A SURPRISE.

By November 1967, Robert McNamara was a man in torment. His tactical qualms about the bombing, which had plagued him since the first months of Rolling Thunder, now plunged him into deep moral despair. He pressed onward despite it, remaining the good soldier, planning sorties from the situation room, fulfilling his duties to the president, flirting with optimism. But at heart he doubted the United States could win the war militarily. He wondered whether it was worth fighting at all. In January 1966, McNamara had asked Dick Goodwin, a visitor to his imposing Pentagon office, "Would [it] make any difference to American security, Dick, if this entire place went communist?" McNamara gestured with a sweep of his arm across a huge hanging map of Asia. Goodwin, stunned, stuttered in response until McNamara cut him off. "It wouldn't make the slightest bit of difference," McNamara declared, and sank deep into his leather chair.

It inevitably brought him into conflict with the president. For some time Johnson had worshiped McNamara, told everyone he wished he could bring McNamara into the White House and hand over the reins. McNamara was Johnson's "Messiah," recalled George Reedy, and the computer printouts compiled by McNamara's brilliant assistants were the Gospels. In the early days of the Johnson presidency, LBJ greeted every statement by his defense secretary with a glow of proprietary pride: McNamara is *mine*; isn't he wonderful? Johnson, said his adviser John Roche, "would have forgiven McNamara almost anything, because he really did give him his devotion."

Almost anything. By 1967 there were two things Johnson could not abide—wobbling on Vietnam and friendship with Bobby Kennedy. McNamara was guilty of both and they appeared to go hand in hand: "Bob McNamara started out being a good man," Johnson later reflected, "but he got worried he was on the wrong side of the war after his Kennedy friends turned against it." It was comforting, somehow, to see things this way. To acknowledge McNamara's doubts was to grant them a terrifying validity: if McNamara was right, the war was wrong. It was better to believe that McNamara's glassy stare at cabinet meetings was the sign of a spirit sapped by Bobby Kennedy, not by a tragic, unending war.

Kennedy, too, had doubted McNamara's loyalty. In 1964 he thought McNamara too quick to bow to his new master. But later, on the golf course in Hyannis Port with Ted Sorensen, Bobby described McNamara as his only true friend left in the administration, the only one who was genuinely loyal to both RFK and LBJ. During the Kennedy presidency, the straight-edged McNamaras, Bob and Margy, were drawn to the sophisticated silliness of Hickory Hill; they traded witty banter or played party games like "Sardines," hiding in coat closets with Bobby and Ethel and Byron White. But the relationship between Kennedy and McNamara had grown closer and more complex over the years; to McNamara's assistant Adam Yarmolinsky, Bobby and Bob seemed like nephew and uncle. Kennedy and McNamara were bound by personality—by energy, intensity, an inner restlessness, and moral indignation. George Reedy said that McNamara was "born with a rather heavy load of guilt." Bobby acquired his.

They shared that guilt over the Vietnam War. McNamara seems to have been completely candid—"extraordinarily indiscreet," said a family friend—with Kennedy about the war, talking to him every few days and handing him unreleased, even classified, materials from the Pentagon. "The reason Kennedy was so up on the war," explained Peter Edelman, "was that he was getting facts from McNamara." Kennedy was careful never to reveal his source or to use the material in public statements. Still, it helped to shape his view of the war—"much too much," according to Adam Walinsky. Nothing infuriated Walinsky like statements that began, "Bob McNamara told me . . ." Didn't the war prove McNamara's fallibility? he asked Kennedy. Wasn't McNamara still doing Johnson's bidding, bombing civilians and the like? "Oh, Adam," Kennedy replied, "you don't have to go through all that. . . ." Whenever he felt caged in by Johnson, RFK wielded McNamara's statistics defensively, as a hedge against speaking out more strongly: "I would certainly want to talk to Bob McNamara before I would say anything like that."

Kennedy did not, however, take McNamara's word at face value. At times they drew very different conclusions from the same evidence. In 1967, McNamara handed Kennedy a stack of Pentagon reports and a confidential memo he had written to the president. Kennedy, in turn, handed it to Joe Dolan, telling him to "take this away to some quiet place and read it." There was no privacy in the office, so Dolan carried the documents to the Senate garage and read them in his car. The memo was an evaluation of the war's progress, and it confused Dolan; the supporting evidence seemed to contradict McNamara's argument. "That's what I thought!" Bobby exclaimed when Dolan returned to the office. McNamara, they agreed, was misinterpreting the information.

Kennedy's older advisers shared Dolan's uneasiness. Ken O'Donnell and Fred Dutton wondered how McNamara "could be so dovish and so pro-Kennedy and so close to Johnson." McNamara was obviously a man of integrity and sincerity; no one doubted that. But there was something disconcerting about his ability to flit back and forth between enemy camps. "It was as if there were a Kennedy-McNamara who said one thing to Kennedy-type people," observed David Halberstam, "and a Johnson-McNamara who said another to Johnson-type people." McNamara primly acknowledged his "difficult position," knowing his friendship with Bobby cost him dearly at the White House. "I wasn't being disloyal to Johnson, but it was clear to me that Johnson might think so," McNamara recalled defiantly. "But that didn't stop me." He and Kennedy continued to share dinner and drinks, play tennis, and meet frequently at Hickory Hill and the Pentagon. If Kennedy took that as some kind of secret alliance, well, it was not McNamara's fault: "Bobby Kennedy," he said, "was a very emotional person."

In later years McNamara insisted he had been "scrupulously careful not to betray the president's confidences or mention anything Bobby could use politically against the president. I never hesitated to tell the president what I thought, and I was quite as open with Bobby about my feelings regarding Vietnam." He was a Johnson man; he was a Kennedy man; he was everybody's man.

"McNamara's problem," Johnson explained later, "was that he began to feel a division in his loyalties. He had always loved the Kennedys; he was more their cup of tea, but he also admired and respected the Presidency. Then, when he came to work for me, I believed he developed a deep affection for me as well, not so deep as the one he held for the Kennedys but deep enough . . . to keep him completely loyal for three long years."

Those years ravaged Robert McNamara. By the summer of 1967 he was clearly laboring under that "load of guilt," and his knees began to buckle. His face was gaunt, his skin mottled, his hair stringy and gray. "Oh, God, he looked awful," said John Roche, who thought McNamara "in very serious psychological condition," barely "hanging on by his fingernails." McNamara's wife was in the hospital with what friends called "Bob's ulcer." After checking up on her by telephone, Johnson turned to Roche and said, "He's a wonderful man, Bob McNamara. He has given just about everything and, you know, we can't afford another Forrestal." Others, too, had begun to whisper about James Forrestal, President Truman's defense secretary, who had leaped from a hospital window in a dark fit of depression. Roche and McPherson watched McNamara's jaw quiver at a White House briefing and wondered whether history, tragically, was repeating itself.

When McNamara was not commanding sympathy he was irritating Johnson with his disloyalty and decay. In August, McNamara's lackluster defense of the bombing in the face of Senate hawks (who demanded the "shackles" be removed from the military) shattered Johnson's confidence. He and McNamara sparred openly in a meeting with Democratic leaders on October 23, provoking Johnson to snap, "We do have differences of opinion." And, hastening the end, which was now imminent, McNamara neatly summarized those differences in a November 1 memo. The views expressed "may be incompatible with your own," he warned the president. Surely, this one was: "Continuation of our present course of action in Southeast Asia would be dangerous, costly in lives, and unsatisfactory to the American people." McNamara recommended a stabilization of troop levels, a halt in the bombing, and the Vietnamization of the war. It was his most radical proposal to date, and McNamara knew it. In essence, he was asking Johnson to fire him. Four weeks later, Johnson obliged.

McNamara had heard about the World Bank job in April, when George Woods, president of the World Bank—the International Bank for Reconstruction and Development—paid a visit to McNamara's private Pentagon dining room. Woods's term at the bank ended in August and it was the prerogative of the American president to name his successor. Woods wondered whether McNamara was interested. In fact he was tantalized by the offer; it was the way out he had long been seeking. The bank's focus on development and security meshed well with McNamara's talents and interests. And since the president of the World Bank must serve his 106 member nations impartially, there would be no speeches, no meetings, no troubling questions about the Vietnam War. McNamara reported the conversation to LBJ, saying he would stay at Defense as long as the president wanted him there.

By August, it began to appear that Johnson did still want him in the hot seat at the Pentagon. Woods's term at the World Bank had expired and then been extended while Johnson stalled and McNamara lobbied. After an August 23 cabinet meeting, McNamara appeared at the office of Joseph Califano, his former assistant, and told him about the World Bank post. "Keep this to yourself," McNamara said sternly. "The only reason I'm telling you is, for God's sake, so you don't tell the President I'm indispensable if he asks you about it."

That was before the disagreements of October, the memo of Novem-

ber 1, and McNamara's physical and emotional collapse. According to
one aide, Johnson was something of a Big Daddy, painfully fond of this
wayward son and determined to rescue him. According to another,
Johnson had conceded defeat, concluding that Bobby Kennedy had
finally cashed his claim on McNamara's soul. "The Kennedys began
pushing him harder and harder," Johnson told Doris Kearns.

> Every day Bobby would call up McNamara, telling him that the war was
> terrible and immoral and that he had to leave. Two months before he left
> he felt like he was a murderer and didn't know how to extricate himself.
> I never felt like a murderer, that's the difference. . . . We can't let the
> Kennedys be peacemakers and us warmakers simply because they came
> from the Charles River.
>
>   After a while, the pressure got so great that Bob couldn't sleep at night.
> I was afraid he might have a nervous breakdown. I loved him and I did-
> n't want to let him go, but he was just short of cracking and I felt it'd be
> a damn unfair thing to force him to stay.

Whatever drove Johnson—pity, concern, or disdain—he clearly could
no longer abide the Nervous Nellie in his Pentagon. McNamara was an
irritant to the Joint Chiefs, an embarrassment on the Hill, and a dangerous liability in the upcoming election. On November 13 the president
called Henry Fowler, his treasury secretary, and told him to make
arrangements with the World Bank. Fowler wanted the job himself, but
Johnson had three choices in mind: "McNamara, McNamara, and
McNamara."

The triple nominee himself had not been told before the news broke.
When it did, McNamara hurried to the Oval Office, received Johnson's
confirmation, and then hurried back to the Pentagon. Moments later,
Bobby Kennedy arrived to urge him to use the important opportunity
he had been given. Decline the World Bank post, Kennedy said. Resign
from the government and tell the press you can no longer serve Lyndon
Johnson in good conscience. Tell the president you can no longer fight
his dirty war. Go out with a blast—"a hell of a blast," McNamara recalled
him saying.

Bobby sat with McNamara for hours, pushing. Edelman suspected
they were talking about 1968. Meanwhile Bobby's political lieutenants
were spreading the story that McNamara was leaving—or being fired—
over the war. At Bobby's prompting, Ted Kennedy took to the Senate
floor and floated the conspiratorial notion that McNamara was being
"transferred." In this way they hoped to turn Johnson's loss into
Kennedy's gain. It was an intoxicating notion—a return to the New
Frontier, its estranged son McNamara returning to the fold, a renewed

alliance against the usurper who had taken a good war and made it bad. McNamara's defection would give Kennedy's dissent the legitimacy it otherwise lacked.

"I wasn't about to do anything that wasn't in my opinion in the national interest," McNamara piously reflected. Sensing this, Kennedy shifted tactics. If McNamara would only refuse the World Bank post and its vow of silence, he need not take a shot at LBJ or the war. Just resign— that was enough for now. Because Bobby knew, as Walinsky pointed out, "sooner or later he'd get him"—McNamara, ever the grand prize.

While Bobby Kennedy talked himself hoarse at the Pentagon, Johnson, for once, did not pick up the telephone. For forty-eight long hours, LBJ remained silent, withholding the Treatment, refusing to compete or to narrow the breach. It was a terrific, almost reckless, gamble. To offend McNamara was to risk it all—Johnson's policy in Vietnam, his claim to the Kennedy legacy, his reelection. McNamara, however drained and discredited, still meant that much; he was Johnson's best and brightest Kennedy man. Could the president possibly endure a joint assault by McNamara and RFK? "You have to give Johnson credit for balls," Walinsky later admitted. "He knew who McNamara was, and he just waited."

Johnson was, as ever, an excellent judge of character. He had sized up Robert McNamara and knew the defense secretary was less a Kennedy man than a company man. McNamara would take what he was given, and he would be grateful for it.

At 11:00 the next night, November 29, Bobby joined Arthur Schlesinger, Pierre Salinger, and a crowd of others at the King Cole Bar in Manhattan. Bobby shared his impression that Johnson had blindsided McNamara by sending up his name without a word of warning. Schlesinger considered McNamara an accomplice. "Wouldn't any self-respecting man," he asked Bobby, "have his resignation on the president's desk half an hour" after the story hit the papers? "Isn't that what you would do?" Frustrated and dismayed, Schlesinger wished McNamara would resign quietly and return to private life. "Why does he have to fall in with LBJ's plan to silence him and cover everything up?"

At about 1:00 A.M. the group broke up and bought the morning's *New York Times*. The headline read, simply, MCNAMARA TAKES WORLD BANK POST. Schlesinger looked at Bobby and thought him surprised and sad. "My God," said a friend of Walinsky's, back in Washington. "[McNamara has] been working for the corporation all his life and he doesn't know what it is to be a free man." McNamara kept silent on the war for almost three decades. In his memoirs he explained, feebly, that as a cabinet officer he served a constituency of one: the president, Lyndon Baines Johnson.

It was an intensely personal defeat for Bobby Kennedy and politically "a big blow," as Edelman believed. Kennedy was infuriated at Johnson's utterly shabby treatment of a loyal officer. At the same time
Kennedy was disappointed by McNamara's servility. In all McNamara's
years of service, he had been given one real chance to alter the course
of the war, and he had let it pass. Johnson was now dangerously free of
a restraining hand ("That, of course, is the way McNamara always portrayed himself to the Senator," said Walinsky). The firing of McNamara
meant that RFK would never reach any accommodation with the president on the war. Perhaps it signaled a coming military escalation. Washington was rife with what Tom Wicker called "the devil theory": the
suspicion that McNamara's departure meant Johnson's "capitulation . . .
to the warlike aims of nameless generals."

Adam Walinsky had few doubts that the real devil was LBJ. In a vitu-
perative, occasionally eloquent, and often melodramatic twenty-page
memo titled "Caesar's Meat," Walinsky penetrated the heart of "this
most elegantly brutal of Lyndon Johnson's political triumphs." The
stakes in this battle were far more, Walinsky argued, than the soul of
Robert McNamara.

> Johnson has given the message to any who would challenge him, espe-
> cially to the heir he still fears and hates. He has said to Robert Kennedy:
> "You think to challenge me. Then watch carefully what I am about to do.
> I will take this man—with all . . . his power and ability and character—I
> will take this man and break him into nothing. I will reach in and tear out
> his spine, and he will say 'thank you, sir.' Indeed I will do more. I will give
> you time to appeal to him—time to offer him another way. . . . But he
> will not follow you, he will choose safe submission even though it means
> he must crawl before me as a penitent. He will be thankful, he will even
> lie to conceal his ignominy; perhaps he will lie to himself. Let him. We,
> you and I, will know the truth."

Walinsky had learned long before not to criticize the senator's friends,
but his memo was unsparing in its documentation of McNamara's moral
cowardice. Walinsky was not looking for a reaction, but the one he got
surprised him: "That's about right," Kennedy said flatly.

When McNamara left the government on February 29, 1968,
Kennedy prepared a short statement to deliver from the Senate floor:
"On many occasions the Secretary of Defense's opinion prevailed but
the fact is, as is well known in this Body, on important occasions he lost."
So had the senator from New York, and badly.

CHAPTER 16

"Later Than We Think"

During the summer of 1967, Bobby Kennedy made a temporary peace with LBJ. Kennedy's political advisers had been urging reconciliation ever since the spring's bombing halt fiasco. In a March 15 memo, Fred Dutton allowed a bit ungenerously that Kennedy's Vietnam speech was "probably politically necessary for the younger constituency that looks to you," but warned Bobby against another "slugging match" with LBJ. Observers were beginning to wonder whether Bobby had any measure of his brother's "cool" and detachment—or whether he was a political hothead perpetually on the verge of eruption. "The appearance of contending with President Johnson during the coming months could only aggrevate [sic] that," Dutton wrote. "For most political figures a rivalry would be useful; but you have long since passed that stage." Dutton reminded him of his obligation to campaign for Johnson in 1968, which was just around the corner.

Bobby had not forgotten. Though he despaired at the thought of campaigning for Johnson, he shrewdly began mending fences. In March he delivered the Gridiron speech—an annual off-the-record duel of wits (or so intended) between one Democrat and one Republican before a chortling Washington press corps. "Ted Sorensen says it is a gamble—it can be a great coup or very dismal," Frank Mankiewicz warned Kennedy in the midst of the Manchester mess. "Considering the news of the past month or so, I would gamble." Kennedy did so, regaling the Gridiron audience with scripted jokes that begged for a drumroll: "[President Johnson and I] had a long serious talk about the possibilities of a cease-fire, the dangers of escalation and the prospects for negotiations. And he promised me the next time we are going to talk about Vietnam.

"You see, all those stories about Mr. Johnson and me not getting along during my brother's years in the White House simply do not square with the facts. We started out during the Kennedy Administration on the best of terms—friendly, close, cordial—but then, as we were leaving the inaugural stands . . ."

If humor did not reduce tensions, Kennedy would try flattery. Soon he agreed to introduce the president at a Democratic dinner on June 3 in New York. Returning that evening from a friend's funeral in London, Kennedy hopped into a limousine and rushed to the Americana Hotel in Manhattan, piecing together two speech drafts—Ted Sorensen's and Adam Walinsky's—in the speeding car and arriving too late to introduce Johnson. Still, Kennedy made his appearance more than an afterthought by praising "the height of [Johnson's] aim, the breadth of his achievements, the record of his past, and the promises of his future." This conciliatory language was obviously more Sorensen's than Walinsky's. Kennedy loyalists were aghast as Bobby continued, declaring that LBJ "has borne the burdens few other men have ever borne in the history of the world, without hope or desire or thought to escape them. He has sought consensus, but he has never shrunk from controversy. He has gained huge popularity, but he has never failed to spend it in pursuit of his beliefs or the interest of his country. . . . In 1964 he won the greatest popular victory in modern times, and with our help he will do so again in 1968."

"How could you say all that?" a friend asked Bobby the next day. Bobby eyed him coldly. "If I hadn't said all those things, that would give Lyndon Johnson the opportunity to blame everything that was going wrong . . . Vietnam, the cities, the race question . . . on that son-of-a-bitch Bobby Kennedy." Nonetheless, Kennedy appeared to have overdone it. On June 15, Schlesinger wrote that Kennedy's hyperbolic introduction "seemed out of character, and that is the one thing you must never be." After all, only two weeks earlier, Kennedy had held forth at Hickory Hill about Johnson's military zeal, his indifference to human life, and his utter imperviousness to moral argument or reason. "How can we possibly survive five more years of Lyndon Johnson?" Bobby had asked Schlesinger. "Five more years of a crazy man?" But Kennedy did not see what he could possibly do to stop him.

Even in their wildest flights of fantasy, Kennedy-watchers never imagined such impotent displays of fury. Hickory Hill, in the public imagination, was the site of cool, Machiavellian scheming and empire-building. Throughout 1967 the press carefully chronicled every Kennedy attack; fevered speculation filled the papers. A quick scan of headlines in *U.S. News & World Report* revealed the political atmosphere:

WILL BOBBY'S FRIENDS TRIP UP LBJ IN '68?
IS ROBERT KENNEDY TRYING TO UPSET LBJ IN '68?
IF BOBBY KENNEDY WERE A CANDIDATE . . .
IF IT NARROWS DOWN TO JOHNSON OR KENNEDY IN '68 . . .

There were so many expectant questions that the answer seemed obvious. Kennedy was running—not in 1972 but in 1968—and every public statement was a declaration of his candidacy. Differences with Johnson were "political sharpshooting." Debates were "a harassing kind of guerrilla warfare." The *Cincinnati Enquirer* described the existence of a secret Senate cabal that plotted to embarrass Johnson and replace him with Kennedy. This, of course, was Kennedy's ultimate objective: "dislodging Mr. Johnson from the White House."

Political cartoonists joined the fray, portraying Bobby as a jack-in-the-box that frightened the president; as "the fairest of them all" in Johnson's "mirror, mirror on the wall"; as a pesky cupid shooting "assorted barbs" into Johnson's backside; as a giant shadow looming over Johnson, trailing him, but ready to overtake him. In a mock comic strip called "Big Lyndon," *MAD* magazine pictured the president leading a cabinet war conference on the feud ("If we don't get 'im to the conference table, this terrible war could go on *forever!*") and sticking pins into a Bobby Kennedy voodoo doll. Mimeographed editions of *MacBird,* Barbara Garson's parody of both *Macbeth* and the Johnson-Kennedy feud, began making the rounds in 1966. According to *Ramparts,* the play quickly became "a favorite of the Ivy League cocktail party circuit." The San Francisco Mime Troupe produced a puppet version with LBJ and RFK at swords' point, as a sort of political Punch and Judy.

Yet to Kennedy supporters across the country, 1968 was becoming very serious business. In February 1967 a group calling itself Citizens for Kennedy-Fulbright (after the two most prominent critics of Johnson's war policy) sent a letter to Democratic leaders, insisting, "Our party's future may be seriously endangered by the renomination of President Johnson in 1968. . . . We believe a more attractive candidate is both necessary and available. That candidate is Robert F. Kennedy, a man who could unify and inspire the Roosevelt coalition. Not only would Senator Kennedy make a stronger and more charismatic candidate than Johnson, he would also make a better party leader, a party leader more attuned to *your* needs." (Marvin Watson had a copy of the letter on Johnson's desk forthwith.) By year's end the group had dropped Fulbright's name from its letterhead and boasted of draft-Kennedy petitions, "anti-Johnson resolutions," and chapters in more than twenty states. The Illinois chapter offered $5 memberships in an advertisement reading, "We are in Vietnam to save face. And this"—a glowering, decrepit caricature of LBJ—"is the face we are saving. Help us change faces. Help us draft Robert Kennedy." In October, Martin Shepard, the group's thirty-two-year-old leader, charged Johnson with "betraying every promise he made" as well as "ruining the country." Shepard called for his resignation.

Citizens for Kennedy—in its various incarnations across the country—was staffed by political amateurs of the New Left, mostly young people opposed to the war. Kennedy himself disavowed the movement, if it was in fact a movement. At the very least it was a growing coalition—strongest in California and on college campuses and including the occasional Stevensonian liberal (this was an irony, as Kennedy voted for Eisenhower in 1956) or disgruntled Democratic official. Press reports rumored the group to be receiving quiet encouragement from state and local party officials, but this was unlikely. Most party professionals disdained the coalition. In autumn 1966, at the peak of RFK's popularity, nearly every Democratic state chairman stated with certainty that Kennedy had no chance against Johnson (and very little against Humphrey). But the professionals were increasingly out of touch with the growing numbers who, when asked to consider "four more years," thought only of more bloodshed abroad and more riots at home.

Disenchantment with LBJ was building to a head in 1967. In August his favorable rating hit 39 percent, the worst of his presidency. In September his disapproval rating (48 percent) outpaced his approval rating (40 percent)—another unwelcome first. Johnson's greatest strength had always been his productivity—no other president had signed so many bills on so many subjects so quickly. But the 90th Congress, elected in November 1966, was far more recalcitrant than what LBJ nostalgically called "the great 89th." Under the constraints of a wartime budget, Congress voiced its first public complaints that LBJ was overreaching; this year, unlike the last, congressional committees ensnared and strangled the president's annual rush of proposals. LBJ spent the spring of 1967 streamlining and correcting existing programs. He also spent it wrangling with governors who bristled at racial integration and complex federal mandates—Johnson's "government by guideline." The New York Times stated it broadly: PRESIDENT FACES MAJOR PROBLEMS.

Greatest among them was the war. Nine thousand Americans died in Vietnam in 1967; sixty thousand were wounded. By summer, LBJ loosened his restraints on the Joint Chiefs and permitted a step-up in bombing, even near the Chinese border. The Times broke with the administration's Vietnam policy in August, complaining that "the rebuilding of slums and other domestic tasks are being sacrificed to the necessity for spending upward of $2 billion a month to feed the Vietnamese conflict." In reaching for foreign policy consensus, Johnson had alienated his liberal base. His miscalculation was most apparent in the divided votes of the Senate Foreign Relations Committee, where the Republicans became his allies and the Democrats dissenters. By identifying himself so personally with the Vietnam War—picking bombing targets, being photographed while leaning over enormous maps of the Mekong River Delta—Johnson repelled his natural constituency. "I voted for him in 1964," Jack Newfield wrote in the *Village Voice* in the spring of 1967, "and now I don't believe a word he says. . . . I am a Democrat, so the thing to do is defeat him next year. . . . At Auschwitz a child who knew he was about to die screamed at a German guard, 'You won't be forgiven anything.' This is my saying the same thing to Lyndon Johnson. He is not my President. This is not my war."

Those who felt the same rushed into the camp of the loyal opposition, which contained more and more Democrats but only one credible candidate: RFK. Kennedy was an alternate pole of attraction because his candidacy simply made sense. Unlike Fulbright or McCarthy or McGovern, Bobby had Kennedy money, Kennedy glamour, the Kennedy name, and the Kennedy organization. But his new constituency was not drawn chiefly to his name or glamour; it was not composed of the sort of fan-club Democrats who bought *Life* magazine and yearned for restoration. It was a serious group, fueled by moral outrage over the war, and it turned to Kennedy because it felt his fervor and because he was the only Democrat who could possibly beat Lyndon Johnson.

Allard Lowenstein was typical of the coalition: a young reformer who years earlier might well have folded his arms and sat out Kennedy's race against Kenneth Keating. Now, at Hickory Hill on the night of September 23, 1967, Lowenstein was appealing to Kennedy to overthrow the president. Kennedy was relaxed, wearing a sweater and a thin strand of beads. "Argue it out," he told the small gathering, and leaned back into the sofa. He listened bemusedly as Lowenstein, sitting cross-legged and shoeless on a stuffed chair, outlined a plan to "dump Johnson." Kennedy approved of the endeavor but did not think himself well suited to it. "I would have a problem if I ran first against Johnson," Bobby told Lowenstein, seriously and a bit sadly. "People would say that I was splitting the party out of ambition and envy. No one would believe that I was doing it because of how I feel about Vietnam and poor people. I think Al is doing the right thing," Kennedy said, turning toward the others in the room, "but I think that someone else will have to be the first to run. It can't be me because of my relationship with Johnson."

Lowenstein looked at Kennedy and for a moment said nothing. This was the sort of flatly political answer Lowenstein had not expected from Kennedy, not anymore. Then Lowenstein said, "The people who think that the future and the honor of this country are at stake because of Vietnam don't give a shit what Mayor Daley and Governor Y and Chairman Z think. We're going to do it, and we're going to win, and it's a shame you're not with us, because you could have been President."

Robert Kennedy respected Lowenstein but was not ready to lead his crusade. ("He took it as seriously as the idea of a priest in Bogotá deposing the Pope," Lowenstein recalled.) Lowenstein sounded like the Young Turks in Kennedy's own Senate office, Edelman and Walinsky. "We all wanted him to run," remembered Melody Miller, a young aide, and they all wanted him to run *now*, not in 1972. The riots and the war had infused the 1968 race with moral urgency. Ron Linton, an advance man in JFK's 1960 campaign and now a fixture in RFK's office, explained, "one principle that was clear in the Kennedy camp was that you strike when you can strike. There wasn't any reason to wait until 1972. We didn't approve of Lyndon Johnson, we didn't think he was doing a particularly good job, and we wanted Bob Kennedy to run for president."

The assumption was universal but largely unsaid in public. Aside from the occasional joke, Kennedy never spoke openly of running for president, and most of the time his staff followed suit. Joe Dolan, who had been aiming for 1968 from the beginning, kept it quiet. "I didn't articulate that to Adam or Peter or anybody. I didn't want anybody to be able to say" that Kennedy was going to run. As usual Walinsky was an exception: after the 1966 midterm elections he wrote Kennedy a memo that said, in essence, Johnson was finished. Johnson was the prisoner of a war that promised only to get bloodier; by 1968 the country would be desperate for moral leadership. If Kennedy failed to carry the banner it would be snatched up by a liberal Republican, probably John Lindsay. "I was just a punk kid, well-known as a bombthrower," Walinsky shrugged in retrospect. Everyone who looked at the memo thought it unrealistic, and Kennedy never mentioned it. But he did show it to Ethel, who was saying privately that Bobby was going to *have* to run against Johnson.

Walinsky broached the subject again a year later in a memo titled "Gratuitous Advice Revisited." Walinsky stated his motives up front: a bit of self-interest and "a deep personal dislike of Lyndon Johnson, not so much as a man as . . . what he represents—everything I distrust and fear in this country and little of what I love and admire." For Walinsky, it was all about Johnson: Johnson's war, Johnson's riots, Johnson's America. "The President of the United States is more than a reflection of his time, he shapes it," Walinsky wrote. "Our time, our America, is being shaped by an ignorant bully." All of this led Walinsky to conclude that "to support Johnson's reelection will be a national tragedy and a personal disaster." He urged the senator to begin escalating his conflict with LBJ to set the stage for a challenge.

A year earlier, Walinsky had been the only Kennedy adviser talking openly about 1968. But the course of the war and the virtual collapse of Johnson's presidency caused Kennedy's political timetable to slide forward imperceptibly; all of a sudden, Walinsky's was no longer a voice in the wilderness. In October, Joe Dolan began sending Kennedy a running countdown to the presidential primaries—with a schedule of filing dates. At his own initiative, Dolan was already calling contacts around the country, speaking at times with his head and the receiver stuck halfway into an empty trashcan so reporters in the office could not hear him. Usually Dolan made the calls from the law offices of Fred Dutton or Milton Gwirtzman. "How are things looking in your state?" he asked local pols. "How does it look for Johnson?" Dolan never asked directly whether they would support Kennedy, but most politicians were evasive. They seemed nervous just to talk to a Kennedy man. "You couldn't pin them down. Everybody was scared shitless."

Still, Kennedy's Senate aides needed little encouragement. "Everything we did was as if he was going to run," Dolan said. "Everything I did with Frank Mankiewicz was done under the assumption that Kennedy was going to run. We never talked about it but we were positioning ourselves—so if he wants to run he can run. That's why I was there! I'd have gone back to Colorado otherwise!"

Kennedy's older advisers—the ones he inherited from JFK—were more cautious than Dolan and Walinsky. In July 1966, Ted Sorensen playfully sketched out nine possible presidential scenarios in "a premature memo to RFK," but not one of them involved a challenge to Johnson. Sorensen was looking toward 1972 (or beyond), and so were the rest of the traditionalists in Kennedy's camp, men like Pierre Salinger and Larry O'Brien and even Ted Kennedy. In 1960 they themselves had been Young Turks, engineering John Kennedy's election as if to spite the political establishment. Now they *were* the establishment—corporate lawyers and consultants with easy access on Capitol Hill and even, in some cases, to Lyndon Johnson's White House. Most of them told Bobby Kennedy not to run because he would lose; and losing was political suicide. After Kennedy's bombing-halt speech, Sorensen told writer Jimmy Breslin that "Bob Kennedy is the only hope in this country for our children and my children. And we can't afford to have him in controversies this early."

Walinsky liked to think that Kennedy had left advisers like Sorensen far behind, that he now considered them quaint but irrelevant. "Those

New Frontier cats were out of the '50s," sneered another Young Turk. "Don't forget that JFK campaigned in '60 on . . . that Cold War crap." But Kennedy was as likely as ever to pick up the phone and call Sorensen or Dutton, the men who shaped that 1960 campaign. Bobby did not always take their advice, but he always sought it. Politics in 1967 were in transition, and RFK was caught between the old and the new.

In the winter of 1967–68 only one thing was clear in Kennedy's mind: life was too unpredictable to make long-term plans, and 1972 was too distant to be considered. Beyond this, the rest was a muddle. Kennedy faced an impossible political dilemma. "You've got the worst of two worlds," Walinsky told him over dinner. "You're against the war but you're for Johnson." Kennedy looked at him in mock wonder and replied, "When did you start getting so wise, Adam?" Kennedy had no real desire to run in 1968, but it was becoming harder for him to defend the administration and remain true to himself or his supporters. When Kennedy spoke at a college in Long Island, a student said the audience had come because of Kennedy's integrity, his courage, and his views on Vietnam and the cities. "Yet you tell us in the next breath that it's your intention to support the president for reelection," the student added. "Whatever happened to the courage and integrity?" A Brooklyn College student put it more bluntly, waving a rubber chicken and a sign renewing the old question, "KENNEDY—HAWK, DOVE, OR CHICKEN?" Joe Dolan thought it was rather funny; Kennedy did not, and snapped, "How would *you* like to be called 'chicken'?" Yet Kennedy kept returning to college campuses, kept inviting their mockery as if it were a form of penitence or masochism. The students' moral fervor was jarring but somehow invigorating.

Kennedy found nothing affirming in the sober wisdom of his political advisers—a steady pessimistic drone that said he would lose, he would split the Democratic party, he would elect Richard Nixon or George Romney. Fred Dutton wrote Kennedy in November 1967 that an open conflict with LBJ would tear the party asunder in 1968 and probably beyond. Walinsky retorted, "I am not old enough to care whether the Democratic Party is split or survives. . . . The Party has meaning only insofar as it satisfies our hopes and desires for the nation." Again, Kennedy admired Walinsky's ideological piety but could not fully embrace it. In an important sense, Democrats would all go down together: Bobby's political suicide would also be the death of antiwar senators like Joe Clark, Wayne Morse, and George McGovern—by running, Kennedy would force them to choose between himself and the president. It was a damnable choice, and anyone siding with Kennedy would be a prime target for presidential retribution. Kennedy calculated he could be responsible for the loss of six Senate seats. "I can't do that," he said.

This feeling of responsibility was not reciprocated. Few prominent Democrats were willing to back a Kennedy challenge. "Everyone seems only interested in taking care of himself," reported McGovern, who canvassed antiwar politicians for Kennedy. "This is the atmosphere Johnson has created." News like this—and instinct—told Kennedy that Sorensen and Dutton were right; running *was* political suicide. At dinner with Ethel and friends, Bobby worried, "if I run, I will go a long way toward proving everything that everybody who doesn't like me has said about me. . . . [That] I've been intending to run all the time, that I've been building up Vietnam as an issue, that I've never accepted Lyndon Johnson as president, that I'm a selfish, ambitious, little s.o.b. that can't wait to get his hands on the White House."

"Now, Bob," Ethel cut in, "you're always talking as though people don't like you. People do like you, and you've got to realize that."

Bobby smiled. "I don't know, Ethel. Sometimes, in moments of depression, I get the idea that there are those around who don't like me." Fred Dutton had just told him so—warning that Bobby's rise in the polls owed less to his own strength than to Johnson's weakness. Johnson could easily exploit Kennedy's lack of a secure base by manipulating the war. The president could increase the bombing or stop it altogether, he could escalate or de-escalate, he could negotiate or stand firm—whatever was required to undercut Kennedy. (Mankiewicz suspected Johnson had been doing this since 1966.) "What bothers me is that I'll be at the mercy of events Johnson can manipulate to his advantage," Kennedy complained. He sketched out a scenario for Walter Lippmann: "Suppose, in the middle of the California primary, when I am attacking him on the war, he should suddenly stop the bombing and go off to Geneva to hold talks with the North Vietnamese. What do I do then? Either I call his action phony, in which case I am lining up with Ho Chi Minh, or else I have to say that all Americans should support the President in his search for peace. In either case, I am likely to lose in California."

Lippmann considered this a moment. "Well," he replied, "if you believe that Johnson's reelection would be a catastrophe for the country . . . the question you must live with is whether you did everything you could to avert this catastrophe."

Lippmann's tough question was one Kennedy could answer with certainty: Johnson's reelection *would be* catastrophe. Racial, ideological, and generational tensions were tearing the country apart and the president seemed incapable of mending it. Kennedy often quoted Yeats's "Second

Coming"—"Things fall apart; the centre cannot hold; / Mere anarchy is loosed upon the world"—and denounced Johnson's blue-ribbon commissions as just another attempt to play politics with rising passions. Unlike Johnson, Kennedy had never delighted in politics for its own sake: politics was a blunt instrument to acquire power, the power to change things for the better. Johnson seemed to have given up on that—and even his beloved Great Society—since he had cashed in his political capital on an unpopular war. Kennedy thought Johnson an expert at controlling people, "the most formidable human being I've ever met." But personal force, Kennedy said, was just a manifestation of weakness. Unable to lead by moral suasion or reason, Johnson resorted to coercion.

Kennedy wanted the White House back. All observers understood this, and some attributed it to messianism or a quest for personal glory or restoration. True, there was the sense of destiny cut short, and many in the Kennedy circle eyed the Oval Office in a proprietary way. The press talked of a Kennedy dynasty. An *Esquire* cover of April 1967 pictured four Kennedys seated in presidential rocking chairs: Jack, Bobby, Ted, and "John-John"—four successive presidencies stretching into the 1990s, broken only by the brief Johnson interregnum. Bobby was too much of a realist for such thoughts, and if he had them he kept it to himself. What he did discuss was ending his own maddening sense of frustration. The frustration was not, in Peter Edelman's view, born of politics or any particular piece of legislation, and was not about Lyndon Johnson thwarting Robert Kennedy. "It was about *big* things," Edelman recalled, "about Lyndon Johnson killing Americans and killing Southeast Asians in Vietnam. *That's* what we were mad at Lyndon Johnson about. About the fact that there was this horrible violence in our cities, and he wasn't responding with sufficient leadership or proposals or resources. So our response was, 'We have to try harder. We have to press our case harder.' " It was the agony of watching Lyndon Johnson and believing "we can do better."

This was RFK's dilemma, as he saw it: politics versus integrity, common sense versus conviction. On the one hand was the political cost of challenging Johnson. On the other was the psychic (and no doubt political) cost of moral abdication. The cartoonist Jules Feiffer captured Kennedy's contradiction perfectly by portraying a television debate between "the Bobby twins":

THE GOOD BOBBY: We're going in there and we're killing South Vietnamese. We're killing children, we're killing women. . . . We're killing innocent people because we don't want to have the war fought on American soil. Do we have that right, here in the United States, to perform these acts because we want to protect ourselves? I very seriously question

whether we have that right. All of us should examine our own con-
sciences on what we are doing in South Vietnam.

THE BAD BOBBY: I will back the Democratic candidate in 1968. I expect
that will be President Johnson.

THE GOOD BOBBY [turning to the Bad Bobby]: I think we're going to have
a difficult time explaining this to ourselves.

By autumn 1967 the Good and Bad Bobbys were tired of debating.
RFK decided to let his advisers fight it out, and asked Pierre Salinger to
convene a meeting of "all my people and all President Kennedy's people." Salinger, Ted Kennedy, Larry O'Brien, Ken O'Donnell, Stephen
Smith, and Ted Sorensen met on October 8 in a New York hotel; Walinsky and Bobby's other young aides were not invited. Bobby, to protect
his "plausible deniability," did not attend either. It was just as well. Nearly everyone present—especially Ted Sorensen—opposed a challenge to
LBJ on the obvious grounds. Salinger "guaranteed" that LBJ was going
to withdraw from the race, but most of the others dismissed this as nonsense. Their only collective recommendations were that Joe Dolan poll
New Hampshire and that Bobby get a haircut. Otherwise, scoffed
O'Donnell, the meeting was "just the most inconclusive bunch of crap
thrown around."

Kennedy's instincts remained at war. His difficulties were compounded by the fact that Allard Lowenstein had finally found a candidate: Senator Eugene McCarthy of Minnesota. "Is it true?" an agitated Kennedy
asked George McGovern on the telephone. If so, "it would make it hard
for all of us later if we wanted to make some other move." Kennedy had
encouraged McCarthy to run as a stalking horse in New Hampshire but
never imagined he would make a real run. Bobby had disdained the
Minnesota senator since 1960, when McCarthy supported Stevenson,
then Johnson, and treated JFK with scorn. Kennedy did not consider
McCarthy a "serious" candidate, but McCarthy's candidacy confounded
any decision Kennedy might make about 1968: if Kennedy stayed out,
his antiwar stance appeared a fraud; if Kennedy jumped in, he seemed an
opportunist. "So [Kennedy] will try to be as little an opportunist as possible (for Kennedy, sort of like being a little pregnant) by smiling beatif-
ically on McCarthy's campaign," Michael Janeway concluded in *The
Atlantic.* During a press "backgrounder" several days after McCarthy's
November 30 announcement, Kennedy insisted that McCarthy wasn't
really pursuing the presidency, he was seeking a debate on Vietnam—and
that, Kennedy maintained, was "quite healthy" for the party and the
country.

"It's all so complicated," Kennedy moaned to Jack Newfield. "I just
don't know what to do." Again he summoned his advisers in what

Schlesinger called "a council of war," at lunch at Bill vanden Heuvel's on Sunday, December 10. Again they settled nothing. Ted Kennedy and Sorensen told Bobby a failed candidacy would damage his leadership of the antiwar movement. O'Donnell called for a symbolic antiwar candidacy. Only Schlesinger and Goodwin believed Kennedy could mount a serious challenge. "It seemed evident that Bobby is sorely tempted," Schlesinger recorded in his journal. "He would in a way like to get into the fight, and he is also deeply fearful of what another Johnson term might do to the world." But at the moment, Kennedy was every bit as fearful of making a wrong move. He put off a decision and told his advisers to keep on brooding.

Three days later, Schlesinger tried to shore up Bobby's flagging spirits with a bit of perspective: "Even should you lose the fight for the nomination (which I do not think you will) you will be vindicated in the end if Johnson is as hopeless as we think he is."

In 1967, Lyndon Johnson was not so much hopeless as skittish. He had lost his consensus on Vietnam, had lost his momentum in Congress, and was losing his ability to step outside the White House without being harassed by demonstrators. The president was becoming a prisoner in the White House. "I wish you would get out more among the people," Harry McPherson pleaded in a memo of May 1967, "and that you would use the occasion to fight for your legislative program.... My feeling is that a few pickets don't hurt much, despite the publicity that attends them, and that what really hurts is the feeling that you are isolated from the people and their problems." What also hurt Johnson in McPherson's estimation was Bobby Kennedy's travels to "Mississippi or the Harlem slums or San Francisco. The fact that he looks bored, and probably doesn't give a damn about what he is seeing, is beside the point. To the concerned voter, certainly to the young, he is 'out among us.' "

The concerned voter was a constant worry now that 1968 approached. White House aide Fred Panzer hit Johnson with a steady barrage of polling data from 1967 onward. Almost weekly, Johnson absorbed Panzer's charts and considered the latest Gallup, Harris, or Quayle ratings. Johnson's pairings with Robert Kennedy excited particular interest—more interest, in fact, than LBJ's pairings with potential Republican rivals. Kennedy's standing, Panzer reported in September, "is not a positive indication of his strength but simply a sign that he is filling the void when LBJ's popularity drops." This was cold comfort to LBJ, whose popularity was dropping steadily. By midyear, Kennedy had recovered from the Manchester and peace feeler debacles and surged ahead of Johnson in the polls. At Thanksgiving 1967, Bobby held his widest lead ever: 52 percent to LBJ's 32 in a Harris survey. Still, Kennedy remained vulnerable on Vietnam (50 percent of Americans thought Kennedy was wrong to propose a bombing halt; 27 thought he was right), and a Gallup poll that week registered Johnson's first gains since summer. Johnson also took heart in the predictions of Richard Scammon, a burly pollster who delivered regular pep talks to the White House staff. "Scammon thinks Bobby Kennedy would be 'crazy' to challenge you in 1968," an aide wrote Johnson after a November meeting, "and then we all speculated as to whether or not he was crazy."

"How *rational* is Bobby?" John Roche mused in a memo to the president. "Unfortunately, I am no psychiatrist." Yet Roche did a reasonable impression: as the second biggest Bobby-hater in Johnson's White House, Roche devoted page after page of virile prose to Bobby's alleged thoughts and schemes. Roche's memos were indispensable reading to the conspiracy-minded president. In April 1967, Roche hypothesized that RFK "has a vested interest in the defeat of the [Democratic] ticket in 1968"—and would bring it down by withholding his support from LBJ. Thus, said Roche, "the Kennedy Corporation must be convinced that if we go down in bankruptcy, *they will go down with us.* This is the only argument that will have the slightest impact on them. The word should get to them by every available channel that if a Republican wins in 1968, the GOP will probably be in for 20 years."

Roche's psychological portrait of Bobby was confused. In December he painted Bobby as blinkered and bewildered. "Bobby Kennedy is sponsoring a 'War of Liberation' against you and your Administration," Roche wrote Johnson. "To date, however, he has kept it at 'Phase I'—random guerrilla attacks. And I have been convinced that he himself has not made up his mind on whether to move on to 'Phase II'—organization of Main Force Units. I still don't think he knows what he is doing. . . . At the risk of sounding ironic, I would suggest that Bobby is no *more* decisive than you are when torn by conflicting sentiments." Only a month later, though, Roche was certain that the futility of running had dawned on Bobby. "Does he realize this?" Roche asked rhetorically. "Of course he does. He is an arrogant little *schmuck* (as we say in Brooklyn), but nobody should underestimate his intelligence. . . . He will play it safe."

Nobody in the White House underestimated Bobby's intelligence, but other aides believed Roche was underestimating Bobby's lust for power. Except Roche, everyone "knew" Bobby was ready to run—his party, president, and own fate be damned. Johnson knew it, too; he always had. He found Roche's memos engrossing, to be sure, but for Johnson the question was not whether Bobby would make a grab at the nomination, but when, and how. Johnson grew obsessed with detecting, interpreting, and then parrying Kennedy's every move. With little happening on

Capitol Hill (aside from a bruising, unsuccessful fight for a tax surcharge), 1967 became a grand game of watching and waiting. "Everything was a plot. Everything!" exclaimed Ken O'Donnell, who was under White House pressure to pledge for Johnson *now,* in mid-1967, before Bobby jumped in.

Johnson's advisers were duly vigilant. Watson served up his familiar menu of political gossip. "M—see me—what is this—" Johnson jotted in the margin when he wanted the full story, which he usually did. J. Edgar Hoover gathered helpful information, such as a report that RFK had installed an active Communist as his political representative in the Midwest—and that among the Communists at the National Conference for New Politics (NCNP) in September were "many pro-ROBERT KENNEDY liberals . . . who were seeking a third [party] ticket as a means of weakening President LYNDON JOHNSON's campaign for re-election in 1968. . . . A great deal of 'KENNEDY money' was reportedly put into the NCNP." White House aides pestered their sources in West Virginia: "What is Bobby up to" in the state? "Nothing," was the answer.

Something or nothing, it mattered little. The president was planning for the worst. In December, Johnson decreed that Kennedy's kind remarks at the June 3 Democratic dinner in New York "ought to go to every National Committeeman and every state chairman. . . . Ask John Criswell [at the DNC] to figure out a way," he told an aide. Despite his landslide victory in 1964, Johnson still considered himself a legislative politician, ill at ease outside Washington. He didn't know the men who pushed the buttons or pulled the levers across the country; Bobby Kennedy did, and that was how Bobby and Jack had humiliated him in 1960. After that lesson Johnson never doubted that the Kennedys ran the best political operation in the history of the Democratic Party.

This last point gave Johnson serious cause for concern, for his own campaign organization was moribund—"absolutely appalling," concluded George Reedy after a brief review of the party apparatus. Reedy walked through the offices of the Democratic National Committee and was aghast. The DNC had been staffed by a skeleton crew since 1965, when Johnson dropped the budget ax on the committee and purged its Kennedy men. Many of the departed had been experts in voter registration. As a parting shot, one leaked a statement to the press that "a National Committee has no claim to existence if it abolishes voter registration. The very willingness to even suspend it for any period of time is appalling." Committee chairman John Bailey was also known as a Kennedy man; Johnson left him in place but cut him off. It became something of a political joke in Washington that Marvin Watson refused

to return Bailey's phone calls. Watson, in all but name, had become the
real party chairman, and reigned with such clumsy imperiousness that he
alienated more contacts than he cultivated. A week after the electoral
disaster of 1966, a journalist pronounced the national committee "a
farce; it has no money, no manpower, no direct pipeline into the [White]
house, and absolutely no control over political appointments." In
Reedy's view, there was "no one around who could run a hot dog stand,
let alone a campaign."

For Johnson, though, a crippled committee had its virtues. "He wanted it weak," recalled Hubert Humphrey. A reporter added, "He wants no
potential rival political power base in the party." No president did. And
of course Kennedy was no ordinary rival. According to popular myth,
Bobby already controlled a government-in-exile, a party-within-the-
party. Democrats wanted Bobby, not LBJ, by their side in 1966, and it
was Bobby's side they would take in 1968. Or so Johnson believed. Postmaster General Larry O'Brien was an obvious choice to revive the party
organization, but Johnson vetoed the appointment: O'Brien was too
close to Kennedy. A weak national committee was no help to anyone,
and Johnson preferred it that way.

Roche disagreed strongly. "Nothing could encourage [Bobby] more
than an atomized Democratic Party Organization—and that is what we
have," he wrote Johnson in December. Roche didn't understand "what
the hell was the matter with Lyndon Johnson" in 1967. In political
terms, the president's behavior was inexplicable, "absolutely absurd."
Johnson was hungry for information on Bobby Kennedy, but when it
came to his own campaign, he was erratic and inattentive. Johnson knew
the drill; it should have been second nature by now. But when his aides
recommended the establishment of Citizens or Businessmen (or Artists
or Scientists) for Johnson groups, the usual campaign fare, LBJ ignored
their memos or returned them with notes saying, "Don't do anything
about this yet."

Johnson's aides were mystified. "Well, maybe he isn't going to run
again," Harry McPherson shrugged. "Oh, come off it," Roche replied.
Neither of them took the idea very seriously. They presumed instead that
Johnson's indifference meant overconfidence, that Johnson felt he could
win without the party's organizational baggage.

O'Brien was less confident. In late September, at Johnson's request, he
prepared a lengthy "White Paper" on the 1968 campaign (Johnson did
not trust O'Brien to run the DNC, but this sort of activity, conducted
within the confines of the White House, was safe enough). "This is not
an election that can be easily won," O'Brien declared. "Our effort must
be massive." He outlined Johnson's main obstacles: the war, the riots,

"splinter group hostility," rising Republican strength in the suburbs, and the weakness of the DNC. O'Brien did not mention Bobby Kennedy; he doubted Bobby would run. Still, someone else might well capitalize on Johnson's unpopularity. The white paper resonated with urgency and closed on a cautionary note: "I believe this goal [reelection] is attainable and that it will be accomplished. We must not, however, lose any of the precious weeks and months that are needed to put into effect the organization of the campaign. . . . The time for decision making is upon us."

"It is later than we think!" echoed Jim Rowe in a memo to Johnson. Apparently, O'Brien's forty-four-page clarion call had roused everyone but the president. Another month passed before Johnson asked O'Brien for another long memo. Should I declare early? What should I do about the primaries? How and when should I establish a campaign organization? Johnson had a long list of anxious questions—as if it had just occurred to him that time was short. Johnson met with his political advisers on the evening of November 3 to discuss O'Brien's latest recommendations, but even O'Brien admitted that the meeting collapsed into "a debacle" after Johnson left the room. Everybody was a "viewer," O'Brien grumbled. Where had the "doers" gone?

McCarthy's declaration four weeks later did nothing to shake Johnson from his complacency. Like Bobby, Johnson deemed McCarthy "not a serious candidate." McCarthy was obscure, intellectual, Midwestern— hardly a threat to Johnson's renomination. If McCarthy, not Kennedy, was the standard-bearer of the Democratic left, LBJ could rest easy. White House aides underrated the McCarthy challenge and even mocked it. "McCarthy is doing so badly," Roche told the president in mid-December, "that I am tempted to float a rumor that he is actually working for you to dispirit the 'peace movement.' " Roche coolly predicted "a couple of real beatings for McCarthy in the early primaries." Johnson's own polls revealed that a hypothetical Kennedy entry cut McCarthy's support to 6 percent.

The real rivalry remained clear. To Reedy, McCarthy's entry signaled only that "Bobby Kennedy was sitting in the wings and waiting nervously to make an entrance." Reedy was a bit worried that enthusiasm for McCarthy would build, but McCarthy had no organization; well-meaning students and antiwar intellectuals were no match for the Kennedy machine. And on December 8, Bill Moyers called the White House to pass along a rumor from Sargent Shriver: Bobby was getting ready to run.

Or was he? Sargent Shriver certainly wasn't privy to Bobby's thinking, which remained utterly confused. "The ordeal continues," Arthur

Schlesinger noted in his journal. It was January 25, 1968, two days after North Korea had seized the U.S. Navy surveillance ship *Pueblo*. President Johnson promptly called up fifteen thousand reservists, and the United States experienced a brief flush of patriotic fervor. Even the dovish Frank Church called the seizure "an act of war." Challenging the commander in chief now seemed more foolish, or seditious, than ever. And just as Johnson appeared to be upping the ante in Vietnam, Kennedy appeared to reach breaking point. Just before the *Pueblo* incident, LBJ appointed Clark Clifford to succeed Robert McNamara. "He might just as well have appointed Attila the Hun!" Kennedy growled at Jack Newfield. But nothing upset Kennedy like his own indecision. "I have never seen RFK so torn about anything," Schlesinger observed. "I do not mean visibly torn, since he preserves his wryness and equanimity through it all, but never so obviously divided." On January 28, Kennedy invited Schlesinger and Goodwin to Hickory Hill. "We have to settle this thing one way or another," Bobby said firmly. But he had also invited a range of celebrities, from John Glenn to Rod Steiger, and it seemed apparent that Bobby was not going to settle anything that evening.

And then it appeared that he had. On January 30, at an annual off-the-record *Christian Science Monitor* breakfast at the National Press Club, Kennedy confessed with a grin that the pressure to run was affecting him "badly, badly." His dissatisfaction with the McCarthy campaign was evident. "I think it is being helpful to President Johnson," he said. Yet Kennedy shrugged off a reporter's challenge to stand for principle over politics, and granted the fifteen columnists and correspondents one glum sentence for attribution: "I have told friends and supporters who are urging me to run that I would not oppose Lyndon Johnson under any foreseeable circumstances." Mankiewicz had persuaded Kennedy to substitute "foreseeable" for "conceivable," but it was foolish to put much stock in semantics. In her *Atlantic* column Elizabeth Drew noted flatly that "if he runs, he runs, and he would not be held by press or public to his earlier disavowals."

Still, this was the end for Adam Walinsky. After fifteen months of urging Kennedy to run, Walinsky had lost heart. He approached Bobby at Hickory Hill and gave his two weeks' notice. "What are you going to do?" Kennedy asked. He was mildly stunned. Walinsky did not know what exactly he was going to do, but he was going to do something about Johnson and the war if Kennedy was not. Things were heating up; Walinsky had friends on the street and in jail. He felt a need to be more actively engaged. "All right," Kennedy said. "I accept that. I understand." He was no less a disappointment to himself.

January 30 was Tet—the Vietnamese New Year. And at the moment Kennedy disavowed his candidacy, eighty thousand Vietcong and North Vietnamese troops were streaming across South Vietnam in the greatest offensive of the war. Insurgents attacked more than one hundred cities. They even burst into the courtyard of the U.S. embassy in Saigon and held positions there for almost seven hours. The overall assault did not surprise American military planners, though its timing did; U.S. forces recovered quickly and dealt a punishing blow to the enemy.

The blow to the American psyche was every bit as severe. The Tet offensive wrenched the credibility gap wide open. During the fighting, even the unflappable CBS anchorman Walter Cronkite was said to have snapped, "What the hell is going on? I thought we were winning the war!" During the fall of 1967, it had been forced smiles all around as the administration waged a massive (and successful) public relations campaign on the war. After Tet, disbelief was widespread and turned quickly to despair. Johnson did not help matters by comparing unrest in Saigon to riots in Detroit: "a few bandits can do that in any city," he said, bizarrely. Televised images contradicted his every word; there was quite evidently no "light at the end of the tunnel." The enemy was strong and determined. Lyndon Johnson was broken and beaten. One could hear it in his voice the morning after Tet, at the annual presidential prayer breakfast at the Shoreham Hotel. "The nights are very long," Johnson said weakly. "The winds are very chill. Our spirits grow weary and restive as the springtime of man seems farther and farther away. I can, and I do, tell you that in these long nights your president prays."

Tet laid bare the lies and false optimism of the administration's policy in Vietnam, and LBJ stood exposed and virtually alone. "The fig leaf was gone," Edelman observed triumphantly. "Tet just *ripped* the fig leaf right off."

Had the Tet offensive occurred before Kennedy's breakfast at the National Press Club, he might have announced his candidacy in the first week of February. "He screwed up! He screwed up!" shouted Edelman, agitated by the memory even decades later. The cruel irony of Kennedy's timing put the senator in a dark funk for days. He avoided committee meetings, ignored phone calls and mail, and stalked his office alone. When the cloud lifted, he faced a flurry of memos offering advice. Daniel Ellsberg's was the most sobering: LBJ, he wrote, was bound to enter the 1968 campaign "with flags flying." Surely, Ellsberg predicted, the next step was invasion of North Vietnam. But what to do? Dutton wrote the senator suggesting a "careful statement" in favor of negotiations.

A statement was forthcoming, but it was hardly careful. On February

7, Bobby sat in his New York apartment with Schlesinger, Goodwin, and Walinsky (who had, at least in effect, rescinded his resignation) and drafted a strong response to Tet. "Johnson can't get away with saying this is a victory for us," he told Walinsky. When Bobby's speechwriters proposed alternate paragraphs, he picked the toughest language every time. The next day, Kennedy addressed a book and author luncheon at Chicago's Ambassador East Hotel—and blasted the administration's policy in Vietnam. "Our enemy," he began, "savagely striking at will across all of South Vietnam, has finally shattered the mask of official illusion with which we have concealed our true circumstances, even from ourselves."

Kennedy had never spoken so passionately about the war. Then he returned to an idea he had broached in his first speech on Vietnam, before the massive troop buildup of July 1965: a political conflict required a political settlement. "We have misconceived the nature of the war," Kennedy told the audience in Chicago. ". . . We have sought to resolve by military might a conflict whose issue depends upon the will and conviction of the South Vietnamese people. It is like sending a lion to halt an epidemic of jungle rot." It was time, he said, for the administration to "face the reality that a military victory is not in sight and that it probably will never come."

KENNEDY ASSERTS U.S. CANNOT WIN, the *New York Times* declared the next morning. And though Kennedy had not mentioned the president by name, reporters knew a direct hit when they had seen one. Bobby's speech was "the most sweeping and detailed indictment of the war and of the Administration's policy yet heard from any leading figure in either party." A "source" close to Kennedy told the paper to expect more speeches like this one, since the senator's decision not to run for president had "freed" him from accusations of opportunism. This was unlikely. The hawkish columnist Joseph Alsop left a message with Kennedy's secretary: "In the last twelve hours I have talked to three friends of [RFK's], none of them particular friends of Lyndon Johnson, and each said to me that, after that speech, they were compelled to regard Bobby Kennedy as a traitor to the United States."

But the speech had buoyed Kennedy's spirits considerably. Attacking the war and LBJ, he had finally felt like himself. When Bobby returned to Washington he found a letter Mankiewicz had placed atop the mounting pile on his desk. It was from Kennedy's friend, the writer Pete Hamill, and it was an eloquent plea to reconsider a run for the presidency:

> If we have LBJ for another four years, there won't be much of a country left. I've heard the arguments about the practical politics. . . . You will destroy the Democratic Party, you will destroy yourself. I say that if you

don't run, you might destroy the Democratic Party; it will end up nationally, the way it has in New York, a party filled with decrepit old bastards .
. . and young hustlers, with blue hair, trying to get their hands on highway contracts. It will be a party that says to millions and millions of people that they don't count, that the decision of 2,000 hack pols does. They
will say that idealism is a cynical joke. . . .

I wanted to remind you that in Watts I didn't see pictures of Malcolm
X or Ron Karenga on the walls. I saw pictures of JFK. That is your capital in the most cynical sense; it is your obligation in another, the obligation of staying true to whatever it was that put those pictures on those
walls. I don't think we can afford five summers of blood. I do know this:
if a 15-year-old kid is given a choice between Rap Brown and RFK, he
might choose the way of sanity. . . . Give that same kid a choice between
Rap Brown and LBJ, and he'll probably reach for his revolver.

In the days that followed, Kennedy carried Hamill's letter in his
attaché case, read it repeatedly, and made his friends read it. He called it
the turning point.

There were other catalysts. George Romney's withdrawal from the race
was one, since it left the beatable Nixon as the likely Republican nominee. Another was the report of LBJ's Commission on Civil Disorders.
In late February its chairman, Governor Otto Kerner of Illinois, delivered his prophecy of an America "moving toward two societies, one
black, one white—separate but unequal." When Johnson appointed the
committee to determine the causes of urban riots in 1967, Kennedy had
been dismissive, but the report impressed him. Its verdict of "white
racism" did not impress Johnson, who refused to acknowledge the
report. "This means that he's not going to do anything about the war and
he's not going to do anything about the cities, either," Kennedy said.

Still, it all came back to the war. That, in Kennedy's judgment, was
why Johnson was ignoring the cities. In early March, Daniel Ellsberg
leaked to Kennedy a top-secret memo by General Wheeler of the Joint
Chiefs. The memo made mention of General Westmoreland's response
to Tet: a request for the deployment of 206,000 additional troops by the
end of 1968. After reading the Wheeler Report, Johnson was dismayed
("as worried as I have ever seen him," said Clark Clifford), but Kennedy
was apoplectic. "And Johnson's calling this war a success?" he shouted at
Ellsberg. Kennedy called Ted Sorensen and said he just didn't see how
Johnson could be "that stupid and that brutal." In fact, Johnson had
rejected the request. But its very existence made it harder for Kennedy
to stand aside.

Or to keep silent. On March 7, during a heated debate on escalation,

Kennedy rose in the Senate chamber and delivered the most biting comments of the day. "Before any further major step is taken in connection with the war, the Senate [must] be consulted," he demanded. He asked whether the United States had a commitment to protect a South Vietnamese regime that suffered from "deep-seated corruption." And for the first time he attacked Johnson publicly: "When this [corruption] was brought to the attention of the President, he replied that there is stealing in Beaumont, Texas. If there is stealing in Beaumont, Texas, it is not bringing about the death of American boys."

Kennedy was running against Lyndon Johnson. He had yet to declare, but he was already running.

When reporter Charles Bartlett returned from New Hampshire in the first week of March, he sat down immediately and wrote a memo to the president. He told Johnson that New Hampshire Democrats, from the rank and file to Governor John King, "were really making a mishmash" of Johnson's primary campaign. It was not an "official" campaign—LBJ was only a write-in candidate—but Bartlett warned that it was becoming excessively negative, even brutal. One Johnson ad even claimed that a vote for Gene McCarthy was a vote for Ho Chi Minh. Unless Johnson's men changed course, the president might well be hurt or embarrassed. In response, Johnson sent Bartlett a cursory thank-you note, and that was all.

Johnson's silence might have been a sign of confidence. In early March, after all, a Roper poll had Johnson beating McCarthy 62 percent to 11 percent (RFK, who was not on the ballot, received 9 percent). Another poll put Johnson's support at 74 percent. There were danger signs, however. In a survey authorized by the White House, McCarthy was shown to be gaining ground—not enough to overcome Johnson, but enough to create "*a press interpreted victory in the state.*" Meanwhile, Johnson's obsession with Kennedy kept him from focusing on the McCarthy challenge. Fearful that Larry O'Brien might stir up a write-in campaign for RFK, the president kept O'Brien far from New Hampshire. Bernie Boutin, Johnson's man in New Hampshire, called O'Brien and apologized for shutting him out. But Boutin had been under strict orders: no communication with O'Brien.

In the final twenty-four hours before the New Hampshire vote the Johnson forces were starting to panic. "It was a chaotic situation," recalled John Roche, who was trying desperately to keep track of events. The night before the vote, Johnson called Roche at about 10:00. "What's Gene going to do?" the president asked.

"Well, his name is on the ballot. Yours isn't," Roche replied. "I can't see how you can keep him under a third."

"No," Johnson corrected, "he'll get 40 percent, at least 40 percent. Every son-of-a-bitch in New Hampshire who's mad at his wife or the postman or anybody is going to vote for Gene McCarthy."

Johnson had it exactly right. Johnson "lost" the New Hampshire primary by polling 49.4 percent to McCarthy's 42.2 percent. What Johnson really lost was not the vote itself, but the game of expectations and the myth of invincibility. All the disaffected—even the war hawks, and there were many in New Hampshire—voted for Gene McCarthy, simply to vote against Lyndon Johnson.

Kennedy wanted to announce his candidacy before the New Hampshire primary, but George McGovern and other friends advised him strongly against it. McCarthy had been trudging through the snows for months. "If you announce, you are going to split the dissenting vote in New Hampshire," McGovern told Bobby. "Then the McCarthy people are going to very legitimately say that you destroyed their day of glory." Kennedy's own polls showed that Johnson would beat him and McCarthy both; anyway, it was far too late for Kennedy to get on the ballot. As a last-minute write-in candidate, Kennedy would invite charges of opportunism—and hurt the cause of peace, he reasoned. He withheld his announcement. Sorensen flew to New Hampshire to dissuade Kennedy supporters from their efforts. Upon Sorensen's return to New York, Kennedy called to thank him. Moments later the White House did the same.

On the day of the primary, Kennedy was in New York for a speaking engagement in the Bronx. He asked Schlesinger and Moyers to join him that night at "21." A year earlier, in January 1967, Moyers had left the White House after two years as a wartime press secretary and de facto chief of staff. He had exhausted himself; and in the process he had exhausted Johnson's trust. The day Moyers resigned, RFK had invited him to lunch at Sans Souci in Washington. A news photographer shot their picture at the restaurant, and when it hit the paper the next day, Johnson exploded with rage. He was sure Kennedy had set it up. After that incident, recalled John Roche, "nothing would ever convince Johnson that Moyers really hadn't been on the Kennedy payroll for years and years." In February 1967, when Moyers became publisher of New York Newsday, the newspaper's staff welcomed him with an enormous luncheon; Moyers, rising to the occasion, quipped that Johnson's parting words had been "Bill, I'll keep an eye on you up there if you'll keep an eye on Bobby." In the months ahead, Moyers tried to do just that, sending Johnson an occasional morsel of anti-Kennedy gossip—even as Moyers grew closer to Kennedy. But the president turned a cold shoulder toward his protégé.

Now, driving uptown to "21," Moyers unburdened himself to Schlesinger. The White House, Moyers said, was "impenetrable"; Johnson had sealed himself off from reality. Inside this "paranoid" bubble the president saw every action and every event as a conspiracy. Everything was politics now, and it was all deeply personal. Though it pained Moyers deeply to say it, he realized that "four more years of Johnson would be ruinous for the country." Johnson, he added, "flees from confrontations. He is willing to take on people like Goldwater and Nixon, to whom he feels superior. But he does not like confrontations when he does not feel superior." Still, Moyers thought Kennedy would make a grave error by running for president—he would lose, embitter his party, and destroy himself.

At "21," Kennedy was surprised and ambivalent about the New Hampshire results. McCarthy was not going to step out of the way, that was now certain. Nonetheless McCarthy had "done a great job in opening the situation up." Arriving in Washington the next day, Kennedy announced that since the Democratic Party was already split, "I am actively reassessing the possibility of whether I will run against President Johnson."

The White House made no official comment. But some of Johnson's advisers admitted that the development might require a review of their campaign plans.

A strange subplot had begun on March 11, the day before the primary. President Johnson agreed to a meeting with Ted Sorensen—a reward of sorts for Sorensen's efforts to cool the Kennedy forces in New Hampshire. In the Oval Office, Johnson treated Sorensen to a virtuoso performance—rambling at great length, unleashing a two-hour torrent of musings, observations, and gripes. "Everything was tied together," Sorensen recalled. "Vietnam . . . the division in the Democratic party; the discussion of his running; the discussion of Bob running; the division in the country." What can I do? Johnson asked. Sorensen suggested an independent, blue-ribbon commission to evaluate what had gone wrong in Vietnam.

"Well, Dick Daley made the same suggestion," Johnson replied agreeably. "If it could be done without undercutting the Secretary of State and without looking to the Communists as though we're throwing in our hand, that might be useful. I'll think about that. You think about names for the commission." They bandied about a few possibilities. "You know, maybe Robert Kennedy should be chairman," Johnson said, shockingly. Sorensen thought Bobby should be a member, not chairman. Neither man linked the commission idea to the Kennedy candidacy that both men knew was coming.

Sorensen was mildly encouraged by the prospect of a change in policy. Kennedy, upon hearing of the discussion, was not. Mayor Daley had made the same suggestion to RFK, but the Kerner Commission was fresh in Kennedy's mind; Kennedy doubted the president would accept a damning report on Vietnam any more readily than one on the riots. The commission smelled like a trap. But in a sense the trap was already sprung: Kennedy could not dismiss a peace proposal out of hand—however unpromising it appeared. "At the last minute Ted had boxed us in," complained Joe Dolan, who along with the Young Turks had been fighting Sorensen's influence all along. Sorensen was the last holdout against Bobby's candidacy, and now Sorensen's proposal was Kennedy's last obstacle. "There's going to have to be something like this commission to keep Bobby out," Sorensen confessed to Johnson's counsel DeVier Pierson.

But whom was Sorensen protecting—Bobby or himself? There was no question that Sorensen considered Bobby's candidacy political suicide. He had said so many times and with increasing insistence. But Sorensen nurtured his own ambitions and, like Bill Moyers, walked a narrow line between LBJ and RFK, between the present and the future. "Ted always wanted a foot in both camps," recalled Pierson. "Ted had his own agenda and did not want to be unnecessarily at cross-purposes with the president. He extended olive branches." At lunch with Pierson in February, Sorensen offered to take an active role in reelecting Johnson, who he judged in "good shape" even in New York. Sorensen promised to help LBJ by "doing everything possible to discourage the 'nut' running the favorable-to-Kennedy slate" in New Hampshire. In a memo to LBJ, Pierson reported that Sorensen "offered to act as a liaison with Bobby and his people to the extent that we want him to do so. It is hard to say how sincere he is," Pierson cautioned, "[but] my own impression is that he feels Bobby's best interests (and his own) are served by less division and more unity in 1968."

Sorensen's commission proposal was a last, flimsy olive branch, a gesture both well-meaning and self-seeking, and Kennedy could not get on with his campaign without addressing it. He "gritted his teeth," recalled Joe Dolan. "He was clearly unhappy about it." "I felt I had to go the last mile, to prove I was not running out of ambition, or some petty feelings about Johnson," Kennedy explained later. Also, "I was not anxious to run if the war could be ended without my running. So the commission idea was something I felt compelled to explore, although I never thought it would happen."

Kennedy met Sorensen at the Pentagon on March 14 to discuss the proposal with Defense Secretary Clark Clifford. Before the morning meeting, Clifford had stopped by the president's bedroom and listened to Johnson rant about Bobby's tricks; keep your guard up, LBJ told Clifford. Now, at the Pentagon, as Bobby went through the motions ("Ending the bloodshed in Vietnam is more important to me than starting a presidential campaign . . ."), Clifford perceived an ultimatum, a "carefully devised plan": call your war a failure or I'll run. Clifford promised to discuss the idea with the president, but as a parting shot told Kennedy his chance of wresting the nomination from LBJ was "zero." If Kennedy was depending on the war to win him the nomination, he would be "grievously disappointed," because the president still controlled the levers of foreign policy. Kennedy calmly replied that he had considered those arguments but planned to run if Johnson did not appoint a commission. Kennedy and Sorensen parted with polite smiles, but confrontation loomed.

At 3:30, Clifford described the meeting to President Johnson, Vice President Humphrey, and Supreme Court Justice Abe Fortas in the small lounge beside the Oval Office. To LBJ, the commission smacked of a political deal. Moreover, Bobby Kennedy's place on such a panel would raise hackles on Capitol Hill and alienate the president's private advisers. It was simply out of the question. Johnson picked up the telephone receiver and listened silently as Clifford called Kennedy and Sorensen. Clifford told them of the president's decision, adding something about a commission's "giving comfort to Hanoi" and "usurping presidential authority." What if I'm not on the commission? Kennedy asked. Clifford told him it made no difference. Three men said their goodbyes, and four men hung up their receivers.

"I came into the office of President prepared to protect the prerogatives and the strength of the office of the Presidency," Johnson explained later, "and I didn't think that our system ever contemplated turning over the functions of Commander-in-Chief to a civilian commission, and to admit to the world and the enemy and to his own country that he didn't believe in what he was doing." This was not revisionism; in the hours after rejecting the proposal, Johnson made this argument quite matter-of-factly. It was a statesman's view, principled and dignified. But it was equally clear to DeVier Pierson that afternoon that Johnson "certainly wasn't going to dabble with Bobby and find him a way out of the race by giving him some socks on policy."

Later that evening, Pierson spoke to Sorensen by telephone. Together they lamented the proposal's demise. "Well, I guess Bob will run now," Sorensen sighed. He sounded defeated. "I suppose I'll have to change hats."

"Change hats?"

"Yes, I'll have to put on my campaign hat. I'm sure you understand I'll have to help Bob if he runs. Even if this does happen, I hope you and I can stay in touch."

Pierson assured him that they would. But both men understood that they were already at odds, and there would be no more olive branches.

CHAPTER 17

RFK vs. LBJ

"I am announcing today my candidacy for the Presidency of the United States."

It was March 16, 1968, and Robert Kennedy stood in the Senate Caucus Room his brother had used for the same purpose only eight years before. Ethel was by Bobby's side, and both looked a bit uneasy. Bobby wore a gold PT-109 clasp on his red and blue tie but conveyed little of Jack's brash confidence. "I do not run for the Presidency merely to oppose any man"—a woman giggled nervously —"but to propose new policies," Bobby declared. As a statement of purpose this was almost apologetic, but Bobby quickly found his form: he added sternly that the nation's "disastrous, divisive policies" in Vietnam and the cities could be changed "only by changing the men who are now making them." Then, quickly, he backed off. Anticipating press criticism, Kennedy insisted:

> My decision reflects no personal animosity or disrespect toward President Johnson. He served President Kennedy with the utmost loyalty and was extremely kind to me and members of my family in the difficult months which followed the events of November 1963. I have often commended his efforts in health, in education, and in many areas, and I have the deepest sympathy for the burden that he carries today. But the issue is not personal. It is our profound differences over where we are heading and what we want to accomplish. . . .
>
> At stake is not simply the leadership of our party or even our country—it is our right to moral leadership on this planet.

In the press conference that followed, Kennedy demonstrated just how difficult it would be to wage a campaign of clashing issues rather than warring personalities. "Every time I have spoken on Vietnam . . .

every time I have spoken on what I think needs to be done as far as the cities are concerned, it's been put in the context of a personal struggle between myself and President Johnson," Kennedy complained to reporters. He insisted, a bit wishfully, that the results from New Hampshire had created a different climate—by exposing divisions that ran deeper than those between himself and Johnson. The primary, Kennedy said, "established that the division that exists in this country [and] the division that exists in the Democratic Party are there, that I haven't brought that about, that what has brought that about is what President Johnson"—he paused—"the *policies* that are being followed by President Johnson."

This was going to be difficult. Attempts to depersonalize the conflict were futile and smacked of insincerity. Kennedy was running a campaign of issues, but the issues were *Johnson's* policies, *Johnson's* worldview, *Johnson's* fallacies, and *Johnson's* deceit. Kennedy was going to have an awful time convincing anyone that his campaign was not a vendetta. Where some saw integrity and conviction, others would surely see spite, ambition, and cruelty. And the press would obliterate Kennedy's careful semantic distinctions: the morning after his announcement, the *New York Times* headline read KENNEDY . . . ATTACKS JOHNSON, not KENNEDY ATTACKS JOHNSON'S POLICIES. "There is evidence," *U.S. News* pronounced solemnly, "to suggest that emotion played a key part in his decision to challenge Mr. Johnson."

As it turned out, the Kennedy-Johnson campaign got nasty and personal very quickly. The White House greeted Kennedy's announcement by leaking details of the Vietnam commission proposal. A White House aide called Kennedy's (it was now Kennedy's, not Sorensen's or Daley's) idea an ultimatum and "the damnedest piece of political blackmail" he had ever heard. "According to the Administration version," reported CBS correspondent Roger Mudd in a special bulletin, "Kennedy demanded as his price of withdrawal that the President go on TV to state that a complete revision of the U.S. war policy was needed, and that the Commission be selected from a list supplied by Kennedy himself." This was not, in fact, the administration's version of the story, which was damaging enough, but by setting the ball of innuendo rolling, the White House had established the tenor of the campaign. KENNEDY MADE JOHNSON OFFER TO FORGO RACE, claimed the *Times*.

"I am surprised," Kennedy retorted on March 17, "that the traditional rules of confidence governing White House conversations are no longer respected by the White House itself." Kennedy gave his own, more accurate version of the commission idea (it was never an official "proposal," he insisted) and answered Johnson's aides in kind: Johnson's

rejection of the commission made it "unmistakably clear to me that so
long as Lyndon B. Johnson was President, our Vietnam policy would
consist of only more war, more troops, more killing, and more senseless
destruction of the country we were supposedly there to save." Bobby hit
Johnson's weakest spot—his credibility. The leak, Bobby said, was an
"incredible distortion," a stark illustration of "why the American people
no longer believe the President."

True enough, but Bobby Kennedy was the one on the defensive—
forced to justify his candidacy to organization Democrats who pictured
the party's ticket going down to defeat in November. The press was
largely a mouthpiece for an outraged establishment. The consensus,
reported *U.S. News,* was that "Senator Kennedy so dislikes Lyndon Johnson that he is willing to risk his future and his party's in an effort to
knock the President out of the White House." Party stalwarts like Mayor
Daley rushed to defend the president. Antiwar Democrats who had
surged into McCarthy's camp after New Hampshire felt bitter and
betrayed. A student volunteer summed up their reaction: "We woke up
after the New Hampshire primary like it was Christmas Day," she
remarked on March 16, hours after Bobby's entry. "And when we went
down to the tree, we found Bobby Kennedy had stolen our presents."
Kennedy's old cohorts like John Kenneth Galbraith and newer ones like
Allard Lowenstein felt too deeply committed to McCarthy to defect.
Others, like Dick Goodwin, lingered a few weeks in the McCarthy
organization and then extracted themselves uncomfortably. Across the
country the reaction was the same: as Joe Dolan had put it months earlier, everybody was still "scared shitless."

There was something liberating, though, about all this hostility; it
freed Kennedy to say what he believed. There was no sense now in being
delicate or politic. "*Hit hard at the Administration,*" one of Kennedy's former aides advised him, and Kennedy did. He let loose the fullness of his
contempt for Lyndon Johnson and, in doing so, finally felt true to his
nature. Frank Mankiewicz coined it the "free-at-last syndrome."
Kennedy's usual release was humor, and on March 18 he filled his first
campaign speech with jabs at Johnson. Referring to the ill-fated Vietnam
commission, Kennedy told students at Kansas State University that "the
problem was that the President and I couldn't agree who should be on
the commission. I wanted Senator Mansfield, Senator Fulbright, and
Senator Morse. . . . And the President, in his own inimitable style, wanted to appoint General Westmoreland, John Wayne, and Martha Raye."
The well-scrubbed students (most of whose haircuts were shorter than
the candidate's) were a bit startled by Kennedy's dry irreverence and
broke into laughter. Then, more seriously, Kennedy turned to the polit-

ical bankruptcy of the South Vietnamese regime. "President Johnson has responded to criticism of corruption in Vietnam by reminding us that there is stealing in Beaumont, Texas," he said, returning to a comment that had irritated him for weeks. "I, for one, do not believe that Beaumont is so corrupt. I do not believe that any public official, in any American city, is engaged in smuggling gold and dope; selling draft deferments or pocketing millions of dollars in U.S. government funds." Later, in an aside: "If no one else will stand up for Beaumont, Texas, I will." The students roared their approval. Three days later at the University of Alabama a young man asked if Kennedy would accept a place on Johnson's ticket. "I said I was for a coalition government in Saigon, not here," Bobby joked.

At times, though, Kennedy's humor drifted toward sarcasm, and he grew positively belligerent in the coming days. At Vanderbilt University in Nashville, Kennedy asked students, "When we are told to forgo all dissent and division, we must ask: who is truly dividing the country? It is not those who call for change, it is those who make present policy." And then, departing from the text, Bobby added with a rising shout, "They are the ones, the President of the United States, President Johnson, they are the ones who divide us!" By the time Kennedy reached Los Angeles this tone of outrage had crept into the script: in a line crafted by Goodwin (though widely attributed to Walinsky), Bobby accused Johnson of "calling on the darker impulses of the American spirit. . . . Integrity, truth, honor, and all the rest seem like words to fill out speeches, rather than guiding principles." The *Kansas City Star* had called it right on the first day of the campaign: NO PUNCHES PULLED.

After the rhetorical flights of Kennedy's Vanderbilt address, Arthur Schlesinger wrote him that "it is a little early in the campaign for that. Let [Johnson] get personal first." Bobby's tone sparked the first serious internal debate of the Kennedy campaign. Edelman recalled much "tactical soul-searching" among Kennedy's advisers: how tough, they asked one other, should Bobby be on Johnson? "There was so much pent-up emotion," said Edelman, that it was hard for Bobby—or his speechwriters or aides—to contain it. Kennedy's older advisers cautioned him and one another. "Bob has to be very careful about the level and character of his attacks on President Johnson," Pierre Salinger lectured in a letter to Ted Kennedy. "There is a tremendous feeling among people who are friendly with the Senator that some of his speeches have been too strident and that Bob should talk positively on the issues and let the President dig his own grave."

Of course, Bobby *had* been talking positively about the issues, but it was the attacks on Johnson that captured the headlines. After three years of making something out of nothing (or very little, anyway), reporters savored each bitter word. Richard Harwood of the *Washington Post* called Kennedy a "demagogue." When Kennedy said that the war had driven young people away from public service and toward pot and protest, Harwood blasted him for "impl[ying] that the President is to blame for the alienation and drug addiction among American youth, for rebelliousness and draft resistance on American campuses, and for the 'anarchists' and rioters in American cities." Kennedy, he said, was seeking nomination by "revolution."

The savage reaction to RFK's candidacy in the press and the warm, enthusiastic crowds on the campaign trail did much to temper Kennedy's tone in the coming days. His mood lifted and his good humor returned; he seemed at ease with himself and his decision. Now, rather than attacking LBJ for unleashing "darker impulses," Kennedy called for "a new birth of those noble and spacious impulses that are the most enduring qualities of the American spirit." Kennedy rejected a speech draft by Schlesinger that recounted "the tragedy of our President" and condemned Johnson for abandoning the principles of Woodrow Wilson, Franklin Roosevelt, Harry Truman, and John F. Kennedy, "the great Democratic Presidents." Instead, Bobby implied that Johnson had abandoned his own promises—"just as they voted so overwhelmingly in 1964, [Americans] want no wider war"—but mentioned neither the president nor even the administration. General disagreements were the most Kennedy would muster at this stage of the race; he had been a consistent supporter of the administration, though LBJ and the press imagined otherwise, and Bobby's campaign researchers had little time in these first frenzied weeks to unearth smaller bones of contention.

Still, Bobby's tactical retreat brought snide headlines. Rowland Evans and Robert Novak gleefully derided "young radicals" disappointed by Kennedy's new refusal to "titillate New Leftists with personal attacks against President Johnson." But Kennedy offset any losses on the left by making gains in the center. At campaign stops the crowds were frenzied, almost terrifying; they grabbed at his hands, his clothes, his hair ("They *loved* to touch his hair for some reason," puzzled an advance man). Kennedy lost a fresh pair of cufflinks at every stop; every night he nursed swollen and bloody hands. Yet he seemed to thrive on the energy of the crowds. "Well," he told a friend, shrugging mildly, "so many people hate me that I've got to give the people that love me a chance to get at me." Older "John Kennedy liberals" began to drift back into his orbit, infusing Bobby's grassroots campaign with wisdom and experience. In late March a Gallup poll of Democrats showed Kennedy surging ahead of Johnson for the first time in a year: 44 percent preferred RFK as their nominee, 41 preferred LBJ. (Only two months earlier, Johnson had beaten Kennedy 52 to 40.) When Gallup accounted for independents and Republicans, Kennedy's lead shot up another five points. *U.S. News* hailed "a brisk start for the Kennedy drive." *Newsweek* canvassed potential delegations and declared, with far greater portent, that LBJ "may be in real danger of being dumped by his own party."

President Johnson watched Kennedy's drive with dismay but with little surprise. Kennedy's entry merits one terse line in Johnson's memoirs: "I had been expecting it." Indeed he had. Johnson had been expecting it from the first days of his presidency. But perhaps the anticipation had been worse than the reality: after years of fearing an open fight, Johnson now seemed to relish it. On the morning of Kennedy's announcement, the president seemed in good humor at a meeting of the National Alliance of Businessmen. "Of course," Johnson observed playfully, "always in this life that we live, you have to take your chances. Some people speculate in gold—a primary metal. And some people just go around speculating in primaries." The audience laughed warmly. "The press asked for my reaction to the recent activities of the Senator from New York," Johnson continued. "I don't want to tell you all of my reactions this morning. But when I read in the paper that he had pushed Henry Ford out of the *Meet the Press* program Sunday, I thought he was going too far. . . ."

The next day, at a meeting of the National Farmers Union in Minneapolis, Johnson was more belligerent, pounding the podium with his big fist. "Make no mistake about it," he declared, "I don't want a man in here to go back thinking otherwise—we are going to win." Johnson was talking about Vietnam, but he was fighting a two-front war now; his audience could not have missed the reference. "We love nothing more than peace," he added, "but we hate nothing more than surrender. . . . We don't plan to let people . . . pressure us and force us to divide our nation in a time of national peril." *Newsweek* described the speech as "a rhetorical barrage aimed ostensibly at Ho Chi Minh but really designed to bring down Kennedy." Several days later the president told a foreign policy conference at the State Department that "today we are the Number One Nation. And we are going to stay the Number One Nation." The message in both speeches was clear: Bobby Kennedy was not going to deter this president from victory in Vietnam.

At a press conference several days later, Johnson took a slight swipe at the Kennedy candidacy: "I would have no comment on Senator Kennedy's entrance other than to say I was not surprised," Johnson told reporters. "And I could have made this statement to you this time last year." This wry aside, dignified but disparaging, suggested that Johnson was ready for the challenge. "You are going to see [Johnson] put up one hell of a fight," a White House official told reporters. Others, though, were apprehensive. "Wait until [Kennedy] starts moving," a Johnson adviser told *U.S. News*. "The Kennedy clan, money galore, untold pressures on every party official, fleets of planes, organization down to the last eyelash. And, along with all this, the Kennedy 'image,' with every Kennedy from Jackie to mother Rose Kennedy making speeches. We know damn well what it will be like. The President has run against Kennedy money before—back in 1960."

The party machinery, however rusty, clicked into gear. Campaign manager Jim Rowe boasted that his staff had called four hundred Democratic politicians across the nation and that 399 committed to LBJ. Citizens for Johnson-Humphrey hustled switchboards and desks into its Watergate office. At first the room was bereft of LBJ campaign posters, but in the interim someone propped up a Bobby Kennedy dartboard—its bull's-eye right between the senator's eyes. Johnson's legislative liaisons canvassed congressional opinion, state by state. They nudged friendly senators to go on the record for LBJ. "I am for the President all the way," replied Scoop Jackson, before telling the same thing to AP and UPI.

Johnson's advisers were concerned lest nudging lead to outright shoving. As Kennedy hit the campaign trail, Rowe drafted a telegram to Democratic Party leaders from Citizens for Johnson-Humphrey: "There are those who seek to divide us, but I urge you to volunteer with us." Yet after several days' canvassing in Massachusetts, Larry O'Brien voiced "deep concerns" about such a "hasty overreaction." In a memo to Johnson on March 19, O'Brien argued that the telegram was "bound to be construed as a nationwide effort for loyalty oaths. . . . The press and some party people would read the telegram as a clear sign of panic. . . . At this early stage, we should not be pointing to those who would divide us. At this point we should let the dividers slug it out among themselves." Harry McPherson warned the president against a "narrowing of tolerance toward those who don't stand at attention for us when we say 'pop to.' . . . Half-way support for you is to be preferred to total support for Bobby; and our rejectees may very well end up over there." Congressional liaison Barefoot Sanders sounded a final cautionary note. "We should continue to plug for floor speeches for the President," he wrote Johnson, "but we should not force Congressmen to decide publicly. The reputation for high-pressure tactics belongs with the Kennedys."

The debate over "loyalty oaths" revealed the extent to which Kennedy's entry energized the president's staff. They had been waiting months for *something* to spur LBJ to action, and now they seemed almost pleased that Bobby had jumped in. "If I ever had any doubts about John-son's running," enthused Rowe, "I would have lost them the day Kennedy announced because he is not about to turn the country over to Bobby." In an instant every White House aide became a political sage; they flooded the president with campaign proposals ranging from the clever to the absurd. John Roche suggested a national committee of "Italo-Americans for Johnson," as "they really hate Bobby." Fred Panzer, calling talk radio a "politically undeveloped medium" full of "great opportunities," recommended that the Democratic National Committee enlist a "Jaw Corps . . . to exercise their jawbones" by calling talk shows and singing Johnson's praises. "Send to [John] Criswell [at the DNC] & ask to get busy," Johnson scrawled on the memo. Two weeks later a jaw corps stood at attention, ready to deliver a chorus of "no"s when Wash-ington's WTOP-AM asked the question "Can the youth of America nominate Bobby Kennedy?"

Most comical of all was George Reedy's suggestion for luring youth away from RFK. "The Citizens Committee," Reedy wrote Johnson, "should organize one of those electric guitar 'musical' groups to travel around to meetings. It is not too difficult to get some kids with long hair and fancy clothes and give them a title such as 'The Black Beards' or 'The White Beards' and turn them lose [sic]. They don't have to be very good musically to get by as long as they have rhythm and make enough noise. I have seen enough of these groups to know that they bring young people out regardless of their political feelings and put them in an enthusiastic mood."

"M—" the president scribbled before passing the memo to Marvin Watson, "this may deserve attention."

The White House had amassed information on the Kennedy family for four years; now it was ready to put it to use. And if Bobby was going to run against Lyndon, Bobby was going to have to run against Jack. Aides eagerly collected John Kennedy's words on Lyndon Johnson, poverty, and Vietnam. Every statement was handpicked and edited to imply that LBJ was the true heir to the Kennedy legacy. Bobby was also going to have to run against his father. Just as they had done in 1960, Johnson's aides dug up Joseph Kennedy's most defeatist, accommoda-tionist statements of 1940, and scoured dime-store biographies for sor-did details of his life. And lastly, Bobby was going to have to run against himself. Aides culled quotes from Bobby's 1962 statement on Vietnam ("We are going to win") and his introductions of LBJ at political dinners and rallies. Copies of the speeches were sent to national committeemen and state chairmen in all fifty states. "I would see to it that recordings of the two or three most forthright Kennedy endorsements of Johnson are played 15 to 20 times a day on the radio in the primary states," McPherson added in a memo to the president. McPherson imagined an introduction: "And now, on behalf of President Johnson, we bring you these words of Senator Robert F. Kennedy. . . ." LBJ was the one with a credibility gap, but perhaps his men could create one for RFK.

As they surveyed potential delegate slates, Johnson's campaign advisers were particularly anxious about New York State. Every other state party organization would pledge automatically to LBJ, while Kennedy hunted for independent support. But in New York, John J. Burns, the state chairman, was solidly behind Kennedy. LBJ's old friend Edwin Weisl, Sr., New York's national committeeman, publicly accused the "Kennedy machine" of bullying local Democratic leaders. Johnson's troops readied for the assault they had expected since 1964; Marvin Watson kept a close eye on local developments, anointing Frank O'Connor as the president's man in New York. When a Humphrey aide reported that "O'Connor is going like a house afire . . . making a real dent in the Kennedy hold on New York," Johnson was grateful. "M—" he wrote, "let's call O'Connor.—L." Other contacts were less optimistic. An assistant to Joseph Resnick, a strongly pro-Johnson candidate for the Senate, complained to John Roche that "the President is in serious trouble in New York State. Although few leaders have actually declared for Kennedy so far, many are ready to jump. . . . There definitely is pro-Johnson sentiment—but dorman[t]. . . . The choice of O'Connor was most ill-advised and disturbing to many people . . . the damage is done." Resnick had troubles of his own: he faced an uphill battle against Eugene Nickerson, Bobby's choice, in a primary race with important repercussions on the state delegation. Another local Johnson man admonished the White House: "If we had moved earlier to insure [sic] New York against Bobby, he could not move."

Watson immersed himself in these internecine struggles, but Johnson's longtime advisers concentrated on the larger fight. Reedy urged LBJ to "remain aloof from the [Kennedy-McCarthy] brawl. [You] must depend on [your] friends for the necessary organizational efforts . . . [and] hope that when the strife is over, the wounds will not be so deep that unity— or at least a substantial degree of unity—is impossible." McPherson, on the other hand, warned Johnson against sitting still. "A moving target is better than a stationary one," McPherson wrote the president on March 18. This contest was about *change*, and that did not bode well for LBJ. McPherson coolly and comprehensively assessed the Kennedy challenge:

> Kennedy offers the change to a dove policy, together with the reputation
> of a tough guy. . . . He will try to "bridge the gap" between young and

old, he will be photographed with Negroes who have criminal records but want to go straight—the tough guys with hearts of gold who can "stop riots." He will try to occupy the same relation to you that his brother Jack occupied to the Eisenhower-Nixon Administration: imagination and vitality vs. staleness and weariness, movement vs. entrenchment, hope of change vs. more of the status quo. We will be defending our programs; he will be attacking the tired bureaucrats who run them. We will point out the good we've done; he will . . . point to the people who have been left out—the Mississippi and Harlem Negroes, the Indians, the Appalachian farmers, etc. He will speak before college groups whom no member of the Administration could address without embarrassment. Many young liberals are bitter about his opportunistic entry into the race after McCarthy's strong showing, but Kennedy is cynical enough to believe that they will forget, given time, razz-ma-tazz, and the development of momentum behind his candidacy. He is right about that.

Kennedy was the candidate of change for change's sake; but McPherson believed that Johnson could fashion himself the candidate of real, substantive change—by scaling down (or appearing to scale down) American involvement in Vietnam, by responding to the Kerner Commission report, and by conveying "movement, candor, [and] dissatisfaction" along with "strength, experience, and achievement—these can win it for you," McPherson concluded.

Overall the campaign picture was confusing and troubling for the president. Some aides told him to stand firm; others warned him to get moving. Some told him to lean on his supporters; others said to back off. Some suggested that Johnson declare his candidacy today; others advised him to stall indefinitely. No consensus emerged—except that Kennedy was a serious threat, far more serious than McCarthy in the long run. And presidential aides, after all, could only do so much; only the candidate, Lyndon Johnson, could answer the serious strategic questions that lingered, unresolved.

Yet there was an odd silence in the Oval Office. LBJ penciled an occasional comment in the margin of a memo, indicating approval or disapproval of an aide's proposal, but otherwise he had little to say about the Kennedy campaign. He held no war councils or roundtables. He gave no marching orders. For four years, Johnson had tracked Bobby Kennedy's smallest and most inconsequential moves—and now that Bobby was finally doing it, finally running against him for president, Johnson seemed distracted, almost uninterested. Johnson's campaign manager was getting panicky—"We should have moved in California by now!" James Rowe wrote the president on the eve of Bobby's declaration, and eleven days later aides were still asking LBJ if *somebody* was going to say *something* to refute Bobby's "indefensible positions."

Lyndon Johnson would leave that to McCarthy, because Lyndon Johnson was no longer running for reelection.

LBJ had been talking about withdrawing from the 1968 race for many months. "I'm going to get out of this," he told friends, advisers, and near-ly everyone he talked to. "A man doesn't have to take this kind of thing." But then, Lyndon Johnson always said something like that when he was running for office—even as a young congressman running for senator. "I got kind of accustomed to it and didn't take it seriously," recalled Ed Weisl. Charles Bartlett did, briefly, when he heard a rumor that Johnson was about to drop out, but Bartlett was a reporter; it was his job to chase down leads. He chased this one straight to the Oval Office and left more convinced than ever that LBJ was ready to take on the problems that gripped America. Among his aides, though, the president was always equivocal about 1968: "Now, if I decide to run this year . . ." he would say, or "I'm not sure I'm going to be a candidate, but if I am . . ." No one attached particular importance to these qualifiers. It was just Johnson's way of talking. A few of the president's associates—John Connally and General Westmoreland, for example—predicted that Johnson was going to step aside. But no one took them seriously, either.

A few others, though, understood the gravity of Johnson's reserva-tions. George Christian, the White House press secretary, enjoyed John-son's complete trust; Christian had come straight from Texas to work for LBJ and, unlike Bill Moyers, had no competing loyalties or tendency to freelance in conversations with the press. In the late summer of 1967, LBJ informed Christian of his wish to withdraw. Johnson never said definitively that he would not run, but he was already focused on the *timing* of a statement and asked Christian to draft one. Christian oblig-ed. Still, LBJ could never find the right time to bow out—there was always something left unfinished, something requiring Johnson's last ounce of political capital; and declaring an end to one's career at a news briefing seemed somehow inappropriate. Perhaps the State of the Union Address in January was a grand enough occasion, a clean break. For a time Johnson fixated on that. He asked Horace Busby, one of his oldest associates, to draft a second statement of withdrawal. Years later, Johnson insisted he had no real intention of delivering it, and merely wanted it in his pocket during the speech "to know it was there." (He later claimed to have left it by his bedside table.) After the State of the Union Address, Johnson climbed into the presidential limousine and turned to George Christian. "I just didn't think I could tell them, 'I want you to pass this, and I want you to pass that,' and then say, 'Get to it. I'm leaving.' " Johnson seemed to be apologizing. From that point onward, in Christian's view, "it was a question of when."

Why, then, the polls, O'Brien's "White Paper," and all the campaign planning? Was it all a charade? Not entirely. Johnson was looking for a way out of the White House; but at same time he was looking for a reason to stay in it—the victory he had promised in Vietnam, a national emergency that required his skills, a sudden groundswell of support, or a country that had returned to its senses. None of these was likely. But they could not be counted out—could they? When Johnson told Christian he wanted out, he meant it. And when he told Bartlett he was ready for the fight ahead, he meant that, too. "Whatever Johnson tells you at any given moment, he thinks is the truth," said George Reedy. Reedy also said that the first victim of a Lyndon Johnson whopper was Lyndon Johnson. In this case, though, it was utterly unclear which statement was the truth and which was the whopper.

In February, Johnson crossed a threshold of sorts when he refused to get on the ballot in New Hampshire. It was a foolish abstention and a recipe for the political embarrassment that followed. "After New Hampshire, everything else was going to be a disaster," recalled Christian. The Wisconsin primary on April 2 was beginning to look like one of those disasters; the Johnson organization in the state was moribund, administration officials were heckled at every appearance, and the president offered little guidance. It was as if Johnson were undermining his own campaign in order to force his own withdrawal.

Bobby Kennedy's entry was another disaster; and then, on March 25 and 26, came LBJ's meeting with his "wise men"—Dean Acheson, George Ball, General Omar Bradley, McGeorge Bundy, Abe Fortas, and others—on Vietnam. In November 1967 the same group had validated LBJ's policy, urging him almost unanimously to stay the course. But Johnson's notes of the March meeting conveyed a dramatically different picture: "can no longer do the job we set out to do. . . . Adjust our course . . . move to disengage." The wise men's candor shattered Johnson's confidence, and he reacted with rage. "Your whole group must have been brainwashed," Johnson snapped at Ball. LBJ collared the CIA and military analysts who briefed the group. "Tell me what you told them!" he shouted. But after two days of brutal briefings, Johnson seemed to understand that disengagement was his only real option in Vietnam. Even another 206,000 troops would not break the stalemate. Sullenly, Johnson retreated to a familiar source of blame. "This," he grumbled, "is caused by the 206,000-troop request, leaks . . . and Bobby Kennedy."

The next day Johnson asked Joe Califano who would win the nomination if he withdrew. "Kennedy," Califano said, and flinched—ready for verbal assault by LBJ. "What's wrong with Bobby?" Johnson mused. "He's made some nasty speeches about me but he's never had to sit here. Anyway, you seem to like his parties." Califano grinned sheepishly. "Bobby would keep fighting for the Great Society programs," Johnson added. "And when he sat in this chair he might have a different view of the war." Califano was stunned; he had certainly never heard this before in LBJ's countless diatribes about Bobby, Bobby, Bobby.

Johnson had lunch with Califano and Harry McPherson the next afternoon. They worked for an hour in the sun on the edge of the Rose Garden, reviewing a television address Johnson planned to deliver on March 31. In earlier drafts it had been a speech about war; but now, after the meeting of the wise men and a heated internal debate, it was becoming a speech about peace. It proposed a bombing halt as a pretext for negotiations—the same notion Johnson had lacerated Kennedy for a year before—as well as a tax surcharge. The president paused and looked at his two aides. "What do you think about my not running for reelection?"

At first McPherson and Califano said nothing, thinking Johnson was merely releasing his frustration. But he returned to the subject and pressed them for a response. "Of course you must run," McPherson said.

"Why? Give me three good reasons why."

They walked back into the Oval Office. "Well, if *I* were you I wouldn't run," McPherson continued. "It's a murderous job, and I see no way to change the things that make it so bad, at least not soon. But I'm not you. You have to run."

Johnson, displeased, shook his head. "That's a conclusion, not a reason," he said. "What would be so bad about my not running? What would happen?"

"For one thing," McPherson replied, "nobody else could get a program through Congress. Nobody else knows how."

"Wrong." Johnson shook his head again. "Any one of 'em—Nixon, McCarthy, Kennedy—could get a program through next year better than I could. They'd be new, and Congress always gives a new man a little cooperation, a little breathing room. I'd be the same old Johnson coming back to the well again, beggin' and pushin' 'em to give me a better bill than last year. No. Congress and I are like an old man and woman who've lived together for a hundred years. We know each other's faults and what little good there is in us. We're tired of each other. Give me another reason."

McPherson appealed to Califano for help, but they were mercifully interrupted by the arrival of Marvin Watson. As McPherson walked Califano to his office, the two men debated whether Johnson was serious. They concluded that he was not. After all, one had only to look at the president's desk that week: reports from Senator Edmund Muskie on the LBJ-RFK race in Maine, a detailed summary of network news coverage of the Kennedy campaign, a breakdown of the Colorado delegation, Las Vegas odds on the nomination (LBJ 7–5, RFK 4–1, McCarthy 8–1). True, Johnson seemed disengaged, but the Johnson campaign went on despite him; Fred Panzer plumbed the polls for Kennedy's weak spots, and the Texans mapped out regional strategies during an excited session at Liz Carpenter's house. The Texans remembered 1960: Johnson might well dally for months, so they had best get started without him.

Meanwhile, a team of speechwriters and advisers labored on Johnson's March 31 speech. After a conversation with pollster Lou Harris, Panzer suggested that LBJ confront Kennedy by inserting this sort of passage: "This is not statesmanship. This is rank opportunism. And the American people know the difference between those who ask what they can do for their country, and those who ask what their country can do for them." But Johnson, striving for statesmanship himself, ignored the suggestion. The speech was not about Bobby. It was about Vietnam and, as Johnson told reporters on the afternoon of March 30, "other questions of some importance." Leaning forward in his chair, looking relaxed and agreeable, LBJ took questions at noon in the Rose Garden. "I think you will get from the speech generally the Government's position and the course that we intend to take," he said.

"Sir, will it be painful?" a reporter asked.

Johnson smiled. "You call me and tell me after you hear it."

An hour before his speech, President Johnson handed the final draft to the U.S. Army Signal Corps man who would put it on the TelePrompTer. "I'm not going to know probably until I get in there whether I'm going to use that speech," Johnson admitted. It was the speech's ending—Christian and Busby's contribution—that he was still unsure about. Perhaps Johnson wanted it included just to know it was there. But thirty-five minutes into the speech, Johnson raised his right hand (a signal to Lady Bird) and intoned slowly and gravely:

With American sons in the fields far away, with America's future under challenge right here at home, with our hopes and the world's hopes for peace in the balance every day, I do not believe that I should devote an hour, or a day, of my time to any personal partisan causes. Or to any duties other than the awesome duties of this office—the Presidency of your country.

Accordingly, I shall not seek, and I will not accept, the nomination of my party for another term as your President.

The Johnson-Kennedy contest lasted fifteen days and was over before it really began.

Robert Kennedy's American Airlines flight from Phoenix arrived at John F. Kennedy International Airport at about 9:50 P.M., just minutes after Johnson's speech concluded. Kennedy, airborne for its duration, had not watched it. A young campaign worker, followed by state Democratic chairman John Burns, darted on board, pushing his way up the aisle, shouting, "The president withdrew, the president withdrew!" Burns offered confirmation: "Johnson isn't running."

"You're kidding," Kennedy muttered. Staggered, he sat back down, trying to gain perspective. He stayed seated in silence while others brushed past him and thrust themselves into a crowd of two hundred screaming supporters at the terminal. "I don't know quite what to say," he finally told reporters. He had not been prepared for this. Ethel murmured something about being astonished.

On the forty-minute drive to his Manhattan apartment, Kennedy uttered only one sentence: "I wonder if he would have done it if I hadn't come in."

Magazines rushed to press with exclusives: WHY HE DID IT. WHY JOHNSON WITHDREW. WHY LBJ IS QUITTING. Most of this was conjecture; political observers were every bit as perplexed as Bobby Kennedy. Not even White House aides and friends of the president knew the answer. Was this Kennedy's greatest political triumph? Had Bobby driven the president of the United States back to the ranch?

Kennedy's friends and advisers certainly thought so. Adam Walinsky watched Johnson's speech alone with Ted Sorensen. They sat quietly taking notes. When Johnson withdrew, Walinsky exploded with joy. "Son of a bitch!" he shouted, leaping from his seat and throwing his pencil to the floor. "We did it!" Roger Wilkins, watching the speech at home, thought that even the first thirty-five minutes were "a reaction to Kennedy," and it went without saying that Johnson's conclusion was "all about Kennedy." Asked later about Kennedy's impact on Johnson's decision, Peter Edelman replied, "Big. Big, big, big. Bigger than that. Huge." Joe Dolan felt vindicated: he had said all along that LBJ was a bully and that bullies ran from fair fights. "Johnson dropped out because Kennedy was going to beat him," said Frank Mankiewicz, "and Johnson knew he was going to be not just defeated but humiliated."

No Kennedy man was willing to share much credit with Eugene McCarthy. Goodwin, who worked on the McCarthy campaign, conceded only that McCarthy "precipitated" the chain of events. Indeed, Larry O'Brien had told the president the night before his withdrawal that McCarthy was about to beat him two to one in the April 2 Wisconsin primary; this news, more than anything, may have convinced Johnson that if he planned to withdraw he had best do it *now*, before his utter humiliation. But even McCarthy had to admit, in retrospect, that Kennedy's entry "may have had some bearing" on the president's withdrawal. After all, White House aides had stated publicly (and quite plausibly) that McCarthy was not a concern, that "McCarthy will be the forgotten man on the inside pages as soon as the Kennedy steamroller gets in motion."

Now the steamroller was undoubtedly rolling. Johnson men, proud and indignant, refused to concede that it had flattened the president; instead, they implied that LBJ had stepped aside to safeguard the public interest. "This," a friend of Johnson's said bitterly, "is better than to stay in the race and have Robert Kennedy take advantage of the unpopularity of the President's policy and personality to undermine the strength and security of this nation." Johnson confessed as much to Hubert Humphrey on April 3: that he simply could not function as president if he was subjected every day to attacks from Nixon, McCarthy, and Kennedy. In the short press conference that had followed Johnson's March 31 speech, a reporter asked if RFK had affected the timing of his decision to withdraw. Yes, the president said, because Kennedy "added to the general situation [of disunity] I talked about that existed in the country."

Of course, there was much more to LBJ's withdrawal than Bobby Kennedy. In 1968, Johnson began to talk about dying young, as his father had. LBJ had stabs of chest pain that concerned him, reminding him of 1955 when he nearly died. "I did not fear death so much as I feared disability," Johnson wrote in his memoirs. At LBJ's request, George Christian prepared a memo on the full picture of how the White House operated after Woodrow Wilson's debilitating stroke. "Could it happen," Johnson wondered aloud, "that I would wind up here in this bed with a stroke, confined from the responsibilities of the job, with men in the field, with great divisions in the country, and have to rely on a staff?" In later years Johnson claimed that the throat polyps removed during his presidency had been malignant.

Whatever the doctors said, there was no doubt that Lyndon Johnson was exhausted, physically and emotionally. "I'm tired," he told a friend on March 31. "I'm tired of feeling rejected by the American people. I'm tired of waking up in the middle of the night worrying about the war.

I'm tired of all these personal attacks on me." The bickering within his own party had embittered him and then finally worn him down. One could see it in his pallid countenance. If any president could be expected to rise above all this enmity, to let it fall like water off his back, that president was not Lyndon Johnson. It ate into his bones like acid. "I always felt that every job I had was really too big for me," LBJ later confessed in an interview by Walter Cronkite. Johnson bemoaned his own "general inability to stimulate, inspire and unite all the people of the country." All those laws, programs, and good works—and all Johnson got credit for was the war, riots, and inflation. "How is it possible," he asked repeatedly, "that all these people could be so ungrateful to me after I had given them so much?"

Lady Bird did not understand, either, but she gently urged Lyndon to stop trying. On a visit to retired congressman Carl Vinson, back home in Georgia after fifty years in the House, Lady Bird said, "See, Lyndon, there's a man who can leave Washington and be happy." But Vinson was an old man; for Johnson to leave now, to abandon willingly the presidency of the United States, seemed sheer cowardice, especially now that Bobby Kennedy was running for the office. Could Johnson leave the White House with his dignity intact?

This concern inspired the myth of Johnson's martyrdom, his political self-sacrifice for the larger cause of national unity. Johnson rightly reasoned that a fight between himself and Kennedy would be brutal, personal, and divisive. It would tear the Democratic Party apart; it would tear the country apart; and the winner (if elected in November) would start his term bloodied and discredited. Though Lyndon Johnson expected victory, he relished neither the fight nor the prize. "The people of this country did not elect me to this office to preside over its erosion," Johnson told an aide, "and I intend to turn [over] this office with all its power intact to the next man who sits in this chair." By withdrawing from the race, Johnson would spare the country inevitable agony. By transcending a bitter campaign, Johnson would become a force of unity rather than division, the president of all the people rather than the candidate of a few. For the first time in his life, Lyndon Johnson would be above politics.

No longer a candidate, Johnson strove wearily for statesmanship. At the regular Tuesday legislative breakfast on April 2, Larry O'Brien asked the president why he had withdrawn as a candidate. "I'm doing everything I humanly can to bring peace," Johnson sighed. He looked old and tired. "But there'll always be those who will say all I care about is politics. So now I've done the one thing that proves it's not politics." He told another aide, "all I'm interested in is doing whatever is necessary to end the war and to protect our boys over there." The more often Johnson said this the deeper his conviction became: he had withdrawn from the race in order to bring the war to an honorable conclusion. "He realized," Bill Moyers argued, "that every move he made toward peace in Vietnam . . . was being interpreted in the American press, and by Kennedy's friends and associates, and probably by Kennedy himself—and indeed in Hanoi—as singularly a political ploy without any substance or sincerity behind it." But by bartering his political future in a deal for peace, Johnson might rewrite his epitaph: martyr, not coward.

Johnson's gestures to Hanoi brought peace talks but not peace to Vietnam. Years later, looking back, LBJ had to confess that his withdrawal from the presidential race was hardly heroic. He did not soar above the political fray. He ran from it. He ran from the press, the intellectuals, the students, and the "traitors." He ran from the war, the riots, and the demonstrations. He ran from McCarthy and Nixon and Wallace. And if there was ever a chance that Johnson might confront this multitude of antagonists, Bobby Kennedy ended it on March 16. Kennedy's candidacy, Johnson explained later, was

> the final straw. The thing I feared from the first day of my Presidency was actually coming true. Robert Kennedy had openly announced his intention to reclaim the throne in the memory of his brother. And the American people, swayed by the magic of the name, were dancing in the streets. The whole situation was unbearable for me.

"Get out of the way," Horace Busby told Johnson. "Let nature take its course." Nature, or the Kennedy steamroller.

Robert Kennedy had never really believed that Lyndon Johnson would withdraw from the race. Bob McNamara had told him to expect it. So had Edelman. "Now, you just can't go on the basis of that," Kennedy replied irritably. And now that Johnson *had* withdrawn, Kennedy could hardly make sense of it. When Kennedy stepped into his apartment at United Nations Plaza on the night of March 31, he was quiet and withdrawn, hardly in the mood for the raucous celebration that erupted after Johnson's speech. The group surrounded him, offering congratulations, but Kennedy shook them off. "The joy is premature," he said with a tight smile. Ethel, refusing to let Bobby spoil the moment, brought out a bottle of Scotch. "Well," she declared, "LBJ never deserved to be President anyway." The mood was so recklessly euphoric that Bobby took William vanden Heuvel aside and asked him to please talk privately to some of their more boisterous colleagues—it was best that the excitement not leak out of the apartment and into tomorrow's newspapers. Reporters had already descended upon 14F UN Plaza.

In another room, Bobby sat beside the telephone. His friend Jim Whittaker called from Los Angeles. "I think it's the best news I've ever heard," Whittaker exclaimed. "Congratulations."

"It's not that easy, Jim," Bobby said. But he did agree that he was the major factor in Johnson's decision.

Bobby quickly learned how difficult Johnson's absence was going to be. He placed three or four calls to Mayor Daley, reached someone in Daley's entourage, and got the clear impression that Daley did not want to talk to him. Kennedy called governors, senators, and mayors. "This obviously creates a changed situation," he said to each one as he woke them from a sound sleep. "I just hope that you keep an open mind until I have a chance to talk to you personally." None of them was particularly responsive; Johnson's withdrawal had been enough news for one night, and it was not very long before Bobby began to wonder whether the calls were actually counterproductive.

Bobby called Larry O'Brien, who days earlier had told a crowd at the National Press Club that "as long as I serve the President, he will have my total loyalty . . . [and] no one understands this better than Bob Kennedy." Kennedy reached O'Brien just before midnight. "I hope I got to you first," Bobby said.

"You did, Bob." (Humphrey would not call for another few minutes.)

"Larry, I'm glad we've kept in touch and I'm glad we understood each other all the way. Your position has always been a fair one and, now that Johnson has made this decision, I hope you'll join me."

O'Brien replied that he would seriously consider it.

"Here we go again, Larry," Kennedy said excitedly. "It's going to be like the old days. You'd better get a good night's sleep tonight because I'm not going to let you sleep from now on. It's a new ball game now."

Meanwhile Arthur Schlesinger and Adam Walinsky traded drafts of a statement for tomorrow's press conference (RFK had originally scheduled it to answer the president on Vietnam). Walinsky wanted to take a tougher line toward the retiring president, but Schlesinger won that debate. The exhausted candidate watched with bleary-eyed disinterest. "Well, work it out," he said before drifting into the bedroom at about 2:00 A.M. The next day, at the Overseas Press Club, RFK read aloud the telegram he had wired the president:

> First of all, let me say that I fervently hope that your new efforts for peace in Vietnam will succeed. Your decision regarding the Presidency subordinates self to country and is truly magnanimous. I respectfully and earnestly request an opportunity to visit with you as soon as possible to discuss how we might work together in the interest of national unity during the coming months.

Kennedy added that the president's decision reflected "both courage and generosity of spirit." As victor, Kennedy could afford to be "truly magnanimous" himself. And if "work[ing] together" seemed a bit much to expect, Kennedy was nonetheless eager for a personal meeting with LBJ. It was important to the country that its two most prominent leaders appear at peace. It was also important to Kennedy's campaign that he open a channel to the White House and its crucial foreign intelligence. Perhaps he might even persuade Johnson that their rivalry was really, in the end, nothing personal.

In the car to the airport Kennedy was subdued, obviously deflated. There had been a *cause* in running against Johnson, he told his young aide Carter Burden. There had been a real challenge, a real adversary, emotion, and even "fun." Now there was mostly disappointment—and nothing but hard work ahead. Bobby foresaw chasing Hubert Humphrey—LBJ's heir apparent—across the country and working twice as hard, but in a campaign stripped of its spirit. Where there had once been passion there was now just sweat. Still, Kennedy felt more certain than ever that the nomination was his.

On the night of March 31, Kennedy's advisers briefly discussed how to shift the tone of their campaign. Overnight Johnson had rendered himself a sympathetic figure, if only temporarily. Kennedy had been prepared for a politically motivated peace offensive and had planned to dismiss it as inadequate. But he had not been prepared for this. Suddenly, said Milton Gwirtzman, "it was a campaign without a theme."

Kennedy's request for a "unity" meeting reached the president after the results of the Wisconsin primary—in which McCarthy won 56 percent of the vote. Johnson received less than a third, and though he was no longer a candidate this was new cause for embitterment. "I won't bother answering that grandstanding little runt," he reportedly said of Kennedy's request.

Johnson soon cooled and invited Kennedy to the White House on April 3. Kennedy, accompanied by Sorensen, arrived shortly after 10:00 A.M. Bobby's hair, recently trimmed at the urgings of his advisers ("Don't pay attention to anything he says," Ted Kennedy told Bobby's barber. "Cut off as much as you can"), was neatly combed; the effect was odd, as if he were a schoolboy being sent to the rector. But seeing Kennedy in the familiar environs of the cabinet room, one could tell how much he had aged since the days of the missile crisis.

LBJ entered the room a few minutes later, trailed by his advisers Walt Rostow and Charlie Murphy, and with little Lyn, his grandson, on his arm. As Lyn scampered out of the room, the men sat down—Kennedy in the vice president's chair, Sorensen at his left, and LBJ and Rostow across the table. Murphy sat several seats away from the president. Johnson opened the conversation by praising Kennedy's cable, sharing Kennedy's wish to be helpful to the nation at this critical time. LBJ reviewed the explosive situation in Saigon and the Middle East, and said it had been very difficult for him to cope with these problems while under constant attack from Kennedy, McCarthy, and Nixon. In the final analysis, though, Johnson doubted he and Kennedy would be very far apart if they sat at the same table.

Now that they did sit at the same table, the two men were surprisingly subdued—even warm. "Your speech," Bobby said, "was magnificent." He apologized that they had not been in closer contact; it "was my fault," he said, and he had always understood that Johnson placed the national interest above all else.

Turning again to Vietnam, Johnson tried to justify having extended the bombing north of the demilitarized zone. The administration's position, he said, had been misunderstood. One of his most serious problems was the willingness of some Americans to play the enemy's game. This was why he had withdrawn from the campaign. It had not been easy to endure the jibes of Kennedy and McCarthy supporters, students, intellectuals, or Negroes ("after all I've done for civil rights and for higher education!"), though they might yet accept his peace proposal at face value. Nor had it been easy with the Joint Chiefs. Johnson had won a partial bombing halt by a vote of three to two, but explained now that if he had pursued a complete cessation he would have lost, four to one. He launched into a detailed review of the military situation. Rostow provided a map, and the men stood and leaned over it as Rostow traced key lines of defense.

"I will be glad for you to make suggestions," Johnson said. "I feel no bitterness or vindictiveness. I want everybody to get together to find a way to stop the killing." Johnson outlined necessary spending cuts, complained of international money problems, and grumbled that the *New York Times* story on Westmoreland's request for 206,000 troops—the leak that Johnson privately blamed on Kennedy—had somehow cost the United States $1 billion in gold reserves, money that should have gone to the cities.

"Where do I stand in the campaign?" Kennedy asked, returning the conversation to politics. "Are you opposed to my effort and will you marshal forces against me?"

Johnson repeated his pronouncement of March 31—that the presidency and politics did not mix. "I'm not that pure," he admitted, "but I'm that scared. The situation of the country is critical." Johnson added that he had not yet talked to any other candidate, and when Humphrey arrived at the White House later that day "I will tell [him] about the same things I'm telling you. I don't know whether he will run or not. If he asks my advice, I won't give it. If I thought I could get into the campaign and hold the country together, I would have run myself," he said, adding, "I am no king maker and don't want to be." But he might, of course, have to disagree with Kennedy tomorrow. Johnson had to keep his options open.

The president assured Bobby that he had never viewed him with contempt. Nor had he ever wanted to become president or vice president. He had joined the ticket in 1960—and given up "the best job I ever had"—only to beat Nixon. And after November 1963, he had never thought of his administration as the Johnson administration, but as a continuation of the Kennedy-Johnson administration. It was still a partnership, a family matter, and he had kept the faith: "Somewhere up there," Johnson said quietly, "President Kennedy would agree that I've done so."

The difficulties between himself and Bobby, Johnson said, had been exaggerated. By imagining a feud, the press had created one. The great divide should never have developed, "and if *you* hadn't left the White House," he said, pointing at Sorensen, "maybe it never would have."

"Will people in your Administration be free to take part in preconvention politics and support candidates?" Sorensen asked.

"I will need to think about that." Johnson said he had no hard-and-fast rule.

Kennedy cut in. "If you decide later to take a position, can we talk to you prior to that?"

"Yes," Johnson replied, "unless I lose my head and pop off. I will try to honor your request."

"I wanted to know because if I should hear reports that you are doing such and such, I want to know whether to believe them," Kennedy explained.

"If I move," Johnson said, "you'll know."

Reviewing his own presidency, Johnson judged that he had achieved more than any other president in civil rights and education. But perhaps it had not been enough. "The next man who sits in this chair will have to do better," he said, in an unconscious echo of a Kennedy refrain.

"You are a brave and dedicated man, Mr. President." The words stuck in Kennedy's throat. For some reason they were inaudible, and he had to repeat himself: "You are a brave and dedicated man."

Johnson wanted Kennedy to know that he did not hate him, he did not even dislike him, and in an important way they would always be partners, leaders of the Kennedy-Johnson team that had been forged in Los Angeles in 1960. The meeting ended after a hundred minutes with heartfelt handshakes all around. All five men felt it had been worthwhile.

Juanita Roberts, Johnson's secretary, walked into the room to bring a message to the president. She cast a spiteful glance at Bobby Kennedy and marveled at how small and sad he looked—small and sad yet somehow still arrogant. What a *little* man you are, Roberts thought. And as she turned and walked from the room she felt terribly ashamed of herself.

"I'm glad it ended on that note," Lyndon Johnson later said of his last conversation with Robert Kennedy, "because in the public mind . . . we were spending a lot of our time conniving and fighting each other. I never spent any of my time doing that, and I don't know how much of his, if any, he spent. But that was the public impression." In his memoirs, Johnson added that "when tragedy struck him down, I was glad that my last meeting with Bobby had been friendly." Any friendliness, though, was quickly fleeting. Eugene McCarthy soon paid a courtesy call to the Oval Office, and when McCarthy mentioned Kennedy, the president said nothing; instead he drew a finger across his throat, silently, in a slitting motion. Later that week, Johnson exploded at press reports of the April 3 meeting with Kennedy and Sorensen, whom, he now charged, had leaked the story to score political points.

Sorensen, meanwhile, still awaited an answer to his question about endorsements—were administration officials free to support candidates in the preconvention period? Ever since the unity meeting Johnson had implied that he personally would remain neutral, but he gave no such order to his cabinet. Labor Secretary Willard Wirtz went to lunch with Humphrey on April 3 and endorsed him the next day. Johnson said nothing. Secretary of Health, Education and Welfare Wilbur Cohen soon did the same. Johnson again said nothing.

Then, three weeks later, on April 23, news wires carried Agriculture Secretary Orville Freeman's endorsement of Hubert Humphrey. Suddenly irritated, Johnson called Joe Califano. "I can't have the government torn apart by Cabinet officers and presidential appointees fighting among themselves about Kennedy, McCarthy and Humphrey." He told Califano to call the cabinet and tell them to "stay out of the race or get out of the government." They were also to stay clear of Humphrey's upcoming campaign luncheon.

"What do you mean, [Johnson] doesn't want involvement?" Freeman barked at Califano. Like Humphrey, Freeman was a Minnesotan; he felt obliged to attend the luncheon. "I've said what I'm going to do and I'm going to do it."

John Schnittker, Freeman's under secretary, had long been a quiet blessing to Robert Kennedy's Senate staff. Schnittker was one of Edelman's discreet contacts in the Johnson administration—mostly for technical assistance on legislation. A day or two after Kennedy's entry, Sorensen asked Schnittker to advise the campaign on agricultural questions. At this point, however, LBJ was still a candidate; and though Schnittker wanted to help he considered it improper. Only after March 31 did Schnittker call the Kennedy campaign and say, "I'll help." He was now ready to leave the government. Kennedy aides saw no reason for him to do that. Schnittker was more valuable inside the Agriculture Department than outside it.

When Schnittker told Freeman of his decision to endorse Kennedy, Freeman urged him against it. It was one thing to back the vice president, quite another to back Bobby Kennedy. "Too much of a confrontation," Freeman said, and it could split open the Agriculture Department. This meant little to Schnittker. If the president wasn't nonpartisan (no one expected him to keep his promise, not with Kennedy in the race), why should Schnittker be? "After discussion with Secretary Freeman," he wrote Johnson on April 25, "I have indicated that I favor Senator Kennedy, and that I am willing to help the Senator secure the nomination in any way consistent with my present responsibilities. I understand this is consistent with your statement to the Cabinet on April 3." Schnittker had attended that meeting and honestly believed that Johnson's neutrality pact applied only to the White House, not the entire executive branch. He concluded: "I indicated to the Secretary that I would be willing to leave the Department if that were necessary, but that in my view, we can operate the Department of Agriculture effectively for the next few months while lending some support to different candidates for the Presidency." Schnittker endorsed Kennedy that morning.

In the afternoon, Schnittker received a call from the president, a patient lecture: you and the others got the wrong idea at that cabinet meeting, Johnson said. If you want to participate in the primaries, get out of the government. LBJ hoped Schnittker wouldn't take his endorsement any further or "make a big thing of it."

Then another endorsement hit the wires: Assistant Secretary of Agriculture John Baker had come out for Humphrey. Johnson, standing as usual beside his clattering ticker, was one of the first to read the news. "Freeman, Schnittker, and John Baker on the line at once and at the same time!" he shouted incomprehensibly while punching his secretary's call button. Freeman and Schnittker, airborne en route to a meeting, were unreachable, so only the unlucky Baker received a presidential phone call. According to Califano, Johnson "verbally whipped the skin off Baker's back" and demanded his resignation. (Later, Califano called Baker privately and told him to forget the whole thing.)

The president was outraged anew when Sorensen called to complain about the "different standard" that applied to Humphrey supporters like Wirtz, Cohen, and Freeman. Why was it acceptable to come out for Humphrey but not for Kennedy? LBJ told Califano to call Sorensen back, spell out the policy of complete neutrality, and make clear that "in no way does the President owe anything to Bobby Kennedy."

Then the president quietly permitted Harry McPherson to advise and write speeches for Hubert Humphrey. "I am aware of the need for discretion," McPherson replied.

"Kennedy now is exposed," a Johnson adviser gleefully told reporters. "He will start to scramble back. He has to start saying nice things about the President." Kennedy, admittedly, was "a little stupefied" after Johnson's withdrawal, according to Peter Edelman. In a sense the campaign had been on autopilot in March. Attacking Johnson—or Johnson's war—was natural and almost effortless for Kennedy. Now, overnight, his stump style was obsolete and his campaign virtually devoid of issues. "Johnson was the war!" Joe Dolan exclaimed in frustration. LBJ had drained the fuel from the Kennedy steamroller. Moreover, the president's peace initiative and Hanoi's encouraging response meant that responsible candidates had to wait, watch, and offer support. "For the moment," Arthur Schlesinger wrote Kennedy on April 3, "the case against military escalation in Vietnam has been won."

In the short term, Johnson's withdrawal was more bane than boon to Bobby Kennedy. Awkwardly and disingenuously, he began to praise the president in public speeches. In Camden, New Jersey, on April 1, Kennedy declared that "we take pride in President Johnson, who brought to final fulfillment the policies of thirty years." (Schlesinger had written the line several days before Johnson's withdrawal as "a bouquet to LBJ" that was never thrown.) The next day in Philadelphia, Kennedy praised the president's "act of leadership and sacrifice. . . . He showed his devotion to his duty, and to the search for peace in Vietnam." Still, Bobby crossed out a line reading "I have had differences with President Johnson—but I regard them as policy, not personal, differences." Perhaps it was best to forget those differences altogether.

It was not going to be easy to shift gears. Even a month later a Kennedy campaign aide reported that the president's abdication "brought a general apathy on most campuses, since he and Vietnam were the principal issues. The only people who remained active and excited . . . were those who had great momentum—i.e. the McCarthy students."

Some advisers, like Schlesinger, saw the contest between Kennedy and McCarthy as the critical one. Others focused on the delegate count and Hubert Humphrey's obvious advantage. Though it was too late for Humphrey to enter the primaries, it mattered little; primaries were an outsider's game, a means to circumvent the party structure, and the vice president was no outsider. He was Lyndon Johnson's proxy and benefi-ciary, and a less inviting target for RFK. "The animus didn't flow against Hubert Humphrey the way it did against Lyndon Johnson," Edelman explained. The Kennedy campaign had lost both its bearings and its sense of purpose.

But only momentarily. On April 4, Robert Kennedy received a bru-tal, unwanted reminder of why he was running for president. He was campaigning in Indiana when word came that Martin Luther King had been shot dead in Memphis. Kennedy recoiled, as if he had been struck physically, and wept. That night, despite the pleas of his advisers, despite the stern warnings of the local police, Kennedy eulogized King at what had been intended as a campaign rally in an Indianapolis ghetto.

Most of the audience had not heard the news. They gasped in horror as Kennedy delivered it. The night was very cold, and Kennedy stood hunched in a black overcoat, his face gaunt, speaking extemporaneously from the depths of his despair:

> In this difficult day, in this difficult time for the United States, it is per-haps well to ask what kind of a nation we are and what direction we want to move in. For those of you who are black . . . you can be filled with bit-terness, with hatred, and a desire for revenge. We can move in that direc-tion as a country, in great polarization—black people amongst black, white people amongst white, filled with hatred toward one another.
>
> Or we can make an effort, as Martin Luther King did, to understand and to comprehend, and to replace that stain of bloodshed that has spread across our land, with an effort to understand with compassion and love. . . .
>
> Let us dedicate ourselves to what the Greeks wrote so many years ago: to tame the savageness of man and to make gentle the life of this world. Let us dedicate ourselves to that, and say a prayer for our country and for our people.

On the night of April 4, Indianapolis was one of the few major Amer-ican cities that did not erupt in flames.

Meanwhile, in Washington, President Johnson delivered a nationally televised address, intoning gravely that "America is shocked and sad-dened by the brutal slaying. . . . I ask every citizen to reject the blind vio-lence that has struck Dr. King. . . . We can achieve nothing by lawlessness and divisiveness." Less than a mile north of the White House, at the People's Drugstore on the corner of 14th and U streets, a group of black store clerks huddled around a radio and listened skeptically to the president's words. "He's a murderer himself," one said. "This will mean a thousand Detroits," another replied. Two hours later, at the same streetcorner, a weeping middle-aged black man heaved a trashcan through a storefront window and sparked a riot—one of a hundred across the country that night. By week's end thirty-seven people were dead. For the first time in history, the White House situation room had monitored battles not overseas but at home, in America's streets, some fewer than fifteen blocks away.

Two eulogies—one anguished but full of hope; the other sorrowful, heartfelt, but somehow hectoring. In the cities, Kennedy's impassioned rhetoric sounded a sharp contrast to Johnson's desperate pleas for peace. The riots had broken Johnson's spirit. "How is it possible, after all we've accomplished?" he asked. Black rage confused him and then angered him, unleashing a torrent of resentment against the criminals, Communists, "hoodlums," and "outside agitators" he perceived behind the unrest. "He never understood black consciousness," judged Roger Wilkins. "He did not understand that generations of heaping inferiority into our souls needed to be purged, and if you're going to put that awful stuff into people, when people begin to expel it, it's not coming out pretty."

But "Kennedy," according to Wilkins, "did understand." RFK recognized—and shared, by the time of King's death—black rage, resentment, and desperation. Like Johnson, Bobby had fought for integration, though at first with little enthusiasm. But in time, the education that had begun during the Freedom Rides, the lessons learned in Northeast Washington and Bedford-Stuyvesant and on the Committee on Juvenile Delinquency, had changed him. He had not metamorphosed, as his critics charged, but he had grown. He was no longer James Baldwin's sullen pupil, folding his arms as others tried to shake him from his complacency. Since then he had witnessed much suffering, he had experienced some of his own, and he struggled to understand. "To understand is not to permit; but to fail to understand is the surest guarantee of failure," he once wrote. In a speech to the National Catholic Conference on Interracial Justice, he argued, "The violent youth of the ghetto is not simply protesting his condition, but making a destructive and self-defeating attempt to assert his worth and dignity as a human being—to tell us that though we may scorn his contribution, we must still respect his power." Kennedy had come to endorse some of the tenets of Black Power—namely, cultural pride and economic self-determination. His Bedford-Stuyvesant project embodied the idea that economic independence was a precursor to real integration.

At King's funeral in Atlanta, Robert Kennedy was hailed as a hero. The president reluctantly stayed at home; the Secret Service and FBI had warned him that this time, he might be the target. Johnson's absence, and Kennedy's presence at the head of the funeral procession, symbolized a changing of the guard. In reality, it had been years since civil rights leaders looked to LBJ as their protector or provider. A younger, more aggressive generation was taking matters into its own hands. At the same time, a good many blacks and whites considered Robert Kennedy to be the nation's last hope for racial reconciliation. John Lewis, a young civil rights activist who had marched with King and campaigned for RFK, spoke for himself and for much of the black community: "After the funeral of Dr. King, I felt I had lost a friend, a big brother, a colleague. Somehow, I said to myself, 'Well, we still have Bobby Kennedy.' And I just snapped out of it like that and got back on the campaign trail."

On the campaign trail, RFK was gaining strength. "Robert Kennedy appears to be in such a dominant position," *U.S. News* reported, "that if he is to be stopped, President Johnson will have to play a part." Of course, LBJ had pledged at his April 3 meeting to stay out of preconvention politics. But the Kennedy camp was convinced that Johnson had broken his pledge and was intervening directly on Humphrey's behalf. "He did every bloody thing possible to stop Bobby," complained Ken O'Donnell. ". . . Whatever weight the White House could lean on, they leaned on all over the country."

Some of Kennedy's advisers even suspected that Humphrey himself was a front—a ventriloquist's dummy in the lap of LBJ, as Humphrey had been so cruelly rendered on the cover of *Esquire* in November 1966. Surely the cunning master politician was planning to spring a surprise on the Democratic Convention. It was almost unthinkable that Johnson would *not* "pull the rabbit out of the hat," as Adam Walinsky put it, and try to recapture the nomination. A greater worry was that Johnson would de-escalate in Vietnam as a campaign tactic, and then re-escalate after election day.

These fears diminished as the campaign progressed. In the Indiana primary, Governor Roger Branigan ran as a favorite son and Humphrey surrogate, boasting to the president he would "knock the blocks off of Robert Kennedy in Indiana." Dolan called Branigan a "stalking horse for Johnson" and rumors circulated that the president was urging key Democrats to hold the line against Bobby. Organized labor in the state seemed unduly hostile to RFK, and Edelman's clear impression "was that the White House was in there for Branigan," stirring up the organization. If so, it was all for naught: on May 7, Kennedy received 42 percent to Branigan's 31 and McCarthy's 27. And thereafter, in Mankiewicz's

view, LBJ's influence amounted to "damned little." A labor drive for
Humphrey in Nebraska failed miserably; Humphrey was not even on the
ballot, and Kennedy crushed McCarthy in the May 14 primary by twenty points. If there was any White House pressure during the primaries,
it was felt not by voters but by organization men. The battle for their
allegiance—and their first-ballot votes at the convention—lay ahead, in
the summer, after Kennedy had finally dispensed with McCarthy. Until
then, concluded Mankiewicz with satisfaction, "nobody really cared
what Lyndon Johnson thought."

Nor does it appear that Lyndon Johnson tried to make them care.
"We were damned interested" in the contest, said a Johnson aide, but
interest did not equal action. Fred Panzer sent Johnson highly detailed
poll data on the Indiana primary, but there is no evidence that Johnson
did anything but read it. LBJ seemed strangely resigned to a Kennedy
presidency. If the voters want another Kennedy, he shrugged, let them
have one.

Johnson had rendered himself a "political eunuch," in Stewart Udall's
words. LBJ had always been the fixer, the deal-maker, the greatest politician in an increasingly antipolitical age. Now he relished his self-con-
ferred status as statesman. In late May, at lunch with the president and
George Christian, a reporter whispered that "Senator Kennedy was buying California voters on street corners," buying staff members' loyalty
with $50,000 salaries, and offering to pay delegates' expenses to Chica-
go. This was the sort of gossip Johnson had thrived on for years. Several
months earlier he might have had Marvin Watson on the telephone to
California, or made the call himself. But today, heavy-lidded, he changed
the subject. "The people who support moderation will prevail in 1968,"
Johnson declared. And he pointed out that most Kennedy and
Humphrey supporters were not, as sometimes portrayed, extremists.

Johnson's political disinterest baffled and aggravated White House
aides. Most were strongly for Humphrey, strongly against Kennedy, and
assumed that Johnson was, too. Yet it was becoming hard to tell. LBJ
ignored aides who urged him to use his new prestige to discredit
Kennedy. When Horace Busby recommended that Johnson assume a
more aggressive public posture ("Bobby, taking advantage of your
restricted movement, has been exploiting the crowd to create an impression he is the *only* figure with 'charisma' "), he did not. When Kennedy
began emphasizing "law and order" in his campaign speeches, and a presidential adviser urged that "*some prominent local persons in the 'primary'
states start a frontal attack on Kennedy to keep in the voters' minds his emotional
over-identification with the rioting elements,*" Johnson did nothing. Kennedy
was the vice president's responsibility. "If the New York Senator is to be

stopped," predicted *U.S. News,* revising its earlier verdict, "Hubert Humphrey will have to do the stopping."

On June 5, at the Ambassador Hotel in Los Angeles, it was a twenty-four-year-old Palestinian immigrant named Sirhan Bishara Sirhan who stopped Robert Kennedy. At 3:31 A.M., Walt Rostow called the president with the horrible news. "Too horrible for words," gasped Lyndon Johnson.

CHAPTER 18

Between Myth and Martyrdom

At 6:00 in the morning, as Robert Kennedy lay dying at the Good Samaritan Hospital in Los Angeles, Lyndon Johnson phoned DeVier Pierson, the White House counsel. "Where's that legislation on Secret Service protection for presidential candidates?" the president demanded.

This struck Pierson as an unusual request at 6:00 A.M., even for LBJ. "It's in my office," he replied.

"Well, come down and get it, and bring it to my bedroom right now," Johnson said grimly. The line clicked and went dead. Only when Pierson's nine-year-old son ran from the television set screaming did Pierson understand that Robert Kennedy had been shot.

In the presidential bedroom, in the hours before dawn, Johnson and his top assistants were already busy with nervous activity. LBJ telephoned members of the Kennedy family to offer his prayers and sympathy. He sent a telegram to Ethel: WE GRIEVE AND PRAY WITH YOU. He ordered troops on alert in Los Angeles and Washington, D.C., to forestall the sort of unrest that had followed the King assassination. "[Washington] is quiet now," Joe Califano reported to LBJ a few hours later, "but [city leaders] are concerned that enough people will get stirred up over the Kennedy slaying . . . that there could be trouble later in the day." This time, though, there was no trouble in the ghetto, just a numb silence that bespoke defeat.

White House aides, meanwhile, worked intently on the legislation pulled from Pierson's files. Several weeks earlier, just after King's murder, Johnson had instructed Pierson to draft a bill granting Secret Service protection to presidential candidates. The bill had stalled on the Hill; Congress refused to consider the issue until the parties had chosen their nominees. But on the morning of June 5, Johnson assigned a Secret Service detail to each remaining candidate. He simply picked up the telephone and did it by presidential fiat, though he had no such authority. Johnson spent much of the morning on the phone urging congressional leaders to pass a law before somebody called him on it. Violence, Johnson told them, was a disease; it was contagious. Without maximum security the campaign was going to be a shoot-out. After the second political assassination in eight weeks, a Johnson aide recalled, "there wasn't going to be a whole lot of argument about it." Congress acted within twenty-four hours.

Reporters had begun to gather in the West Wing briefing room. LBJ's press secretary George Christian held them off with a brief statement issued in Johnson's name:

> There are no words equal to the horror of this tragedy. Our thoughts and our prayers are with Senator Kennedy, his family, and the other victims.
>
> All America prays for his recovery. We also pray that divisiveness and violence be driven from the hearts of men everywhere.

There was really very little else to be said. It was unseemly to eulogize a man who was not yet dead, though the networks' frequent medical bulletins made it clear that Kennedy was dying, slowly.

Hours later, at lunch with Califano, Christian, and McPherson, Johnson dwelt upon Kennedy's condition and the brutality that plagued America. Johnson was "as concerned and thoughtful as I ever remember him," Califano later judged, but it was obvious from Johnson's look of disbelief that he had not begun to make sense of the tragedy. He was alternately subdued, traumatized, and terribly agitated. During lunch, when an aide informed him that Kennedy was near death, Johnson sighed heavily. "God help the mother of those boys," he said. "Thank God He's given her such faith that she can withstand the tragedies the Good Lord has seen fit to subject her to." Johnson retired to the bedroom for his afternoon nap but was unable to sleep. He clicked on the television, watched it in silence. All networks carried the weary image of Frank Mankiewicz, who gave periodic updates to the cameras at Good Samaritan.

Johnson's grief was more complicated, or conflicted, than Mankiewicz's. As McPherson later observed, Johnson "must have been filled with a hundred competing emotions." Chief among them were horror and anguish. "It didn't matter whether you liked Bobby Kennedy or not," George Christian recalled. "It was a traumatic experience." Lyndon Johnson talked about and talked to the grieving Kennedys; characteristically, though, he could not help but think about himself. He told aides that violence clung to him—not to the Kennedys, but to him— like barnacles. Johnson had but seven months left as president and would consider himself lucky to live through them. He was terrified of meeting the same fate as the Kennedys and King. LBJ had been in the motorcade in Dallas and heard the gunshots that could have taken him down as well, if a Secret Service agent had not thrown himself atop the vice president. And now, with so much hatred loose in the country, Johnson felt vulnerable even in the White House. The number of would-be assailants leaping the gates (before being apprehended by the Secret Service) had skyrocketed since the Kennedy years. Johnson asked his aides to prepare a memo on the mounting threats to his personal safety.

Johnson's role in history was also in jeopardy. Weeks earlier a political cartoonist had sketched a respectable, leather-bound volume labeled *The Johnson Years* flanked—and dwarfed—by majestic bookends labeled *JFK* and *RFK*. The cartoon heralded a second Kennedy presidency, but now its symbolism was even more poignant: Lyndon Johnson's presidency began and was ending in the blood of a Kennedy. It was a cruel symmetry. In a memo to LBJ a few days after the assassination, George Christian worried that in its "aftermath . . . [there] may be a diminishing of public recognition of your contributions as President." Johnson was forever trapped between myth, martyrdom, and what might have been. "It would have been hard on me to watch Bobby march to 'Hail to the Chief,' " Johnson reflected later with obvious bitterness, "but I almost wish he had become President so the country could finally see a flesh-and-blood Kennedy grappling with the daily work of the presidency and all the inevitable disappointments, instead of their storybook image of great heroes who, because they were dead, could make anything anyone wanted happen."

When Christian had released a four-sentence statement in the president's name at 6:45 A.M., reporters assumed Johnson himself would have more to say later. Or would he? Well into the evening Johnson fought off suggestions that he make a televised address. He had never been much of a performer in front of the cameras. He could not pretend to any love for Robert F. Kennedy, and a tearful presidential tribute could only widen the credibility gap. Johnson wondered aloud whether another written statement might be enough, but every adviser told him no, it would not, and that he would appear callous if he did not speak for himself. In the end they prevailed upon Johnson that, as Clark Clifford later put it, "he *had* to set aside his own feelings and speak against the forces of hatred."

Aides set about drafting an appropriate message of condolence for the death that had not yet occurred. The president, meanwhile, had drinks with Senators Everett Dirksen and Mike Mansfield and urged them not to launch congressional investigations into the shooting. Investigations, Johnson argued, would only divide the country and cause pain to the Kennedys. And it was not as if the Warren Commission had really resolved anything. Instead, as if by habit, Johnson proposed a commission on violence—to explore not the circumstances of Kennedy's death but "the whys." LBJ knew the public had grown weary of his constant commissions, commissions to study this or look into that—and rightly so, Johnson admitted. But for the time being they would all have to suspend disbelief, including their president. Dirksen and Mansfield nodded agreement.

In the final hours before his televised address, Johnson and a handful of advisers grappled with the brief text. The speech was scheduled for 10:00 P.M., but Johnson felt he should not go on the air until Kennedy had died. As aides scrambled to meet the networks' prime-time deadline, the Secret Service provided the president with minute-by-minute updates on Kennedy's condition: "8:50 P.M. EDT. Heart getting weaker." It was not yet a wake but a macabre waiting game. "Johnson was kind of scurrying around," remembered DeVier Pierson, "and then Kennedy didn't die. He just lingered on and on."

At 10:07, Johnson somberly decided to go ahead. "My fellow citizens," the president began, reading from the TelePrompTer in the Fish Room,

> I speak to you tonight not only as your President, but as a fellow American who is shocked and dismayed, as you are, by the attempt on Senator Kennedy's life. . . .
>
> We do not know the reasons that inspired the attack on Senator Kennedy. We know only that a brilliant career of public service has been brutally interrupted; that a young leader of uncommon energy and dedication, who has served his country tirelessly and well, and whose voice and example have touched millions throughout the world, has been senselessly and horribly stricken.
>
> At this moment, the outcome is still in the balance. We pray to God that He will spare Robert Kennedy. . . . The Kennedy family has endured sorrow enough, and we pray that this family may be spared more anguish.
>
> Tonight this Nation faces once again the consequences of lawlessness, hatred, and unreason in its midst. It would be wrong, it would be self-deceptive, to ignore the connection between that lawlessness and hatred and this act of violence. It would be just as wrong, and just as self-deceptive, to conclude from this act that our country itself is sick. . . . Two hundred million Americans did not strike down Robert Kennedy last night any more than they struck down President John F. Kennedy in 1963 or Dr. Martin Luther King in April of this year.

But those awful events give us ample warning that in a climate of
extremism, of disrespect for law, of contempt for the rights of others, violence may bring down the very best among us. . . .
Let us put an end to violence and to the preaching of violence.

Johnson announced the appointment of a National Commission on
the Causes and Prevention of Violence and then, after some closing
words of consolation, retired to the Oval Office to rework the gun control bill Congress had gutted three weeks earlier.

The White House press corps took measure of the man and his staff
and observed the somber faces in the hallways of the West Wing; that
night they filed reports of the president's sincerity. Journalists outside the
briefing room were less convinced. *The Nation* promptly denounced the
president's address as "perfunctory and platitudinous" and argued that
Johnson, in his search for the causes of violence, had typically failed to
look inward. Instead "he responds to events with programmed jerks that
are faithfully echoed in the articulated jerks of his platform delivery.
That," the editors concluded, "is what Robert Kennedy was fighting."

Late that night, Johnson sat in the small study off the Oval Office with
Califano, McPherson, and Pierson. A steward wandered around, asking
ineffectually if anyone wanted a drink. The group, like family members
waiting downstairs for an ailing relative to die, talked disjointedly about
mundanities. At 1:00 in the morning the president wanted dinner. He
convened Califano, Christian, McPherson, and Larry Temple for a sober
roundtable in the mansion. Repeatedly Johnson picked up the telephone
attached under the table and asked the Secret Service man at the other
end: "Is he dead yet?" At other times he nudged Califano and gestured
to the phone in the next room. Califano knew what Johnson wanted
and shuffled off to call Larry Levinson, again and again. Levinson was
relaying messages from the Secret Service in Los Angeles to Califano,
who confided in a muffled voice, "The President's pacing back and
forth, saying, 'I've got to know. Is he dead? Is he dead yet?' "

Levinson was taken aback and grew angry. "Joe, is this something that
he's *wishing* to have happen? Why is he asking it that way?"

Califano had no answers. "I couldn't tell," he recalled, "because Johnson didn't know, whether he hoped or feared the answer would be yes
or no."

At 5:01 A.M. on June 6, the answer was yes, Robert Kennedy was
dead.

That morning Lyndon Johnson read a brief eulogy and declared a day
of national mourning. "Robert Kennedy," he said,

affirmed this country—affirmed the essential decency of its people, their longing for peace, their desire to improve conditions of life for all.

During his life, he knew far more than his share of personal tragedy.

Yet he never abandoned his faith in America. He never lost his confidence in the spiritual strength of ordinary men and women. . . .

Our public life is diminished by his loss.

Yet at the same time Johnson was full of worry that the Kennedy family would request the highest honor to a deceased public servant—a state funeral, with the body lying in state in the Capitol Rotunda. Thankfully, the family decided that the body should instead lie in state at St. Patrick's Cathedral in New York. After the funeral Mass on June 8, Kennedy's body would be carried by train to Washington and buried at Arlington National Cemetery, beside his brother's grave. This, too, alarmed Johnson. The Secret Service advised the president to stay at home rather than attract aspiring assassins. Johnson, in any case, had no wish to enter a church full of grieving Kennedy partisans who had despised him, LBJ, the unfortunate survivor, for nearly a decade.

Johnson was equally concerned—or offended—by Bobby Kennedy's burial site. On the morning of June 6, within hours of Kennedy's death, within hours of declaring Kennedy "a noble and compassionate leader, a good and faithful servant of the people," the president phoned Clark Clifford and demanded to know whether Bobby had the right to be buried at Arlington. "I was stunned," Clifford recalled. "I was dumbfounded." The president's call marked "one of the saddest experiences in my long friendship" with Lyndon Johnson. True, the cemetery was increasingly crowded and RFK was neither a president nor a war hero. But it was not as if Robert Kennedy were undeserving of the honor. Johnson seemed to be fishing for a regulation to keep Bobby out of Arlington, however "irrelevant" the defense secretary considered such regulations to be. Clifford reported that LBJ had clear discretion to bury Bobby in the Kennedy plot at Arlington. To deny the family's wishes was therefore not only cruel, it was politically reckless. Johnson bowed, begrudgingly, to this advice.

Bitterness lingered on both sides. On the night of June 6, members of RFK's Senate staff contacted Loyd Hackler of the White House press office and asked for transcripts of the president's 10:00 statement. Hackler said that the press office was closed, though he would be glad to leave copies at the gate with a White House guard. A Kennedy aide curtly retorted that Hackler should personally bring them to the Senate Office Building. Struggling to remain as courteous as possible, Hackler agreed. Later he reflected that Kennedy's staff "wanted to blame Lyndon Johnson" for the assassination. "Their whole attitude was to blame Lyndon Johnson."

The next evening, Kennedy aides made arrangements for the funeral service and train to Washington. An agenda of the meeting records the question: "Should President Johnson, Mrs. Johnson, Vice President Humphrey be invited?" But there was more here to consider than politics or egos; there was national unity. If death did not dissolve a personal grudge, then there could be little hope for a country torn by division. Johnson (and Lady Bird and the Humphreys) were invited to pay their respects.

Those who had sought in vain to bridge the gap between Johnson and the Kennedys continued their struggle. Califano and Robert McNamara appealed to Johnson on the matter of Bobby's burial site. Bill Moyers called Kennedy's moribund campaign headquarters on L Street in Washington and declared, "I will do anything to help. I will even come and make coffee." The ordained Baptist minister arrived shortly to soothe weary souls and field incoming press calls; and on the evening of Kennedy's burial, Moyers spoke movingly to those who remained at their posts to the end. It was, he said, their final act of service. Then he left to buy candles for a burial that would take place after dark.

On the morning of June 8, a few minutes before the 10:00 A.M. funeral service began, President Johnson and Joe Califano walked humbly into St. Patrick's Cathedral.

"It was a difficult entrance," recalled Califano. The pews were lined with tense faces contorted by grief and, in Califano's view, by anger—anger at Lyndon Johnson. If there was indeed a climate of violence in the country, some mourners reasoned, President Johnson had engendered it. The bombs and mines and napalm in Vietnam attested to that, and the fires in America's cities were testament to another losing war, the one against poverty. The church was filled with men who had once intended—even expected—to change all that by driving LBJ from the White House and putting Robert Kennedy in his place. "Johnson knew all this," Califano reflected. "I could *feel* it as we walked down the aisle." After the services Johnson slipped out as quickly and quietly as he had entered, and flew back to Washington.

A light rain fell that evening as the president's limousine left the White House and sped toward Union Station, arriving shortly before Kennedy's funeral train, right around 9:00. While friends and family members loaded Kennedy's casket into the rear of the hearse, the Johnsons stood respectfully aside with the Humphreys. The president then spoke briefly with Ethel, Ted, and Bobby Jr. and made a slow, grim march toward his limousine. The car slipped discreetly into the middle of the procession, fifteenth in line as the mourners drove toward Arlington Cemetery, pausing briefly at the Justice Department and again at the Lincoln Memorial. Along the way Johnson spoke softly about Rose Kennedy. "That woman," he said, "has suffered more than anyone I know. Her religious faith is what brings her through these tragedies." Lady Bird placed her hand on Lyndon's arm as tears welled up in his eyes.

At the cemetery, the Johnsons stood beside the Kennedys and recited the Lord's Prayer; they knelt on the damp artificial grass with Ethel as she prayed at the grave; and at Ethel's courteous suggestion they left the cemetery ahead of the family, just before 11:00. During the ride to the White House, Johnson spoke not a single word. He left the car and climbed the stairs to the living quarters in silence, and did not emerge until the morning.

On June 19, in a handwritten note, Ethel Kennedy expressed her gratitude to LBJ:

> You and Mrs. Johnson have done so much to help my family and me in the past days. You were both so kind and generous and I shall always remember with deep gratitude your warm and immediate assistance. . . . Your kindnesses, both known and unknown, were many, but they were all surpassed by the feeling of personal human sympathy which you and Mrs. Johnson gave to my children and me and the entire Kennedy family.
>
> We shall always be grateful to you, Mr. President, for honoring Bobby by being at his funeral, by meeting the train in Washington and by accompanying us to Arlington. I shall always remember the goodness of heart which prompted your thoughtfulness, your kindness and your help.
>
> Love, Ethel.

LBJ—"genuinely touched," Califano recalled—wrote back promptly.

> Thank God you have so many who love you nearby, that you have been blessed with so many fine children, and with a strong affirmative spirit in yourself. If there is ever anything I can do to help you or yours in the future, Ethel, I hope you will let me know. So long as I have the power to help, please know that I have the desire to do so.

But first Johnson had his own needs to consider. In a memo to the president, Liz Carpenter, Lady Bird's press secretary, expressed worry that another political assassination and another public funeral had left the country "brainwashed by high drama." For the time being, that drama had eclipsed Johnson's less sensational achievements. "We need some

quick dramatic actions," Carpenter concluded, "that show you are coping with the issue of violence." Approvingly, the president forwarded the
memo to George Christian, who suggested a big push on law and order
and gun control.

Johnson had already introduced a gun control bill, on June 6. In fact,
he had been introducing gun control bills for years with little success.
But now, as he had done so skillfully in 1963 and 1964, Johnson sought
to turn tragedy into legislative triumph. "The hour has come," Johnson
declared on June 6, "for Congress to enact a strong and effective gun
control law, covering the full range of lethal weapons." He proposed a
ban on all mail-order and out-of-state sales of handguns, shotguns, and
rifles and on the sale of guns to minors. He called for the national registration of guns and the licensing of gun owners.

These reforms, Johnson hoped, would be the lasting legacy of Robert
Kennedy's assassination. But by October, when LBJ eventually signed the
Gun Control Act, congressional allies of the gun lobby had stripped the
bill of its provisions for owner licensing and gun registration. Johnson
claimed partial victory—Congress had, at least, ended "murder by mail
order" and sales to minors—but he did not claim it in the name of
Robert Kennedy. In 1964, Johnson had been careful to credit every
stunning achievement to the memory of "our beloved President
Kennedy." But Robert Kennedy had not been president and he was not,
to LBJ, beloved.

In June, LBJ had offered Ethel Kennedy his solemn pledge to do "anything I can do to help you or yours." She made only one request, delivered to Johnson by Robert McNamara: that the federal government help
fund a permanent gravesite for Robert Kennedy beside his brother's.
According to the Defense Department, Bobby's resting place at Arlington was no more than a "temporary location." Naturally, Ethel wanted a
more permanent arrangement, and she commissioned the international-
ly renowned architect I. M. Pei to design a memorial. That was the family's prerogative, fulfilled at the family's expense (more than $500,000).
Ethel merely asked the government to approve the plan and maintain
the landscape—foliage, access roads, and the like.

It was a small, "seemingly routine" request, judged Clark Clifford, the
secretary of defense, and he approved the plan. Paul Nitze, Clifford's
deputy, reported to LBJ that "following the same policy that applied in
the case of President Kennedy, it is appropriate for the government to
fund walkways and other elements of the design incorporated for the use
and convenience of the public." Nitze added that the government's
proper share for maintenance of RFK's gravesite was $431,000, 42 per-

cent of the overall cost (compared to $1,770,000, 76 percent of the total cost for JFK's). That sum was already covered by the Pentagon's budget for fiscal year 1970.

But nothing regarding Robert Kennedy had ever been routine, and LBJ refused to discuss it. Clifford, McNamara, and Califano visited him repeatedly, each urging that he approve Ethel's request, and the president turned them away. He refused to request the $431,000 in his 1968 supplemental budget, his 1969 budget, his 1969 supplemental budget, or his 1970 budget. At the LBJ Ranch on Christmas Eve, the president reviewed a memo outlining the costs of the gravesite in some detail and then told Califano to get even more detail.

On January 12, 1969, during President Johnson's last weekend at Camp David, the Kennedys' intermediaries extracted a victory of sorts: LBJ instructed the Bureau of the Budget to add $431,000 to the president's contingency fund for 1970. Lyndon Johnson, of course, was not going to be president in 1970. He had left the matter to his successor. And in a final, petty display of bitterness undiminished by tragedy, LBJ omitted specific mention of the Kennedy grave from his budget.

Friday, January 17, 1969, was "LBJ Day"—Lyndon Johnson's last full weekday as president. On the floor of the Senate, Edward Kennedy rose to praise Johnson's accomplishments and to bid farewell to his family's troubles with LBJ. "The circumstances which brought President Johnson to the office he has held made it inevitable that there would be speculations about strained relations between him and my family," said the senator, hastening to add that any differences between LBJ and RFK "came not from personal grievances but from the obligation of men in public life to discharge their responsibilities to the people of the United States as they saw them and from what at the time were fundamental differences over important public policies. I know," Ted Kennedy concluded, "that President Johnson understood this, and history will as well."

President Johnson himself was feeling equally magnanimous. "I don't hold a thing against anyone in this town, or anywhere else," Johnson insisted to a packed auditorium at the National Press Club five days later. "There is not a Republican in the Senate or House that is man enough for me to dislike or hate—or a Democrat, either!"

Robert F. Kennedy's final resting place lies within the rolling sweep of Arlington National Cemetery, not far above the banks of the Potomac River. Several miles south, at the bottom corner of the District of Columbia, the Potomac meets the Anacostia, along which stands another public tribute: Robert F. Kennedy Memorial Stadium. If Johnson required any final proof that even after Bobby's death there remained

Kennedy men in his midst, covertly and gleefully subverting "the Johnson interest," RFK Stadium was it.

The idea was Bill Geoghegan's. Geoghegan, a wry Washington lawyer, had served under Bobby Kennedy at the Justice Department. David Black was LBJ's under secretary of the interior and one of Geoghegan's closest friends. Black had never met Kennedy, but had, like so many other young members of the Johnson administration, admired him from afar. In December 1968, Black and his wife had dinner at the Geoghegans' and talked about the presidential transition. "Before you leave the administration," Geoghegan said, half-joking, "there's something you ought to do—as a favor to me and all Kennedy people. Name D.C. Stadium after Robert F. Kennedy."

"What does Interior have to do with that?" Black asked. Geoghegan reminded him that the fifty-thousand-seat D.C. Stadium—home of baseball's Washington Senators and football's Washington Redskins—was built in the late 1950s in Anacostia Park. Like all park areas in the District, Anacostia was national parkland, and therefore under Interior's jurisdiction. Secretary of the Interior Stewart Udall—a John Kennedy appointee, and never a Johnson favorite—could rename the stadium by administrative fiat. To Geoghegan, "RFK Stadium" had a natural ring: RFK had been an athlete (a football player, even) and, more important, had been deeply committed to the District, especially its poorest citizens, many of whom inhabited tiny row houses in the stadium's shadow.

By noon the following Monday, Black had checked Geoghegan's proposal with Udall and the department's top lawyer. Both were enthusiastic if a bit uneasy. Udall had the authority; that was clear. It was equally clear that LBJ would regard "RFK Stadium" in the District as he would a land mine in his anteroom. Udall, who was then sparring with Johnson over a proposal to add millions of acres to the national park system, considered the idea delightfully mutinous. "He knew," recalled an assistant, "it would piss Johnson off immensely." There was particular irony in rumors that Johnson wanted the stadium named for himself—LBJ Stadium.

"Run with it," Udall told Black. Of course, Black would have to tread lightly to avoid stirring LBJ. "It was agreed to keep this absolutely confined, to keep the 'conspiracy' closely guarded," Geoghegan explained later. The handful of "conspirators" also agreed to delay action until the very last weekend of the Johnson presidency, when they would present LBJ with a *fait accompli.*

On Saturday, January 18, less than forty-eight hours before the inauguration of Richard Nixon, David Black submitted his proposal to the three-man D.C. Armory Board, which operated the stadium on behalf of the National Park Service. This was a mere formality. In less than ten minutes the board's chairman pronounced the new name "a good thing," and all three men voted aye. Udall signed the action into law that afternoon. "Like his brother," Udall declared, "Robert Kennedy left a mark on the nation's capital. Bob was spartan in his adherence to physical fitness, he loved the out-of-doors, he loved people and he gloried in the competition of sports." Udall then left for the Justice Department to witness the unveiling of a bust of Robert Kennedy.

When Udall returned to Interior his eyes were red and full of water, his voice hoarse and heavy. Don't bother calling the press about RFK Stadium, Udall instructed Charlie Boatner, his press aide; I've already done it. "Did you tell the White House?" Boatner asked, aghast. Boatner was an old Fort Worth journalist, a friend of Johnson's since the 1950s. Scornfully, he believed that Udall was trying to work his way back into "the Kennedy scheme."

"I didn't have to tell the White House," Udall replied.

"I know that," Boatner said, increasingly agitated, "but do you think it was the political thing to do, [naming] it without telling the White House?"

It was politically provocative, even hostile, and Udall well understood it. Word reached the Oval Office not by messenger, memo, or telephone but by news ticker. Johnson, blindsided by a member of his own cabinet, "reacted accordingly," as George Christian recalled. Enraged, Johnson called his interior secretary and, according to David Black, "really called Udall on the carpet . . . really chewed his ass." And on Monday morning, as LBJ dressed for the inauguration ceremony, he gave Udall's proposed land grants a cursory glance, signed the small grants, and rejected the big ones—including a million-acre grant in Udall's home state of Arizona.

"If I had named the stadium after Lyndon Johnson," a bitter Udall told friends, "we would have had all seven million acres."

Among Kennedy partisans, this became popular lore in later years, passed along with a bemused shake of the head and the question: Can you believe Johnson could be so petty? Sadly, it was utterly believable. In fairness, Johnson's rejection of the land grants had less to do with RFK Stadium than with Udall's shoddy homework on the Hill and his clumsy attempts to force LBJ's hand on the parklands. But to David Black and numerous others, it remained a clear "cause and effect proposition." To spite the memory of Robert Kennedy, President Johnson had denied the nation an enduring gift.

By the end of January the incoming administration of Richard Nixon had "discovered" an unidentified $431,000 in the budget for fiscal year

1970 and readily authorized a permanent gravesite for Robert F. Kennedy. President Nixon, said press secretary Ronald Ziegler, was "favorably disposed to the proposal."

Epilogue

Lyndon Johnson wrote in his memoirs that his troubled relationship with Robert Kennedy "was not so much a question of issues. . . . Perhaps his political ambitions were part of the problem. Maybe it was just a matter of chemistry." Of course, it was all of these things—issues, politics, personalities—and there is no simple equation to determine what mattered most. Issues divided personalities, grudges stoked policy disputes, honest differences created political opportunities and vice versa. Where a "grudge" ended and an "honest difference" began was anyone's guess.

The distinction, though, is important in what it says about these two men. As Johnson's memoirs reveal, his antagonism to RFK was firstly personal and ultimately political. It was not at heart a dispute over policy in Vietnam, the war on poverty, or competing visions of the Kennedy legacy. "On most matters of national importance we had similar views," Johnson wrote. "We even agreed on Vietnam for a long time." In fact they had never really agreed, but Johnson was hardly schooled in or concerned with the nuances of RFK's counterinsurgency theory. Johnson's perception of Kennedy was forever rooted in 1962, when the attorney general stood in the Saigon airport and pledged to "do what is necessary" to defend South Vietnam. That pledge fell to Johnson to fulfill, and the burden broke him. He could never accept Kennedy's subsequent retreat as anything but tactical, driven by the basest political motives.

In Johnson's wartime lexicon, "principled opposition" was an oxymoron. When Congressman Tip O'Neill split with the administration on Vietnam—relatively late, in September 1967—Johnson dressed him down in the Oval Office. "Tip, what kind of a son-of-a-bitch are you?" Johnson shouted. As O'Neill justified himself, unburdening a conscience

465

weary and troubled by the war, Johnson was almost baffled by the congressman's sincerity. "Is that what you think?" Johnson asked. "I thought you did this for political reasons." It was a revelation for the president: "You're doing this," he repeated, seemingly awestruck, "because you really believe it." If LBJ appeared forgiving, it was because he and O'Neill were friendly and, more important, O'Neill agreed to keep quiet on the war. Johnson and Kennedy had no such relationship and, certainly, no such understanding. To LBJ, Kennedy's changing views constituted betrayal, not evolution.

Perhaps Johnson resented Kennedy's freedom to evolve. Kennedy was not president: he could ruminate endlessly, he could propose alternative policies, but he did not have to commit himself to a particular course of action. Except on matters concerning New York State, Kennedy was under little pressure actually to *do* anything, so long as he articulated problems and appeared in constant motion. Kennedy could call for an end to the war, but only Johnson could end it. Thus Johnson's burden, in his own, jaundiced view, became Kennedy's political opportunity. LBJ wallowed too deeply in self-pity to perceive that Kennedy's opposition to the war was hurting Kennedy, not Johnson, in the polls.

This was typical of LBJ. Behind every Kennedy position, he perceived a Kennedy scheme. "His major weakness," George Reedy said of Johnson, "is [his] assumption that . . . every move that people make has to have a logical purpose," has to fit neatly into a secret agenda. As majority leader, Johnson had been more perceptive than this. His great skill, as one aide put it, had been to understand "what makes men do things." Neither envy nor contempt then blinded Johnson to a man's motive. After all, the Senate was full of men he disliked—Paul Douglas of Illinois was self-righteous, William Proxmire of Wisconsin was an ingrate, Albert Gore of Tennessee was inflexibly liberal—and though the majority leader could not control these colleagues he could, most of the time, manage them. But the presidency was different from the Senate leadership. The power of the executive was far greater, but harder for Johnson to wield. As Fred Dutton observed, LBJ was a born "inside operator. He understood a finite system magnificently. He never learned to deal . . . with an unlimited environment of variables, whether it was the American electorate or the international scene. He needed to have a chess board." When LBJ complained in 1960 that he lacked "the training or the temperament for the presidency," it had the ring of disingenuousness, but in four years Johnson himself had come to believe it. And if the presidency was not the Senate, Bobby Kennedy was not Douglas, Proxmire, or Gore. Bobby was *harder,* somehow; he could not be bent or mastered. LBJ sought men's vulnerabilities, and in Kennedy he found none.

Kennedy was not susceptible to Johnson's charm, flattery, or intimidation. Kennedy did not fear Johnson—Johnson feared Kennedy, and hated him for it.

Of course, Johnson had hated him almost from the beginning, before Bobby had any independent power, back when Bobby was only part (or engineer) of a larger Kennedy machine. Here Johnson's "bad chemistry" thesis is more persuasive. Bobby Kennedy had always been an easy man to hate. As late as May 1967, Gallup revealed RFK's "intensely dislike" rating among the public to be more than 50 percent higher than LBJ's. In 1968, James Reston noted that "you can't even ride with the Irish cabbies in Boston without hearing some vicious remark about Bobby's policies or his person. . . . The opposition to him is personal, almost chemical, and sometimes borders on the irrational." Throughout his presidency, LBJ was often seized by this sort of irrationality. Again, it had not always been so: during his Senate years Johnson had bounced back resiliently, apparently undiminished by any setback. He was sensitive to slights, but never known to "twist the knife in anybody," as Harry McPherson put it. Johnson's axiom was pragmatism: "Before you do anything," Johnson once lectured an aide, "your last thought ought to be 'I've got to live with the son-of-a-bitch.' " But as president, McPherson recalled, LBJ "developed more of a feeling of ornery independence . . . and would not embrace people whom he felt bitterly toward." Ornery independence, or bitter isolation. Johnson, who had always held back from a final assault upon a man's dignity, routinely assaulted Kennedy's.

Still, "bad chemistry" is an insufficient explanation of Johnson's war against Kennedy. It was in fact not hatred but fear of Kennedy that defined Johnson's often phobic presidency. LBJ's feelings of political illegitimacy, virtual paranoia, self-pity, his willful blindness—Kennedy brought Johnson's deepest fears and most self-destructive tendencies to the surface. It was as if he were created to remind Johnson that his political hold was never secure, his claim to the presidency was never legitimate, and his place in history was never assured. As Bobby came to embody Johnson's worst fears, Bobby himself became Johnson's worst fear. What began as bad chemistry came to represent all the forces that brought Johnson's downfall. The great irony of Johnson's presidency is that by antagonizing Kennedy needlessly, by twisting the knife, Johnson pushed Kennedy inexorably toward the one thing Johnson feared most: a challenge in 1968.

Kennedy always denied that his clash with Johnson was a matter of personalities. He denied it so frequently and vehemently that he seemed to believe it himself. Melody Miller learned this in December 1966 when she attended a Christmas party at Hickory Hill. The twenty-year-old Miller was an occasional aide; she worked for Kennedy during her vacations from Penn State. Spotting her from across the room, Kennedy approached, warmly welcomed her back, and began to "really give me the third degree" about the state of campus politics, Miller recalled. She told Kennedy that students were growing restless in their concern about Vietnam. Part of the problem, she confided, was that students "were not particularly enamored of Lyndon Johnson." Johnson was backward; he was boorish.

Kennedy looked at her darkly and said, "That's an unacceptable reason to be against Lyndon Johnson." That was the word she would always remember: *unacceptable.* Criticizing policies, Kennedy implied, was one thing; mocking accents and regionalisms was quite another. After all, there were plenty of acceptable reasons to be against Lyndon Johnson.

Evidently this was a very different RFK from the one who had tossed about a Johnson voodoo doll at Hickory Hill in the early sixties. In those days Kennedy's distaste for Johnson was deeply personal and visceral. From their first encounters, he saw Johnson as more than a political adversary—LBJ was a glad-handing, deal-making, old-style adversary who not only broke his promises (namely, his pledge not to interfere with John Kennedy's campaign for president) but also made scurrilous charges (about Joseph Kennedy's politics and JFK's health). In Bobby's uncharitable estimation, LBJ was everything that he hated: a phony, a liar, a moral coward. This was a political battle that Bobby Kennedy took personally. He took most battles personally: whether they came from Roy Cohn or Jimmy Hoffa or Lyndon Johnson, any challenges—to himself, his family, or his ideals—were a personal affront.

In one sense John Kennedy's assassination changed nothing. Bobby continued to take offense at most misunderstandings with LBJ, even describing him as "an animal in many ways." But in another sense the assassination changed everything. With JFK's death, Johnson had inherited what was most precious to Bobby: the Kennedy legacy. Accordingly, Bobby's animus shifted—from Johnson's personality to his policies. By Christmas 1966 it was entirely in character for Kennedy to chastise a young aide for making gibes at Johnson, because the feud now was about so much more than mannerisms. It was about the war, the cities, the racial divide, and the generation gap.

Was this a new Robert Kennedy? LBJ did not think so. He believed that Kennedy cultivated issues carefully and cynically, driving little wedges into Johnson's coalition. If so, then the feud was not a question of issues; it was a question of politics driven by a personal vendetta. But Johnson was only partly correct. He was right to describe RFK as a

political creature—canny, competitive, and successful, neither fully altruistic nor ascetic, eager for the spotlight and the credit. It was not happenstance that by 1968 Kennedy had assembled what Peter Edelman
called the legislative "guts of a presidential campaign." Kennedy's mounting political challenge to Johnson was evident to all.

Still, as *The Nation* pointed out during the rural hunger crisis of 1967,
"Robert Kennedy could put aside personal politics—for mercy's sake."
He supported the Great Society even when its funding and philosophy
struck him as inadequate. He backed the administration in 65 percent of
all roll-call votes, not a terribly high number but more than Eugene
McCarthy, LBJ's first challenger in 1968. And though displays of loyalty
paid political dividends, Kennedy supported Johnson not only when it
was wise, but when it was, in his view, right. Kennedy was capable of
admitting, as he did in 1964, that "I think his reaction on a lot of things
is correct."

A lot of things, but not the war. For Kennedy, the feud was all about
the war. "The rest," said Adam Walinsky, "was prologue." It was the war,
not a vendetta, that propelled Kennedy into outright opposition. It was
Johnson's apparent misuse of power, not simply his possession of the
presidency, that sparked the Kennedy challenge. In December 1967, as
his advisers debated a run for the White House, Kennedy halted a conversation concerning his future and the party's future. "He did think
another factor should be weighed," Arthur Schlesinger recorded in his
journal, "i.e., the country. He was not sure whether the country or the
world could survive five more years of Johnson." Whether it was arrogance, messianism, or the simple truth, Kennedy ultimately believed he
was the only one capable of stopping Johnson, and when he concluded
that the country could not survive another Johnson presidency, he
entered the race. His convictions and his contempt for LBJ had never
been more inextricably bound.

Some Johnson partisans grumbled that Kennedy's contempt shaped
his convictions, not the reverse. "Subconsciously," George Reedy later
asserted, "Bobby developed the antiwar issue because it was anti-Johnson." But even Kennedy's friends were not privy to his subconscious, and
the evidence does not confirm Reedy's claim. Kennedy often *skirted*
issues like the war precisely because they were anti-Johnson, or were
portrayed as such. The inevitable "feud" headlines inhibited Kennedy,
not only because they made him look ruthless and petty but also because
they obscured real differences on important issues. Had Johnson died in
1965 and Hubert Humphrey escalated the war, Kennedy, freed of the
feud, might well have grown more strident in his opposition. To argue
otherwise is to embrace one of Johnson's contradictory caricatures of

RFK: that everything he did sprang from either a cool, rational, electoral calculus or a hateful vengeance. In fact Kennedy was both shrewd and earnest, cautious and reckless, and callous and compassionate. He was, in his complexity, more like Lyndon Johnson than either man imagined.

The feud that helped define the public lives of LBJ and RFK also helped shape the two greatest national undertakings of their times—the war on poverty and the war in Vietnam. Consumed by contempt for Kennedy, Johnson transformed a potential ally into an archenemy, rendering the poverty program an imbalanced, unworkable amalgam of his own New Deal grandiosity and Kennedy's insurgent community activism. Johnson's homefront "war" thus degenerated, tragically, into a series of skirmishes—many of the ugliest and most brutal within the same camp. "How can they be so petty?" Kennedy asked a friend in 1967, after the administration had undercut his ghetto development plan and introduced its own less ambitious bill. "They didn't even try to work something out together. To them it's all just politics." Together Johnson and Kennedy could not have eradicated poverty in America, but the political power and moral force of their united effort could have shaken its foundations.

If the feud weakened the war effort at home, it may have intensified it abroad. "Ho Chi Minh," Johnson reflected, "was [trying] to win in Washington . . . to win in the homes of this country what he could not win from the men out there" in uniform. In this sense, Bobby Kennedy was as dangerous an opponent as Ho, or more. And in the battle for public opinion, only Bobby, not Ho (or Fulbright or McCarthy), could hold Johnson accountable to the Kennedy legacy. Every time Bobby spoke a word of dissent it begged the question: what would Jack have done? Although Johnson had surrounded himself with JFK's best and brightest—Bundy, McNamara, Rostow, Rusk—Bobby seemed far better qualified to answer that question. Between John Kennedy's policy and Johnson's, Bobby said flatly in 1967, "there is a contradiction." And if changing policies meant conceding Bobby's point, Lyndon Johnson would stay the course.

It is impossible to say whether Johnson would have pursued a different path in Vietnam had RFK remained either silent or supportive. But it can be said with certainty that Robert Kennedy was a significant psychological element in Johnson's thinking about the war—one of many elements, to be sure, but a crucial one. "Kennedy's mere existence intensified Johnson's terror of withdrawing from Vietnam," Doris Kearns concluded after months of discussions with LBJ. Johnson told her that if he had withdrawn from Vietnam, the dovish Bobby Kennedy would have turned hawk, "telling everyone," Johnson said, "that I had betrayed John Kennedy's commitment. That I had let a democracy fall into the hands of the Communists. That I was a coward. An unmanly man. A man without a spine. Oh, I could see it coming, all right." Was this a deep-seated fear, a clever rationale, or both? With Johnson one could never be sure.

As Johnson and Kennedy became ever more bitter enemies, they divided constituencies they once shared, weakening their party by forcing its members to choose between them. They exposed and exacerbated the growing divide within the Democratic Party and American politics in general. But were they becoming different kinds of Democrats? According to Kennedy's supporters he was a man of (or ahead of) his time, beyond LBJ, even "beyond liberalism." Apostles of the so-called New Politics claimed Kennedy as their "avatar" and LBJ as their "antichrist."

The New Politics, a term very much in vogue in the late 1960s, was notoriously ill defined—"Silly Putty," scoffed one political analyst. But by any definition Kennedy was its god, and Johnson—not the racist demagogue George Wallace, or the premier hawk, General William Westmoreland—its devil. To partisans on either side, the clash between Johnson and Kennedy was as elemental as that between good and evil. Of course, on the continuum of American politics, ranging from left to right, Kennedy and Johnson were not terribly far apart. They agreed on the fundamentals. Both men accepted America's right to intervene deeply in world affairs and its obligation to counter Communist aggression abroad. They shared a faith in the redemptive role of government at home. They rejected the New Left's anticapitalist critique and firmly believed that the American political system held the keys to its own renewal. "At this point," wrote a disappointed Robert Scheer in the left-wing magazine *Ramparts* in 1967, "Kennedy's program for America differs in no essential way from that of LBJ or any other mainstream politician."

But this charge, like the god/devil dichotomy, was a bit overheated. Though LBJ represented the status quo in some ways, he was hardly conventional: his hubris and vision distinguished him as the most activist president since Franklin Roosevelt. Johnson installed the most innovative thinkers on his task forces, pumping their pilot programs full of federal funds. "He tried so avidly to embrace the new," recalled Adam Walinsky admiringly. "Lyndon was much bolder about civil rights legislation, for example, than the Kennedys ever would have been." But then the riots broke Johnson's spirit, and the war drained the coffers and killed his credibility. And Bobby Kennedy drew the spotlight, if he had not always held it. By 1968, Johnson seemed spent, a relic, the archetype of a stubborn, dogmatic, dying brand of liberalism. And Bobby Kennedy, in the nine years since he carried a secret deal for the Democratic nomination to the LBJ Ranch, had seemed to travel very far indeed. He had been in constant motion—creating a new image, laboring to build a new coalition, and posing new questions and new ideas.

Image was not everything, but it was surely important. To the emerging advocates of the New Politics, Johnson's style was almost as objectionable as the war. Jack Newfield wrote that "the New Class . . . abhorred [Johnson's] deceitfulness, his corniness, his crudity." And in an age enthralled (or appalled) by youth, LBJ seemed out of step. He was at ease with high school students, 4-H clubs, Boys' Nation—clean-cut, hardworking kids who bought into the system. But the college students, the demonstrators, the long-hairs in their blue jeans, baffled Johnson. He could not understand their naked hostility toward a system—and a president—that had given them so much, from better schools to bigger scholarships. "Don't they realize I'm really one of them?" he asked plaintively in his retirement. "I always hated cops when I was a kid, and just like them I dropped out of school and took off for California. I'm not some conformist middle-class personality. I could never be bureaucratized." This was truer than the students imagined. The real LBJ was no organization man, no McNamara. The real LBJ was sarcastic and caustic and suspicious of authority. As if to prove it, when he retired to his ranch, LBJ grew his hair long and unruly.

Bobby Kennedy's hair was almost perpetually shaggy, but, more important, he was young, direct, and dynamic; and he evoked the anger, irony, and moral stridency of the New Politics. Every public rebuff by the administration lent the former attorney general a "rebel" air. Like many young Americans, he felt frustrated and alienated. And like them he read (on occasion) the *Village Voice* and Tom Hayden's *Rebellion in Newark*; gamely, he listened to records by Bob Dylan and Jefferson Airplane, as if sampling a curious ethnic cuisine. If there was a whiff of radical chic about listening to "White Rabbit" in a penthouse apartment, Kennedy was not so much trendy as insatiably curious, and reports of these "experiments" gave him a certain street credibility among the young and disaffected. "They respond to his hangups," wrote journalist Penn Kimball in 1968.

Posturing, though, was less important than party-building. Johnson had done little of that, purposefully leaving the Democratic National Committee weak and underfunded, too impotent for insurgency. LBJ's "politics of consensus" were also foundering. Few Republicans who voted Democratic in 1964 had been truly for Johnson; they had been against Goldwater, and they did not switch party allegiance after that.

Indeed, the yearly spectacle of burning and looting in America's cities cost Johnson much of his conservative support just as the war cost him the liberals. In this environment, consensus was a fantasy. And though Johnson held on to the unions and the South, the Democratic base even there was cracking.

"I think there has to be a new kind of coalition to keep the Democratic party going, and to keep the country together," Kennedy told Newfield during the 1968 campaign. ". . . We have to write off the unions and the South now, and replace them with Negroes, blue-collar whites, and the kids. If we can do that, we've got a chance to do something. We have to convince the Negroes and poor whites that they have common interests. If we can reconcile those two hostile groups, and then add the kids, we can really turn this country around." If Kennedy was in fact writing off the unions and the South, it was largely because they had already written him off. But Kennedy had never much liked union bosses anyway. Instead he courted rank-and-file members. Many businessmen were for LBJ, but Kennedy, like his father, had always considered them "sons of bitches"; despite public-private enterprises like Bedford-Stuyvesant, in 1968 Kennedy sought converts in the tenements, not the boardrooms. Coalition politics, as a friend of Kennedy's commented, had become "a floating crap game" and Kennedy was hovering around the perimeters, watching the game evolve and trying to get a sense of the rules, if there were any. As the traditional Democratic alliance fragmented, Kennedy scrambled for the pieces that fit his own political needs and personal temperament. Blacks and working-class whites, antiwar liberals and moderates—they were Kennedy's natural constituencies and his only chance at success in 1968.

The Democratic disaffected had lost faith in LBJ, despite all he had done or tried to do, and he had lost faith in them. He took their attraction to Kennedy as a deeply personal affront. Consumed by the war and bitterly resentful of black "subversives," Johnson effectively cut poverty and civil rights from his agenda. By 1967, he spoke less of hope and progress than of safe streets and crime control—"euphemisms," scoffed Pat Moynihan, "for the forcible repression of black violence." When the President's Commission on Civil Disorders proposed a range of "traditional" policies to quiet urban unrest, LBJ refused even to read the report. A burgeoning backlog of task force reports collected dust; Johnson ignored some, rebuffed others, and even suppressed one (on rural poverty, a "Kennedy issue"). In 1968, Moynihan likened Johnson's domestic agenda to the Alliance for Progress: "a vast and noble commitment now pretty much in mothballs."

Kennedy, too, was losing his taste for vast commitments, but for different reasons. The wartime budget precluded grandiose, Johnsonian programs, and perhaps, Kennedy thought, this was for the best. "We had learned enough about bureaucracies," Walinsky later explained, "to make us profoundly distrustful of the notion that the government could do more than set a direction or create a set of incentives and opportunities." As the flaws in the Great Society began to mount, Kennedy became the first Democrat of real prominence to acknowledge the limits of government action—the first to argue that traditional, centralized solutions were not working and, perhaps, could not work. "Reliance on government," Kennedy declared, "is dependence and what the people in our ghettos need is . . . independence, not the charity and favor of their fellow citizens, but equal claim of right and equal power to enforce those claims." He endorsed direct, noncategorical federal aid to state and local governments—an early notion of "block grants" borrowed from House Republicans. In 1967, the left-wing *Ramparts* compared him to Ronald Reagan. Kennedy was eroding the distinction between liberal and conservative; if he subscribed to any particular doctrine it was pragmatism—infused with characteristic moral urgency.

Kennedy offered few solutions. But he was asking the right questions, the ones that LBJ was becoming too rigid or resentful to ask. Did the government create opportunity or stifle it? Was the domino theory defunct? How did one weigh the national interest against human anguish? Kennedy had begun an essential, agonizing reappraisal of government action at home and intervention abroad. He promised to reform what Johnson had done, not to undo it. He had not toppled Lyndon Johnson but transcended him.

Thirty years later, the Johnson-Kennedy antagonism continues to cast a long shadow over American politics. In 1992, Bill Clinton ran for president as a self-styled "New Democrat," a self-proclaimed heir to Robert Kennedy's progressive yet pragmatic brand of liberalism. Clinton's nomination at the Democratic National Convention followed a twenty-minute documentary film on RFK. On the eve of his inauguration, Clinton knelt beside Kennedy's grave at Arlington. Then, within months, the new president seemed charged by a faith in government that rivaled Lyndon Johnson's: Clinton's proposed system of universal health care might well have been designed by one of LBJ's task forces. That debt, of course, went unacknowledged. The Great Society, like Lyndon Johnson himself, stood now largely in ill repute, victim of their own bloated expectations, their manifest failings, and the harshness of Republican rhetoric. Mindful of this and of the scars of Vietnam, Clinton never once invoked Johnson's name.

The failure of the Clinton health plan—and, two years later, the debate among Democrats over a Republican welfare reform bill—revealed a party deeply at odds with itself over the role of government and the efficacy of its programs. Some Democrats, evoking Kennedy's concern for those on the margins, also echoed his suspicion of centralization and disdain for bureaucracy. They crafted gradual, targeted, piecemeal reforms. Others held fast to Johnson's belief that only big government can protect citizens from the vicissitudes of the free market and, as he put it, "remedy the public failures which are at the root of so many human ills."

Robert Kennedy, by his courage and his martyrdom, had long ago won the hearts of Democrats. But Lyndon Johnson had by no means relinquished the battle for their souls.

Notes

INTRODUCTION

3 *"mean, bitter, vicious"*: Edwin O. Guthman and Jeffrey Shulman, eds., *Robert Kennedy: In His Own Words* (New York: Bantam, 1988): 417.

3 *"grandstanding little runt"*: Arthur M. Schlesinger, Jr., *Robert Kennedy and His Times* (New York: Ballantine, 1978): 933.

3 *Lyndon Johnson and Bobby Kennedy*: Most of Robert Kennedy's friends and colleagues called him "Bob." As one friend recalled, " 'Bobby' was reserved for two classes of people: . . . members of the family and those who tried to appear as if they knew him well, and didn't." Detractors like LBJ also delighted in using RFK's childhood diminutive. Yet Robert Kennedy in the public imagination was consistently (and often affectionately) "Bobby." As "Robert" remains a bit formal and "Bob" unfamiliar, I bow to common parlance. The journalist Penn Kimball noted in 1968, "To call him by a name different from that invariably used by his family and elder brother seems as false to most Americans as to call Babe Ruth 'George.' " Geoghegan OH, JFKL; Penn Kimball, *Bobby Kennedy and the New Politics* (Englewood Cliffs, NJ: Prentice-Hall, 1968): 3.

4 *"You're lucky you've been born poor"*: Hugh Sidey, "He Makes a Truce with a Man He Almost Came to Hate—LBJ," *Life*, Nov. 18, 1966: 39; Sidey OH, LBJL.

4 *Kennedy spoke in monosyllables*: Schlesinger, *Robert Kennedy*, 47.

4 *"a matter of chemistry"*: Lyndon Baines Johnson, *The Vantage Point: Perspectives of the Presidency, 1963–1969* (New York: Holt, Rinehart & Winston, 1971): 539.

4 *neither man saw real combat*: See Robert A. Caro, *The Years of Lyndon Johnson: Means of Ascent* (New York: Knopf, 1990): 33–43; and Schlesinger, 55–66.

4 *"snot-nosed kid"*: Paul R. Henggeler, *In His Steps: Lyndon Johnson and the Kennedy Mystique* (Chicago: Ivan R. Dee, 1991): 62.

4 *"my ancestors were teachers"*: Robert Dallek, *Lone Star Rising: Lyndon Johnson and His Times, 1908–1960* (New York: Oxford University Press, 1991): 14.

4 *the Johnson family's fortunes*: Ibid., 28, 31, 48.

4 *The Johnsons earned a certain notoriety*: Robert A. Caro, *The Years of Lyndon Johnson: Path to Power* (New York: Knopf, 1982): xvii–xviii, 83, 96–7.

4 *the boyhood homes of Robert Francis Kennedy*: Schlesinger, *Robert Kennedy*, 12.

5 *the Kennedys were newcomers*: Johnson's English and Scottish ancestors arrived in America as early as the mid-eighteenth century; John Johnson, LBJ's great-great-grandfather, fought for American independence. Kennedy's great-grandparents emigrated from Ireland a century later. Dallek, 14, 16; Schlesinger, 4–5; Nigel Hamilton, *JFK: Reckless Youth* (New York: Random House, 1992): 12, 15, 20–23.

5 *"used his money to free us"*: Schlesinger, *Robert Kennedy*, 21.

5 *Johnson dogged his father's footsteps*: Dallek, *Lone Star Rising*, 50.

5 *"reason you right out of your shoes"*: Georgia C. Edgeworth, quoted in *ibid.*, 52.

5 *Bobby's grandfather Honey Fitz*: Schlesinger, *Robert Kennedy*, 5, 7, 15–16, 45.

6 *"You can't get any work out of a politician"*: Ibid., 101–2.

6 *"a hell of a way"*: Udall interview.

6 *"You couldn't help but like him"*: James H. Rowe, Jr., quoted in Dallek, *Lone Star Rising,* 163.

6 *"On many important occasions"*: Helen Gahagan Douglas (D-CA), quoted in *ibid.*, 278. On LBJ's ideological flexibility, see *ibid.*, 275–8.

6 *Bobby had always been sensitive*: Schlesinger, *Robert Kennedy*, 128.

6 *"Just fierce!"*: Spalding OH, JFKL.

6 *the Kennedys played touch football*: Lawrence F. O'Brien, *No Final Victories: A Life in Politics—from John F. Kennedy to Watergate* (Garden City, NY: Doubleday, 1974): 45–6.

7 *Johnson, too, was easily wounded*: Dallek, *Lone Star Rising,* 42, 354; Reedy OH, LBJL.

7 *At a radio and television correspondents' dinner*: Huntley OH, LBJL.

7 *"an underdog in sports"*: David Hackett, quoted in Schlesinger, *Robert Kennedy*, 49–50.

7 *Sam Johnson took up unpopular causes*: Dallek, *Lone Star Rising,* 48–9, 169, 275–6.

7 *"Some men," Johnson reflected*: Doris Kearns, *Lyndon Johnson and the American Dream* (New York: Harper & Row, 1976): 54.

8 *"A successful investigation of Sputnik"*: Schlesinger, *Robert Kennedy*, 161.

9 *"anyone who writes with certainty"*: Edwin O. Guthman, *We Band of Brothers* (New York: Harper & Row, 1971): 251.

9 *Observations are scattered*: The same may be said of oral history interviews and, specifically, recollections of exact conversations. In assembling this narrative history I have naturally relied upon both—for while it may be impossible for participants to recall the exact words of long-ago conversations, it remains possible to recall the essence of a conversation. Still, I use participants' recollections with discretion, matching one credible source with others where possible, and I do not "reconstruct" or "imagine" any conversations.

9 *after a White House dance*: Schlesinger, *Robert Kennedy*, 672.

CHAPTER 1: PRELUDE TO A FEUD

10 *Bobby Kennedy's overnight stay*: Dallek, *Lone Star Rising,* 559; Rowland Evans and Robert Novak, *Lyndon B. Johnson: The Exercise of Power* (New York: Signet, 1968): 262; Bobby Baker with Larry L. King, *Wheeling and Dealing: Confessions of a Capitol Hill Operator* (New York: W. W. Norton, 1978): 42–3.

11 *"Mr. Johnson took to the Senate"*: Merle Miller, *Lyndon: An Oral Biography* (New York: G. P. Putnam's Sons, 1980): 141(emphasis in original).

11 *Johnson secured a largely ceremonial, procedural post*: Bruce J. Schulman, *Lyndon B. Johnson and American Liberalism: A Brief Biography with Documents* (Boston: Bedford Books, 1995): 42–3.

11 *Johnson's hold over his colleagues*: Evans and Novak, 104.

12 *Humphrey of Minnesota would slink*: Rowe OH, LBJL.

12 *The Johnson Treatment was partly intuitive*: Kearns, 122–4; Dallek, *Lone Star Rising*, 474–5.

12 *"He was sort of like a cowboy"*: Humphrey OH, LBJL.

12 *"He played it like an organ"*: Sidey OH, LBJL.

12 *Johnson's mastery of the Senate*: Harry C. McPherson, *A Political Education* (Boston: Little, Brown, 1972): 122; Schulman, 42, 45–6; Dallek, *Lone Star Rising*, 361–3.

12 *In Sidey's view*: Sidey OH, LBJL.

12 *Yet Johnson maintained great respect*: Dallek, *Lone Star Rising*, 426–7, 433–8; Schulman, 46–7.

13 *"On any major piece of legislation"*: Evans and Novak, 112 (emphasis in original); Cater OH, LBJL; McPherson, 158–9.

13 *"These were glory years"*: Daniel Patrick Moynihan, foreword to McPherson, xiii–xiv.

13 *"I'm bursting with pride"*: Clifford OH, LBJL.

13 *LBJ's status as congressional colossus*: McPherson, 123–4.

13 *If any ambition surpassed Johnson's reach*: Schulman, 49–50.

13 *Yet a formidable obstacle*: Ibid., 51–3; Dallek, *Lone Star Rising*, 496–7.

14 *Johnson had promoted himself*: In 1956, LBJ made a tentative, ill-fated native son's grab at the Democratic nomination for president, but he had yet to be "tested" in any real sense. See Dallek, *Lone Star Rising*, 488–93, 501–7.

14 *1959 found LBJ in low spirits*: Theodore H. White, *The Making of the President 1960* (New York: New American Library, 1961): 155; McPherson, 168–70; Dallek, *Lone Star Rising*, 547–57.

14 *As 1960 approached*: Dallek, *Lone Star Rising*, 547–57.

15 *"everybody in the Senate"*: Dallek, *Lone Star Rising*, 562.

15 *Plagued by fears of another heart attack*: Paul K. Conkin, *Big Daddy from the Pedernales* (Boston: Twayne, 1986): 146.

15 *he told his friend Jim Rowe*: Rowe OH, LBJL.

15 *"He wanted it so much"*: Ibid.; Dallek, *Lone Star Rising*, 544.

15 *"I don't want to get a bug"*: Evans and Novak, 261, 263.

15 *"There are times when my heart"*: Cater OH, LBJL.

15 *Past political scares loomed*: Johnson defeated popular Texas Governor Coke Stevenson in a Senate primary that Robert Caro has persuasively argued was "stolen" by LBJ, whose partisans likely stuffed a number of ballots. See Caro, *Means of Ascent*.

16 *Nor did Johnson wish to forfeit*: Dallek, *Lone Star Rising*, 546; Christian interview.

16 *He scattered campaign funds*: Evans and Novak, 263.

16 *He spoke often in the Northeast*: Dallek, *Lone Star Rising*, 545–6.

16 *Governor Edmund "Pat" Brown of California*: Dutton OH, LBJL.

16 *"All this talk about my candidacy"*: Dallek, *Lone Star Rising*, 545–6.

17 *Throughout 1959, Johnson and his aides*: Ibid.

17 *Senator Joseph McCarthy of Wisconsin*: David M. Oshinsky, *A Conspiracy So Immense: The World of Joe McCarthy* (New York: Free Press, 1983): 252–3; Schlesinger, *Robert Kennedy*, 106–9.

18 *McCarthy and Cohn quickly plunged*: Guthman, 16; Schlesinger, *Robert Kennedy*, 101; Oshinsky, 295–8.

18 *"much more credence . . . than normal"*: Schlesinger, *Robert Kennedy*, 112.

18 *Cohn's petulance had been troubling*: Ibid., 113.

18 *"McCarthy was out of his mind"*: Guthman, 18–19.

18 *"wanted so desperately to be liked"*: Schlesinger, *Robert Kennedy*, 114; Kenneth O'Donnell and K. LeMoyne Billings in Jean Stein interviews, George Plimpton, ed., *American Journey: The Times of Robert Kennedy* (London: Andre Deutsch, 1971): 49–51.

18 *Kennedy returned to the subcommittee staff*: Oshinsky, 361, 401–2, 467–8.

19 *"Tell Jackson we're going to get him"*: Schlesinger, *Robert Kennedy*, 121. The expletive was deleted by a previous storyteller.

19 *a more fruitful field of inquiry*: Ibid., 137, 144; Guthman, 8.

19 *The counsel's office*: Schlesinger, *Robert Kennedy*, 144–6.

20 *"more concerned with what corruption"*: Guthman, 9–10.

20 *Bobby's energy and wry levity*: Pierre Salinger, *With Kennedy* (London: Jonathan Cape, 1966): 19; Salinger OH, JFKL.

20 *"I've seen a lot counsels here"*: Schlesinger, *Robert Kennedy*, 146; Guthman, 70.

20 *Teamsters president Dave Beck*: Salinger OH; Schlesinger, *Robert Kennedy*, 147–9; Guthman, 52–3.

21 *"about the finest job"*: Schlesinger, *Robert Kennedy*, 159.

21 *"My biggest problem as counsel"*: Ibid., 161.

21 *Some political observers*: Ibid., 160–61; Guthman, 55–6.

21 *A Berkeley professor wrote*: Schlesinger, *Robert Kennedy*, 160; Guthman, 8–9.

21 *"got his jollies playing God"*: Schlesinger, *Robert Kennedy*, 174.

22 *"it was the investigation of Beck"*: Guthman, 8; Schlesinger, *Robert Kennedy*, 165.

22 *"Look at him"*: Schlesinger, *Robert Kennedy*, 169–71.

22 *"Candor compels me"*: Ibid., 163–5.

23 *"Jack Kennedy is the first Irish Brahmin"*: Ibid.

23 *Bobby "was neither a natural athlete"*: Ibid., 49.

23 *The Court of St. James's*: The American embassy in London, where Joseph Kennedy served as ambassador from March 1938 to December 1940.

23 *"Bobby's a tough one"*: Schlesinger, *Robert Kennedy*, 104–5.

23 *"were really different generations"*: Billings quoted in Stein interview, Plimpton, ed., 40. Bobby garners only ten mentions in Nigel Hamilton's 900-page biography of JFK to age twenty-nine.

23 *JFK's 1952 Senate race*: O'Donnell quoted in Plimpton, ed., 40–41.

24 *"If you're not going to work"*: Schlesinger, *Robert Kennedy*, 101–3.

24 *"I don't think [Jack] was aware"*: Plimpton, ed., 40.

24 *"almost nothing to do with the operations"*: Feldman interview.

24 *a disheveled paperboy*: English OH, JFKL.

24 *"didn't think of him as a political genius"*: White and Linton interviews.

25 *When the brothers talked politics*: Feldman interview.

25 *Kennedy told columnist Joseph Alsop*: Joseph W. Alsop with Adam Platt, *"I've Seen the Best of It": Memoirs* (New York: W. W. Norton, 1992): 411–12.

25 *"other worlds outside the chamber"*: McPherson, 41–2; Rowe OH, LBJL.

25 *"You're better off than you ever were"*: Plimpton, ed., 65.

25 *JFK might well be the candidate*: Gerald S. and Deborah H. Strober, *"Let Us Begin Anew": An Oral History of the Kennedy Presidency* (New York: HarperCollins, 1993): 1–2; White, *Making 1960*, 67.

25 *"If the Convention ever went"*: White, *Making 1960*, 69–70.

26 *"We knew how it would turn out"*: Ibid., 68–9.

26 *"the final assault plan"*: Ibid.

26 *"Bobby and I ran around"*: Plimpton, ed., 64–5.

26 *"first and only choice"*: Theodore C. Sorensen, *Kennedy* (New York: Harper & Row, 1965): 35, 117.

26 *sixteen of JFK's most important advisers*: White, *Making 1960*, 65, 68–70.

27 *Arthur Schlesinger observed*: Schlesinger, *Robert Kennedy*, 207; Tydings OH, JFKL.

27 *"the baroque tendencies of politics"*: Plimpton, ed., 67–8.

27 *"Bob came out of that campaign"*: Linton interview.

27 *Bobby's standard of performance*: Bernard Boutin in Strober, ed., 6.

28 *"I know nothing about it"*: Transcript of telephone conversation between LBJ and Bill Arbogast, May 24, 1960, 12:45 A.M., "1960," Notes and Transcripts, Box 1, LBJL.

28 *"Just let me do it my way"*: Baker, 119; Marks OH, LBJL.

28 *"we wanted to get out"*: Reedy OH, LBJL.

28 *Jenkins, and the up-and-coming Texas politician*: Jenkins OH, LBJL.

28 *"I've already done everything"*: Baker, 119.

28 *Local Texas politicians*: Rowe OH, LBJL; White, *Making 1960*, 57.

29 *"Senator Humphrey is our big rival"*: Schlesinger, *Robert Kennedy*, 208; Humphrey OH, LBJL.

29 *" 'can't win' bullshit"*: Baker, 121.

29 *"Johnson had a lot to lose"*: Carpenter OH, LBJL; Weisl, Jr., OH, LBJL; Baker, 119.

29 *a conspiracy of "red hots"*: Baker, 45.

29 *his role in the Senate*: McPherson, 51, 177–8; McPherson OH, LBJL.

29 *"a real awakening in American politics"*: Humphrey OH, LBJL.

29 *"they suddenly started to realize"*: O'Donnell OH, LBJL.

30 *"Even I knew better"*: McPherson, 178; Baker, 120; McGovern OH, LBJL.

30 *In Fred Dutton's view*: Dutton OH, LBJL.

30 *Reedy typed a memo*: Dallek, *One Star Rising*, 566 (emphasis in original).

30 *"tell him for me"*: Henggeler, 25–6.

30 *Kennedy intrigued Johnson*: Jenkins OH.

31 *"Jack was doing these incredibly brave things"*: Robert Kintner, quoted in Miller, 343.

31 *Kennedy's womanizing, too*: Baker, 76–7; McPherson interview.

31 *an uncommon interest in the junior senator*: Reedy OH; McPherson OH; LBJ to JFK, Jan. 6, 1954, WHFN-JFK, Box 4, LBJL; Henggeler, 25–8.

31 *"one of the proudest moments"*: LBJ to JFK, Aug. 23, 1956, WHFN-JFK, Box 4, LBJL.

31 *"how proud I am"*: Rowe OH, LBJL; Jenkins OH; LBJ to Joseph P. Kennedy, Aug. 25, 1956, WHFN, Box 5, LBJL.

32 *Joe made a striking offer:* Copyright deposit, unpublished manuscript, "Rendezvous with Democracy: The Memoirs of 'Tommy the Cork' " by Thomas G. Corcoran with Phillip Kopper, p. c/4–9, Corcoran Papers, Box 586A, Library of Congress; Corcoran to LBJ, Oct. 9, 1965, Corcoran Papers, Box 66.

32 *Johnson saw Joe's offer:* Dallek, *Lone Star Rising,* 490–91.

32 *Johnson-Kennedy "dream ticket":* Evans and Novak, 278.

32 *Johnson became solicitous:* Henggeler, 28–30.

32 *pre-presidential jostling brought old resentments:* Krock OH, LBJL; Henggeler, 30–31.

33 *"they were contenders":* Dungan OH, LBJL.

33 *A conversation in March 1958:* O'Neill OH, LBJL; Tip O'Neill with William Novak, *Man of the House: The Life and Political Memoirs of Speaker Tip O'Neill* (New York: Random House, 1987): 101.

33 *Johnson and Sam Rayburn ridiculed Kennedy:* Evans and Novak, 277.

33 *Johnson's loyalists toiled for Humphrey:* Humphrey OH, LBJL; Dallek, *Lone Star Rising,* 566–7.

33 *At the Washington premiere:* Baker, 118–19.

33 *"What are the possibilities":* Rowe OH, LBJL.

34 *"this Catholicism thing":* Transcript of telephone conversation between LBJ and Amon Carter, May 12, 1960, 12:45 A.M., Notes and Transcripts of Johnson Conversations, Box 1, LBJL.

34 *"when it gets down to the nut-cuttin' ":* Baker, 121; Sorensen interview.

34 *He went on the attack:* White, *Making 1960,* 157; Dallek, *Lone Star Rising,* 568–9; Baker, 45.

34 *In a conversation with Peter Lisagor:* Lisagor OH, JFKL; Dallek, *Lone Star Rising,* 572.

35 *the unspeakable truth:* Edwards OH, LBJL; *New York Times,* July 5, 1960: 19.

35 *The news was explosive:* Edwards OH; Herbert S. Parmet, *JFK: The Presidency of John F. Kennedy* (New York: Dial Press, 1983): 18; Clifford interview; Salinger, 40–41; Dallek, *Lone Star Rising,* 572; *New York Times,* July 5, 1960.

35 *doctors had been administering cortisone:* Richard Reeves, *President Kennedy: Profile of Power* (New York: Simon & Schuster, 1993): 24, 42.

36 *Kennedy would blithely outlast the mud-slinging:* Feldman OH, JFKL.

36 *To JFK's campaign staff:* Feldman OH; *New York Times,* July 5, 1960; Feldman interview.

36 *declared himself a candidate:* Chronology of Events Leading up to the 1960 Convention, Pre-Presidential Diary, Box 1, LBJL; *New York Times,* July 6, 1960: 1.

36 *"the sorriest, nastiest [hotel]":* Jacobsen OH, LBJL.

37 *Johnson and Jim Rowe:* Rowe OH, LBJL; Rowe OH, JFKL.

37 *"get it over with":* Reedy OH; Rowe OH, LBJL.

37 *"I think you should know":* Salinger OH.

37 *LBJ raised the sinister specter:* *New York Times,* July 8, 1960: 11.

37 *Bobby Kennedy charged mysteriously:* *New York Times,* July 9, 1960: 1, 8.

38 *Johnson had gone on the record:* Oshinsky, 74–80, 199, 476, 491; Dallek, *Lone Star Rising,* 456–8; Baker, 93.

38 *"Each of us must decide":* Oshinsky, 490–1; Dallek, *Lone Star Rising,* 458; Jenkins OH.

38 *Bobby was a "liberal fascist"*: Clifford, 395; Jenkins OH.

39 *"a fallen-away Kennedy"*: Carpenter interview.

39 *"I was never any Chamberlain"*: *New York Times*, July 14, 1960: 15.

39 *Kennedy spoke of the comment*: Harris OH, JFKL.

39 *Johnson invited Jack Kennedy to debate*: Dallek, *Lone Star Rising*, 573; Valenti OH, LBJL; Sidey OH, JFKL; Roche OH, LBJL.

39 *Johnson continued to press Adlai Stevenson*: Dallek, *Lone Star Rising*, 573; Dutton OH, LBJL.

39 *"He had that look"*: Plimpton, ed., 72.

40 *Baker saw the look*: Baker, 118.

40 *"Whenever you see Bobby"*: Plimpton, ed., 72.

40 *"I want you to release"*: Brown OH, LBJL.

40 *At their headquarters*: Plimpton, ed., 67–8; Schlesinger, *Robert Kennedy*, 221.

40 *"gay, relaxed and possibly relieved"*: LBJ diary entry, July 13, 1960, Pre-Presidential Diary, Box 1, LBJL.

40 *he sat dejectedly in his suite*: Boatner OH, LBJL; White, *Making 1960*, 195.

CHAPTER 2: THE AFFRONT

41 *"Time and years will eventually hammer"*: White, *Making 1960*, 198.

41 *"There were only three"*: Guthman, 78.

42 *Press secretary Pierre Salinger confessed*: Salinger, 42.

42 *"Possible Vice Presidential Nominees"*: Sorensen to JFK and RFK, June 29, 1960, Sorensen Files, Box 25, JFKL.

42 *Sorensen and John Kennedy kept*: Sorensen interview; Sorensen, *Kennedy*, 186; Evans and Novak, 276.

42 *As the convention drew closer*: Sorensen and Feldman interviews; Clifford OH, LBJL; James A. Wechsler, "The Two-Front War: Johnson vs. Kennedy," *Progressive*, May 1967: 22; Schlesinger, *Robert Kennedy*, 223.

43 *"that is a very iffy question"*: *New York Times*, July 4, 1960, 1, 4.

43 *"I have been prepared"*: Dallek, *Lone Star Rising*, 576.

43 *"Certainly," Kennedy said*: *New York Times*, July 9, 1960, 8.

43 *Bobby Kennedy and his campaign staff*: Schlesinger, *Robert Kennedy*, 223; Clifford interview; Dooley OH, JFKL.

43 *Symington was palatable, labor's choice*: Conway OH, JFKL.

43 *"He did not disturb"*: McPherson, 39–40; Linton interview.

43 *"He's my choice"*: Guthman, 74–6; Linton interview; Boatner OH, LBJL.

44 *JFK's thinking on the vice presidency*: Rostow interview; Rostow OH, LBJL; Graham OH, LBJL.

44 *On Sunday night, July 10*: White, *Making 1960*, 199.

44 *At Kennedy's suite the next night*: "Notes on the 1960 Democratic Convention" ("Graham Memorandum"), July 19 and 24, 1960, "Phil Graham," Archives Reference File, LBJL; Alsop, 427–8; Graham OH.

44 *Tommy Corcoran caught JFK*: Corcoran, "Rendezvous with Democracy," p. c/12–14.

45 *O'Neill passed along*: O'Neill, 93–5; O'Neill OH, LBJL.

45 *"We thought our party was over"*: Jenkins OH, LBJL; Boatner OH; Baker, 122–3.

45 *LBJ seemed to dread an offer:* White, *Making 1960,* 199; Dallek, *Lone Star Rising,* 574–5.

45 *"No, I won't go along":* Dallek, *Lone Star Rising,* 576; Transcript of telephone conversation between LBJ and Congressman Carl Vinson, Dec. 2, 1963 (Document 22), "December 1963 [1 of 3]," Recordings and Transcripts of Telephone Conversations and Meetings, Box 1, LBJL.

45 *Rayburn declared himself a convert:* Boggs OH, LBJL; Baker, 127–8; LBJ-Vinson telephone conversation, Dec. 2, 1963.

46 *"it is inconceivable":* Dallek, *Lone Star Rising,* 576; Boatner OH.

46 *"Texas is going to be very unhappy":* John Connally with Mickey Herskowitz, *In History's Shadow: An American Odyssey* (New York: Hyperion, 1993): 163.

46 *Johnson's effectiveness as leader:* Dallek, *Lone Star Rising,* 577; Jenkins OH.

46 *"fettered, on [a] leash":* Valenti OH, LBJL; McPherson, 179.

47 *"Power is where power goes":* Rowe OH, LBJL.

47 *"He was thinking":* Evans and Novak, 281.

47 *This was Lady Bird's hope:* Valenti OH, LBJL; Evans and Novak, 282.

47 *an escape from sectionalism:* Arthur M. Schlesinger, Jr., *A Thousand Days: John F. Kennedy in the White House* (Boston: Houghton Mifflin, 1965): 47–8; McPherson OH.

48 *In the Kennedy suite:* Evans and Novak, 278; Dutton OH, LBJL.

48 *"the most indecisive time":* RFK OH, JFKL.

48 *Salinger stepped across the hall:* Salinger interview; Salinger OH, JFKL; Salinger, 44.

48 *Johnson "said some rather nasty things":* RFK OH.

49 *"contempt for Johnson as majority leader":* Sidey OH, LBJL (emphasis added).

49 *"You just won't believe it":* RFK OH.

49 *Boggs thought it quite clear:* Boggs OH; O'Neill, 95.

49 *"it is a trap of history":* Theodore H. White, *The Making of the President 1964* (New York: New American Library, 1965): 186.

50 *"a question of semantics":* Sorensen interview.

50 *"I didn't really offer":* Bartlett OH, LBJL. Myer Feldman considers the "offer" to be a feeler misconstrued by LBJ. Feldman OH, JFKL.

50 *"Jack Kennedy's offer at the morning conference":* Baker, 128.

50 *unaware of JFK's flirtations:* When Bobby Baker hinted to Sorensen about a Kennedy-Johnson ticket, neither Sorensen nor JFK confided this information to RFK. Whether this was an oversight or due to the nature of the information—LBJ was openly despised by RFK—it is apparent that RFK was not briefed on all political intelligence pertaining to LBJ and the vice presidency. Sorensen, *Kennedy,* 186; Evans and Novak, 276.

50 *"We both promised each other":* RFK OH.

50 *initial misgivings were compounded:* Boggs OH; O'Donnell OH, LBJL; Schlesinger, *Robert Kennedy,* 224–5.

51 *"Did it occur to you":* Schlesinger, *Robert Kennedy,* 225.

51 *labor leaders filed into Kennedy's suite:* Conway OH; Plimpton, ed., 71–2; White, *Making 1960,* 202; Guthman, 47.

51 *"All hell broke loose":* Humphrey OH; Graham OH; Udall OH, LBJL; Manatos OH, LBJL; Schlesinger OH, LBJL.

51 *"Who'd want to be Vice President":* Jacobsen OH, LBJL; Roberts OH, LBJL; Sanders OH, LBJL; Boatner OH.

52 *"Get me my .38"*: Dallek, *Lone Star Rising*, 579; Baker, 126.

52 *"Jack changed his mind"*: RFK OH.

52 *"Whatever it is"*: Connally, 164; Graham memo.

52 *"just sort of to feel him out"*: RFK OH; Salinger, 46; Sorensen interview.

52 *"Lyndon just can't accept"*: Connally, 164; Baker, 128; Graham memo.

52 *Graham sat nervously*: Graham memo.

53 *By Connally's account*: RFK remembers only two visits, the first and last of the three recounted here. But Graham's account appears to corroborate Connally's: Graham writes that between those two visits, "LBJ sent for me to say that Bobby Kennedy had been *back down* to see Rayburn some twenty minutes before (say, roughly, 3:00) and had said Jack would phone directly." Graham memo (emphasis added).

53 *Johnson's vote for the Taft-Hartley bill*: On Taft-Hartley, see James T. Patterson, *Grand Expectations: The United States, 1945–1974* (New York: Oxford University Press, 1996): 50–52.

53 *"Bobby, there is no point"*: Connally, 164–5; LBJ diary entry, July 14, 1960, Pre-Presidential Diary, Box 1, LBJL; Graham memo; Baker, 129.

53 *Thirty minutes passed*: Graham memo.

53 *"Do you really want me?"*: Rowe OH, LBJL.

53 *"I went down to see"*: RFK OH.

54 *In a room down the hall*: Graham memo; Rowe OH, LBJL.

54 *The room was a tumult*: Graham memo; Baker, 129.

54 *"Bobby is down here"*: Graham memo.

55 *"Jim, don't you think"*: Rowe OH, LBJL.

55 *Lyndon and Lady Bird Johnson stood*: Graham memo.

55 *"I just got a call"*: RFK OH.

55 *As it turned out, it was disastrous*: Connally, 166; Baker, 130.

56 *Johnson's friends joined in*: Connally, 166; Alsop, 428; Graham memo.

56 *"Phil didn't know us then"*: Graham OH; RFK OH.

56 *"with the close relationship"*: RFK OH.

56 *"people become extremely emotional"*: Reedy OH, LBJL.

56 *The party's liberals sullenly acquiesced*: Conway OH; O'Donnell OH.

57 *at the ornate Spanish mansion*: Bartlett OH; Plimpton, ed., 72; Schlesinger, *Thousand Days*, 58.

57 *Salinger returned to his office*: Salinger, 44–5.

58 *Jim Rowe expected*: Dallek, *Lone Star Rising*, 583.

58 *passions had cooled substantially*: Ibid., 583.

58 *"Lyndon was just as anxious"*: Feldman interview; Reedy OH.

58 *"Our paths only crossed a few times"*: Reedy OH; Rowe OH, LBJL.

58 *the "Kennedy girls"*: Carpenter OH, LBJL; "Off to Texas," UPI wire report, Aug. 29, 1960, LBJL.

58 *"These towns couldn't possibly have these names"*: Carpenter OH.

59 *"We loved every minute"*: Ethel Kennedy to Lady Bird Johnson, n.d., 1960, WHFN-RFK, Box 6, LBJL.

59 *"your sense of humor"*: Lady Bird Johnson to Ethel Kennedy, Nov. 10, 1960, WHFN-RFK, Box 6.

59 *"I hear that you have an interesting story"*: Lisagor OH, JFKL.

59 *Bobby took no issue with Johnson's conduct*: Feldman interview.

59 *"Tell Jack that we'll ride it through"*: Schlesinger, *Thousand Days*, 74.

59 *"Why his staff did not kill him"*: Dallek, *Lone Star Rising*, 586–7; Evans and Novak, 297; Feldman interview; Dutton OH, LBJL; Reedy OH, LBJL.

60 *Even his Texan advisers*: Jacobsen OH.

60 *"we are getting outstanding favorable reaction"*: Telegram, RFK to LBJ, October 21, 1960, Senate Political Files, Box 260, JFKL.

60 *"Lady Bird carried Texas"*: Carpenter OH; Dallek, *Lone Star Rising*, 588. RFK may also have been referring to an ugly incident on November 4 at the Adolphus Hotel in Dallas, where a frenzied right-wing mob spat and yelled at the Johnsons and hit Lady Bird in the head with a picket sign. The incident sparked a wave of sympathy across Texas and the South. Dallek, *Lone Star Rising*, 587; Carpenter OH.

60 *"That Minnesota boy"*: Carpenter OH.

60 *"There was no jubilation"*: Miller, 273.

60 *At 7:00 the next morning*: Carpenter OH.

60 *"If Jack Kennedy gets elected"*: "No. 2 Man Lyndon Baines Johnson," *Newsweek*, Oct. 31, 1960: 25.

CHAPTER 3: THE VICE PRESIDENT AND THE ASSISTANT PRESIDENT

61 *"I am vice president"*: Schlesinger, *Thousand Days*, 703.

61 *"the vice presidency is to become a center"*: "Lyndon Johnson—a New Kind of Vice President," *U.S. News & World Report*, Jan. 23, 1961: 51.

61 *"The restless and able Mr. Johnson"*: Tom Wicker, "LBJ in Search of His New Frontier," *New York Times*, March 19, 1961: 29.

61 *"will be very important"*: "Lyndon Johnson."

62 *Headlines heralded*: "No. 2 Man Lyndon Baines Johnson," *Newsweek*, Oct. 31, 1960: 25.

62 *"Bobby, I've been thinking"*: Baker, 133–4.

62 *Humphrey thought it perfectly obvious*: Baker, 134; Evans and Novak, 306; Humphrey OH, LBJL.

63 *On January 3, 1961*: Baker, 135; Evans and Novak, 307–8.

63 *"We might as well ask Jack Kennedy"*: Miller, 276.

63 *46 to 17*: "LBJ's Changed Role," *Time*, Feb. 23, 1962: 25.

63 *"Those bastards sandbagged me"*: Baker, 135; Miller, 276.

64 *Johnson began to probe the boundaries*: Katzenbach OH, LBJL.

64 *a Johnson aide drafted an executive order*: Evans and Novak, 308; Schlesinger OH, LBJL.

64 *John Kennedy was astonished*: Schlesinger OH; Evans and Novak, 309; Salinger, 63.

65 *"It is Bobby"*: "Enter Bobby Kennedy—New Man-to-See in Changing Washington," *Newsweek*, Nov. 21, 1960: 32.

65 *"I had to do something on my own"*: Schlesinger, *Robert Kennedy*, 246.

65 *"I said I didn't want to be Attorney General"*: Ibid., 247.

65 *"dying to do it"*: Tremblay OH, JFKL.

65 *"Bobby we'll make Attorney General"*: Schlesinger, *Robert Kennedy*, 248.

65 *"It is simply not good enough"*: New York Times, Nov. 23, 1960.

65 *The president-elect . . . enlisted Clark Clifford*: Clark M. Clifford with Richard Holbrooke, *Counsel to the President: A Memoir* (New York: Random House, 1991): 545.

65 *"It's the only thing"*: Reeves, 29.

66 *"I need to know"*: Schlesinger, *Robert Kennedy,* 250–2; Reeves, 29.

66 *Alexander Bickel of* The New Republic: Schlesinger, *Robert Kennedy,* 251–2.

66 *"snot-nosed little son-of-a-bitch"*: Baker, 138–9.

66 *shepherd Bobby's nomination through the confirmation process*: Ibid.

67 *"We've got to make a real crusade"*: Ibid.

67 *Johnson recommenced the Treatment*: Ibid., 139; Schlesinger, *Robert Kennedy,* 253.

68 *He had prepared intently*: Schlesinger, *Robert Kennedy,* 253.

68 *Johnson lobbied tirelessly*: Baker, 139–40.

68 *Johnson's advocates credited him*: Baker, 136; Schlesinger, *Robert Kennedy,* 253.

69 *the new attorney general*: Schlesinger, *Robert Kennedy,* 255–7; Schlesinger, *Thousand Days,* 696.

69 *"Bob never pauses to regroup"*: Dolan OH, JFKL.

70 *"titles meant nothing"*: Geoghegan OH, JFKL.

70 *the old abruptness resurfaced*: Schlesinger, *Robert Kennedy,* 258–61.

70 *"We've got to do something"*: Reeves, 83; Schlesinger, *Thousand Days,* 259.

71 *He attended all key meetings*: William Beecher, "Brother Bobby," *Wall Street Journal,* Feb. 6, 1962: 1.

71 *Presidential aide Richard Goodwin*: Reeves, 103–5.

71 *at the home of Averell Harriman*: Evans OH, JFKL; Harriman OH, JFKL; Reeves, 347n.

72 *their language a series of coded grunts*: Schlesinger, *Thousand Days,* 692, 700–1.

72 *Bobby's direct phone line*: Beecher, "Brother Bobby."

72 *"If Jack Kennedy wanted"*: Penn Kimball, "He Builds His Own Kennedy Identity and the Power Flows Freely to Him," *Life,* Nov. 18, 1966: 136.

72 *"Do you want the opinion"*: Feldman interview.

72 *The Bay of Pigs debacle*: Reeves, 103, 180–81, 264; Max Holland, "After Thirty Years: Making Sense of the Assassination," *Reviews in American History* 22, vol. 2, June 1994: 195.

73 *"sharp step-up"*: Beecher, "Brother Bobby."

73 *Bobby oversaw a regular gathering*: Reeves, 264; Holland, "After Thirty Years," 195–6.

73 *Rusk considered him petulant*: Rusk OH, JFKL.

73 *Robert Kennedy's more exuberant ideas*: Ibid.

73 *Bobby's ideas were mulled over*: Rostow OH, JFKL.

73 *Rusk's personnel battles with Robert Kennedy*: Dean Rusk with Richard Rusk and Daniel S. Papp, *As I Saw It* (New York: W. W. Norton, 1990): 336; Rusk OH, JFKL.

73 *"Let Bobby have his say"*: Rusk, 275, 336.

73 *General Clay*: Reeves, 223.

74 *"a political phenomenon"*: Paul O'Neil, "The No. 2 Man in Washington," *Life,* Jan. 26, 1962: 76. Harry Hopkins was FDR's secretary of commerce and most important adviser. Sherman Adams was Eisenhower's chief aide.

74 *"number two man"*: "Role of Robert Kennedy: No. 2 Man in Washington," *U.S.*

News & World Report, July 10, 1961: 43; " 'Bobby' Kennedy: Is He the 'Assistant President'?" *U.S. News & World Report,* Feb. 19, 1962: 52.

74 *"Nothing big goes on":* O'Neil, "No. 2 Man."

74 U.S. News *outlined RFK's legerdemain:* " 'Bobby' Kennedy."

74 *"who really makes foreign policy":* "Who Really Makes Foreign Policy," *U.S. News & World Report,* Feb. 18, 1963: 33–5.

74 *Some officials sought to underplay:* Beecher, "Brother Bobby"; " 'Bobby' Kennedy."

74 U.S. News *was reporting Bobby's frequent mention: U.S. News & World Report,* Feb. 19, 1962: 49, 51–2.

75 *"Up, way up":* "No. 2," *Time,* May 5, 1961: 14.

75 *the few stories on the vice president:* "LBJ's Changed Role," *Time,* Feb. 23, 1962: 25; Ward S. Just, "What Ever Happened to Lyndon Johnson?" *Reporter,* Jan. 17, 1963: 28.

75 *"trips around the world":* Kearns, 164.

75 *Charlie Boatner, a Johnson aide:* Boatner OH, LBJL.

76 *As majority leader. Ibid.*

76 *If the matter at hand . . . concerned Texas:* White interview; White OH, LBJL.

76 *"I was no particular confidant":* Yarmolinsky OH, LBJL.

76 *"No one knew quite what to do":* Clifford, 390.

76 *"I don't know what to do with Lyndon":* Krock OH, LBJL; RFK OH, JFKL; Dungan OH, LBJL.

77 *To avoid conflicts:* Tom Wicker, "LBJ in Search of His New Frontier," *New York Times,* March 19, 1961: 123–4; Wicker OH, JFKL; Dutton OH, LBJL.

77 *"I want you to know one thing":* O'Donnell OH, LBJL.

77 *He demanded that every request:* Joseph A. Califano, Jr., *The Triumph and Tragedy of Lyndon Johnson: The White House Years* (New York: Simon & Schuster, 1991): 64.

77 *"wouldn't give him the time of day":* White interview.

77 *what Johnson's staff perceived:* Valenti OH, LBJL.

77 *"enormously impressed with themselves":* Bartlett OH, LBJL.

77 *Robert Kennedy communicated as much:* Feldman interview.

77 *"I've got a date":* Nicholas Lemann, *The Promised Land: The Great Black Migration and How It Changed America* (New York: Knopf, 1991): 138–9.

78 *The president's instructions were clear:* Schlesinger, *Thousand Days,* 704; Bartlett OH.

78 *"Where is the vice president":* O'Brien OH, LBJL.

78 *"President Kennedy,"* Time *reported:* "LBJ's Changed Role."

78 *Johnson was often excluded:* Dungan OH; White interview.

78 *top assistant on civil rights:* White interview.

79 *LBJ was rarely given more than five minutes:* Califano, 64.

79 *"It was a terrible thing":* White interview; White OH, LBJL.

79 *JFK had Bobby Kennedy phone:* Evans and Novak, 313; Bartlett OH.

79 *Yet even when present:* Evans and Novak, 310; Reedy OH, LBJL.

79 *The press, as usual, made bold predictions:* "LBJ's Changed Role"; Just, "What Ever Happened"; Wicker, "LBJ in Search."

80 *the White House issued an executive order:* "Executive Order 10925, Establishing the President's Committee on Equal Employment Opportunity," March 7, 1961, Lee White Papers, Box 20, JFKL; Schlesinger, *Thousand Days,* 933.

80 *Even while touring Afghanistan*: D. P. Moynihan, foreword to McPherson, xvi.

80 *the vice president took consistent pride*: Just, "What Ever Happened"; Reedy OH; McPherson OH, LBJL.

80 *"I think this can be"*: JFK to LBJ, Feb. 7, 1962, Vice Presidential Masters, Box 29, LBJL.

80 *As chairman, Johnson was reluctant*: Reedy OH.

81 *LBJ's old colleagues pressured him*: Evans and Novak, 317–18.

81 *aides drafted a planned executive order*: Harris Wofford to Ted Sorensen, Dick Goodwin, Fred Dutton, and Burke Marshall, Sept. 11, 1961; Katzenbach to White, Dec. 1, 1961; Wofford to White, Oct. 23, 1961, White Papers, Box 20.

81 *"Let's make it fashionable"*: Evans and Novak, 317–18 (emphasis in original).

81 *Johnson was fighting to preserve*: Just, "What Ever Happened."

81 *"one of the great phonies"*: James N. Giglio, *The Presidency of John F. Kennedy* (Lawrence, KS: University of Kansas Press, 1991): 172; Conway OH, JFKL; Evans and Novak, 317–18. President Kennedy appointed Goldberg to the United States Supreme Court in the summer of 1962.

82 *"I am looking forward to cooperating"*: LBJ to RFK, March 31, 1961, VP Papers, Box 27, LBJL.

82 *"It certainly shows"*: RFK to LBJ, May 8, 1962, WHFN-RFK, Box 6, LBJL.

82 *"I am satisfied"*: JFK to LBJ, August 22, 1962, VP Papers, Box 27; Giglio, 173.

82 *"it wasn't worth a damn"*: Katzenbach OH, JFKL.

82 *Bobby shared organized labor's suspicion*: White interview; White OH, LBJL.

82 *"What the hell are they doing"*: Giglio, 173; White interview.

82 *He preferred to send his delegate*: Seigenthaler OH, JFKL.

82 *"It was things like this"*: Hobart Taylor OH, LBJL.

83 *the committee was full of good talkers*: Seigenthaler OH.

83 *"There was an awful lot of propaganda"*: RFK OH; White interview.

83 *"The number . . . was shockingly high"*: RFK OH; Guthman and Shulman, eds., 151, 153; Giglio, 172. Johnson was so infuriated by the investigation he refused to speak to Wirtz for months.

83 *"It was a matter of great concern"*: RFK OH.

83 *"an effective organization"*: Ibid.

83 *"Oh, he almost had a fit"*: Ibid.

84 *White had held on to the draft executive order*: White OH, LBJL; White OH, JFKL.

84 *"The country was in absolute turmoil"*: Marshall OH, LBJL.

84 *when the CEEO met on May 29, 1963*: Schlesinger, *Robert Kennedy*, 360.

85 *"I'd gone into . . . every federal office"*: Marshall OH, JFKL.

85 *the next CEEO meeting*: Lawson OH, JFKL.

85 *"rather a blabbermouth"*: RFK OH.

85 *Webb gave a measured, optimistic presentation*: Korth OH, LBJL; Schlesinger, *Robert Kennedy*, 360.

85 *Bobby turned now to Hobart Taylor*: Conway OH.

86 *"He went over the whole thing again"*: Lawson OH.

86 *"after completely humiliating Webb"*: Conway OH; Lawson OH. This handshake was enough to earn Conway Johnson's eternal enmity.

86 *In the days that followed*: Wilkins interview; Edison Dictaphone recording of telephone conversation between LBJ and Sorensen, June 3, 1963, LBJL; LBJ,

recorded interview by Walter Cronkite, CBS News Special, Feb. 1, 1973, LBJL.

86 *"having a difficult time with Johnson"*: Schlesinger, *Robert Kennedy*, 361–2.

86 *Just after the meeting*: Lawson OH; Evans and Novak, 317–18; Schlesinger, *Thousand Days*, 934–5.

87 *White detected jockeying*: White OH, LBJL.

87 *"the sharpest disputes"*: RFK OH.

CHAPTER 4: TWO HEIRS APPARENT

88 *"He was crushed by the loss"*: Baker, 148–9.

88 *His first trip set the pattern*: Carpenter OH, LBJL.

88 *the image was the same*: Reedy OH, LBJL; Evans and Novak, 326–9.

89 *embassy cables testified*: Evans and Novak, 328; Dutton OH, LBJL; Rusk OH, JFKL.

89 *Kennedy dispatched Johnson to Southeast Asia*: Carpenter OH; Evans and Novak, 320–21; Bartlett OH, LBJL; Dolan interview, 1990.

89 *during his meeting with . . . Diem*: Reedy OH; Evans and Novak, 321–3; Ellen J. Hammer, *A Death in November: America in Vietnam, 1963* (New York: Oxford University Press, 1987): 34–5.

89 *Johnson's analysis was concise*: Kearns, 168; Reedy OH.

90 *"the single best speech on foreign aid"*: Rostow interview; Rostow OH, LBJL.

90 *vice president in West Berlin*: Evans and Novak, 324–5; Schlesinger OH, LBJL.

90 *He acquitted himself brilliantly*: Evans and Novak, 325.

90 *"Put that issue aside"*: Rostow OH.

90 *Kennedy wanted Johnson to share*: Evans and Novak, 313.

91 *"He absorbed briefings in expert fashion"*: Rusk, 331–2.

91 *When the president tried to absolve Johnson*: Ibid., 209.

91 *"We had the impression"*: Schlesinger, *Robert Kennedy*, 508.

91 *Johnson tried for days to convince*: Baker, 145.

91 *mysterious "White House insiders"*: "Vice President Johnson Carves a New Career," *U.S. News & World Report*, Aug. 21, 1961: 57–8.

91 *"general policy of never speaking"*: LBJ, recorded interview by William J. Jorden, LBJL.

91 *"a listening role"*: Maxwell Taylor OH, LBJL.

92 *"used to laugh about it"*: RFK OH, JFKL.

92 *officers' training school at Harvard*: Schlesinger, *Robert Kennedy*, 65–6. RFK finally got overseas in February 1946, but only got as far as Guantánamo Bay, where the bored nineteen-year-old apprentice seaman sat aboard the inactive destroyer *Joseph P. Kennedy, Jr.* for almost four months. He was honorably discharged on May 30.

92 *lasting, fundamental impressions of the ExComm members*: Walinsky interview; Walinsky OH, JFKL; Tremblay OH, JFKL. The ExComm also included Rusk; McNamara; Sorensen; CIA Director John McCone; Secretary of the Treasury Douglas Dillon; National Security Adviser McGeorge Bundy; Under Secretary of State George Ball; Deputy Under Secretary of State U. Alexis Johnson; General Maxwell Taylor, JCS chairman; Edward Martin, assistant secretary of state

for Latin America; Llewellyn Thompson, adviser on Russian affairs; Deputy Secretary of Defense Roswell Gilpatric; Assistant Secretary of Defense Paul Nitze; and, less consistently, Ken O'Donnell; UN Ambassador Adlai Stevenson; Chip Bohlen, preceding Thompson's arrival on day two; and Don Wilson, deputy director of the U.S. Information Agency. A number of others made brief appearances. Robert F. Kennedy, *Thirteen Days: A Memoir of the Cuban Missile Crisis* (New York: W. W. Norton, 1969): 8.

92 *"You're going to kill"*: Off-the-record meeting on Cuba, Oct. 16, 1962, 11:50 A.M.–12:57 P.M., McGeorge Bundy Transcript of Audiotape 28.1, p. 21, Presidential Recordings, President's Office Files, JFK Papers, JFKL; Reeves, 378, 385–6.

92 *"I had always had a feeling"*: Plimpton, ed., 135.

92 *Bobby helped defuse tensions*: Sorensen OH, JFKL; Plimpton, ed., 138.

92 *Not all were impressed*: Rusk, 231–2; Reeves, 378, 397.

93 *"in looking forward to the future"*: Reeves, 381.

93 *Bobby argued for a "quarantine"*: Reeves, 385.

93 *"You have the recommendation"*: Rusk, 234.

93 *"I realize it's a breach of faith"*: Transcript of Audiotape 28.1, 20; Reeves, 374.

94 *"I would like to hear"*: Transcript of Audiotape 28.1, 20.

94 *"Well, uh, the, uh"*: Off-the-record meeting on Cuba, Oct. 16, 1962, 6:30–7:55 P.M., Transcript of Audiotapes 28.2 and 28A.1, 30; Sorensen interview.

94 *"Johnson never made any suggestions"*: RFK OH.

94 *"the beginnings, perhaps"*: R. F. Kennedy, *Thirteen Days*, 68.

94 *The second letter*: Reeves, 413.

94 *"hostages of the Soviet Union"*: R. F. Kennedy, 73.

94 *By now it was clear*: Reeves, 415–16.

95 *By midafternoon on October 27*: Transcript of meeting 41A.1, Oct. 27, 1962, pp. 52–3; Summary Record of NSC Exec Comm Committee Meeting No. 8, Oct. 27, 1962, 4:00 P.M., NSF Meetings and Memoranda, Box 316, JFKL; Reeves, 419.

95 *"We were afraid . . . he'd never offer this"*: Transcript of meeting 41A.1, 54–60.

96 *"We can't very well invade Cuba"*: Transcript of meeting 42.1, 63–7; Reeves, 419–20.

96 *During the next two hours*: Reeves, 420; R. F. Kennedy, 86–7.

96 *The ExComm reconvened at 9:00 P.M.*: Transcript of meeting 42.2, 82; Reeves, 422–3.

97 *The Soviet response*: Reeves, 423–4, 455–6; R. F. Kennedy, 88.

97 *"the night I should go to the theater"*: R. F. Kennedy, 88.

97 *"I would go, too"*: Schlesinger, *Robert Kennedy*, 566.

97 *"he would circulate and whine"*: RFK OH.

97 *Saturday night, October 27*: Reeves, 422.

97 *"angry, or worried"*: Sorensen interview.

98 *Robert Kennedy rarely spoke of this view*: Walinsky interview.

98 *Baker understood Johnson's nostalgia*: Baker, 144.

98 *Johnson had walked into the Senate cloakroom*: McPherson OH, LBJL.

98 *"vacant and gray"*: Kearns, 165.

99 *he usually demurred*: Feldman interview; Dutton OH, LBJL; Just, "What Ever Happened"; Sorensen interview.

99 *"couldn't have been better"*: Dutton OH, LBJL.

99 *Mike Manatos, President Kennedy's Senate liaison*: Manatos OH, LBJL.

99 *"I didn't do what I should have"*: LBJ, recorded interview by Walter Cronkite, CBS News Special, broadcast Jan. 27, 1972, LBJL.

99 *"Lyndon has no chits"*: Just, "What Ever Happened."

99 *Kennedy never understood Johnson's loss of influence*: Dungan OH, LBJL; Sorensen interview; Feldman OH, JFKL.

99 *"thought Lyndon had an ego"*: Feldman OH. Also see Michael P. Riccards, "Rare Counsel: Kennedy, Johnson and the Civil Rights Bill of 1963," *Presidential Studies Quarterly*, Summer 1981: 398n.

99 *"President Kennedy . . . didn't feel"*: LBJ, Cronkite's interview.

100 *Johnson complained to Harry McPherson*: McPherson OH. Ironically, O'Brien wished for more of Johnson's support but thought it improper to ask. Among cabinet members, O'Brien considered himself an equal, and felt perfectly comfortable saying, "Here's what I think you ought to do." But he thought it unseemly to be giving direction to the vice president of the United States; the most a congressional liaison could do was keep the vice president abreast of the issues and allow him to determine his own course of action. O'Brien OH, LBJL.

100 *the president simply threw up his hands*: Reeves, 276–7.

100 *"out of his element"*: Baker, 141–2; McPherson, 48.

100 *"We've got all the minnows"*: McPherson, 48; McPherson OH.

100 *"those kids . . . from the White House"*: Baker, 142.

100 *a telephone conversation with Sorensen*: LBJ-Sorensen conversation, 5–6, LBJL.

100 *"did not have nearly as much"*: Sorensen interview.

101 *"evangelical force"*: Schlesinger OH, LBJL.

101 *"a lot of homework to do"*: Roberts OH, LBJL.

101 *"Now, I want to make it clear"*: LBJ-Sorensen telephone conversation, 7–8.

101 *"I don't think it's been thought through"*: Ibid., 9–12.

102 *"the minimum we can ask for"*: Ibid., 6–8.

102 *With regard to the attack itself*: Ibid., 2, 19.

102 *"One hundred years ago"*: L. B. Johnson, 156–7; Rostow interview.

102 *"the Negroes are tired"*: LBJ-Sorensen telephone conversation, 3, 8.

102 *"these risks are great"*: Ibid., 4–5.

103 *a series of memos to Sorensen*: LBJ to Sorensen, June 10, 1963, Sorensen Papers, Box 30, JFKL; Riccards, 396–7.

103 *"some good ideas"*: RFK OH; Sorensen interview.

103 *"confronted primarily with a moral issue"*: Theodore C. Sorensen, ed., *"Let the Word Go Forth": The Speeches, Statements, and Writings of John F. Kennedy* (New York: Delacorte, 1988): 194; Riccards, 397; Katzenbach OH, LBJL.

103 *an afternoon swim at the Elms*: McPherson OH.

103 *LBJ grew indignant*: Time, Feb. 23, 1962: 25; LBJ, Cronkite's interview.

103 *The superficial splendor of Camelot*: White OH, LBJL; Conkin, 137; Richard N. Goodwin, *Remembering America: A Voice from the Sixties* (Boston: Little, Brown, 1988): 298.

104 *"by Kennedy people for other Kennedy people"*: Elizabeth Gatov, quoted in Miller, 279.

104 *one of Ethel Kennedy's master lists*: Ethel Kennedy, Telephone Message, March 13, 1961, Telephone Messages, Box 1, JFKL.

104 *"nobody was terribly interested"*: Miller, 278–9.

104 *Johnson jokes and Johnson stories*: Linton interview.

104 *"Whatever happened to Lyndon"*: "Bobby for Veep?" *Time*, March 20, 1964: 21.

104 *"just awful . . . it was inexcusable"*: Sidey OH, LBJL.

104 *an LBJ voodoo doll*: Hugh Sidey, "He Makes a Truce with a Man He Almost Came to Hate—LBJ," *Life*, Nov. 18, 1966: 38.

104 *In November 1963, at a stag party*: Linton interview.

105 *"There were always people"*: Alsop OH, JFKL.

105 *"Dear Bobby"*: LBJ to RFK, Sept, 25, 1963, VP Papers, Box 27, LBJL.

105 *"brooding and bottling up"*: Baker, 144.

105 *LBJ vented the "emotional fallout"*: McPherson, 191.

105 *weekly vice presidential staff meetings*: Boatner OH, LBJL.

105 *Every day brought a new complaint*: Baker, 144.

106 *"Johnson was a good actor"*: Linton interview; McPherson, 191.

106 *"I am constantly amazed"*: LBJ to JFK, Aug. 30, 1963, VP Masters, VP Papers, Box 29, LBJL.

106 *a guest at the LBJ Ranch spoke negatively*: Valenti OH, LBJL.

106 *"certain fondness"*: Schlesinger, *Robert Kennedy,* 669–70; Dolan interview.

106 *"Every time I came"*: Schlesinger, *Robert Kennedy,* 670.

106 *"the president, by necessity"*: Schlesinger, *Thousand Days,* 703.

106 *incapable of blaming John Kennedy*: Kearns, 163.

106 *The president's Johnson stories*: Bartlett OH.

107 *"President Kennedy," Johnson said*: LBJ, Cronkite's interview.

107 *Johnson's hatred and fear*: James A. Wechsler, "The Two-Front War: Johnson vs. Kennedy," *Progressive*, May 1967: 23; Schlesinger, *Robert Kennedy*, 671; Baker, 144.

107 *making a mockery*: McPherson, 191; Valenti OH, LBJL; Baker, 144; Califano, 295.

107 *"Every time they have a conference"*: Miller, 305.

107 *Speaking to reporters on October 16, 1963*: Schlesinger, *Robert Kennedy*, 671.

107 *"would have offended anyone"*: White OH, LBJL.

107 *Bobby darted past him*: Clifford, 389–90; Califano, 64.

108 *Headlines did tell*: "No. 2 Man Lyndon Baines Johnson," *Newsweek*, Oct. 31, 1960: 25; "Role of Robert Kennedy: No. 2 Man in Washington," *U.S. News & World Report*, July 10, 1961: 43; Tom Wicker, "LBJ in Search of His New Frontier," *New York Times*, March 19, 1961: 29; Just, "What Ever Happened," 28.

108 *"I never heard Bob"*: Schlesinger, *Robert Kennedy,* 673.

108 *"If your brother is president"*: McPherson interview.

108 *"never heard him accuse"*: Katzenbach and RFK, quoted in Schlesinger, *Robert Kennedy,* 673; Katzenbach OH, JFKL.

109 *"how lucky he was"*: RFK OH.

109 *"wasn't very helpful"*: Guthman and Shulman, eds., 23, 215.

109 *"genuine contempt for liars"*: Paul O'Neil, "The No. 2 Man in Washington," *Life,* Jan. 26, 1962: 78.

109 *"just interested in helping John Kennedy"*: RFK OH.

110 *"Why don't you like me"*: Schlesinger, *Robert Kennedy,* 672.

110 *the first strategy session*: Schlesinger, *Thousand Days,* 1018.

110 *"What is the Vice President's standing"*: "The Vice President's Chances in '64," *U.S. News & World Report*, Feb. 25, 1963: 14. The magazine determined "the answer to both questions—in the view of most observers—is: 'Good.' "

110 *Was he, in fact, to be dumped*: Schlesinger, *Thousand Days*, 1019; *Robert Kennedy*, 671.

110 *"I think [JFK] admired him"*: RFK OH; Bartlett OH.

110 *The brothers expressed unease*: Schlesinger, *A Thousand Days*, 1018. Interior Secretary Stewart Udall remembered no "comments from anybody about dumping Johnson in 1964." Udall OH, LBJL.

110 *LBJ never sought assurances*: LBJ, Cronkite's interview; Wechsler, "Two-Front War"; Weisl, Sr., OH, LBJL.

111 *He hinted very strongly*: Freeman OH, LBJL; Boatner OH.

111 *"The public . . . has already forgotten"*: Gore Vidal, "The Best Man 1968," *Esquire*, March 1963: 59; McPherson OH; Valenti OH, LBJL.

111 *"As the days passed"*: RFK OH.

112 *The idea of a Kennedy dynasty*: Bartlett OH. Cigarette case described in "The Bobby Phenomenon," *Newsweek*, Oct. 24, 1966: 37.

112 *a second John Kennedy administration*: RFK indicated some interest in taking a post other than attorney general, perhaps in defense or foreign affairs, but both seemed unlikely. To be McNamara's number two would be to concentrate far too much power in the Defense Department; as Under Secretary of State RFK would undermine Rusk's position. There was simply no sub-cabinet position he could assume. Gwirtzman OH, JFKL.

112 *"It seems inevitable"*: Vidal, "Best Man," 60–61. Still, Vidal was no booster of Robert Kennedy. He feared RFK would be "a dangerously authoritarian-minded President."

113 *The trip was primarily a fund-raiser*: Schlesinger, *Thousand Days*, 1019.

113 *"how irritated he was"*: Schlesinger, *Robert Kennedy*, 654.

CHAPTER 5: A HEAVY RECKONING

114 *At 3:00 P.M. on November 22, 1963*: Schlesinger, *Robert Kennedy*, 656; William Manchester, *The Death of a President* (New York: Harper & Row, 1967): 268–9.

115 *"I'll be glad to find out"*: Manchester, 269–72.

115 *"very businesslike, although"*: LBJ, recorded interview by Walter Cronkite, CBS News Special, May 6, 1970, LBJL.

115 *There was no need*: Manchester, 324–5.

115 *Kennedy steeled himself*: Ibid., 386–7.

116 *Johnson stood impassively*: Schlesinger, *Robert Kennedy*, 657–8; Valenti OH, LBJL.

116 *What can I do but turn*: Manchester, 387.

116 *"the natural thing to do"*: LBJ, Cronkite's interview.

116 *"[Bobby] ran," Johnson said*: Schlesinger, *Robert Kennedy*, 675.

116 *Other observers thought*: Manchester, 387.

116 *"There were four or five"*: RFK OH.

116 *"What raced through my mind"*: Recording of telephone conversation between LBJ and Bill Moyers, Dec. 26, 1966, 10:17 A.M., Tape 66.02, Recordings of

Telephone Conversations, White House Series, Recordings and Transcripts of Conversations and Meetings, LBJL.

117 *"None of us had any idea"*: O'Brien OH, LBJL.

117 *"Mrs. Kennedy and Kenny O'Donnell"*: Evans and Novak, 336.

117 *"The attorney general wants"*: Manchester, 314, 319.

117 *He remembered giving his official judgment*: Ibid., 319–20; Bartlett OH, LBJL; O'Brien OH.

117 *"incapable of telling the truth"*: RFK OH.

118 *The stories were legion*: Manchester's *Death of a President* provides essentially a verbatim account of the reflections of embittered Kennedy aides. On the resulting controversy, see Chapter 14.

118 *"McHugh said that Lyndon"*: Schlesinger, *Robert Kennedy*, 675.

118 *"I didn't see any hostility"*: Valenti interview.

118 *Neither did reporter Charles Bartlett*: Bartlett OH; Miller, 320; Carter OH, LBJL.

118 *Kennedy went to the Oval Office*: RFK OH; Schlesinger, *Robert Kennedy*, 676.

119 *Now, as Bobby told a friend*: Seigenthaler OH, JFKL.

119 *"During all of that period"*: LBJ, recorded interview by William J. Jorden, LBJL.

119 *This was manifestly untrue*: The president and Lady Bird willingly gave Jackie Kennedy as long as she needed (until December 7, as it turned out) to move out of the White House before they moved into it; but Johnson conducted business in the Oval Office from his first day as president.

119 *"For millions of Americans"*: Kearns, 170.

120 *"1. The President is dead"*: Memorandum, "Remarks to the Cabinet—2:30 P.M., the Cabinet Room, Nov. 23, 1963," Special File on the JFK Assassination, Box 1, LBJL.

120 *"Gentlemen, the president"*: Manchester, 475.

120 *"he could hardly countenance"*: Freeman OH, LBJL.

120 *"A nice little statement"*: Schlesinger, *Robert Kennedy*, 676–7.

120 *Cabinet members later called it*: Manchester, 476–7.

121 *"We won't go in"*: Schlesinger, 676–7; Manchester, 477n.

121 *The next flashpoint*: Schlesinger, *Robert Kennedy*, 677.

121 *"Why does he tell you"*: Manchester, 480.

121 *"Bob prefers you wait"*: Ibid.

121 *Johnson delivered a masterful address*: Tom Wicker, "Johnson Bids Congress Enact Civil Rights Bill with Speed . . ." and "Transcript of President Johnson's Address Before the Joint Session of Congress," *New York Times*, Nov. 28, 1963: 1, 20.

122 *"pale, somber and inscrutable"*: Schlesinger, *Robert Kennedy*, 677; Anthony Lewis, "From Johnson, the Homely Touch," *New York Times*, Nov. 28, 1963: 20.

122 *"People just don't realize"*: Schlesinger, *Robert Kennedy*, 657.

122 *probably Bill Moyers*: Memorandum of Conversation, 3:30 P.M., Nov. 27, 1963, Special File on the JFK Assassination, Box 1. There is no indication of its author, but since Bill Moyers initiated the meeting, he probably prepared the president for it. Moyers was RFK's main liaison to the Oval Office and probably the only Johnson aide with such detailed knowledge of Bobby's feelings.

123 *"Your people are talking"*: Manchester, 639.

123 *This was not true*: RFK OH; Seigenthaler OH; Schlesinger, *Robert Kennedy*, 677;

"Kennedy Family—Johnson Contacts," WHFN, Box 5, LBJL.

123 *Johnson felt at his best*: LBJ, Cronkite's interview.

123 *"In a sense," wrote Stewart Alsop*: Stewart Alsop, "Johnson Takes Over: The Untold Story," *Saturday Evening Post*, Feb. 15, 1964: 18.

124 *"I've just finished a two-hour session"*: Transcript of telephone conversation between LBJ and Clark Clifford, Dec. 4, 1963, 6:25 P.M., Document 56, Recordings and Transcripts of Telephone Conversations and Meetings, Box 1, LBJL.

124 *"Public sentiment will be on his side"*: Henggeler, 75.

124 *"didn't feel like seeing him"*: RFK OH.

124 *"I'm not mentally equipped"*: Goodwin, 295.

125 *"How many Americans"*: Max Holland, "After Thirty Years: Making Sense of the Assassination," *Reviews in American History* 22, vol. 2, June 1994: 193.

125 *"I hope this has nothing"*: Evan Thomas, "Bobby Kennedy's War on Castro," *Washington Monthly*, Dec. 1995: 28.

126 *conspiracy theories were as rife*: Holland, "The Key to the Warren Report," *American Heritage*, Nov. 1995: 52, 54.

126 *"hindsight began early"*: Manchester.

126 *the arrest of Lee Harvey Oswald*: Holland, "Key," 54.

126 *"We are prepared to . . . answer in kind"*: Schlesinger, *Robert Kennedy*, 589.

127 *A French journalist*: Jean Daniel, "When Castro Heard the News," *New Republic*, Dec. 7, 1963. Daniel, a French reporter, was interviewing Castro when the first reports reached Cuba.

127 *Embittered Oswald deeply*: Holland, "After Thirty Years," 197.

127 *"there can be no long-term living"*: *Alleged Assassination Plots Involving Foreign Leaders: An Interim Report of the Senate Select Committee to Study Governmental Operations with Respect to Intelligence Activities* (hereafter, *"Assassination Report"*), 94 Cong., 1 Sess., Nov. 20, 1975: 135–6.

127 *"in some way or other removed"*: *Ibid.*, 136, 139.

127 *Still, Castro's presence*: Holland, "After Thirty Years," 195–6; Reeves, 264.

128 *"the driving force"*: Harris Wofford, *Of Kennedys and Kings: Making Sense of the Sixties* (New York: Farrar, Straus & Giroux, 1980): 386; *Assassination Report*, 144, 150–51; Holland, "After Thirty Years," 196.

128 *"a rogue elephant"*: Arthur M. Schlesinger, Jr., "An Open Letter to Bill Moyers," *Wall Street Journal*, July 5, 1977: 10.

128 *Robert Kennedy found out*: *Ibid.*

128 *"If you have seen Mr. Kennedy's eyes"*: *Assassination Report*, 133.

129 *Schlesinger and Bill Moyers*: Schlesinger, "Open Letter"; Schlesinger interview; letter, Schlesinger to author, Feb. 4, 1997.

129 *Richard Helms testified*: *Assassination Report*, 134–5.

129 *assassination was authorized implicitly*: It appeared authorized, at least, to those who wished it to be. Helms's executive assistant, the man who briefed RFK on the CIA/Mafia plots, disputed the notion that talks with Robert Kennedy carried any such subtext. *Ibid.*, 142.

129 *"It was made abundantly clear"*: *Ibid.*, 141, 148–51.

129 *administration officials, at those same Senate hearings*: *Ibid.*, 134–5.

129 *"The conspiratorial atmosphere"*: *Supplementary Detailed Staff Reports on Intelligence*

Activities and the Rights of Americans, Book III, *Final Report of the Senate Select Committee to Study Governmental Operations with Respect to Intelligence Activities* (hereafter, "*Final Report*"), 94 Cong., 2 Sess., April 23, 1976: 59.

130 *Several accounts suggest*: Schlesinger, *Robert Kennedy,* 664–5; Holland, "Key," 62. Also see Wofford, 384–9.

130 *McCone later concluded*: Holland, "After Thirty Years," 200–1.

130 "*perceived so much hatred*": Schlesinger, *Robert Kennedy,* 664; Holland, "Key," 62. "I never thought it was the Cubans," Kennedy told Dick Goodwin in 1966, "If anyone was involved it was organized crime," Goodwin, 465.

130 "*There's so much bitterness*": Guthman, 244.

130 *Bobby flirted with existentialism*: Holland, "After Thirty Years," 200; Schlesinger, *Robert Kennedy,* 665–7.

131 *when Richard Helms testified*: Final Report, 71.

131 "*We had a hand in killing him*": Hammer, 309.

131 *LBJ told Pierre Salinger*: RFK OH.

131 "*whether [Oswald] was connected*": Recording of telephone conversation between LBJ and J. Edgar Hoover, Nov. 29, 1963, 1:40 P.M., Tape K6311.04, PNO 15, LBJL; Recording of telephone conversation between LBJ and Senator Richard Russell, Nov. 29, 1963, 4:05 P.M., Tape K6311.05, PNO 7, Recordings of Telephone Conversations, White House Series, Recordings and Transcripts of Conversations and Meetings, LBJL.

132 "*inner political instinct*": Valenti interviewed on *Nightline,* ABC, Dec. 1, 1993, Transcript #3268.

132 "*President Kennedy tried to get Castro*": Shortly after assuming the presidency, LBJ ordered a halt to all covert activity aimed at Castro's ouster or assassination. Califano, 295.

132 "*Consideration was given*": Rosen to Cartha DeLoach, Feb. 15, 1967, in *Final Report,* 82.

132 "*You know this story*": Recording of telephone conversation between LBJ and Ramsey Clark, Feb. 18, 1967, 10:39 A.M., Tape K67.02, LBJL.

133 *LBJ took a call from . . . Connally*: Recording of telephone conversation between LBJ and John Connally, March 2, 1967, 9:22 P.M., Tape K67.02.

133 "*the president had instructed that the FBI*": DeLoach to Clyde Tolson, March 17, 1967, in *Final Report,* 82–3.

134 "*damned Murder Incorporated*": Garry Wills, *The Kennedy Imprisonment: A Meditation on Power* (Boston: Atlantic Monthly Press/Little, Brown, 1981): 103.

135 "*Texas, my home*": Kearns, 170.

135 " '*They,*' of course, were the Texans": D. P. Moynihan, foreword to McPherson, xviii.

135 "*I'll help as best I can*": Manchester, 321, 385–6; O'Brien OH.

135 "*unconscious argument . . . that Johnson*": Schlesinger, *Robert Kennedy,* 819.

136 "*What wounds me*": Manchester, 316.

136 "*Was Dallas to blame*": "Dallas Asks Why It Happened," *New York Times,* Nov. 23, 1963: 2; John Herbers, "Dallas Divided over Its Future," *New York Times,* Nov. 28, 1963: 27.

136 "*In the tranquil autumn of 1963*": Manchester, 3.

137 "*Absolutely, absolutely*": Dungan OH, LBJL.

137 *even Dungan had to concede*: Ibid.; Schlesinger OH, LBJL.

137 *"We always have a split"*: Jacobsen OH, LBJL; Reedy OH. Once in Texas, John Kennedy gave little indication that the great Democratic feud was anything but a minor irritant. Cliff Carter (a Johnson man) of the Democratic National Committee remembered "no concerted or great effort to try to cement relations" between the warring parties. "It may have been hoped that this would be one of the fringe benefits" of the president's visit, but the key items on the agenda were raising money and approval ratings. For the Austin dinner, the president's staff approved table arrangements that placed the governor high on the dais with Kennedy and Johnson; the senator sat at a lower table. There was no pretense of delicate diplomacy. And when LBJ tried to smooth a clash over who would ride with the president, Kennedy intervened, telling Connally and Yarborough bluntly: "You'll ride this way or you won't ride." Jacobsen OH; Carter OH; Jenkins OH.

137 *Connally aide Larry Temple*: Temple OH, LBJL.

138 *insist upon a fund-raising trip*: Ibid.; Jacobsen OH; Valenti OH, LBJL; Boggs OH, LBJL.

138 *a certain embarrassment*: Recording of telephone conversation between LBJ and Katzenbach, Jan. 25, 1967, 7:45 P.M., Tape 67.01, LBJL.

138 *"That's a great myth"*: Recording of telephone conversation between LBJ and Kintner, Dec. 20, 1966, 7:57 A.M., Tape 66.01, LBJL; LBJ-Katzenbach conversation. By his own account, Johnson was every bit as recalcitrant as the governor. "Matter of fact, I tried to postpone [the trip], told [JFK] our popularity is too low," he insisted later. "I put him off several months and Connally put him off several months, didn't want him to come, told him it was a mistake for him to come! And he finally called Connally . . . secretly, [from] the White House! And didn't tell me anything about it!" Privately, in the Oval Office, the president confided to Connally why Lyndon Johnson was not present: "the Vice President," Kennedy told him, "is not enthusiastic." Recording of telephone conversation between LBJ and Katzenbach, Dec. 5, 1966, 10:46 A.M., Tape 66.01, LBJL; LBJ-Kintner conversation; LBJ-Katzenbach conversation, Jan. 25, 1967.

138 *"Just before the president went to Texas"*: RFK OH; Schlesinger, *Robert Kennedy*, 654; Clark OH, LBJL.

CHAPTER 6: UNEASY ALLIANCE

139 *displays of unity*: Telegrams, LBJ to RFK, Jan. 1, 1964, and RFK to LBJ, Jan. 4, 1964, WHFN-RFK, Box 6, LBJL.

139 *It typified his efforts*: Clifford OH, LBJL; Dungan OH, LBJL; Schlesinger OH, LBJL.

140 *"I've always liked Lyndon"*: Bartlett OH, LBJL.

140 *"the United States of Kennedy"*: McPherson OH, LBJL.

140 *Bobby rebuffed or misinterpreted*: Katzenbach OH, LBJL.

140 *At Hobe Sound, Florida*: Salinger OH, JFKL.

140 *"beginning to be poisoned"*: Gwirtzman OH, JFKL.

140 *"Stay, for God's sakes"*: O'Brien OH, LBJL.

140 *"the rapid departure"*: Clifford, 390.

141 *"I needed that White House staff"*: Kearns, 177–8; White interview.

141 *"the potential for internecine warfare"*: McPherson OH.

141 *"Suddenly they were outsiders"*: Kearns, 175.

141 *"I don't know anybody"*: Dungan OH.

141 *no Johnson government-in-exile*: Pierson OH, LBJL; Christian interview.

142 *the Johnson Pitch worked*: White OH, LBJL; Dutton OH, LBJL.

142 *"We came down to be with Kennedy"*: Manatos OH, LBJL.

142 *"the White House staff was a personal extension"*: Schlesinger OH.

142 *"Here was a Cabinet member"*: Manchester, 475.

143 *"the Harvard lunch"*: Manchester, 474.

143 *"unfortunate, unnecessary, and highly emotional"*: Sorensen interview.

143 *thought he was nuts"*: White OH, LBJL.

143 *Salinger found it hard*: Salinger interview.

143 *LBJ's longtime secretary, Juanita Roberts*: Roberts OH, LBJL.

144 *"a totally new man"*: Sidey OH, LBJL; Dutton OH.

144 *"moved heaven and earth"*: O'Brien OH.

144 *White suspected Johnson had bullied*: White OH, LBJL.

144 *staff relations were correct*: Feldman interview; Reedy OH, LBJL; Dungan OH; Valenti OH, LBJL.

144 *Even Jackie, in his view*: Salinger OH.

144 *"he revealed it plenty"*: Krock OH, LBJL.

144 *"Those touch football boys"*: Hugh Sidey, "He Makes a Truce with the Man He Almost Came to Hate—LBJ," *Life*, Nov. 18, 1966: 38–9.

144 *Years later, Johnson openly rued*: Boatner OH, LBJL.

145 *Kennedy dominated LBJ's attention*: Eric Goldman, *The Tragedy of Lyndon Johnson* (New York: Dell, 1968): 196–200.

145 *"key figure in the great transition"*: Stewart Alsop, "Johnson Takes Over: The Untold Story," *Saturday Evening Post*, Feb. 15, 1964: 18.

145 *"You're going to have trouble"*: Corcoran, "Rendezvous with Democracy," pp. a/16–18.

145 *The affable O'Brien*: O'Brien OH.

146 *LBJ called presidential counsel Lee White*: White interview; White OH, LBJL.

146 *In January the president released a review*: Guthman, 252.

146 *"I have two daughters"*: Schlesinger, *Robert Kennedy*, 414; McPherson, 24–5; Baker.

146 *"a mechanism that cranked"*: Miller, 295–6.

146 *Baker's tight coil of personal debts*: Miller, 297.

147 *"No doubt [Johnson] should have tried"*: McPherson, 200.

147 *"They said [Baker] deceived me"*: Recording of telephone conversation between LBJ and Ramsey Clark, Jan. 25, 1967, 8:22 P.M., Tape 67.01, Recordings of Telephone Conversations, White House Series, Recordings and Transcripts of Conversations and Meetings, LBJL.

147 *"one of the most inept things"*: Reedy OH.

147 *There was little doubt*: Baker, 175–6, 183; Henggeler, 63.

148 *"I didn't really follow it"*: RFK OH, JFKL; Rogovin OH, LBJL. Larry O'Brien's experience most likely bears this out. If Kennedy had in fact known the details

of the Baker case before their public disclosure, he would surely have informed O'Brien, the administration's congressional liaison. "Either it would have been made known to me or it damned well should have," said O'Brien. O'Brien OH.

148 *RFK explored the Johnson connection*: Schlesinger, *Robert Kennedy*, 414; Bartlett OH.

148 *RFK made a surprising phone call*: Baker, 183.

148 *"I just wanted to assure him"*: RFK OH.

149 *"a feeling . . . among Johnson friends"*: " 'Bobby' Kennedy on LBJ's '64 Ticket?" *U.S. News & World Report*, March 23, 1964: 42–4.

149 *Justice as the enemy within*: Marshall OH, JFKL; Rogovin OH.

149 *"There's a double standard"*: LBJ-Clark conversation, Jan. 25, 1967. Nicholas Katzenbach did indeed invite "aggressive" attorneys to pursue the matter, but demanded they be fair as well. He wanted the department's case—or lack thereof—to be beyond reproach. In fact, if there was special treatment of the Baker case, either before or during Johnson's presidency, it was that Justice handled it with kid gloves. Rogovin thought its handling "clearly abnormal." Justice Department officials, he argues, were paralyzed by fears that any action would be seen as directed by the White House. Katzenbach OH; Rogovin OH.

149 *"a kickback pure and simple"*: Baker, 196; Goldwater campaign bumper sticker, author's collection.

149 *a federal grand jury indicted*: Miller, 299.

150 *"Johnson felt defensive and protective"*: McPherson OH.

150 *"Lyndon Johnson's Justice Department"*: Baker, 196.

150 *Johnson shrugged his shoulders*: According to Baker, Johnson told him in October 1972, "All that was within me wanted to come to your aid. But Bobby Kennedy would have crucified me, the Republicans would have crucified me, the press would have crucified me. . . . I knew it would be politically disastrous, and perhaps even legally disastrous." Baker, 267.

150 *LBJ would summon Salinger*: Salinger interview; Salinger OH.

151 *he dispatched RFK to East Asia*: Guthman, 247; Schlesinger, *Robert Kennedy*, 683.

151 *"Where did the Post"*: Recording of telephone conversation between LBJ and McGeorge Bundy, Jan. 13, 1964, 1:05 P.M., Tape 6401.13, cit. no. 1342; recording of telephone conversation between LBJ and Richard Russell, Jan. 10, 1964, 1:25 P.M., Tape 6401.11, cit. no. 1305.

151 *By some accounts*: O'Brien OH; Goodwin, 247; Schlesinger, *Robert Kennedy*, 683–4.

151 *"very, very frank with Sukarno"*: Michael Forrestal, quoted in Schlesinger, *Robert Kennedy*, 685.

152 *Washington on January 28*: Guthman, 247, 250–51; Rusk OH, JFKL.

152 *"Bob concluded otherwise"*: Guthman, 251, 253.

152 *"There were tasks to perform"*: Johnson, 12.

152 *"We were like a bunch of cattle"*: Kearns, 172.

153 *Johnson's grip on the reins*: Evans and Novak, 360–61.

153 *Califano failed to pick up his POTUS . . . line*: Califano, 25–6.

153 *Johnson's "two-shift day"*: Schulman, 67.

153 *a newly expansive spirit*: McPherson, 216; Richard Strout, "TRB from Washington," *New Republic*, May 2, 1964; Evans and Novak, 367.

154 *"what the hell's the presidency for"*: Schulman, 67; Evans and Novak, 360–82; Henggeler, 67.

154 *"It was the damnedest performance"*: McPherson OH.

154 *"the period of mourning"*: *New York Times*, March 22, 1964.

154 *"the most perfectly equipped"*: Edmund Morris, *The Rise of Theodore Roosevelt* (New York: Ballantine, 1979): 17.

154 *"After I finished"*: LBJ, recorded interview by Walter Cronkite, CBS News Special, May 6, 1970, LBJL.

155 *"We're very important to Johnson now"*: Goodwin, 295.

155 *"It's really the worst matter"*: Schlesinger, *Robert Kennedy*, 686.

155 *"A traffic violation"*: Guthman and Shulman, eds., 407–8.

155 *"he sounded like Barry Goldwater"*: Ibid., 408.

156 *It was Mann*: Mann was in fact returning to the post from which JFK had removed him. LBJ appointed Mann as assistant secretary of state for inter-American affairs, the same position Mann held under President Eisenhower. When Salinger announced Mann's reappointment on December 14, 1963, Schlesinger sent a copy of the briefing statement to Goodwin with a note attached: "R.I.P." Kennedy's Alliance for Progress, in Schlesinger's view, was as good as dead, and Goodwin was inclined to agree. Goodwin, 245; Schlesinger interview; Schlesinger to RFK, Dec. 15, 1963, SC/PF, Box 11, JFKL.

156 *"They're tryin' to run"*: Recording of telephone conversation between LBJ and Russell, March 9, 1964, 9:45 P.M., Tape 6403.07, cit. no. 2441; Guthman and Shulman, eds., 412; Schlesinger, *Robert Kennedy*, 682.

157 *"Johnson paid one iota"*: Katzenbach OH, JFKL.

157 *"I have this feeling"*: Schlesinger, *Robert Kennedy*, 687.

157 *At a Justice Department party*: Ibid., 687–8.

157 *Robert Kennedy was tired*: "I'm tired of chasing people. I want to go on now to something else," RFK said in 1964. "Bobby Kennedy's Future," *U.S. News & World Report*, July 13, 1964: 36.

157 *"Where are we going to get the votes"*: Guthman and Shulman, eds., 204–5, 210.

157 *"I felt not only did I want"*: Ibid., 211.

158 *"Those running for office"*: Giglio, 166–8; Kenneth O'Reilly, *Nixon's Piano: Presidents and Racial Politics from Washington to Clinton* (New York: Free Press, 1995): 190, 200–3.

158 *In the summer of 1961*: O'Reilly, 205.

158 *Soon Bobby was involved*: O'Reilly, 204, 211–17; Schlesinger, *Robert Kennedy*, 317, 322; Guthman, 166, 175; Taylor Branch, *Parting the Waters: America in the King Years, 1954–63* (New York: Simon & Schuster, 1988): 412–20; 426–7, 434, 469; Guthman and Shulman, eds., 97.

159 *"You can say that it would be"*: Guthman and Shulman, eds., 100.

159 *In practice, Kennedy was less reluctant*: Giglio, 176–9, 182; Branch, 648–53, 656–8, 660–9; Schlesinger, *Robert Kennedy*, 355–60.

159 *The intensity of the outburst*: Schlesinger, *Robert Kennedy*, 358–60; Guthman and Shulman, eds., 204.

160 *"if I didn't get out in front"*: Kearns, 191.

160 *"I never had any bigotry"*: Ibid., 230–31.

160 *"I'm not prejudiced nor ever was"*: Ibid., 232; Evans and Novak, 376–7.

160 *"No compromises on civil rights"*: Goodwin, 257–8.

161 *"I'll do on the bill"*: RFK OH; Recording of telephone conversations between LBJ and O'Brien, March 6, 1964, 7:20 P.M., Tape 6403.03, cit. no. 2367.

161 *"if we were not going to obtain"*: RFK OH.

162 *"Yeah, it was very nice"*: Recording of telephone conversation between LBJ and RFK, Feb. 10, 1964, 6:30 and 9:07 P.M., Tapes 6402.13 and 6402.14, cit. nos. 2003 and 2034.

163 *"They'd lose it substantially"*: RFK OH.

163 *"We just made such a fuss"*: Ibid. Memos and phone logs show frequent contact between RFK and LBJ on the bill's progress. RFK to LBJ, May 21 and June 5, 1964, WHFN-RFK, Box 6.

163 *He demoralized the weary Southerners*: Evans and Novak, 379; Kearns, 192.

163 *"We all knew that"*: RFK OH.

164 *"get down here and start civil-righting"*: Kearns, 192; Henggeler, 113.

164 *"No one knew why"*: Schlesinger, *Robert Kennedy,* 696.

164 *"Everett Dirksen liked President Kennedy"*: RFK OH.

164 *"We could have beaten Kennedy"*: Henggeler, 114.

164 *he was right to protest*: Evans and Novak, 378.

165 *Johnson signed the 1964 Civil Rights Act*: Schlesinger, *Robert Kennedy,* 696; "The Kennedys," episode 3, *American Experience,* WGBH-Thames Television.

165 *"Our enthusiasm—that of Dr. King"*: Schlesinger, *Robert Kennedy,* 696.

166 *he framed it along with a photograph*: Lemann, *Promised Land,* 184–5. Bill Geoghegan and other Kennedy aides have the same picture and inscription hanging in their offices. Geoghegan interview.

166 *Poverty was one of those concerns*: Lemann, *Promised Land,* 142; Mark I. Gelfand, "The War on Poverty," in Robert A. Divine, ed., *The Johnson Years,* vol. 1, *Foreign Policy, the Great Society, and the White House* (Lawrence, KS: University of Kansas Press, 1981): 127; Lemann, "The Unfinished War (I)," *Atlantic,* December 1988: 39; Lampman OH, LBJL.

166 *"Push ahead full-tilt"*: James T. Patterson, *America's Struggle Against Poverty, 1900–1985* (Cambridge, MA: Harvard University Press, 1986): 134; L. B. Johnson, 71; Gelfand, "War on Poverty," 128.

167 *an "alarming increase" in juvenile delinquency*: Schlesinger, *Robert Kennedy,* 440–41; Lemann, *Promised Land,* 123–5; Sugarman OH, LBJL.

167 *"Bobby best understood things"*: Schlesinger, *Robert Kennedy,* 442, 448; Hackett OH, JFKL; Sugarman OH; Hackett in Conference Transcript of Group Discussion of the Kennedy Administration Urban Poverty Programs and Policies, Brandeis University, June 16–17, 1973, JFKL: 37–8.

167 *PCJD staff members*: Lemann, "Unfinished War (I)," 43; Lemann, *Promised Land,* 133.

167 *"We felt that you could spend"*: Hackett OH. The PCJD, in any case, had a paltry endowment—no more than $3 million. Merrick OH, LBJL.

167 *The committee held that government*: Patterson, 127–9; Hackett OH; Daniel Knapp and Kenneth Polk, *Scouting the War on Poverty: Social Reform Politics in the Kennedy Administration* (Lexington, MA: Heath Lexington Books, 1971): 111–12.

168 "*He had this sort of* concrete *idea*": Lemann, *Promised Land,* 143–4 (emphasis in original).

168 "*Few things that Robert Kennedy had touched*": Daniel Patrick Moynihan, *Maximum Feasible Misunderstanding* (New York: Free Press, 1969): 80.

168 "*If [Johnson had] said no to it*": Lemann, *Promised Land,* 144.

168 "*What we said,*" Hackett recalled: Schlesinger, *Robert Kennedy,* 688.

168 *he weighed in with a memo to LBJ*: Emphasis in original. The six urban areas were Boston, MA; Kanawha County, WV; Los Angeles, CA; New York, NY; St. Louis, MO; and Washington, DC. Memorandum, "Anti-Poverty Program," RFK to LBJ, Jan. 16, 1964, Bill Moyers Office Files, Box 39, LBJL. As David Hackett wrote to Kenneth O'Donnell, it must be noted that "the Attorney General (*briefly*) saw a draft of this memorandum before his departure for Japan. He wanted it forwarded with a note indicating that it had been approved in general but not signed by him" (emphasis in original). Hackett to O'Donnell, Jan. 16, 1964, Moyers Files, Box 39.

169 "*seriously consider[ed] heading*" *the antipoverty effort*: Schlesinger, *Robert Kennedy,* 689.

169 *Johnson's choice of Shriver*: Gelfand, "War on Poverty," 131; Gordon OH, LBJL; Lemann, *Promised Land,* 114, 145–6; O'Reilly, 195.

169 "*Sarge was no close pal*": Walinsky OH, JFKL; Pollak OH, LBJL; Sanders OH, LBJL.

169 "*It'll never fly*": Lemann, *Promised Land,* 147; Sundquist OH, LBJL.

170 "*I'm sure politically [Shriver] was right*": Gordon OH.

170 "*Bob won every argument*": Hackett OH; Yarmolinsky OH, LBJL; Horowitz OH, LBJL; Schlei OH, LBJL. Schlei was RFK's chief contact on the drafting team.

170 *Shriver led a mission to Hickory Hill*: Lemann, *Promised Land,* 149, 152–3.

170 *As the drafting process continued*: Ibid., 149, 153; Lampman OH, LBJL.

170 *a host of other programs*: One of them, VISTA (a domestic Peace Corps), was inserted into the mix at Bobby Kennedy's insistence. Shriver, fearing opposition on the Hill and, perhaps, a rival to the overseas Peace Corps (still under his leadership), opposed VISTA's inclusion. Kennedy evidently won that argument too. Pollak OH; Hackett OH.

170 *an unworkable amalgam*: On LBJ's impatience see Patterson, *America's Struggle,* 140–41; Gelfand, "War on Poverty," 131–2. On the marginalization of Kennedy men see Pollak OH; Hackett OH; Poverty Conference Transcript, 229–30.

170 "*the bill was a mishmash*": O'Neill, 185.

171 *a surprisingly wide margin*: The final House vote was 226–185. Califano, 76.

171 "*I haven't had many personal dealings*": RFK OH.

171 *they won the sympathy of RFK*: Guthman, 257.

171 "*They're all scared, of course*": Guthman and Shulman, eds., 412.

171 "*side of him in his relationship*": RFK OH.

172 "*I thought that they felt*": Ibid.

172 "*a favorite of the president*": Ibid.

172 "*That's what makes me so bitter*": Ibid.

172 "*important to what my relationship*": Ibid.

173 "*affected by what was written*": Ibid.

174 *"It's just fantastic"*: Ibid.

174 *"It was a curious attitude"*: Clifford OH.

174 *"have a drink at night and swim"*: RFK OH.

174 *"There [were] a number of people"*: Gwirtzman OH, JFKL.

175 *"Bobby was absolutely convinced"*: Miller, 388.

175 *another widened it*: Gwirtzman OH.

175 *"Some [were] within the government"*: Guthman, 257.

175 *remain in public service*: Ibid., 253.

CHAPTER 7: THE BOBBY PROBLEM

176 *Robert Kennedy's only plan*: Guthman, 253; Dutton OH, JFKL.

176 *"It's too early for me"*: Evans OH, JFKL.

176 *"What does [Johnson] know"*: Goodwin, 244, 254.

177 *"The important thing is to do something"*: William vanden Heuvel and Milton Gwirtzman, *On His Own: Robert F. Kennedy, 1964–1968* (New York: Doubleday, 1970): 9.

177 *"I haven't thought it through"*: Goodwin, 246–7.

178 *"It would be an unpleasant relationship"*: RFK OH.

178 *"I think it's possible"*: Katzenbach OH, JFKL; vanden Heuvel and Gwirtzman, 7–8.

179 *Bobby knew that Johnson did not want*: vanden Heuvel and Gwirtzman, 7–8.

179 *Bobby presumed that a Vice President Kennedy*: Dutton OH.

179 *advisers implored Bobby to claim*: Gwirtzman OH, JFKL.

179 *Ken O'Donnell, while refusing*: O'Donnell OH, LBJL.

179 *"He just felt the weight"*: Marshall OH, JFKL.

179 *"If there is some way"*: Guthman, 284.

179 *Gwirtzman to write a memo*: Memorandum, Gwirtzman to RFK, n.d. [probably June 1964], Gwirtzman Papers, Box 5, JFKL; Gwirtzman OH.

180 *Ted Kennedy and Steve Smith agreed*: O'Donnell OH.

180 *something akin to horror*: Salinger OH, JFKL.

180 *Bobby railed at Larry O'Brien*: O'Brien OH, LBJL.

180 *"If Lyndon Johnson hadn't been"*: Guthman, 283–4.

181 *"If I was in the United States Senate"*: Guthman and Shulman, eds., 416, 427; RFK OH.

181 *"I don't think that Bobby"*: Spalding OH, JFKL.

182 *"I think he's hysterical"*: RFK OH.

182 *"the Bobby problem"*: Kearns, 196–200; O'Donnell OH.

182 *"as soon as I opened the papers"*: Kearns, 199–200.

182 *"the pulling and tugging"*: Jack Valenti, *A Very Human President* (New York: W. W. Norton, 1975): 128.

182 *"I don't want to go down"*: O'Donnell OH.

183 *"With Bobby on the ticket"*: Kearns, 200; Clifford, 396; Recording of office conversation between LBJ and O'Donnell (prior to telephone conversation between LBJ and Bundy), Feb. 12, 1964, 10:25 A.M., Tape 6402.15, cit. no. 2057.

183 *"if I need Robert Kennedy"*: O'Donnell OH; "The Vice Presidential Derby," *Nation*, Feb. 10, 1964: 130.

183 *Corbin was Bobby Kennedy's watchdog*: Gwirtzman OH; O'Donnell OH; Dolan interview, 1994; Evans OH.

183 *"If you have a job"*: Helen Keyes quoted in Jean Stein interview, Plimpton, ed., 69; Evans OH; Gwirtzman OH.

184 *"stay in Washington for 16 years"*: "Bobby for Veep?" *Time*, March 20, 1964: 21.

184 *the drumbeat for Bobby began*: *New York Times*, Aug. 23, 1964: 83; "As the Buildup Begins for Robert Kennedy," *U.S. News & World Report*, Feb. 10, 1964: 38.

184 *"didn't do this to embarrass Johnson"*: *Time*, March 20, 1964: 21.

184 *"to stage a big Kennedy show"*: Bartlett OH, LBJL.

184 *Corbin's contacts in New Hampshire*: Joseph A. Loftus, " 'Draft Kennedy' Unit Files in Wisconsin," *New York Times*, March 11, 1964: 1; *Time*, March 20, 1964: 21.

184 *Corbin's ham-fisted tactics*: Harold Faber, ed., *The Road to the White House* (New York: New York Times, 1965): 117; Carter OH, LBJL.

184 *Cliff Carter, Johnson's key man*: Carter OH.

185 *"the Attorney General has said"*: Faber, ed., 117.

185 *Bobby issued his disclaimers*: Alan L. Otten, "The Bobby Kennedy Dilemma," *Wall Street Journal*, March 13, 1964: 8.

185 *Johnson knew well enough*: Faber, ed., 117; Recording of telephone conversation between LBJ and Carter, Feb. 12, 1964, 9:52 A.M., Tape 6402.15, cit. no. 2056; O'Donnell OH.

186 *"It was a bitter, mean conversation"*: RFK OH; Bartlett OH (emphasis added).

186 *"He was loyal to President Kennedy"*: RFK OH; Seigenthaler OH, JFKL.

186 *"He was appointed by President Kennedy"*: RFK OH; Goodwin, 248.

186 *Johnson was momentarily unnerved*: Recording of telephone conversations between LBJ and Carter, Richard Maguire, and O'Donnell, Feb. 11, 1964, 5:21 P.M., Tape 6402.14, cit. no. 2050; LBJ and Carter, Feb. 10, 1964, 8:15 P.M., Tape 6402.13, cit. no. 2006; and LBJ and John Bailey, Feb. 11, 1964, 5:20 P.M., Tape 6402.14, cit. no. 2047; Guthman, 254; Goodwin, 248.

187 *"very indiscreet about the fact"*: RFK OH.

187 *Johnson, meanwhile, vented*: LBJ-Carter-Maguire-O'Donnell conversation, Feb. 11, 1964.

188 *"Walter Jenkins told me"*: Memorandum, C. D. DeLoach to J. Edgar Hoover, Jan. 15, 1964, JEH Official and Confidential #92.

188 *FBI documents referred to Corbin*: Memorandum, "Paul Corbin also known as Paul Kobrinsky," Jan. 15, 1964, JEH O&C #92; Recording of telephone conversation between LBJ and Carter, Feb. 12, 1964, 9:52 A.M., Tape 6402.15, cit. no. 2056; DeLoach–Hoover memo. These FBI "name checks," sometimes prepared at a president's behest and other times at the Bureau's initiative, included anything anyone had ever told the FBI about the individual in question. Charges were often unsubstantiated; "raw" files were full of misinformation. *Hearings Before the Senate, Select Committee to Study Governmental Operations with Respect to Intelligence Activities*, Vol. 6, *FBI*, Dec. 3, 1975: 161.

188 *The head of the FBI*: Richard Gid Powers, *Secrecy and Power: The Life of J. Edgar Hoover* (New York: Free Press, 1987): 390–2, 397; RFK OH; Schlesinger OH,

LBJL. Hoover's hatred of RFK dated back to Kennedy's tenure on the Rackets Committee, when the young counsel proposed a national crime commission. Hoover, jealously protective of his professional turf, indignantly vetoed the idea. Drew Pearson and Jack Anderson, "Hoover-RFK Conflict Started Early," *Washington Post*, Dec. 15, 1966: F19.

188 *"mak[ing] a fuss over him"*: RFK OH.

189 *The two men had been friends*: Powers, 394; Reeves, 288.

189 *"to really stick it in"*: Guthman OH, JFKL; RFK OH; Powers, 397.

189 *"We've gotten a lot of letters"*: Recording of telephone conversation between LBJ and J. Edgar Hoover, Nov. 29, 1963, 1:40 P.M., Tape K6311.04, PNO 15.

190 *"You're more than the head"*: Ibid.

190 *"ha[s] more confidence in me"*: Memorandum, Hoover to Tolson *et al.*, Nov. 29, 1963, JEH O&C #92.

190 *"Hoover used to send over"*: RFK OH.

190 *"There was always somebody"*: Bartlett OH.

190 *On February 6, 1964*: Richard G. Held to Hoover, Feb. 10, 1964, JEH O&C #92.

191 *the president, who griped about it*: Guthman, 257–8; Memorandum, DeLoach to Hoover, March 6, 1964, JEH O&C #92 (emphasis added).

192 *"both he and the President"*: Memorandum, DeLoach to Hoover, March 9, 1964, JEH O&C #92.

192 *DeLoach reported more suspicious activity*: Memorandum, DeLoach to John P. Mohr, March 20, 1964, JEH O&C #92.

192 *"If Guthman, Katzenbach or anyone"*: DeLoach–Mohr memo.

192 *March 10 in New Hampshire*: Faber, ed., 117. Guthman credits LBJ with 29,630 and RFK with 25,861; *U.S. News* puts it at 29,635 for LBJ and 25,861 for RFK. Guthman, 256; " 'Bobby' Kennedy on LBJ's '64 Ticket?" *U.S. News & World Report*, March 23, 1964: 42.

192 *"The 4,223-vote difference"*: Time, March 20, 1964: 21.

192 *"Draft RFK for Vice President"*: Ibid.; " 'Bobby' Kennedy on LBJ's '64 Ticket?"; Carter OH.

193 *MacArthur advised Bobby*: Guthman, 256–7.

193 *"couched in terms"*: Otten, "Bobby Kennedy Dilemma."

193 *A Gallup poll of April 12*: George H. Gallup, *The Gallup Poll: Public Opinion 1935–1971*, vol. 3, *1959–1971* (New York: Random House, 1972): 1860, 1874–5.

193 *Bobby threw himself into the pursuit*: Guthman, 270.

193 *"acting more and more like a candidate"*: Otten, "Bobby Kennedy Dilemma"; Ben Bradlee, " 'What's Bobby Going to Do?'—An Informal Talk with RFK," *Newsweek*, July 6, 1964; Schlesinger, *Robert Kennedy*, 707–8.

193 *"The attorney general's callin' me"*: Recording of telephone conversation between LBJ and Moyers, April 23, 1964, 6:03 P.M., Tape 6404.12, cit. no. 3122; Recording of telephone conversation between LBJ and Mann, May 5, 1964, 6:40 P.M., Tape 6405.02, cit. no. 3348.

194 *the addition of Poland*: Dutton OH.

194 *"I had thought that the State Department"*: Recording of telephone conversation between LBJ and RFK, June 18, 1964, 8:58 P.M., Tape 6406.11, cit. no. 3784.

195 *"I don't want him sayin' "*: Recording of office conversation between LBJ and

Bundy (prior to telephone conversation between LBJ and RFK), June 18, 1964, 9:02 P.M., Tape 6406.11, cit. no. 3785.

195 *Cracow and Warsaw*: Gwirtzman OH; "Bobby Kennedy's Future," *U.S. News & World Report*, July 13, 1964: 38.

195 *near frenzy of press excitement*: Ibid.; Bradlee, "What's Kennedy Going to Do?"; Otten, "Bobby Kennedy Dilemma."

196 *"I should think I'd be the last man"*: Bradlee, "What's Kennedy Going to Do?" 24.

196 *"I'd like to harness all the energy"*: Ibid.

196 *"the Attorney General seemed to feel"*: "Bobby Kennedy's Future," 37.

196 *"These things have a way"*: Bradlee, "What's Kennedy Going to Do?" 25; O'Brien OH.

197 *"He let it be known"*: Gwirtzman OH.

197 *"To what extent"*: Otten, "Bobby Kennedy Dilemma"; " 'Bobby' Kennedy on LBJ's '64 Ticket?" 43.

197 *"Lyndon always thought"*: " 'Bobby' Kennedy on LBJ's '64 Ticket?" 43–4.

197 *the political press, prodded by Johnson*: Ibid., 44; James Reston, "The Odd Silence Between Johnson and Kennedy," *New York Times*, March 11, 1964: 38; "As Johnson Really Takes Over . . ." *U.S. News & World Report*, April 6, 1964: 32.

198 *counted himself out*: R. W. Apple, Jr., "How Kennedy Did It: 27 Days of Hard Politicking," *New York Times*, August 26, 1964: 30.

198 *Bobby mentioned offhandedly to John Seigenthaler*: Seigenthaler OH.

198 *"I just wanted to make sure"*: RFK to LBJ, n.d. [probably June 11, 1964], WHFN-RFK, Box 6, LBJL.

198 *Lodge's departure amid growing instability*: Robert S. McNamara with Brian VanDeMark, *In Retrospect: The Tragedy and Lessons of Vietnam* (New York: Times Books, 1995): 123.

199 *At Clark Clifford's office*: Clifford, 395; Roger Hilsman in Stein interview, Plimpton, ed., 205; Sorensen interview.

199 *"I just wanted you to know"*: Recording of telephone conversation between LBJ and RFK, June 11, 1964, 6:11 P.M., Tape 6406.06, cit. no. 3699.

199 *"I would be accusing myself"*: Valenti, 141; Rostow interview.

200 *"No, no, I don't want to say that"*: Recording of telephone conversation between LBJ and Bundy, June 17, 1964, 6:38 P.M., Tape 6406.09, cit. no. 3759; Recording of telephone conversation between LBJ and James Reston, June 17, 1964, 6:58 P.M., Tape 6406.09, cit. no. 3761.

201 *Bundy and Robert McNamara also volunteered*: McNamara, 123.

201 *Johnson's approval ratings*: Gallup, 1855, 1859, 1865–6, 1869, 1874, 1880, 1885, 1901, 1903, 1911; Recording of telephone conversation between LBJ and John McCormack, March 7, 1964, 12:30 P.M., Tape 6403.04, cit. no. 2387.

201 *"If they try to push Bobby Kennedy"*: Kearns, 201; Recording of telephone conversation between LBJ and Weisl, Sr., Feb. 5, 1964, 6:24 P.M., Tape 6402.06, cit. no. 1901. In December 1963, 16 percent of Democrats would have liked to see just that, preferring Robert Kennedy as their party's presidential nominee in 1964. But Johnson, boasting a commanding lead of 68 percent, had little to fear. (No others polled above 5 percent.) Gallup, 1854.

201 *rank-and-file Democrats*: The first poll is dated May 31, 1964, the second June 24. Gallup, 1883, 1888–9.

202 *"asinine and premature"*: *Time*, March 20, 1964: 22.

202 *Even among the JFK holdovers*: Carter OH.

202 *polls indicating that Bobby's presence*: Only 4 percent of Southern Democrats would vote Republican if Humphrey was on the ticket. "Now—a Lyndon Johnson Party," *Newsweek*, Aug. 10, 1964, p. 18.

202 *The question plagued Johnson*: Valenti OH, LBJL.

202 *offered the spot to Secretary McNamara*: McNamara, 123–4.

203 *"a Kennedy without . . . having a bad Kennedy"*: RFK OH; Kintner OH, LBJL; Christian interview; Pierson OH; Telephone conversation between LBJ and Katzenbach, Jan. 25, 1967, 7:45 P.M., Tape K67.01.

203 *"if you are going to take a Kennedy"*: Miller, 387.

203 *"doesn't make a hell of a lot"*: RFK OH; Gallup, 1883, 1888–9.

203 *"Just remember, Bill"*: Goodwin, 296.

204 *Cliff Carter insisted*: Clifford, 396; Carter OH.

204 *final blow to Bobby's hopes*: Miller, 389; Goodwin, 298.

204 *"The Goldwater nomination"*: "The President's Campaign Objectives," July [23,] 1964, PL/Kennedy, Robert, Box 26, LBJL. The author is unlisted but is certainly Clifford, by his own account and others'. Clifford OH, LBJL.

204 *"He's going to tell me"*: Guthman, 280.

205 *There are two accounts*: White, *Making 1964*, 316.

205 *"I have asked you to come over"*: "Memorandum," n.d., WHFN-RFK, Box 6, LBJL. That autumn at the ranch, LBJ handed these pages to Jack Valenti for safekeeping, saying, "They're important for my memoirs." He obviously intended this memo, and not Clifford's more politically candid talking points, to be the official record of events. "DT to vm," Sept. 30, 1964, WHFN-RFK, Box 6.

205 *"evoke bitter memories"*: Clifford, 396.

206 *"He wanted me to know"*: Schlesinger, *Robert Kennedy*, 711–13.

206 *two men made tentative steps*: "Memorandum"; Schlesinger, *Robert Kennedy*, 712–13. Officially, the meeting lasted from 1:09 to 2:11 P.M. WHFN-RFK, Box 6.

207 *Bobby's parting words*: "The President's Campaign Objectives"; White, *Making 1964*, 317–18.

207 *a punch to the mouth*: Wilkins interview; O'Brien OH; Califano, 296; Schlesinger, *Robert Kennedy*, 713.

207 *"miffed, disappointed and relieved"*: Schlesinger, *Robert Kennedy*, 713.

207 *"a Machiavellian turncoat"*: "Now—a Lyndon Johnson Party," 19.

207 *Torn by conflicting loyalties*: vanden Heuvel and Gwirtzman, 11–12; Gwirtzman OH; White, *Making 1964*, 318.

207 *Johnson, for his part, believed*: Harriman OH, JFKL.

208 *White walked into the Oval Office*: White interview; White OH, LBJL.

208 *a midday press conference*: "Transcript of President's News Conference on Foreign and Domestic Affairs" and Tom Wicker, "President Bars Kennedy, Five Others from Ticket; Humphrey, McCarthy Lead," *New York Times*, July 31, 1964: 8.

208 *In the White House that afternoon*: Wicker, "President Bars Kennedy."

208 *"our amusement at these journalistic fantasies"*: Clifford, 397; Clifford interview.

208 *"In reference to the selection"*: White House Press Release, July 30, 1964, WHFN-RFK, Box 6.

208 *As Johnson retired*: Wicker, "President Bars Kennedy"; "Why the President Crossed Six Men off the List as Possible Running Mates," *U.S. News & World*

Report, Aug. 10, 1964: 14–15. According to Deke DeLoach, the president ordered him to the White House that day to determine whether seventy-two pro-Kennedy telegrams were "the real thing" or had been "cooked up" by "Bobby's people." DeLoach believed the latter. Cartha "Deke" DeLoach, *Hoover's FBI: The Inside Story by Hoover's Trusted Lieutenant* (Washington, D.C.: Regnery, 1995): 383–4.

209 *"Mr. Johnson's decision"*: Wicker, "President Bars Kennedy"; "Now—a Lyndon Johnson Party."

209 *"As I have always said"*: vanden Heuvel and Gwirtzman, 12.

209 *"Now that damn albatross"*: Miller, 389; White, 315–17; Goldman, 236–7.

210 *"he would do better"*: Miller, 389.

210 *"stunned semi-idiot"*: Alsop OH, LBJL.

210 *Kennedy, who stormed back*: Goldman, 237; Edelman OH, JFKL. Later, when his sense of humor returned, Bobby told of Johnson's "shallow duplicity" with a certain glee. Edelman OH.

210 *"He tells so many lies"*: Schlesinger, *Robert Kennedy*, 715.

210 *"Now I have to decide"*: Guthman, 281–2.

CHAPTER 8: GET ON THE JOHNSON-KENNEDY TEAM

211 *"27 days of hard politicking"*: R. W. Apple, Jr., "How Kennedy Did It: 27 Days of Hard Politicking," *New York Times*, Aug. 26, 1964: 1, 30.

211 *taken from Kenneth B. Keating*: Faber, ed., 224.

211 *"most discredited of machine hacks"*: Editorial, "The Kennedy Blitzkrieg," *New York Times*, Aug. 22, 1964: 20.

211 *Kennedy's chief aide*: "Alter Ego of Kennedys, Stephen Edward Smith," *New York Times*, Aug. 26, 1964: 30.

212 *"If this was a steamroller"*: Ibid.

212 *New York's zealous Reform Democrats*: Guthman, 288.

212 *"We will never board"*: R. W. Apple, Jr., "Kennedy Opposed by 27 Reformers," *New York Times*, Aug. 23, 1964: 1; Apple, "Kennedy Awaits Mayor's Support," *New York Times*, Aug. 21, 1964: 11; Apple, "Stratton Assails Race by Kennedy," *New York Times*, Aug. 27, 1964: 25.

212 *"Bobby-come-lately"*: "Kennedy Blitzkrieg." After RFK's announcement the *Times* offered a more tempered view: "He has demonstrated in the last four years that he is a man of capacity, energy and resolution. He has also demonstrated less engaging qualities of ruthlessness in pursuit of his goals." Editorial, "Mr. Kennedy Declares," *New York Times*, Aug. 26, 1964: 38.

213 *within the Liberal Party*: *New York Times*, Aug. 26, 1964: 30; *New York Times*, Aug. 27, 1964: 25; Schlesinger, *Robert Kennedy*, 719.

213 *"Mayor Wagner doesn't like"*: Harriman quoted in Carpenter to LBJ, Aug. 6, 1964, WHCF-Name File, Box 97, LBJL.

213 *"LBJ has very special feelings"*: "Robert Kennedy and New York: Decision Point," *Newsweek*, Aug. 24, 1964: 25–7.

213 *Kennedy led the early polls*: Schlesinger, *Robert Kennedy*, 719–20; Warren Weaver, Jr., "Keating Welcomes Kennedy to State; Offers a Guidebook," *New York Times*, Aug. 26, 1964: 1.

213 *In late August, Johnson gave Wagner*: Marjorie Hunter, "Johnson Signs Bill to Fight

Poverty; Pledges New Era," *New York Times*, Aug. 21, 1964: 1, 11; Guthman, 288; *New York Times*, Aug. 22, 1964: 20.

214 *"I think I shall respond"*: RFK to Peter Lisagor, in Schlesinger, *Robert Kennedy*, 718; "The Magic of Memory," *Time*, Sept. 4, 1964: 29.

214 *"The search for enduring peace"*: "Kennedy Enters Race for Senate," *New York Times*, Aug. 26, 1964: 1; "Kennedy's Statement on His Candidacy," *New York Times*, Aug. 26, 1964: 30; *Newsweek*, Sept. 7, 1964: 29.

214 *"It was going to be a routine convention"*: O'Brien OH, LBJL.

214 *"What if the memorial movie"*: Paul Healy, "Capitol Stuff," *New York Daily News*, July 21, 1964: 4; Henggeler, 80.

215 *LBJ struggled to safeguard*: White, *Making 1964*, 314; "Now—a Lyndon Johnson Party," 19; "LBJ: 'I Ask for a Mandate to Begin,' " *Newsweek*, Sept. 7, 1964: 28.

215 *"You might as well"*: O'Brien OH.

215 *"was he was afraid"*: O'Donnell OH, LBJL.

216 *Johnson had Hoover's FBI men*: *Hearings Before the Senate Select Committee to Study Governmental Operations with Respect to Intelligence Activities*, 94 Cong., 2 Sess., Vol. 6, *Federal Bureau of Investigation*, Nov. 18, 19, Dec. 2, 3, 9, 10 and 11, 1975: 178, 189.

216 *The request had come*: Powers, 398; *Hearings*, 163, 175; Memorandum, "Special Squad, Atlantic City, New Jersey, Democratic National Convention, Aug. 22–28, 1964," C. D. DeLoach to J. P. Mohr, Aug. 29, 1964, Exhibit 39, *Hearings*, 495.

216 *During the week*: DeLoach to Bill Moyers, Sept. 10, 1964, Exhibit 41, *Hearings*, 179, 496, 510; DeLoach, *Hoover's FBI*: 3–11.

216 *The tidbits were turned up*: *Hearings*, 163, 495–6.

216 *a Senate Subcommittee investigated*: Memorandum, H. N. Bassett to Callahan, Jan. 20, 1975, Exhibit 40–1, *Hearings*, 506; Schlesinger, *Robert Kennedy*, 715–16.

217 *"This is not a sectional choice"*: "The Man Who Quit Kicking the Wall," *Time*, Sept. 4, 1964: 22; Miller, 391–2.

217 *"I assumed it would be Bobby"*: LBJ, recorded interview by Walter Cronkite, CBS News Special, Dec. 27, 1969, LBJL.

217 *"You know, I'm not sure"*: Salinger interview; Salinger OH, JFKL.

218 *LBJ paced the south lawn*: Reedy OH, LBJL; Reedy interview.

218 *In response to Johnson's sorrowful note*: LBJ, Cronkite's interview; Goodwin, 301.

219 *The afternoon prior to his introduction*: "Man Who Quit Kicking the Wall," 29; R. W. Apple, Jr., "Kennedy Gets an Ovation; Recalls Ideals of Brother," *New York Times*, Aug. 28, 1964: 14; Seigenthaler OH, JFKL.

219 *residents of the Pageant Motel*: Nan Robertson, "Residents of the White House Move into a Motel," *New York Times*, Aug. 25, 1964: 23; O'Brien OH; Linton interview.

219 *Backstage, Bobby and John Seigenthaler*: Seigenthaler OH; "The Kennedys," *American Experience*, WGBH-Thames Television, 1992.

220 *"Just let it go"*: "The Kennedys."

220 *For sixteen cathartic minutes*: *New York Times*, Aug. 28, 1964: 1; *Time*, Sept. 4, 1964: 29; " 'In Love with Night,' " *Newsweek*, Sept. 7, 1964: 28; Edwin O. Guthman and C. Richard Allen, eds., *RFK: Collected Speeches* (New York: Viking, 1993): 114–17; Schlesinger, *Robert Kennedy*, 718; White, *Making 1964*, 348. The exact length of the ovation is unclear and probably unimportant. In any case, I use

the *New York Times'* count, sixteen minutes. But *Time* clocked it at thirteen minutes, and Theodore White and Arthur Schlesinger at twenty-two.

220 *"When I think of President Kennedy"*: Guthman and Allen, 116. "See?" barked one Chicago delegate at another. "I bet nobody else could quote Shakespeare to a Democratic Convention and get away with it. I feel sorry for this guy Keating." White, *Making 1964,* 348.

221 *"Let us now turn to our task"*: *Public Papers of the Presidents of the United States: Lyndon B. Johnson* (hereafter *"Public Papers, LBJ"*), vol. 2, 1963–64 (Washington, D.C., 1965): 1009–13; *New York Times,* Aug. 28, 1964: 14; *Time,* Sept. 4, 1964: 19B.

221 *"the emotional storm loosed"*: *Newsweek,* Sept. 7, 1964: 28; White, *Making 1964,* 348–9.

221 *"I leave with great pride"*: RFK to LBJ, Sept. 3, 1964, WHFN-RFK, Box 6, LBJL.

222 *"It is with regret"*: LBJ to RFK, Sept. 3, 1964, WHFN-RFK, Box 6.

222 *"He was in trouble"*: English OH, JFKL; Guthman, 287, 296; Edelman OH, JFKL; Nolan OH, JFKL; Schlesinger, *Robert Kennedy,* 721.

222 *The resulting campaign*: Guthman, 294; Schlesinger, *Robert Kennedy,* 722–3.

223 *New York belonged to Lyndon*: Guthman, 298; Weisl, Jr., OH, LBJL; Cater OH, LBJL.

223 *In the fall*: English OH; Nolan OH; Guthman, 298, 303; Schlesinger OH, LBJL; Schlesinger to RFK, Oct. 9, 1964, Milton Gwirtzman Papers, Box 5, JFKL; Nolan OH; Leaflet, "Robert Kennedy Talks About the Issues," and pamphlet, "Let's Put Bob Kennedy to Work for New York," in Edelman Papers, Box 9, JFKL; Guthman, 298, 303.

223 *an uneasy alliance*: English OH; Mondale OH, JFKL.

224 *At Kennedy's headquarters*: Dolan interview, 1990; Bill Haddad to RFK, Oct. 11, 1964, 1964 RFK Senate Campaign, Box 37, JFKL.

224 *"Dick Goodwin and Mike Feldman both"*: Schlesinger to RFK, Oct. 9, 1964; Moynihan to RFK, Aug. 19 and Sept. 21, 1964, Staff Files of Angie Novello, 1964 RFK Senate Campaign, Box 37. On Moynihan and LBJ, see Chapter 12.

224 *The president granted Adlai*: Moyers to Adlai Stevenson, Oct. 16, 1964, WHCF Conference File-Name File, Box 147, LBJL.

224 *Finances, like endorsements*: Gwirtzman OH, JFKL; Katzenbach OH, JFKL.

225 *"One kid said to another"*: Haddad to RFK, Oct. 11, 1964; Schlesinger to RFK, Oct. 9, 1964; Gwirtzman OH.

225 *As Lyndon Johnson planned*: O'Brien OH; O'Donnell OH.

225 *"it in"*: McPherson interview.

225 *President Johnson made his triumphant appearance*: Nolan OH; Homer Bigart, "Johnson Pledges Moves to Lessen World Tensions," *New York Times,* Oct. 15, 1964: 1, 30.

226 *"President Johnson . . . threw his arm"*: Laymond Robinson, "President Greets Kennedy Warmly," *New York Times,* Oct. 15, 1964: 1, 31.

226 *That evening, LBJ called Bobby*: R. W. Apple, Jr., "President Takes Unnoticed Trip," *New York Times,* Oct. 15, 1964: 1, 30.

226 *The Johnson-Kennedy blitzkrieg*: "Whereabouts of Candidates," *New York Times,* Oct. 15, 1964: 23; Laymond Robinson, "Kennedy Cheered with President," *New York Times,* Oct. 16, 1964; *Public Papers, LBJ,* vol. 2, 1337–47.

227 *"The United States needs a young"*: "Remarks by President Lyndon B. Johnson, Street Corner Rally, Albee Square, Brooklyn, New York, October 16 [sic], 1964," RFK Senate Papers, 1964 Campaign, Box 23, JFKL; *Public Papers, LBJ,* vol. 2, 1347–8.

227 *"signed at least as many autographs"*: *New York Times,* Oct. 16, 1964.

227 *Johnson returned to New York*: R. W. Apple, Jr., "Kennedy Steps In as Pinch Speaker," and Peter Kihss, "Johnson Hailed by 18,000 in Campaign Windup Here; He Asks Kennedy Victory," *New York Times,* Nov. 1, 1964: 1, 82; Nickerson OH, JFKL.

228 *the October 7 arrest of Walter Jenkins*: Jenkins had been arrested once before, in 1959, for "disorderly conduct (pervert)," in the vague but brutal code of the time. It did not make the papers. But in 1964, after the Republicans' tipoff, word leaked of Jenkins's arrest and subsequent hospitalization (for "nervous exhaustion") and scandal erupted. Gleeful Goldwater forces fulminated against a supposed cover-up and the need for a "moral" administration. James Reston, a bit prematurely, declared the scandal a "setback" for LBJ. (It was promptly bumped off the front page by a major shakeup in the Kremlin.) More important, Jenkins's departure and humiliation dealt a severe blow to the White House staff and to the Johnsons personally. LBJ spoke strongly and publicly on Jenkins's behalf, citing his service of twenty-five years and his "personal dedication, devotion and tireless labor." He and Lady Bird offered the Jenkins family "our love and prayers," but the president ordered Jenkins's resignation and an FBI investigation intended to spare the White House further embarrassment. Max Frankel, "President's Aide Quits on Report of Morals Case," Charles Mohr, "Goldwater Says Morality Is Demanded by the Nation," and James Reston, "Setback for Johnson," *New York Times,* Oct. 15, 1964: 1, 31; Tom Wicker, "Johnson Denies Jenkins Cover-up; Sets FBI Inquiry," and "Storm Center in Capital: Walter Wilson Jenkins," *New York Times,* Oct. 16, 1964: 1, 20.

228 *The FBI, which had tried*: Powers, 399.

228 *"It was the same material"*: RFK OH (emphasis in original).

228 *This time, though, Johnson's indiscretion*: Nickerson OH.

228 *Johnson deposited Kennedy in Belmont Park*: *New York Times,* Nov. 1, 1964: 1, 82; *Public Papers, LBJ,* vol. 2, 1558–61.

229 *"Kennedy will win"*: Earl Mazo, "Democrats Count on a Johnson Sweep to Help Full Slate in New York, New Jersey and Connecticut; Kennedy May Benefit," *New York Times,* Nov. 1, 1964: 81.

229 *Election day, November 3, 1964*: Kennedy received 3,823,749 votes to Keating's 3,104,056; Johnson tallied 4,913,156 (68.6 percent) to Goldwater's 2,243,559 (31.3 percent). Faber, ed., 295–6; Guthman, 311; vanden Heuvel and Gwirtzman, 54; R. W. Apple, Jr., "Kennedy Edge 6–5," *New York Times,* Nov. 4, 1964: 1.

229 *On the penultimate day*: "Kennedy Discusses Campaign Tactics," *New York Times,* Nov. 5, 1964: 31.

229 *There were other factors*: Guthman, 303–10; Tom Wicker, "Johnson Swamps Goldwater and Kennedy Beats Keating; Democrats Win Legislature," *New York Times,* Nov. 4, 1964: 1.

230 *At New York's Statler Hilton Hotel*: Peter Kihss, "Kennedy Greeted by Adulation of Screaming, Youthful Crowds," *New York Times,* Nov. 4, 1964: 27.

230 *"If my brother was alive"*: Schlesinger, *Robert Kennedy,* 729.

230 *when he stepped onto the dais*: *New York Times*, Nov. 4, 1964: 27; Transcript, RFK Speech, Election Night Coverage, CBS, Nov. 4, 1964, W. Averell Harriman Papers, Box 479, Library of Congress Manuscript Collection.

230 *He did not thank Lyndon Johnson*: George Lois, the Manhattan ad man who concocted the "Get on the Johnson, Humphrey, Kennedy team" slogan for the campaign, also designed covers for *Esquire*. In November 1965, the magazine's cover pictured LBJ wearing a suit of medieval armor. "Jack Kennedy was a prince among men. How do you feel about Lyndon Johnson?" the editors asked waggishly. The day the issue hit the newstands, Lois received a bottle of wine and a note from RFK: "Dear George, I see you finally got off the Johnson-Humphrey team. Love the *Esquire* cover!" George Lois, *Covering the '60s: George Lois, the Esquire Era* (New York: Monacelli, 1996): 28–9.

230 *"Bobby thanked the postmasters"*: Carpenter interview; Valenti, 150.

231 *"This is more than a victory"*: *New York Times*, Nov. 4, 1964: 1, 22; *Public Papers, LBJ*, vol. 2, 1578–82.

231 *Dolan was still in Washington*: Dolan interview, 1994; Guthman, 304.

231 *Guthman called Dolan at 6:00*: Dolan interview.

232 *"The President stated"*: DeLoach to Hoover, Nov. 13, 1964, RFK File #77-51387-[illegible], vols. 11–12, FBI.

232 *Hoover quickly engaged the IRS*: SAC, WFO to Hoover, Nov. 24, 1964, RFK File #77-36282-31. Johnson's telltale cursive "L," penned by LBJ or (as in this case) by his secretary, is on the document to indicate he had read it.

232 *It was already too late*: Dolan interview.

232 *"none of the other individuals"*: Memorandum, "Joseph Francis Dolan, Assistant Deputy Attorney General," W.V. Cleveland to Mr. Evans, Nov. 23, 1964, RFK File #77-36282. I thank Joe Dolan for making these files, obtained by FOIA request, available to me. Also, Hoover to Moyers, Dec. 2, 1964, RFK File #77-36282-33.

CHAPTER 9: "LITTLE POTSHOTS"

233 *When Robert Kennedy entered*: Evans OH, JFKL; Dun Gifford in Jean Stein interview, Plimpton, ed., 183.

233 *"conscious of the fact"*: Edelman OH, JFKL.

234 *"that streak of fatalism"*: Walinsky interview; Walinsky OH, JFKL.

234 *"head of the Kennedy wing"*: Guthman and Shulman, eds., 416.

234 *a memo of November 7, 1964*: Memorandum, "Legislative programs and strategy for new session," Walinsky to RFK, Nov. 7, 1964, Walinsky Papers, Box 24, JFKL.

234 *"The Great Society"*: *Public Papers, LBJ*, vol. 1, 1963–64, 704–7.

235 *It was almost utopian*: Schulman, 81–2; Allen Matusow, *The Unraveling of America: A History of Liberalism in the 1960s* (New York: Harper & Row, 1984): 153.

235 *"Medicare for the old"*: Kearns, 216.

236 *"getting everything through the Congress"*: Patterson, *Grand Expectations*, 564.

236 *Members of Congress*: Kearns, 217; Patterson, *Grand Expectations*, 563; Cater OH, LBJL; McPherson, 268.

236 *"There is but one way"*: Kearns, 226.

236 *As always, this knowledge*: Patterson, *Grand Expectations*, 564; Schulman, 88.

236 *Johnson had done well*: Schulman, 91; Goodwin, 288; Patterson, *Grand Expectations*, 569; Kearns, 235.

236 *Maximum output in minimum time*: Kearns, 216–19; Schulman, 94.

236 *"I always knew that the greatest bigots"*: Goodwin, 281.

236 *"an almost universal suspension of disbelief"*: Goodwin, 281–4; Graham OH, LBJL; Reedy OH, LBJL.

236 *"It didn't really seem to matter"*: McPherson interview.

236 *scrambling to keep pace*: Edelman interview; Walinsky OH.

238 *Appalachian regional development bill*: Walinsky OH; Edelman interview; Memorandum, "Senator Robert F. Kennedy's Record on Key Votes, 1965–1967," Edelman Papers, Box 10, JFKL.

238 *destined to be a bit player*: "Senator Robert F. Kennedy's Record"; Schulman, 91; Schlesinger, *Robert Kennedy*, 838; Edelman OH; Memorandum, "Senator Robert F. Kennedy was the sole or principal sponsor of the following legislation enacted by 89th Congress (1965–1966)," June 26, 1967, Edelman Papers, Box 7.

238 *Elementary and Secondary Education Act*: Hugh Davis Graham, "The Transformation of Federal Education Policy," in Divine, ed., *Johnson Years*, vol. 1, 155–6, 162–3; Schulman, 89.

239 *"You started with a base of support"*: Walinsky interview.

239 *Soon there was creeping doubt*: Walinsky OH.

239 *"What is an educationally deprived child"*: Matusow, 222–3.

239 *they crafted an evaluation procedure*: In practice, said Walinsky, evaluation "was just a constant struggle." Teachers' unions refused to cooperate by testing any child, teacher, class, or school individually. Sensing their resistance, the Department of Health, Education, and Welfare took its time developing standards for testing, finally agreeing only to test large samples, not individuals. The first results came back in the fall of 1968, after RFK's assassination, and showed, according to Hugh Davis Graham, that "Kennedy's suspicions were well founded." The 1968 study revealed that the "limited, hard evidence that does exist on attempts to improve the educational performance of low status children by providing additional money and services is devastatingly pessimistic." Students in federally funded samples appeared to perform marginally worse than control groups. And thereafter, said Walinsky, "there were schools all over America with closets full of abandoned audio-visual equipment," the educational fad of the day and the chief outlet for ESEA grants. Again, Kennedy's hunch was correct: school boards dominated by middle-class conservative bureaucrats proved unwilling to reorient schools to the needs of their poorest students. A 1966 poll revealed 70 percent of district superintendents opposed to allocating ESEA funds on the basis of poverty. Walinsky interview; Walinsky OH; Graham, 171; Matusow, 223.

240 *On Medicare, three months later*: Matusow, 226–7, 231; Patterson, *Grand Expectations*, 573–6.

240 *Kennedy did nothing to impede*: Walinsky interview.

240 *"I was too naive"*: Ibid.

240 *At Edelman's initiative*: Edelman OH; Memorandum, "Senator Robert F. Kennedy . . ."

241 *the concept of community action*: Lemann, *Promised Land*, 151, 153; James A. Morone, *The Democratic Wish* (New York: Basic Books, 1990): 225; Pollak OH, LBJL.

241 *Yet no one intended the poor:* Schlei OH, LBJL; Gordon OH, LBJL; Yarmolinsky OH, LBJL.

241 *But the fighting:* Patterson, *America's Struggle,* 146; Lemann, *Promised Land,* 164–7.

241 *"we ought not to be":* Memorandum, "Poverty Program: Opposition from the Mayors," Charles L. Schultze to LBJ, Sept. 18, 1965, Moyers Office Files, Box 56 (emphasis in original).

241 *Meanwhile the embattled OEO:* Patterson, *America's Struggle,* 147; Editorial, "Poverty Scramble," *New York Times,* Nov. 9, 1965: 42.

241 *"Something quite odd":* Memorandum, "The District of Columbia and Poverty," Rowe to LBJ, June 29, 1965, Moyers Office Files, Box 56. The activist was James Banks, director of the United Planning Organization.

242 *Johnson was already concerned about Bobby's inroads:* Califano, 79; Morone, 241; Patterson, *America's Struggle,* 143; Clipping, Henry J. Taylor, "Shriver a Headache for LBJ?" *New York World-Telegram,* Feb. 4, 1966: 26, in Joseph Dolan Papers, Box 1, JFKL.

243 *"Marvin: Start keeping me a file":* LBJ to Watson, Dec. 7, 1966, attached to clipping, Edward A. Lahey, "Kennedy Session Surprise," *Fort Worth Star-Telegram,* Dec. 4, 1966: 7-A, in Watson Office Files, Box 25; Doug Nobles to Watson, Jan. 27, 1967, in Watson Office Files, Box 31; Califano, 80; Lemann, "The Unfinished War (II)," *Atlantic,* January 1989: 55; also, Cohen OH, LBJL.

243 *LBJ asked Califano "in the strictest confidence":* The president instead plucked the successful programs from OEO's grasp one by one and dropped the ineffective ones entirely. Califano, 80. On LBJ's imprisonment, see Knapp and Polk, 14.

243 *Kennedy had few friends in OEO:* Peter Edelman considered OEO staffed by "such really awful guys that it [was] very hard to relate to them." Edelman OH; Yarmolinsky OH.

244 *Publicly Kennedy had no comment:* Edelman OH.

244 *"and some of the far-out":* McPherson to LBJ, May 18, 1966, McPherson Office Files, Box 52, LBJL.

244 *"We've got Bobby":* Recording of telephone conversation between LBJ and Katzenbach, Jan. 25, 1967, 7:45 P.M., Tape K67.01, Recordings of Telephone Conversations, White House Series, Recordings and Transcripts of Conversations and Meetings, LBJL.

244 *Model Cities, a five-to-ten-year:* Califano, 115; Lemann, *Promised Land,* 187; Patterson, *America's Struggle,* 148. On the political pliability of HUD, see McPherson OH. On the mayors, see Merrick OH, LBJL.

245 *"It's too little":* Lemann, *Promised Land,* 187.

245 *"Our present policies": Federal Role in Urban Affairs: Hearings Before the Subcommittee on Executive Reorganization of the Committee on Government Operations, U.S. Senate,* 89 Cong., 2 Sess., Part 1: 45, 47–59.

245 *"I don't know whether we delude ourselves": Ibid.,* 145–6, 187; Part 3, 764.

246 *"We have done more": Ibid.,* Part 2, 430, 451.

246 *President Johnson thought the hearings:* Califano, 134.

246 *"Johnson felt he went":* Humphrey later insisted that had he been in the Senate in 1966 he would have supported RFK and Ribicoff, not the president. Humphrey OH, JFKL; Califano, 134.

246 *"entire play in the Ribicoff hearings":* Henry Wilson to Kintner, Aug. 26, 1966, WHCF Name File, Kennedy, Robert F., Box 98, LBJL; McPherson to LBJ,

Sept. 2, 1966, McPherson Office Files, Box 52.

246 *"In the last two weeks"*: Editorial, "Our Suffering Cities and the Senators," *Washington Star*, Aug. 28, 1966.

247 *On the morning of December 12*: Robert B. Semple, Jr., "Kennedy Defends Johnson on Poor," *New York Times*, Dec. 13, 1966: 1, 42.

247 *Kennedy's energies were elsewhere*: Walinsky OH; Walinsky interview; Levinson interview.

248 *"When in two or three years"*: Memorandum, "Harlem and Bedford-Stuyvesant," Dave Hackett and Tom Johnston to RFK, Aug. 27, 1965, Gwirtzman Papers, Box 5, JFKL; Guthman and Shulman, 204; Dolan interview, 1994.

248 *"anti-business reputation"*: Carl Solberg, *Hubert Humphrey* (New York: W. W. Norton, 1984): 259.

248 *"I share . . . many hostilities"*: Goodwin to RFK, ca. Feb. 2, 1966, SC/PF, Box 4, JFKL.

248 *On December 10, 1966, Kennedy announced*: Steven V. Roberts, "Redevelopment Plan Set for Bedford-Stuyvesant," *New York Times*, Dec. 11, 1966: 1, 88; Schmidt OH, JFKL; Burden OH, JFKL.

248 *Kennedy's Bedford-Stuyvesant program*: Lemann, *Promised Land*, 193, 198; Levinson interview; John Roche to Watson, Jan. 24, 1967, WHCF Name File, Box 98, LBJL; Moynihan to RFK, July 20, 1967, SC/PF, Box 8, JFKL. By offering the program to 150 congressional districts, Johnson locked up 150 votes in the House—and abandoned the experimental nature of Model (originally, "Demonstration") Cities.

249 *"will be regarded as one"*: L. B. Johnson, 330; Roberts, "Redevelopment Plan."

249 *Model Cities did not last*: Lemann, *Promised Land*, 198, 251; Patterson, *Grand Expectations*, 648–9; Watson OH, JFKL; Schlesinger, *Robert Kennedy*, 849.

250 *In the long run*: Lemann, "The Myth of Community Development," *New York Times Magazine*, Jan. 9, 1994: 60; Schlesinger, *Robert Kennedy*, 850n.

CHAPTER 10: A WIDER WAR

251 *During the night of February 6, 1965*: George C. Herring, *America's Longest War: The United States and Vietnam, 1950–1975*, 2nd ed. (New York: Knopf, 1986): 128–9; L. B. Johnson, 124–5; Goodwin, 368.

251 *Kennedy received a letter*: William Proxmire to RFK, Feb. 27, 1965, Legislative Subject Files, Box 46, RFK Senate Papers, JFKL.

251 *"We must understand"*: Guthman, 318–19.

253 *"we're not going to win"*: Schlesinger, *Robert Kennedy*, 785.

253 *"We are going to win in Vietnam"*: *New York Times*, Feb. 19, 1962: 1.

253 *It was an adequate statement*: Schlesinger, *Robert Kennedy*, 784; Dutton OH, LBJL.

254 *"these brilliant, young, great"*: Plimpton, ed., 202–3.

254 *"got into the guerrilla war business"*: Rostow OH, JFKL. Michael Forrestal believed the term "counterinsurgency" may have been RFK's. See Plimpton, ed., 205–9.

254 *As a theory, counterinsurgency*: Schlesinger, *Robert Kennedy*, 500–502.

254 *By the summer of 1963*: Guthman, 318; Schlesinger, *Robert Kennedy*, 502; Hammer, 32–3.

255 *South Vietnam tumbled swiftly downward*: Herring, *America's Longest War,* 95–7.

255 *"Was the United States capable"*: Plimpton, ed., 207.

255 *"a garden path to tragedy"*: Reeves, 576–7.

256 *the fate of Diem*: *New York Times,* Feb. 19, 1962; Reeves, 587; Herring, *America's Longest War,* 90, 96.

256 *In late August*: Herring, 97–8; Reeves, 561–3; RFK OH.

256 *the coup was on*: Hammer, 206; McNamara, 63; Reeves, 590–91; Herring, *America's Longest War,* 100.

257 *In the late afternoon of October 29*: Bromley Smith, "Memorandum of Conference with the President, October 29, 1963, 4:20 P.M., Subject: Vietnam," NSF Meetings and Memoranda, Box 317, JFKL; Reeves, 640–41; Hammer, 274–5.

258 *In the days that followed, President Kennedy*: Herring, 105; Reeves, 644–9.

258 *At 9:00 A.M. the next morning*: Reeves, 649; Plimpton, ed., 207.

258 *When Roger Hilsman returned*: Plimpton, ed., 204; Herring, 93.

259 *Johnson had never shown much interest*: Dallek, *Lone Star Rising,* 443–4; Goodwin, 369.

259 *Kennedy sent him to Saigon*: see Chapter 4; Hammer, 34–5.

259 *In October, JFK asked General Taylor*: Maxwell Taylor OH, LBJL; Herring, 81–3.

259 *"I don't recall any substantial difference"*: LBJ, recorded interview by William J. Jorden, OH, LBJL.

260 *"Lyndon Johnson was against"*: RFK OH.

260 *usually, he followed Jack's*: Rusk detected no policy differences on Vietnam between LBJ and JFK. "Both of them looked upon Vietnam as an important place and looked upon the SEATO [Southeast Asia Treaty Organization] treaty as an important commitment. Both of them hoped that the South Vietnamese would be able to do this job more or less on their own." Rusk OH, JFKL.

260 *"grabbed a big juicy worm"*: Hammer, 312; Herring, *America's Longest War,* 110.

260 *"From November '63 until July '65"*: LBJ, Jorden's interview.

261 *"solid phalanx"*: Clifford OH, LBJL.

261 *"Everything I knew about history"*: Kearns, 252.

261 *"little piss-ant country"*: Patterson, *Grand Expectations,* 609; Herring, "The War in Vietnam," in Divine, ed., vol. 1, 28; L. B. Johnson, 152; Kearns, 252–3.

262 *"Being quite frank about it"*: Recording of telephone conversation between LBJ and RFK, May 28, 1964, 11:45 A.M., Tape 6405.11, cit. nos. 3539–40.

263 *"We went through the plan"*: Recording of telephone conversation between LBJ and RFK, June 9, 1964, 12:25 P.M., Tape 6406.03, cit. no. 3646.

264 *"Lyndon Johnson was an agreeable man"*: Recording of telephone conversation between LBJ and McNamara, June 18, 1964, 11:11 A.M., Tape 6406.10, cit. no. 3767; Kearns, 259; Hugh Sidey, *A Very Personal Presidency: Lyndon Johnson in the White House* (New York: Atheneum, 1968): 211.

264 *"If I ran out"*: LBJ, Jorden's interview; Herring, *America's Longest War,* 122; Goodwin, 355; Kearns, 282–5.

265 *In February 1965, when American B-52s*: Herring, "War in Vietnam," 39–40; Herring, *America's Longest War,* 142; Patterson, *Grand Expectations,* 608; McPherson, 393–4.

265 *In late April 1965*: L. B. Johnson, 136–7; LBJ, Jorden's interview.

266 *Bobby Kennedy, too, scoffed*: Schlesinger, *Robert Kennedy,* 745–6; Walter LaFeber,

"Latin American Policy," in Divine, ed., vol. 1, 74–5.

266 *"Wendell [Pigman] and I are all concerned"*: Walinsky to RFK, May 5, 1965, Legislative Subject File, Box 46.

267 *"Such a course would involve"*: "Remarks of Senator Robert F. Kennedy on Vietnam and the Dominican Republic," May 6, 1965, *Congressional Record*, 89 Cong., 1 Sess.; Schlesinger, *Robert Kennedy,* 745–6, 786–7.

268 *an outburst of criticism about Latin America*: Schlesinger, *Robert Kennedy,* 746; LaFeber, "Latin American Policy," 77–8, 84.

268 *On the basis of this one speech*: "The 'Liberal' Break with Johnson," *U.S. News & World Report*, May 24, 1965: 35–6; Tom Wicker, "Kennedys and Johnson," *New York Times*, June 24, 1965: 16.

269 *"I am awfully glad"*: Dolan to RFK, May 27, 1965, Dolan Papers, Box 1, JFKL.

270 *"a major, thoughtful talk"*: Dutton to RFK, May 12, 1965, RFK SC/PF, Box 3, JFKL; Guthman and Allen, eds., 217–18.

270 *"an inordinate faith"*: Walinsky OH.

270 *"Adam fought a very lonely battle"*: Gwirtzman OH, JFKL.

270 *Walinsky's differences with RFK*: Walinsky OH.

271 *"thoughtful and constructive"*: E. W. Kenworthy, "Kennedy Proposes Treaty to Check Nuclear Spread," *New York Times*, June 24, 1965: 1, 16.

271 *"President Kennedy saw this clearly"*: Ibid.; Guthman and Allen, eds., 218–22.

271 *Clinton Anderson, Democratic senator*: Kenworthy, "Kennedy Proposes."

272 *the anniversary of the United Nations*: Goodwin, 397–8.

272 *a peevish wake-up call to Walinsky*: Walinsky OH.

272 *"left the strong implication"*: Kenworthy, "Kennedy Proposes"; Editorial, *New York Times*, June 23, 1965.

273 *In Saigon, political leadership*: Herring, *America's Longest War*, 136–7; Patterson, *Grand Expectations,* 612. The analyst was William Bundy of the State Department.

273 *Once again, the manifest weakness*: Herring, *America's Longest War*, 137–8.

273 *"We know, ourselves"*: McNamara, 192, 200–201.

273 *In a memo signed by Bundy*: Ibid., 204; Kearns, 280–81.

274 *McNamara's most salient piece of advice*: Yet McNamara did not press the argument. "I don't know that you want to go that far and I'm not pressing you to," McNamara told LBJ, bullying himself into submission. "It's my judgment that you should. But my judgment may be in error here." McNamara, 201.

274 *On July 28, Lyndon Johnson announced*: Herring, *America's Longest War*, 133, 140; Patterson, *Grand Expectations,* 613–14.

274 *Kennedy weighed the costs of keeping silent*: Walinsky OH; Schlesinger, *Robert Kennedy,* 787; Guthman and Allen, eds., 275.

275 *On July 8 . . . Sherwin Markman*: Markman OH, LBJL; Guthman and Allen, eds., 275.

275 *"another Kennedy vs. Johnson issue"*: Watson to LBJ, July 8, 1965, WHFN-RFK, Box 6.

275 *Markman jumped in a taxi*: Markman OH; Guthman and Allen, eds., 275; Markman to Watson, July 8, 1965, WHFN-RFK, Box 6.

276 *"The essence of successful counterinsurgency"*: Guthman and Allen, eds., 276–80.

276 *"the man who kept me"*: Markman OH; Guthman and Allen, eds., 280.

276 "*Bobby, Schlesinger, Teddy White, et al.*": Memorandum, "Newsmen, Conversations," Horace Busby to LBJ, July 20, 1965, and Busby to LBJ, June 30, 1965, Busby Office Files, Box 51, LBJL.

CHAPTER 11: HAWK, DOVE, OR CHICKEN?

277 *In the fall of 1965*: Goodwin, 433; Walter LaFeber, "Latin American Policy," 63–6, 71–3; Guthman and Allen, eds., 223–4.

277 *When Bobby Kennedy accepted*: Schlesinger, *Robert Kennedy*, 754–5; Walinsky OH, JFKL.

278 *Therein lay the political audacity*: Walinsky OH; McPherson, 321–2.

278 "*What kind of briefing*": Schlesinger, *Robert Kennedy*, 747.

278 *Judging by Vaughn's performance*: Ibid.; Walinsky OH.

279 "*In the first place*": Schlesinger, *Robert Kennedy*, 748.

279 "*wither tree branches*": Walinsky OH; Mankiewicz OH, LBJL (emphasis added).

279 *Kennedy expressed further concern*: Mankiewicz OH; LaFeber, 71, 80; Schlesinger, *Robert Kennedy*, 748–9.

279 "*I am not thinking of running*": "Children Cry Viva As Robert Kennedy Visits Peru's Cuzco," *New York Times*, Nov. 12, 1965: 23; Schlesinger, *Robert Kennedy*, 749–50; Goodwin, 435–8.

280 "*an unofficial, privately financed*": Mankiewicz interview; "Children Cry Viva"; Schlesinger, *Robert Kennedy*, 749–50; Goodwin, 435–8.

280 *On November 20, in Brazil*: Schlesinger, *Robert Kennedy*, 752.

280 *an unnamed source was tracking Bobby's travels*: Unsigned memorandum, "Impressions of RFK South American Tour," n.d. [November 1965], WHFN-RFK, Box 6, LBJL; Goodwin, 421, 434, 454–5.

280 "*Someone suggested privately*": Memorandum, "Impressions."

282 "*perhaps less from personal preference*": "Kennedy's Course," *Nation*, Dec. 6, 1965: 430; Schlesinger, 753.

282 *The press also charged Bobby*: Mankiewicz interview; Mankiewicz OH.

282 "*business determined the internal policy*": Schlesinger, *Robert Kennedy*, 755.

283 *A Senate speech of May 9 and 10, 1966*: Guthman and Allen, eds., 227; Richard Eder, "Kennedy Bids U.S. Aid Latin Change," *New York Times*, May 10, 1966: 1; Eder, "Kennedy Cautions on U.S. Policy of Opposing Latin 'Communists,' " *New York Times*, May 11, 1966: 18.

283 "*I support the effort that's being made*": "Kennedy Rejects a National Race," *New York Times*, Aug. 26, 1965: 18.

284 *Walinsky typed out a memo*: Draft memorandum, "Conduct of the War in South Vietnam," RFK [Walinsky] to LBJ, July 21, 1965, Walinsky Papers, Box 16; Author telephone conversation with Walinsky, April 15, 1996.

284 "*If a person feels that strongly*": Schlesinger, *Robert Kennedy*, 789; Transcript, "Los Angeles Blood Speech," Nov. 5, 1965, Legislative Subject Files, Box 46, RFK Senate Papers, JFKL.

284 *important speech at Johns Hopkins*: L. B. Johnson, 133; Paul L. Montgomery, "Vietnam Debated by Intellectuals," *New York Times*, Jan. 16, 1966: 5.

284 *in November 1965, a special Italian mission*: David Kraslow and Stuart H. Loory, *The Secret Search for Peace in Vietnam* (New York: Random House, 1968):

127–34; Schlesinger, *Robert Kennedy*, 790.

284 *"Why didn't we accept the Fanfani message"*: Schlesinger, *Robert Kennedy*, 791.

285 *"We have been too optimistic"*: Larry Berman, *Lyndon Johnson's War: The Road to Stalemate in Vietnam* (New York: W. W. Norton, 1989): 12; Schlesinger, *Robert Kennedy*, 791–2.

285 *Hoping to steel Johnson*: Hugh Sidey, "He Makes a Truce with a Man He Almost Came to Hate—LBJ," *Life*, Nov. 18, 1966: 39.

285 *"[think] of you and your responsibilities"*: RFK to LBJ, Jan. 1966, WHFN-RFK, Box 6, LBJL.

286 *"Your warm letter arrived"*: LBJ to RFK, Jan. 27, 1966, WHFN-RFK, Box 6. Later, in April 1967, Johnson's secretary asked whether she might have Bobby's original letter framed: "We could do it like the Thomas Jefferson letter so all four pages could be seen and read without handling. It would be a nice subtle thing." Weeks passed with no response from the president; Bobby's letter yellowed in its file folder. mjdr to LBJ, April 1967, WHFN-RFK, Box 6.

286 *Thirty-seven days of waiting*: Berman, 12.

286 *"If we regard bombing"*: Guthman and Allen, eds., 281–2.

286 *In 1965, a diplomatic attempt*: Schlesinger, *Robert Kennedy*, 788–9, 793.

287 *This belief left Kennedy isolated*: "The Kennedy Caper," *Newsweek*, March 7, 1966: 24; L. B. Johnson, 242–5; Berman, 9–10; Edelman OH, JFKL.

287 *But as others led the debate*: Guthman and Allen, eds., 281–2; Edelman OH.

287 *"too much junketing"*: Dutton to RFK, Feb. 8, 1966, SC/PF, Box 3, JFKL.

288 *Bobby dialed Dick Goodwin's number*: Goodwin, 453–4.

288 *Later that afternoon, Goodwin read*: Guthman and Allen, eds., 282.

288 *Cavalierly, he even drew an "X"*: Speech draft, ca. Feb. 19, 1966, Legislative Subject Files, Box 47, RFK Senate Papers, JFKL; Barthelmes OH, JFKL.

288 *"If you have any thoughts"*: RFK to McNamara, Feb. 18, 1966, RFK SC/PF, 1964–1968, Box 6, JFKL.

289 *"can choose any form of government"*: Newspaper clipping, Andrew J. Glass, "In the Nation," *New York Herald-Tribune*, Feb. 25, 1966, Legislative Subject Files, Box 47.

289 *"Do you think there's any news"*: Barthelmes OH.

289 *"There are three routes"*: Guthman and Allen, eds., 282–6.

289 *in the question-and-answer session*: E. W. Kenworthy, "Kennedy Bids U.S. Offer Vietcong a Role in Saigon," *New York Times*, Feb. 20, 1966: 1–2; "Viet Coalition Rule, Including Viet Cong, Urged by Kennedy," *Washington Post*, Feb. 20, 1966: A1, 16; "Kennedy Supports Johnson on Viet Nam but Still Differs," *Washington Star*, Feb. 23, 1966: A5.

290 *"Do you speak for the White House"*: "Bobby Disclaims Certain Blessing," *Washington Post*, Feb. 20, 1966: A16.

290 *The frenzy that followed*: Guthman and Allen, eds., 286; "Kennedy Caper," 25.

290 *"Most feel Senator B. Kennedy"*: Unsigned memo to LBJ, February 21, 1966, WHCF Name File, Kennedy, Robert F., Box 98, LBJL; Christian interview; Rusk OH, JFKL; Reedy interview.

290 *Johnson ordered his marshals to attack*: Tom Wicker, "Humphrey Scores Kennedy's Plan on Vietcong Role," *New York Times*, Feb. 21, 1966: 1. For all his thunder, Humphrey later claimed to be secretly sympathetic toward Bobby's view (if not

toward Bobby). But Humphrey's doubts about escalation in 1965 had earned him a months–long silent treatment by LBJ and reeducation by military advisers. Humphrey was back in favor and eager to stay there. Schlesinger, *Robert Kennedy,* 794; Humphrey OH, JFKL; Richard Eder, "Ball and Bundy Score Idea," *New York Times,* Feb. 21, 1966: 20; "White House Stands on View on Vietcong," *New York Times,* Feb. 20, 1966: 2.

291 *Stunned and beleaguered, Kennedy returned*: Edelman interview; Edelman in Plimpton, ed., 212; Edelman OH.

291 *The next morning, February 22*: Unsigned White House memo, n.d. [February 1966], WHFN-RFK, Box 6.

291 *took a phone call from Moyers*: Walinsky interview.

291 *"It was not that I thought"*: "Transcript of a Press Conference Held by Senator Robert F. Kennedy, at 5:00 P.M., Senate Office Building, Washington, D.C., Feb. 22, 1966," Walinsky Papers, Senate Subject File, 1965–68, Box 17, JFKL; "Kennedy Supports Johnson." Rusk, however, hastened to add, "I do not myself believe that the South Vietnamese people in genuinely free elections would be the first people in history voluntarily to elect a Communist regime to power." Kennedy might well have asked, in this case, what inspired the fuss about including the NLF in pre-election talks. Arthur Krock, "In the Nation: Robert Kennedy's Proposal," *New York Times,* Feb. 22, 1966: 22.

291 *the troubling matter of General Taylor*: Schlesinger, *Robert Kennedy,* 795.

292 *"There is enormous confusion"*: Moyers to LBJ, February 22, 1966, WHFN-RFK, Box 6; "Kennedy Supports Johnson."

292 *"if Senator Kennedy did not propose"*: "Kennedy Supports Johnson."

292 *the Freedom House dinner*: John D. Pomfret, "Johnson Denies 'Blind Escalation' in Vietnam War," *New York Times,* Feb. 24, 1966: 1, 16.

292 *Bobby, who had never suggested*: The old New Dealer was David Lilienthal. Schlesinger, *Robert Kennedy,* 795; James A. Wechsler, "LBJ and RFK," *New York Post,* Feb. 24, 1966: 24; Pomfret, "Johnson Denies."

293 *"the Kennedy-Johnson controversy"*: Editorial, "The Kennedy-Johnson Debate," *New York Times,* Feb. 27, 1966; Editorial, "Coalition in Vietnam," *New York Times,* Feb. 22, 1966: 22; "Kennedy vs. Kennedy," *Washington Post,* March 1, 1966; "Kennedy on Kennedy," *Washington Post,* March 2, 1966.

293 *a "major gain" for a new breed*: David S. Broder, "Kennedy's Vietnam Plea Spurs Popularity on Democratic Left," *New York Times,* Feb. 21, 1966: 1, 18; *Newsweek,* March 7, 1966: 25.

293 *"I know there has been such talk"*: Original transcript, "Interview with Senator Robert F. Kennedy," *U.S. News & World Report,* Feb. 25, 1966, Legislative Subject Files, Box 47.

293 *"Keep stating your position"*: Dutton to RFK, Feb. 23, 1966, SC/PF, Box 3; Draft statement, Feb. 26, 1966, Legislative Subject Files, Box 47; Walinsky OH.

294 *Before Bobby's appearance on CBS*: Schlesinger, *Robert Kennedy,* 795.

294 *Walinsky was right*: Walinsky OH.

294 *"Statements that are made"*: Richard Halloran, "Humphrey, RFK Tangle on Vietcong," *Washington Post,* Feb. 28, 1966: A1, 8.

294 *An hour later, Vice President Humphrey*: Ibid.; Schlesinger, *Robert Kennedy,* 795-7.

295 *Billy Don Moyers*: "Man with Many Hats, Billy Don Moyers," *New York Times,*

Dec. 15, 1966: 54; Evans and Novak, 299.

295 *the best favor Johnson could do*: White OH, LBJL; White interview; "Man with Many Hats"; Valenti OH, LBJL; Goodwin, 267.

295 *His mastery of budget issues*: Wood OH, LBJL.

296 *Moyers developed his own network of contacts*: George Herring, *LBJ and Vietnam: A Different Kind of War* (Austin, TX: University of Texas Press, 1994): 10–11; Christian OH, LBJL.

296 *"one of the most remarkable collectors"*: "Man with Many Hats."

296 *"Anybody that understands the relationship"*: Reedy OH.

296 *Still, Johnson's treatment of Moyers*: Christian OH; McPherson OH, LBJL.

296 *"A smart fellow"*: RFK OH, JFKL.

297 *Kennedy was probably less interested*: Seigenthaler OH, JFKL. Even Schlesinger thought Kennedy's view unfair. "Rusk," he said, "was a man of great, though highly blinkered, intelligence and very rational and concise in his presentation of things." Schlesinger OH, LBJL.

297 *"It was terrifically frustrating"*: Guthman and Shulman, eds., 10–11, 44–5, 287.

297 *"I love that Dean"*: Rusk, 327, 333; Schlesinger OH; Califano, 38n.

297 *"Bobby Kennedy came down"*: LBJ, recorded interview by William J. Jorden, LBJL.

298 *"God . . . he was on the phone"*: Dolan interview, 1990, 1994; Gwirtzman OH, JFKL; Mankiewicz OH. A year before becoming Kennedy's press secretary, Mankiewicz was already awestruck by Moyers's performance: "If you had anything to do with the President's speech last night (and it occurs to me you may have), you should be very proud of yourself. I have not seen or heard an address which moved me as much since the days of FDR, and I was a very young and impressionable fellow then." Mankiewicz to Moyers, March 16, 1965, Mankiewicz Papers, Box 34, JFKL.

298 *"[Johnson] had assigned me"*: Moyers, recorded interview by Robert Dallek, May 14, 1997, Washington, DC, transcript courtesy Robert Dallek; Evans OH, JFKL; "LBJ vs. RFK?" *Newsweek*, June 13, 1966: 35; Christian OH; Christian interview.

298 *"That's the trouble"*: Henggeler, 169; Christian OH.

298 *Johnson's other concerns about his press secretary*: Jacobsen OH, LBJL; Reedy OH; Christian OH; Larry Berman, "Johnson and the White House Staff," in Divine, ed., vol. 1, 192–3.

298 *Moyers fretted openly*: Christian interview; Carpenter OH, LBJL.

298 *Moyers played increasingly to Johnson's prejudices*: Moyers to LBJ, Sept. 10, 1966, and attached clipping, Peregrine Worthstone, "A Kennedy in Tarnished Armour," London *Daily Telegraph*, Sept. 4, 1966, Watson Papers, Box 25, LBJL.

299 *"I think it is important for the President"*: Moyers to Rostow, September 30, 1966, Moyers Office Files, Box 12. On the similar efforts of Moyers's staff, see Hayes Redmon to Moyers, Sept. 2 and Oct. 4, 1966, Moyers Files, Box 12.

299 *"Moyers was reaching out"*: Bartlett OH, LBJL; Weisl, Jr., OH, LBJL; Christian interview.

299 *Wayne Morse moved*: Eugene J. McCarthy, *Up 'Til Now: A Memoir* (San Diego: Harcourt Brace Jovanovich, 1987): 184. The only five senators to support the amendment were Morse, Fulbright, Gruening, McCarthy, and Milton R.

Young.

299 *Edelman noted with regret*: Schlesinger, *Robert Kennedy*, 797; Edelman OH; Max Frankel, "Alternative in Vietnam," *New York Times*, April 25, 1966.

299 *On April 27, after four days of clashes*: E. W. Kenworthy, "Kennedy Assails Sanctuary Policy," and "Text of Kennedy Statement on Bombing in Vietnam," *New York Times*, April 28, 1966: 1–2.

300 *"Senator Kennedy was quite effective"*: Kintner to LBJ, April 28, 1966, WHCF Confidential File-Name File, Box 147, LBJL (emphasis added).

300 *That Sunday, May 1, Javits appeared*: Richard Witkin, "Javits Bows Out of Albany Race; Seeks Role in '68," *New York Times*, May 2, 1966: 1, 28.

300 *"Senator Robert F. Kennedy has applied"*: Watson to LBJ, March 5, 1966, Watson Office Files, Box 25.

300 *At the invitation of the anti-apartheid*: Schlesinger, *Robert Kennedy*, 800–1.

300 *keeping tabs on Kennedy's itinerary*: Redmon to Moyers, May 14, 1966, Moyers Office Files, Box 12.

300 *"lay the foundation"*: Moyers to LBJ, May 26, 1966, 3:10 A.M., Country File, Africa, General, National Security File, Box 76, LBJL.

301 *"I spoke directly of enforced inequality"*: L. B. Johnson, 353; White House Press Release, "Remarks of the President at White House Reception Celebrating the Third Anniversary of the Organization of African Union," May 26, 1966, Country File, Africa, General, NSF, Box 76; Schlesinger, *Robert Kennedy*, 801.

301 *"[Kennedy] arrives in Johannesburg"*: Redmon to Moyers, May 14, 1966.

301 *"shared determination to wipe away"*: Guthman and Allen, eds., 231–46; Schlesinger, *Robert Kennedy*, 802–6.

302 *"Kennedy's voice is already strong enough"*: "The Kennedy Safari," *Nation*, July 4, 1966: 2–3.

302 *"unique, if difficult, opportunity"*: Memorandum, "Check List of African Problems," Rick Haynes to Rostow, June 8, 1966, Files of Ulric Haynes, NSF, LBJL; Memorandum, "Senator Robert Kennedy's statements in Africa," Rostow to LBJ, June 21, 1966, Appointment File (Diary Backup), Box 37, LBJL.

302 *In July 1966, Dick Goodwin sipped*: Goodwin, 463–4.

303 *"Don't engage in a running attack"*: Dutton to RFK, Feb. 23, 1966; Schlesinger, *Robert Kennedy*, 822–3; Walinsky interview.

303 *Bobby's silence bespoke*: Mankiewicz OH; Walinsky OH; Schlesinger, *Robert Kennedy*, 798.

303 *"You haven't said anything"*: Jack Newfield, *Robert Kennedy: A Memoir* (New York: New American Library, 1969): 128.

304 *"Time and again Kennedy tried"*: Author telephone conversation with Walinsky, April 15, 1996.

304 *"He tried talking privately"*: Edelman OH.

304 *"despair and fatalism"*: Schlesinger to RFK, Jan. 23, 1967, Walinsky Papers, Box 18.

CHAPTER 12: ALL-OUT LOYALTY

305 *"What . . . are the basic impressions"*: Dutton to RFK, July 29, 1965, SC/PF, Box 3, JFKL.

305 *intense (and growing) fascination*: Warren Weaver, Jr., "Will the Real Robert

Kennedy Stand Up?" *New York Times Magazine,* June 20, 1965: 8–9+. The poll was taken from Oct. 29 to Nov. 2, 1965, and released on Nov. 28. Gallup, 1972–3.

305 *"receives more mail"*: "Another Kennedy Seeks the Presidency: Inside Story of New York Senator's Plans," *U.S. News & World Report,* June 27, 1966: 56–61; " 'Kennedy for President'—A Buildup Starts for '72," *U.S. News & World Report,* May 10, 1965: 49–50.

306 *The buildup, observers declared:* " 'Kennedy for President.' "

306 *Prematurely, the press hailed Bobby's emergence:* Tom Wicker, "Kennedys and Johnson," 16; "Why 'Liberals' Grumble about LBJ," *U.S. News & World Report,* July 5, 1965: 41; James Reston, "The Education of Robert Kennedy," *New York Times,* Nov. 11, 1965: 6.

306 *Most congressional press secretaries:* Barthelmes OH, JFKL; Schlesinger, *Robert Kennedy,* 730; Mankiewicz interview; Arthur Krock, "In the Nation: 'He'll Prent [sic] It' Just the Same," *New York Times,* May 26, 1966: A46.

307 *Kennedy pored over:* Salinger interview; Guthman OH, JFKL; Barthelmes OH; Dutton to RFK, July 29, 1965; Mankiewicz interview.

307 *"The press . . . did not convey":* Edelman OH, JFKL; Mankiewicz interview; Barthelmes OH.

307 *Ted Kennedy's dinner-dance:* Art Buchwald, *Son of the Great Society* (New York: G. P. Putnam's Sons, 1966): 85–6; Gwirtzman OH.

308 *According to Walinsky:* Walinsky OH, JFKL.

308 *"that son-of-a-bitch":* Dolan interview, 1990; Rosemary McBride to Dolan, Feb. 17, 1966, WHCF Name File, Box 98, LBJL. Him and Her were a tragic pair. Her died in January 1965 after swallowing a rock on the White House grounds. Him was crushed under the wheels of a staff car on the South Lawn in June 1966. "White House Auto Kills President's Favorite Dog," *Washington Post,* June 16, 1966: A3.

308 *Walinsky took a pencil:* "Every One Counts: The Democratic Campaign Handbook 1966," Walinsky Papers, Box 2, JFKL; Dolan interview, 1994; "R. Kennedy's Aide Attacks U.S. Policy," *Washington Post,* June 19, 1966: A18; Phil Casey, "Africa's Concern about U.S. Cited by Kennedy on Return," *Washington Post,* June 20, 1966: A7.

309 *calling Johnson "the president":* Walinsky OH; Dolan interview, 1990; Evans OH, JFKL; Goodwin, 415; Edelman and Walinsky interviews; Barthelmes OH; Walinsky OH.

309 *Kennedy would not contribute to it:* Walinsky OH; Dolan interview, 1994.

309 *Johnson knew this, and it frightened him:* Kearns, 213.

309 *"Next to LBJ":* "Another Kennedy Seeks the Presidency."

310 *"Johnson's mythogenic capacity":* "The Kennedy Legend and the Johnson Performance," *Time,* Nov. 26, 1965: 30–31.

310 *LBJ considered his own public image:* McPherson OH, LBJL; David Culbert, "Johnson and the Media," in Divine, ed., vol. 1, 214–17, 228, 231, 237.

310 *Advisers encouraged Johnson:* McPherson to LBJ, April 28, 1966, McPherson Office Files, Box 52, LBJL; Markman OH, LBJL; Rostow OH, LBJL; McPherson OH.

310 *When Lyndon Johnson did allow himself:* Henggeler, 133–4. See Henggeler,

131–42, for a detailed account of crafting the Johnson image.

311 *White House press aides contrived*: Ibid., 134, 140–41.

311 *Awestruck aides bragged*: White OH, LBJL; McPherson OH; Rusk, 333.

311 *"overbred smart alecks"*: Kearns, 122; Henggeler, 133–4; "Will Bobby's Friends Trip Up LBJ in '68?" *U.S. News & World Report*, April 10, 1967: 53–4.

311 *Reedy was often infuriated*: Reedy interview; Weisl, Sr. OH, LBJL; McPherson, 294.

312 *Johnson set out to co-opt*: Henggeler, 136–9; Cater OH, LBJL; Huntley OH, LBJL; McPherson OH; Goldman, 514.

312 *"More perhaps than other people"*: "Failure of a Mission," *Nation*, Sept. 19, 1966: 236.

312 *Brandeis University's John Roche*: McPherson, 270–73; Roche OH, LBJL.

312 *"Hickory Hill seminars"*: Penn Kimball, "He Builds His Own Kennedy Identity and the Power Flows Freely to Him," *Life*, Nov. 18, 1966: 139.

313 *"at least one major, exciting personal adventure"*: Dutton to RFK, April 6, 1966, SC/PF, Box 3.

313 *"picture of President Johnson in a bathing suit"*: Henggeler, 141–2.

313 *"scrutinized the daily papers"*: Goodwin, 271.

314 *"you could never convince"*: Cater OH; Pierson OH, LBJL; Kintner OH, LBJL; "Another Kennedy Seeks the Presidency." "You spoke to me," Kintner reminded the president, "about an article in *Newsweek* called 'Is It Superman? No, It's LBJ.' In all honesty . . . I did not have the same reaction you did. I thought the article was favorable." Kintner to LBJ, Feb. 27, 1967, FG1, Box 14, LBJL.

314 *"Kennedy press zealots"*: *New York Times*, July 12, 1960: 20.

314 *Johnson ordered the FBI to investigate*: Recording of telephone conversations between LBJ and Reedy, June 9, 1964, 3:29 P.M. and 8:34 P.M., Tape 6406.04, cit. nos. 3647–48; Author telephone conversation with John Barron; Memorandum, "Re: The 'Washington Evening Star's' Animosity Towards the President," DeLoach to Tolson, June 17, 1965, J. Edgar Hoover Official and Confidential File #92; Memorandum, "Peter Lisagor 'Chicago Daily News' Information Concerning," R. E. Wick to DeLoach, March 3, 1966, JEH O&C File #92. The memo follows up on Johnson's request to Hoover for information on Lisagor and the source of Lisagor's leaks. See memorandum for official confidential files, J. E. Hoover, Feb. 25, 1966.

314 *"Kennedy has been able to plant stories"*: Hoover to Tolson, Belmont *et al.*, Sept. 2, 1965, FBI File #77-51387-1792, vols. 11–12.

314 *At private dinners with Chet Huntley*: Huntley OH; Sidey OH, LBJL. Johnson's aides were not so sure the president could trust Huntley, either: when Huntley privately expressed his support of the war, Jack Valenti was shocked. Valenti wrote Marvin Watson that "this, of course, is in contrast to what many of us believed to be the truth—I had heard Huntley was in the other fellow's [RFK's] camp." Valenti to Watson, Feb. 25, 1968, Watson Files, Box 31, LBJL.

315 *"They thought they had a buffoon"*: McPherson OH; Sidey OH.

315 *The venomous talk trickled back*: Henggeler, 168; McPherson OH; Alsop OH, LBJL; Huntley OH.

315 *"They spread the doubt"*: Goodwin, 405; Pierson OH; Henggeler, 181–2.

316 *"Let's start working"*: Carpenter to LBJ, April 1, 1966, WHFN-RFK, Box 6,

LBJL.

316 *In a clumsy attempt*: Henggeler, 182–5, 194; Larry Berman, "Johnson and the White House Staff," in Divine, ed., vol. 1, 192–3.

316 *"His regionalism, accent"*: Redmon to Moyers, June 9, 1966, Moyers Files, Box 12, LBJL.

316 *"Not a sparrow fell"*: Roche OH; LBJ, recorded interview by Walter Cronkite, CBS News Special, May 6, 1970, LBJL; Kintner OH.

317 *Johnson could never trust the Kennedy men*: Dutton OH, JFKL; Roche OH.

317 *"Do you know there are some disloyal"*: Goodwin, 394–6.

317 *He inserted a hardcore Johnson loyalist*: Boatner OH, LBJL; Rogovin OH, LBJL.

317 *overlapping spheres of influence*: Pierson interview; McPherson to LBJ, Aug. 31, 1966, and Aug. 11, 1966, 11:40 A.M., McPherson Files, Box 52, LBJL.

318 *By 1965, loyalty had become*: Cohen OH, LBJL; Black interview; Black OH, LBJL.

318 *Daniel Patrick Moynihan had lifted*: McPherson to LBJ, June 24, 1965, 12:45 P.M., McPherson Files, Box 52; Douglas Schoen, *Pat: A Biography of Daniel Patrick Moynihan* (New York: Harper & Row, 1979): 74.

319 *Moynihan began spending weekends*: McPherson to LBJ, June 24, 1965, 12:45 P.M.; Schoen, 84–91, 108–9; McPherson OH.

319 *"Nobody in the country"*: McPherson to Moyers, May 19, 1965, McPherson Files, Box 51.

319 *"the most imaginative man"*: McPherson to LBJ, June 14, 1965, McPherson Files, Box 52.

319 *the* New York Times *had just reported*: Schoen, 94–5.

319 *a remarkable pair of memoranda*: McPherson to LBJ, June 24, 1965, 12:45 P.M.; Memorandum, "Thoughts on Bobby Kennedy and loyalty," McPherson to LBJ, June 24, 1965, 6:00 P.M., McPherson Files, Box 21.

321 *The memo achieved none of these things*: McPherson OH; McPherson to LBJ, July 7, 1965, McPherson Files, Box 52.

321 *LBJ's appointment of Roger Wilkins*: Wilkins interview; Wilkins, *A Man's Life: An Autobiography* (New York: Simon & Schuster, 1982): 103.

322 *In late 1965, Attorney General Nicholas Katzenbach*: Wilkins interview.

322 *As the hearings approached*: Ibid.

322 *"Johnson just didn't want Bob Kennedy"*: Schlesinger, *Robert Kennedy,* 740.

322 *Wilkins ignored the messages*: Wilkins interview; "A Panel in Senate Backs Rights Aide: Roger Wilkins Approved by Commerce Committee," *New York Times,* Jan. 26, 1966: 17.

323 *"poise and . . . calm judgment"*: White House Press Release, "Remarks of the President and Hon. John T. Connor, Secretary of Commerce, at Swearing-In Ceremony for Roger Wilkins as Director of Community Relations Service in the Theater," Feb. 4, 1966, Folder "Roger Wilkins D-DC," John Macy Office Files, LBJL.

323 *"the son of a bitch"*: Wilkins interview.

323 *Solicitor General Thurgood Marshall*: Ibid. Wilkins recaptured Johnson's goodwill quite accidentally, by defending his policies on an obscure Sunday-morning TV show. LBJ was watching only because the show's host was Cokie Boggs (the future Cokie Roberts), daughter of Johnson's friend Congressman Hale Boggs. Wilkins interview.

323 *"Johnson's paranoia used to get"*: Roche OH; Goodwin, 393.

324 *"Bobby saw his chance"*: Goodwin, 405–6.

324 *"infecting the entire process"*: Ibid., 392–409.

325 *Bobby Kennedy—and the conventional wisdom*: Seigenthaler OH, JFKL; Dungan OH, LBJL; Alan Otten, "The Consenting Advisors," *Wall Street Journal*, Feb. 27, 1967; Berman in Divine, ed., vol. 1, 206–7; Roche OH; Pierson OH.

325 *Yet none could completely resist*: McPherson OH; Boatner OH; Valenti OH, JFKL; Pollak OH, LBJL.

325 *An average day in the Johnson White House*: Valenti, 163; Christian OH; Loyd Hackler OH, LBJL; McPherson, 157; Cater OH; Rowe OH, LBJL; McPherson to LBJ, June 18, 1965, McPherson Files, Box 52.

326 *"I don't know why he wanted"*: Christian interview.

326 *Marvin J. Watson was a Texas businessman*: White interview; White OH; Goodwin, 387; Pierson OH; McPherson, 251–2.

326 *Watson was his dealer*: The "Robert Kennedy" folder in Box 25 of Marvin Watson's Office Files holds a treasure trove of purported political intelligence. See, for example, Cliff Carter to Watson, July 18, 1966; LBJ to Watson, Dec. 7, 1966; Invitation, " 'Kennedy in '68' Cocktail Party, Citizens for Kennedy in '68," Oct. 8, 1967; C. R. Smith to Warren Woodward, Jan. 15, 1968; Woodward to Watson, Jan. 16, 1968; and attached clippings, Watson Files, Box 25. Also, Watson to LBJ, May 18, 1965, WHFN-RFK, Box 6.

327 *Watson cannot shoulder all the blame*: Califano to LBJ, Dec. 8, 1967, WHCF-Name File, Kennedy, Robert F., Box 98, LBJL; Al M. to Moyers, Feb. 20, 1967, and Christian to LBJ, Feb. 24, 1967, PL/Kennedy, Robert F., Box 26, LBJL; McPherson to LBJ, Nov. 2, 1967, McPherson Files, Box 53; McPherson OH.

327 *"you tend to view everything"*: McPherson OH.

CHAPTER 13: SHADOWBOXING

328 *"This nation is mighty enough"*: Schulman, 234; Califano, 119; "The Bobby Phenomenon," *Newsweek*, Oct. 24, 1966: 36.

328 *Kennedy uneasily approved every appropriation*: Unsigned and undated memorandum, "Senator Robert F. Kennedy's Record on Key Votes, 1965–1967," Peter Edelman Papers, Box 10, JFKL.

328 *In mid-October, Kennedy brazenly pressed*: "Bobby Phenomenon"; Edelman OH, JFKL.

329 *"if [Kennedy] really wanted to win"*: "Bobby Phenomenon"; Richard Reeves, "The People Around Bobby," *New York Times Magazine*, Feb. 12, 1967: 88–9; Coleman OH, JFKL; Mankiewicz OH, LBJL.

329 *a spotlight on rural hunger*: "Slow Starvation Seen in Mississippi," *New York Times*, April 26, 1967: 28; Gelfand, "War on Poverty," 140–41.

329 *On April 9, 1967, Kennedy*: Editorial, "Grudge Fight," *Nation*, May 22, 1967: 644; Mankiewicz OH; Wright quoted in Plimpton, ed, 124. To publicize his war on poverty, LBJ visited a poor Appalachian household in 1965. "They seemed real happy to talk with me and I felt real good about that," Johnson recalled. "Then as I walked out, I noticed two pictures on the wall. One was Jesus Christ on the cross. The other was John Kennedy. I felt as if I'd been slapped in the face." Goodwin, 248.

330 *When Kennedy did go back to Washington*: Freeman did, however, immediately send a representative to Mississippi. Schlesinger, *Robert Kennedy*, 855–6; LBJ to Califano, April 17, 1967, 6:15 P.M., and Califano to LBJ, April 17, 1967, 6:35 P.M., WHCF, WE9 Ex, Box 29, LBJL.

330 *"I just don't know"*: In his farewell budget message to Congress in January 1969, LBJ endorsed a larger appropriation for food stamps. By this time, the gesture was meaningless. Gelfand, *War on Poverty*, 140–41.

330 *"Why would he respond so coldly"*: "Grudge Fight."

331 *"as an attack by Kennedy"*: Schlesinger, *Robert Kennedy*, 856–7; Edelman interview; "Grudge Fight." A *Des Moines Register* reporter calculated that LBJ thereafter rejected at least a dozen successive staff appeals for food aid reform.

331 *"The two bills were incredibly intricate"*: Newfield, 104–5; Levinson interview.

331 *"the creation of new jobs"*: Newfield, 104–5; Edelman interview; Schmidt OH, JFKL.

332 *"Johnson put a whole task force"*: Edelman OH; Newfield, 105–6; Monroe W. Karmin, " 'Follow the Leader' as Played by LBJ," *Wall Street Journal*, March 7, 1968.

332 *Bobby marshaled some former JFK advisers*: Newfield, 106; Mankiewicz OH.

332 *"HUD and Treasury are primed"*: Levinson to LBJ, March 19, 1968, WHCF-Name File, Kennedy, Robert F., Box 98, LBJL; Levinson interview; Karmin, " 'Follow the Leader' "; Newfield, 105–6.

333 *"How can they be so petty"*: Newfield, 106. In January 1968, Califano began discussions with two Kennedy advisers, but presidential politics made mutual trust impossible. The talks broke down quickly.

333 *Later in the summer of 1967*: Edelman interview; Edelman OH; Coleman OH.

333 *Other leaks confirmed*: Edelman interview; Edelman OH; Coleman OH.

333 *"When you have a hundred thousand"*: John Gardner OH, LBJL; Edelman interview. Schnittker forwarded helpful critiques on speeches and made policy recommendations to Edelman. Edelman Papers, Box 1, JFKL.

334 *"you had to be careful"*: Linton interview.

334 *It was draining*: Edelman interview; Mankiewicz OH; Guthman and Shulman, eds., 211.

334 *"at least one or two bills"*: Dutton to RFK, April 6, 1966, RFK SC/PF, Box 3, JFKL; Edelman and Walinsky interviews.

334 *"We were laying the groundwork"*: Edelman interview.

335 *"Long range planning"*: "Bobby Phenomenon"; Mankiewicz interview.

335 *Joe Califano reflected*: Califano, 296.

335 *"little potshots"*: Recording of telephone conversation between LBJ and Katzenbach, Jan. 27, 1967, 7:45 P.M., Tape K67.01, Recordings of Telephone Conversations, White House Series, Recordings and Transcripts of Conversations and Meetings, LBJL; Califano, 158.

335 *Bobby was not a team player*: Nimetz, Edelman, and Mankiewicz interviews.

336 *more inclined to support Johnson*: Dolan interview, 1994; Tydings OH, JFKL. Senator Tydings, however, recalled one instance when RFK might have opposed an administration bill for contrarian purposes only: a minor amendment to the Presidential Election Campaign Fund Act. Tydings surmised that "if his brother had been President he would [have] support[ed] it." Tydings OH; also, Bellinger to Fred Panzer, March 29, 1968, Panzer Office Files, Box 372, LBJL.

336 *the press characterized minor steps*: "Bobby Kennedy: New Thoughts About Tackling LBJ in '68?" *U.S. News & World Report*, Sept. 11, 1967: 20.

336 *"Contrary to what may be"*: "Another Kennedy Seeks the Presidency," *U.S. News & World Report*, June 27, 1966: 58; Bellinger to Panzer, March 29, 1968. Eugene McCarthy supported LBJ in 62 percent of roll-call votes in 1965, 64 percent in 1966 and 56 percent in 1967; Ted Kennedy's numbers were 75, 71, and 68 percent. Unsigned and undated memorandum, "Voting Patterns," Edelman Papers, Box 10.

336 *a private White House study*: At 84 percent, McCarthy was an even stronger supporter. Unsigned and undated memorandum, "Select Senate Votes, 90th Congress—First Session, Breakdown of Voting by Senators Robert Kennedy and Eugene McCarthy," Panzer Files, Box 372.

336 *"Don Quixote may have been"*: Memorandum, "Issues for Attention," Dolan to RFK, November 21, 1967, Walinsky Papers, Box 2, JFKL (emphasis in original); Dutton to RFK, Dec. 8, 1966, SC/PF, Box 3.

336 *"It is the speeches"*: "Another Kennedy."

337 *In the state of New York*: "State Leaders in New Spotlight," and Warren Weaver, Jr., "New Political Chieftains Emerging in Two State Parties in Wake of Election Upheaval; Kennedy Viewed as a New Power," *New York Times*, Nov. 5, 1964: 37–8.

337 *These were high expectations*: Gwirtzman OH, JFKL; William V. Shannon, *The Heir Apparent: Robert Kennedy and the Struggle for Power* (New York: Macmillan, 1967): 147; Schlesinger, *Robert Kennedy*, 808–9; Newfield, 142–3.

337 *Moreover, any takeover*: Schlesinger, *Robert Kennedy*, 809; Walton OH, JFKL.

338 *Kennedy had certain obligations*: Newfield, 143–4; Blumenthal OH, JFKL; Gwirtzman OH.

338 *in January 1965, Kennedy stumbled*: Shannon, 148–50; Newfield, 146–7; vanden Heuvel interview; Gwirtzman OH; English OH, JFKL.

338 *In truth, Kennedy's intervention*: English OH; "Wagner, Rocky and the Kennedy Act," Editorial, *Nation*, Feb. 22, 1965: 184–5; Warren Weaver, Jr., "Will the Real Robert Kennedy Please Stand Up?" *New York Times*, June 20, 1965: VI, 9.

338 *the White House followed the internecine battles*: Schlesinger, *Robert Kennedy*, 809.

339 *Johnson installed Edwin Weisl, Sr.*: *Newsweek*, Sept. 7, 1964: 29; vanden Heuvel interview.

339 *As committeeman, Weisl wielded*: Weisl, Jr., OH, LBJL; English OH; Nickerson OH, JFKL.

339 *"Mr. Johnson may not want"*: "Kennedy Family: Another Chapter," *U.S. News & World Report*, Nov. 16, 1964: 48; Katzenbach OH, JFKL; Javits OH, JFKL; English OH.

339 *Johnson savored sweet vengeance*: Baker, 144, 146–7; Manchester, 4; LBJ to RFK, Sept. 7, 1961, VP Papers, VP Masters, Box 29, LBJL; Dungan OH.

340 *A typically shrewd maneuver*: Katzenbach interview; Memorandum, "Re: Thurgood Marshall's Replacement on the Second Circuit," Katzenbach to LBJ, July 14, 1965, Katzenbach Papers, Box 13, JFKL.

340 *Wilfred Feinberg, a man of merit*: Jeffrey B. Morris, *Federal Justice in the Second Circuit: A History of the United States Courts in New York, Connecticut and Vermont, 1787–1987* (New York: Second Circuit Historical Committee, 1987): 176, 181; Katzenbach interview.

341 *"You don't seem to understand"*: Richard Reeves, "Kennedy: Two Years After His Election," *New York Times*, Nov. 14, 1966: 1, 44; Watson to LBJ, Oct. 13, 1966, WHCF-Name File, Box 98, LBJL; Katzenbach OH.

341 *"one of the few pro-Administration figures"*: Unsigned memo to Watson, and Memorandum, "The Howard Samuels Flap," William Connell to Watson, Aug. 11, 1967, Watson Files, Box 25, LBJL; English OH.

341 *Johnson's policy in New York State*: Connell to Watson, April 11, 197; Editorial, "The Kennedy Touch," *Washington Star*, July 1, 1966; "Will the Real Robert Kennedy"; "Kennedy: Two Years After."

341 *Kennedy dodged, or botched, every power play*: Shannon, 156–67; vanden Heuvel interview; Shannon, 168–76; Schlesinger, *Robert Kennedy,* 808–10; Gwirtzman OH; Editorial, "Revolt in Manhattan," *New York Times*, May 26, 1966: 46; "Kennedy Touch."

342 *Kennedy's interest in New York politics*: Shannon, 147–8, 201–4; Newfield, 142; Schlesinger interview; Javits OH; English OH; Coleman OH.

342 *By March, several Democrats*: Jerry Bruno to RFK, April 12, 1966, Gwirtzman Papers, Box 6, JFKL; Shannon, 177; Gwirtzman OH; Blumenthal OH; Nickerson OH; Memorandum, "Candidate for American Specialists Grant: Eugene H. Nickerson," John Pressly Kennedy to McPherson, March 29, 1965, McPherson Files, Box 7, LBJL. The Johnson administration had sent, among others, Chief Justice Earl Warren to Africa; the speaker of the California assembly, Jesse Unruh, to East Asia; and the presidents of Young Democrats and Young Republicans to Europe.

343 *"Under ordinary circumstances"*: McPherson to LBJ, March 31, 1965, McPherson Files, Box 52; McPherson to Moyers, April 13, 1965, McPherson Files, Box 7.

343 *"How do you know Nickerson's a candidate"*: McPherson to LBJ, April 14, 1965, McPherson Files, Box 52.

343 *"I am still playing dumb"*: McPherson to Moyers, April 19 and 21, 1965, McPherson Files, Box 7. In July Nickerson paid his own way to Europe. Nickerson to RFK, July 30, 1965, SC/PF, Box 8, JFKL; Nickerson OH.

343 *"the Kennedy organization . . . is working"*: Redmon to Moyers, July 11, 1966, Watson Files, Box 25. Moyers placed the Redmon memo in LBJ's night reading.

343 *"1) Deny the Democratic governorship"*: Memorandum, "The emerging pattern in New York," William Connell to Watson, July 30, 1966, Watson Files, Box 12.

344 *Nor was Nickerson in RFK's pocket*: Gwirtzman OH; English OH; Shannon, 188–9, 199–201; Memorandum, "Gubernatorial Race—New York State," Bruno to RFK, April 12, 1966; vanden Heuvel interview.

344 *By late 1966 Kennedy had established himself*: "Kennedy: Two Years After." On RFK's fund-raising skills, see English OH.

344 *In the autumn of 1966 the Kennedy challenge*: "Bobby Phenomenon," 30; Gallup, 2023. In an August 21 Gallup poll, Democrats preferred RFK over LBJ 40 to 38 percent; independents favored RFK 38 to 24 percent. McNamara and Humphrey, the only other contenders, languished far behind.

344 *Johnson's popularity rating skidded*: "How Much of the Way with LBJ?" *U.S. News & World Report*, Sept. 26, 1966: 25, 27.

344 *"We need help wherever"*: "Bobby Phenomenon." Later, Governor Brown wished

he hadn't invited Kennedy at all. When Kennedy stumped for Brown in the contest against Republican Ronald Reagan, "people crowded around to see [Kennedy]," Brown recalled. "I was old hat." He wondered if Bobby had come for his own benefit rather than Brown's. Kennedy's aides, Brown complained later, "were very domineering." They followed their own agenda and "spent money like drunken sailors and then billed us for it." Brown OH, LBJL.

345 *California was one of many states*: In California, Thomas W. Braden and former Texan Lloyd N. Hand competed for the lieutenant governorship. Braden had managed JFK's 1960 campaign in southern California. Hand was President Johnson's chief of protocol. (The current lieutenant governor, Glenn Anderson, defeated them both.) In Wisconsin, "There was really only one national issue that loomed large . . . Robert F. Kennedy," reported *Newsweek*. In the race for governor, Lieutenant Governor Patrick J. Lucey advertised his close friendship with Bobby. He won a big victory over David Carley, the state's national committeeman and the Johnson/Humphrey favorite. In Massachusetts, Kenneth O'Donnell faced Edward J. McCormack, Jr., in the gubernatorial primary. McCormack was a nephew of House Speaker John McCormack, a powerful Johnson ally. O'Donnell, of course, was John Kennedy's dedicated appointments secretary—and a sure loser in the primary. Bobby backed him halfheartedly, Ted Kennedy remained aloof, and O'Donnell lost. And in Georgia, State Senator Jimmy Carter placed third in the primary for governor. Carter reportedly had strong Kennedy backing. Ellis Arnall, a former Georgia governor and a liberal on civil rights, defeated Carter (a moderate) and Lester Maddox (a segregationist). "Had [Carter] made the runoff," *U.S. News* indicated, "there would have been a clear-cut test of sentiment as between Johnson and Kennedy. Those close to the Kennedy people said the plan was to picture Mr. Arnall as a 'Johnson man.' " "Just Ahead—First Real Clues to the 1966 Elections," *U.S. News & World Report*, May 2, 1966: 31–2; "Changes Ahead? What Primaries Tell," *U.S. News & World Report*, Sept. 26, 1966: 40; "Politics: Prevailing Winds," *Newsweek*, Sept. 26, 1966: 31.

345 *Johnson and Kennedy themselves backed off*: The president made clear he was not backing Governor Haydon Burns in the Florida primary no matter what Burns said. Kennedy called Michigan party leaders to disavow a former aide's efforts in the primary there. Meg Greenfield, "LBJ and the Democrats," *Reporter*, June 2, 1966: 13.

345 *Obscure local races*: Holmes M. Alexander, "RFK: How He's Building His Own Party," *Nation's Business*, July 1966: 38–9; Editorial, "Tennessee Testing Ground," *Commercial Appeal*, April 13, 1966: 6; "Just Ahead."

345 *"I rather doubt we will"*: Carter to Watson, June 7, 1965, WHCF Confidential File-Name File, Box 147, LBJL.

345 *Kennedy in fact did nothing*: Dolan to RFK, Jan. 4, 1966, Dolan Papers, Box 1, JFKL; Dutton to RFK, April 6, 1966, SC/PF, Box 3.

345 *As Bobby barnstormed*: "On the Campaign Trail with Robert Kennedy," *U.S. News & World Report*, Nov. 7, 1966: 40; Richard L. Strout, "New Yorkers Applaud Johnson, Squeal at Kennedy," *Christian Science Monitor*, Aug. 22, 1966; "Politics: Prevailing Winds." John Kenneth Galbraith read newspaper reports of Bobby's "thin" speeches fleshed out by lengthy tributes to JFK. "I deplore this,"

Galbraith wrote him in September, "and believe it also poor politics. In politics there is no substitute for discussion of issues. . . . Hard substance is the Kennedy style." Couching his criticism in a bit of charm, Galbraith signed his letter "Yours didactically, pedantically, gratuitously but affectionately." Galbraith to RFK, Sept. 22, 1966, SC/PF, Box 4.

345 *Johnson's large, vibrant crowds:* "How Much of the Way with LBJ?"; Strout, "New Yorkers Applaud"; "Welcome to the Vineyard," *Newsweek,* Oct. 24, 1966: 38.

346 *On August 21:* Strout, "New Yorkers Applaud"; "Welcome to the Vineyard"; "On the Campaign Trail."

346 *A Herblock cartoon: Washington Post,* Aug. 25, 1966; Max Frankel, "Johnson off the Stump This Time," *New York Times,* Oct. 2, 1966.

346 *As election day approached:* Lewis L. Gould, "Never a Deep Partisan: Lyndon Johnson and the Democratic Party, 1963–1969," in Divine, ed., *The Johnson Years,* vol. 3, *LBJ at Home and Abroad* (Lawrenceville, KS: University of Kansas Press, 1994): 32–3; Califano, 153.

347 *On November 8, 1966, voters:* Gould, 33–4; Warren Weaver, Jr., "Governors Link Loss to Johnson," *New York Times,* December 16, 1966: 1, 25; "RFK Says He Helped Elect 39 of 76 Nominees," *New York Times,* Nov. 14, 1966: 44.

347 *Johnson refrained from bragging:* Unsigned memorandum, n.d., Watson Files, Box 23; "Governors Link Loss."

347 *John Bailey was a "Kennedy man":* Bobby Kennedy, in fact, was in no way enamored of Bailey. Gwirtzman OH; "He Drives to Bring About 'The Restoration,' " *Life,* Nov. 18, 1966: 37. On Johnson and the DNC, see Gould, 21–36, 44–6; Berman, "Johnson and the White House Staff," in Divine, ed., vol. 1, 200; Udall OH, LBJL; Weisl, Jr., OH.

347 *"a brand-new ball game":* Memorandum, "66-68," Mankiewicz to RFK, n.d. [November 1966], Mankiewicz Papers, Box 42, JFKL.

348 *Kennedy refused to join in:* Gwirtzman to RFK, n.d., Gwirtzman Papers, Box 5, JFKL; "Welcome to the Vineyard," 35; Schlesinger, *Robert Kennedy,* 817.

CHAPTER 14: MALAPROPAGANDA

349 *tapping his telephone:* Dolan interview, 1990.

349 *The practice of wiretapping telephone lines:* Schlesinger, *Robert Kennedy,* 818; Katzenbach interview; *Hearings Before the Senate Select Committee to Study Governmental Operations with Respect to Intelligence Activities,* Dec. 3, 1975, Vol. 6, *FBI:* 162–3, 166, 199–200; Califano, 276; DeLoach, *Hoover's FBI,* 48–59.

349 *"[Long] is out to get Bobby":* Schlesinger, *Robert Kennedy,* 818, 1086.

350 *"While his heart and guts":* Macy, as chairman of the Civil Service Commission, was LBJ's watchdog on personnel. James J. Best, "Who Talked to the President When?" *Political Science Quarterly,* Fall 1988: 538; Graham, "The Transformation of Federal Education Policy," in Divine, ed., vol. 1, 169–70; Katzenbach interview; O'Donnell OH, LBJL; Katzenbach to Hoover, July 28, 1965, and Hoover to Katzenbach, July 29, 1965, Katzenbach Papers, Box 10, JFKL.

350 *Katzenbach envisioned a shooting match:* Katzenbach interview; Memorandum, "Re: Installation of Wire Taps and Microphones, Addendum," DeLoach to Tolson, Dec. 20, 1965, FBI File #77-51387-1800, vols. 11–12; DeLoach to Tolson,

Jan. 21, 1966, FBI File #77-51387-1810, vols. 11–12.

350 *DeLoach feigned sympathy*: Rogovin OH, LBJL; Katzenbach interview; DeLoach to Tolson, March 3, 1966, JEH O&C File #92; Memorandum, "Re: Installation of Wire Tapes and Microphones, Disclaimers by Attorney General Katzenbach and Former Attorney General Kennedy," DeLoach to Tolson, Dec. 20, 1965, File #77-51387-1800, vols. 11–12. In late 1966, Katzenbach became under secretary of state—at his own initiative, according to Katzenbach. LBJ "sincerely refused" the request for months, claiming Katzenbach's departure would hurt the Justice Department's civil rights effort. But Ed Weisl, Jr., asserted that Ramsey Clark made false accusations about Katzenbach's loyalty; more than anything else this undermined LBJ's confidence in Katzenbach and led to his replacement by Clark. Either way, in retrospect Katzenbach judged his move "probably a mistake." He would have been happier if he had remained attorney general. Weisl, Jr., OH, LBJL; Katzenbach interview.

350 *the successful prosecution of Fred R. Black, Jr.*: Rogovin OH; Katzenbach interview.

351 *"this is a damn important matter"*: Schlesinger, *Robert Kennedy*, 817–18.

351 *"All right, Nick"*: Katzenbach interview.

351 *Long seized upon the Katzenbach memo*: Fred P. Graham, "Hoover Asserts Robert Kennedy Aided Buggings," and "Texts of Letters on Wiretap Controversy," *New York Times*, Dec. 11, 1966: 1, 84.

351 *"You can get a comment"*: Ibid.; Courtney A. Evans to RFK, Feb. 17, 1966, Gwirtzman Papers, Box 5, JFKL; Max Frankel, "President Aloof in Bugging Feud," *New York Times*, Dec. 13, 1966: 39.

352 *"made Hoover absolutely furious"*: Katzenbach interview; Clipping, Robert E. Thompson, "Johnson Sidesteps RFK-Hoover Row," *New York World Journal Tribune*, Dec. 13, 1966, Mankiewicz Papers, Box 37.

352 *"There is little doubt"*: Powers, 397.

352 Washington Post *reporter Richard Harwood*: Rosenthal later became editorial-page editor of the *New York Times*. Harwood, "RFK Barred Bugging in 1962 Memo," *Washington Post,* Dec. 15, 1966: A1; Califano, 188; Recording of telephone conversation between LBJ and Abe Fortas, Dec. 17, 1966, 10:45 A.M., Tape 66.01, Recordings of Telephone Conversations, White House Series, Recordings and Transcripts of Conversations and Meetings, LBJL.

352 *Publicly, Johnson was more circumspect*: James Reston, "The Kennedy-Hoover Controversy," *New York Times*, Dec. 14, 1966: 46; Clipping, David Kraslow, "Johnson Sidesteps Queries on Hoover, Kennedy Dispute," *Los Angeles Times*, Dec. 13, 1966, Mankiewicz Papers, Box 37; Califano, 188.

353 *"anathema to him"*: McPherson OH, LBJL; Califano, 187.

353 *Johnson was surreptitiously recording*: Califano, 187–8; Powers, 399.

353 *"Lyndon talks about that [FBI] information"*: RFK OH, JFKL.

353 *in his State of the Union Address*: Califano, 183, 188; "Texas Ueber Alles," *Nation*, Jan. 30, 1967: 132; Clipping, "LBJ Wiretap Blast Seen Aimed at RFK," *New York Post*, March 23, 1967, Mankiewicz Papers, Box 37; Mankiewicz OH, LBJL.

354 *"It was a mistake from the beginning"*: Guthman, 313; John Corry, *The Manchester Affair* (New York: G. P. Putnam's Sons, 1967): 18–20; Wills, 104.

354 *William Manchester, a mildly accomplished writer*: Corry, 21–23, 29–32; Wills, 104–6.

354 *"I'm not under any obligation"*: Manchester to Valenti, Nov. 5, 1964; Valenti to LBJ, Nov. 9, 1964; Valenti to LBJ, Aug. 31, 1965, Special File on the Assassination of John F. Kennedy, Box 1, LBJL.

355 *"He could not bear"*: Manchester, xii–xiii; Recording of telephone conversation between LBJ and Moyers, Dec. 26, 1966, 10:17 A.M., Tape 66.02, LBJL; Corry, 54–6; Schlesinger, *Robert Kennedy,* 818; Manchester, 310.

355 *"deer-hunting incident"*: Corry, 56–7; Manchester, 118–19.

355 *"of defining the book"*: Schlesinger, *Robert Kennedy,* 819; Corry, 61–2.

356 *"Frankly, gentlemen," he wrote*: Corry, 61–2; Schlesinger, *Robert Kennedy,* 819–20.

356 *In subsequent drafts*: Manchester, 118–19; Schlesinger, *Robert Kennedy,* 820–21; Walinsky OH, JFKL.

356 *Jackie tightened Bobby's bind*: Columnist William S. White in Schlesinger, *Robert Kennedy,* 821; "Widow Dismayed by Kennedy Book," *New York Times,* Dec. 11, 1966: 1, 39; Corry, "Mrs. Kennedy Will Seek an Injunction to Block Book About the Assassination," *New York Times,* Dec. 15, 1966: 1, 36; Editorial, " 'Authorized' History," *New York Times,* Dec. 16, 1966: 46; "Growing Rift of LBJ and Kennedys: Behind the Furor over a Book," *U.S. News & World Report,* Jan. 2, 1967: 22–7.

357 *"forty-six mean, vicious errors"*: Recording of telephone conversation between LBJ and Katzenbach, Dec. 5, 1966, 10:46 A.M., Tape 66.01.

357 *"Somebody really ought to be"*: Recording of telephone conversation between LBJ and Fortas, Dec. 17, 1966, 10:45 A.M., Tape 66.01.

358 *Over the next few weeks*: Jacobsen to LBJ, n.d., and "Jacobsen Analysis, Manchester Book," n.d. [both December 1966], Manchester File, Special File on the Assassination of John F. Kennedy, Box 1.

358 *"It is just a manufactured lie"*: LBJ-Katzenbach conversation.

358 *"He said, 'I hate' "*: Recording of telephone conversation between LBJ and Moyers, December 26, 1966, 10:17 A.M., Tape 66.02.

358 *"I slumped, had a vapor inhaler"*: LBJ-Fortas conversation.

359 *" 'He sprawled out' "*: Recording of telephone conversation between LBJ and Kintner, Dec. 20, 1966, 7:57 A.M., Tape 66.01.

359 *"I [never said] a son-of-a-bitchin' word"*: Recording of telephone conversation between LBJ and Moyers, Dec. 26, 1966, 11:46 A.M. [?], Tape 66.02.

359 *the usual surrogates*: Kintner to LBJ, Dec. 16, 1966, PU 2-6/Manchester, LBJL; Corry, 55–6; *U.S. News & World Report,* April 1, 1968.

359 *"The Kennedy 'corporation' "*: Roche to LBJ, Dec. 23, 1966, Manchester File.

360 *"that we are equipped by experience"*: LBJ-Moyers conversation, Dec. 26, 1966, 10:17 A.M.

360 *"the perpetrator of the fraud"*: LBJ-Fortas conversation. It was Ken O'Donnell, in fact, who spread many of the most damaging stories about LBJ. But Manchester's text was almost as rough on O'Donnell as it was on Johnson, and when the affair erupted O'Donnell offered to make a public statement defending LBJ. Johnson's adviser Jim Rowe cautioned that O'Donnell's offer might be a Kennedy plot to "get off the hook." Rowe to LBJ, Dec. 15, 1966, PU 2-6/Manchester.

360 *a Washington-wide conspiracy*: Ibid.; LBJ-Moyers conversation, Dec. 26, 1966, 10:17

A.M. Johnson was shadowboxing. Bartlett, in fact, wrote a scathing review of Manchester's "prejudice[d]," "ugly" book. Bartlett, "A Disloyal Book," *Chicago Sun-Times* press release, n.d., PU 2-6/Manchester, Box 86.

361 *"Ask Kay," Johnson pleaded*: LBJ-Moyers conversation, Dec. 26, 1966, 10:17 A.M.

361 *"Bobby is having his governors jump"*: LBJ-Fortas conversation. In 1966–67, Kennedy men released a flood of memoirs and, more damaging to LBJ, a steady stream of critiques of the war. "Bobby Kennedy had nothing to do with it," said Schlesinger later. In addition to Sorensen's *Kennedy*, LBJ is probably referring to Schlesinger's *The Bitter Heritage* and, indirectly, Goodwin's *Triumph or Tragedy: Reflections on Vietnam* and John Kenneth Galbraith's *How to Control the Military.* Schlesinger interview; Schlesinger, *Robert Kennedy,* 797.

361 *the policy of silence*: Liz Carpenter recalls the diligence with which the official silence was kept. Roche repeatedly urged *"absolute silence."* Carpenter OH, LBJL; Roche to LBJ, Jan. 23, 1967, Manchester File.

361 *"I will not discuss"*: LBJ-Moyers conversation, Dec. 26, 1966, 11:46 A.M.; LBJ-Moyers conversation, Dec. 26, 1966, 10:17 A.M.

361 *"in general the matter"*: Mankiewicz to RFK, Feb. 3, 1967, Mankiewicz Papers, Box 42; Henry Raymont, "Kennedy Delays Book of Speeches," *New York Times,* March 1, 1967: 1, 25.

362 "MANCHESTER BOOK DULLS": George Gallup, "Manchester Book Dulls RFK Star," *Washington Post,* March 26, 1967: A6; Joe B. Frantz to LBJ, Jan. 10, 1967, PU 2-6/Manchester; George Christian to LBJ, Jan. 13 and Feb. 9, 1967; Press release, "WRAL-TV Viewpoint," Jesse Helms, Executive Vice Chairman and Vice Chairman of the Board, Jan. 19, 1967; Califano to LBJ, Feb. 20, 1967, PU 2-6/Manchester; Elmer Bendiner, "History and Malapropaganda," *Nation,* April 17, 1967: 501; Gore Vidal, *United States: Essays 1952–1992* (New York: Random House, 1993): 807.

362 *"As a result of this Manchester crap"*: Recording of telephone conversation between LBJ and Clark, Jan. 25, 1967, 8:22 P.M., Tape K67.01; LBJ-Katzenbach conversation; Gallup, "Manchester Book Dulls RFK Star."

363 *"I never saw such an arrogant fella"*: LBJ-Clark conversation; "The Swinging Senator," *Nation,* Feb. 20, 1967: 226–7.

363 *Kennedy's ten days in Europe*: vanden Heuvel interview.

363 "SUNDAY GALLUP POLL WILL SHOW": Schlesinger, *Robert Kennedy,* 823.

363 *his meeting on February 1*: Kraslow and Loory, 175–8.

364 *Kennedy had difficulty following*: Schlesinger, *Robert Kennedy,* 824–5; Kraslow and Loory, 201; vanden Heuvel in Plimpton, ed., 216.

364 *That night Frank Mankiewicz called*: Plimpton, ed., 217; Schlesinger, *Robert Kennedy,* 824–5; Kraslow and Loory, 201.

364 *These private peace feelers*: American officials counted as many as two thousand separate attempts—private and otherwise—to initiate peace talks between 1965 and 1967. Herring, *America's Longest War,* 164–5; Herring, *LBJ and Vietnam,* 104, 110–13.

365 *threw them off balance*: Schlesinger, *Robert Kennedy,* 826; Rusk OH, JFKL; Berman, 22–8.

365 *Yet there was a cable*: Katzenbach and vanden Heuvel interviews; Mankiewicz

OH; Schlesinger, *Robert Kennedy,* 825; Katzenbach OH.

365 *Monday morning, February 6*: Katzenbach interview; Kraslow and Loory, 201–2.

366 *the Oval Office meeting*: Katzenbach and Rostow interviews; O'Donnell OH; Schlesinger, *Robert Kennedy,* 826–7; Kraslow and Loory, 202.

366 *"I'll destroy you"*: Schlesinger, *Robert Kennedy,* 826–7; Kraslow and Loory, 202–3; Mankiewicz in Plimpton, ed., 217; Newfield, 131–2.

367 *"I did not bring home"*: J. Y. Smith, "Kennedy Sees LBJ, Denies Peace Role," *Washington Post,* Feb. 7, 1967: A1; mjdr to LBJ, March 10, 1967, and "Partial transcript of Senator Robert Kennedy's Press Conference in West Lobby of White House—Feb. 6, 1967," WHFN-RFK, Box 6, LBJL.

367 *"You know . . . what I've been through"*: Edelman OH, JFKL; Mankiewicz interview; Walinsky OH; Kraslow and Loory, 204–5; Schlesinger, *Robert Kennedy,* 828.

367 *Rostow summoned Kay Graham*: Graham OH, LBJL; Herring, *LBJ and Vietnam,* 114; Rostow to LBJ, Feb. 14, 1967, Folder "Sen. Robert Kennedy's Position on Vietnam—Analysis of," NSF, Files of W. W. Rostow, Box 8, LBJL; Evans and Novak, "Restlessness of Kennedy Is a Factor," *Washington Post,* Feb. 10, 1967: A17; "Swinging Senator."

368 *In fact, peace in Vietnam*: Herring, *America's Longest War,* 164–5; Herring, "The War in Vietnam," in Divine, ed., vol. 1, 46–8.

368 *Meanwhile, the war itself*: Herring, *America's Longest War,* 145–56 ; Patterson, *Grand Expectations,* 595–6; Guthman and Allen, eds., 288.

368 *Nonetheless, growing public concern*: Charles DeBenedetti, "Lyndon Johnson and the Antiwar Opposition," in Divine, ed., *The Johnson Years,* vol. 2: *Vietnam, the Environment, and Science* (Lawrenceville, KS: University of Kansas Press, 1987): 28–9, 39.

369 *The tide of public opinion*: Schlesinger, *Robert Kennedy,* 824.

369 *"Not Morse, who is querulous"*: Memorandum, "Comments on Viet Nam Draft," Mankiewicz to RFK, Feb. 27, 1967, Mankiewicz Papers, Box 44.

369 *"We have striven to isolate China"*: "RFK's New Moves to Stand Apart from LBJ," *U.S. News & World Report,* Feb. 20, 1967: 21; Schlesinger, *Robert Kennedy,* 828–9.

369 *the White House was indignant*: "RFK's New Moves."

CHAPTER 15: PRAISING BRUTUS

370 *Kennedy clicked on the tiny television*: Guthman and Allen, eds., 290–91.

370 *On February 17*: Schlesinger, *Robert Kennedy,* 830; Clifford OH, LBJL.

370 *the bombing campaign*: Berman, *Lyndon Johnson's War,* 12, 24–5, 40–41, 48–9, 51–3.

371 *Johnson continued to regard*: Kearns, 264; Berman, *Lyndon Johnson's War,* 41, 71; Herring, "The War in Vietnam," 39–40.

371 *Now, with Kennedy's challenge imminent*: Schlesinger, *Robert Kennedy,* 830; Teleconference transcript, Harriman and RFK, 6:00 P.M., Feb. 27, 1967, Harriman Papers, Box 480, Manuscript Collection, Library of Congress.

372 *"It's going to hurt me"*: Schlesinger, *Robert Kennedy,* 830.

372 *Younger staff members*: Edelman in Plimpton, ed., 212; Memorandum, "Comments on Viet Nam Draft," Mankiewicz to RFK, Feb. 27, 1967, Mankiewicz Papers, Box 44, JFKL.

372 *March 1, the night before its delivery*: Guthman and Allen, eds., 291–2; Plimpton,

ed., 212–13.

372 *"Three Presidents have taken action"*: Guthman and Allen, eds., 292–8; Hedrick Smith, "Kennedy Asks Suspension of U.S. Air Raids on North; Administration Unmoved," *New York Times*, March 3, 1967: 1, 10.

373 *"He talked today"*: Recording of telephone conversation between LBJ and John Connally, March 2, 1967, 9:22 P.M., Tape K67.02, Recordings of Telephone Conversations, White House Series, Recordings and Transcripts of Conversations and Meetings, LBJL.

373 *kept Bobby off the network news*: "That taught us a lesson," remembered Mankiewicz. "We always went over and recorded first after that." Mankiewicz OH, LBJL.

373 *Jackson called RFK neither hawk nor dove*: *New York Times*, March 3, 1967: 10.

374 *"While Senator Kennedy has . . . a popular idea"*: Kintner to LBJ, March 2, 1967, 6:00 P.M., FG1, Box 14, LBJL; Benjamin Welles, "Rusk Recalls Hostile Acts After Past Bombing Halts," *New York Times*, March 3, 1967: 1, 11.

374 *"nothing will come of [American diplomacy]"*: "Men at War: RFK vs. LBJ," *Newsweek*, March 13, 1967: 33–4; Max Frankel, "President Faces . . . " *New York Times*, March 4, 1967: 3.

374 *a traveling, freewheeling sideshow spectacle*: "Ferment on Vietnam," *New York Times*, March 5, 1967: IV, 1E; *Public Papers, LBJ*, vol. 1, 1967, 259–70; Mankiewicz OH; Kintner to LBJ, 5:30 P.M., FG1, Box 14.

375 *"The American people should know"*: "Transcript of the President's News Conference," *New York Times*, March 3, 1967: 14.

375 *In a March 4 interview*: Hedrick Smith, "Kennedy Disputes Rusk and Defends Peace Bid as New," *New York Times*, March 5, 1967: 1, 6.

375 *he had won the battle*: *New York Times*, March 4, 1967: 3; "A Coalition for Peace," *Nation*, March 20, 1967: 356; "Men at War: RFK vs. LBJ"; Editorial, "The Vietnam Debate," *New York Times*, March 3, 1967: 34.

376 *"ignored his policy suggestions"*: Guthman and Allen, eds., 298.

376 *he ordered a secret policy review*: Rostow interview.

376 *"I cannot read this speech"*: Memorandum, "RFK Speech," Jorden to Rostow, March 3, 1967, Folder "Sen. Robert Kennedy's Position on Vietnam—Analysis of," NSF, Files of W. W. Rostow, Box 8, LBJL.

376 *Rostow displayed the same bias*: Memorandum, "Senator Robert Kennedy's Proposal of March 2, 1967," Rostow to LBJ, March 9, 1967, 10:30 A.M., and Rostow to LBJ, March 3, 1967, NSF, Files of W. W. Rostow, Box 8; Rostow interview.

376 *"The main difficulty"*: Rusk to LBJ, March 10, 1967, and memorandum, "Senator R. F. Kennedy's Position on Viet-Nam Policy," General Maxwell Taylor to LBJ, March 9, 1967, NSF, Files of W. W. Rostow, Box 8.

377 *"The prognosis is bad"*: Berman, *Lyndon Johnson's War*, 12–16; Herring, *America's Longest War*, 177; Herring, *LBJ and Vietnam*, 11.

377 *McNamara's March 9 memo*: McNamara to LBJ, March 9, 1967, NSF, Files of W. W. Rostow, Box 8.

377 *McNamara was out of step*: David Halberstam, *The Best and the Brightest* (New York: Random House, 1972): 784.

378 *"Their war with each other"*: James Reston, "Johnson and Kennedy on Vietnam," *New York Times*, March 5, 1967: IV, 8B; "Men at War: RFK vs. LBJ."

378 "*I don't think really the question*": Transcript, *Today*, "Senator Robert F. Kennedy Interviewed," March 7, 1967, NSF, Name File, Box 5, LBJL; "Brother Supports Senator," *New York Times*, March 5, 1967: 6.

378 *The press was full of eager speculation*: "Will Bobby's Friends Trip Up LBJ in '68," *U.S. News & World Report*, April 10, 1967: 53–4; "Brother Supports Senator." Even Nixon weighed in against RFK: "Johnson is right and Kennedy is wrong," he declared on March 5, adding that Bobby's "proposals are not new [and] . . . have the effect of prolonging the war by encouraging the enemy." "Nixon Says Robert Kennedy Is Wrong About the War," *New York Times*, March 6, 1967: 10.

379 "*aggravate your Senate colleagues*": Memorandum, "Steps in Support of your Viet Nam Statements," Dutton to RFK, Feb. 23, 1966, SC/PF, Box 3, JFKL; Mankiewicz OH; "LBJ and RFK—Now a Sharper Rift on War," *U.S. News & World Report*, March 13, 1967: 14; LBJ-Connally conversation; "Vietnam Debate"; "Rift in Congress over War Widens," *New York Times*, March 4, 1967: 1, 3.

379 *a "peace bloc"*: Rostow to LBJ and Associated Press summary of *Izvestia* report, March 4, 1967, NSF Country File—Vietnam, Box 211/212, LBJL; McGovern OH, LBJL.

379 *happier on his own*: Mankiewicz OH; Walinsky OH, JFKL; "The Democratic Rebels in Congress," *Nation*, Oct. 10, 1966: 341–2; Tydings OH, JFKL.

380 *Both houses of Congress*: Herring, "War in Vietnam," 40.

380 "*They're up there on the sidelines*": LBJ, recorded interview by Walter Cronkite, CBS News Special, Feb. 6, 1970, LBJL.

380 *As James Reston noted*: Reston, "Washington: Johnson and Fulbright," *New York Times*, Jan. 26, 1966: 36.

380 "*war was everything*": McPherson OH, LBJL; Sanders OH, LBJL.

380 *Johnson cut off his critics*: McGovern OH; O'Neill OH, LBJL; O'Neill, 194–9.

381 *Fulbright infuriated him*: Pierson interview; McNamara, 259.

381 "*Why is it they never find*": DeBenedetti in Divine, ed., vol. 2, 32–5; LBJ, Cronkite's interview; James A. Wechsler, "The Two Front War: Johnson vs. Kennedy," *Progressive*, May 1967: 21; Kearns, 316–17.

381 *On March 21, he released*: John W. Finney, "Note by Johnson Evoked a Rebuff from Ho Chi Minh," *New York Times*, March 22, 1967: 1.

382 "*I can only wish*": Harold Gal, "Kennedy Critical of Johnson Again," *New York Times*, March 22, 1967: 1, 10.

382 "*should have been, and still could be*": Memorandum, "Viet Nam War," Dolan to RFK, March 22, 1967, Dolan Papers, Box 1, JFKL.

382 *president dragged a weary and perplexed team*: Edelman OH, JFKL; Max Frankel, "Guam Talks End; President Voices Hope and Caution," *New York Times*, March 21, 1967: 1; Frankel, "President Home from Guam Talk," *New York Times*, March 22, 1967: 1, 11; "Ky Stole the Show," *Nation*, April 3, 1967: 418–19.

383 *On April 24, after the United States bombed*: E. W. Kenworthy, "McGovern Leads a Senate Attack upon Escalation," and "Excerpts from Senate Exchange on Vietnam War," *New York Times*, April 26, 1967: 1, 8–9.

383 *elections in South Vietnam*: Herring, *America's Longest War*, 159–60; Berman, 79; Robert F. Kennedy, *To Seek a Newer World* (New York: Doubleday, 1967): 188–93.

383 *"He felt so strongly"*: Greenfield OH, JFKL.

384 *Kennedy and Jacob Javits*: Hedrick Smith, "Senators Deplore 'Fraud' in Vote Drive in Vietnam," *New York Times*, Aug. 12, 1967: 1,2.

384 *the pacification (Revolutionary Development) program*: Ibid.; Herring, *America's Longest War*, 157–9; Herring, "War in Vietnam," 45–6.

384 *"free, honest and effective"*: Smith, "Senators Deplore 'Fraud.' "

384 *On September 3, Johnson's team*: Berman, *Lyndon Johnson's War*, 79–80; Herring, *America's Longest War*, 160; Ellsberg interview.

385 *In a Gallup poll*: The first poll results were issued Oct. 1, 1967; the second, Oct. 22. Nixon beat Johnson 49 to 45 percent and beat Kennedy 48 to 47, while Rockefeller crushed Johnson, 54 to 40, and slipped by Kennedy, 47 to 46. Gallup, 2083, 2086–7.

385 *In October 1967 Kennedy met Daniel Ellsberg*: Ellsberg interview.

385 *Kennedy invited Ellsberg*: Ibid. Bobby had said the same thing—that he preferred a "Laos-type" solution in Vietnam—to New Leftist Tom Hayden earlier that year. Schlesinger, *Robert Kennedy*, 829.

386 *In 1961, facing the overthrow*: Rostow OH, JFKL; Herring, *America's Longest War*, 77–9, 82; Parmet, 133–55; Giglio, 64–8.

386 *"What made your brother"*: Ellsberg interview; Schlesinger, *Robert Kennedy*, 756.

386 *"We['ve] turned, we've switched"*: Peter Grose, "Kennedy Asserts Johnson Shifted U.S. Aim in Vietnam," *New York Times*, Nov. 27, 1967: 1, 15.

387 *"the never-never land"*: Editorial, "Kennedy vs. Kennedy," *New York Times*, Nov. 28, 1967: 46.

388 *"It is their war"*: John Herbers, "President Kennedy's Vietnam Aim Debated Again," *New York Times*, Nov. 28, 1967: 4.

388 *The loss of South Vietnam*: Herring, *America's Longest War*, 80–82.

388 *Humphrey cheerfully defended*: Grose, "Kennedy Asserts Johnson."

388 *Former Kennedy men like Rusk*: Rostow OH, LBJL; Rusk OH, JFKL; Herring, "War in Vietnam," 37–8.

389 *A banner headline*: Edwin L. Dale, Jr., "M'Namara Is Named by U.S. to Head the World Bank; Johnson Move a Surprise," *New York Times*, Nov. 28, 1967: 1.

389 *"Would [it] make any difference"*: Goodwin, 453.

389 *McNamara was Johnson's "Messiah"*: Reedy OH, LBJL; Deborah Shapley, *Promise and Power: The Life and Times of Robert McNamara* (Boston: Little, Brown, 1993): 277–85; Roche OH, LBJL.

389 *"Bob McNamara started out"*: Baker, 265; Clifford, 457.

390 *In 1964 he thought McNamara*: Sorensen OH, JFKL; Shapley, 91; Elizabeth Stevens and Adam Yarmolinsky in Plimpton, ed., 162, 210; Spalding OH, JFKL; Reedy interview.

390 *They shared that guilt*: Edelman OH; Walinsky interview; Walinsky OH.

390 *In 1967, McNamara handed Kennedy*: Dolan interview, 1994.

391 *Kennedy's older advisers*: Dutton OH, JFKL; Halberstam, *Best and Brightest*, 768.

391 *McNamara primly acknowledged*: Shapley, 409–10; McNamara, 260; LBJ quoted in Kearns, 320.

391 *Those years ravaged Robert McNamara*: Shapley, 408; Roche OH; Clifford, 456–7; Temple OH, LBJL; Schlesinger, *Robert Kennedy*, 883–4; Berman, *Lyndon Johnson's War*, 72–3, 90.

392 *a November 1 memo*: McNamara, 307–9.
392 *the World Bank job*: Shapley, 416–17. George Christian reports that McNamara mentioned the job to LBJ on several occasions. Christian OH, LBJL.
392 *"The only reason I'm telling you"*: Califano, 249.
393 *According to one aide*: Roche OH. The second aide was Lieutenant General Robert Ginsburgh, a former military assistant to Rostow. Shapley, 436–7.
393 *"The Kennedys began pushing"*: Kearns, 320–21.
393 *he clearly could no longer abide*: Halberstam, *Best and Brightest,* 783–4; Shapley, 436–7; Edelman OH; McNamara, 312–13.
393 *McNamara hurried to the Oval Office*: Schlesinger interview; Shapley, 437–9.
393 *Bobby sat with McNamara*: Edelman OH; Roche OH; Shapley, 438–9; E. W. Kenworthy, "M'Namara Shift Queried in Senate," *New York Times*, Nov. 29, 1967: 17; Edelman OH.
394 *"But I wasn't about to"*: Shapley, 439; Walinsky interview.
394 *For 48 long hours*: Walinsky and Schlesinger interviews; Max Frankel, "Major Shift in Capital," *New York Times*, Nov. 28, 1967: 2.
394 *At 11:00 the next night*: Schlesinger, *Robert Kennedy,* 884; Shapley, 439–40; Walinsky OH; McNamara, 314.
395 *an intensely personal defeat*: Edelman, Walinsky, and Mankiewicz interviews; Max Frankel, "M'Namara Takes World Bank Post; War Shift Denied," and Tom Wicker, "McNamara and the Devil Theory," *New York Times*, Nov. 30, 1967: 1, 16, 46.
395 *"this most elegantly brutal"*: Walinsky, "Caesar's Meat," n.d. [November–December 1967], 2, 17–18, appendix to Walinsky OH; RFK quoted in Walinsky OH.
395 *"On many occasions"*: Speech draft, Feb. 29, 1968, SC/PF, Box 8, JFKL. Before he left the Department of Defense, McNamara visited Larry O'Brien's White House office to "make a strong pitch that Bobby should run for president," as O'Brien recalled. O'Brien said that the dispute over war policy should be resolved internally, but McNamara insisted that no change would come unless RFK became president. Still, McNamara did not endorse Kennedy until two weeks after Johnson's withdrawal. O'Brien OH; Shapley, 466–7.

CHAPTER 16: "LATER THAN WE THINK"

396 *"probably politically necessary"*: Dutton to RFK, March 15, 1967, SC/PF, Box 3, JFKL.
396 *the Gridiron speech*: Guthman, 315; Mankiewicz to RFK, Jan. 3, 1967, Mankiewicz Papers, Box 42, JFKL.
397 *a Democratic dinner on June 3*: Schlesinger, *Robert Kennedy,* 836; Mankiewicz OH, LBJL; Transcript, "Remarks of Honorable Robert F. Kennedy, United States Senator from the State of New York, at Democrat State Committee Dinner, at the Americana Hotel, New York City, June 3, 1967," WHFN-RFK, Box 6, LBJL.
397 *"How could you say all that"*: Schlesinger, *Robert Kennedy,* 836; Schlesinger to RFK, June 19, 1967, SC/PF, Box 11.
397 *A quick scan of headlines*: "Will Bobby's Friends Trip Up LBJ in '68?" *U.S. News & World Report,* April 10, 1967: 53–4; "Is Robert Kennedy Trying to Upset LBJ in '68?" *U.S. News & World Report,* Oct. 2, 1967: 39–40; "If Bobby Kennedy

Were a Candidate . . . " *U.S. News & World Report*, March 13, 1967: 14; "If It Narrows Down to Johnson or Kennedy in '68 . . ." *U.S. News & World Report*, Feb. 6, 1967: 13.

398 *Kennedy was running*: "Will Bobby's Friends Trip Up LBJ"; "Is Robert Kennedy Trying"; *Cincinnati Enquirer* report cited in Holmes M. Alexander, "RFK: How He's Building His Own Party," *Nation's Business*, July 1966: 54.

398 *Political cartoonists joined*: Cartoon Collection, Boxes 1–2, LBJL; Watson Files, Box 25; "The Bobby Phenomenon," *Newsweek*, Oct. 24, 1966: 35; *MAD About the Sixties: The Best of the Decade* (Boston: Little, Brown, 1995); Barbara Garson, *MacBird* (Berkeley: Grassy Knoll, 1966); *Ramparts*, Dec. 1966: 1, 27–38.

398 *"Citizens for Kennedy-Fulbright"*: Letter, Dr. Martin Shepard, Regional Coordinator, "Citizens for Kennedy-Fulbright," February 7, 1967, PL/Kennedy, Robert F., Box 28, LBJL; Letter, Martin Shepard and Charles O. Porter to Congressman Bill Karth, April 28, 1967, WHFN-RFK, Box 6. The second letter shows LBJ's (in this case, his secretary's) cursive "L," indicating the president had read it. Also, pamphlet, "Citizens for Kennedy-Fulbright in 1968," n.d., WHFN-RFK, Box 6; Political advertisement, Illinois chapter of CFKF, n.d., PL/Kennedy, Box 26; "Kennedy's Backers to Continue Efforts," *New York Times*, Oct. 29, 1967: 67.

399 *staffed by political amateurs*: "Is Robert Kennedy Trying"; Schlesinger, *Robert Kennedy*, 146; David Halberstam, *The Unfinished Odyssey of Robert Kennedy* (New York: Random House, 1968): 9–10; "What Party Leaders Think of Bobby Kennedy's Future," *U.S. News & World Report*, Sept. 26, 1966: 54–6.

399 *Disenchantment with LBJ*: Lewis L. Gould, "Never a Deep Partisan: Lyndon Johnson and the Democratic Party, 1963–1969," in Divine, ed., vol. 3, 37; Gallup, 2078–9; Max Frankel, "President Faces Major Problems," *New York Times*, March 4, 1967: 3.

399 *Greatest among them was the war*: Califano, 247–8; Robert Dallek, *Hail to the Chief: The Making and Unmaking of American Presidents* (New York: Hyperion, 1996): 122–4; Newfield, 176–7.

400 *Kennedy was an alternate pole*: Halberstam, *Unfinished Odyssey*, 10–12, 32–3. Also McGovern OH, LBJL.

400 *Allard Lowenstein was typical*: Halberstam, *Unfinished Odyssey*, 3–4; Newfield, 186; David Harris, *Dreams Die Hard: Three Men's Journey through the Sixties* (San Francisco: Mercury House, 1993): 202–3; William H. Chafe, *Never Stop Running: Allard Lowenstein and the Struggle to Save American Liberalism* (New York: Basic Books, 1993): 270–1.

401 *Robert Kennedy respected Lowenstein*: English OH, JFKL; Harris, 193; Miller and Linton interviews.

401 *The assumption was universal*: Walton OH, JFKL; Dolan interview, 1994; Walinsky interview; Walinsky OH, JFKL; Halberstam, *Unfinished Odyssey*, 45; Ethel's views discussed in O'Brien, 219, and Walinsky OH.

401 *"a deep personal dislike"*: Memorandum, "Gratuitous Advice Revisited," Walinsky to RFK, n.d. [late 1967], SC/PF, Box 20, JFKL.

402 *A year earlier Walinsky*: Edelman OH, JFKL; Memorandum, "1968 Presidential Primary Filing Date Schedule," Dolan to RFK, Oct. 24, 1967, Dolan Papers, Box 1, JFKL; Dolan interview; Gwirtzman OH, JFKL; Dutton OH, JFKL.

402 *"Everything we did"*: Dolan interview.

402 *"a premature memo"*: "Angie," Kennedy scribbled to his secretary, "will you keep this document—Don't forget to take it with you when you close—RFK." Memorandum, "Three Principles of Democratic Presidential Politics: A Premature Memo to RFK," Sorensen to RFK, July 1966, Gwirtzman Papers, Box 5, JFKL.

402 *the rest of the traditionalists*: Halberstam, *Unfinished Odyssey*, 47–9.

402 *"Those New Frontier cats"*: Lewis Chester, Godfrey Hodgson, and Bruce Page, *An American Melodrama: The Presidential Campaign of 1968* (London: Deutsch, 1969): 111–12; Walinsky OH.

403 *In the winter of 1967–68*: Schlesinger, *Robert Kennedy*, 901. "Bob Kennedy developed after Dallas a sense of the unpredictability of things," Schlesinger recalled, "which made long-term planning absolutely impossible for him. I think no one would have been less surprised by the manner of his death than he. . . . Man against fate was very much his sense of life, plus the existentialist view that man defines himself by his choices. He knew the risks he was running; he saw no choice but to run them. There was a sense of fatality about it all." Plimpton, ed., 145–6.

403 *"You've got the worst"*: Walinsky OH; Schmidt OH, JFKL; Dolan interview, 1990.

403 *a steady pessimistic drone*: Mankiewicz OH; Dutton to RFK, Nov. 3, 1967, SC/PF, Box 3; Walinsky to RFK [late 1967]; Schlesinger, *Robert Kennedy*, 899–900. After Kennedy declared for president he asked for McGovern's endorsement. "Well, Bob," McGovern recalled telling him, "I've taken the view so far because I'm up for reelection this time that I shouldn't make any public endorsements, but if you come to my state I'll introduce you in such a way that everybody will understand where my sympathies are." Kennedy was understanding and grateful. On the night of his assassination he won the South Dakota primary. McGovern OH.

404 *"Everyone seems only interested"*: Schlesinger, *Robert Kennedy*, 899.

404 *"if I run, I will go"*: Benno Schmidt and his wife, Nancy, were present at the dinner. Schmidt OH, JFKL; Dutton to RFK, Nov. 3, 1967; Schlesinger, *Robert Kennedy*, 900; Mankiewicz interview.

404 *"What bothers me"*: Schlesinger, *Robert Kennedy*, 900–901.

405 *"Things fall apart"*: RFK, "Topics: 'Things Fall Apart; the Center Cannot Hold . . .' " *New York Times*, Feb. 10, 1968: 32; Walinsky to RFK [late 1967]; Greenfield OH, JFKL; Theodore H. White, *The Making of the President 1968* (New York: Atheneum, 1969): 155–7, 161; Goodwin, 415; Edelman OH; Marshall OH, JFKL.

405 *Kennedy wanted the White House*: Edelman, Mankiewicz, and Schlesinger interviews; Lois, 51. In September 1965, *U.S. News* examined the permutations of "the Kennedy brothers' dream." Before Dallas, the magazine surmised, the Kennedys envisioned three successive two-term presidencies: JFK, RFK, EMK. After November 1963, it was two vice presidential terms for RFK, two presidential terms for RFK, and two presidential terms for EMK. After LBJ barred RFK from the 1964 ticket, the goal allegedly became two successive two-term presidencies beginning in 1972. "The Kennedy Brothers' Dream—A New Chapter," *U.S. News & World Report*, Sept. 14, 1965: 33–5.

405 *"the Bobby twins"*: Cartoon, Jules Feiffer, "The Bobby Twins, Episode 2," *New Republic*, Feb. 10, 1968: 34; also in Halberstam, *Unfinished Odyssey*, 57–8.

406 *Salinger to convene a meeting*: Salinger interview; O'Donnell quoted in Schlesinger, *Robert Kennedy*, 891; White, *Making 1968*, 158.

406 *Kennedy's instincts remained*: RFK and McGovern quoted in Schlesinger, *Robert Kennedy*, 887–8; Michael C. Janeway, "Washington Report," *Atlantic*, January 1968: 6; Sorensen OH, JFKL; Halberstam, *Unfinished Odyssey*, 17; Goodwin, 480–81; Memorandum, "Re: McCarthy Backgrounder," Dec. 4, 1967, Gwirtzman Papers, Box 5.

406 *"It's all so complicated"*: Newfield, 196; Chester *et al.*, 114–15; Schlesinger, *Robert Kennedy*, 894–5.

407 *"Even should you lose"*: Schlesinger to RFK, Dec. 13, 1967, SC/PF, Box 11.

407 *"I wish you would get out"*: McPherson to LBJ, May 12, 1967, FG1, Box 14, LBJL. On LBJ's sense of siege, see Califano, 257–8; Kearns, 311–12.

407 *a steady barrage of polling data*: See Panzer Office Files, Box 397-9, LBJL, specifically, Memoranda, "Advance Gallup [Poll] for Sunday, October 1, 1967" and "Analysis of Harris Survey, Nov. 27, 1967," Panzer to LBJ, Sept. 29 and Nov. 27, 1967, Panzer Files, Box 398. Despite the fact that this file is full of Harris and Gallup polls sent directly and almost weekly to LBJ, it also contains Panzer's frequent caveats about the unreliability of poll data in general. In fact, LBJ had Panzer draft phony letters from "citizens" to George Gallup questioning his methodology and results. Panzer also dismissed Louis Harris as "very close to the Kennedy camp in 1960." Still, LBJ devoured every number that came his way, haranguing aides on the phone with demographic breakdowns. Panzer to LBJ, Oct. 7 and 16, 1967, Box 398; Memorandum, "The President and the Polls," Panzer to LBJ, Feb. 17, 1967, Box 398; Recording of telephone conversation between LBJ and Clark, Jan. 25, 1967, 8:22 P.M., Tape K67.01.

408 *Still, Kennedy remained vulnerable*: "One Polls Finds Gain by Johnson; Kennedy Widens Lead in Second," *New York Times*, Nov. 27, 1967: 14; Ben Wattenberg to LBJ, Nov. 21, 1967, Watson Files, Box 25; Levinson interview. "As [Kennedy] takes a position to the left of the President on Vietnam, he is also taking himself out of the main stream of public opinion," Panzer observed excitedly in March. Panzer to LBJ, March 3, 1967, CF-RFK, LBJL.

408 *"How rational is Bobby"*: Roche to LBJ, April 18 and Dec. 18, 1967, Watson Files, Box 29 (emphasis in originals). Like Roche, Jim Rowe was "convinced that Bobby Kennedy has made a political judgment that he cannot take the ticket from you in 1968; or, that, if he could, it would inevitably result in a shattered Democratic Party which would go down to defeat . . . and destroy Bobby forever." Rowe too advised that an emissary appeal to Bobby's *"self-interest,"* to tell Bobby that his future depended upon "support[ing] Johnson actively as far as [his] integrity will allow." Rowe suggested that Larry O'Brien, Stewart Udall, or Robert McNamara make the pitch—as "Cabinet members who are close to Bobby, and yet, I think, . . . loyal to you." Memorandum, "Bobby Kennedy," Rowe to LBJ, Jan. 16, 1968, Watson Files, Box 30.

408 *"Bobby Kennedy is sponsoring"*: Roche to LBJ, Jan. 26, 1968, Watson Files, Box 25 (emphasis in original).

408 *aides believed Roche was underestimating*: Roche OH; Kearns, 312–13; O'Donnell

OH, LBJL.

409 *Watson served up*: See Watson Files, Box 25. LBJ note on letter, John Criswell to Watson, March 15, 1967, Watson Files, Box 25; SAC, Chicago, to Hoover, Nov. 22, 1967, FBI File #77-51387, vols. 14–15; Memorandum, "Politics and West Virginia," Rowe to LBJ, May 31, 1967, Watson Files, Box 30. Rowe's source complained that administration officials are "always calling him to ask what Bobby is up to."

409 *"ought to go to every National Committeeman"*: LBJ to Ben Wattenberg, Dec. 10, 1967, Watson Files, Box 25; Roche to LBJ, Feb. 20, 1967, Watson Files, Box 29; Christian interview.

409 *"absolutely appalling"*: Reedy OH, LBJL; Gould, "Never a Deep Partisan," 28–34; Freeman OH, LBJL; Reedy interview.

410 *"He wanted it weak"*: Hubert H. Humphrey, *The Education of a Public Man: My Life and Politics*, ed. Norman Sherman (Garden City, NY: Doubleday, 1976): 364–5; Gould, "Never a Deep Partisan," 34, 36. Gould adds: "One reason for Johnson's suspicion of the Democratic National Committee was that he saw it as a means through which Kennedy might challenge his power."

410 *"Nothing could encourage"*: Roche to LBJ, Dec. 4, 1967; Roche OH; McPherson OH, LBJL.

410 *a lengthy "White Paper"*: Memorandum, "A White Paper for the President on the 1968 Presidential Campaign," Lawrence O'Brien, Sept. 29, 1967, 1, 26–29, 32, 36, 42, 44, Watson Files, Box 28; O'Brien OH, LBJL (emphasis in original).

411 *"It is later than we think"*: Memorandum, "Notes and Comments on: 'A White Paper . . .' " James Rowe, n.d., Watson Files, Box 28; O'Brien to LBJ, Nov. 3, 1967, and O'Brien to Watson, Nov. 7, 1967, Watson Files, Box 28; O'Brien, 215.

411 *McCarthy's declaration*: McPherson, 427; Gould, "Never a Deep Partisan," 37–8, 51n; Roche to LBJ, Dec. 18, 1967, Watson Files, Box 29.

411 *"Bobby Kennedy was sitting"*: Reedy OH; Califano to LBJ, Dec. 8, 1967, WHCF Name File, Kennedy, Robert F., Box 98, LBJL. Of course, both Shriver and Moyers were suspect in the White House because of their ties to RFK. The rumor offered a welcome opportunity for both men to recapture Johnson's good graces.

411 *"The ordeal continues"*: Schlesinger, *Robert Kennedy*, 902; Berman, *Lyndon Johnson's War*, 144–5; Chester *et al.*, 107; Schlesinger, *Robert Kennedy*, 902–3.

412 *Christian Science Monitor breakfast*: Chester *et al.*, 106–7.

412 *"if he runs, he runs"*: Elizabeth B. Drew, "Washington Report," *Atlantic*, April 1968: 4.

412 *the end for Adam Walinsky*: Walinsky OH.

413 *January 30 was Tet*: Herring, *America's Longest War*, 186–90; Berman, *Lyndon Johnson's War*, 145–9.

413 *"What the hell"*: Herring, *America's Longest War*, 191. Prompted by Tet, Cronkite traveled to Vietnam to investigate. A month after the offensive he delivered his famous and damning conclusion: "It seems now more certain than ever that the bloody experience of Vietnam is to end in a stalemate." Watching the broadcast, LBJ turned to George Christian and said wistfully that if he had lost Cronkite he had lost the country. David Culbert, "Johnson and the Media," in Divine, ed., vol. 1, 223–7.

413 *public relations campaign on the war*: See Berman, *Lyndon Johnson's War*, 114–19,

138; Herring, "War in Vietnam," 51.

413 *"a few bandits"*: Berman, *Lyndon Johnson's War*, 149.

413 *"The fig leaf was gone"*: Edelman interview.

413 *a dark funk*: Newfield, 204; Memorandum, "Thai/Ellsberg Comments on the January Asian Crisis," Daniel Ellsberg, Jan. 31, 1968, Walinsky Papers, Box 19, JFKL; Ellsberg interview; Dutton to RFK, Jan. 31, 1968, SC/PF, Box 3.

413 *On February 7, Bobby sat*: Newfield, 205; Schlesinger, *Robert Kennedy*, 905.

414 *"Our enemy,"* he began: "Excerpts from Text of Kennedy Speech," and Tom Wicker, "Kennedy Asserts U.S. Cannot Win," *New York Times*, Feb. 8, 1968: 1, 12.

414 *"In the last twelve hours"*: Schlesinger, *Robert Kennedy*, 905.

414 *"If we have LBJ"*: Hamill letter reprinted in Newfield, 206–8 (emphasis in original).

415 *There were other catalysts*: Newfield, 210; Schlesinger, *Robert Kennedy*, 908–9.

415 *it all came back to the war*: Walinsky interview; Schlesinger OH, LBJL; Berman, *Lyndon Johnson's War*, 171–2; Ellsberg interview; Sorensen OH. On March 10, when Neil Sheehan and Hedrick Smith broke the story in the *New York Times*, the reaction in Congress was explosive. Though Ellsberg had leaked the Wheeler Report to RFK only, Sheehan later told Ellsberg quite firmly that Kennedy's office had not leaked it to the *Times*. Sheehan implied that the leak came from elsewhere on the Hill. It had never before occurred to Ellsberg to leak confidential materials to the press, but as the controversy raged, he realized, "that's powerful." Three years later, Ellsberg leaked the Pentagon Papers—a top-secret, 7,000-page government report on America's involvement in Vietnam—to the *Times*. Ellsberg interview.

416 *"Before any further major step"*: John W. Finney, "Criticism of War Widens in Senate on Build-up Issue," *New York Times*, March 8, 1968: 1,8; Schlesinger, *Robert Kennedy*, 905–6.

416 *When reporter Charles Bartlett*: Bartlett OH, LBJL.

416 *a Roper poll*: Panzer to LBJ, March 4, 1968, Panzer Files, Box 397; Larry Berman, "Johnson and the White House Staff," in Divine, ed., vol. 1, 204–5 (emphasis in original).

416 *Bernie Boutin, Johnson's man*: O'Brien, 221; O'Brien OH.

416 *In the final twenty-four hours*: O'Brien, 221; Roche OH.

417 *Johnson "lost" the New Hampshire primary*: Gould, 39; "Poll Finds Vote for McCarthy Was Anti-Johnson, Not Antiwar," *New York Times*, March 18, 1968: 50.

417 *"If you announce"*: McGovern OH; Dolan (1990) and Salinger interviews; Theodore C. Sorensen, *The Kennedy Legacy* (New York: Macmillan, 1969): 133.

417 *On the day of the primary*: Schlesinger, *Robert Kennedy*, 911; Roche OH.

417 *"Bill, I'll keep an eye"*: Carroll Kilpatrick, "Moyers Quits White House Job," *Washington Post*, Dec. 15, 1966: A1; Max Frankel, "Moyers Resigning as Johnson's Aide to Head Newsday," *New York Times*, Dec. 15, 1966: 1, 54; Terence Smith, "Moyers Honored at L.I. Luncheon," *New York Times*, Feb. 18, 1967. Moyers's tips are referred to in Al M. to Moyers, Feb. 20, 1967, and Christian to LBJ, Feb. 24, 1967, PL/Kennedy, Robert F., Box 26, LBJL; Califano to LBJ, Dec. 8, 1967, WHCF Name File, Kennedy, Robert F., Box 98, LBJL. In July 1967, Kennedy invited Moyers and his wife on a five-day cruise off the Maine coast (there is no record of whether Moyers accepted). RFK to Moyers, July 20, 1967, SC/PF, Box 8, JFKL.

418 *Now, driving uptown*: Schlesinger, *Robert Kennedy*, 911–12.

418 *Kennedy was surprised: Ibid.*; John Herbers, "Kennedy Is Ready to Run; Says Vote for M'Carthy Discloses Split in Party," *New York Times*, March 14, 1968: 1, 30.

418 *A strange subplot*: Sorensen interview; Sorensen, *Kennedy Legacy*, 133–6; Schlesinger, *Robert Kennedy*, 914; Sorensen OH; Newfield, 216.

419 *whom was Sorensen protecting*: Pierson interview; Pierson OH, LBJL; Pierson to LBJ, Feb. 5, 1968, Watson Files, Box 12.

419 *"gritted his teeth"*: Schlesinger, *Robert Kennedy*, 915; Newfield, 217. If Bobby was unhappy, Fred Dutton was outraged. In an angry memo Dutton reminded Bobby that Johnson could not be trusted, that Johnson could undo any concession six months down the line. "You are dealing not just with Viet Nam but with the psychology and personality of a particular man," Dutton wrote Bobby, adding, "I do not believe anyone can really do business with Lyndon Johnson." Dutton left Bobby with a question: "Is the [commission] offer really just an escape hatch to avoid your having to chose [sic] between running and not running—or find a safe haven for awhile?" Dutton to RFK, n.d. [March 13 or 14, 1968], Gwirtzman Papers, Box 5.

420 *Kennedy met Sorensen*: Sorensen, *Kennedy Legacy*, 137–8; Clifford, 502–3; Clifford OH, LBJL; Clifford interview.

420 *Clifford promised to discuss*: "Memorandum of Conference with Senator Robert Kennedy and Theodore C. Sorensen," Clifford, March 14, 1968, WHFN-RFK, Box 6; Clifford, 503–4.

420 *At 3:30, Clifford described*: "Memorandum . . ."; Clifford, 504–5. There is an interesting discrepancy between Clifford's contemporaneous memo and his memoirs. In the memo of March 14, 1968, Clifford lists LBJ's three objections to the commission: first, it would appear a political deal; second, it would upset his advisers; and third, Kennedy's presence would invite opposition on the Hill. Yet in his memoirs, Clifford cites only one of these objections—to a "political deal"—and adds three concerns found nowhere in his detailed account of March 14: first, "comfort to Hanoi"; second, "usurp[ing] Presidential authority"; and third, that Kennedy's proposed commission members were all known opponents of the war. One must assume that the reasons Johnson gave Clifford and the reasons Clifford gave Kennedy for rejecting the committee were not entirely in sync.

420 *"I came into the office"*: LBJ, recorded interview by Cronkite, CBS News Special, Dec. 27, 1969, LBJL; Pierson interview.

421 *"Well, I guess Bob will run"*: "Transcript of telephone conversation between DeVier Pierson at the White House and Ted Sorensen at Senator Robert F. Kennedy's office, Thursday, March 14, 1968, 6:15 P.M.," Pierson, March 14, 1968, WHFN-RFK, Box 6; Pierson interview; Pierson to LBJ, March 14, 1968, WHFN-RFK, Box 6.

CHAPTER 17: RFK VS. LBJ

422 *"I am announcing"*: "Statement of Senator Robert F. Kennedy, Washington, D.C., March 16, 1968," Edelman Papers, Box 11, JFKL; Wicker, "Kennedy to Make

Three Primary Races; Attacks Johnson," *New York Times*, March 17, 1968: 1; laughing woman referred to in Richard Reeves, "The Making of a Candidate, 1968," *New York Times Magazine*, March 31, 1968: 25; Jules Witcover, *85 Days: The Last Campaign of Robert Kennedy* (New York: Quill, 1969): 86–7.

422 *"Every time I have spoken"*: "Transcript, 3/16 RFK Announcement, Senate Caucus," 1968 Presidential Campaign Files, Media Division, Box 3, JFKL (emphasis added).

423 *the press would obliterate*: Wicker, "Kennedy to Make Three Primary Races"; "Can McCarthy and Bobby Stop LBJ?" *U.S. News & World Report*, April 1, 1968: 27.

423 *The White House greeted Kennedy's announcement*: Sorensen OH, JFKL; CBS broadcast transcribed in Tom Johnson to LBJ, and Jim Jones to LBJ, March 17, 1968, WHFN-RFK, Box 6, LBJL. White House aide Jones scribbled a curt "NO" next to the paragraph on "the Administration version." Also, Wicker, "Kennedy Made Johnson Offer to Forgo Race," *New York Times*, March 18, 1968: 1.

423 *"I am surprised"*: "Statement of Senator Robert F. Kennedy, March 17, 1968," Edelman Papers, Box 11; Wicker, "Kennedy Made Johnson Offer."

424 *Kennedy was the one on the defensive*: "Can McCarthy and Bobby Stop LBJ"; White, *Making 1968*, 90; Schlesinger, *Robert Kennedy*, 922–3; Goodwin, 527.

424 *"Hit hard at the Administration"*: Memorandum, "Suggestions on McCarthy," John W. Douglas to RFK, March 18, 1968, Edelman Papers, Box 13 (emphasis in original); Schlesinger, *Robert Kennedy*, 927; Newfield, 232; Clipping, John R. Cauley, "No Punches Pulled by Kennedy," *Kansas Star*, March 18, 1968, in 1968 Campaign Papers, Research Division: Subject File, Box 56; "Statement by Senator Robert F. Kennedy, Alfred M. Landon Lecture Series, Kansas State University, Ahern Fieldhouse, Manhattan, Kansas, March 18, 1968, 10:00 A.M.," Edelman Papers, Box 11; Newfield, 236; Witcover, 103–5.

425 *"When we are told"*: "Address by Senator Robert F. Kennedy, Values Symposium, Vanderbilt University, Nashville, Tennessee, March 21, 1968," Edelman Papers, Box 11; Newfield, 236, 240; Cauley, "No Punches Pulled"; Witcover, 116–17.

425 *"it is a little early"*: Schlesinger to RFK, March 27, 1968, Edelman Papers, Box 11; Edelman interview; Walinsky OH, JFKL; Dutton OH, JFKL; Edelman OH, JFKL; Salinger to Edward Kennedy, March 28, 1968, Gwirtzman Papers, Box 5, JFKL.

426 *Richard Harwood of the* Washington Post: Schlesinger, *Robert Kennedy*, 927–8.

426 *"a new birth"*: Press Release, "Excerpts of Senator Robert F. Kennedy, Democratic State Party Dinner, Hotel Biltmore, Phoenix, Arizona, March 30, 1968," 1968 Campaign Files, Speeches and Press Releases, Box 4; Speech draft for Arizona address, Schlesinger, 1968 Campaign Files, Speechwriters Division, Box 3, JFKL; Gwirtzman OH, JFKL.

426 *Rowland Evans and Robert Novak*: Evans and Novak, "Kennedy Disappoints Young Radicals by Softened Attack on War and LBJ," *Washington Post*, March 28, 1968.

426 *gains in the center*: Schlesinger, *Robert Kennedy*, 929; Gallup, 2104, 2112; "Gallup (late March) impact of Kennedy Candidacy," Panzer Files, Box 377; "A Brisk

Start for the Kennedy Drive," *U.S. News & World Report*, April 1, 1968: 10. In a hypothetical two-man race, Democrats still preferred Johnson to McCarthy 59 to 29 percent in late March. Gallup, 2112.

427 *"I had been expecting it"*: L. B. Johnson, 538; Pierson OH, LBJL.

427 *"always in this life"*: *Public Papers, LBJ*, vol. 1, 1968–69, 402–5.

427 *"Make no mistake about it"*: Kearns, 338–9; Henggeler, 237–8.

427 *"I would have no comment"*: *Public Papers, LBJ*, vol. 1, 1968–69, 433–4; "The Rivals," *Newsweek*, April 8, 1968: 35–6.

428 *"You are going to see"*: Clipping, Robert J. Donovan, "Johnson Bides His Time in Kennedy Feud," *New York Post*, March 20, 1968, in 1968 Campaign Files, Press Division, Box 11, JFKL; "LBJ's Mood in Times of Trouble," *U.S. News & World Report*, April 8, 1968: 69.

428 *The party machinery*: Donovan, "Johnson Bides His Time." Rowe kept quiet his concern over the group's antiwar sentiment (Memorandum, "Peace with Honor in Vietnam," Rowe to LBJ, March 19, 1968, Watson Files, Box 30). Also White, *Making 1968*, 113; Citizens for Johnson-Humphrey mentioned in "Kennedy Unit Opens Headquarters, Johnson Forces Expand Theirs," *Washington Post*, March 27, 1968; Memorandum, Mike Manatos, March 16, 1968, Watson Files, Box 25.

428 *Johnson's advisers were concerned*: "Draft telegram to Democratic Party leaders from James Rowe and Larry O'Brien, National Citizens for Johnson-Humphrey," n.d., John Criswell to Watson, March 18, 1968, and O'Brien to LBJ, March 19, 1968, Watson Files, Box 28; McPherson to LBJ, March 19, 1968, McPherson Files, Box 53; Sanders to LBJ, March 22, 1968, PL/Kennedy, Robert F., Box 26.

428 *Kennedy's entry energized*: Rowe quoted in Kearns, 339; Roche to Watson, March 26, 1968, Watson Files, Box 29; Panzer to LBJ, March 14, 1968, and Panzer to Watson, March 28, 1968, Watson Files, Box 28.

429 *"The Citizens Committee"*: Reedy to LBJ, March 29, 1968, Watson Files, Box 28. Another administration official thought Johnson should use Kennedy's youthful following against him. "Pictures of youngsters touseling his hair and grabbing his cuff links are reminiscent of the Sinatra-Presley syndrome and could be used to identify him with the bobby socks mania of the past. Can you imagine John F. Kennedy permitting people to ruffle his hair and manhandle him? Do people really want a President whom they can pinch, pull, squeeze and hug?" Memorandum, Bill Crook, Assistant Director of OEO, to Watson, March 27, 1968, PL/Kennedy, Robert F., Box 26.

429 *The White House had amassed information*: See Panzer Files, Box 371; Jones to Watson and Watson to Jones, March 30, 1968, PL/Kennedy, Box 26; McPherson to LBJ, March 18, 1968, McPherson Files, Box 53; McPherson to Watson, March 18, 1968, McPherson Files, Box 51. McPherson called the president's attention to this quote from a biography of Joseph Kennedy: " 'Kennedy, a diligent gatherer of facts, regularly yielded to his innate pessimism and pushed the facts to extreme—and erroneous—conclusions. . . . In his hurt pride, he seized every opportunity to restate his conclusions in terms calculated to jolt Washington out of its indifference.' One shouldn't carry the analogy too far," McPherson added, "but as Joe once said, 'Bobby and I think alike.' " McPherson to LBJ, March 22, 1968, WHFN-RFK, Box 6.

430 *anxious about New York State*: Gus Tyler to Watson, March 21, 1968, Watson Files, Box 29; "A Look Inside the Johnson-Kennedy Contest," *U.S. News & World Report*, April 8, 1968: 48–50; Rowe to Watson, March 19, 1968, Watson Files, Box 29; Memorandum, "New York and the O'Connor Operation," William Connell to Cecil Burney, and LBJ to Watson, March 27, 1968, PL/Kennedy, Box 26; Dan Roewer to Roche, March 23, 1968, Watson Files, Box 13; Thomas P. Ronan, "State Democrats Name Nickerson for Senate Race," *New York Times*, March 31, 1968: 1, 35; Ernest Goldstein to Watson, March 15, 1968, Watson Files, Box 12.

430 *"remain aloof from the [Kennedy-McCarthy] brawl"*: Reedy to LBJ, March 16, 1968, Watson Files, Box 28. The memo was addressed to LBJ, but Reedy referred to the President in the third person.

430 *"A moving target"*: McPherson to LBJ, March 18, 1968.

431 *an odd silence in the Oval Office*: Califano, 265; Rowe to LBJ, March 15, 1968, Watson Files, Box 30; Temple to LBJ, March 26, 1968, Watson Files, Box 25.

432 *"I'm going to get out"*: Rowe OH, LBJL; Weisl, Sr., OH, LBJL; Bartlett OH, LBJL; Pierson OH; Westmoreland's prediction in Berman, *Lyndon Johnson's War*, 122; Connally's in Temple OH, LBJL.

432 *Christian, the White House press secretary*: Christian OH, LBJL; LBJ, recorded interview by Walter Cronkite, CBS News Special, Dec. 27, 1969; Christian interview.

433 *Johnson was looking for a way out*: Christian interview; Reedy OH.

433 *"After New Hampshire"*: Christian interview; O'Brien, 225–6, 229–30.

433 *LBJ's meeting with his "wise men"*: Berman, *Lyndon Johnson's War*, 100–101, 194–201; David Fromkin, "Lyndon Johnson and Foreign Policy: What the New Documents Show," *Foreign Affairs*, January/February 1995: 169.

434 *The next day Johnson asked Joe Califano*: Schlesinger, *Robert Kennedy*, 930.

434 *Johnson had lunch*: Califano, 265; McPherson, 427, 436–7; Clifford OH, LBJL.

434 *"What do you think"*: McPherson, 427–8; Califano, 265–6; McPherson interview.

435 *the president's desk that week*: Califano to LBJ, March 27, 1968, Loyd Hackler to LBJ, March 25, 1968, Sanders to LBJ, March 25, 1968, John Gonella to LBJ, March 22, 1968, all in PL/Kennedy, Box 26; Panzer to LBJ, March 30, 1968, Watson Files, Box 28; Christian interview.

435 *"This is not statesmanship"*: Panzer to LBJ, March 30, 1968, Watson Files, Box 28.

435 *"questions of some importance"*: Frankel, "Johnson to Talk to Nation Tonight on Vietnam War," and "Text of White House Statement and Transcript of Johnson's News Conference," *New York Times*, March 31, 1968: 1, 38; Temple OH, LBJL.

435 *An hour before his speech*: *Public Papers, LBJ*, vol. 1, 1968–69, 469–76; Wicker, "Johnson Says He Won't Run," Sylvan Fox, "Political Chiefs Stunned; Kennedy Sets News Parley," and "Transcript of the President's Address on the Vietnam War and His Political Plans," *New York Times*, April 1, 1968: 1, 26–7.

436 *Robert Kennedy's American Airlines flight*: Homer Bigart, "Kennedy, Told News on Plane, Sits in Silence amid the Hubbub," *New York Times*, April 1, 1968: 27; Newfield, 244; Witcover, 126–7.

436 *Magazines rushed to press*: "Why He Did It—What Now," *Newsweek*, April 15, 1968: 43.

436 *Kennedy's friends and advisers*: Walinsky OH; Wilkins, Edelman, Dolan (1990) and

Mankiewicz interviews.

437 *No Kennedy man was willing*: Goodwin in Plimpton, ed., 242; O'Brien, 229.

437 *"may have had some bearing"*: McCarthy, 187; "Look Inside the Johnson-Kennedy Contest."

437 *Johnson men, proud:* "Look Inside the Johnson-Kennedy Contest"; "Memorandum of Conversation, Wednesday, April 3, 1968," Rostow, April 5, 1968, Appointment File (Diary Backup), Box 94, LBJL; *Public Papers*, 477.

437 *much more to LBJ's withdrawal*: Christian interview; L. B. Johnson, 425; LBJ, Cronkite's interview; Baker, 262–3. Nonetheless, George Reedy claims to have been personally close to Johnson's doctors and "quite confident that [LBJ's withdrawal] had nothing to do with his health." Reedy interview; Reedy OH.

437 *Johnson was exhausted:* "Why He Did It"; "Why Johnson Withdrew," *U.S. News & World Report*, April 15, 1968: 39–41; "Why LBJ Is Quitting," *U.S. News & World Report*, July 22, 1968: 25–7; LBJ, Cronkite's interview; Kearns, 340–3; McPherson OH.

438 *Lady Bird did not understand:* "The Renunciation," *Time*, April 12, 1968: 22; Christian OH; LBJ, Cronkite's interview.

438 *the myth of Johnson's martyrdom*: LBJ quoted by Moyers in Michael Janeway's interview, "Bill Moyers Talks About LBJ, Power, Poverty, War, and the Young," *Atlantic*, July 1968: 37.

438 *strove wearily for statesmanship*: O'Brien, 233; Temple OH; Moyers in Plimpton, ed., 218; Kearns, 346–7.

439 *"the final straw"*: Kearns, 343.

439 *"Get out of the way"*: Christian interview.

439 *Kennedy had never really believed*: Gwirtzman OH; Edelman OH; Burden OH, JFKL; Newfield, 244; Ethel Kennedy and vanden Heuvel quoted in vanden Heuvel to Gwirtzman, Oct. 27, 1968, Gwirtzman Papers, Box 5; *New York Times*, April 1: 1968: 27; Chester *et al.*, 6.

440 *"I think it's the best news"*: Whittaker OH, JFKL.

440 *Bobby quickly learned*: Gwirtzman OH; vanden Heuvel to Gwirtzman, Oct. 27, 1968.

440 *Bobby called Larry O'Brien*: Kennedy teased O'Brien before the speech: "I was wondering what you were going to say about me. . . . I thought maybe you'd have something nice to say about me" (O'Brien OH, LBJL). Watson to LBJ, March 20, 1968, including press release, "Remarks by Postmaster General Lawrence J. O'Brien, National Press Club Luncheon, Washington, D.C., March 20, 1968—12:30 P.M.," Watson Files, Box 28; O'Brien, 232; O'Brien OH.

440 *Meanwhile Arthur Schlesinger and Adam Walinsky*: RFK to LBJ, March 31, 1968, SC/PF, Box 23, JFKL; Copy of telegram, RFK to LBJ, April 1, 1968, WHFN-RFK, Box 6, LBJL; "Statement of Senator Robert F. Kennedy, Overseas Press Club," April 1, 1968, Edelman Papers, Box 11; Gwirtzman OH.

441 *In the car*: Burden OH; vanden Heuvel to Gwirtzman, Oct. 27, 1968; Gwirtzman OH.

441 *"I won't bother answering"*: Schlesinger, *Robert Kennedy*, 933.

441 *"Don't pay attention"*: Ibid., 921.

441 *LBJ entered the cabinet room*: Presidential Diary, April 3, 1968, WHFN-RFK, Box 6. According to George Christian, LBJ conducted the meeting in the cabinet

room in order to record it secretly—to get commitments on tape. Johnson later discovered that RFK had worn a scrambler, and the tape was "just garbage!" The machine was not broken; it recorded Johnson's meetings with other candidates perfectly well. Christian says that Rostow later confirmed (or did not deny) this version of events. Sorensen considers the charge "ridiculous" and rather hilarious. Christian and Sorensen interviews.

442 *"Your speech,"* Bobby said: "Memorandum of Conversation: The President, Senator Robert F. Kennedy, Theodore Sorensen, Charles Murphy, and W. W. Rostow, 10:00 A.M., April 3, 1968," Rostow, n.d., and Draft, "Notes on Meeting of the President with Senator Robert Kennedy, April 3, 1968," Charles S. Murphy, April 4, 1968, WHFN-RFK, Box 6; Sorensen and Rostow interviews; Sorensen OH, JFKL; Sorensen, *Kennedy Legacy,* 146–7; Rostow OH, LBJL.

444 *Juanita Roberts, Johnson's secretary*: Roberts OH, LBJL.

444 *"I'm glad it ended"*: LBJ, Cronkite's interview; L. B. Johnson, 539.

444 *McCarthy soon paid a courtesy call*: McCarthy, 196; Levinson interview.

444 *were administration officials free*: Califano, 291–2; Schnittker OH, LBJL; Freeman OH, LBJL.

445 *Schnittker, Freeman's under secretary*: Edelman interview; Schnittker OH.

445 *When Schnittker told Freeman*: Schnittker OH; Freeman OH; Schnittker to LBJ, April 25, 1968, PL/Kennedy, Box 26, LBJL; Schnittker OH.

445 *another endorsement hit the wires*: Califano, 292–3; Memorandum, "Phone Call from Ted Sorenson [sic]," Murphy to LBJ, April 26, 1968, PL/Kennedy, Box 26; Schnittker OH; Freeman OH.

446 *"I am aware"*: McPherson to LBJ, April 24 and May 14, 1968, McPherson Files, Box 53; and McPherson to Humphrey, May 15, 1968, McPherson Files, Box 51. It must be added, however, that LBJ did little to support Humphrey beyond lending him a few presidential aides. LBJ, apprehensive that Humphrey would repudiate the administration's policy in Vietnam, regarded his vice president with deep ambivalence. "We didn't do anywhere near as much as the White House could do," complained McPherson. "The machinery of government was not transformed . . . from neutral-bureaucratic to partisan-political. And the president would not bend." Johnson's silence was so protracted that observers began to wonder whether LBJ preferred Nixon to Humphrey. In fact, LBJ despised Nixon and may have preferred New York Governor Nelson Rockefeller, a Republican, to all other candidates. Temple OH; McPherson OH; McPherson, 448–9; Califano, 289–91.

446 *"Kennedy now is exposed"*: "Why Johnson Withdrew"; Edelman OH; Dolan (1994) and Edelman interviews; Schlesinger to RFK, April 3, 1968, SC/PF, Box 11.

446 *more bane than boon*: Speech drafts, March 30 and April 1, 1968, and Speech to Democratic City Committee, Convention Hall, Philadelphia, PA, April 2, 1968, RFK Speeches, 1965–1968, Reading Copies, Box 9, JFKL.

446 *"brought a general apathy"*: "Memoranda: to Campaign Headquarters," Jim Flug to Sorensen, Salinger *et al.*, May 1, 1968, 1968 Presidential Campaign Files, Youth/Student Division Subject File, Box 5; Schlesinger to RFK, April 3, 1968; Edelman OH.

447 *He was campaigning in Indiana*: Newfield, 246.

447 *"In this difficult day"*: Schlesinger, *Robert Kennedy,* 939–40.

447 *"America is shocked"*: Chester *et al.,* 16–17.

448 *"How is it possible"*: Kearns, 305; O'Reilly, 256, 269.

448 *"He never understood"*: *The American Experience: LBJ,* WGBH-Television.

448 *"Kennedy . . . did understand"*: Wilkins interview; Brian Dooley, *Robert Kennedy: The Final Years* (New York: St. Martin's, 1996): 36–8.

448 *"To understand is not to permit"*: RFK, *To Seek a Newer World,* 21; Schlesinger, *Robert Kennedy,* 844.

449 *At King's funeral*: Califano, 282; *The American Experience: The Kennedys.*

449 *"Robert Kennedy appears"*: "Who Will It Be in November?" *U.S. News & World Report,* April 15, 1968: 36; O'Donnell OH, LBJL.

449 *Some of Kennedy's advisers*: Walinsky OH; Lois, 16.

449 *These fears diminished*: Dolan (1994), Edelman, and Mankiewicz interviews; Mankiewicz OH, LBJL; primary results in Schlesinger, *Robert Kennedy,* 949, 955.

450 *"We were damned interested"*: Markman OH, LBJL; Branigan quoted in Watson to LBJ, April 2, 1968, WHCF Name File, Box 98, LBJL; Memorandum, "Indiana Interpretation," Panzer to LBJ, May 10, 1968, Panzer Files, Box 397; McPherson OH.

450 *"political eunuch"*: Udall interview; "Meeting of the President with Robert Spivack, May 23, 1968," George Christian, Christian Office Files, Box 1, LBJL.

450 *Johnson's political disinterest*: Memorandum, "Personal Appearances," Busby to LBJ, April 26, 1968, PL/Kennedy, Box 26 (emphasis in original). For a similar suggestion see Panzer to Jones and Temple, April 26, 1968, PL/Kennedy, Box 26; Unsigned memorandum to LBJ, May 9, 1968, PL/Kennedy, Box 26 (emphasis in original); "Who Will It Be in November."

451 *"Too horrible for words"*: Califano, 297.

Chapter 18: Between Myth and Martyrdom

452 *Johnson phoned DeVier Pierson*: Pierson interview; Pierson OH, LBJL.

452 *In the presidential bedroom*: Christian OH, LBJL; Telegram, LBJ and Lady Bird Johnson to Ethel Kennedy, June 5, 1968, WHFN–RFK, Box 6, LBJL.

452 *"[Washington] is quiet now"*: Califano, to LBJ, June 5, 1968, 10:15 A.M., WHFN–RFK, Box 6; Califano, 297.

452 *White House aides, meanwhile*: Temple OH, LBJL; Pierson interview; Christian OH.

453 *"there wasn't going to be a whole lot"*: Temple OH; Califano, 297n.

453 *"There are no words equal"*: *Public Papers, LBJ,* vol. 1, 1968–69, 691; Pierson OH; Christian OH.

453 *Hours later, at lunch*: Califano, 298; disbelief recalled in Pierson interview.

453 *"A hundred competing emotions"*: McPherson OH, LBJL; Christian OH; Frankel, "Johnson and Kennedy Family Face a New Tragedy Together," *New York Times,* June 9, 1968: 55.

454 *LBJ had been in the motorcade*: Manchester, 166; Levinson interview.

454 *Weeks earlier a political cartoonist*: Bill Mauldin, *Chicago Sun-Times,* April 17, 1968. The caption is, "Bookends?"

454 *George Christian worried*: Christian to LBJ, June 10, 1968, FG1, Box 18, LBJL.

454 *"It would have been hard"*: Kearns, 350. Clark Clifford writes that after RFK's death, "more deeply than before, Lyndon Johnson feared that history would always trap him between the martyred Kennedys." Clifford, 545.

454 *"he* had *to set aside his own feelings"*: Clifford, 545 (emphasis in original).

454 *Aides set about drafting*: Califano, 298; McPherson, 381; Temple OH.

455 *In the final hours*: Pierson OH; Califano, 298; Clinton J. Hill, SAIC-USSS, to LBJ, June 5, 1968, 8:58 P.M., WHFN-RFK, Box 6; Pierson interview.

455 *"My fellow citizens"*: Public Papers, LBJ, vol. 1, 1968–69, 691–3.

456 *rework the gun control bill*: Pierson OH; Califano, 299.

456 *The White House press corps*: Christian OH. Tom Johnson (who later became president of CNN) suggested on June 5 that LBJ's active role in managing the crisis of Kennedy's shooting "would make a good feature." LBJ apparently disagreed. Tom Johnson to LBJ, June 5, 1968, FG 1, Box 18, LBJL.

456 *The Nation promptly denounced*: " 'For God's Sake,' " Nation, June 17, 1968: 779–80.

456 *Johnson sat in the small study*: Pierson interview; Califano, 299–300; Levinson interview.

456 *Califano had no answers*: Califano, 300.

456 *"Robert Kennedy," he said*: Public Papers, LBJ, vol. 1, 1968–69, 693.

457 *Johnson was full of worry*: Califano, 300.

457 *the president phoned Clark Clifford*: Clifford, 545–6. "That was a very delicate situation, and I wondered whether I should even mention it [in *Counsel to the President*]," Clifford explained in 1994. "I don't want to go on any further than I did in the book." Clifford interview.

457 *LBJ had clear discretion*: Jones to LBJ, June 6, 1968, WHFN-RFK, Box 6.

457 *RFK's Senate staff contacted Loyd Hackler*: Hackler OH, LBJL.

458 *An agenda of the meeting*: Agenda, "Evening Meeting, 8 P.M.," June 6, 1968, Youth/Student Division: Subject File, Box 5, 1968 Presidential Campaign, RFK Senate Papers, JFKL.

458 *Califano and Robert McNamara appealed*: Clifford, 546.

458 *Bill Moyers called*: Miller interview.

458 *On the morning of June 8*: Califano, 301.

458 *"It was a difficult entrance"*: Ibid. (emphasis in original).

458 *A light rain fell*: Bob Fleming memo, "President's Funeral Participation," June 10, 1968, WHFN-RFK, Box 6; Califano, 302.

459 *At the cemetery*: Fleming memo; Califano, 302.

459 *"You and Mrs. Johnson"*: Ethel Kennedy to LBJ, June 19, 1968, WHFN-RFK, Box 6. Several days later, Jackie Kennedy wrote the Johnsons: "I do thank you so much for your wire about Bobby—and for all you did, in those sad days—to make it possible for him to be laid to rest with all the love and care and nobility that meant so much to those who loved him—Sometimes there are no words to say things—only this—I am deeply grateful—Thank you—as ever, Jackie." Jacqueline Kennedy to LBJ and Lady Bird Johnson, June 22, 1968, FE 3-1/Kennedy, Robert F., LBJL.

459 *"Thank God you have so many"*: LBJ to Ethel Kennedy, June 19, 1968, WHFN-RFK, Box 6; Califano, 303.

459 *"brainwashed by high drama"*: Carpenter to LBJ and Lady Bird, June 9, 1968;

LBJ's handwritten note, n.d.; Christian to LBJ, June 10, 1968, FG 1, Box 18.

460 *Johnson had already introduced a gun control bill*: *Public Papers, LBJ*, vol. 1, 1968–69, 694–5; Califano, 304.

460 *She made only one request*: Paul H. Nitze to LBJ, Dec. 21, 1968, WHFN-RFK, Box 6; Clifford, 546.

461 *LBJ refused to discuss it*: Clifford, 546.

461 *LBJ Ranch on Christmas*: Jones, note, Jan. 4, 1968 [*sic*; actually 1969], WHFN-RFK, Box 6.

461 *LBJ instructed the Bureau*: Clifford, 546; "Johnson Budget Aids a Kennedy Memorial," *New York Times*, Feb. 1, 1969: 14.

461 *"The circumstances which brought"*: "Senator Kennedy Lays Rift with Johnson to Policy," *Washington Post*, Jan. 18, 1969: A12.

461 *"I don't hold a thing"*: Lyle Denniston, "'All Is Forgotten': Johnson Bids Good-by to the Nation's Press," *Washington Star*, Jan. 18, 1969: A1.

462 *The idea was Bill Geoghegan's*: Black and Geoghegan interviews.

462 *Udall, who was then sparring*: Udall interview.

462 *"it would piss Johnson off"*: Garside and Geoghegan interviews.

462 *"Run with it"*: Black and Geoghegan interviews.

462 *the three-man D.C. Armory Board*: Black interview; "DC Stadium's Name Changed to Robert Kennedy," *Washington Star*, Jan. 18, 1969: A1; Morris Siegel, "Stadium Renamed for Robert Kennedy," *Washington Star*, Jan. 19, 1969: B1; "DC Stadium Renamed for R.F. Kennedy," *Washington Post*, Jan. 19, 1969: A1.

463 *Udall returned to Interior*: Boatner OH, LBJL.

463 *"[Johnson] reacted accordingly"*: Christian OH; Black interview. The renaming was also bound to raise hackles in Congress—a reflexive concern of LBJ's, even in his last days as president. As an outgoing president he had pledged not to take any binding executive actions during the transition. Though the rechristening hardly mattered in any practical sense, it was *symbolically* important and appeared (even if it was not) an encroachment on congressional powers. Sure enough, before day's end, Republicans on the Hill grumbled that they might well change the name again—to Eisenhower Stadium. *Ibid.*

463 *Udall's proposed land grants*: Pierson OH; Robert Waters, "LBJ Weighs Big Park Expansion," *Washington Star*, Jan. 19, 1969: A1; Thomas Nolan, "LBJ Trims and Signs Park Plan," *Washington Star*, Jan. 20, 1969: A1.

463 *"If I had named the stadium"*: "The Ex-President: Bitter Aftertaste," *Newsweek*, Feb. 3, 1969: 32.

463 *Among Kennedy partisans*: Black, Geoghegan, Mankiewicz, Udall, and White interviews.

464 *"favorably disposed to the proposal"*: "Nixon Backs Route Plans to Robert Kennedy's Grave," *New York Times*, Feb. 2, 1969: 53.

Epilogue

465 *"not so much a question of issues"*: L. B. Johnson, 539.

465 *"On most matters of national importance"*: *Ibid.*

465 *"do what is necessary"*: *New York Times*, Feb. 19, 1962: 1.

465 *Tip O'Neill split with the administration*: O'Neill, 196–9.

466 *"His major weakness"*: Reedy OH; Cater OH; McPherson OH; Dallek, *Lone Star Rising*, 430, 548; Dutton OH, LBJL.

466 *LBJ sought men's vulnerabilities*: Doris Kearns posits that RFK challenged Johnson's very notions of manliness: unlike JFK, whom Johnson deemed a "weak and pallid" intellectual, Bobby climbed mountains, rode rapids, and fathered many children—though he also read and quoted poetry and took long, reflective walks. According to Kearns, LBJ classified men as either "doers" or "thinkers." JFK was obviously the latter, but RFK, to Johnson's great astonishment, managed to be both. Kearns, 201.

467 *Gallup revealed RFK's "intensely dislike" rating*: Gallup, 2063. RFK's "highly unfavorable" rating was 13 percent to LBJ's 8 percent. Johnson's "highly favorable" rating was 34 percent to Kennedy's 30—a sign that antiwar sentiment had yet to crystallize by spring 1967.

467 *"you can't even ride"*: *New York Times*, April 24, 1968: 46; McPherson OH, LBJL; LBJ quoted in Goodwin, 260.

467 *Melody Miller learned this*: Miller interview.

468 *"an animal in many ways"*: Guthman and Shulman, eds., 417.

469 *"guts of a presidential campaign"*: Edelman interview.

469 *"Robert Kennedy could put aside personal politics"*: Editorial, "Grudge Fight," *Nation*, May 22, 1967: 644; Unsigned and undated memorandum, "Voting Patterns," Edelman Papers, Box 10, JFKL; RFK OH, JFKL. From 1965 to 1967, McCarthy supported LBJ in 60 percent of roll-call votes.

469 *"The rest . . . was prologue"*: Walinsky interview.

469 *"He did think another factor"*: Schlesinger, *Robert Kennedy*, 894–5.

469 *"Bobby developed the antiwar issue"*: Reedy interview.

470 *"How can they be so petty"*: Newfield, 106.

470 *"Ho Chi Minh"*: LBJ, recorded interview by Walter Cronkite, CBS News Special, Feb. 6, 1970, LBJL.

470 *"there is a contradiction"*: Robert Scheer, "A Political Portrait of Robert Kennedy," *Ramparts*, February 1967: 16.

470 *"Kennedy's mere existence"*: Kearns, 259. Also see Bruce Kuklick, *The Good Ruler: From Herbert Hoover to Richard Nixon* (New Brunswick, NJ: Rutgers University Press, 1988): 128.

471 *"telling everyone," Johnson imagined*: Kearns, 253.

471 *"beyond liberalism"*: Ronald Emery Lee, "The Rhetoric of the 'New Politics': A Case Study of Robert F. Kennedy's 1968 Presidential Campaign," unpublished Ph.D. dissertation, University of Iowa, 1981: 35.

471 *"Silly Putty"*: unidentified analyst quoted in Lee, 1–2.

471 *"At this point"*: Scheer, "Political Portrait of Robert Kennedy."

471 *"He tried so avidly"*: Walinsky interview.

472 *"the New Class . . . abhorred"*: Ibid., 175; McPherson OH; Reedy OH.

472 *"Don't they realize"*: Kearns, 333–4.

472 *like them he read . . . the* Village Voice: Newfield, 39, 49; Kimball, 20–23, 75.

472 *LBJ's "politics of consensus"*: See Dallek, *Hail to the Chief,* 122–4.

473 *"a new kind of coalition"*: Newfield, 253.

473 *appealed to rank-and-file members*: Dooley, 45–55.

473 *"a floating crap game"*: Leonard Duhl in Plimpton, ed., 148.

473 *"forcible repression of black violence"*: Moynihan, "The Democrats, Kennedy and the Murder of Dr. King," *Commentary*, May 1968: 20. The suppressed report was "The People Left Behind," produced in September 1967 by the President's Advisory Commission on Rural Poverty.

474 *"We had learned enough"*: Walinsky interview.

474 *"Reliance on government"*: Scheer, "Political Portrait of Robert Kennedy"; Moynihan, "The Democrats," 24; Wicker, "In the Nation: The Real Questions About Welfare," *New York Times*, May 11, 1967; Goodwin, "Has Anybody Seen the Democratic Party?" *New York Times Magazine*, Aug. 25, 1996: 35.

Bibliography

MANUSCRIPT COLLECTIONS

Lyndon Baines Johnson Library, Austin, Texas

Archives Reference File
  Phil Graham
  Robert F. Kennedy
  1960 Campaign
Democratic National Committee Papers
National Security File
  Country File
  Country File, Vietnam
  Files of McGeorge Bundy
  Files of Walt W. Rostow
  Memos to the President: McGeorge Bundy, Walt W. Rostow
  Name File
  Subject File
Office Files of the White House Aides
  Horace Busby, Jr.
  Joseph A. Califano, Jr.
  S. Douglass Cater
  George Christian
  James C. Gaither
  Richard N. Goodwin
  Walter W. Jenkins
  James R. Jones
  Robert E. Kintner
  Lawrence E. Levinson
  Harry C. McPherson

John W. Macy, Jr.
Mike Manatos
Bill D. Moyers
Lawrence F. O'Brien
Kenneth O'Donnell
Frederick Panzer
DeVier Pierson
George Reedy
Pierre Salinger
Hobart Taylor, Jr.
Larry E. Temple
W. Marvin Watson
Ben Wattenberg
Lee C. White
Pre-Presidential Papers
   Appointment Files: Diary and Diary Backup
   Notes and Transcripts of Conversations
   Senate Masters
   Senate Political Files
   Vice Presidential Masters
   Working Papers of the President's Committee on Equal Employment Opportunity
Special Files
   Administrative Histories
   Cartoon Collection
   Diaries and Appointment Logs
   Handwriting File
   Office of the President File
   Presidential Aircraft Manifests and Logs
   Recordings and Transcripts of Conversations and Meetings
   Special File on the Assassination of John F. Kennedy
   Statements of Lyndon B. Johnson
   Tom Johnson's Notes of Meetings
   White House Famous Names
White House Central Files
   Appointment Files: Daily Diary and Diary Backup
   Confidential File
   Name File
   Subject Files

John Fitzgerald Kennedy Library, Boston, Massachusetts

Gerald J. Bruno Papers
McGeorge Bundy Papers
Joseph Dolan Papers
Peter Edelman Papers
Myer Feldman Papers
Milton Gwirtzman Papers
Thomas M. Johnston Papers

Nicholas DeB. Katzenbach Papers
John Fitzgerald Kennedy Papers
Central Name File
National Security Files
President's Office Files: Presidential Recordings, 1961–1962
White House Central Files
Robert Francis Kennedy Papers
Pre-Administration Papers, 1937–1960
Attorney General Papers, 1961–1964
Senate Papers, 1964–1968
Presidential Campaign Papers, 1968
Frank Mankiewicz Papers
Burke Marshall Papers
Pierre Salinger Papers
Arthur M. Schlesinger, Jr., Papers
Theodore C. Sorensen Papers
William J. vanden Heuvel Papers
Adam Walinsky Papers
Lee C. White Papers

Library of Congress, Washington, DC

Thomas G. Corcoran Papers
W. Averell Harriman Papers
Joseph L. Rauh Papers

PERSONAL INTERVIEWS

David Black, telephone interview, Sept. 28, 1995
Elizabeth Carpenter, telephone interview, Oct. 2, 1994
George Christian, Austin, TX, Nov. 11, 1994
Clark M. Clifford, Washington, DC, Aug. 8, 1994
Joseph Dolan, Denver, CO, Aug. 14, 1990, and Aug. 15, 1994
Peter Edelman, Washington, DC, June 1, 1994
Daniel Ellsberg, Washington, DC, June 23, 1995
Myer Feldman, telephone interview, Sept. 9, 1994
Grenville Garside, telephone interview, Sept. 16, 1994
William A. Geoghegan, Washington, DC, Sept. 16, 1994
Nicholas deB. Katzenbach, Washington, DC, March 14, 1996
Lawrence E. Levinson, Washington, DC, Oct. 25, 1994
Ron M. Linton, Washington, DC, Sept. 7, 1994
Frank Mankiewicz, Washington, DC, May 23, 1994
Harry C. McPherson, Washington, DC, Aug. 2, 1990
Melody Miller, Washington, DC, Oct. 13, 1995
Matthew Nimetz, New York, NY, Nov. 23, 1994
W. DeVier Pierson, Washington, DC, Aug. 3, 1994
George Reedy, telephone interview, Feb. 11, 1996
Walt W. Rostow, Austin, TX, Nov. 17, 1994

Dean Rusk, telephone interview, March 15, 1994
Pierre Salinger, Washington, DC, June 28, 1994
Arthur M. Schlesinger, Jr., New York, NY, Oct. 24, 1995
Theodore C. Sorensen, New York, NY, Nov. 23, 1994
Stewart Udall, Washington, DC, Oct. 11, 1995
Jack Valenti, telephone interview, July 31, 1990
William J. vanden Heuvel, Washington, DC, March 5, 1996
Adam Walinsky, New York, NY, Nov. 28, 1994
Lee C. White, Washington, DC, July 26, 1994
Roger Wilkins, Washington, DC, July 13, 1994

ORAL HISTORIES

Lyndon Baines Johnson Library, Austin, Texas

Clifford L. Alexander, Jr., Nov. 1, 1971; Feb. 17, 1972; June 4, 1973
Stewart Alsop, July 15, 1969
Charles L. Bartlett, May 6, 1969
David S. Black, Nov. 12, 1968
Charles K. Boatner, Dec. 17, 1968; May 21, 1969; June 1 and 2, 1976
Hale Boggs, March 13 and 27, 1969
Edmund G. "Pat" Brown, Sr., Feb. 20, 1969; Aug. 19, 1970
Elizabeth S. Carpenter, Dec. 3, 1968; April 4, May 15, and Aug. 27, 1969; Feb. 2, 1971
Clifton C. Carter, Oct. 1, 9, 15, and 30, 1968
Hodding Carter, Nov. 8, 1968
S. Douglass Cater, April 29 and May 8, 1969; May 26, 1974; April 24, 1981
Oscar L. Chapman, Aug. 15 and Oct. 2, 1972
George E. Christian, Nov. 11, 1968; Dec. 4, 1969; Feb. 27 and June 30, 1970; July 1, 1971
Ramsey Clark, Oct. 30, 1968
Clark M. Clifford, March 17, July 2 and 14, Aug. 7, and Dec. 15, 1969; April 24 and June 16, 1970
Wilbur J. Cohen, Dec. 8, 1968; March 2 and May 10, 1969
Jack T. Conway, Aug. 13, 1980
Ralph A. Dungan, April 18, 1969
Frederick G. Dutton, Aug. 4, 1969
India Edwards, Feb. 4, 1969
Orville L. Freeman, Feb. 14, March 12, and July 21, 1969
John W. Gardner, Dec. 20, 1971
Arthur J. Goldberg, March 23, 1983
Kermit Gordon, April 8, 1969
Katharine Graham, March 13, 1969
Charles M. Haar, June 14, 1971
Loyd Hackler, May 28 and June 2, 1969
Robert L. Hardesty, March 26, 1969
Walter Heller, Feb. 20, 1970, and Dec. 21, 1971
Luther H. Hodges, Sr., Oct. 10, 1970

Harold W. Horowitz, Feb. 23, 1983

Hubert H. Humphrey, Aug. 17, 1971; June 20 and 21, 1977

Chester R. "Chet" Huntley, May 12, 1969

Jake Jacobsen, May 27, 1969

Walter Jenkins, Aug. 24, 1971; July 12, 1984

Lyndon Baines Johnson, recorded interviews by Walter Cronkite, CBS News Specials, broadcast on Dec. 27, 1969; Feb. 6 and May 6, 1970; Jan. 27, 1972; and Feb. 1, 1973

————, recorded interview by William J. Jorden, Aug. 12, 1969

———— and Theodore C. Sorensen, telephone conversation, Edison Dictaphone Recording, June 3, 1963

Nicholas deB. Katzenbach, Nov. 12 and 23 and Dec. 11, 1968

William P. Kelly, April 4, 11, and 16, 1969

Robert E. Kintner, July 13, 1972

Fred Korth, March 7, 1969

Arthur Krock, Nov. 21, 1968

Robert J. Lampman, May 24, 1983

Mike Manatos, Aug. 25, 1969

Frank Mankiewicz, May 1 and 5, 1969

Sherwin J. Markman, May 21, 1969

Leonard Marks, June 15, 1970

Burke Marshall, Oct. 28, 1968

John A. McCone, Aug. 19, 1970

John W. McCormack, Sept. 23, 1968

George McGovern, April 30, 1969

Harry C. McPherson, Dec. 5 and 19, 1968; Jan. 19, March 24, and April 9, 1969

Samuel V. Merrick, Sept. 28, 1981

Charles S. Murphy, May 7 and 29, 1969

Lawrence F. O'Brien, Sept. 18, Oct. 29 and 30, and Dec. 4 and 5, 1985; Feb. 11 and 12, April 8 and 9, June 25, July 24 and 25, Sept. 10 and 11, Nov. 20 and 21, and Dec. 17 and 18, 1986; April 22 and 23, June 18 and 19, July 21 and 22, Aug. 25 and 26, Sept. 23 and 24, Nov. 3 and 4, and Dec. 10 and 11, 1987

Kenneth O'Donnell, July 23, 1969

Jacqueline Kennedy Onassis, Jan. 11, 1974

Thomas P. "Tip" O'Neill, Jan. 28, 1976

Wright Patman, Aug. 11, 1972

W. DeVier Pierson, March 19, 20 and 27, 1969

Stephen J. Pollak, Jan. 27, 29, 30 and 31, 1969

George E. Reedy, Dec. 12, 19, and 20, 1968; Feb. 14, 1972; June 7, 1975

Juanita Roberts, Aug. 29 and Oct. 17, 1969

John P. Roche, July 16, 1970

Mitchell Rogovin, Oct. 23, 1968

Eugene V. Rostow, Dec. 2, 1968

Walt W. Rostow, March 21, 1969

James H. Rowe, Jr., Sept. 9 and 16 and Dec. 16, 1969

Dean Rusk, July 28 and Sept. 26, 1969; Jan. 2 and March 8, 1970

Harold "Barefoot" Sanders, March 24 and Nov. 3, 1969

Norbert A. Schlei, May 15, 1980
Arthur M. Schlesinger, Jr., Nov. 4, 1971
John A. Schnittker, Nov. 21, 1968
Hugh Sidey, July 22, 1971
Jule M. Sugarman, March 14, 1969
James L. Sundquist, April 7, 1969
James Symington, July 14 and Sept. 17, 1969; Nov. 3, 1971
Hobart Taylor, Jr., Jan. 6 and Feb. 14, 1969
General Maxwell D. Taylor, Jan. 9 and Feb. 10, 1969; June 1 and Sept. 14, 1981
Larry Temple, June 11, 12, and 26 and Aug. 7, 11, and 13, 1970
Stewart L. Udall, April 18, May 19, July 29, Oct. 31, and Dec. 16, 1969
Jack Valenti, June 14 and Oct. 18, 1969; Feb. 19 and March 3, 1971; July 12, 1972
Ben J. Wattenberg, Nov. 23 and 29, 1968
Robert C. Weaver, Nov. 19, 1968
Edwin Weisl, Jr., Oct. 30, 1968; May 23, 1969
Edwin Weisl, Sr., May 13, 1969
Lee C. White, Sept. 28, 1970; Feb. 18, March 2 and 3, and Nov. 2, 1971
Robert C. Wood, Oct. 19, 1968
Adam Yarmolinsky, July 13, 1970; Oct. 21 and 22, 1980

John Fitzgerald Kennedy Library, Boston, Massachusetts

Joseph Alsop, June 18 and 26, 1964; Oct. 29, 1979
William Attwood, Nov. 8, 1965
Wes Barthelmes, May 20, 1969
Abraham D. Beame, June 27, 1978
Albert H. Blumenthal, Dec. 14, 1973; July 1, 1974; Oct. 10, 1975; Nov. 23, 1976
Hale Boggs, May 10, 1964
Carter Burden, Feb. 13, 1974
David Burke, Dec. 8, 1971
Frank Burns, April 17, 1970
Oscar C. Carr, Jr., May 6 and 7, 1969
Barbara Coleman, Dec. 8, 1969; Jan. 9, 1970
Jack T. Conway, April 10 and 11 and Dec. 29, 1972
Gerard Doherty, Feb. 3, 1972
Joseph Dolan, July 8, 1964
Francis X. Dooley, March 9, 1976
Frederick G. Dutton, Nov. 18, 1969
Peter Edelman, July 15 and 29, Aug. 4, and Dec. 12, 1969; Jan. 3 and Feb. 21, 1970;
    Feb. 13, 1973
John English, Nov. 3 and 25 and Dec. 19, 1969; Feb. 3, 1970
Myer "Mike" Feldman, Jan. 23, Feb. 27, March 6, 13, and 27, April 10, May 29, Aug.
    6, Sept. 20, and Dec. 11, 1966; July 29 and Aug. 26, 1967; Jan. 6 and Sept. 21, 1968
William A. Geoghegan, Feb. 17, 1966
K. Dun Gifford, Nov. 22, 1971; Jan. 5, 1973
Jeff Greenfield, Dec. 10, 1969
Edwin O. Guthman, Feb. 21, 1968
David Hackett, July 22 and Oct. 21, 1970
W. Averell Harriman, March 13, 1970

Fred Harris, July 29, 1970

Brooks Hays, May and June 1964

Joseph C. Houghteling, June 19, 1969

Hubert H. Humphrey, March 30, 1970

Eli Jacobs, Oct. 27, 1976; Sept. 6 and 20, 1979

Jacob Javits, June 19 and April 10, 1970; June 7, 1973

Nicholas deB. Katzenbach, Oct. 8, 1969

Robert F. Kennedy, Feb. 29, March 1, April 13 and 30, May 14, and Dec. 4, 6, and 22, 1964; Feb. 27, 1965; July 20 and Aug. 1, 1967

Jerome Kretchmer, July 19, 1973

Marjorie McKenzie Lawson, Oct. 25 and Nov. 14, 1965

Anthony Lewis, July 23, 1970

Peter Lisagor, April 22 and May 12, 1966

Allard K. Lowenstein, April 23 and Dec. 2, 1969

Patrick J. Lucey, Jan. 6, 1972

Mike Manatos, Oct. 30, 1970

Burke Marshall, Jan. 19 and 20, 1970

Samuel V. Merrick, Oct. 17 and Nov. 4, 1966

Walter Mondale, May 17 and Aug. 3, 1973

Esther Newberg, May 22, 1969

Eugene H. Nickerson, Nov. 30, 1971

John E. Nolan, May 11 and Nov. 11, 1971; Jan. 18, 1972

Wendell Pigman, June 9, 1969

Poverty and Urban Policy, Conference Transcript of Group Discussion of the Kennedy Administration Urban Poverty Programs and Policies, Brandeis University, June 16 and 17, 1973

E. Barrett Prettyman, Jr., June 5, 1969

John R. Reilly, Oct. 22 and 29 and Dec. 16, 1970; Feb. 22, 1973

Teno Roncalio, Dec. 20, 1965

Walt W. Rostow, April 11, 1964

James H. Rowe, Jr., May 10, 1964

Dean Rusk, Dec. 2 and 9, 1969; Feb. 19, March 13 and 30, April 27, May 13, and July 21, 1970

Pierre Salinger, July 19 and Aug. 10, 1965; May 26, 1969; April 18, 1970

Benno C. Schmidt, July 17, 1969

Hugh Sidey, April 7, 1964

John Seigenthaler, June 5 and July 1, 1970

Stephen E. Smith, April 16, 1970

Theodore C. Sorensen, March 26, April 6 and 15, and May 3 and 20, 1964; March 21, 1969; July 23, 1970

Charles Spalding, March 22, 1969

Stuart Symington, Aug. 18 and Sept. 4, 1964

Hobart Taylor, Jr., Jan. 11, 1967

Gerald Tremblay, Jan. 8, 1970

Joseph D. Tydings, May 3 and Sept. 29, 1971; May 8, 1973

Stewart L. Udall, Jan. 12, Feb. 16, March 12, April 7, May 20, June 2, July 6, and Sept. 17, 1970

Jack Valenti, May 25, 1982

Robert Wagner, Nov. 2, 1967
Adam Walinsky, Nov. 29 and 30, 1969; May 22, 1972; Oct. 5 and 30 and Dec. 14,
    1973; Feb. 12, July 3, and Dec. 4, 1974; March 12 and Nov. 22, 1976; July 3, 1978;
    Sept. 7, 1979
William Walton, May 14, 1970
Thomas J. Watson, Jan. 6, 1970
Lee C. White, May 25, 26, and 28, 1964; Jan. 9, March 17, April 9, and May 11, 1970
James W. Whittaker, April 25 and 26 and Nov. 13, 1969
Thomas G. Wicker, Jan. 27 and March 22, 1966

BOOKS

*Alleged Assassination Plots Involving Foreign Leaders: An Interim Report of the Senate
    Select Committee to Study Governmental Operations with Respect to Intelligence Activi-
    ties,* 94 Cong., 1 Sess., Nov. 20, 1975.
Alsop, Joseph W., with Adam Platt. *"I've Seen the Best of It": Memoirs.* New York: W. W.
    Norton, 1992.
Baker, Bobby, with Larry L. King. *Wheeling and Dealing: Confessions of a Capitol Hill
    Operator.* New York: W. W. Norton, 1978.
Bell, Jack. *The Johnson Treatment: How Lyndon B. Johnson Took Over the Presidency and
    Made It His Own.* New York: Harper & Row, 1965.
Berman, Larry. *Lyndon Johnson's War: The Road to Stalemate in Vietnam.* New York:
    W. W. Norton, 1989.
Branch, Taylor. *Parting the Waters: America in the King Years, 1954-63.* New York:
    Simon & Schuster, 1988.
Brinkley, Alan. *The End of Reform: New Deal Liberalism in Recession and War.* New
    York: Vintage, 1995.
Buchwald, Art. *Son of the Great Society.* New York: G. P. Putnam's Sons, 1966.
Burns, James McGregor, ed. *To Heal and to Build: The Programs of President Lyndon B.
    Johnson.* New York: McGraw-Hill, 1968.
Califano, Joseph A., Jr. *The Triumph and Tragedy of Lyndon Johnson: The White House
    Years.* New York: Simon & Schuster, 1991.
Caro, Robert A. *The Years of Lyndon Johnson: Means of Ascent.* New York: Knopf, 1990.
————. *The Years of Lyndon Johnson: The Path to Power.* New York: Knopf, 1983.
Carpenter, Liz. *Ruffles and Flourishes.* Garden City, NY: Doubleday, 1970.
Chafe, William Henry. *Never Stop Running: Allard Lowenstein and the Struggle to Save
    American Liberalism.* New York: Basic Books, 1993.
Chester, Lewis, Godfrey Hodgson, and Bruce Page. *An American Melodrama: The Pres-
    idential Campaign of 1968.* London: Deutsch, 1969.
Christian, George. *The President Steps Down: A Personal Memoir of the Transfer of Power.*
    New York: Macmillan, 1970.
Clifford, Clark M., with Richard Holbrooke. *Counsel to the President: A Memoir.* New
    York: Random House, 1991.
Conkin, Paul K. *Big Daddy from the Pedernales: Lyndon Baines Johnson.* Boston:
    Twayne, 1986.
Connally, John, with Mickey Herskowitz. *In History's Shadow: An American Odyssey.*
    New York: Hyperion, 1993.

Corry, John. *The Manchester Affair.* New York: G. P. Putnam's Sons, 1967.

Dallek, Robert. *Hail to the Chief: The Making and Unmaking of American Presidents.* New York: Hyperion, 1996.

————. *Lone Star Rising: Lyndon Johnson and His Times, 1908-1960.* New York: Oxford University Press, 1991.

Davie, Michael. *LBJ: A Foreign Observer's Viewpoint.* New York: Duell, Sloan & Pearce, 1966.

DeLoach, Cartha "Deke." *Hoover's FBI: The Inside Story by Hoover's Trusted Lieutenant.* Washington, DC: Regnery, 1995.

Divine, Robert A., ed. *The Johnson Years.* 3 vols. Vol. 1, *Foreign Policy, the Great Society and the White House.* Vol. 2, *Vietnam, the Environment, and Science.* Vol. 3, *LBJ at Home and Abroad.* Lawrenceville, KS: University of Kansas Press, 1981, 1987, 1994.

Dooley, Brian. *Robert Kennedy: The Final Years.* New York: St. Martin's, 1996.

Dugger, Ronnie. *The Politician: The Life and Times of Lyndon Johnson.* New York: W. W. Norton, 1982.

Evans, Rowland, and Robert Novak. *Lyndon B. Johnson: The Exercise of Power.* New York: Signet, 1968.

Faber, Harold, ed. *The Road to the White House.* New York: New York Times, 1965.

Federal Role in Urban Affairs: Hearings Before the Subcommittee on Executive Reorganization of the Committee on Government Operations, U.S. Senate, 89 Cong., 2 Sess., Parts 1-5, Aug. 15-19, 22-26, and 29-31 and Sept. 1, 1966.

Gallup, George H. *The Gallup Poll: Public Opinion, 1935-1971.* Vol. 3, 1959-1971. New York: Random House, 1972.

Garson, Barbara. *MacBird.* Berkeley: Grassy Knoll Press, 1966.

Giglio, James N. *The Presidency of John F. Kennedy.* Lawrenceville, KS: University of Kansas Press, 1991.

Goldman, Eric F. *The Tragedy of Lyndon Johnson.* New York: Dell, 1968.

Goodwin, Richard N. *Remembering America: A Voice from the Sixties.* Boston: Little, Brown, 1988.

Guthman, Edwin O. *We Band of Brothers.* New York: Harper & Row, 1971.

———— and C. Richard Allen, eds. *RFK: Collected Speeches.* New York: Viking, 1993.

———— and Jeffrey Shulman, eds. *Robert Kennedy: In His Own Words.* New York: Bantam, 1988.

Halberstam, David. *The Best and the Brightest.* New York: Random House, 1972.

————. *The Unfinished Odyssey of Robert Kennedy.* New York: Random House, 1968.

Hamilton, Nigel. *JFK: Reckless Youth.* New York: Random House, 1992.

Hammer, Ellen J. *A Death in November: America in Vietnam, 1963.* New York: Oxford University Press, 1987.

Harris, David. *Dreams Die Hard: Three Men's Journey through the Sixties.* New York: St. Martin's, 1982.

Hayden, Tom. *Reunion: A Memoir.* New York: Collier, 1989.

Hearings Before the Senate Select Committee to Study Governmental Operations with Respect to Intelligence Activities, 94 Cong., 2 Sess., Vol. 6, *Federal Bureau of Investigation,* Nov. 18, 19, Dec. 2, 3, 9, 10, and 11, 1975.

Henggeler, Paul R. *In His Steps: Lyndon Johnson and the Kennedy Mystique.* Chicago: Ivan R. Dee, 1991.

Herring, George C. *America's Longest War: The United States and Vietnam, 1950-1975.*

2nd ed. New York: Knopf, 1986.

———. *LBJ and Vietnam: A Different Kind of War.* Austin, TX: University of Texas Press, 1994.

Hodgson, Godfrey. *America in Our Time.* New York: Vintage, 1978.

Humphrey, Hubert H. *The Education of a Public Man: My Life and Politics.* Ed. Norman Sherman. Garden City, NY: Doubleday, 1976.

The Investigation of the Assassination of President John F. Kennedy: Performance of the Intelligence Agencies, Book V, *Final Report of the Senate Select Committee to Study Governmental Operations with Respect to Intelligence Activities,* 94 Cong., 2 Sess., April 23, 1976.

Johnson, Lady Bird. *A White House Diary.* New York: Holt, Rinehart & Winston, 1970.

Johnson, Lyndon Baines. *The Vantage Point: Perspectives of the Presidency, 1963-1969.* New York: Holt, Rinehart and Winston, 1971.

Kearns, Doris. *Lyndon Johnson and the American Dream.* New York: Harper & Row, 1976.

Kennedy, John F. *The Strategy of Peace.* New York: Harper & Brothers, 1960.

Kennedy, Robert F. *Thirteen Days: A Memoir of the Cuban Missile Crisis.* New York: W. W. Norton, 1969.

———. *To Seek a Newer World.* New York: Doubleday, 1967.

Kimball, Penn. *Bobby Kennedy and the New Politics.* Englewood Cliffs, NJ: Prentice-Hall, 1968.

Knapp, Daniel, and Kenneth Polk. *Scouting the War on Poverty: Social Reform Politics in the Kennedy Administration.* Lexington, MA: Heath Lexington Books, 1971.

Kraslow, David, and Stuart H. Loory. *The Secret Search for Peace in Vietnam.* New York: Random House, 1968.

Kuklick, Bruce. *The Good Ruler: From Herbert Hoover to Richard Nixon.* New Brunswick, NJ: Rutgers University Press, 1988.

Larner, Jeremy. *Nobody Knows: Reflections on the McCarthy Campaign of 1968.* New York: Macmillan, 1970.

Lasky, Victor. *Robert F. Kennedy: The Myth and the Man.* New York: Trident, 1968.

Lemann, Nicholas. *The Promised Land: The Great Black Migration and How It Changed America.* New York: Knopf, 1991.

Levitan, Sar A. *The Great Society's Poor Law: A New Approach to Poverty.* Baltimore: Johns Hopkins Press, 1969.

Lincoln, Evelyn. *Kennedy and Johnson.* New York: Holt, Rinehart & Winston, 1968.

Lois, George. *Covering the '60s: George Lois, The Esquire Era.* New York: Monacelli, 1996.

MAD About the Sixties: The Best of the Decade. Boston: Little, Brown, 1995.

Manchester, William. *The Death of a President.* New York: Harper & Row, 1967.

Mann, Robert. *The Walls of Jericho: Lyndon Johnson, Hubert Humphrey, Richard Russell and the Struggle for Civil Rights.* New York: Harcourt Brace, 1996.

Matusow, Allen J. *The Unraveling of America: A History of Liberalism in the 1960s.* New York: Harper & Row, 1986.

McCarthy, Eugene J. *Up 'Til Now: A Memoir.* San Diego: Harcourt Brace Jovanovich, 1987.

———. *The Year of the People.* Garden City, NY: Doubleday, 1969.

McNamara, Robert S., with Brian VanDeMark. *In Retrospect: The Tragedy and Lessons of Vietnam*. New York: Times Books, 1995.

McPherson, Harry C. *A Political Education*. Boston: Little, Brown, 1972.

Miller, Merle. *Lyndon: An Oral Biography*. New York: G. P. Putnam's Sons, 1980.

Mooney, Booth. *The Lyndon Johnson Story*. New York: Farrar, Straus & Cudahy, 1956.

Morone, James A. *The Democratic Wish*. New York: Basic Books, 1990.

Morris, Edmund. *The Rise of Theodore Roosevelt*. New York: Ballantine, 1979.

Morris, Jeffrey B. *Federal Justice in the Second Circuit: A History of the United States Courts in New York, Connecticut and Vermont, 1787-1987*. New York: Second Circuit Historical Committee, 1987.

Moynihan, Daniel P. *Maximum Feasible Misunderstanding*. New York: Free Press, 1969.

Newfield, Jack. *Robert Kennedy: A Memoir*. New York: New American Library, 1969.

O'Brien, Lawrence F. *No Final Victories: A Life in Politics—from John F. Kennedy to Watergate*. Garden City, NY: Doubleday, 1974.

O'Neill, Tip, with William Novak. *Man of the House: The Life and Political Memoirs of Speaker Tip O'Neill*. New York: Random House, 1987.

O'Reilly, Kenneth. *Nixon's Piano: Presidents and Racial Politics from Washington to Clinton*. New York: Free Press, 1995.

Oshinsky, David M. *A Conspiracy So Immense: The World of Joe McCarthy*. New York: Free Press, 1983.

Parmet, Herbert S. *JFK: The Presidency of John F. Kennedy*. New York: Dial Press, 1983.

Patterson, James T. *America's Struggle Against Poverty, 1900-1985*. Cambridge, MA: Harvard University Press, 1986.

———. *Grand Expectations: The United States, 1945-1974*. New York: Oxford University Press, 1996.

Plimpton, George, ed., and Jean Stein, interviewer. *American Journey: The Times of Robert Kennedy*. London: Andre Deutsch, 1971.

Powers, Richard Gid. *Secrecy and Power: The Life of J. Edgar Hoover*. New York: Free Press, 1987.

Public Papers of the Presidents of the United States: Lyndon B. Johnson, 1963-69. 10 vols. Washington, DC: U.S. Government Printing Office, 1965-70.

Reedy, George E. *Lyndon B. Johnson, a Memoir*. New York: Andrews & McMeel, 1982.

Reeves, Richard. *President Kennedy: Profile of Power*. New York: Simon & Schuster, 1993.

Rusk, Dean, with Richard Rusk and Daniel S. Papp. *As I Saw It*. New York: W. W. Norton, 1990.

Salinger, Pierre. *With Kennedy*. London: Jonathan Cape, 1966.

Schlesinger, Arthur M., Jr. *Robert Kennedy and His Times*. New York: Ballantine, 1978.

———. *A Thousand Days: John F. Kennedy in the White House*. Boston: Houghton Mifflin, 1965.

Schoen, Douglas. *Pat: A Biography of Daniel Patrick Moynihan*. New York: Harper & Row, 1979.

Schulman, Bruce J. *Lyndon B. Johnson and American Liberalism: A Brief Biography with Documents*. Boston: Bedford Books, 1995.

Shannon, William V. *The Heir Apparent: Robert Kennedy and the Struggle for Power*. New York: Macmillan, 1967.

Shapley, Deborah. *Promise and Power: The Life and Times of Robert McNamara.* Boston: Little, Brown, 1993.

Sidey, Hugh. *A Very Personal Presidency: Lyndon Johnson in the White House.* New York: Atheneum, 1968.

Solberg, Carl. *Hubert Humphrey.* New York: W. W. Norton, 1984.

Sorensen, Theodore C. *Kennedy.* New York: Harper & Row, 1965.

————. *The Kennedy Legacy.* New York: Macmillan, 1969.

————, ed. *"Let the Word Go Forth": The Speeches, Statements, and Writings of John F. Kennedy.* New York: Delacorte, 1988.

Strober, Gerald S. and Deborah H. *"Let Us Begin Anew": An Oral History of the Kennedy Presidency.* New York: HarperCollins, 1993.

Supplementary Detailed Staff Reports on Intelligence Activities and the Rights of Americans, Book III, *Final Report of the Senate Select Committee to Study Governmental Operations with Respect to Intelligence Activities,* 94 Cong., 2 Sess., April 23, 1976.

Thomas, Evan. *The Very Best Men.* New York: Simon & Schuster, 1995.

Toledano, Ralph de. *R.F.K.: The Man Who Would Be President.* New York: G. P. Putnam's Sons, 1967.

Valenti, Jack. *A Very Human President.* New York: W. W. Norton, 1975.

vanden Heuvel, William, and Milton Gwirtzman. *On His Own: Robert F. Kennedy, 1964-1968.* New York: Doubleday, 1970.

Vidal, Gore. *United States: Essays, 1952-1992.* New York: Random House, 1993.

White, Theodore H. *The Making of the President 1960.* New York: New American Library, 1961.

————. *The Making of the President 1964.* New York: New American Library, 1965.

————. *The Making of the President 1968.* New York: Atheneum, 1969.

Wickenden, Dorothy, ed. *The New Republic Reader: Eighty Years of Opinion and Debate.* New York: Basic Books, 1994.

Wicker, Tom. *JFK and LBJ: The Influence of Personality on Politics.* New York: Morrow, 1968.

Wilkins, Roger W. *A Man's Life: An Autobiography.* New York: Simon & Schuster, 1982.

Wills, Garry. *The Kennedy Imprisonment: A Meditation on Power.* Boston: Atlantic Monthly Press/Little, Brown, 1981.

Witcover, Jules. *85 Days: The Last Campaign of Robert Kennedy.* New York: Quill, 1969.

Wofford, Harris. *Of Kennedys and Kings: Making Sense of the Sixties.* New York: Farrar, Straus & Giroux, 1980.

Zarefsky, David. *President Johnson's War on Poverty: Rhetoric and History.* University, AL: University of Alabama Press, 1985.

JOURNAL ARTICLES

Altschuler, Bruce E. "Kennedy Decides to Run: 1968." *Presidential Studies Quarterly,* Summer 1980: 348-52.

Best, James J. "Who Talked to the President When?" *Political Science Quarterly,* Fall 1988: 531-45.

Dallek, Robert. "Lyndon Johnson and Vietnam: The Making of a Tragedy." *Diplomatic History,* Spring 1996: 147-62.

Fromkin, David. "Lyndon Johnson and Foreign Policy: What the New Documents Show." *Foreign Affairs,* January/February 1995: 161-70.

Holland, Max. "After Thirty Years: Making Sense of the Assassination." *Reviews in American History,* June 1994: 191-209.

Riccards, Michael. "Rare Counsel: Kennedy, Johnson and the Civil Rights Bill of 1963." *Presidential Studies Quarterly,* Summer 1981: 395-8.

UNPUBLISHED PAPERS AND THESES

Lee, Ronald Emery. "The Rhetoric of the 'New Politics': A Case Study of Robert F. Kennedy's 1968 Presidential Campaign." Unpublished Ph.D. dissertation. University of Iowa, 1981.

Martin, Marilyn Ann. " 'The Politics of Restoration': The Rhetorical Vision of Camelot and Robert F. Kennedy's 1968 Campaign." Unpublished M.A. thesis. University of North Texas, 1989.

Sanders, Frederick Clarke, Jr. "The Rhetorical Strategies of Senator Robert Kennedy and Senator Eugene McCarthy in the 1968 Presidential Primaries." Unpublished Ph.D. dissertation. University of Oregon, 1973.

Index